Life Line

Life Line

by

Judy Falck-Madsen

ACKNOWLEDGMENTS

I would like to express my heartfelt thanks to Jane Denham Cornish, Renée Farrington and Carla Rolde for all their help in researching this book, and to my husband, Finn, our daughter, Lani, and son, Bjørn, for their unflagging support while I was writing it.

For those who are interested in knowing more about the prisoners of the Japanese and General MacArthur's personality, I highly recommend Gavan Daw's book, "Prisoners of the Japanese" and William Manchester's "American Caesar".

© July 2005 – Judy Falck-Madsen
Cover illustration: Anthony Owen
Typesetting and layout: Books on Demand GmbH
Production: Books on Demand GmbH, Norderstedt, Germany
Publishing: Books on Demand GmbH, København, Danmark
This book is an on-Demand-product

Table of contents

Prologue	7
Jane	10
Hollywood – 1929	19
Donda	31
Vivian	65
Mickey Meets Vivian	77
Pacific Paradise	104
Hard Times	121
A Fresh Start	132
A Roll of the Dice	150
Diamond Head – 1941	160
The Philippines	168
Pearl Harbor	182
Bataan and the Rock	189
The Fall of Bataan	220
Evacuation	235
Las Vegas – 1942	243
Carbanatuan	262
On the Home Front	275
Hell Ships	308
Donda's House	316
Slave Labor at Narumi	324
Las Vegas – 1946	353
Post-War Hawaii	373
The Final Curtain	417
Epilogue	478
Bibliography	480

Prologue

The wind is howling on the western side of the house, throwing rain against the mullion windows, and I find I cannot sleep as snatches of memory nag my consciousness, prompting me to tell a story whose plot I do not yet know. Memories, so vivid that it is as if they have had a life of their own during all these years while I have grown older, are like pieces to a puzzle. If I try to put them down, hold them still on sheets of paper, perhaps they will form a meaningful picture, one I can look at with some satisfaction and then tuck it away.

Intermixed with the impressions of my lifetime are the vivid images of my parents, dancing to a different tune. In a bygone time, they lived their lives to the lyrics of Cole Porter. The world seemed a pretty place, where one could spin golden dreams and feel the intoxication that comes from moods not shattered by ugly realities. Faraway places were not scenes of vast conflicts, poverty, and maimed survivors. Exploring the wilderness was unmarred by the discovery of a candy wrapper or empty beer can. In Hollywood, the skies were always blue, and snow-capped mountains rose crystal clear behind acres of fruit orchards. To be poor in America was to be miserable, but not without aspirations. The only limits to dreams were the boundaries of one's imagination.

In the endless stream of humanity, there are certain individuals who are pushed out of the mainstream by the sheer force of the multitudes, and they become unpredictable small elements whose course is interesting to observe, even if it peters out in the sand. My parents, Mickey and Vivian, were like that. My life is like water dripping on the proverbial stone; theirs were like small shooting stars that streaked across the hemisphere, making one catch one's breath with a moment's excitement, before they vanished forever in the vastness of eternity.

My hair is turning gray, and it is strange to catch sight of myself in a mirror and realize that I am seeing a woman much older than my mother and father were when their lives were snuffed out. I have taken the safe paths; they ventured into the unknown. Would they have wished for anything different for themselves if they had known the outcome of their daring?

If I try to resurrect them on paper, I have, along with my memories, only a stack of old letters, some newspaper clippings, my mother's movie stills, my father's one brief message allowed to pass out of a Japanese prison camp during the war, and old photographs, enigmatically static.

* * * * *

Each generation is linked to the ones preceding it. To understand a person, it is useful to know something about those people who had something to do with shaping that person's character, and, in my fathers and mother's cases, two women are the strongest recent links: My mother's mother and my father's mother. However, except for their strength of character, these two women could not have been more dissimilar.

We called my maternal grandmother, Donda. She was warm and caring. She lived by the Golden Rule and forgave all those who were unable to do the same. She was never lonely; her house was filled with people who needed her for her sympathy and for her willingness to share a good laugh. During a long lifetime, she had witnessed much suffering, and her faded brown eyes were serene with wisdom. She mourned when Franklin Delano Roosevelt died, and she voted Democrat as long as she cherished a belief that the Democrats could change things. Without bitterness, she became a 'sofa-voter' when she decided that she was old enough to stop believing her vote would make a difference. Her hands were gnarled with hard work, with blue veins prominent on skin that looked as fragile as rice paper. She had been a beauty, and the twinkle in her eyes gave a hint of the attention she had enjoyed before she grew so old. To me, she was too wonderful to be judged by ordinary criteria.

My father's mother was the exact opposite. Jane Jones was vain, ambitious, self-centered, and argumentative. She had learned that money was power, and she had contempt for anyone who didn't share her convictions. Except for her possessive loves, her world was business and politics. She was a dyed-in-the-wool Republican, both due to her temperament and because she found it expedient to be associated with the party that ruled Nevada.. Even when she was older, she was justly proud of her fine figure. With straight back and lifted chin, she appeared rather haughty and indifferent to anyone she didn't choose to charm. She dressed in nicely tailored black suits with creamy white silk blouses, black kid gloves, and black pumps. To complete her image, she drove a shiny black Packard and carried in her handbag at all times a couple of hundred dollar bills (an impressive sum of money in the early forties) to uphold her belief that everyone has his price.

As much as I loved Donda, I disliked Jane. However, she did have two things in common with Donda: She loved her only son as much as Donda loved all her many children, and both women had chosen to make their ways without the help of a man, no small accomplishment in the early part of the twentieth century.

Each woman was unique, but they were also part of an intricate design called family. The wonder is whether these designs take shape much like crystals are formed – according to a predestined pattern, or whether we should believe that we shape them ourselves.

To tell a tale, so many years later, about two people whose fates ran together, one sees the whole of the matter. The two families were like intertwining vines, their individual parts climbing and developing such as do all things in nature. There were those segments which were the stems, furnishing the sap for further growth, and those segments which were doomed to shrivel, overshadowed by other, more hardy branches. Love was the nourishing factor, and the American concept of freedom for the individual was the force that made the vigorous growth unpredictable.

One cannot see one's own part in the design of things, but if one looks at the rest, it is clear that as long as the trunk is kept intact, and the stems and tendrils are allowed to develop, each part contributes to the ultimate result. Nothing is wasted, for all of it serves to form a magnificent complexity, as exciting as any work of art. I'll start my narration with Jane, an especially hardy stalk in this unpruned vine.

This is to my children and grandchildren, whom my parents, Vivian and Mickey Owen, never got to see.

Jane

Jane's family traveled west in a covered wagon. People were moving westward by the thousands, and their numbers were swallowed up in the vastness of the land. There were many types who drifted west. Some were younger sons from families with too many mouths to feed, men who had left farmlands that spread along the Atlantic seaboard. Others went west after the upheavals of the Civil War – men with gaunt faces and meager possessions who had everything to win and precious little to lose.

Some men were spurred on because they were dreamers or adventurers, or because they had made a mess of their lives back where they had started. It was usually the men who decided to hit the trail. The women who followed them grew strong, if they endured, by coping with unaccustomed hardships and giving birth in desolate regions, far away from helpful mothers and sisters.

Certain individuals are restless by nature and others content to stay put. In Jane's family, the restlessness seems to have been an inborn trait, for it didn't rise from need. Her grandfather was a prosperous merchant in Indiana, but his five sons spread in all directions, following an urge to seek their own fortunes. Jane's father, William Dunaway, was the only son who went west, in search of "wood and water," the two things he claimed were needed for farming or ranching.

Jane's mother, Margaret, was half Cherokee Indian. Her grandparents had been driven from their rich farmlands, along with the Cherokees from Georgia, North and South Carolina, and Tennessee, to the bleak stretches carved out for them in Indian Territory, in Oklahoma. Thousands had died on the way, and those who survived never put down deep roots in the alien land.

There was nothing gentle in William's face, and the placid expression on Margaret's face leads one to believe that she was resigned to taking him for what he was. Margaret's own mother, born with the cruel legacy of the displaced, had learned not to make demands on her purebred American-Indian parents. Robbed of the richness of the Cherokee culture, they lived out their lifetimes like people whose souls had already departed this earth. Their daughter married a white man to escape the hopelessness of her people, and, now, Margaret, too, was married to a white man, uncomplainingly following him in his pursuit of a white man's dream.

Jane was born in 1885, in Forestberg, Texas, the first of six children. Two more girls, Flossie and Ella, had been born by 1889, when word got out that there was going to be a land rush in Oklahoma. Three million acres were thrown open to homesteading. (Ironically, they were acres taken from the land promised to Indians – the land that had been given to Jane's mother's Cherokee grandparents.) When the start gun was fired, fifty thousand people stampeded for a parcel of that land.

William decided to try his luck, because he was running out of wood where they were; however, by the time they had packed their belongings into their covered wagon and crossed the Red River, the race was already over. The Dunaways arrived two days too late. Fortunately, there were those who had been more eager than wise, and William soon found someone willing to trade his plot of land for a cow.

When the excitement of the race was over, William was still left with the nagging feeling that there was something better somewhere farther along the trail. In fact, it was never long before he began to feel fenced in or heard rumors of a place with better water and wood.

Three more children were born in Oklahoma. Each new birth meant one more mouth to feed, and their fortunes continued to decline, as William discovered that people in the same boat as he was got there first and took the best land.

Over the years, Jane saw the smooth skin on her mother's face turned to leather by the desert sun and the dry prairie winds, but Jane herself grew up loving the plains and deserts, despite all hardships. She had the look of the west, her green eyes deep-set, shaped by looking at wide-open spaces across great distances, into the glare of the sun and the bite of the wind. She loved those lands for the feeling of freedom one gets from empty plains and bare mountains. The West was where all men felt equal, and an attractive woman enjoyed the status of being a scarcity. It was a breeding place for free spirits and rough ways, and five of the children of this wandering man turned out head-strong and resourceful. Only the baby of the family, Joy, was gentle, because she grew up in the shelter of her sibling flock.

Jane's character was formed while watching her father grasp the reins that held the family's destiny and obstinately drive them on, showing no concern for her mother's comfort. While her mother possessed the stoicism of the half-breed, Jane inherited the white man's urge to mold his environment into something he could control. She started to make plans for her future, and she vowed to herself that no man would tell her what to do.

Things started looking up when William got a job as Marshal of Potawatami County, Oklahoma. However, the story goes that enforcing the law didn't interfere with seducing other men's wives, and he died of a heart attack while riding across a pasture, heading for the cool shade with a willing woman. (Considering that William's own father had remarried when he was seventy-nine, one tends to give credence to this rumor.)

After his death, William's family ended up as mere sharecroppers in Holdenville, Oklahoma, doing grueling work without the rewards that come from ownership. Jane hated the backbreaking labor and hated the way sharecroppers were treated by those who owned the land. Being the eldest, she felt the full responsibility of their fate. She was determined that she would make a different future for herself, and she fed her ambition with plans for self-improvement. There was instilled in her a burning desire to be free and yet avoid the mistakes her father made by being a rambling man. The answer to getting ahead in the world was not just being able to grab what you wanted, but to be able to hold on to it. Owning property was the key to controlling one's destiny, she decided.

As soon as Jane and her equally attractive sister, Flossie, could fend for themselves, their mother took the youngest children and moved to Canon City, Colorado, where she had family, and she showed her preferences by staying put the rest of her days.

In the early 1900's, a woman's only chance for honest employment, other than domestic work, was to be a teacher, a nurse, or a secretary. Jane's father's wanderlust prevented her getting any more than the most rudimentary education. Still, as an adult, she proved able to make her way in a man's world, showing them up at their own games. Letters she wrote illustrate her sound business acumen. Type-written, they are tangible evidence that she continued to set goals and seek skills that would give her an advantage in rising above the more predictable fates of a woman on her own.

Eventually, she married a good-natured cowboy, named Ed Owen, but his was a life of following the herds. When Ed was home, her sharp tongue drove him out of the house, and there were plenty of pretty women who were willing to cheer him up. The marriage didn't last, but being alone seemed to have suited Jane fine. She had fallen for Ed's looks, but she had no patience with his lack of ambition, and she was astute enough to see there would be no great future if they stayed together.

The only tangible result of their short-lived union was a baby boy, born in 1908, and she had to raise him on her own. She named her son Vincent Voyne, setting him apart from the other rough and tumble Okies. He was a winning child, handsome and bright, with a sunny disposition, and the name didn't stick. Later, when his blonde hair had turned dark, and his blue eyes danced with mischief, he was nicknamed Mickey, as in the term, 'an Irish Mick,' a name that suited him well.

Lost in the recesses of family memory is knowledge about a second brief marriage to someone who took her to Florida where Mickey spent part of his childhood. This mysterious marriage to a man named Jones might have given Jane a start in making a fortune, but, later, she proved on her own that she didn't need men to assure her continued success. She learned to drive a hard bargain in business deals, just like a man, but she also used her female attributes to her advantage. She had dimples in her cheeks, hair that fell naturally into soft curls, and coquettish Southern charm.

Life as a sharecropper had made her tough, and she knew how people could take advantage of you as soon as they saw a chink in your armor. Therefore, she usually had a male associate somewhere in the background, just to be on the safe side if the going got rough, but she chose men she could steer.

She made it her policy to buy property with a possibility for rentals, thus insuring a steady income, enough to be well-dressed and to see that there was nothing material lacking in her son's life. Some relatives said it wasn't good for a boy to be raised by an indulgent mother, but they couldn't help but like Mickey and figured he wasn't to blame for his mother's fancy notions. If they expected him to be spoiled, his ready smile and candid blue eyes soon disarmed them. He brought a spark of life to the dullest company, for he had a God-given capacity for fun. He loved the many places he and his mother lived and all the people they met, as she restlessly pulled up stakes, letting her good nose for opportunity lead her to new pastures.

Through the nomad existence Mickey led with his mother, he tasted life in many exotic settings. It was a childhood that prepared him well for the bizarre experiences awaiting him in his future.

Like so many single mothers, she talked to her son far more than a boy is willing to listen, reasoning with him, when a firm hand from a role model might have been more effective. Even as a small boy he could give the appearance of listening intently while his thoughts were elsewhere and of evading her ambitious programs for his own improvement. He also learned to rely on her bailing him out when the chips were down. She could have a vile temper and was stern and judgmental, but she adored her only child and was blind to his faults.

In America the dream of success was a religion, and Jane was a devoted disciple. Everything she learned was remembered, and she acquired a degree of polish one would not have imagined possible for a woman of her background. She felt strongly that she was destined to succeed, and her idea of success was a grand one – one that would stretch into the future through her son and his offspring.

While Jane worked hard to provide the framework for Mickey's development into a great man, her very strength made it possible for him to be easy-going. He himself was ambitious, but he was too fun loving and had enjoyed too much comfort while growing up to possess the sort of drive characteristic for Jane and her siblings. Rather than developing the traits necessary for pursuing success, he learned to think of himself as someone belonging to a breed born to succeed. It should be something that fell into his lap, simply because he was qualified.

He would never fully appreciate the effort it took for Jane to lift herself out of the strata where her rambling father and passive mother had landed her. Only her siblings could appreciate and understand the amount of energy it took to climb a steep mountain in search of a place in the sun. Once she was there, Jane looked down on much of the rest of the world and judged them to be inferior. Mickey, on the other hand, liked everyone, and everyone liked him. This amiability would have been an asset in a more settled life if balanced by a firm upbringing, but it was the seed to a mercurial character in the sort of floating existence he had with his doting mother.

The self-assurance Mickey acquired, thanks to Jane's aspirations, put him in touch with people whose immediate forefathers didn't have to struggle to earn the money necessary for the next step up on the road to achievement. For Jane, money was the lubricant for the machine she set in motion, something too important to be taken for granted. For Mickey, it was a commodity he had never been without.

Mickey inherited the generous nature of the father he hadn't known, and he liked nothing better than to please. At an early age, he became aware of the favorable effect he had on those around him, and like an actor, he was stimulated by giving others pleasure. When he was a small boy, the most important person to please was his mother, and it became a habit to exaggerate the good things Jane liked to hear. She adored him, and he basked in her love and approval. A critical assessment of Mickey's character could have warned her that he was likely to become a con artist.

Jane's independent spirit endowed him with an innate disrespect for authority, but she soon discovered that his own independence led him in different directions than those she had planned for him. He had an artist's eye for what he considered important in life. Moreover, her unflagging ambition kept her busy and left him with a good deal of space to pursue the many pleasures that fill a boy's world.

In order to please her and still have the freedom to explore a fascinating mixture of people, he perfected the art of telling white lies. Mickey had a lively imagination anyway, and to invent a tall tale became second nature to him, sparing him the hassle of listening to a tiresome harangue if she learned that he was hanging about with 'trash' or not living up to the standards she was striving to achieve for him.

Learning came easily to him, and it was tempting to coast on talent, rather than diligently shape an assignment. Typical was an episode when a favorite grammar school teacher praised him for his homework but said that he should work harder. "You are clever enough that you should have had an 'A' for this assignment, rather than the 'B' I'm obliged to give you, Vincent," she said with a smile of encouragement. "I can see clearly that you didn't spend much time writing this paper."

Mickey walked home from school, carrying his school books in a leather strap, running a stick along a picket fence and stopping up to watch a gull glide against a clear blue sky. In this general state of well being, the teacher's backhanded praise took wing and turned into a vision. Arriving home and seeing his mother, he wanted to draw her into this happy mood and see her smile.

She looked up when she heard the front door slam shut and saw him toss his schoolbooks onto the hallway table. She smiled with pleasure when she saw him standing in the doorway, an adorable boy with earnest blue eyes. She had no truck for people who addressed children in a manner unlike they would an adult, and she sounded very serious when she asked Mickey about his day at school.

His face lit up when he told her that his teacher had said his paper was the best one turned in. He watched for the desired effect, and, seeing her smile, he embroidered even more on the truth and added, "She gave me an A!"

Jane beamed with pride and but told him she wasn't surprised. "The rest of those children can't hold a candle to you, and I expect you to do well." She turned her attention back to a financial plan she was making and didn't object at all when he ran outside to play, claiming he had no homework.

Although Jane wouldn't impress one as being warm, she was intensely loyal to the many near and distant relatives who were fanned out in most of the states west of the Mississippi. She liked to take Mickey with her to visit these diamonds in the rough, all of them fiercely independent no matter what status they had in society. Loving them taught Mickey to be tolerant of all sorts of people and to be aware of those special qualities that a man at the bottom of the social ladder could have. He was too much a hedonist to have ambitions as a reformer, but he would always be aware of social injustice and the struggles of those whose background he shared.

Despite his truly democratic nature, the pleasure of the status he enjoyed as the son of a woman of means was in no way wasted on him. When he was still quite young, Jane started sending him on errands, believing that to be a good part of his development. He liked the special treatment he received from the haberdasher or the owner of the general store when he called for something his mother had ordered. He liked the feeling he got when he said, "Put it on the bill," and could leave without the inconvenience of paying money and receiving change. His friends were invariably impressed.

Jane's intentions were good, but what she succeeded in doing was to ingrain in him the habit of 'putting things on the bill', with payment being a vague transaction taken care of sometime in the future.

Things Mickey later said about his childhood remain, like splashes of color on an abstract canvas. He told of gathering alligator eggs in Florida's swamps, to be sold as small, newly hatched pets. He also gave a spine-tingling description of surviving a hurricane, having found refuge during the aftermath of floods, on the hood of a car in which lay two young ladies who were stone dead.

In 1923, when Mickey was fifteen, he and Jane suddenly showed up at her mother's place in Colorado and settled down for a few years. Times were hard for workers and farmers, but Jane was driving a swanky Hutmobile, the first car owned by anyone in the family.

Mickey finished high school in Colorado, and, besides being popular, he demonstrated a great talent for always being the center of attention. "Don't try to outshine the sun. It was here first," was the advice affectionately given him in the school yearbook. He was remembered as always being in the limelight and with such a winning personality that his peers found his popularity to be well deserved. Everyone expected him to go far in whatever he chose to do.

He went to college in Florida, where he developed a feeling for the winds of history, a taste for good literature, and an insatiable thirst for knowledge in all fields. All of it pleased him, but he didn't pin himself down to just one single endeavor. His zest for life didn't leave him time to go into depth. It appeared that the world was his oyster, and with irrepressible good spirits he explored all aspects of pleasure. He read voraciously, feeding his imagination with dreams beyond the usual American ideals. Egged on by his mother's great expectations, he grew up confident that he was capable of any future he could imagine.

Jane was no fool and gradually became aware of a certain weakness in his character, a lack of a sense of responsibility, but she was also captivated by his quick wit and was ever ready to make excuses for his frivolous behavior. She liked to blame his many youthful escapades on the company he kept, refusing to believe that he himself had an irresponsible streak.

She was in California when Mickey finished college. Her younger sister, Ella, was terminally ill, and Jane and Flossie moved in with her to nurse her. Ella lived in the town of Hawthorne where their brother, Jordan, had opened the latest in a string of funeral parlors that stretched from Los Angeles to this one-horse town, where he could find the space that everyone in the family seemed to yearn for.

It was the first time in years that Flossie and Jane were stationery enough to take stock of the family's fortunes, and they were pleased to see how well Jordan had done for himself. It was by chance that he ended up in undertaking, but they could see that was a sure-fire way for a man to make money, no matter how other things were going. He was tall and handsome, with a grave demeanor, the sort of man who made a bereaved person feel good. He hadn't hit thirty, but he was already a pillar of the community.

Mickey blew into town, bursting with energy and full of self-confidence, shaking the harmony in Jordan's sphere. Jane had plans for Mickey to go to law school, but once he got to Hawthorne, he sweet-talked her into letting him get a job in Hollywood while he pondered his future. He was intoxicated with the possibilities the world presented and couldn't wait to taste life away from the restrictions of an institution of learning.

Hollywood, the new film capitol and the playground of the West, sounded like something right up his alley. He had met a pretty co-ed back in Florida, and she dreamed of trying to get into pictures. Maybe that would be something for him, too, he thought. Wisely, he didn't mention any of this to his mother as she argued that he should continue his studies.

Flossie witnessed the discussion with detached amusement. The gadfly of the family, she was between divorces and could well understand Mickey's desire to kick up his heels. She liked her young nephew and thought it would do him good to get a first-hand look at 'sin city.' Jane was coddling him, and Flossie wholeheartedly supported the idea of Mickey trying his fortunes on his own. Playfully, she put in her two bits, saying, "Let him give it a shot, Jane. Mickey could always work for Jordan if all else failed."

Mickey shot a mock look of reproach at Flossie. Jordan's sense of self-importance rendered him oblivious to the comic element in a man named 'Dunaway' making a fortune as a mortician, but his disrespectful nephew had a hard time keeping a straight face whenever Jordan's business was mentioned. Right now, Mickey knew he had to appease his mother, however, and he chose to brush past Flossie's remark.

With blithe self-assurance, he said, "I'm sure there must be some sort of work for a college graduate. I can always go to law school later on. Or I might prefer to study medicine. At any rate, it wouldn't be so bad if I got a job and paid my own way through graduate school."

Jane gave it some thought. During these years of the Great Depression, nothing seemed like a cut-and-dried formula for doing well. At any rate, she had to put her own plans on a back burner while she devoted herself to nursing her sister, Ella.. It might be just as well if he discovered what it's like to fend for himself, she mused. Right now, her biggest fear was that some pretty young thing would turn his head before he was ready for it, and on his own, he wouldn't have much money for courting young ladies.

In 1929 America was full of people down and out, but in that vast land there always lingered a feeling of hope, a belief that one's fortune lay on the other side of the hill or across the river. The desperate and the adventurous moved on, and the resolute knew how to dig in their heels and exploit that which was closest at hand. Hollywood was a world of its own, the land of make-believe. Sure, there was unemployment like everywhere else, but there was also a buzz of excitement, even for those on the fringes of the movie industry. During hard times, the business of making dreams has favorable conditions.

As for Jordan, he had always taken a critical view of this cocky nephew. One look at Jane's handsome son, with merriment written all over his face, and he knew he wouldn't be able to use him out front in the funeral parlor. Not only that, he could not afford to have his own reputation jeopardized by any shenanigans done by his nephew, and Mickey had been with them no more than a few days when he seemed to know everyone in town. Jordan was actually relieved when Mickey confided in him that he was going to Hollywood and try his luck. Things seemed so much more peaceful when he was alone with his sisters, basking in their admiration.

"Well, don't get your hopes too high. You'll soon find out how hard it is to get a job. You can come back here if you want to, and I'll put you to work in the back."

Mickey knew what that involved, and he would any day prefer the smell of perfume in Hollywood to the smell of formaldehyde in one of Dunaway's stiffs.

* * * * *

Hollywood – 1929

Mickey checked into a boarding house in Los Angeles and went out to a 'greasy spoon' to grab a bite to eat. As soon as he arrived in Hollywood, he noticed a prevalence of pretty faces, and the waitress behind the counter was a cute little thing with honey-blonde curls, big blue eyes, and dimples in her cheeks. Things were quiet in the diner, and Mickey flirted with her to pass the time of day. When he told her he was looking for work, she seemed to study him before she said anything.

"What are you lookin' for?" she asked, as she gave the counter a perfunctory wipe with a damp cloth. "You're not planning to be a movie star, are you?" she said, teasingly.

"No, of course not," he insisted, as if the thought had never occurred to him. "I'm a writer. It doesn't matter what I do. Everything counts for experience."

This caught her interest, and she looked him over with a bit more respect. She was used to good-looking guys coming in and chatting her up, but this one wasn't run of the mill.

She bit her lower lip and gave it some thought. Mickey noticed how smooth the skin was on her cheek. "Maybe you could think about it, and I could come back later and walk you home," he said, putting a generous tip on the counter. An evening with her would be better than sitting around the boarding house with a bunch of old crows, he thought.

"Hey!" she said, as he approached the door, "I'm off in ten minutes. Wait around, and you can follow me home and meet my brother, Gus. He might be able to help you out."

She chatted amiably with Mickey as they walked along straight streets with monotonously similar bungalows and small front lawns. Her name was Sally, and while she was working in the diner she hoped some talent scout would discover her.

She lived with her family in a neat, shingled house on Alameda Avenue. It had been a hot day, and her brother, Gus, was sitting in the shade of a porch that ran the length of the front of the house. He stood up when he saw his sister coming up the walk with a stranger and looked at Mickey with curiosity. Gus was a big, burly guy, but he had a nice smile and looked like he wouldn't hurt a fly.

Sally introduced Mickey to her brother, and when they shook hands, Mickey's disappeared in the big grasp of Gus' paw. Clearly, Gus had used his hands for hard work, but now he was happy to be an ambulance driver. As luck would have it, one of the other drivers had just been fired, and he told Mickey they needed an experienced driver right away.

"Hey, that's me!" said Mickey, enthusiastically. He had been driving his mother's cars since he was big enough to reach the pedals. He drove effortlessly, and he loved speed. He and Gus hit it off right away, shared a few beers, and arranged to meet the next day at the hospital.

Mickey had no trouble being hired. Just to make a good impression, he told them that he wanted to study medicine and thought a stint as an ambulance driver would be good experience. He started work right away, and the newness of the work made it exciting.

"Actually, maybe I should be a doctor," he thought. That was one of the options Jane was in a habit of considering when she talked about his future. The notion of him curing some rich old dowager who would gratefully pair him off with her beautiful daughter flashed through his ever active fantasy, like a bright penny tossed into a wishing well.

In Los Angeles in those days, most people died at home, and those who were taken to hospitals were usually in pretty bad shape. He soon discovered that an ambulance driver saw life inside out. He learned to judge how much chance he had of getting a patient to the hospital before he or she died, and he learned to drive like a bat out of hell when he thought there was a chance of saving someone. He became accustomed to seeing real suffering and seeing the anguish of the patient's family who had to stay behind and watch the ambulance drive away. Most people regarded hospitals as a point of no return, and worry was written all over their faces.

He and Gus often worked together, and Gus liked him for his cheerful kidding. However, he noticed that even though Mickey seemed to take everything as one big joke, he had a way of making people feel good when they needed a kind word, and he had a sixth sense for what to do until they could get to a doctor. More than once he saved a person's life by prompt action when they got to the scene of an accident.

One night they were called to the site of a car wreck in Pasadena. An open coupe had collided with a palm tree on a quiet street where the wealthy had their spacious homes. A young lady lay unconscious on the parkway. She was like an expensive trinket, tossed carelessly aside, her beaded chiffon dress glittering in the streetlight. A man in a tuxedo crouched alongside her, nervously dragging on a cigarette. He was slightly bald and wore a chunky ring with a large diamond on his pinkie finger. A couple of policemen stood by their squad car, strangely passive, like they were waiting for orders.

The balding man stood up and started to babble a lot of information when Gus and Mickey jumped out of the ambulance. He had been sobered by the accident, but he reeked of booze. Mickey pushed him aside and kneeled down beside the girl, feeling her pulse. They gently lifted her unto a stretcher, Mickey putting a hand under her head to be sure her neck remained straight. Her blonde hair was like silk, as soft as a child's, but it was matted with blood on one side. "She has a nasty cut on her head, but it doesn't look too deep," Mickey said to Gus, ignoring the man who had looked like he was afraid to get his dress shirt stained.

Before they drove off, the man gave Mickey his card, saying, "Look buddy, I won't be able to come by and check on her, if you know what I mean. The officers there and I have decided to keep this thing quiet. But she's a good kid. I'll make it worth your while if you'll make sure she's treated well and give me a call tomorrow."

Mickey took a close look at him. What a bastard, he thought. Probably cheating on the old lady. Out loud, he said, "Sure, we'll take good care of her."

Gus was disgusted. "You see that sort of thing all the time in this town. A pretty girl mixed up with some old geezer, hoping he'll make her a movie star. I'll bet that was one of the big wigs from the studios."

Mickey got out the card when they had wheeled the girl into emergency, and Gus was right. Scott Wilson, Fox Studios. Seemed to ring a bell. Maybe this would be a good chance to get a foot in the door, Mickey thought.

The next day, he checked on the girl first thing in the morning. She was going to be all right, but she would have to stay in the hospital a few days. Mickey asked if there was anyone she wanted him to notify. "Do you have any family here?"

She shook her head, but looked at him hopefully. "How's Mr. Wilson? He was driving. Is he okay?"

Mickey assured her that the driver hadn't been hurt and wondered what she felt about him not being by her side. "Yeah. He said we should be sure that you get good care, and asked me to let him know how you are."

She knew then that he wouldn't be coming around to see her. They were all alike, these Hollywood tycoons – Promise the world and turn their backs on you as soon as there is any trouble. Thank God her face hadn't been messed up. Maybe she should go back home and get married to her high school flame.

Mickey watched her face and could read her thoughts. "Cheer up. I don't think he'll be coming to see you, but he's picking up the tab, and it looked like he would be full of gratitude if you keep quiet about him being drunk when he ploughed into that tree, if you get my drift."

She gave Mickey a weak smile and said, "You can make use of that information if you want. I think I've been cured of Hollywood dreams. It's time I go back to Kansas and settle down. I'm lucky I've just ruined my stockings and a twenty-dollar dress. A few more hours with that guy and I wouldn't have much to call my own."

Mickey decided not to call Wilson, but to drop in on him the next day, before he started his shift. He dressed carefully, putting on a suit that would make it clear he was no ordinary ambulance driver. When he got to the gate at Fox, he showed Wilson's card to the guard and was pointed in the direction of the building where the top executives had their offices.

Once inside the door, he was confident it would be easy to capture Mr. Wilson's interest. A secretary knocked on Scott Wilson's door, and Mickey walked into an office that reflected the man's importance.

Whether it was because of a bad conscience or because Mickey made a good impression, Wilson welcomed him cordially, and Mickey took an unprejudiced look at him. He wasn't all that bad a guy, Mickey decided. If you tried to understand things from both points of view, you could see what a temptation it was for some of these hot shots to score with the many young hopefuls who were throwing themselves on the mercy of Hollywood.

While Mickey reported on the condition of the young lady who was injured, Wilson tried to size up the situation, wondering what the price might be for this little affair being kept under wraps.

Mickey sensed that Wilson was studying him and took advantage of this shift in attention to change the subject. "This is the first time I've been on studio property, Mr. Wilson. This must be about the most dynamic business in the world right now. What are the chances of a person getting a job out here?"

"Well, that depends on what you're good at or what you want." He paused, like a poker player trying to guess the other player's hand and let Mickey do the talking. It was with a feeling of relief that he heard Mickey say he wanted badly to work where movies are made and was willing to start at any sort of job.

There were a dozen people pounding on the door each day, looking for a job, but there was something about Mickey that made Wilson think he would be useful. In any case, it was a modest price for keeping him quiet.

"I'll tell you what. I know you're a college kid and probably ambitious as hell, but I'll give you work if you're willing to start at the bottom and show what you're worth. You've got a job if you show up tomorrow at the gate and tell Joe that you're the new messenger boy. Report to John MacMahoney, and he'll tell you what to do."

Mickey thought for a second, knowing it wouldn't sound too good if he told Jane he was just a messenger boy. But what the hell, there were plenty of people who were big shots who started out sweeping floors. It would put him where he could be noticed, and he could drive ambulances at night, to make extra money. Without further hesitation, he said, "Thanks a lot Mr. Wilson. That's great. What time should I be here?"

That first week on work was enough to get Mickey hooked on the atmosphere. His new boss, John MacMahoney was an all 'round nice guy. His associates called him Mac, and he told Mickey to do the same. He made sure Mickey had plenty to do so he would have a good chance of staying on.

Being around the sets was addictive. On the very first day, he was asked to deliver a message to Jean Harlow. When he knocked on her door, she called out in an off-hand manner for him to come on in.

She was sitting at her dressing table, leaning forward to look in the large mirror as she removed makeup from her flawless skin. Her blonde hair was pale as a halo, and her skin had the healthy glow of natural beauty. When Mickey stepped closer, she looked at him with a tantalizing look, and, for once, he was tongue-tied. Aware of the effect she was having, she smiled, amused, and reached out a hand to take the message. She was stark naked.

The studio stars of the thirties were of a special breed. To all appearances, the make-believe atmosphere that enveloped them like a lustrous bubble served to protect them from the ugliness of real life. In those more naive days, it was possible to create and maintain an illusion, and even those who weren't stars could be caught up in the effect of the illusion. It suited Mickey well, with his imagination and his flair for stepping into any role that matched the scene.

He became accustomed to seeing in life-size the people who loomed on the silver screen, and he loved the pool of talent that surrounded these stars: The musicians, the chorus girls, the writers, and the clever technicians. They were like a wonderful bunch of whiz kids, being kept in line by the cool-headed businessmen who saw movies only as a commercial product.

On the surface, the place was oozing with glamour. People in costumes and celebrities were everywhere. William Fox had taken the big step and embraced talkies, and the challenges were enormous. The poetic, sketchy scripts of the silent screen had to be replaced with scripts written like plays, with dialogue and special effects and music. A good many of the scriptwriters for the silent movies were women, but now teams were put together composed mostly of men who were used to writing for the stage.

There was plenty of room for quick-thinking, innovative people who could solve the problems that cropped up when sound was added to photography. For example, if a woman wearing silk stockings crossed her legs on set, the microphones picked it up like the sound of a cyclone, and the scene had to be done over again. In the search for a place to make talkies without the distracting sounds of the real world, the desert became a popular place to shoot movies. There the crews didn't have to worry about traffic sounds, but work outside the studios also meant a bigger crew to do everything, from moving all the necessary equipment to furnishing meals.

Another problem was the whirring noise of the cameras, and in the beginning that was eliminated by putting the cameraman in a padded, airtight box. Obviously this had its disadvantages. When the temperatures rose on the desert, the cameraman in his padded box roasted. At one desert session, the cameraman passed out, and the crew discovered that the temperature in his box was 150 degrees Fahrenheit.

Of course, not all scripts were suited to a desert shoot, and soundproof stages had to be improvised, with mattresses wired to the walls.

Then there were the sounds that were desirable. With considerable ingenuity, techniques were discovered to produce the sounds called for by the manuscript: Halved coconut shells pounded on a pad to imitate horse hooves, sheet metal to make the sound of thunder, cardboard ripping to sound like the collapse of a building.

When Hollywood embraced the new concept of sound, it was no longer enough for a star to have the right face and gestures. A good speaking voice was pre-requisite, and the actors and actresses imported from Broadway lent an extra dimension of worldliness to the untamed Hollywood scene.

Mickey was intrigued with it all, and he couldn't have arrived on the scene at a better time. He wasn't burdened with the prejudices the old school of filmmakers had, like those who thought of talkies as a passing fad, something inartistic and destructive. They lamented the fact that so many stars of the silent screen had to be discarded because of the transition and resented the new type of talent that was being imported from Broadway.

There were many other changes. As is always the case with change, something new swept out most of what had been established, but one man's loss was another man's gain. All over America, musicians who had earned a living in cinema theaters, providing live music for the silent screen, were fired, as theaters were wired for sound. These performing artists joined the ranks of unemployed, while business ventures providing sound equipment flourished. Mickey was a man of the times, quick to laud the latest development. Like with most transitions, there would be a constant stream of new inventions and new opportunities to make money. He loved the dynamics of it all, the repercussions of a whole new chapter being written in the history of America.

He thrived in this world of fantasy, making himself available all over the place, and soon he knew every Tom, Dick and Harry, both the big shots and the small folks at Fox. Mac had kept an eye on his protégé and was aware of Mickey's popularity. Not only did everyone like him, he was sharp as a tack.

An avid reader, Mickey kept up with publications about what was current on live stage. He knew everything anyone needed to know about who was starring on Broadway, and who was writing the plays. Fox was turning out movies at a rate that called for constant expansion, and clearly, Mickey could be useful. He'd be a natural as casting director, Mac thought.

* * * * *

Mickey sat at Mac's smooth, mahogany desk and leaned back comfortably in the leather chair. I wouldn't mind having a set-up like this, he told himself, as his eyes swept over the wall of autographed photos of film stars.

Kate, the secretary who had ushered him into MacMahoney's office popped her head in the doorway and said, "Here he comes, Mickey," shaking her head affectionately when she saw what cheek he had. He jumped nimbly to his feet and flashed her a grateful smile, moving away from the desk to stand at a respectful distance.

"Well, at least you look respectable," she added, taking in his well-groomed appearance, from the spiffy shoes to the starched shirt and bow tie. For a moment she looked into his incredibly blue eyes and longed to run her fingers through his dark wavy hair, like she had the night before. Instead, she blushed and quickly stepped aside just as John MacMahoney made his entrance.

He had decided to call Mickey into his office and offer him an assignment as casting director for a western that had to be put together in record time. "I've got Rex Harrison lined up, but can you get hold of the rest of the cast? I want them ready to start shooting by the beginning of next week."

Mickey was elated. Now he could tell his mother he was casting director. That ought to satisfy her. He could quit his job as ambulance driver. From now on the sky's the limit, he thought happily.

The assignments followed fast and thick. Mickey loved his job, and parties were an important part of the routine. It was there one made the contacts necessary to fill roles, and before long, he was on first name basis with some of the hottest talent in Hollywood. With all its eccentricities, social life in Hollywood was a colorful and exhilarating scene, and Mickey took to it like a duck to water.

To feed Mickey's dreams, there were tales of success all around him. He saw some of his friends become big stars fast and got to know others who were already famous when they were imported from the East Coast. He saw that people with relatively little talent could be turned into celebrities overnight, with the right type of publicity. Everything seemed possible, and it was easy to forget the fact that there were masses of unemployed adults and hungry children throughout America.

Not long after he got his job as casting director, Jane's sister Ellen, died, and Jane announced that she would join Mickey in Hollywood. In those days it was taken for granted that a son took care of his mother if she was alone, and, although Jane could take care of herself, she doubted that Mickey could. Besides, she liked to feel needed. Flossie certainly didn't need her – She left Hawthorne as soon as the funeral was over and was gallivanting about, staying at nudist colonies and dating a handsome man who claimed to be an Indian chief.

Jane knew enough about the type of life Mickey was leading in Hollywood to worry about how he would handle his success, and she decided that if he was going to make something out of such a good start, he needed a stable home base. The first step would be to buy a house for them. She wanted something pretentious enough to further his career, but sensible enough to be a good investment. Money was no hindrance. Jane had never trusted the boom in the stock market. Her investments were always in property, the one thing she had a gut feeling for, and she had little sympathy for all the fools who had lost their shirts on stocks the day the bubble burst. The way things were during this depression, she thought, a piece of property would be Mickey's best insurance for the future.

She found a four-bedroom house near Van Nuys and busied herself furnishing it. Because he was so laid-back, Mickey easily fell into line when she showed up to take over his life – He was out on the town too much to pay much attention to where he lived. He easily resumed the old pattern of letting her take care of their finances. Making a budget didn't really interest him. Besides, although he was making good money, he was usually short of cash by the end of the week. Money was never a problem when Jane was around, but he didn't analyze the whys and wherefores. With his earnings added to her accumulation of capital, they had a comfortable life with nice clothes. If he was short on cash once in awhile, he could always count on her to tide him over.

Not only was it common practice for a son to support his mother, other family members also looked to the one who had struck it lucky, hoping for a helping hand during hard times. Mickey's cousin, Jack Dunaway, came to California to seek his fortune and was driving busses for a measly forty cents an hour when Mickey gave him a job in the movies. Fox Studios needed cowboys for the Westerns they were cranking out regularly, and Mickey asked Jack whether he was still good on horseback. Jack said yes, and from then on, he was part of a twelve-man team who played in nearly every western made by Fox. At seventy dollars a week, he earned more in one day than he could during an entire week of driving a bus.

When Mickey did the casting job for "The Fall of Pompeii," he needed chariot drivers and thought of Flossie. Taller than average and a skilled horsewoman, she was garbed out as an Amazon and raced a chariot in one memorable scene. (He also got her a part in 'Warrior's Husband', but there she caused a problem by upstaging the star, who insisted she be taken off the set.)

In the 1930's Fox controlled more than 500 theaters in the United States and 450 abroad. They made money even on movies turned out by the competitor. While bread lines grew and families pulled together to try to ride the storm, the relative extravagance of going to the movies offered the main relief in a dismal scene. People wanted to escape for a couple of hours into an imaginary world with fabulously rich sheiks, implausible romances, and predictable westerns.

Movie stars were immensely wealthy, compared to the man in the street, but their excessive lifestyles provided a welcome contrast to the dreary expectations of the unemployed. America was still the land of hope, and, instead of causing resentment, witnessing the over-night fame of a person in movie land was confirmation that dreams could come true.

Jane didn't like Hollywood, but she saw life there as a wonderful opportunity to achieve all the things that she had learned were important during her early years with an uncertain future. With her careful management, she could mold Mickey into the kind of man who would have it all. While he submerged himself in the intoxicating brew of Hollywood, she gloated over his future possibilities.

The years of traveling with Jane and coaching from her had given Mickey enough refinement to make it possible for him to fit into any sort of society. Inspired by those who made a living acting out roles, he easily slipped into a multitude of roles that Hollywood offered off stage. He even subconsciously adjusted his speech to whomever he was addressing. With his superiors, he was the serious young man with the intelligent answers. With workmen or cowpokes, he was the down-to-earth, easily approached regular guy. And with the famous actors who made it in Hollywood because of special talents or a certain charisma, he was the sort of person they could turn to, for understanding and encouragement or for a good night on the town.

He learned that under the surface of many a successful star lurked a deep sense of insecurity, and that their fame seldom gave them the inner calm and happiness that he had encountered in more humble walks of life. He formed an ambition of milking the scene for what he could and retiring early to a paradise of his own making, a dream he shared with Jim Cagney, who became a good friend.

Cagney came out to Hollywood from a successful career on Broadway, and Mickey was impressed with his skilful approach to his work. He had a sincerity and loyalty that wasn't all that common in Hollywood, and he was devoted to the pretty little chorus girl he had married. Seeing how much fun they had, Mickey began to think how nice it would be if he were married, too.

Jane didn't mind when he ran about town with a half a dozen different women, but she wasn't at all happy when he started seeing one particular chorus girl on a regular basis. However, when she tried to question Mickey about the girl, he wasn't very communicative. He just said she was a "heck of a lot of fun."

"Well, it's alright to have fun, sugah, but I hope you find a young lady someday who can be the sort of wife a man can be proud of. Seems to me a whole lot of these gals are just a trifle vulgar."

Mickey knew perfectly well that Dell wasn't the sort of girl his mother had in mind, but he liked her for her honesty. He had seen enough of movie stars and women aspiring to stardom to know that they didn't usually have Dell's down-to-earth, easy-going love for life. Besides, she was a fabulous dancer and had curves all in the right places.

Mickey's work as a casting director furnished a good excuse for being a man about town. He loved a party, and he could always count on Dell to come along as an attractive date. What he especially appreciated about her was that she didn't seem to have a jealous bone in her body. Once they were on the scene, he could feel free to float and establish all the connections he might find useful then or at a later date.

There were wild, zany parties, and the booze flowed freely. With his boundless energy, Mickey was often among those who kept a good session going by moving on to a new party, and Dell was always able to keep up with him.

Jane watched for the small signs that would indicate where the affair was going. When she finally met Dell, she could see this little chorus girl was more serious than Mickey was. Funny how men never seemed to be aware of an attractive woman being more than just superficially interested, she thought. Of course, she knew that was part of the technique of a woman who had something on the ball. The best way to scare a man off was to overtly show one's interest.

Jane tried to warn Mickey, but he laughed and told her that Dell was no more interested in settling down than he was.

Like any young man, Mickey had a healthy urge to get beyond the petting stage with Dell, but like most sensible young ladies, she knew that once she gave in to her own warm desires, there might be hell to pay. Each time they were together, their kisses became more intense, and they were both left gasping for air. Mickey liked to drive his convertible up to Mulhulland Drive before taking Dell home.

He put the top down and pulled her close to him while they both gazed up at a star-studded sky. He had played around plenty and knew just how to make the right moves. Dell was swept along by his smooth approach, but at the last crucial moment, she stopped him, gently but with the hint of a promise. Eventually, Mickey was desperate to get her to bed.

After one particularly memorable evening, a party with the cast and crew to celebrate the final day of filming, Mickey and Dell ended up at the mansion of one of the big stars of the day. The embers of an all-night party were re-kindled with bacon and eggs washed down with screwdrivers and plenty of black coffee.

It was a party that lasted two days, and on the morning of the third day, Mickey woke up in a strange bed with Dell sleeping beside him. He had a vague recollection of all the events that had taken place, but he pushed his thoughts aside and began to nuzzle her ear.

Dell opened her eyes and smiled at him. In a flash, it dawned on Mickey with crystal-clear clarity that they were in a hotel in Las Vegas. They had been hitched the night before. He had a fleeting compunction involving his mother and what she was going to say, but right now, he was more interested in enjoying the moment.

On the drive back to Hollywood, they both agreed that for now it would be best to go on as usual. No one at the studio needed to know they were married just yet, and they would have to figure out what to do about Mickey's mother and Dell's mother, both of whom depended on their offspring.

When Mickey dropped Dell off at the apartment she shared with her widowed mother, he lifted her chin and kissed her on the mouth. Then he smiled and said, "This probably wasn't too smart a move, but we sure had a helluva good time this weekend. I'll be back this evening and we can make some plans." Then he headed on home.

Jane was furious when Mickey told her what had happened. "You can get it annulled. You were too drunk to know what you were doing, going up there with that wild bunch of friends. That woman has wanted to get her claws on you ever since you started taking her out. She's not your kind at all, Mickey."

Mickey defended Dell and said it was his idea to go to Vegas. He was genuinely fond of Dell, and he couldn't see any reason why it couldn't work out. The only problem was that he and his mother had joint ownership of the house. Dell would have to move in with them, and he wondered how that was going to be. But, heck, he was earning good money. He could tell her it would only be until they could find something else.

What he didn't realize was that Jane had taken her precautions. She saw how money went through Mickey's hands like sand in an hourglass. Just in case something unexpected happened, she had been putting money aside for Mickey, but the account was in her name. He would have a hard time if he thinks he can do without me, she thought.

Donda

If life is a stage, the setting for Vivian's life couldn't have been more different than was Mickey's. Looking back, it is odd to think that they ever met. To tell the tale of the events that led up to that meeting involves many players, for in the life of Vivian's mother, Donda, there was a swing door, and through it came a rich cast of characters. Jane's story had her only son as a focal point. Donda had to share her love evenly among seven children and the many people who followed in their wake. She wasn't driven by an ambition similar to Jane's. Her temperament was such that she was destined to take life as it came, using love and laughter to patch up her wounds. However, like Mickey, Vivian's story can only be told with her mother as a catalyst.

Donda was born Martha Morgan, in Joy Prairie, Morgan County, Illinois, in 1877. Her parents died of consumption when she was a small child, and she and her younger twin brothers were raised by their maternal grandmother, a formidable woman who wore a black patch to cover her one blind eye.

Grandmother Smart was a farmwoman, with no illusions about avoiding the hurdles in life. She gained a shrewd wisdom from knowing about the land and domestic animals, those things that made the difference between starvation and prosperity. She also knew that a beautiful girl had good trading value as long as she remained pure, and she guarded over her young charge to make sure she didn't lose her value.

When Donda blossomed into womanhood, Grandmother Smart began to worry about living long enough to secure her grandchild's future. She was a practical woman who had never been distracted by romantic notions, and, without any qualms, she agreed to marry Donda off to a prosperous farmer, named Charles Silcox. He was the oldest of four brothers, and the family had good rich farmlands that could provide well for generations to come. Not only that, Charles' father, James, had bought a mill during the Civil War, thereby increasing his fortune considerably. All his enterprises were enough to keep his four sons employed and provide a relatively genteel life for his daughters.

Donda had just turned sixteen and was blissfully unaware of the facts of life. Charles was thirty-one, a handsome man, but one without social graces. He chose a wife with a farmer's eye; Donda was like a prize filly, strong enough to be useful and attractive enough to show off on Sunday. It hadn't occurred to his innocent young bride that there were choices in life, and she was quite willing to go along with the plans others made for her. Being pretty and capable, she never felt the need to set abstract goals, but lived in the present, content with her lot.

The wedding was in January, when deep snow blanketed the earth, a time of year often favored for such occasions by farmers in those days, for it didn't conflict with working the soil or harvesting. The only pre-nuptial excitement Donda felt was over the pretty dress she was to wear for the occasion. Without any clear idea of what marriage entailed, and having been raised by an old grandmother who kept close tabs on her, she obediently accepted the groom with the respect he otherwise commanded in the community. She had an affectionate nature and liked this nice person she was to marry, but physical love between a man and woman was something she had not contemplated.

For most young country people, courting took place at box socials or dances and on country lanes. If they decided to marry, a chaste snuggling under a blanket (called 'spooning'), within the house of the bride-to-be's parents, was accepted. However, it wasn't Donda's fate to have her senses awakened by such innocent customs.

The house that was to be theirs after the wedding was not yet finished, and Charles took his bride to the house he shared with his parents and two of his brothers. The wedding night was mortifying for the young bride. She was attacked by her husband and startled by the hoots and hollers of his boisterous friends who made a row outside the bedroom window with the traditional "shivaree," a noisy serenade to accompany a bride's initiation into the adult world. Bewildered as she must have been after the humiliation of a wedding night she wasn't prepared for and the embarrassing realization that the men who stood outside in the snow knew what had transpired, she faced those cold winter months without a complaint, assuming that hers must be the fate of all women, and that there was no call for complaining.

Dazed, she felt the silence of the frozen world around her like a wall that had closed her in with strangers. It was an orderly farm, and the hours when there was daylight were filled with the many chores designated as woman's work. Sleep at night was like sleep of the dead. One day followed the next, without idle time to speculate about her fate, and she came to accept that her life had formed itself like she imagined had been the destiny of the generations before her. The years would pass with the cycles of the seasons, the births, and the unavoidable nocturnal struggles with the man in her life.

Nine months after the wedding, a daughter was born. Donda was seventeen a week prior to the birth. She spent the next fourteen years producing babies as a shield against her husband's assaults, for she soon discovered that he was basically a decent man who felt obliged to refrain from his marital rights while she was visibly pregnant or keeping the latest born in their bed to nurse at night. Being ignorant of what one could expect of life, she wasn't unhappy with her lot. She accepted her marriage as the way of life, was pleased with her handsome brood, and grew taller than her husband, with the posture of a woman whose spirit is not broken.

While the confusion she experienced that first year faded and was replaced with the sense of purpose that maternity brings, Charles became the bewildered one. He continued to experience these primal urges to possess her body and the aftermath of guilt for having inflicted himself on her against her will. He persisted, knowing it was his right, but more and more frequently he escaped afterwards, into the oblivion of a drinking bout, trying to numb the longings in his soul for something he couldn't name. He didn't dwell on his own feelings, however, but busied himself with the farm.

Both of them were proud of their offspring…Beulah, the lovely first born who was normal until the age of ten when scarlet fever resulted in encephalitis, leaving her mentally retarded, Albert and Elmo, the handsome brothers, shy Marcia, with the frail looks of an angel, Vivian, whose beauty even then made her stand out, her glowing complexion set off by dark hair and enchanting hazel eyes that turned to green when the light shifted, and Bobbie and Elsie, both irresistibly pretty, with large blue eyes and blonde hair.

One can almost predict the character of a child born into a large family, according to when he or she arrived. Of all Donda's children, Vivian was most blessed. She was the fifth child, born three years after her sister, Marcia – time enough to make her a welcome addition, with siblings old enough to look forward to her arrival. From the very beginning, she was wrapped in their love, making it easy for her to be self-confident and out-going. Without having to try, she became the darling of the family.

Donda's life took on meaning through high standards in her housekeeping, her renown for cooking, and her reputation for keeping her large family well groomed. She sewed all the frocks her girls wore and enjoyed everyone's compliments when she paraded them at church each Sunday. With capable hands she could keep her house spotless, wring the neck of a chicken for dinner, bottle a winter's supply of fruit and vegetables, salt down meat, and feed a dozen extra hired hands. A good sense of humor and a natural compassion for others shaped her character into that of a wise and understanding person and pre-ordained her to a long life of giving and caring. Their farm was in Morgan County, and Donda's father had been a Morgan. Family ties were strong, both in Charles' and Donda's families, and her knowledge of human nature grew as the years passed and her life was interweaved with her near and distant relatives.

Her good looks didn't fade, and Charles encouraged her to buy pretty dresses. She had a gift for dressing well and was tall enough to look grand in the elaborate hats and flattering gowns of the age. Her children were bursting with pride when she made an appearance at their one-room school at the end of the lane.

The teacher, Mr. Haze, was a strict man who paced the room with a hickory stick in his hand when he wasn't sitting behind his desk. Pupils who were punished were expected to place a hand on the upturned palm of the teacher's hand, in order to make the blow sharper when he whacked their hands with the stick. Vivian enjoyed the feeling of security that came with having older siblings close at hand. Once, the teacher singled her out for having talked out of turn. Knowing what to expect, she trembled as she placed her small hand on his. He raised the stick, but as he brought it down to strike her hand, she panicked and pulled it away, with the result that he hit his own hand smartly. Furious, he would have given it another try, but Vivian's brother, Elmo, left his place at the back of the classroom, and hurried to put his arm protectively around Vivian's shoulder.

She looked up at Elmo with a tearful smile, and he said, "Don't worry, Sis. No one is ever gonna hurt you." It was the first time, but far from the last time, that she remembered experiencing the strength of a family.

Charles was a hard-working man, quiet by nature, but his character changed drastically when he went on a bender with his brothers. They made their own cider, let it ferment, and by freezing it in the snow, they got a product called 'jack cider', where the water was frozen off, leaving a concentrate of alcohol. Polishing off a jug of jack cider was a male ritual, and the four brothers would become boisterously happy. However, his occasional bouts of imbibing didn't serve to forge a closer link to the woman who shared his life.

Once, he tangled with a skunk on his way home, and smelled to high heaven. Donda sternly demanded that he stand outside in the snow and remove all his clothing to be burned, and he meekly submitted, accepting the fact the house was her domain. Usually, however, she humored him, helped him to bed, and refrained from chiding him when he woke the next day with a heavy head. She considered his getting drunk to be a male right.

Whether she was drawing water from the well or taking a box lunch out to the field hands, Donda was never too busy to rejoice in the beauty of the land. Not being one to seek a word of comfort in the Bible, she could flush out a dreary mood by looking at a flock of birds throwing themselves like a silk scarf across a windy sky. Often, it was Vivian who dogged her mother's footsteps, and she learned to share this love for nature's beauty.

It was a good life, but, except for sudden accidents or windfalls, it was a predictable one. Then the two youngest of Charles' brothers, Chester and Bill, grew restless and decided to leave farming. They had more book learning than Charles did, and they announced that they were going West, to see what life might have in store for them out there. By now, California was on everyone's lips, and they heard tales of mild weather and trees laden with golden oranges. Soon after they left, their parents followed them to California and bought a grocery store in Upland, leaving the running of the farm entirely to Charles and his brother, Jim.

Donda's children thrived, except for Marcia who was always ill with ear infections. With her gentle ways and fragile looks, she seemed like a will of the wisp with one foot in heaven. During one of her bouts with fever, she saw clearly a vision of Christ, glowing on the green background of the pulled-down shade at the bedroom window. Pleased, she said He smiled and beckoned for her to follow Him. That same year, her face lit up in ecstasy when she saw Halley's comet streak across the sky, and she excitedly asked her mother and father whether it was a sign for her. In a family without strong religious traditions, but with a goodly share of superstitions, such tendencies in a child of theirs only produced a fear that they were going to lose her.

There was precious little one could do in those days when a child took ill. Many were the remedies, but Marcia's earaches were recurrent. Her father even tried blowing pipe smoke into her ear, something that distracted her a bit but proved to be ineffectual. With Marcia's failing health as an excuse, Charles decided he too would move his family to California, convinced that her health would improve in the balmy climate.

The year was 1911, and Vivian was eight years old. She loved the farm, with its hired hands, stock of animals, and the stream and pond that gave her and her brothers and sisters so many happy hours. It was sad to think of leaving everything familiar, but she had learned not to question the wisdom of decisions made by her parents. During the hectic days that followed, she went sadly about, saying goodbye to the animals she loved and lingering at her favorite hiding places. She was young enough to be exempted from the chores that might have made farming less appealing, and old enough to know the pleasure of gathering hen-warm eggs or picking sun-ripe berries.

Donda found her pining out back, where a chicken-wire platform provided nesting space for the turkeys. She loved each of her children equally, but she felt a special bond to Vivian who, right from the beginning, seemed to have inherited Donda's zest for life. Vivian was sitting on an apple crate that had served as a table when the girls played house. Donda lifted her up and sat down with her on her lap.

It was always such a pleasure to look at this child, she thought, admiring the way Vivian's hair curled softly around her face. She took Vivian's tiny hand in hers, and squeezed it gently, knowing instinctively why she needed comforting. "Penny for your thoughts," Donda said kindly.

Vivian snuggled closer to her mother, and when she answered there was a tremble in her voice. "Do we have to leave, Mommy?"

It was a quiet moment amidst the hustle and bustle of the big move, and, through Vivian, Donda was suddenly overwhelmed by the thought of all they would be leaving behind. The very idea of going to California was so tantalizing that she hadn't stopped to think about what she would miss, no matter how much she might come to like their new home. With a feeling of great sadness, she pictured the many faces she might never see again.

For now, however, she had to brush aside this flood of doubt and comfort Vivian. This was not a time for regrets – There was no turning back. She tried to sound bright and cheerful as she told Vivian how wonderful everything would be in California. "We will never have to worry about staying warm for the winter, and Pa will not have to work anymore. We will all be together, and, who knows? Maybe the whole family will come out to join us when they hear how grand things are."

"I wish nothing would ever change," Vivian said wistfully, but then she jumped down from her mother's lap and seemed to have forgotten feeling sad.

"Well, that bit of sadness certainly disappeared quickly!" Donda said, with surprise in her voice.

"I just remembered that I won't have to go back to school and see horrible old Mr. Haze," Vivian said happily.

When the Silcoxes moved to California, they did not have to face the hardships that the Dunaways encountered when they made the trek westward in a covered wagon. Charles and Donda freighted all their worldly possessions by train and settled in nicely in Upland, near his brothers and parents. Unlike William Dunaway, they weren't seeking adventure, but a gentle climate and a farmer's dream of an easy life.

The house they bought was newly built, a large wooden structure, with an orchard and enough land to grow their own vegetables and keep some animals. With careful planning, they knew they would be well off. There was still an income from the farmlands back in Illinois that Charles' younger brother James was managing, and soon their sons would be old enough to find work.

Charles built pens for a nice collection of poultry: Ducks, chickens and turkeys. He plotted out a sizeable kitchen garden and marveled over the fact that the growing season stretched throughout the calendar year. It looked like they had landed in the Garden of Eden.

* * * * *

Just as storms sculpt the land, adversities shape the course of our lives. The most commonplace activity becomes significant when linked with some great misfortune. Always an economic housewife, Donda let nothing go to waste. They had a good crop of cabbage, and she had spent the afternoon making sauerkraut, enough to last the family throughout winter. She had carefully pounded each layer of thinly shredded cabbage with salt, forcing juices to form brine. Pleased with the result, she placed a limestone on top, to weight it down and flavor it, covered her work with a clean cloth, and put a lid on the barrel. Albert had come home from work, and she asked him to carry the barrel down into the dugout cellar by the kitchen door.

The process always took longer than she thought it would. It was getting late, and she realized that she would have to hurry to have dinner ready on time. She loved her new kitchen, and it was a pleasure to use the stove. The old wood stove that she had used back East was replaced with modern gas burners that had only to be lit.

Vivian came into the kitchen and asked when dinner would be ready, and Donda told her it wouldn't be long. "Why don't you practice that little tune you have been learning on the piano until we're ready to eat?" she suggested.

She heard Vivian's footsteps as she scampered off to play the piano they had brought out from Illinois. As Vivian picked out the simple melody, Donda hummed along, smiling, her hands busy with preparations for the evening meal.

She soon had a pot full of potatoes boiling on the back burner and made thin slices of calves' liver while she heated grease in a big skillet to fry them in. The grease in the pan was a trifle too hot when she threw in the first slices of liver, and they seemed to explode. Globs of hot grease splashed on the oilcloth that covered the wall in back of the stove.

She was cross with herself for being careless and turned to the sink to grab a cloth and wipe away the grease. Without warning, the flames from under the pot of potatoes caught hold of the oilcloth, and when she turned back from the sink, the wall was a sheet of flames. Terrified, she backed away and ran outside to pump water into a pail, yelling for help at the same time.

The family came running from all directions, but the heat was too great for them to approach the kitchen. The small brigade they could form to the water pump was pathetically inadequate. The flames were already too high for anyone to get near the fire, and buckets of water fetched from the pump were of no more use than spitting in the wind. Because the house was built in wood, there was nothing to delay the flames from spreading.

Donda's prime concern was to take a count of the family members, and suddenly they realized that Vivian was missing. With panic in their voices, they yelled for her, and Albert stared in horror when he saw his sister pounding on a downstairs bedroom window. During the commotion, she had rushed back into the house in an attempt to salvage what she treasured most – her mother's gowns. She stood in the only spot not engulfed in flames and clutched all the dresses she could hold. Al ran to break the window and lift her out, while tangles of slippery chiffon and silk in soft colors billowed above her small arms. He managed to pull her free, but in breaking the window to get Vivian out, the draft of air fed the flames, destroying whatever was left in the house. One elegant gown was caught on the windowsill, and it ignited, the seed pearls on its bodice popping in the heat. Donda shuddered, thinking of what might have been Vivian's fate.

By now the fire department had arrived, and the nearest neighbors had rushed to the scene and milled helplessly about. There was no insurance, and all that was saved was Donda's Sunday best and the barrel of sauerkraut.

It has been said that California is the only state in the Union where one can freeze to death under a rose bush in full bloom. The family was without a roof over their heads and with precious few possessions, but there is an American tradition of helping. Charles parents and his brothers didn't have room for them, but before nightfall, they were all settled wherever there was space with their neighbors. Until they could rebuild, they would have to live on charity, scattered about among kind friends.

During this period of hardship, Vivian stayed with a family who opened her eyes to a whole new world. The man was a lawyer, and he and his wife had only two little girls. The wife didn't have to work hard like Donda did to take care of her big family, and, in Vivian's eyes, the girls were treated like princesses. They each got new shoes and clothes whenever they needed something – Not like Vivian's family, where everything was passed down until it wore out. There were so many pretty things in their house, things Vivian had never seen. She wouldn't have traded her family for anything in the world, but she took in every detail in this temporary dwelling, storing impressions away that would come to the surface later in life.

A new way of thinking was revealed to Donda, too. People met in church and at the general store and became friends, but it was different when you lived with them. You learned their habits. The family who had taken in Charles and Donda, along with Bobbie and Elsie, had something other than the inevitable Bible in their home. For the first time in her life, Donda was exposed to the penny novels of the day, and she became aware of romantic love, a notion that had never occurred to her. With good common sense, she remained resigned to her own fate, but she couldn't help but daydream and wonder.

Nearly a year passed before they could move into a new house, one in Lomita, smaller than the last, and makeshift without the furniture from Illinois.

After they settled in, Charles found himself at loose ends. All his life he had been a farmer, and he had been good at making a living off the land. Following the move, he felt he had lost his identity, for he was no longer in control. They chose Lomita because land was cheap there, but it was a rural, backwater community. When the Silcoxes moved there, most people were earning a living truck farming, but, for a farmer from Illinois, it was dismal to see that one had to live with periods of draught. A family's fortune was dependent on having a well that wouldn't dry up. The world as he had known it, with knowledge founded on a lifetime of living with the seasons, was lost in this new location. Here, there was temperate weather, but with a constant worry about water.

Friends and Charles' family gave them what they needed for housekeeping, but they no longer had money in the bank. Everything had been used on the new house. They had to earn a living, and, without marketable skills, their future didn't look bright. It was a turning point for Charles. Untrained for work other than farming, and too old to make the effort of building up a sizeable truck farm, he was forced to take the odd job, and the only work he was sure of getting was roadwork. It wasn't easier than farming, and neither was it as rewarding. While his parents prospered with their general store, and Chester made good money running Upland's first automobile agency, Charles could only see his future as a downhill slide.

Donda busied herself with the universal chores of housekeeping, not seeming to need him in her adjustment to the new life. Feeling inadequate, he imagined criticism and turned more and more frequently to drink as balm to his raw nerves. Without making a fuss, Donda started to take in other people's laundry. Her indestructible optimism and faith in the family served only to make him feel even more that he was shrinking in importance.

He started drinking heavily, and drink made him ill tempered. Albert was doing roadwork with him to make his contribution, and he, too, was taking on his father's rough ways. On payday, father and son drank together, and it became clear that Albert had inherited his father's tendency to fly into rages when he was drunk. Donda worried that it would end with a brawl between Charles and his son. It was as if the family were sitting on a keg of dynamite. Nothing was left of their former life in Illinois, where work and pleasure fell into a rhythm as sure as the changing seasons.

Charles had always been a quiet man and gentle with his children, but his behavior was no longer predictable. The family was nervous when he stayed away from home and tense when he returned. Donda learned to accept this change in Charles, not knowing how she could help him out of it. He was like a stranger in their midst, for he had been so different, back East. He didn't understand any better than they what was happening to him and was incapable of controlling his moods.

Vivian was the apple of her father's eye, and, no matter what his mood, he was always gentle with her. Still, she was old enough to sense the conflict between her parents. She grew serious and wise beyond her years, but the years in which her family's fortunes were better had formed her personality. She was convinced that things would get better.

One memorable Thanksgiving, Charles came home late. Having given him up for the day, the family was already seated around the table. Donda had done her best to set a pretty table, hoping this traditional feast would make them forget their present misfortunes, at least for a day. She had worked since dawn, making the dishes they always ate at Thanksgiving; however, the festive air was forced, and it vanished instantly when Charles came home.

As he staggered through the door, the room became charged with tension. Vivian looked at her father, and her eyes were huge with alarm. His clothes were dirty, and he looked like he had been in a skirmish or fallen down. She felt like crying. She loved him so much, but she didn't understand why he was behaving so differently from the way he had back on the farm.

Sensing trouble, Donda bit her tongue and didn't scold him. His mouth was twisted in a bitter grimace, and his blue eyes were blood-shot. He reeked of corn whisky and ale. His speech was slurred when he started to talk, and his voice sounded unfamiliarly harsh and loud in the stillness of the room.

"Why's everybody so gall darned quiet?" he snapped, turning to Donda. "Is this the kind of welcome a man can expect on Thanksgiving? Sure as hell isn't much fun to come home," he mumbled.

Elmo said, "Come on and sit down, Pa. We thought we had better start without you so the food doesn't get cold."

Ignoring Elmo, Charles stared at Donda who stood motionless with a platter in her hands. The tilt of her chin and the mask she wore to conceal her emotions made his frustration boil over. He sensed that her silence was due to contempt, and he felt an urge to shatter her composure.

"What makes you think we can afford such a fancy dinner?" he said, angrily. With strong hands, he grasped one end of the lace-edged tablecloth and jerked with all his might, sending platters with all the wonderful food crashing to the floor. The golden brown turkey, the creamy mashed potatoes, cranberry sauce, carefully arranged garnishes, candied sweet potatoes, colorful salads, it was all in a heap, covered with broken crockery and the cut flowers that had been so lovely in the center of the table. Horrified, the family was mesmerized by the sight of a plate that rolled on its edge towards the door, wobbled, and landed with a bang when it fell.

Donda was furious. Without a word, she bent down, removed her slipper, and hit him neatly in the forehead. Dark red blood gushed from the place where the heel had struck him.

Stunned, Charles turned and left the room, slamming the door. No one spoke as they listened to him stagger upstairs to throw himself on the bed, fully clothed.

Vivian felt like her world was crumbling. She loved her dad as much as she always had, but she wished he wouldn't make life so difficult.

Donda immediately felt remorse at having hurt Charles, and, more so, at having shown him up before his grown sons. Beneath her anger was the knowledge that he was a decent man who deserved a better fate. Her angry blow had been spontaneous, but she knew that he wasn't the sort of man who would have struck her back.

More than Charles' forehead had suffered a blow. He was fifty-two years old, a man out of his element and vulnerable, and his wife was thirty-six, feeling at her prime. Even if she had felt a great love for him, there was nothing she could have done to reassure him, and the more he misbehaved, the less devoted she felt. This time he knew he had stepped over the line. When he sobered up, he was ready to listen to reason, and his parents intervened. It was agreed that he should be committed to Patton, a place that treated alcoholics. They would pay for his stay.

It didn't help. Charles never shirked his role as a provider, but during a period when he was without work, he drank himself into a stupor. Again Donda appealed to the elder Silcoxes to see to it that he was committed to Patton, and they agreed.

It was summer, the family's expenses were minimal, and without having to worry about Charles and his moods, Donda enjoyed the peacefulness that fell over the household. One day, she took the girls with her to pick blackberries beside the dirt road. It was hot, and she had rolled back her sleeves. A metal pail was swinging from her arm, and she had tucked her long skirt into the top of her boots to keep it from getting dusty.

Vivian stopped picking berries when she noticed a tall man, smartly clad in a white summer suit. He strolled over to where Donda was, and he tipped his straw hat and greeted her, stopping up to pass the time of day. He was blonde, but his face was deeply tanned. Donda guessed him to be about forty, but it was hard to tell; he looked different from anyone she knew.

He commented on the quality of the lush berries that season. He seemed in no hurry, and stood watching her with a friendly smile, studying her. Looking at her slim waist and graceful movements, he wouldn't have guessed that she had given birth to seven children. She deftly picked the ripe berries, expertly, without crushing them. Her cheeks were flushed and stray tendrils had pulled loose from the thick mass of dark hair piled high on her head. She wasn't in the habit of being self-conscious, but she sensed his pleasure in watching her and felt light-hearted and happy. She was too unspoiled to read anything personal into his interest.

He made small talk, putting her at ease, and when he had left, she found herself thinking about him far more than was suitable. On the other hand, in such a quiet little town, anyone new caused a sensation, especially someone as incongruous as he. She encountered him often in the weeks that followed, when she walked to the general store or on the way to visits with the neighbors. These innocent encounters were always along country roads, with no one in sight, and she tried to tell herself that they weren't of importance. She kept his acquaintance a secret from Charles when she visited him at Patton, instinctively knowing that he might not like her talking with a strange man.

Sensing that something unusual was happening, Vivian felt uneasy. Children will always resent their mother getting attention from outside the family, even when they are too young to know what that attention might mean. She watched her mother closely and was leery of the stranger long before her mother became aware of his interest in her person.

Donda was told that the man was a doctor from out East. He seemed to have enough money, but he no longer practiced, and no one knew why. She was intrigued with him, because, from their chats, she learned that he had traveled to so many faraway places, something that in her eyes made him very sophisticated. One look at his hands told her that he had never known hard work. His handsome chiseled features had a melancholic look that struck a chord of sympathy in her kind nature.

Dr. Lowentrout left his place daily for a stroll, and, after his first encounter with Donda, he found that he was planning these excursions with the hope of catching a glimpse of her.

Then summer waned, and she didn't see him anymore. She asked Mrs. Taylor, whose house was not far from the long driveway leading to Lowentrout's place, whether she had seen the doctor and was told that he was ill.

"He doesn't leave the house. My boy does errands for him, but he doesn't seem to want much, except for fresh milk. He's such a gentleman, but I think it's strange he doesn't have any family here. Some people say he isn't really a doctor, but he set my Tom's arm when it was broke, and he has a doctor's black satchel."

Donda decided to take Vivian along and look in on Dr. Lowentrout. It would only be neighborly, and, in honesty, she missed those brief encounters with him. She filled a basket with fruit from the garden and a fresh loaf of bread and set out in the afternoon when cool shadows fell across the dusty road.

The doctor's house stood well back from the road, in a setting too rustic to make the air of neglect obvious. There were a few steps up to a porch that ran the length of the house, making it pleasantly shady. There were shutters on the windows, and these were closed, giving the place an abandoned air. She knocked at the door, and he took so long to answer that she had turned and was leaving when he called her name. He was standing behind the screen door. His voice was hoarse, and she was taken aback by his appearance. He looked thinner and drawn. She thought he might be embarrassed to be seen looking so disheveled, but he opened the door and asked her in.

She hesitated, suddenly unsure of her own intentions, but she wasn't a timid person, and her curiosity got the better of her. She stepped inside, Vivian slipping in quietly behind her. Vivian was round-eyed with interest. Everything about the doctor was so intriguing, she thought. The living room was dark and looked like it hadn't been dusted for a long time. Books and periodicals were strewn about everywhere, and there were soiled glasses here and there.

"We heard that you haven't been well and thought we should see if there is anything we can do for you," Donda said lamely, feeling awkward at finding him so unkempt.

He seemed amused and watched her awhile before he answered, "Oh, I'm well enough today, Mrs. Silcox. Sit down, stay awhile…You're like a breath of fresh air." His eyes looked feverish, and he needed a shave.

He swept some papers off the sofa and indicated that she and Vivian could sit there. He then sat on an easy chair facing them, his back to the light that came through the doorway to an adjacent room. His face was in shadows. Donda felt like she was being watched, without being able to see his facial expressions clearly.

She glanced at Vivian, and as if reading her thoughts, he explained, "You needn't worry that I have anything contagious. It's an old ailment that you will never suffer from," and he laughed as if it were a joke of his.

She asked if there was anything he needed, and whether he had anyone who could help him, glancing around the disorderly room as she spoke.

"No. I once had a wife, but I'm no longer burdened with her or society. You might say I'm a free man, but that, of course, is a matter of opinion. What about you? Have you ever thought what it would be like to be free?" he asked, playfully.

She put an arm around Vivian, giving her a hug, and replied, "No. I don't think I would want that."

Suddenly, he blurted out, "What a pity that such a gorgeous woman should be wasting away out here in the sticks, Mrs. Silcox!"

Embarrassed, she changed the subject, asking him whether he would like for her to come around and do some cleaning for him until he was stronger. She missed Charles' income while he was ill. Surely Charles wouldn't object to anything she could contribute. Besides, with him in Patton, he need never know.

Lowentrout said he would like that. It wasn't because he really cared about his surroundings, but he found her fascinating. Vivian didn't know why, but she felt a sense of anxiety when she saw the way the doctor looked at her mother.

It was the beginning of a period when Donda spent several hours a week, putting order into Dr. Lowentrout's house, and he spent an equal amount of time putting ideas into her head. It was harmless enough, but once the mind has been prepared for new thoughts, it is difficult to predict human actions.

It was days later that Donda learned that his affliction was due to periodic bouts of taking morphine. He himself didn't seem capable of a clear explanation as to how he had fallen into an addiction, but, being a doctor, it wasn't difficult for him to obtain his supply. When he lapsed into misuse, he lost track of time, spending days in darkness, sustaining himself with glasses of cold milk. Donda was puzzled that anyone that intelligent could be so self-destructive, but his behavior fit into her notion of him as a law unto himself. However, during the weeks that she came regularly to his house, he avoided drugs and awakened Donda's curiosity to thoughts that had nothing to do with domestic skills.

In 1911, the State of California had given women the vote. It was more than just a mandate to take a part in politics; it was an act that made some of them more aware of themselves as equal partners in a marriage. Breaking away from the Eastern ties, followed by the loss of their worldly possessions made Donda ripe for change, and, already then, California was a place where ideas took off faster than they did in other parts of the country.

Charles came home when the demons that alcohol had unleashed faded into the background. He was ready to resume the form of life they now had, but for Donda, there was no going back. The doctor had broadened her horizons and opened her eyes to the possibility of taking charge of her own future. He had told her that an alcoholic like Charles will always fall into disuse when the pressure builds up, and Donda figured he knew what he was talking about, judging from Lowentrout's own addiction.

She no longer was ready to accept the little that she and Charles had in common. Habits he had which she had tolerated bothered her, now that she could compare him to the doctor.

Maybe she could strike out on her own with the younger children and try to make a decent life for herself while she still had her looks. She had longings she tried to avoid defining, but she knew they could never be fulfilled with Charles by her side.

She had become aware of the fact that her looks were an asset, but she knew how transient looks are. She thought of Dolly, Charles' younger sister and the beauty of the family, whose face had been ruined shortly before the family moved West. The horse pulling her sulky had shied where there was roadwork, rearing on its hind legs and tipping the vehicle. Dolly was thrown out on a sheet of hot tar. She survived, but the pattern of her crocheted shawl was permanently etched into one side of her face. Poor Dolly made a prison of her home after that, avoiding the curiosity and the sympathy of strangers and friends.

Donda pulled herself back to the present and thought about her own situation. With Charles at home, mental doors were shutting, and she had a premonition of life with Charles being her prison one day.

There are three reasons for a woman to stay with a husband she doesn't love. She'll stay if she has young children and can't fend for them on her own. She'll stay if she's afraid of losing the home and material comforts she and her husband have acquired together, or she'll stay if she is lacking the courage to do anything else. Donda had courage, and the family's run on bad luck had taken away the security she would otherwise have been sacrificing.

As for the children who need a father, the youngest child, Elsie, had been born in 1908. By then Donda was firm enough in her opinions that she could arrange to have her own will with Charles most of the time. She cunningly kept Elsie in the marital bed longer than she had the other children, and in that way, her last-born served as a shield between Donda and Charles. She had made up her mind not to have any more pregnancies, and without new additions to the family, she was freer than she ever had been.

In 1917, encouraged by Dr. Lowentrout and inspired by the times, Donda decided to leave Charles. Albert was already married, a shotgun wedding that wasn't off to a very auspicious start, although Donda loved his bride. Marcia, who was seventeen, stayed with her father to keep house for him. Donda took Elmo, Beulah, Vivian, Bobbie, and Elsie with her.

They went to East Los Angeles, where Donda contacted a woman whom the doctor had said would help her with a place to stay and finding work. Elmo got work at the shipyards in San Pedro and helped to support the family. The court ordered Charles to pay alimony.

They moved into a two-story duplex, on a street where there were small gardens and not many trees. It was a far cry from the home they had left in Illinois; however, everything that had happened since they had come to California had rendered Vivian's dreams of the farm into a vague memory, too far distant to be painful. The family had been a unit during her most formative years, and she had faith that things would get better.

For her younger sisters, the transition was not as easy. They had forgotten the good years and fell into the habit of expecting the worst. Elsie and Bobbie grew up with the stigma of not having many memories of better times. Charles soon decided to flee from California to Nevada, where he couldn't be pursued to pay alimony. He found work in Reno, well out of reach. Not being one to waste time and energy moaning over her plight, which she reckoned was, after all, her own doing, Donda took on all the work that was necessary to feed her daughters, with Elmo chipping in all of his earnings. Marcia joined them and worked in a drugstore at the ice cream counter. It meant that the girls were very much alone during the daytime, and Donda was happy that there were kindly neighbors who kept an eye on them. Of course, Beulah was there, but she was like a small child herself when it came to being in charge.

It wasn't long before Dr. Lowentrout made an appearance and occupied lodgings in the basement. With his contempt of established morality, he had served to inspire Donda to break with her past, but his lapses into morphine-induced stupors didn't allow for very practical guidance.

Vivian was blossoming into a beauty and quickly made friends in school. She was given the role of a bride in the annual school play, and the excitement of her first taste of acting kept her mind off the pain of seeing her parents split up. Her popularity made things easier, drawing her out of the home scene. She found herself dreaming of the future, rather than longing for the past.

The only work Donda could get was as a cook in a lunch counter, and that didn't provide enough income to subsist. She supplemented that with work at a laundry, hard work that left little energy for dreams of a better life. Her sparse leisure hours were filled with doing laundry she took in privately and with keeping her family fed and clothed. Their home was no longer kept tidy. Bobbie and Elsie grew up ashamed of their poverty, teased by neighborhood children whose mothers didn't have to work.

Bobbie was eleven, a good little girl who never gave her mother reason to believe that she was unhappy. Elsie was only eight, young enough to be formed by the motley individuals who peopled their lives from the time they left Lomita. She became street-wise, with a sharp tongue and quick reply to anyone who tried to push her around. Like children all over the world, when deprived of the contrivances used to stimulate their imaginations, she found stimulus in the daily encounters with the world around her, a world teeming with the sort of characters who have always tended to flock to Southern California.

The police were on Dr. Lowentrout's trail. He had passed off false prescriptions to get his drugs, and his stay in Donda's basement turned out to be a brief one. Donda no longer had the doctor to feed her fantasy, but she struggled on, too busy to fret about whether or not she had made the right decision in leaving Charles. She had at any rate stopped thinking of him as a shelter from a storm. Hard times were forcing more and more people into a desperate struggle to survive, and she was grateful that she had a strong constitution and capable hands.

Even at that, Donda was too kind-hearted to turn someone away whom she deemed needed help more than she did. One of her twin brothers turned up out of the blue, and she gave him a place to stay. The other brother, Archie, had a good job, but this one, Arthur, was the twin from the dark side of the mirror. He had been in prison, put away for robbery, but he was released because he was mortally ill with tuberculosis. While he stayed with Donda's family, coughing and spitting up blood, he was too weak to work. His only pleasure was taking Bobbie by the hand and going to the matinees. They spent each afternoon in the dark movie theatre, Bobbie blissfully unaware of the danger of contagion, enjoying the flight of fancy produced on the silver screen.

Hope is a gift. It is a state of mind that is attainable to some people and not to others, regardless of their circumstances. With Donda, hope was eternally green. Through all her troubles, she kept sight of others who were worse off and was thankful for her blessings. She was grateful that her brood was healthy. Even Marcia no longer suffered from the colds she had in Illinois. Surely they would run into a streak of good luck. "Lord knows that's what it will take, but things are bound to get better," she liked to say to Elmo who had taken on the role of the man in the family.

Then one day she received an official-looking letter from a law firm in Illinois. In it, Donda was informed that a parcel of land back in Illinois had been sold, and according to the terms of her divorce, half of the money would be hers.

She could hardly believe her good fortune. Laying the letter on the table, she let her mind wander back to Illinois, picturing the land that had been sold. It lay far from the farmhouse and barn. It looked fertile, with lush meadow grass, but the ground water was high, and it was often late in the spring before they could plough those acres. They had finally left it fallow, using it for grazing, and she smiled, remembering all the trouble it caused when their milk cows wandered into an area where wild garlic grew, rendering their milk undrinkable for days. Strange – now that land had sold for a handsome price. The town had expanded, and someone bought it up to build new houses. I suppose they will have to drain it, she mused.

Usually, she tried not to think about Illinois. When they made the decision to come to

California, they knew they wouldn't be able to travel back for a good many years, maybe never. Remembering all her loved ones tugged at her heart, but she was good at writing letters. No matter how busy she was, she kept in touch with family, and the replies to her letters were full of news about the people she knew. The scenes left behind remained static in her mind, and now she realized that one day everything back there would actually look different, too.

Fearful that she might have misread the letter, she picked it up again and read it through carefully. Slowly, she allowed herself to absorb the good news. She thought of all the things the children needed, all the things she might do to make things a little easier. Life had taught her to be cautious, and she told herself that before the money was in her hand, she wouldn't think about it. Then, if it really did come through, well, she would put it in the bank and take her time deciding how to use it.

She was too excited to merely go on about the housework and decided to drop in on her neighbor, Mrs. Martin. Donda put the laundry to soak, and told the girls she was going next door, asking Vivian to come and get her if any problems arose.

Ella Martin was always pleased to get a visit from her younger neighbor, and they chatted easily over a cup of coffee. It was difficult to judge Ella's age. She dyed her hair, and her face was too plump to be lined. She was a handsome woman, and she clearly liked Donda, whom she considered to be very attractive, a nice addition to the neighborhood. She often talked about her son and implied that he and Donda would make a good match. Donda hadn't met the son, but he was there on this occasion, visiting for a few days.

Unaware of his presence, Donda knocked at the door to the small parlor where Ella usually sat, mending or altering clothes for paying customers. When the door was opened, Donda found herself face to face with a handsome stranger.

He smiled at seeing such a lovely lady on the doorstep. Donda was forty-one, not at all young by the standards of those days, but she looked much younger. She was taller than most and had the carriage of a real lady. The steam from the laundry had given her a rosy glow, and wisps of hair framed her face softly.

"Oh, I'm sorry. I didn't know you had company," she said to Ella, smiling at the man and turning to leave.

Ella stepped forward and motioned for her to come in. "That's alright," the older woman said, "it's just my son, come to stay with me a few days. Glad you came by ... I wanted him to meet you."

"How do you do? My name's Dave," he said, in a deep, vibrant voice.

They insisted Donda stay and made her feel so much at home, that before she had left, she had shared with them her good news. She immediately felt foolish, talking about money that wasn't even hers yet, but they both seemed so pleased on her behalf. Dave made her feel like they had known each other for years.

"Well, I have to leave now," Donda said. "I have a batch of clothes to finish and hang up tonight. I promised they would be delivered by tomorrow evening."

Dave Martin looked surprised. "A woman of your caliber shouldn't have to do work like that," he said earnestly.

Donda laughed at that and said, "I don't mind, really. At least it's honest work, and there are plenty of people going without."

"I hope all your work will leave some time for me to see you before I take off again," Dave said smoothly.

Donda blushed, pleased that he was interested, but flustered over an unaccustomed situation. The men she encountered at work liked to jest with her, but they all went home to wives or were too young for her. He looked like such a gentleman. He wore French cuffs with gold cuff links, a dark three-piece suit, and he was tall. It was the first time she recalled feeling all aflutter with a man. Then she reminded herself that she was no spring chicken and had a flock of children to feed. Not likely to attract a man like that, she thought, as she thanked them for coffee and hurried home.

However, Dave was very much attracted. What Donda didn't know was that Dave was always interested in a woman with a bit of money, and if he found someone as pretty as Donda, it didn't matter that it wasn't a great sum. After she left, he sat calculating in his mind what could be done with the amount she had mentioned. It would be enough to buy a car and establish a new address, enough to give him wind in his sails. He never lacked ideas as to how he would manage, but having failed so dismally in his last scheme, he did lack start capital.

He stayed on at his mother's. During the following weeks, he found it was fun flirting with this refreshingly uncomplicated woman. Unsophisticated, she swallowed whole everything he told her, but she was bright enough to make talking with her interesting. Most intriguing of all, he could sense that nothing in her past life had awakened the sensuality he knew most women had, regardless of what type they appeared to be. If he had a special talent, it was his ability to arouse a woman's desire, and he knew that Donda would be worth the effort. He looked at her with his confident, bedroom eyes, and she felt a shiver up and down her spine, unlike anything she had experienced in all those years of marriage.

He decided that he would woo and win her. She had enough imagination to be lured by his pipe dreams, but the countrywoman's pragmatism, which meant that he wouldn't have to worry about her becoming troublesome. Once they had set up housekeeping together, it should be an easy matter to convince her that she should have that half-wit daughter put in a home, and that left just three girls at home. Sons could present more of a problem, but he wanted to move up to the Bay Area anyway, and that would be too far for their interference. His handsome face was like something molded out of marble, as he sat in his mother's parlor, planning the future.

Donda was so impressed with Dave that she readily accepted his vague explanations about making a living as a writer. That fit in very well with his cultivated air. "I do occasional journalistic assignments for quick cash," he said, "but I am working on a novel that I hope will go over big."

Donda smiled approvingly. That explained why he spent so much time around the house. His mother had said that he had been back East but didn't like the climate.

Even though she had long hours of work each day, Donda bloomed. She found she had unbounded energy and was never too tired to squeeze in the more and more frequent hours she and Dave had together, falling into conversation as she passed his mother's house, or going for evening strolls in the nearby park. Vivian was old enough to be left in charge, and her younger sisters were good, used to fending for themselves from the recent years of hardship when they learned to understand that their mother had to work. They were happy, seeing her relaxed. They were unaware that Dave was anything more than a nice man visiting his mother.

Donda looked at herself in the mirror and could see the transformation that was taking place. "They say there's nothing like a fire in an old barn," she thought with a bit of trepidation. She was too excited by Dave to stop herself from thinking about him every waking hour, but she was also a bit afraid. She didn't want to do anything that would be a bad example for her girls.

Dave soon wiped away all her concern when he proposed marriage. She was crazy with longing for him, but now she knew she could hold out until they were man and wife. He told her his plan to move to San Francisco, and she gladly consented. This was just the sort of man she had dreamed about when she read those penny novels. She had to pinch herself to make sure she wasn't dreaming. Her happiness knew no bounds, and she was too smitten to question his plans. He was very good at planning. He, too, was excited about the prospect of finally possessing this gorgeous creature.

Donda's money came through, and she put it in the bank for safekeeping. There was so much to do to prepare for her life with Dave and she wanted to leave that money until she knew what needs she would have in her new home.

Feeling awkward, Donda didn't tell her family about their plans. It was somehow embarrassing to admit that she was going to be a bride now, when Marcia was almost old enough to get married. Just as well to let them know after she and Dave tied the knot.

They were married at a quiet civil service and were to leave for San Francisco the following week. They spent their wedding night at the Ambassador in luxury. Donda had never dreamed that she could feel such ecstasy.

With the marriage certificate in hand, Dave was able to get access to Donda's account and buy his dream car. Vivian was sitting on the porch with Donda when Dave pulled up to the curb in it. She would never forget it. It was a magnificent, sleek, black Hutmobile, with a custom made Landau top. Donda was as excited as the girls, not knowing that the car was something obtained with her money. (Ironically, it was the same type luxury car that Jane would soon be sporting in Colorado, the difference being that no man could ever take advantage of her money.)

Donda was devastated when she found out he had emptied her bank account. With a feeling of fear, she realized that she really knew nothing about this man's character, other than what a doting mother had told her.

Dave reassured her, saying, "I wanted to surprise you! I couldn't put out the cash myself right now, but we will have far more than that when I sell my book. You don't need that money, now that I will be taking care of you, and think what a grand time we can have, driving up to San Francisco. We'll arrive in style, and that is the sort of life I want you to have from now on," he said, looking down at her lovingly and pulling her closer to him.

Again, Donda was aware of her own lack of sophistication. Of course a man like Dave would consider that sum of money nothing out of the ordinary! She deliberately tucked away her anger and disappointment, along with a niggling feeling that she had made a big mistake in trusting him. Like a person who has found herself on a train headed for the wrong destination, she decided to make the best of things and enjoy the trip. Done was done, and she would just have to hope for the best.

They left the very next day for San Francisco, with Beulah, Vivian, and Bobbie in tow. Marcia went to stay with her Uncle Chess and his wife. Donda prudently decided to leave Elsie with Albert and his wife. After all, Dave was used to bachelor life, and she thought it best if they were settled before she brought her most unruly daughter into their home. Vivian was the only one who could be excited about the prospect of moving to San Francisco with all its allure. She was fifteen, old enough to find a job once they got there and step into the exciting world of adults.

* * * * *

As soon as they settled in, Dave Martin showed his true colors. The first thing he did was to insist that Beulah be put in an insane asylum.

He brought it up one morning, just after breakfast. Donda had sent Beulah out back to hang out the wash. It was one of the household chores Beulah really liked to do, but there was a brisk wind, making the sheets flap, and she was having trouble putting the pegs on the line.

"I'd better go help," Donda said to Dave. "Poor Beulah is so afraid of dropping anything and getting it dirty."

Dave put a hand out to stop her from getting up from the table. "I've been giving it a lot of thought," he said, in a matter-of-fact tone, "and I think it will be for the best if Beulah is put in a home. She's far too much of an encumbrance for you."

Startled, Donda felt angry tears stinging her eyes and refused to talk about it. Dave let the subject drop for a day or two, but he brought it up again, one night after the girls had gone to bed.

"You must realize, darling, that I'm thinking of what is best for Beulah. The day will come when we won't be able to take care of her, and she would be better off having become accustomed to other surroundings." His voice was smooth and reasonable. Donda always found it difficult to sound logical when she objected to what he had to say. Her arguments were emotional, and she wasn't clever with words.

There was, of course, some truth in what he said, but he hadn't come from a big family. She knew that there would always be a brother or sister who would look after Beulah. "You're wrong, Dave. In our family, we take care of each other. Beulah will always have a home, and I've never considered her a burden. Why, she can help out with a lot of things around the house." She studied his face for a reaction, but his handsome features were like a mask.

"Well, I haven't wanted to come right out and say this, but there is another reason for my wanting to make a change. You must realize that for a man in my position, it is an embarrassment to have someone in the household who is retarded. In the life we will be leading, she will be a stumbling block." His voice was cold, and Donda felt the first tinge of panic. She looked at him in surprise. Could this be the same man who had so much praise for her offspring while he was courting her?

She pursed her lips together and busied herself with some mending. There was a lump in her throat, and she felt ill with agitation. Her feelings were too strong to allow for a discussion of the matter, and, a little later, she said she felt very tired and was going to bed. For once she hoped he wouldn't follow her right away. When he did retire, she pretended to be asleep, her back turned to his side of the bed, but she had a troubled night, wide awake, filled with grief, as she imagined how frightened Beulah would be if she were placed in a home.

The next morning, when Beulah was setting the table, Donda tried looking at her with Dave's eyes. Her thick hair was bobbed straight across, a style chosen for practicality, for anything else would be too difficult for Beulah to manage herself. As usual, her petticoat was hanging a little below her dress, her belt having hitched the dress up above the waistline. She had buttoned her sweater wrong, and though she was clean, she certainly did look sloppy. Beulah felt her mother's eyes upon her and, always devoted, smiled the innocent smile of a small child, despite her twenty-five years. Donda smiled back sadly, feeling ashamed that she could even look at Beulah critically.

How often she had pondered what had gone wrong with her first-born. Just before Beulah's birth, Donda had gone out back to draw water from the well. It was a new well, and they hadn't built proper sides around it. She had stepped onto the planks that covered the hole and lowered the pail down into the cold water. One plank broke, throwing her off balance, and she found herself standing in the bottom, waist-deep in water, with no way to scale the steep sides. It was nearly an hour before the men came in from the fields and helped her out, and she gave birth that evening, a month premature. She remembered what a beautiful little girl Beulah had been and how proud she had been of her when she was a baby. During her early years, she was quiet and timid, but there was nothing at that time to indicate that she was retarded.

Had her early birth marked her later development? Or was it liked Doc Benson had said, that Beulah should have had her adenoids removed when she was six? Charles didn't believe in doctors and had refused to have it done, Donda recalled. No, she shouldn't blame Charles, she thought. Beulah had never been right after she had scarlet fever when she was ten. Donda remembered how relieved she was when the epidemic had passed, and all her children were alive. Vivian had come close to dying, climbing out of bed in her delirium and walking barefooted in the snow, calling "Mommy" in the freezing wind. Maybe the fever went into Beulah's brain like Dr. Lowentrout once said. Whatever the reason, she felt it was her responsibility to shelter Beulah, as the child who never would grow up. She was determined to protect her, as she always had done.

This soon became increasingly difficult to do. By now Donda realized that Dave had no money when he married her, and what was hers had nearly all been used on the car and the move. During the first few months, she had been lulled into complacency by the sophisticated ease with which he mapped out their daily life. They had moved into a furnished house, and Donda had not an inkling of the fact that they were living on credit.

He had led her to believe that he made a good living as a writer, but he didn't seem to be selling anything he wrote. Donda's perpetual optimism made her think that this was just a temporary lapse. It was difficult for her to judge how much of an effort he was making, but she soon discovered that he had a different attitude towards money than hers.

When she asked him for money to buy groceries, Dave told her to open an account with the local merchants. "It's much more sensible, because my income varies according to what articles I sell. People are used to doing business that way in this area."

Donda had an inborn aversion to asking for credit, and no one in her family had ever owed money. Rather than argue with him about it, she put on her hat and gloves and found a job at a lunch counter. While she was toiling away all day long, he was at home, immaculately dressed, sitting by his typewriter or staring off into space to gather his thoughts. He took the car and was gone for hours, leaving it to be accepted and understood that he was out making contacts. As long as she insisted that bills be paid, it was clear that Donda would have to keep working, until something Dave wrote could be sold, and he kept assuring her that success was just around the corner. "Once I sell this manuscript, everything else will be easy."

Since Donda was gone most of the day, and Dave was home, she began to worry about whether he was unkind to Beulah the many hours they were alone. Beulah seemed nervous, unlike her usual self.

It wasn't just Beulah. Donda couldn't help but notice that Vivian and Bobbie were also avoiding their stepfather. They were good girls, and she couldn't see why he should be so strict with them. She was disconcerted that his attitude towards them had changed so much after the wedding.

She began to regret having married him, but he would sense her mood and smoothly brush away her doubts, later in the evening, when they were alone. He lit the old charm, wooing her with his easy smile and the sound of his voice. She had never known such a desire. It robbed her of all common sense, and she avoided any thoughts that would put him in a bad light. "Perhaps it is just nerves. He'll be happier and easier to get along with when he starts earning some money."

Still, she worried, and finally she relented and decided to put Beulah in a home. She had a nagging fear that Beulah might come to harm, being alone with Dave all day. His attitude was so negative, and she knew he wouldn't keep an eye on her, as one should. It troubled her that Beulah was so attracted to men. As trusting as she was, someone could take advantage of her if she weren't supervised. Maybe he's right, and they will be able to help her more than I have, she thought. At least she would be out of harm's way, and it doesn't have to be permanent.

It was a dreadful day for Donda, when they drove Beulah to the home for the feeble-minded. Beulah loved going for an outing in the car, and Donda explained to her that they were going to see some people she thought Beulah might like.

"Dave and I are going away for a little trip, and these people have said that you can stay there while we're gone. It will be nice for you to make some friends, honey, and if you don't like it there, we'll come to take you home." Donda looked anxiously at Beulah's face, but it was placid, as usual, and she was too pleased about wearing her best dress and going somewhere in the car to be alarmed about what Donda was trying to tell her.

Donda told herself that she was being silly to be so unhappy. Dave was undoubtedly right. It would be good for Beulah to be with people like herself, and they wouldn't have to worry about anything happening to her.

She herself didn't know anything about asylums and she didn't want to ask anyone. Somehow she felt ashamed. Even Dave's mother had once hinted about a home for Beulah. Donda didn't have their schooling and was aware of it. If she was going to be happy with Dave, she couldn't act like an ignorant farmer's wife all her days.

The home was located out in Sonoma County, and the big gates that opened onto a long drive up to the main building made it look inviting. Dave parked the car at the bottom of the steps leading up to the main entrance and told Donda to wait in the car with Beulah until he had gone inside and announced their arrival.

He returned a few minutes later with a white-clad nurse and a man who looked like he might be one of the doctors. They were both smiling and greeted Donda and Beulah in a friendly manner. Donda began to relax, thinking it wasn't nearly as bad as she had expected. She got out of the car and helped Beulah get out, telling her to greet the people.

Beulah had never known anything but kindness. Her brothers and sisters had protected her from being teased by any other children as they were growing up, and once her schooling had been abandoned, she had always been with her family. She smiled trustingly and allowed the two strangers to take her by the arm and lead her away. Childlike, she resisted when the man started to take her suitcase, and she clutched it in front of her as they walked up the stairs.

"It's best if we leave while she has her attention on them," Dave said, hurrying Donda into the car and running around to the driver's side. He started up the motor and drove quickly away. Donda looked back and saw that the big oak door had already been shut, with Beulah on the inside.

She wanted to cry but knew that Dave would think her silly. "After all," she told herself, "it is a lovely place, and they looked very nice." She had planned to go inside and look things over before leaving Beulah there, but Dave took charge so unexpectedly, and everything had happened so fast. She wondered whether he had arranged the way things transpired before they had even come out there. He was always in control, and right now she resented it; however, she reminded herself that she had found that quality so attractive when she met him.

She stole a glance at him but couldn't read his thoughts. Her throat was tight, and she didn't dare talk for fear of breaking down. The only comforting thought was that she would simply come out and take Beulah away if she was unhappy.

It was as if Dave had read her thoughts. Without looking in her direction, he told Donda that the doctor had said it would be best if they didn't pay a visit the first few months. "Patients are much happier if they are given a chance to settle in."

* * * * *

Vivian was sick at heart when she learned that Beulah had gone away. Her oldest sister was like a much-loved pet, always devoted, and even-tempered. What she lacked in comprehension she made up for in loyalty and affection.

Meanwhile, Vivian and Bobbie had not only discovered that their stepfather was unreasonably strict, they didn't like the way he looked at them. They hurried out of the room if they found themselves alone with him, instinctively shying away from his touch. Donda tried to make apologies for his behavior, but Vivian knew it was his fault that Beulah had to leave, and she was furious. Still, her mother was the same person she had always loved, and she didn't want to take it out on her. She was clearly trying to make the best of a bad situation.

Under the circumstances, both girls had to leave school at an early age to earn a living, but they were eager to enter the adult world. Vivian was sixteen, and she found a job, in San Francisco, as a clerk for Southern Pacific Railroads. At fourteen, Bobbie went to work behind the candy counter for Woolworth's. With so much changed, they no longer felt that they belonged in their mother's home, and they asked her to let them move out on their own. Donda felt she had little choice but to give them her blessing even though they were both so young.

The year was 1919. There were no safety nets, but life was a great adventure for two confident young ladies. They lived at the YWCA at first, but that meant having to eat all their meals out. When Bobbie got a better job with the telephone company, they moved to a small apartment in Oakland. Now they could do their own cooking and save money, though Vivian had to commute by tram and ferry each day to San Francisco.

For Vivian and Bobbie life was full of hope. The future was an unknown quantity, and they were blessed with the American conviction that dreams can come true, no matter how humble one's background. For most women back then, a promising marriage was the best ticket to the good life – even more so for girls whose families couldn't afford to give them a higher education. Donda had brought up her daughters well, and they knew that the only way to catch an attractive husband was to protect one's virtue. Even at such a vulnerable age, they were too ambitious to fall into the many pitfalls that could destroy a girl's reputation.

The unwritten rules were stringent. Young men protected the group of girls they intended as future wives and took advantage of girls who were classified as easy. Donda had made sure that her girls left home with an unshakable belief that giving in to a man's fancy was a sure-fire way to either get pregnant or struck by lightning, and the only hope for a good match was to remain a virgin.

They were a pretty pair: Vivian, with her porcelain complexion, green eyes and shiny dark hair, was vivacious and graceful, and Bobbie, a lovely blonde with great blue eyes, was grave and trusting. They were so young, but in those days there was no transitional period between childhood and being a young adult. They were both lady-like by nature. Vivian, being the oldest was more self-assured, but Bobbie kept up with her by dressing to look older, her soft hair swept up under the fancy hats of those days. Much to Donda's relief, the two girls proved that they could manage well on their own.

San Francisco is a magical city. Perched on so many hills, overlooking one of the most beautiful bays in the world, it was the perfect setting for spinning dreams. Its cool climate made it a place for fashion. For Bobbie and Vivian, it was wonderful fun to pool their salaries and feel that life was good when it meant wearing a new hat, or stepping out in a becoming new frock. Their mother had taught them to sew, and they were clever at copying the latest fashion from dresses in shop windows.

Vivian started dating Rudy soon after she went to work. She met him at Southern Pacific, where Rudy had a good position in bookings. He was very handsome, but she sometimes wished he weren't so serious. His father had been a country doctor and died of overwork when Rudy was still young. The dutiful son took his father's place as the breadwinner for his mother and sister, becoming a responsible provider overnight.

Vivian loved to dance, and she liked to be admired. Rudy didn't like dancing, and, for a while, Vivian dated a few other young men. She was chosen to adorn the cover of a Southern Pacific magazine, and there were plenty of suitors from the office. None were as considerate as Rudy, however. People said they made such a handsome pair, and Vivian began to think that perhaps it was hopeless to wish for someone who was perfect in every way. He wasn't as exciting as she would have liked, but she came to depend more and more on him.

For Rudy it had been love at first sight, and he was determined to win her. Under his quiet surface, he was the one who was capable of a consuming passion. He had never known anyone quite like her. She was like a bright beam of sunshine. He never tired of watching her as she talked easily with the other employees, her natural warmth animating everyone who captured her attention, from the cleaning staff to the other secretaries or the dark-suited men in the executive offices.

Vivian had a dream of the good life and an eye for the material things that went with it. Rudy knew that she loved nice things, and he wanted to give her everything she desired. Once they started dating steadily he began to give her beautiful gifts, knowing that each gift accepted was a chink in her armor, for he had made it clear he wanted to marry her. With her old-fashioned upbringing she knew that she shouldn't accept gifts from a man, but she pushed aside the thought. After all, Rudy never demanded anything in return.

Once a month, Bobbie and Vivian took the train to Sonoma to visit poor Beulah. The inviting exterior of the main building was a sham. Once past the clean reception rooms, one entered departments that were all but pleasant. It was a grotesque place of tormented souls and apathetic neglect.

The girls were frightened and appalled the first time they were there. There were inmates too far gone to realize that they were sitting in their own filth. A tough crew of caretakers in the other departments replaced the smooth-talking staff of professionals in the front building. Beulah wasn't with friends as Donda had imagined she would be. They found her sitting on the edge of her bed, with a blank look on her face. She seemed much worse off, being among inmates who were so clearly insane.

Beulah was so docile that they didn't have any trouble getting permission to take her off the grounds of the home when they came to visit. They hated being around the other inmates and the rough staff. When they came, they brought a basket of food and took their sister out in the beautiful countryside to share a picnic lunch with her. She cried when they had to leave, and Vivian and Bobbie were silent during the long train ride home, feeling miserable and wishing that theirs was a happier family. It took a whole day to go and see her. They wouldn't be able to do it more than once a month, but they clung to the hope that Beulah could not keep very good track of time.

For Donda, the separation from Beulah was even worse. However, she stuck to her promise not to visit her in the beginning, partly to avoid making Dave cross and partly because she was afraid she wouldn't be able to leave her in that place one more time. It helped that the girls went to see her.

"How is she?" Donda asked, anxiously, when they had been there the first time. "Did she ask for me? Has she made any friends?" She was still under the delusion that the place was run like a home. After all, Beulah was retarded, not insane.

Already wise beyond her years, Vivian knew how hard it was for her mother, and she nudged Bobbie not to say anything as she told a white lie. "She'll be alright, Ma. We have to give it a chance, and she looked well."

They were sitting in the kitchen, having a glass of cool lemonade. Donda looked tired. She had worked all day at the lunch counter, stopping by the butcher's on the way home to pick up a piece of meat for supper. It wasn't exactly the sort of life Dave had promised her.

Dave was sitting in the living room, impeccably dressed as always, apparently concentrating on words he was writing on a lined yellow pad. "How is Dave doing with his book?" Vivian asked in a low voice, nodding in his direction.

Donda had to admit that she didn't know. "But give it time," she said, defensively, and Vivian didn't pursue the subject. She knew her mother's adage: "You've made your bed. Now lie in it."

Actually, Donda was reaching a turning point. A year and a half of living with Dave had been enough to quench the passion she had felt for him during that breathtaking beginning. He still wasn't making any headway with his writing. She no longer cared where he went during the daytime, being too tired when she came home from a long day at the diner to want his company anyway.

I should never have left Charles, she thought sadly, but she had never thought things would turn out the way they did. It had seemed unfair that she shouldn't experience the pleasures in life that were described in penny novels and on the silent screen. Now that she found herself in a second bad marriage, she wondered whether all she had done to her family was worth it. At least Charles tried to be a good provider. When she decided to leave him, she had felt she had to act while she was still attractive and young enough to have hopes for a new beginning, but now she had learned that she really had only a fuzzy idea of what that start should have been. Why was it that so much in life depended on a man, and she had to have the bad luck of being stuck with two who let her down?

When she finally visited Beulah, Donda realized what a mistake it had been to let Dave talk her into putting her in a home. Seeing Beulah so miserable was enough to make her decide to pack up and leave Dave. It wasn't because she couldn't stand her own situation anymore, but she couldn't bear to see what was happening to her family.

She knew that he would be able to argue her out of it if he caught her in time; therefore, she planned her escape well, buying a train ticket in advance and arranging to pick up Beulah before continuing to Los Angeles. Ever since the fire, her possessions were few, and they could be left with the girls. The car would have to be left behind and written off as a loss, she thought bitterly. It would have made an escape easier, but she didn't even know how to drive it.

In order to obtain a release for Beulah, Donda had to sign a paper permitting the sanatorium to sterilize her. She knew very well that would be for the best, but she felt guilty having to add one more thing to Beulah's suffering. Feeble-minded though Beulah was, she had always hoped she would some day marry and have children.

Donda had learned her lesson, but it had cost her dearly. She would be worse off than ever when she returned to Southern California. Dave had run through all her money, and her family was scattered. She would be reunited with Beulah and little Elsie, but Vivian and Bobbie had good jobs and wouldn't want to leave the Bay Area.

Donda made a successful getaway, but she never filed for divorce, fearing that Dave Martin would find her if she did. (Years later, an FBI agent knocked on her door, trying to locate Dave to arrest him for bigamy and fraud.)

* * * * *

Rudy's habit of trying to win Vivian's hand with gifts escalated. First, he bought her a jade ring in a rich gold setting, telling her that he loved to see her in green, to match her eyes. When they had been dating for a year, he gave her a dainty platinum watch, set with diamonds, to remind her that he thought of her every minute of the day. She couldn't help but be influenced by the other girls at work who thought Rudy was a dream come true.

She missed her family terribly, but she knew her chances to do well were better in San Francisco. She saved all the money she could, and one half a year after Donda's escape, Vivian had saved enough money to take the train and go down to Los Angeles for a visit.

Elmo had rented a house in Los Angeles, and Donda and Beulah moved in with him when Donda left Dave. Elsie came to live with them, too, but her stay with her big brother, Albert, and his wife and their boys had done something to her. She had a wild streak and no longer seemed the trusting child she had been before Donda left her there.

The twenties were desperate times for many people. While great fortunes were made, the little guy was often trampled in the process. It was also a time of movement, and California was like a magnet for people with wild dreams and for people who had failed elsewhere. Donda's plight was no worse than many of her neighbors'.

The vast difference between the very rich and the poor tore the very fabric of America. Rich people flaunted their wealth, convinced that one's station in life was a reward from God and believing that the jobless, the migrant workers, and the wretched children were all part of God's plan. People who might have made a difference to these appalling conditions also put their faith in God and fought the symptoms of this sick society, rather than the illness.

It is in light of that attitude that one can understand why there was no progress in passing legislation that would have made a safety net for the sick or unemployed in the United States at that time, although the temperance movement gained enough political clout to get the Eighteenth Amendment passed. That was the notorious amendment that spelled out prohibition.

Prohibition was like waving a red flag at the stubbornly independent Americans. People who had never even tried liquor before abolition were interested in trying it now. Ever since the Boston Tea Party, Americans had taken pride in not being told what to do, and prohibition made the conditions ripe for a whole new inventory of law circumvention.

An oilman, a rigger named Jeb, owned the big house where Donda lived with Elmo, Beulah and Elsie. He was an old geezer with crude manners and a heart of gold. He took a shine to Donda right off, but knew he wouldn't have a chance with her.

Jeb saw how hard Donda had to work just to make ends meet. She went back to her laundry work, the only steady work she could get, and evenings she worked at a diner a few blocks away. It was tough going for her to support herself, and she had too much pride to accept any handouts. Jeb felt sorry for her, and, in pondering ideas for helping her, he got what he figured was a brainstorm.

"How 'bout you and me openin' up a tea parlor, Donda? You know, one of them fancy places where one can spend an afternoon drinking homemade hooch. All we need, here in the parlor, is one of them grammyphone players, and, hell, maybe a potted palm, where the ladies can pour out the stuff if they don't like it much. Elmo told me you folks used to make wine and cider back in Illinois. Can't you just do the same thing here? You can use the bathtub. I even know someone who can set us up with a still."

Well, Donda never did have much respect for laws that just deprived people from having fun. She wasn't one for drink herself, but even though she had suffered a drunken husband, she couldn't see that a law against drinking would have been much help. People like her folks always had known how to make alcoholic beverages. She told Jeb she thought it was a terrific idea, and that was the start of her venture with bootlegging.

Whatever they brewed in the bathtub, they distilled, but they also made wine in big glass flacons. When the wine was mature, they had young Elsie siphon it off into jugs or other less conspicuous containers to be delivered to various contacts around town. She was a gangly kid of thirteen who had seen enough of life to be pretty street-wise. To siphon the wine, she had to suck on a rubber hose that had one end stuck in the brew, and she soon developed a taste for the glow she felt when she had been filling up jugs.

When Vivian arrived in Los Angeles, she knew nothing of her mother's latest venture. Elmo and Donda were waiting on the platform when the train rolled into the Los Angeles Terminal. Donda was overjoyed to see Vivian. With pride, she took in every detail about Vivian's appearance. She was wearing a smart new outfit, and she looked so ladylike and poised.

"You're looking prettier than ever, honey," she said as she gave her a hug. Suddenly, Donda felt misgivings about what Vivian would think of her new business. She had never had the time or leisure to worry about how she appeared to others. She was good about writing to Vivian and Bobbie, but she brushed lightly over details about Jeb and the 'tea parlor'.

Vivian was so happy to see her family that she could only chuckle about her mother's escapades. The most important thing was that Beulah was back in their midst.

Fortunately, Elmo was doing all right. By working at the shipyards during the First World War, Elmo had been exempt from the draft, and the war drove some wages up to unprecedented heights. During most of the time that his mother had spent in the Bay Area he had worked on a freighter that sailed between San Pedro and Honolulu. However, he wanted to move up in the world, and seeing how many men who worked around the docks suffered from back trouble and other aches and pains gave him the idea of studying to be a chiropractor. To get a degree, he worked hard during the day and attended evening classes.

The most wonderful news was that Marcia was happily married. While she lived with her Uncle Chess and his wife she had a job in the local drugstore, a place that was popular with young people who liked to hang out at the ice cream parlor. She was pretty, with an innocent, wide-eyed look, but she was too shy to strike up a conversation with any of the boys who liked to come there. Elmo had suggested that she become a pen pal to one of the doughboys who were off fighting the trench war in Europe. Writing a letter was much easier for her than any direct contact, and she became great friends with a soldier named Lester.

For a year they corresponded, and then one day, after the Armistice, a handsome young man in uniform turned up at the drugstore and asked if she was Marcia. She recognized Lester at once from the photograph he had sent her, and all her shyness was forgotten in the rush of pleasure at seeing him in the flesh, safe and sound.

Their letters had paved the way for romance, and they soon got married. Lester was lucky to find a job as chauffeur for a rich lady in Pasadena, and with the job was a nice little cottage on the grounds. It wasn't far from where Donda lived, and Vivian loved visiting Marcia and Lester and seeing how happy they were together. Their small cottage was such a cozy place, and Marcia even had a small garden to grow some flowers and keep a few chickens.

Vivian stayed for a week, loving every minute of being with her family, but she was convinced more than ever that she had better hopes for a good future in San Francisco. As much as she loved her mother, she knew that she didn't want to be part of a lifestyle so far removed from her dreams. Unless, of course, she met someone like Marcia's husband. Vivian was so pleased to see Marcia glowing with love, with a man who was clearly devoted to her. If I could find someone like Lester, Vivian thought, I wouldn't care whether or not he was rich or poor.

Donda had slipped down the ladder of respectability, but the times were such that she could melt into the masses of people who thought about daily survival more than social status or long-term dreams. As is typical for hard times, close family ties were forged, and, with little to give, each one developed a generosity far greater than is usually seen among people who have great wealth. For Donda, it was a lesson in getting back to basics. She knew now that those whom she loved mattered more to her than satisfying her own fancy notions of a life she would like to have.

The difficult times also taught each one in Donda's large family the importance of paying one's bills. In the land of opportunity, owing money was tantamount to losing one's freedom. Better to starve today than to live on borrowed money and get into the clutches of someone better off. They pulled in their belts, and learned to be inventive, while outwardly trying to keep up appearances in order to be ready for any luck that might come their way. And through it all, no matter how down and out they were, Donda always gave the family strength. She was like a rock in her unwavering belief that people were basically good, and that everything would turn out well in the end.

Thus, out of the school of hard knocks, Jane and Donda drew totally opposite lessons. For some undefined reason, it didn't occur to either of them to accept a fate of remaining poor, but they had completely different notions of a ticket out of poverty. Whereas Jane was bent upon forging her own destiny through clever enterprise and self-improvement, Donda counted on the winds of good fortune blowing her way. Jane put her faith in Republicanism, while Donda, whose family were Republicans back in Illinois when they were in the chips, turned her back on that party when she was down on her luck and turned Democrat, trusting that party to eke out fair conditions for each and everyone. She left the rest to luck. Their lives would prove that there is no right answer, but whatever you do in life's ongoing play affects the act that follows.

The act that followed theirs was Vivian's and Mickey's.

Vivian

Rudy patiently courted Vivian. It wasn't until Vivian was twenty, in 1923, that she finally consented to become engaged to him. She converted to Catholicism to please Rudy, but her conversion posed no problems. Religious tolerance was characteristic of her large, pragmatic family, and it was easy for her to transfer an already genuine belief in God to another faith. It also suited Vivian's temperament. She had a romantic nature, and a theatrical sense. The rituals and atmosphere of the church appealed to her and lifted her above the shabbiness of life as it had taken form since the family left their farm in the East.

Upon becoming engaged, Rudy gave her a lovely diamond, a carat brilliant with twenty-one tiny diamonds in a platinum setting. It was stunning and looked so right on her slender hand.

She still had a yearning for something indefinable, a feeling like the soaring of the soul when great music is heard. Rudy was every mother-in-law's dream, but the feelings she had thought would come with love weren't there. She knew he would be a good husband and provider and a good father for the children she hoped they would have. Her romantic notions about her future life with Rudy were to do with the framework to their marriage, not Rudy's personality. Always decent and correct, he represented the sort of life she longed for, with nice things in a proper home. Anyway, she hadn't been out with anyone better than Rudy.

She held out her hand, watching the play of sunlight on the many-faceted diamond, and she shrugged off any doubts. One thing is what you read in storybooks, she told herself, and another is real life. She knew that Rudy would always keep her safe from the drudgery of poverty, and she genuinely liked him for his reliably good character. Their future together could only be good.

Vivian and Rudy set the wedding date for May 1924. A photographer captured the beauty of the bride, her sister, Bobbie, and their mother, who looked young enough to have been an older sister, dressed in the loose-fitting, elaborately embroidered silk and chiffon dresses of the time.

With his usual flair for finding the perfect gift, Rudy gave Vivian a leather suitcase filled with handmade silk and satin lingerie to wear for their honeymoon. However, aside from the pleasure she took from luxurious things, her feelings for Rudy were just as calm after the wedding night as they had been during the long engagement. He was her very best friend, but she still didn't experience the romantic feelings that Valentino evoked on the silent screen.

Soon afterwards, Bobbie married Armand, a handsome young man whose parents were both

French. Armand worked for Bergen Lines, a Norwegian steamship company, a job similar to Rudy's, and he and Rudy became good friends. They both were serious, ambitious, and devoted to their young wives. Only one thing puzzled Armand. He knew he was making more money than Rudy, and he wondered why Rudy always had more to spend. He and Bobbie had dinner at Vivian and Rudy's every other week, and he couldn't help but notice that there was always something new in their apartment. Rudy continued to shower Vivian with exquisite presents. Armand couldn't figure out how he managed it, but it would have been rude to ask.

Then, two years after their marriage, without any warning, Vivian and Rudy quite suddenly moved to Los Angeles. It came as a shock to Bobbie and Armand that they hadn't been told anything beforehand about the move. They had otherwise been so close. A move of that distance was too far to stay in close touch, and the questions they would like to have asked Vivian they had to ponder themselves.

In Armand's job with the steamship business, he did business with a fellow named Ron Biggins, one of Rudy's old colleagues at the Southern Pacific. One day, when Armand was visiting Ron, he was asked what he thought about Rudy being fired. Embarrassed, Armand had to admit that he didn't know Rudy had been fired.

"Yeah. We found out that he's been chiseling money. We've known about it for a long time, but it wasn't until last month that we were able to trace it to Rudy. Can you imagine that? He doesn't look like the type who would do somethin' like that."

Armand was thunderstruck. Ron droned on, filling him in on the details, but he really didn't want to know. How could a decent guy like Rudy stoop so low? If they had known he needed money, why the devil didn't he say so? Maybe they could have helped out.

That evening he told Bobbie, and together they tried to imagine when it had all started. Both Rudy and Vivian had always seemed so self-confident that they could never have imagined that there was any trouble in store for them. "I wonder if Vivian knows," Bobbie mused.

"Maybe not. He could have just told her he got the sack. Plenty of people are without jobs these days. One thing for sure, he'll have a tough time finding anything in L.A. Scratch most businesses, and you'll find a connection to the Southern Pacific. He'll be blacklisted from any work with them."

They never did learn whether or not Vivian knew. The sudden move was never discussed, and Bobbie and Armand were too discreet to ask. San Francisco and Los Angeles were a world apart, and it was long before Bobbie saw Vivian again.

* * * * *

The same loyalty that Vivian had always felt towards her family, she felt towards Rudy. Her heart went out to him when she saw how miserable he was when he lost his job. It was her idea to move to Los Angeles. She couldn't bear to let Bobbie and Armand and their friends in San Francisco see them as failures. She knew that her mother would be just the same towards Rudy, no matter what had happened, and they could make a new beginning. That was the wonderful thing about America. One could always wipe the slate clean.

Uncomplaining, she accepted that they were in for tough times and took comfort in the fact that she would be reunited with her large family. Vivian had developed a habit of looking upon the positive and ignoring the negative. She took after her mother and had a solid faith that something good would come of everything bad.

It was just like Armand had predicted. Rudy had a hard time finding work. He finally resorted to selling vacuum cleaners, door to door, until he was lucky enough to land a job with the gas company.

Donda had closed down her tea parlor. Things started getting too rough, and anyway, life was easier now that all her brood were old enough to manage on their own. Elsie took whatever job she could get, but dreamed of going to Beauty College. They had all learned to make do on small means. Donda was a whiz at turning out delectable dishes from cuts of meat and vegetables that no one else would buy.

Elmo had finished his studies to be a chiropractor and set up practice at the harbor in San Pedro. He proved to be right about the number of stevedores who needed a back adjustment, and because he was someone they knew, they flocked to him for treatments. He knew that Rudy's father had been a doctor, and he asked Rudy whether or not he had ever thought about learning to be a chiropractor. Elmo loved his new profession and was convinced it was the best way to help people get well.

"It doesn't take as long as being an M.D., and you can work during the day and study in the evenings. There's good money in it afterwards, and I think it helps a lot of people who can't be helped even by osteopaths," Elmo explained.

Rudy liked Elmo's idea, and with a desperation born of need, he worked tirelessly, holding down his job during the daytime and, at nighttime, studying to be a chiropractor, hoping for a future that could block out his past. Vivian was happy to be close to her mother again and didn't seem to miss the nice place they had in San Francisco, but he was miserable, not being able to keep her in the style he felt she deserved.

Rudy had boasted that his wife would never have to work, but Vivian offered to get a job, saying that it would only be until he was finished with his studies. Before Rudy had consented, however, she discovered that she was pregnant. She was glowing with good health, and all their problems seemed unimportant, as she lapsed into the cocoon-like state a wanted pregnancy can bring.

Late in 1926, a little girl was stillborn during the eighth month. Vivian grieved and felt that her life again had veered off the path she had so carefully mapped out – First, Rudy losing his job, and now the worst loss of all, the loss of a baby. She carefully packed the tiny garments she had so joyfully collected, and gave them away, not being able to bear the sight of them.

Only the dark circles under her eyes hinted at the sleepless nights and the anguish she was feeling, during those weeks after losing the baby. She kept a protective shell around her innermost feelings and never let her disappointment show, even to those who were closest to her, but she was a contemplative person who faced life's problems and tried to find a solution to them, or that failing, a philosophy that would make those problems understandable. She prided herself on not ever complaining. Besides, Marcia was expecting, and it wouldn't do to cast a shadow on her happiness by mourning, she thought.

Of all Donda's offspring, Marcia was the one who demanded the least of her existence, living in the present and untroubled by the future. While Vivian was trying to come to terms with her loss, Marcia was weeding a bed of flowers by the path that led to the cottage where she and Lester had lived since they got married. She smiled as she felt the baby stir inside her womb, and she straightened her back and looked with satisfaction at the mixture of pansies and forget-me-nots freed from being choked by devil grass. Her first pregnancy had ended in a miscarriage, but she told herself that this time nothing would go wrong. Despite her disappointment when she lost the baby, Marcia remained sunny and happy, because she was so much in love. Her good disposition was like balm to Lester who sometimes suffered from dark depressions after those months in the trenches during the war.

Marcia liked the old dowager who employed them, but somehow didn't feel as comfortable around the woman's daughter. The daughter, Barbara Lamont, was a divorcee and had come home to lick her wounds. She was an attractive girl, but with a hard look about her. Restless and bored, she had nothing else to do than seek amusement. Still, Marcia didn't think anything was amiss when Barbara started demanding Lester's services more and more often.

Barbara often wanted him to drive her long distances, to Santa Barbara or Palm Springs where she had friends. Marcia was too naive to suspect another woman of being interested in her handsome husband, but Lester had the uncomfortable sensation that the woman fancied him. During these outings, she sometimes sat up front, claiming that riding in the back made her queasy. She got in the habit of speaking to him about personal matters, and though it made him uncomfortable at first, he eventually became accustomed to her ways, chalking it up to being one of the conditions of the job.

Marcia suddenly remembered that Lester would be coming home soon, and she went inside to start dinner. From the kitchen window she saw him when he walked up the path, and she felt that same flutter of excitement that she always did when she caught sight of him. He looked troubled about something, and she hoped he wasn't getting into one of his dark moods. She hurried to open the door before he got to it. He smiled as he put his arm around her and kissed her on the mouth, flicking his cap neatly onto the coat rack at the same time.

After they had eaten dinner, he mentioned that Barbara Lamont had told him to take her down to Hidden Lake early the next morning. "She said she has invited some girlfriend of hers along for a picnic."

He grumbled to Marcia as he put on his uniform the next morning. "I might be back late tonight, honey," he said. "One trouble with this dippy dame is that she doesn't have any concept of time. I wish she had something more important to do than gallivant around the countryside."

Marcia watched him with pride as he strode across the lawn towards the big house. He was wearing the blue shirt that was part of his uniform, his jacket thrown carelessly over one shoulder and the cap in his hand. She felt blessed to be married to a man who could give her so much pleasure, the joy she felt when she noticed small details, like the color of his hair in the sunlight or the sharp creases on the back of his shirt and the way he walked. She busied herself as soon as he was out of sight. She loved keeping their cottage neat as a pin and tending the chickens they kept in their small back yard, and it was nicer to get things done during the cool morning hours.

Lester sauntered over to the garage and put on his uniform jacket and cap before he got into the car and backed it out. When he got to the big house he went around back to the kitchen, to pick up a hamper with delicious smells seeping out from under the lid. He brought the car around front, and while he waited for his employer's daughter, he leaned against it, idly watching a peacock preen its feathers on the immaculately tended green lawn. The sky was blue, and it would be a hot day.

He heard Barbara saying goodbye to her mother and straightened to open the door for her as she came down the front stairs. She brushed against him as she climbed into the car, and he noticed her perfume. As she usually did when her mother was watching from the window, she sat in the back, busying herself with something in her handbag while Lester got behind the wheel and slowly drove down their long drive.

She was quiet, as the big car purred smoothly along Pasadena's wide streets. As usual, when they got a few blocks away from home, she asked him to stop and waited for him to open her door when she moved to sit up front.

As he started the motor, she told him they wouldn't be picking up her friend after all. "I'm not in the mood. Cook had already prepared the picnic lunch though, and I couldn't see why we couldn't just go to Hidden Lake anyway and eat it before driving back."

"Won't your friend be worried when we don't show up?" Lester asked, nervously.

"Don't you worry about that. It was to be a surprise. I hadn't said we were coming," she replied smoothly. "No one has to know, and don't tell me you wouldn't enjoy a good lunch."

Lester felt stiff and awkward. He knew this was all wrong, but jobs were hard to come by, and he didn't want to offend her by being prudish. Besides – What could he say that wouldn't make him sound like a fool?

He was by now well aware of the daughter's feelings about him, and he knew instinctively that it would be embarrassing for her if he let on that he knew. She could easily get him sacked, and where would he go then? All these thoughts milled about in his head, and he came to the conclusion that the best course was to continue to balance on this tight rope that her unorthodox behavior had stretched out for him. Who knows? She might otherwise get him fired by claiming that it was *he* who had been improper in his behavior. Damned upper class. There was no figuring them out.

He thought guiltily of Marcia and her unstinted devotion to him; she would never understand if he got involved with another woman. Still, with Marcia pregnant again, he couldn't imagine how they would manage if he lost his job. It would mean not only being without work, but they would also lose their lodgings.

He had managed to keep a polite distance to the daughter up to then, but there was something all wrong about the mood today. Deep inside he knew that if he shared the picnic lunch, they both would have crossed over an invisible barrier. He felt hot in his high-collared uniform jacket and beads of perspiration broke out on his forehead as he worried over the predicament in which he found himself.

It was a long drive, and Barbara chatted away, apparently oblivious to his discomfort. When they got to the shimmering lake, they parked in the shade of a live oak tree. They were miles from the nearest house, and the only sounds were those of a jay scolding from the branches above. She asked him to fetch the hamper from the car and watched him as he spread the things out on a checked cloth. She had removed her linen bolero, and her arms were bare in a scoop-necked blouse. She had a diamond pendant at her throat, and it flashed in the sunlight that filtered through the branches above. She was the exact opposite of Marcia, and he could see that some men would be attracted to her sultry good looks. A bit too overpowering for my taste, he thought to himself.

The lunch was delicious, prepared by her mother's excellent cook. There was a good bottle of Chablis to go with succulent pieces of chicken, home-baked rolls wrapped in crisp white napkins to keep fresh, and choice fruit. Lester was unaccustomed to wine, and he quickly felt warmth suffuse his body, blocking out worries about the trap that was closing around him. Their hands brushed several times during the meal. Hers were well tended, unmarred by any work, his brown and strong, with the slender fingers of a sensitive man.

The sound of crickets was loud in the dry heat, and her voice seemed to come from a distance when she told him to relax and take off his jacket and loosen his tie. The heat had faded the blueness of the sky, and the air didn't stir. Her brashness usually made him uncomfortable, but today he felt that he had come too far for it to matter whether he kept up the pretence of being with a superior. It was miles to the nearest house, miles from real life. No one to see them.

Afterwards, he couldn't or didn't want to recall exactly what happened, but all the way home, he was enveloped with the blackness of guilt. They had made love there, under the tree and bathed in the lake afterwards. Added to his guilt was the humiliating feeling that, although he was the man, it was he who had been seduced. It made him feel dirty.

Marcia's trusting face and affectionate hug when he came home later than usual that evening made things worse. He knew he couldn't tell her what had happened. He bottled up his feelings and hoped that something would happen to save him from what he could foresee would be a long series of betrayals.

This continued for some time, Barbara becoming increasingly flagrant in her passion for her chauffeur, and Lester increasingly weighted down with an overwhelming guilt. The physical pleasure he got from his trysts with Barbara made him feel like an animal. He couldn't develop affection for her, but when he was with her, he didn't have the will power to resist an erotic gratification.

Marcia's pregnancy ended in another miscarriage, and sad though they were, Lester felt he would finally be free to make a break with Barbara and risk losing his job. The next time she planned one of their excursions, he told her that he couldn't go on deceiving Marcia.

Not believing that she was being rejected, Barbara thought their different stations in society bothered him. By now she was obsessed with him, and she blurted out that she would marry him if he would throw Marcia over. She refused to believe him when he told her that he loved Marcia more than he could ever love anyone else.

When finally he convinced her he was serious, she became angry and reminded him that she had taken pictures of him half-undressed the last time they had been together. "I'll show them to your timid little wife and let her make the choice," she threatened. Lester felt cowardly as he smoothed her feathers and told her to forget about their disagreement.

He was entangled in a sticky web. The more he struggled to get free, the more firmly he was held fast. He knew Marcia would forgive him if she learned the truth, but things would never again be the same. If only they could just leave, go somewhere Barbara couldn't find them. But that would take planning, if he wanted to pull it off without Marcia asking too many questions, and where could he find another job when half of America seemed to be unemployed? He parked the car in the garage and closed the heavy door. His mind was cluttered with dark thoughts, and he was incapable of seeing beyond them.

Unsuspecting, Marcia had planned a romantic evening for him. She had fixed his favorite dinner, set the table with flowers and candles, and changed into the dress he liked best on her. Looking at her, with her innocent smile, and feeling the warmth of her kiss, he felt more miserable than ever. He started to say something, but ended by excusing himself to change clothes.

Lester had given Marcia a Model A Ford with a rumble seat to make it easier for her to see her family when he was working. After dinner, he suggested that they go for a ride over to see her mother and Elmo. It was a lovely evening for a drive. The dark silhouettes of the palm trees that lined the streets were brushed with silver where the full moon reflected off their fronds. Marcia had never felt happier as she nestled beside his lean body in their small coupe, the beauty of the still evening touching her with its magic. The moonlight was so bright that she would always remember it as a night when one could see everything clearly. Lester was quiet, but that wasn't unusual.

Their unexpected arrival at Donda's was a pleasant surprise. Albert was there, too, and he and Elmo asked Lester to sit with them and have a beer, while Marcia and her mother were in the kitchen making some coffee. It was a tranquil domestic scene like on so many other occasions.

After a few minutes of talk, Lester said that he wanted to get something in the car and excused himself. A minute later, they all heard a shot. Al and Elmo rushed outside and found Lester, a gun in his hand and half his face blown off.

Somehow an ambulance was called, and somehow they managed to keep Marcia from seeing Lester and the bloody remains of his face. Mercifully, he died a few hours later, leaving his young widow devastated and grieving to the point of distraction. Marcia collapsed and for months she wavered between life and death, not wanting to live and unable to die. She moved in with her mother and listlessly allowed Donda to care for her, but she couldn't eat and the family watched her waste away. Close though they were, Vivian could find no words to comfort her sister. She realized that all her problems were minor compared to Marcia's tragic loss.

Most cruel of all was the day Marcia learned about Lester's affair with Barbara. Barbara showed up at Donda's one day on the pretence of being interested in Marcia's well being. Instead, she took out a photograph of Lester, sitting on the grass, his shirt open at the neck. The photo was smudged with Barbara's lipstick, and she taunted Marcia, claiming that Lester was hers. She was like a demented woman. Donda threw Barbara out of the house, but the harm had been done.

Donda had begun to lose hope for Marcia when a neighbor asked to see her. She was a woman who had always liked Marcia, and she thought she could help her. She introduced Donda's distraught daughter to Christian Science, and through this new faith, Marcia struggled back to the land of the living.

If ever she felt a leaning towards self-pity, Vivian thought of Marcia's fate and wondered at the change that had taken place in her. From the timid, grief-stricken person she had been, she was transformed to a woman with an inner strength that lit up her face, like a faith in another world had made the sorrows of this one unimportant. No one else in the family turned to religion, but they were all pleased and relieved to see what it had done for Marcia.

Vivian's ambition to make a perfect life didn't leave her for long. She didn't like to admit failure, even to herself. She had always been singled out for her striking good looks and other people's expectations nurtured in her a desire to rise above the ordinary. Though she was kind and undemanding of others, she set very high goals for herself. If anything proved a woman's worth in those days, it was the role of mother. Her own mother had given birth to seven children. Bobbie had a bouncing baby boy. How could Vivian and Marcia ever have foreseen that they would have any trouble bearing children? The thought was so devastating that she pushed it into the deepest recesses of her mind. She disciplined herself to stop thinking about a home with children, and channeled her energy into other daydreams.

That was when she decided to get into the movies. She had already made lots of friends in Hollywood, and one of them was a girl who worked as an extra for Paramount Studios. She kept telling Vivian that she was so pretty she should be in the movies, and when Vivian said she wanted work, it was an easy matter to join the large group of extras needed for a film.

At first, Rudy was opposed, but she convinced him that she had to get out of the house to forget about the baby. He knew how much she had suffered, and he reluctantly agreed, even though it worried him that she would be mixing with the zany Hollywood crowd.

The agency she contacted liked her right away, and she had no trouble getting a start. She took the stage name of Vivian Martin and was soon a popular choice for bit parts at the major studios. There was good money even in being an extra, for they were paid for all the hours they stood around waiting for the big scene. Dozens of movies were churned out in those years, and Vivian established herself as someone who was a reliable extra. She had her choice of bit parts – playing the maid to screen divas, quick scenes with a chorus line, comedies with a bevy of pretty girls lined up for a beauty contest, or walk-on parts for cloak girls and secretaries. Bit actors had to buy their own costumes, and the studios liked to hire someone they knew would have the know-how to choose the right outfit for the role.

She worked on Maurice Chevalier's first American picture, "Innocents of Paris," and while she had no delusions about her own talent, she started to feel at home among the up and coming actors and actresses of the time.

Vivian turned over all the money she earned to Rudy, pleased to be able to help out. In the beginning, the money was secondary anyway; what she liked was the excitement of being on set with the famous actors and actresses of those times. Each day she was called out, she met interesting people. Hollywood was a melting pot of types, and she loved the atmosphere behind the scene, along with the easy friendships, capricious though they were.

She discovered that a lot of the girls were trying to sleep their way up to fame. It amazed her that some of them were willing to sell themselves to a long line of men, in an effort to get to the top. Old-timers pointed out to her star actresses who had begun with a cameraman and worked their way up to a producer. Gossip was rampant, and those who made it had to endure all the snide remarks from those clawing their way up from the rear. She occasionally thought about what a thin line separated her from those few who made it to the top, but having no great talent, she knew what price stardom would cost. It wasn't a prospect that appealed to Vivian. She was content to treat making movies like any other job.

It was natural that she and Rudy grew apart. They were spending their days in two different worlds, and his evenings were spent at school. To make matters worse, the old Rudy had changed. What happened in San Francisco had marked him. He hadn't intended to steal from the firm; it was something he lapsed into gradually, thinking that he would be able to pay it back. When so many months passed without his theft being discovered, he began to nurture the hope that the money he took never would come to light, and he kept promising himself that this one time would be the last.

That terrible day of reckoning, when he was called into the boss' office and was shown proof of his embezzlement, he was dumbfounded by the extent of it. His knees went weak, and he wondered whether they would put him in jail. His mind raced with possible excuses, but he stared at Mr. Combs without being able to speak.

Combs had always liked Rudy and admired him for all that he had done for his mother and sister. He also liked that pretty young bride of his. It was a darned shame that things had gone so far. Putting Rudy in jail wouldn't recover the money, and if he were any judge of character, this sort of thing would never happen again. When he called Rudy into his office, he had already decided not to press charges, but he had no choice but to fire him.

He was right. Rudy never did a dishonest act in his life after that, but he had also learned not to spend more than he had earned. Not only was he careful, he was cautious to the point of being miserly. He carefully monitored every penny that Vivian spent, and as her earnings increased, she became more and more annoyed with his stinginess. She loved nice clothes and had expensive taste. It was easy for her to convince herself that her good luck in landing bit parts in pictures was dependent upon her looking nice.

One morning she was dressed to meet on the set for "Crazy About Dames". She stood in front of the mirror in their small hallway, adjusting a smart little hat she had bought to match a soft green dress with a white organdy collar. Rudy's face was reflected in the mirror, as he stood behind her, studying her. She turned and asked, "What?! Is something the matter?"

"Isn't that another new hat? You just bought one a few days ago." He sounded peevish, and Vivian's quick temper flared.

"Well, so what! It's springtime, and I needed a few new things for the season. Honestly, Rudy! I can't show up at Fox looking like a charwoman, unless that's the part they've offered me."

It was seldom they quarreled, but now she felt like clearing the air and telling him that she was beginning to resent handing over all her earnings to him and having to ask for handouts. "I even have to ask you for car fare to get to work," she complained.

He was miserable when she was angry, and they patched it up, agreeing that she would chip in a small part of her earnings for their living expenses until he could open up a practice, and she could keep the rest in an account of her own.

After that, Vivian was surprised to see how quickly her account built up. It wasn't long before she could buy a car, making it so much simpler to get back and forth from the studios. She bought herself a snazzy little gray Plymouth convertible, and along with it a feeling of total independence. Meanwhile, she and Rudy continued to grow apart.

Finally, after ten years of marriage, she made up her mind to move out. Rudy had finished his studies and opened a practice in Los Angeles, and Vivian was earning enough to live comfortably on her own. It was wrenching for Rudy, but they parted amicably. Vivian had come to realize that what she felt for Rudy was the love that comes from a long-standing friendship, while Rudy loved her too much to spoil with angry words his hopes that she would come back to him.

Mickey Meets Vivian

Vivian found an apartment in the Hollywood Hills, in a building with a hundred steps leading down to the street. A large studio window gave her a view that swept over the valley below, and she felt literally lifted above the drabness of ordinary life. She was thirty-one years old, at the peak of her beauty and with the grace and poise that comes with maturity.

For the first time in her life, she had everything under control. She felt light years away from that depressing period when she watched her family's fortunes decline. She looked around her new home. Rudy had been generous and insisted that she take with her the things which could give her a good start, and her flair for making effects with fabrics had turned the apartment into a place with style and charm.

Her calico cat with its snowy white paws rubbed against her legs and purred. She picked him up and held him as she continued to gaze out the window, stroking his thick fur. "You like it here, too, don't you?" she said, looking into the cat's large inscrutable eyes.

At last things were going well for the whole family, she thought contentedly. Elmo was getting a reputation as a good chiropractor, referred to as "Doc" by a rapidly growing group of patients. He married Poli, a woman who was a talented commercial artist and a very clever businesswoman, insuring his financial success. Donda still lived on 2nd Avenue in Los Angeles, but gone were the days when she had to earn a living in a laundry or with her 'tea parlor,' now that Doc was able to support himself as well as her and Beulah.

Elsie had blossomed into a very pretty girl, and after racing about town in the fast lane with young George Raft and some of the wilder side of the movie set, she had married a policeman and settled down to housekeeping. Marcia was re-married to a jazz musician named Eddie Church. He would never be able to take Lester's place, but he loved Marcia and was a good provider.

Bobbie and Armand still lived in San Francisco. Vivian had traveled north alone to see them, but being with them turned out to be awkward, knowing they didn't approve of divorce. Bobbie was expecting a second child. Their first little boy was nearly six years old and reminded her of the grief she felt when her own child was stillborn. The very orderliness of their marriage jarred her feeling of confidence in the path she had chosen, and she was relieved to get back to the mad dash life in Hollywood.

Now that she had left Rudy, she felt no compunctions about going out on the town. Elsie's policeman husband was captain of the vice squad and often on duty at night. He didn't mind if the two sisters went out together to grand Hollywood parties, or during the daytime, to the popular lunch spots around town. They shared a love for dancing and a yen for adventure. Vivian was having more fun than she had experienced in a long time, and she had a good income to indulge her longing for beautiful things.

It was wonderful, after years of being careful, to treat herself to an occasional bottle of expensive perfume or a lovely new gown. This is a grand life, she thought, happily. There were plenty of men who asked her out, and she was old enough not to be taken in by the lines they fed a gal. If she met Mister Right she might give marriage another try, but if not, she seemed to be able to manage very well on her own.

However, as time passed, the luster of the Hollywood social scene soon tarnished for Vivian. She sometimes wondered whether success made people peculiar or whether peculiar people were more likely to be successful in Hollywood. She was glad she was too savvy to fall for the offers made to girls from the studios, but on one occasion she couldn't resist a gimmick to earn some easy money. The word was around that any attractive actress who wanted to pick up a hundred dollars could do so, with no strings attached, just by meeting up at an address in Beverly Hills on a pre-arranged afternoon. Whoever participated had to make a promise that she would tell no one what transpired.

"Sounds pretty bizarre to me," Vivian said to Lois, the cute little redheaded chorus girl who told her about it. "Nothing in this world is for free. You mean to say that you didn't have to take off your clothes or do anything nasty?"

"I promise!" Lois said. "Go on – Give it a try. All you have to do is call this number. A man will answer who is someone's personal secretary. He sounds real classy. He'll make an appointment for you to come. Oh, and you have to wear a black dress and a hat with a black veil, but honest, you won't have to take anything off! Just remember, you mustn't tell anyone what it's all about, or you'll spoil it for the rest of the girls. No foolin' – I did it, and I wouldn't give you a bum steer."

A hundred dollars was a heck of a lot of money, she thought, as she mulled the idea over in her mind. She was sure Donda would tell her to steer clear, but shoot, she knew how to take care of herself. Lois had promised her there was nothing dangerous or dirty. Her curiosity piqued, Vivian dialed the number. Just as Lois had said, the man who answered sounded like a gentleman and asked her kindly which afternoon she would prefer.

Encouraged by the fact that she should come in the afternoon and not at nighttime, she set an appointment for the next week.

The gates were open when she drove up the long drive to a mansion surrounded by an impressive park. She parked the car and, getting out, walked a bit hesitatingly to an imposing front door. She was dressed in a black wool crêpe dress, with a small, matching hat, the black veil gathered up smartly by the band. She wore short black kid gloves, and carried her handbag tucked under her arm. The sunny afternoon and her apparel stiffened her resolve. It didn't seem different than the feeling she would have if she were meeting up for a job interview.

Nevertheless, her heart was pounding when she picked up the heavy brass ring that served as a door knocker and let it fall, listening to it resonate in the quiet surroundings. Almost immediately, an English butler, dressed in tails, opened the door.

"Good day, Madam. Won't you come in?" he said in a detached way with a cultivated accent, his eyes absolutely impersonal. "Please follow me. You are expected."

He led the way across the polished floor of an enormous front hall that ended in a sweeping stairway. The high ceiling was elaborately decorated in stucco, and the room was rich even though it was nearly void of furniture. Doors to various parts of the house opened into the hallway, but one of them was shut. They stopped in front of that door, and the butler turned to quickly inspect her attire. Smiling his approval, he opened the door and then stepped back, asking her to enter. She felt startled when she heard the door shut softly behind her.

The room was submerged in darkness, and the contrast from the brightly lit hallway was so great that at first she stood still, trying to get her bearings. Her throat felt dry, but she reminded herself that if the other girls could get through this so could she. She saw that there was something at the other end of the spacious room, bathed in dim light. Taking a few steps forward, she thought it looked like a casket. She went closer, curious now as to what in the world was arranged for her. She tiptoed to avoid the sharp click of her high heels on the bare floor.

It was a casket, placed on a raised platform and banked by flowers, like it would be in a funeral parlor. Boldly, she went forward until she could step up and peer inside. There, in the padded satin dressing of the mahogany casket, was an old man, stark naked, spattered with something that looked like blood. The blue veins stood out on his white skin, and he looked very much dead. Suddenly, he opened his eyes and sat up smiling. Involuntarily, Vivian let out a scream. She almost fell off the platform as she turned and ran to the door, grabbing the doorknob and wrenching it open.

Nonplussed, the butler stood on the other side of the door, a small silver tray in his hand, with a hundred-dollar bill on it. "Thank you, Madam. Here is your payment."

It was such a relief to be outside again in the warm California sunshine. She was still shaking when she sat behind the wheel and began to laugh, embarrassed and relieved. She tucked the bill into her purse and drove off as if she were pursued. She had promised not to tell anyone about it, and now she knew why. For an old man who got his kicks out of hearing a woman scream, the set-up would be ruined if anyone knew what to expect. They needn't worry, she thought. I would be too mortified to admit that I was part of such a weird charade.

So much for the high and mighty of the Hollywood scene, she mused. She knew she would be likely to see this same man, dressed to the nines, cow-towed to by a whole army of studio people, but he had given Vivian a look at the chip in his veneer. Quite a big chip, too, she thought grimly.

Although she laughed it off, she didn't want to remember the perverse scene. She pushed to the back of her mind the nagging thought that she might have strengthened that dirty old man's conviction that people like her would do anything for money.

She admired her mother for being so open about her life and shortcomings, but when things were too close to home, Vivian was ambiguous in her thoughts about the ugly side of life. Later, she could laugh with Elsie about the episode, but she would never dream of telling Bobbie what she had done.

Now, looking out of the window of her apartment at the lush vegetation, newly washed by a welcome rain, she sighed with contentment. She didn't have any work at the studio that day, and she stretched lazily, like the cat, relishing the feeling of being well groomed, well fed, and free.

The phone rang, and a man with a very attractive voice asked if he could speak with Vivian Martin.

"I'm Vivian Martin. Who's calling?"

"This is Mickey Owen. I'm a Casting Director at Fox Studios. I saw you the other day on the set of 'Harmony at Home'. Right now I'm casting a film starring Bob Ames and Robert Harrison, and I think I have a part for you."

Vivian free-lanced at various studios, but there had been a string of jobs at Fox Studios, and she recognized Mickey's name. "That sounds good," she replied. "It would of course depend on when you plan to start shooting."

"If you could stop by my office tomorrow when you get through on the set, we can discuss details, and I can tell you about the script," Mickey said.

She agreed to drop by and thanked him for his call. Pleased, she hummed, as she got ready for her bath and an early night in bed. It would be exciting to be a big star, but there certainly were advantages to playing bit parts. For one thing, she didn't have to worry if she took a part in a movie that turned out a flop. For a star, that could mean the end of her career. Stars under contract were little better than slaves to the studios, obliged as they were to turn out a certain number of films without always having the option to turn down a script. Having small parts also meant that she could work in a lot of different movies, and she always liked meeting new people.

The next day, while chatting with the girls on the set, Vivian mentioned that she might be staying on at Fox a bit longer. "Do you know Mickey Owen?" she asked Gladys, a garrulous hairdresser who knew everyone who worked there and most of the studio scuttlebutt.

"Sure. Everyone knows Mickey. He has a personality that charms everyone, male, female or anything in between. He's a real Romeo, but he's such a nice guy that even the gals he's dumped talk nicely about him. He started out here as a messenger boy, but everyone likes him so well that it wasn't long before he had worked his way up to the top. He's been doing real well as casting director. He got married to a cute chorus girl last year, but the rumor is that they split up."

Her curiosity piqued, Vivian looked forward to their meeting that afternoon. She was still wearing the costume she had used on the set that day, a flapper-style sleeveless dress in yellow with a Peter pan collar and a pleated, plaid skirt in matching yellow and gray. The secretary looked up as she came into Mickey's front office, and when Vivian said who she was, she was told to go right on in.

Well, at least he isn't one of these characters who like to play the big shot by keeping you waiting in the front office, she thought, as she tapped lightly on the door and stepped inside.

Quick in his movements, Mickey spun on his heel and greeted her with a smile. He had been standing by the window, studying stills, and he looked at her as he had the faces in the photographs, with a professional objectivity. For an instant, all went quiet as he felt the impact of her beauty. He had seen her at a distance, and he had studied her face in the black and white stills, but he was unprepared for seeing her close up, in the flesh. Her hair was almost black, her eyes an indefinable hazel that shifted to green when she moved in the light. Her skin was flawless, with a warm flush on her cheek. Not a tall man, he noticed with pleasure that she was petite.

Poised, she introduced herself and reminded him that he had asked her to come by. That brief moment of time being suspended was broken, and he became his usual bustling self, coming around to the other side of his desk, and indicating a chair for her to sit on. He preferred to perch on the edge of his desk when he did sit still, but the impression she had was of someone who was full of energy, quick as mercury.

He filled her in on the plot of the film he was casting. It was titled "Nix on Dames," and there was already a good comedy cast put together. Vivian liked working on comedies. She had become friendly with so many bit players, and the mood in Hollywood was of relaxed fun while great quantities of low-budget movies were turned out each month. She readily agreed to take a small part in this one when she found it wouldn't conflict with her other commitments.

"That's splendid," Mickey said. "Now how 'bout dinner?"

She thought about what Gladys had said and couldn't help but get a kick out of how fast he made a move. He was even more attractive than she had imagined, and it was tempting to accept; however, she was smart enough to know that in the relaxed atmosphere of Hollywood, it paid not to throw all caution to the wind. If he really wanted to take her out, he could work a bit harder at it.

"That would be nice," she said primly, "but I have plans for this evening." She smiled at him, secretly hoping that he would find another opportunity to ask her out.

"Then at least let me drive you home," he quickly offered.

"Thank you, but I have my car on the lot." If this were a duel, she had just said, "Touché!"

He looked at her and shook his head, chuckling under his breath. This one wasn't going to be easy. "Well, at least let me walk you to your car," he said brightly. "I don't give up easily."

They walked out to the parking lot, and he helped her into her car. He was intrigued. She was different from the run of the mill actress. He had watched her in her scene with William Collier, an old-time pro, and his professional eye could pick out her lack of real talent for acting. What he detected now was a much more important talent in his opinion, an ability to come across as a real lady, without sacrificing that warm spark of life. Fire and ice. After she left, he couldn't get her off his mind.

He went back to his office and puttered around an hour or so, delaying the moment when he would have to face going home. His mother and Dell no longer even pretended to hit it off. Having two battling females under the same roof was turning into a hassle, and he found himself procrastinating more and more often, claiming that he had work at the studio and would be late.

Jane objected to his choice from day one, but Dell argued that his mother would object to anyone who came into his life. Dell was the sexiest gal he had ever met and a good sport to boot, but from the moment she moved in and life became complicated, some of the shine went off her attributes.

Jane was right about one thing: He realized now that his main motive for marrying Dell was to take her to bed. Still, things might have been different if they had moved into a place of their own, but Jane made sense when she insisted on them staying with her and saving up. For some reason, Mickey never seemed to save up anything on his own.

He felt sorry for Dell, having to cope with his mother. The artificial atmosphere of the film industry suited him better than the drudgery of domestic relations, and, without a chance in hell of maintaining an atmosphere of romance while living in the same house as his mother, Dell no longer had the same appeal. In his mind they were already divorced, and all that remained were the unpleasant details of disentangling their lives.

He toyed with the thought of driving out to the Coconut Grove. He could always say he had to meet one of the bosses out there and get his opinion on the film they were doing. However, he thought better of it, knowing how much Dell hated being alone with his mother.

When he got back to the house, Jane was cloying sweet in her greeting, and a look at Dell told him there had been a row. She followed him when he went into the bedroom and she shut the door behind her.

"Mickey, if I have to spend any more time under the same roof as your mother, I'm gonna' go nuts. You promised me months ago we'd get a place of our own."

Mickey felt a pang of sympathy for her. He knew what it would be like to be cooped up with his mother and didn't envy her. She no longer resembled the fun-loving gal he met two years ago. It was like all the starch had gone out of her.

Dell thought she had played her cards right when she went for Mickey. She could tell even then that he would be hard to pry away from his mother, but she didn't know how hard. She knew moving would have made a difference for their chances, but his economy was so tied up with his damned mother that she had come to the realization that they couldn't just split out. Mickey kept saying they would move as soon as he saved up enough, but Jane was right about one thing. He couldn't save a dime. To Dell he always made excuses, like "You don't get anywhere in Hollywood being a skinflint." The biggest problem was that Mickey had a way of making his excuses sound plausible.

"You know I want to move out, honey, but first I have to scrape together enough money. My options right now are nil."

"Well, my patience is nil," Dell retorted. "If you really love me, you'll understand that another day in this house and I'll not be left with an ounce of self-respect. You should hear the way your mother talks to me when you're not around."

Mickey believed her. He could hear the snide innuendoes Jane slyly got across even when he was there. He knew she would do anything to break up their marriage, and somehow she had managed to turn Dell into someone he felt less eager to fight for. Maybe it would be best for the poor kid if she tried her luck somewhere else. He looked at her without reassuring her of his love.

After what seemed like a long silence, Dell said softly, "Alright, Mickey, that was just a test. I've lost hope that you are ever going to untie the apron strings. We've had a hell of a lot of fun while it lasted, and I'd rather remember that than to stay around here and get bitter. I'm moving in with my mother again. If you figure out that you want me more than you want that old battleaxe, you know where to find me."

She loved Mickey too much to be angry with him for not standing up for her. Jane was too formidable a foe to be beaten by the likes of her. She could see that Mickey was miserable seeing her unhappy, but he was so conditioned to include his mother in his life that Dell figured it would take a stronger woman than she was to free him from Jane's grasp. Meanwhile, she wanted to get back to being the happy-go-lucky gal she was before she got herself into this mess. She picked up the phone on the nightstand beside the bed and dialed her sister's number. She asked to be picked up as if it had been pre-arranged. Taking a suitcase from the closet, she quickly threw in enough clothes to tide her over.

When her sister honked, Mickey was still sitting on the bed, looking dejected. She kissed him lightly on the cheek as she left the room, saying "Let me know when your mother is away, and I'll borrow my brother-in-law's car to pick up the rest of my things. Buck up, Mickey. I'll be so happy to get away from that old biddy that you shouldn't worry about me."

Jane made a show of busying herself in the kitchen when Dell came sailing through. "I hope to God someone pries him away from you someday," she spat out as she passed by. She slammed the door and hurried out to the street before Jane could scorch her with a reply.

God, how I hate that woman, Dell thought. As much as she had wanted Mickey, she couldn't help but feel a tremendous sense of relief now that she had left at last. It was a good thing my sister convinced me of the futility of staying on in hopes that things would change, she thought. If Mickey really loves me, he'll realize he has to move out to get me back.

Mickey, however, was still sitting on the bed, relishing the thought that a tremendous burden had just been lifted off his back. He couldn't resist Dell when she was a barrel of fun, but it had been a long time since they had a good laugh together. He reminisced about their honeymoon, that week spent at Big Bear, and smiled, recalling how great it was to make love as much as he wanted and as often as he wanted. They stayed in a small cabin and only emerged for meals. It was off-season, and the place had been all but deserted, but when they got back to Hollywood, the newness started to fade. She was a swell gal, but she couldn't hold a candle to someone like Vivian.

Better not show Jane I'm relieved, he thought. She'll just crow about it and tell me she was right all along. If I act dejected, she'll give me some rope for a while. He started to whistle as he changed clothes and stopped himself, looking in the mirror for the proper facial expression to present to Jane. He knew her well enough to figure out that she would be putty in his hands if she thought there was any chance that he would run after Dell. Might as well let her steam awhile and take advantage of the situation.

Jane was alert when he came into the kitchen, wondering what had taken place. "I don't know what got into Del," she said sweetly. "Seems to me she flies off the handle over any bitty little thing."

"Well, Jane, you must have outdone yourself this time. It takes a lot to get Dell's goat. She's about the most even-tempered person I know."

"She might be even-tempered, but she's not good enough for you," Jane retorted. "She won't listen to a word I say about how she could improve herself, and she thinks just because she's married to you it gives her the right to make changes around here."

Mickey interrupted her, knowing that she was just getting warmed up and would go on for hours if she first got a good start. "Dell's left, so I guess you don't have to worry about her making any changes."

He poured himself a drink and walked out on the patio, giving his mother time to let that bit of information sink in.

Jane was delighted, but she knew she had to be cautious. She couldn't let Mickey see that she had planned to drive Dell off ever since the day she met her. Such a simple little gal had no place in the plans she had made for her son. He needed to develop more before he would be ready for a wife, and when that day came, she wanted him to find a woman who would be an asset to him. It's no good crowing now, she thought. If I leave him alone for a few days, he will see for himself how much nicer it is with just the two of us being here.

As they sat down to dinner, Mickey was already planning a party for the weekend. With Jane away for the weekend and Dell out of the house, he could hardly wait to celebrate.

* * * * *

Back at the studio on Monday, he found himself constantly going to the window, hoping to get a glimpse of Vivian. Once he saw her with a flock of extras, and she happened to look up, smiling back when he waved. He made a mental note of what time of day it was, and checking the progress of the film she was working on, he knew that she would be likely to pass by at approximately the same time the next day.

This time, he made a point of being there, and she stopped when he greeted her. It was a hot day, and she had been on the set for hours, but she looked cool and tidy.

"Bing Crosby invited me to bring a date and come to an informal party this Friday. Do you think I could persuade you to join me?" he asked, figuring that Bing's name would carry a bit of weight.

Mickey had been on Vivian's mind more than once during the weekend, but she had decided that she ought to stay clear. For one thing, as far as she could gather, he was married. However, she hesitated. Maybe that was just a rumor. Bing was known for his parties, and where he was there was usually good music.

Seeing her hesitate, Mickey hurried to explain that there would be a lot of fun people there, and, he said with a mischievous look in his eyes, "I promise to get you home early, if that's what you're worrying about."

She felt her resistance melting but decided to make sure he wasn't married. "It sounds like fun, Mr. Owen, but aren't you a married man?" she said boldly.

He liked her for being straightforward. It seemed to be a rare trait in Hollywood, as rare as lasting marriages. Looking sad, he admitted that he was married, "But I'm afraid it was a big mistake. My wife and I have separated. We've decided to call it quits while it's still easy to break up."

That sounded fair enough for Vivian. She could easily sympathize with how it was to be married and not really be married. That had been the trouble with Rudy, and her moving out was just an admission of something that happened long before they called it quits.

"I'd like to come," she said. "What time shall I be ready?"

He arranged to pick her up at eight p.m. They parted, and as he walked away, he felt that familiar sense of pure happiness bubble up inside him, like it always had when he was about to take a step in a new direction.

The party at Bing's was enough to break the ice. He tried to make a pass at her when he took her home, but was promptly rejected. Quickly backing off, he apologized, telling her in a winning way that she was so irresistible that he had a hard time staying in line.

"Will you drive to Malibu with me next weekend and join the same crowd for a beach party?" he asked.

"I'd like that," she said with a smile, liking that he was asking. Who could resist someone like Mickey? "But hands off, agreed?" she said firmly.

"Scouts honor." He nimbly skipped down the many steps to his car and drove off with a big smile pasted on his face.

The following Saturday, Mickey arrived in the early evening. He was casual in ducks and a blue and white striped, short-sleeved shirt, open at the neck. His blue eyes were striking against his tan face, and she liked the smile wrinkles that were at the corners of his eyes. She was ready to go and stepped outside before he reached her door.

Mickey stopped and stood gazing at her when she said hello, smiling at her with an approving look, as if to say "You're just the way I expected you to be". His touch was light on her arm as they went down the steps to his car, but she felt very much aware of the contact.

He had borrowed a swanky car from his friend, Willy Best, the black comedian. Willy talked him into it, telling him it guaranteed success with the ladies.

"Quite an impressive car, you have," she said as he opened the door for her. It was a black convertible, and the interior had the rich smell of new leather.

With a mischievous glance at her, he said "Willie Best loaned it to me ... He said that this might be just the ticket to melt your cold heart."

She smiled in spite of herself, and, as he got in behind the wheel, she noticed the pleasing scent of soap and after-shave.

"And," he continued, "he also said that you're a pretty classy dame ... Not immune to the taste of champagne." With that, he reached in the back and picked up a champagne cooler with a bottle neatly nestled in chipped ice. From the glove compartment, he took two tall glasses and eased the cork out of the bottle, quickly pouring the golden, frothy wine into the glasses and giving her the first glass. She felt a current of pleasure run through her body when their fingers touched, as he put the stemmed glass in her hand.

"To your health, my beauty." He looked at her over the edge of the glass, with laughter in his eyes, but with something more, a direct look that went right to the heart of her and made it skip a beat.

Flustered, she was afraid her voice would betray her when she tried to make a joking remark about him being as dangerous as his reputation. She reminded herself of her determination not to let this evening get out of control, but she could see that she was up against more than she had bargained for. Her reserve was second nature to Vivian. Her background built it up. Forced to learn to take care of herself at an early age, she knew that America was not only the land of opportunity, but also the land of opportunists. Still, it was quite a challenge to ignore the sensations produced by Mickey's presence.

She was relieved when they drove off, and the conversation turned to small talk about the studio and people they both knew, but she couldn't shake off the feeling that she was wrapped up in some delicious spell. He asked her to hold his glass while he drove, and each time he reached for it to take a sip, taking his eyes momentarily off the road to make contact with hers, their hands touched, making her feel giddy with a sensual delight. He drove effortlessly, deftly steering the luxurious car over the winding road.

Vivian loved champagne, but she decided to be cautious and sipped it slowly. The conversation flowed smoothly. They talked of life's dreams and of things they liked. It was as if they were old friends, one of those rare meetings of mind that are tangibly stimulating. She wondered whether he was like this with everyone, or if there really was something special taking place.

They drove towards a flaming sunset, and when it grew dark, he stopped and put up the top. There was a feeling of intimacy in the closed car, as they drove on, enveloped in darkness, except for the lights from the dashboard and the glow from the tip of his cigarette. Vivian didn't want the drive to come to an end. Right now, it was enough to bask in the simple magic of this nebulous contact.

Malibu was the 'in' place for the fun-loving Hollywood crowd. Referred to as mad and merry Malibu, there was a whole string of celebrities who owned places right on the beach, and their parties were famous. When Mickey and Vivian arrived, the others were already there, gathered around a campfire on the beach. Mickey and Vivian joined them just as they had all decided to take a swim. They ran up to the house to change into swimsuits and chased each other across the broad belt of white sand to the water's edge.

Having come from the heart of America, far from the sea, none of Donda's family was a good swimmer, but Vivian loved the surf and waded out as far as she could and still touch bottom. There was a full moon, but the water was inky darkness, and she felt a sudden panic, not liking that she couldn't see what might be in the water with her.

Mickey was in his element and boldly dove in, swimming underwater with swift strokes in the direction where Vivian had gone. She was gazing at the path of the moon on the water when she felt her ankles gripped by two strong hands, and Mickey emerged and took her in his arms. He laughed at the startled look on her face, and then his eyes were serious as he looked at her for what seemed like a long moment before he kissed her, tenderly on the mouth.

Caught off her guard, the sensation was too delicious to resist at first, but then she came to her senses. She didn't want him to get the impression that she was someone easy. She gently pulled herself free and quickly looked around to see whether or not anyone had seen them.

It was too late, though. He knew she had enjoyed that kiss and was already planning when he might be able to steal the next one.

"Brr. It's colder than I expected," Vivian said, as she waded through the surf towards the beach. She ran ahead and grabbed her towel to dry off, anticipating that he would otherwise use this opportunity to help her.

Later the party moved indoors, where they sat in front of an open fireplace, drinking and exchanging the light banter that comes easily to people who spend so much time together both at work and play. They were an appealing lot, the sort of people who gravitate towards a Mecca for cinema or theater. Mickey had so many friends it seemed, and even those who hadn't become famous were charming and talented.

Vivian sat on a sofa, and Mickey placed himself at her feet, leaning against the armrest where he could feel the warmth of her leg. She wondered whether people could detect the electric charges that were passing between them, but it was a lively crowd, too sophisticated to be concerned. She reminded herself that she had decided to be firm with Mickey and not let things get out of hand. There were too many things she didn't know about him, and a gal was a real fool if she let a man get the upper hand too soon.

During the next few weeks, Mickey scarcely thought about Dell. He noticed one evening that she had been by during the daytime and picked up her belongings. It was indicative of what sort of marriage they had that there was so little change once her things were gone. All the furniture belonged to Jane, and Dell had never had a ghost of a chance to put her stamp on the home.

Mickey still had a soft spot for her, but right now he was so intrigued with Vivian Martin that his thoughts of Dell were fleeting. He had never met anyone like Vivian. It wasn't just her looks that appealed to him. She had a quick mind and the same appetite for life that he himself had. It always puzzled him that so many people seemed to have such narrow horizons, but Vivian was interested in all aspects of life. He was careful not to rush her, savoring every moment they spent together and fearful lest she should stop seeing him. For once, he realized he was up against a real challenge.

The next time they were together was an afternoon when he asked her to stop by his office to talk about another part. She got there just as Phyllis, his secretary, was leaving. Mickey was in the anteroom, and Vivian noticed the jovial tone between the two of them. She mentally chalked this up as another winning quality of Mickey's.

They went into his office, and she sank down into an over-stuffed leather chair with a sigh of comfort. She had been on her feet all day in high heels, and it felt good to sit down.

The room was in shadows, with the sky turning red outside the big, plate-glass window facing the studio lots. Except for the occasional closing of a door and distant chatter, it was quiet in the building. People must have taken off early for the weekend, she thought to herself.

Mickey came over and sat on the arm of the chair and, with his index finger, carefully outlined the smooth contour of her cheek. He knew from experience that he could get farther with a woman if he didn't do anything to make her start worrying about her hair or clothing being mussed. It suited him. He was a sensual person who savored the small details about a woman, like a gourmet relishes spices.

They lost track of time as their petting became more intense. Mickey knew for sure – He was head over heels in love and nothing else mattered. It was Vivian who broke off, insisted that she had to be going, but he knew it was only a matter of time before she would be his. This was different though. He wanted more than just a lay.

In her car, driving home, Vivian drove by instinct. She found it impossible to concentrate on anything. Her body had taken control of her mind, and she was too steeped in the sensations of the evening to pursue a serious thought. Though she still managed to keep Mickey from stepping over the line, she knew she wasn't going to be able to resist him much longer.

He took her dancing at the Trocadero that weekend, and they both knew that they were biding time until afterwards when he would spend the night at her apartment. Vivian threw caution to the wind and let herself be swept up in the excitement of that evening and the many nights to follow.

Afterwards, she was upset. Her life had veered out of control. When she was with Mickey, she found herself in a delightful sphere where nothing mattered but the moment. She didn't doubt his love for her, and she knew that in his mind they were already married. That didn't help her feelings of propriety. She hated worrying about whether the neighbors saw him leaving her place in the early hours before dawn, and she dreaded the day when one of her family might come barging in when he was with her. Even Rudy seemed to know what was going on, and though he knew better than to say anything, she was embarrassed to think that he might disapprove.

Mickey laughed at her discomfort. She had never known anyone so unconventional, and while this trait explained part of the excitement of being with him, it embarrassed her when others were involved. What am I doing anyway, she thought. He's five years younger than I am, and as zany as he is he's still tied down to that dreadful mother of his, whether he likes to admit it or not. She was annoyed that things had got out of hand when there was so much about their relationship that left her in doubt.

On the other hand, she longed to be with him when they were apart. Finally she decided that it would be easier to explore their feelings for each other if they could really be alone. She felt an urge to remove herself from the present scene, move somewhere quiet and somehow get her life back to the pleasant orderliness she had enjoyed for what seemed like such a short time, before she met Mickey. She started perusing the ads for houses, hoping to find something less accessible than her present apartment, and one day she saw something that had all the appeal of a real change. It was a mountain cabin in Laurel Canyon, a thousand feet up in the hills.

She called the real estate agent and arranged a meeting for the very next day. It was a fine spring morning, and she left the top down on her car as she drove past the imposing mansions in the foothills, up the winding road through Laurel Canyon where the hills were etched sharply against a bright blue sky. Recent showers had tinged everything with the fresh green of springtime, and the air was fragrant with the scent of wild flowers and sage. The roadside was a wilderness of tangled growth, alive with hummingbirds and jays, mocking birds and pigeons, and she felt the happiness one experiences when the start of an adventure is blessed by good weather. The scenery reminded her of happy moments from her childhood, when her family lived in the countryside.

Bob McKewin, the real estate agent, was already there, leaning against his parked car with a bored expression. A sale like this didn't really have his interest. The property would only appeal to a type who liked outdoor living, and there was far more money in selling something in Beverly Hills. The very stillness of the place seemed to make time stand still in a way that was a trifle unnerving to someone who liked business at a fast pace. He straightened up when he heard Vivian approach and waved a greeting. When she stepped out of her car and smiled, he whistled under his breath in surprise. She was definitely not the type he had expected to show up to see a rustic mountain cabin. Dressed smartly in a lavender-blue ensemble, she was stunning. Mentally dismissing the probability of making a sale, he wondered whether he could get up the nerve to ask her out to dinner. She was wearing a big diamond, he noticed, but no wedding ring.

Vivian could hardly conceal her excitement when she saw the house. There was a garage, built into the hillside and level with the road. The cabin was perched above, with a steep flight of rustic steps, leading from the left side of the garage to the back door, and a winding path of steps, over terraces to the front door.

She was enchanted with the place from the moment she laid eyes on it, charmed by everything...from the heavy, oak front door, to the shingled roof. There was a small living room, with a smooth tiled floor that was the color of red bricks. The walls and low, beamed ceiling were knotty pine. At the end of the room, large windows framed a vista of the deep canyon and sheer hillsides.

There was a small kitchen, like a ship's galley, with a door out onto a terrace, shaded by a large pepper tree that grew on a smooth plateau. Beyond that was a sheer drop-off, studded here and there with tall stalks of yucca, 'candles of God', with their creamy clusters of flowers, standing out against the gray-green tangle of chemise brush, greasewood, and manzanita.

Through French doors there was a screened sun porch facing the road. She opened them, letting in the fragrant mountain air. There was space enough for a cot, and she thought how nice it would be to sleep there on a hot summer night.

Smiling with pleasure, she stepped back into the living room and walked to the other end of the cottage where there was a lovely bathroom, with peach colored fixtures, and beyond that a sunlit bedroom. She didn't hesitate. "I'll take it," she said to the surprised agent.

Poor Rudy, she thought, when she told him the news. He had come by just after she got home. She had already signed the papers. He seemed genuinely distressed. Ironically, he, whom she considered so prudent, was a true romantic. He had never stopped loving her.

With his characteristic cautiousness, he clucked disapproval of the cabin in Laurel Canyon. "The place will be crawling with rattle snakes, there's poison ivy everywhere, and it's miles from stores, not to mention the fact that there won't be a neighbor in sight." He shook his head and couldn't comprehend how a woman who adored the feeling of silk and the scent of expensive perfumes could want to live like a gypsy in the hills.

She didn't try to explain, but she realized that his inability to understand this side of her was the key to their incompatibility. Mickey, she knew, would be as excited as she was.

* * * * *

By moving to the isolated cabin, Vivian threw down her last barrier. It was the perfect love nest, and Mickey used any pretence he could think of to escape Jane's scrutiny and spend a night with Vivian.

His biggest hurdle was the fact that his car broke down, and he needed to buy a new one. Seeing it as an opportunity to get a leash on him, Jane said he could use hers until he had put aside some money. At first he had not found it to be a problem – They seldom needed her car at the same time, but now that Vivian had moved, a car was a necessity. Furthermore, Jane had a sneaking suspicion there was something afoot and used all her cunning to put hurdles in the way of him falling into a new trap.

She fumed inwardly, knowing he just wasn't ready for marriage. It was too soon. Dell's leaving put Jane's plans for Mickey right back on track, but everything going for him would be wasted if someone else came along and turned his head. Jane knew what elements counted for striking it rich, and a man's chances were far greater if he could reach a secure high place before he got shackled down with a wife and family. If only she could keep a tight rein on him until he learned to be prudent!

She made it a practice to use the car all the time, forcing Mickey to tell her his plans if he wanted to have it. It irritated the hell out of Mickey. Even cousin Jack has his own car for gawd's sake, he thought. He remembered with irritation the night he had to ask Jack to drive him out to Laurel Canyon. Vivian had been madder at hops with him for saying he didn't like her seeing Rudy, and he was desperate to make up with her, but Jane was off on one of her jaunts to 'the high country' as she put it.

He had instructed Jack to kill the motor down the road from Vivian's and wait while Mickey knocked on her bedroom window. "If I don't come back to the car before an hour is up, take it as a sign that I'm back in her good graces and just go on home," he said.

Jack had almost fallen asleep, waiting to see whether or not Mickey was forgiven. Later, when Vivian found out Jack had driven Mickey up there and would know he had spent the night, she was mad all over again.

The solution to Mickey's car problems came when he got the idea of 'borrowing' cars from the studio's car pool. His hedonistic nature, coupled with the fact that Jane had never denied him anything he wanted, left him totally lacking in a sense of property. Tangible things were there for the using – like props that were useful in the world as a stage. Being an only child, he had never found it necessary to think in terms of 'yours' and 'mine.' Generous to a fault, he was also capable of giving things away which didn't belong to him or borrowing things without asking. More than once he gave away things that belonged to Jane in order to gain favor with a childhood sweetheart. Now that he was a big shot at the studios there was a treasure-trove of temptations. He didn't hesitate to shower friends and family with the trappings of filmmaking, fabulous velvet drapes or other furnishings that had been used on the sets of the films he cast.

Such details were of little importance in the overall picture, for vast amounts of props were needed for most of the films. However, Mickey was on thin ice when he started to eye the collection of magnificent cars that were often left standing on the studio lot during weekends. Anyone could see that the studio's executives didn't need those cars before Monday morning when they returned from their luxurious retreats in Palm Springs or Santa Barbara, he reasoned.

Sometimes he was told to take one of the cars to pick up a celebrity at the train when they came out from the East Coast to star in one of Fox's pictures. He knew which cars were available, and the man who was hired to keep them clean and in working order knew Mickey. It was easy for him to get in the habit of borrowing one of those when he found himself in a spot. He made sure they were back in place before the weekend was over, and so far no one had noticed.

He got away with this maneuver until one weekend when Vivian had a part in a western, and scenes were being shot on the desert. Mickey arranged to meet her on the shoot and take her to Death Valley Scotty's castle afterwards. Scotty was an old friend of Jane's, and Vivian was bound to be impressed with Scotty's place. They would have a whole blissful weekend together.

When he discovered that Jane would be gone with the car that same weekend, he knew he would have to scrounge around for wheels. He was well aware of Vivian's misgivings about their relationship, and he didn't like to give her the impression that he was not a man of the world, with everything under control. Willy Best wasn't in town, so that angle was out, and as luck would have it, there were slim pickings among the staff cars. Then he spotted the limousine that Fox Studio reserved for visiting VIP's.

As far as he could see, it was just going to be standing idle that weekend. It was a honey of a car, a Rolls Royce that could seat seven in elegant comfort. He started thinking about whom he could invite to join them and got all excited about the plans the car was inspiring.

They had a fabulous weekend. The friends Mickey invited were well known in Hollywood, and it didn't occur to Vivian that Mickey wasn't authorized to take the luxurious car from the studio. When he dropped her off at her place late Sunday evening, he felt he had come closer to winning her over. Without a care in the world, he idly drove the car back to the studio and parked it where it belonged.

*****

Zanuck was furious. It wasn't just the fact that the car wasn't there when he needed it, but the general lax attitude that annoyed him. He always had found that damned casting director to be too cocky for his own good. He passed the word around that as soon as Mickey showed up, he wanted to see him in his office immediately.

Mickey bounced in around nine, sporting his usual exuberant mood. "Hi, Phyllis! How's my favorite secretary?" he said, breezing by her on the way into his office.

"Oh, oh, wait a minute, Mickey. Mr. Zanuck is on the war path, and you're going to have a hard time smoothing his feathers."

Still smiling, Mickey's eyes went round in an expression of surprise. "No kidding? Did he mention what's the matter?"

"You're going to need all your charm. He seems to think that you borrowed his favorite limo for a long weekend."

"Hells bells. I was sure no one would miss it," Mickey muttered as he straightened his bow tie and headed for Zanuck's office.

He tried to think of a good approach for explaining his misdemeanor, but it was a short walk to Darryl Zanuck's office. He arrived not having come up with a good idea and decided the best thing to do was to let Zanuck bawl him out and then take it from there.

The look on Zanuck's secretary's face wasn't encouraging, and for once, Mickey was subdued when he knocked on Zanuck's door. He thought of William Fox and how well they had hit it off, but Fox had run into a string of bad luck. He over-invested during the transition from silent to talking movies, and a serious car crash and the stock market crash of '29 had just about finished him off. In '35 Zanuck took over to save a sinking ship, and he was another kettle of fish. Things had tightened up, and everyone but Mickey was watching out.

"Good morning, Mr. Zanuck. I was told that you wanted to see me," Mickey intoned innocently.

Zanuck was standing behind his desk, and he shuffled through some papers, not looking at Mickey immediately. There was an ominous silence, and when he spoke, his voice was cold. He went right to the point.

"No one authorized you to take the studio limo over the weekend." Mickey started to offer an explanation, but he was cut off. "I don't care what sort of harebrained excuse you have. This outfit is in the red, and it's people like you who got it that way. I've had a look at your expense account, and it seems to me that casting can be done without so much wining and dining. This isn't the first time I've called you on the carpet for expenses. I know you had a lot of freedom before I came, but all that has to stop if I'm going to get Fox back in the running. You're fired! Miss Berlin will see that a check is made out for anything we owe you. I want you to clear your office today."

Mickey was flabbergasted. He was too surprised to protest. He just walked out, past the secretary, and straight back to his office, shutting the door without uttering a word.

"Jesus! I've done it now," he said, shaking his head.

Phyllis was dying of curiosity. She knocked softly on the door and heard Mickey tell her to come on in.

"What happened, Mickey? Zanuck had a hizzy fit when he got to work this morning and got wind that it was you who took the car."

"Yeah. I guess he meant it. He gave me the sack."

"You're kidding! Damn the luck. He could at least have given you another chance." Phyllis, always loyal, was working herself into a state.

Mickey was touched and amused to see her so mad on his behalf. He knew that in all fairness he didn't have any call to be angry.

"Don't worry about me, Phyllis. Zanuck feels like he has to set an example, and I was the chosen one."

Phyllis left the room, and Mickey stood beside his desk. He ran his eyes over the inventory, thinking about how much he had enjoyed his climb up to the job of casting director. He walked over to the window and looked out at the busy scene below, prop men moving things to different sets and actresses all dolled up, milling around. He would miss it, but his mind was already tackling the problem of what to do now. He could hear Jane harping that all this trouble was due to him getting mixed up with Vivian and trying to impress her.

Suddenly, he walked across the room and stuck his head out the door, saying, "Phyllis, honey, would you do me one last favor and get hold of Steve Frazer over at RKO?"

By afternoon that same day he had landed a job as casting director at RKO. Of course, he hadn't mentioned the fact that he had been fired at Fox.

* * * * *

Having landed on his feet, Mickey began to work up the same enthusiasm for RKO that he had felt at Fox Studios. With stars like Katherine Hepburn and Spencer Tracey under contract, there were some good films being turned out. Walt Disney was about to sign a contract for RKO to distribute his clever cartoons, and Mickey thought the chances looked great at his new place of employment.

Now that Vivian lived in the canyon, he discovered another side to her that made him love her even more. She could be his glamorous companion for a Hollywood party, and she just as easily fell into the role of the down-to-earth gal who loved to dig out undergrowth and plant flowers on her terraced garden.

One weekend he took her on a camping trip, and she gamely ate the charred potatoes he had roasted in a bonfire. She was as appealing as a child, with a black smudge on her nose. When the fire had burnt out, they lay wrapped in a warm quilt, gazing at the splendor of the desert sky. In the clear air, the stars were dazzling, so big and bright that one felt drawn into their midst, afloat in the universe.

At times like that Vivian could forget all caution and feel like there was a union of their souls. Still, part of her held back when Mickey spoke of being together forever. He had proposed to her so many times, and she always turned him down. It nagged her that he was dependent on his mother, and she could more easily have accepted his crazy behavior if he had enough money to turn his back on the establishment. Life had taught her that you were only free to have fun if you had paid the rent. Mickey seemed to have no concept of taking care of money.

Being involved with Mickey was like being in a whirlwind, with little time left for serious thinking. A new springtime came, and Vivian awoke each morning filled with joy at the beauty of the canyon. She thought less and less about the future, being content to relish the present.

At first, it was more with a sense of wonder than alarm that Vivian realized that she was pregnant. After the miscarriage of Rudy's and her baby, she had ruled out having children. With Rudy, it was easy to do, because he was so obsessed with building up security. Now she realized that her longing for children had never died, and she felt a grateful acceptance of her condition, regardless of conventions. She and Mickey weren't married, but she knew how much he wanted her. She felt her indecisiveness had been resolved for her by fate. Now there was no turning back.

That evening she told Mickey the news, and he behaved like a madman. He whooped with joy, took her in his arms, and planted a big kiss on her lips. His eyes sparkled, and there was no doubt in her mind that he wanted this baby as much as she did.

"But Mickey, it's going to be so embarrassing – me getting pregnant out of wedlock," she said, remembering suddenly the practical side of the issue. "Now I'm sorry I've been so difficult. Everyone is going to be counting the months, and they'll all know what's been going on. What'll your mother think?"

He laughed. "I don't give a damn about what anyone thinks, as long as I have you." Noticing that she looked truly concerned, he changed his tone. "If it worries you, we can go somewhere else until after the birth. I've got a friend in Hawaii who can fix us up with a cheap place to live. We'll be too far away for anyone to worry about the date of the baby's arrival."

Ever since her brother, Doc, had sailed to the islands on a freighter, Vivian had wanted to go there. It sounded like a marvelous idea. "But I haven't even bothered to file for divorce from Rudy. I only have separation papers. And what about you and Dell?"

"No problem. We'll go down to Mexico and take care of it in a hurry. In fact, we can get a divorce and get married all at one go." He was bursting with joy, and he promised her he would do anything for her happiness.

* * * * *

Jane suspected that Mickey was serious about a woman, and she had asked him several times whether he wouldn't like to bring his 'lady friend' around. He didn't want her scaring off Vivian like she did Dell, and he always found some excuse for it not being just that day.

Now that Vivian had consented to marry him, he couldn't delay the inevitable, but he arranged for the three of them to have lunch at The Brown Derby. That way, he figured, neither Jane nor Vivian would be defending her own turf.

Jane and Mickey were sitting at the table he had ordered when Vivian joined them. Jane had her back to the entrance, but by the look of rapture on Mickey's face, she knew that Vivian had made her appearance.

Jane half-turned and watched her walking towards them. She was stunning in a gray suit, fitted at the waist, with a stole trimmed with silver fox fur. Jane scrutinized every detail, making an immediate estimate of her dress, her jewelry, her elegant shoes and handbag, and the whiff of Chanel No. 5 when she stood alongside of them. Warning bells started to ring, and she returned Vivian's warm greeting with an immaculately courteous, but guarded 'how do you do.'

Within less than a minute, Jane had put Vivian in the category of real competition, someone who would interfere with the carefully laid plans she had for her only son. It was abundantly clear that Vivian was a woman with a mind of her own, and Jane wondered how old Vivian must be to have achieved such poise.

Mickey's mother didn't have a cut and dry picture of what her future daughter-in-law should be, but she did have a sure-fire instinct for what she shouldn't be. If Mickey married Vivian, she could picture the two of them vanishing out of her life, threatening all the plans she had for building the foundation for a dynasty.

Jane pushed first impressions to the back of her mind while she concentrated on using her Southern charm. She said sweetly, "Ah've been wonderin' who the young lady is who's takin' so much of Mickey's time," and Vivian noticed that Jane's smile didn't reach her eyes.

Vivian was shrewd enough to pick up on the implied criticism in Jane's remark, but she smiled guilelessly and chose to ignore it, a reaction that convinced Jane she was up against no ordinary competition. Behind a smokescreen of small talk, she studied Vivian, looking for subtle hints of how to gain the advantage over this new threat to her relationship with Mickey.

Before Mickey could order, Jane took command and asked Vivian what she would like. Vivian could see the change that took place when Mickey's mother was present. Donda had said once that you can guess what a man will be like as a husband when you saw him with his mother. In Mickey's case, however, she couldn't be sure. He seemed to be used to Jane ruling the roost, but his even-tempered indifference gave the appearance of putting him outside his mother's reach.

Their first encounter passed peacefully enough, but both women came away from it convinced that theirs would not be a close relationship.

Jane was, therefore, wary when Mickey said he planned a trip to Mexico for the following week. She frowned, thinking he should be buckling down to stay in the good graces of his new bosses. Things came too easy to him, and these days there were plenty of people who didn't have a dime to their names.

She couldn't help but gloat when she saw how quickly RKO snatched him up, but it worried her that he was so cocky. If he didn't watch out his luck could change. It's that damned woman, she thought. Ever since he got mixed up with her, he can't think straight.

"Well, I'm taking a trip to Scottie's." Jane said. "I need to get away from these city streets. I already told him I'm coming so I hope you can do without the car."

Mickey knew damned well that Jane had an instinct for when to make things difficult for him. She figured tying up the car would make him toe the line, and there wasn't anything he could do about it.

They could just take off in Vivian's roadster, but he hated to admit to Vivian that Jane was pulling the shots. Vivian would needle him about letting his mother run his life. As always, when he felt his back against a wall, he grabbed for the first solution to his problem that came to his quick mind. He would simply use his old ploy of borrowing a studio car.

That cute little secretary in Selznik's office could warn him if there were any promotions coming up where the car was needed. It was a fluke that he loused up at Fox over a car. This time he wouldn't make the mistake of taking one that was so noticeable as the limousine had been.

However, when word got around that he and Vivian were going to Mexico to get hitched, a bunch of friends wanted to go down there with them. It turned into a crazy weekend so typical of Hollywood, and Mickey threw all caution to the wind and took a limo filled with party-makers.

* * * * *

During the drive down to Mexico the limousine became a rolling bar with singing and laughter accompanying the clinking of glasses. They crossed the Mexico border in the early afternoon.

Vivian and the rest of the gals wanted to freshen up when they had checked in, but the men said they would reconnoiter the place and find out where they should have dinner. Mickey knew Vivian would be fit to be tied if he didn't take care of the divorce papers, and the matter was easily settled in a tacky little office. There was time to kill, and the men found a cozy little dive with mariachi music and a swinging party, Mexican style. It was the perfect setting for Mickey's mood, accentuated by his discovering the fun of drinking tequila with salt and lemon. In the exuberant scene, all sense of time disappeared. He was having the time of his life, full of love for Vivian and for the moment, plus an exorbitant amount of tequila. Finally, someone in his party had the presence of mind to suggest that they should return to their hotel and the ladies.

When they got there, roaring with laughter, they had to help Mickey to his room. He seemed alright and said he would see them as soon as he had showered and shaved. However, eyeing the bed, he thought that it would do him good to lie down just for a minute. He stretched out, closed his eyes, and, with a smile of his face, passed out cold. The next thing he knew, Vivian was hopping mad, their friends were awkwardly trying to avoid taking sides, and they piled into the car to head home without having tied the knot. Vivian returned to Hollywood, too furious to be concerned about being unwed and pregnant.

* * * * *

Back at the studio on Monday morning, it seemed like the sky was falling on him. Not only was he in the doghouse with Vivian, he lost his job. Those cats from back East seemed to be all over the place, tightening up the studios, and they found out he had taken a car to Mexico for private use. Maybe the studio bosses shared gossip. At any rate, he now was washed out at RKO as well as Fox.

Never lacking in self-confidence, he didn't waste time worrying about the future. In a flash, he mentally mapped out a plan to leave as soon as possible for Hawaii and rely on his usual good luck to help him land on his feet.

It took all of Mickey's charm to convince Vivian that she should let him have a second chance. She finally agreed when he promised that the wedding ceremony would take place at sea on the way to Hawaii. Hopefully he wouldn't be able to get into trouble if he was cooped up on an ocean liner, she thought. They decided to wind things up in Hollywood and leave as soon as possible.

Jane had been furious, and she said he was through in Hollywood. Maybe she was right, but he shrugged it off. Nothing mattered to him now that Vivian was willing to share her life with him. They had something together that beat anything Hollywood could offer. He had never been happier.

Going to Hawaii would solve everything. Vivian saw it as the perfect answer for getting out from under Jane's influence. Besides, Mickey rationalized, Hollywood seemed stale after he had worked his way to the top and was no longer dazzled by the glamorous façade. The fun was going out of filmmaking now that the studio heads were in it just for the money.

California seemed to be way out ahead with any new development, and he thought he could use what he had learned there to make plenty of money anywhere else in the world. John MacMahoney had retired to the islands with a bundle of cash he made on real estate in Hollywood. He found he couldn't stay idle, however, and he started selling real estate in Honolulu. Excitedly, Mickey thought of turning to him for help.

Mickey wrote to him that he and Vivian had decided to go to the islands, and as soon as their tickets were ordered he wired Mac, telling him they would leave with the next sailing of the Lurline. Mickey asked his old mentor to find them a place for a honeymoon, "preferably an honest-to-God little grass shack on the beach, Mac."

To everyone who knew her, it seemed all rather sudden when Vivian announced that she was marrying Mickey after all, and that they were going to the Hawaiian Islands for an extended stay. She didn't even tell Donda about being pregnant. Luckily, it wasn't showing yet. She knew her mother wouldn't be judgmental, but she felt a bit superstitious. She was scared stiff something might go wrong. After all, she had one stillbirth, and Marcia and Elsie had been just as unlucky countless times. Maybe it was a family flaw.

"But, Vivian, what about your job?" Donda said. "You've been doing so well and earning so much money. Don't you hate to leave right now?" Donda liked Mickey, but she wasn't blind to his faults. She had become aware of his casual attitude towards money, and she knew he wouldn't change.

"Don't worry, Ma. I'll keep up my dues for the Screen Actors Guild. I can always get back in later. I've got a nice tidy sum saved up that I'll keep for a rainy day, and Mickey says he has enough to last us for a good long holiday or until he can find something over there. You know I've always wanted to go to the islands. I have a buyer for my car, and Marcia and Eddie said they want to buy my place in Laurel Canyon. That should tide me over if we run into problems."

Jane was fuming when she learned of Mickey's plans. "Of all the hare-brained ideas, this takes the cake," she said angrily. "Look what we've built up here, Mickey. You can't be serious about wanting to throw it all away. What will you two live on in that place? And what about me? I've invested a lot of time and money to make a decent home for you."

Mickey had known Jane would be hopping mad, but the idea that she really needed him didn't ring true. If anyone could get by, it was his mother. As for his prospects, he had plenty of schemes to work on in the islands. Luck had a way of landing in his lap, and he couldn't see why that should change now when he had found the woman he always dreamed of.

His old boss, Mac, and a rich college pal, Walter Dillingham, were good contacts to have in Honolulu. Mickey also had a dream of doing some writing, scripts for movies, and Vivian encouraged him. Hell, he had seen enough numbskulls get rich with less on the ball than he had. He was confident that he and Vivian would soon be sitting pretty.

While Jane half-listened to Mickey paint what he thought was a convincing picture of how they would get by, she thought, grimly, "Mickey could sell sand in the Sahara, but he's not fooling me."

Meanwhile, she was figuring out her next move. She could see right away that there was no changing Mickey's mind, and she knew darned good and well that he was too much under Vivian's spell to be swayed by a poor, self-sacrificing mother. It seemed like no matter how much she knocked herself out, he would never really appreciate what she was doing for him.

She had counted on Mickey's good earnings to be the start of a fortune, but things had been spinning out of control ever since he got mixed up with that actress. Jane mentally added up her own assets. Mickey would drain their bank account to get a stake for the islands, but she could sell the house. She figured she should easily be able to salvage enough to invest in a new venture.

One thing for sure, she wanted to show this town her heels. She thought with longing of Nevada. She had never felt at home in Hollywood. She liked a place where there was still a taste of the raw west, and in such a place she was always at an advantage.

These Hollywood gals couldn't hold a candle to me if they tried to make a go of it where there were honest cowhands and rugged living, she thought with pride. It would be good to turn her back on tinsel city and all these phony people. As soon as she settled things here she would get in the car and drive up to Reno. Property was cheap there. She reckoned she could buy a place big enough to earn a living on rentals.

With characteristic grit, Jane faced a new future. Let's just see how long that sophisticated young lady who has turned Mickey's head can manage with him before they both come running to me for help, she told herself smugly. However, with that thought she suddenly remembered warning words her mother had once said: "A daughter you have for all your life. A son is yours 'til he takes a wife." Thinking about that made her realize that it would be very unwise to let Vivian and Mickey leave for the islands on a bad note. She was smart enough to know when to make a change in strategy if she eyed a risk of losing a battle.

Mickey was relieved when she completely reversed her attitude of disapproval and seemed to embrace Vivian as the daughter-in-law she always had wanted. She even gave Vivian a diamond ring. He had never known his mother to wear much jewelry, but she had a nice little collection of good pieces, and she had at one point acquired a solitaire diamond in a gold setting. Proposing that they dined out once before Mickey and Vivian's departure, Jane presented the ring to Vivian and said she would think of Vivian as the daughter she never had.

Vivian embraced Jane warmly, touched by her kindness. It just shows how wrong you can be about a person, she thought, grateful that Mickey's mother proved to be someone she would be able to love.

Pacific Paradise

Mickey and Vivian sailed from Los Angeles on the Lurline, in March, 1936. It was a dream trip, right from the moment they got on board and broke out a magnum of champagne to share with a few close friends and those of Vivian's family who had come to see them off. The well-wishers left reluctantly when it was time to sail and stood waving gaily beneath the shower of colored streamers thrown over the side by the passengers. Donda was sad that Vivian was going so far away, but she covered up her feelings with a smile. For a moment, time stood still, and the festive scene was etched in Vivian's memory as she looked down at their up-turned faces. She wondered what life had in store for all of them and for her and Mickey. In such a lovely setting she couldn't picture anything but a wonderful future.

Mickey thought Vivian had never looked more beautiful as she stood at the railing, cheeks flushed and eyes bright with happiness. He could hardly wait to get her back to the cabin to make love before dinner. He had contacted the captain and arranged for them to be married at sea like he had promised Vivian, but for Mickey the wedding ceremony was superfluous. He felt that he was married to Vivian from the first moment he told her he loved her. He knew she wouldn't be happy, however, until the formalities were in order, and a ceremony at sea, with the captain in his white uniform, was more his style than a reverend in a church.

The captain found them to be such a charming couple that he included them in his party. The eight days aboard ship passed quickly in a blur of pleasant sensations. The deep blue of the Pacific put a world between them and the hectic life they had left behind, and each day brought them closer to what everyone had said was a paradise on earth.

They fell in love with Oahu as soon as they set foot there. Friendly natives covered them with fragrant leis, and everywhere they looked they saw smiling faces. Mac had come to greet them and put them up at the Royal Hawaiian, a beautiful pink building right on Waikiki Beach.

He had made arrangements to accommodate Mickey's wild idea of spending some time in a grass shack, and Vivian was delighted, always being game for something out of the ordinary. Mac loaned them a car to drive to the windward side of the island, and they arranged to put their trunks into storage. All they needed for the present could be put into a small valise and a couple of beach bags.

The drive over the Pali left them speechless. Even in their wildest imagination, they hadn't believed the beauty of the island would be so overwhelming, and the small grass shack on the beach at Kawela Bay was just what Mickey had hoped for, a poet's dream of a honeymoon hideaway.

Without any distractions, they melted into their surroundings, soaking up sensations and distancing themselves from the values of the fast-moving society of Hollywood. Secluded as they were, they could enjoy the beach, feeling like they were the only people in the world. The water was as warm as the air, clear as a bell, and, by the reef, teeming with beautifully colored tropical fish. Nightfall came suddenly, but the air remained balmy, and they sat for hours, looking at the night sky or watching the moon rise over the sea.

On early mornings, they walked far down the beach and met villagers who threw fishing nets out on the water, pulling them in rhythmically, filled with fish. The natives called this form of fishing a 'hookilau,' and generously offered to share their catch with Mickey and Vivian. They struck up a friendship with these kindly Hawaiians and learned much from them about the ways of the islands. No one seemed to be in a hurry, and there was a gentleness about these handsome people that Vivian took to right away.

When Captain Cook came to the islands in 1778, he found a large and flourishing population, supported by a highly efficient system of agriculture. Because of the abundance of food and good drinking water, the Hawaiian Islands became an important port of call for whalers in need of fresh supplies. Unfortunately, this contact with foreigners and their diseases was to decimate the Hawaiian population, and once their numbers were reduced, there was no longer any reason to work hard to maintain their farms. Those Hawaiians who survived could easily feed themselves with the bounty of the islands – The seas were teeming with fish and there were coconuts and fresh fruit all year around. Mickey found their lack of ambition to be altogether rational.

The villagers introduced Mickey and Vivian to poi, the Hawaiian staple that was made from pounding taro roots. They learned to eat it with their fingers and were taught by the natives to call it one-finger, two-finger, or three-finger poi, according to how many days old it was and its thickness. It was especially delicious when eaten with another island specialty, lomi-lomi salmon.

Nothing ingratiates a foreigner more than an acceptance of local food, and the Hawaiians were pleased with these white people, 'haoles,' who liked their food. They invited Vivian and Mickey to join them for a luau celebrating a wedding for two young people from the village. An entire day was used for the preparation of this feast, and Vivian was intrigued to learn that they were going to roast a wild boar, wrapped in green ti leaves and lowered into a pit that was dug on the beach and lined with blistering hot stones. The bundle was buried with sand, and when the roast was dug up, hours later, it had a delicious aroma and fell succulently off the bones.

The feast was served under the light of a full moon and a row of torches. Everything was appetizingly laid out on fresh green ti leaves. Each part of the menu was delicious, and the custard-like pudding made from coconut was a perfect dessert.

Mickey and Vivian were hardly using any money, and, at first, neither one of them bothered to think about tomorrow. Today was so perfect. Away from the Hollywood scene, Mickey revealed aspects to his personality that Vivian hadn't discovered. She was already impressed with the amount of knowledge he had acquired while seemingly being constantly in search of fun. No detail was too small to catch his interest. Now, in this quiet hideaway, he spent the same amount of energy exploring the new surroundings as he had playing the social circuit. He would apparently never be bored, no matter in what sort of environment he found himself.

His enthusiasm was contagious, and his adaptability gave her a feeling of security, for in this environment, adaptability was a more valuable asset than those skills needed for a successful business career. She forgot her qualms about marrying someone who could be so irresponsible and felt that together they could have a rich and meaningful life.

They both agreed that they should stay in the islands and try to make a future there. The ideal climate and the beauty of Oahu were all anyone could wish for here on Earth. Mickey had never been happier. He relished watching Vivian, the deft movements of her hands, the graceful way she stretched out on the white sand, the way her eyes changed color as she sat and watched the sea and sky. When her soft, round belly started to swell, he excitedly imagined the baby that was growing inside her and was filled with wonder at a process so beautiful.

As her pregnancy advanced, however, Vivian decided the honeymoon was over and told Mickey that they would have to look for a house.

He thought at first she was joking, but a look at her expression told him that she was serious. He laughed and said, "This is perfect, darling! What more could we want? We'll bring up our child without all the paraphernalia of a conventional home." They were lying on the beach, in the shade of a coconut tree. Mickey ran his hand over her hip and down her leg, thinking if life went on like this forever, he would die happy.

"You know we can't stay here with a baby," Vivian said, sitting up and facing him. "How would I be able to wash diapers, and what would we do if it pours down rain? Water seeps through the roof of our shack like it would through an old dishcloth."

He smiled, lazily, and turned his attention to caressing her back. "A kid doesn't need diapers in this climate. We can let the baby run naked. Look at Keola's family. They are healthy and happy in their ramshackle place."

Vivian looked closely at Mickey to see whether or not he was serious. It was hard to tell, but she was alarmed at the thought of not having everything in order when a baby arrives. Then she remembered the grief she felt when she lost her first baby, and it occurred to her that it might be a mistake to get a nursery ready in advance.

Still, she thought that they must have a decent house to live in. She had loved their holiday, but now she felt a nesting instinct. Mickey would just have to accept the conventional side of her personality.

"No, Mickey," she said, firmly, "we're going to have to make a move. And if we want to stay here in the islands, we need to find a livelihood." She still didn't really know how much money Mickey had pulled out of California. It was so confusing, what with his money being tied up with that mother of his.

Sensing her mood, Mickey sat up, too. Always quick to get interested in a new idea, Mickey decided it would be a splendid to find a nice little place to call their own. Besides, I'll need to get settled if I'm going to start writing, he thought.

They bought a used car, and they found a house in Haleiwa for $25.00 a month and paid three months in advance. There was a small hospital at Kahuku, and Vivian liked the elderly doctor who would be attending the birth.

Mickey and Vivian worked well together, painting the cottage and fixing up old furniture that they found in their drives around the island. He bought a typewriter, and the two of them spent hours trying to turn out a manuscript for a film. All those years in the business had given Mickey plenty of experience in knowing what sort of story could sell, and he had always imagined it would be easy for him to write something himself.

Vivian was good at offering criticism and suggestions, and they made a promising start on a story. At first she was very excited about their chances for success. She was convinced that he could make a go of it. He had such a way with words, and he had read so much.

He soon discovered, however, that it was very tedious to put down all the details that were part of a good story with dialogue. Besides, it went too slowly. He thought about the sessions some of Hollywood's best writers had when they were trying to hammer out a manuscript, and now he understood why they often had to work in a team. It was hard to keep up steam, no matter how good the idea seemed at first.

He turned around and worked the material into a short story that could be published here and now, thinking that would give him wind in his sails. Mickey sent it off to The Saturday Evening Post and waited impatiently for a reply. At long last, his first rejection slip arrived in the mail. It became clear to him that he needed to learn more about the tools of writing, and he enrolled in a correspondence course devised by a Mrs. Brandeis and buckled down to following the exercises recommended by her.

Days passed, and while it nagged Vivian that Mickey didn't seem to have any definite income in sight, his relaxed attitude lulled her into thinking there was no crisis just ahead. He had been such a success at the studios that she didn't doubt he would come through. He was amazingly good at keeping up with trends and was constantly coming up with ideas for ways to make a living if he failed as a writer. With his winning personality, it should be easy for him to get a backer once he settled on an idea that he was willing to go all out for, she thought.

While Mickey diligently plugged away on his typewriter, Vivian waited, absorbing the beauty of their surroundings and the soothing quality of a perfect climate. She walked outside barefooted and stood looking at the sea. She wiggled her toes, enjoying the feeling of the warm sand that covered her feet. Some Hawaiians were on surfboards farther down the beach where a break in the reef made for rolling waves. She stretched and sighed, feeling very much alive and full of joy. So far she and Mickey weren't exactly taking the islands by storm, but she was too happy to worry about it more than a few minutes each day.

Vivian was healthy and calm. Even during the last month of pregnancy, Mickey thought she was a feast for the eye. She went into labor at the end of October, and he rushed her off to the hospital at Kahuku. He paced the lanai that ran around the small hospital, beside himself with worry that something might go wrong. When he saw her afterwards, radiant with their baby in her arms, he was ecstatic.

They named their son Anthony St. Alwyn and nicknamed him Tony. He was a beautiful and easy baby. Mickey couldn't get enough of holding him, and Vivian proved to be a natural as a mother. She was thirty-three and had been worried that she was too old to start a family, but her doubts proved to be unfounded, and she relaxed, enjoying the feeling of fulfillment that comes with breast-feeding a baby.

Because of Vivian's loss of a baby when she was married to Rudy, she and Mickey had hardly dared to talk about this child before he was born. Now they found that they could spend hours making plans for the sort of life they hoped he would have and how they would bring him up. They talked about what a child needs and what he deserves. They both agreed that Tony should never be punished in anger, but that he should have a firm upbringing. They believed that the first six years of a child's life were the most crucial, and that love was the most important ingredient of those formative years. All doubts Vivian might have had about whether she should have let Mickey seduce her were swept away, now that they were really a family, and she saw what a wonderful father he would be.

While Vivian was pre-occupied with Tony, Mickey knew he had to do something quick or they would run out of money. He decided to look up his old college chum, Walter, to see whether he could be any help.

"Walter ought to know some leads," he told Vivian confidently. "The guy comes from one of the Big Five here in the islands, and those families have nearly everything tied up tight as a tick."

The so-called Big Five were those families whose ancestors got in on the ground floor as missionaries when the destiny of the Hawaiian Islands was being shaped. Since his arrival on Oahu, Mickey had observed that the Big Five controlled 96% of the sugar crop, and inevitably, everything worth controlling was associated with sugar – Banking, insurance, utilities, wholesale and retail merchandising, island railroads, and all shipments in and out of the islands. Mickey had discovered that Walter's family really did have clout, and he assumed that Walter himself should have the best connections.

Walter was delighted to hear from Mickey and told him to come out and see him at his parents' spectacular spread out on Diamond Head. Describing it to Vivian, later that evening, Mickey was able to relate in detail the house and grounds. He was intoxicated with the beauty of the place and the lifestyle it represented.

"Walter is just as much of a playboy now as he was during his fraternity days in Florida, and it's clear as a bell that if it weren't for a family sense of duty, he wouldn't have to do a lick of work."

Like many islanders, Walter suffered from the occasional bout of 'island fever,' and it was a pleasant diversion to include in his crowd an attractive couple fresh out of Hollywood. One thing led to the next, and before they knew what was happening, Vivian and Mickey were swept up in a whirl of social activities with a fast crowd who had no concept of what it meant to be low in funds. Everyone was so friendly, and they were invited out constantly.

It added to their popularity that many of the Hollywood celebrities of those days looked them up when passing through the islands. Sometimes Mickey was tempted to turn back to his old métier. Johnny Weissmuller came to film yet another of his Tarzan films and invited Vivian and Mickey to bring Tony along and watch the shooting of a scene. There was an atmosphere that took them back a few years and reminded them of the good days with the studios, but afterwards, talking with Johnny, they knew they had made the right choice – to leave when they did.

Up until that point, Vivian had loved the peace and quiet of their new life on Oahu, but she also liked a good party. Escaping to the islands had been a good idea, but as soon as they made new contacts, they found themselves drawn back into the scene they both knew so well. Social contacts were like an elixir to Mickey, and he eyed countless ways to make money now that he was meeting the right people. However, it was clear that if they were to move in those circles, they would have to find a house more suited to entertaining, one closer to Honolulu.

Mickey easily convinced himself that they should be able to afford the move. He hadn't played with an open hand, and Vivian still didn't have a clear idea of how much money they had in reserve. Mickey knew that it would only buy them another couple of months, but he didn't doubt for a moment that something good would come his way.

By now Mickey had laid aside his writing. If he had a future as a writer, he sure didn't have time to find out right now. You could send off a manuscript and waste months waiting for a rejection slip. The next best bet was advertising. There was big money in it, and he had scads of ideas. Besides, so far there wasn't much competition.

He flitted about all over town, sizing up opportunities, but he soon realized that he had a much better chance for doing well if he had a sleeping partner who could give him a cash injection. He decided to go to Mac and sell him on the idea of investing money in a public relations firm.

Mac was getting up in years, and it amused him to watch his young protégé in action. He had a soft spot for Mickey. Besides, he got to know Mickey's mother before he left Hollywood, and he knew how badly she wanted her son to get ahead in life. She was one impressive lady, he thought, but Mickey sure didn't inherit her head for business. Still, it seemed to Mac that Mickey never ran out of steam. It would be fun to see him stir things up here in the islands, Mac thought, chuckling. He wrote out a handsome check and told Mickey to consider it a loan that didn't have to be paid back right away.

With Mac backing him, Mickey could now start up with a bang. The only trouble was that during those months of running around making contacts he had used a hell of a lot of money, and most of it was on the cuff. He would have to make the rounds and pay his bar bills, or he would have a hard time getting any credit when he was in business. He cashed the check, figuring he could put most of it in the bank the next day.

It felt good to pay what he owed, and everywhere he went he got a warm welcome. It was only natural that he also paid for a round of drinks wherever there were some friends to share his good luck.

He had on quite a glow by the time he headed home. Vivian had been a bit short-tempered lately, but she's going to be happy now, he thought. She was busy putting Tony to bed, so he went into their bedroom to get into some shorts. A wad of bills was sticking out of his pocket when he hung up his trousers, and he fished around to get all the money and count it up.

The blood rushed to his head when he realized that there wasn't nearly as much left as there should be. Christ, he thought, did I lose it? His mind raced over the places he had been as he tried to recall just what he had spent during the course of an afternoon. It dawned on him that he couldn't account for all of it.

He contemplated the possibility that someone lifted some bills out of his pocket, but, hell no, I was only with friends, he thought. No one would do that. Whatever the case, the fact was that he had used a big chunk out of Mac's money. It was a puzzle to him, because he had gone out on the town in Hollywood, to some of the best places, and he always seemed to have enough. By reflex, he thought of Jane, but for once he didn't have her to tide him over.

Vivian was through telling Tony a story, and Mickey joined them to kiss him goodnight. "Don't get him stirred up now, Mickey," she said, trying to be stern. "He's kept me busy all day, and I need a rest."

Mickey brushed Tony's cheek with the back of his hand and said, "Sleep tight, Butch," before obediently following Vivian into the living room.

They hardly spoke as they ate dinner. Mickey seemed pre-occupied, and Vivian didn't know how to broach the subject of what irritated her. She could see that he had been drinking, and her voice was a trifle sharp when she asked him where he had been all day.

"I went to see Mac," Mickey told her. "I sold him on the idea of me doing advertising." He glanced at Vivian and saw how pleased she was, and he continued, "He's putting up money for me to open an office in Honolulu."

Vivian looked jubilant. She had felt confident something would turn up. Mickey hesitated, not sure of how to break the news about the money, but then he took the plunge, knowing there was no way out. She was too likely to talk with Mac and find out anyway.

"The trouble is, I've been putting things on the cuff since we moved. I stopped by the Waikiki Tavern to pay my bill, and everyone and his dog started hitting me for the money I owe them. I still have enough to rent some office space and hook up a phone, but I've used up some of the money I needed to tide us over while I get something up and running." Seeing the expression on her face, he quickly added, "But don't worry. I've got enough. We'll just have to be careful."

Vivian was exasperated. Why did Mickey have to play the big shot and put things on the tab all over town? No wonder his mother held the purse strings when he was in Hollywood. She started to tell him off, but he was already headed for bed and fell asleep as soon as his head was on the pillow.

He woke up in the morning and reached for Vivian, but she wasn't there. She took Tony to the beach every morning, and they had already left the house. Sober and slightly worse for the wear, Mickey made some coffee and sat on the porch trying to plan his next move. He felt cornered, and he was sorely tempted to ask Jane for help. He thought about the day he left her in Hollywood and wondered how well-off she was by now.

When Mickey and Vivian left for the islands, Jane had the house and car, but hardly any cash. A fleeting twinge of conscience told him he had left her in the lurch, but he quickly dismissed that idea. Hadn't she told him not to worry about her? She had said she could manage, and he had never seen her anything but prosperous.

In fact, it wasn't long after they split up that she wrote from Reno saying she had bought a place big enough to rent out rooms. In her letter she sounded like she was making money and had good options for the future.

He wasn't surprised. No one could manage money better than Jane. He hated to ask her for help, but the more he thought about it, the bigger the temptation. To turn to Jane for money was a habit too ingrained to cause him much speculation. He went back into the house and put a piece of paper in the typewriter to write her a letter, which he ended by explaining his acute need for some cash.

* * * * *

Jane couldn't help but gloat when Mickey wrote to her and confided that he hadn't yet had a break in the islands. He assured her that he had several irons in the fire and something would pan out any day, but right now he was close to being broke.

The news of the baby's birth had furnished her with an explanation for Mickey's behavior ever since he announced he was going to the islands. It became clear to her that he had got himself in a mess, through no fault of his own, she reckoned, and now he was beginning to realize that he couldn't manage without his mother's sound advice.

As soon as she had read his letter, she sent him a money order for $25.00, enough to pay their rent for a month she figured. She enclosed it in a letter implying that Vivian was a poor manager and they would be better off coming back to the States where she, Jane, could help them get ahead. Once the letter was posted, she felt good. The money order was her declaration of devotion to this impulsive, charming, and sometimes trying son of hers.

"I knew that sophisticated wife of his wouldn't be able to manage," Jane thought, smugly.

When Mickey received her letter, he just skimmed the contents. He was disappointed that the money order wasn't bigger, but he hadn't really been open with Jane about how much he needed. He had found a small office from which he could operate and was working hard to chase down business, but there were so many expenses involved in getting started. He had to have a phone installed, of course, and he ordered stationery that was visually appealing. Money was going out, but very little was coming in.

He was very quiet one evening, and Vivian asked him whether there was something worrying him. He had a distant look in his eyes, as he sat thinking about how much he should tell her about his present predicament. She knew that he received a letter from Jane, but he hadn't told her that it was in reply to his request for a loan. She'd be madder than hops if she knew, he thought. Maybe it was time to make a clean break, put his cards on the table, and hope she won't give up on me, he thought.

"I haven't wanted to make you worry, darling, but to be honest, it's taking a lot of money to get started, and I'm just about broke. It's only temporary though," he hurried to say. "I've already got business lined up."

Vivian couldn't help but think about the fact that if he would resign himself to an ordinary job, of course he could have found something to tide them over. Right now the security was tempting, but she did understand what made him the way he was. She knew how he felt about the sort of life where a man was chained to a desk six days a week. He had never known anything but freedom, and she really couldn't picture him sitting on a porch, resting up during a two-week vacation each year. Besides, she was just as bad. She wanted something bigger and better than the ordinary Joe had to settle for. They had both tasted the sweet life and preferred to live on dreams and hope for a run of good luck.

He looked so miserable that Vivian felt like comforting him. "I'm not stupid, Mickey. I knew things weren't happening as fast as you hoped. Don't worry," she said, taking his hand. "Something will come along our way ... We'll manage. Maybe I can find a job, if we can get a girl to take care of Tony half day." She was tempted to ease his mind by telling him that she had a savings account in the states, but something told her to keep that to herself in case things got worse.

"It's right now, I'm worried about, sweetheart. Hell's bells...I'm strapped for cash. I owe money at the garage for the last time they had to change a gasket. There is a bill lying around from the telephone company, and if I don't pay this month's electricity, they'll cut it off. I didn't tell you, because I was sure things would work out." Mickey saw her face cloud over and hurried to tell her his idea for a temporary solution to their problems. "Darling, I couldn't bear it if you lose faith in me." He took her hand and kissed her fingers, waiting for her to encourage him to go on.

Being mad wasn't going to solve anything, and Vivian tried to suppress her anger. Who was she trying to kid, anyway? she thought to herself. Knowing Mickey, she could have figured out that he hadn't paid those bills, but he stuffed them in his pocket when he left for the little office he had opened. "I don't know when you will ever learn, Mickey, but right now we have to do something. We're in this together."

He brightened up, hearing her say that, and put forth an idea he had to pawn the diamond his mother had given her – "Just long enough to tide us over."

Vivian was relieved that he suggested that diamond and not the one she had from Rudy, but she didn't think it was right to do so unless they wrote and told Jane about it. Without saying so, she thought to herself that maybe Jane would offer to send them a loan, if she knew how strapped they were.

The next day, when Mickey left the house, Vivian was straightening up and found Jane's letter in the pocket of his shirt. She was curious as to just what Jane might have written to Mickey and how much she knew about their predicament, and she unfolded it and let her eyes skim the contents. What struck her was that Jane seemed to imply that all his woes were due to having an extravagant wife! Of all the nerve, she thought. Damned that woman. As far as she could figure, Mickey's problems were all his own fault and simply reflected the sort of upbringing Jane had given him.

Honest to Pete, she fumed; no one in my family gets out of control with money. She sat right down and wrote a letter to Jane, giving her a piece of her mind about the criticism Jane had dished out and telling her that Mickey's problems were due to his having been spoiled by an ambitious mother. Lastly, she asked permission to pawn the ring Jane had given her. Having read Jane's criticism, she felt no qualms about doing so now.

Jane answered promptly. In a typewritten letter she claimed that the problems Vivian was experiencing were nothing unusual for a woman during the second year of marriage when the romance wears off. She said that she was more than willing to again take over the role of managing Mickey whenever Vivian realized that she couldn't cut the mustard.

She went on to write, *"I know Mickey has a lot of ego, but so have you. When a young woman writes a letter to an older woman it is ego that makes her start the letter with 'I want to set you straight.' Furthermore, if your income allows you to live in a house that costs $10.00 per month, then live in a ten-dollar house instead of a $35.00 house. As for the ring, you have my permission to sell that diamond and use the money any way you want. I've known exactly what is wrong with Mickey and have known it all these years he has wasted, and I could have made him see the light* *if there had not been so much static. His mother was doing a fine job, and he was popular and appreciated by the heads of the studios, until a very pretty, charming, unsophisticated little lady came along and thought the mother was an old fossil and that she could do a better job. It took her two and one half years to get him loose from his mother, but she finally accomplished it. That was the first weakening link in the boy's character. Then along came a more beautiful, charming and very sophisticated lady who decided she wanted the job of molding this boy's character."*

Jane went on describing what she thought had happened to her beloved son: *"These two girls convinced this boy that his mother was not doing him any good and made him think that he was one of God's own chosen. He got so he really believed what the various people whom he thought were friends told him. He got so far away from his mother and her ability to keep him thinking straight that he went completely haywire, as they say in Hollywood. Now the girl who last undertook the job, seems to have found it was too big for her. I just want to say that the mother in this story is willing to take over where she left off."*

The storm blew over. Jane's ring was sold, but, again, by the time the most pressing of Mickey's debts around town were paid off, he had very little left. He hadn't slain the wolf that was howling at the door, but merely delayed his coming in.

Since his start in advertising wasn't quite as he had planned, he had to supplement his income by getting involved in starting up a company that Walter's family was payrolling – A production of papaya nectar. With that and trying to drum up business for his advertising venture, he was burning the candle at both ends. Vivian watched from the sidelines and realized that where Mickey was concerned it was always difficult to say what was work and what was play.

After that, Vivian was glad that she had enough money left of her nest egg to buy passage back to the states if things didn't improve. She lay awake at night, torn between the dreams she and Mickey had invented and the lure of going back to California where she could call the shots. Life had taught her that there is no excuse for just rolling over and letting problems flatten you out.

If there was one thing that went right, it was Mickey's role as a father. He never tired of playing with the baby, and Tony lit up all over when his father came into the room. The warm air and water on Oahu created a perfect environment for a baby's growth and development, and Tony was a bright-eyed, agile little tyke who immediately won everyone's heart.

Mickey trained him to be fearless, tossing him into the air to be caught in his strong arms. The coral reef created a safe body of clear, calm waters, and Mickey dropped Tony in over his head as soon as he was old enough to crawl. He immediately responded by dog paddling, surfacing with a surprised look followed by an ecstatic smile. He was a natural water baby. By the time he was eleven months, he was walking, and he climbed up on things like a little monkey. While Vivian was inclined to be more cautious than Mickey, she agreed with him that a child was stronger if he wasn't over-protected and couldn't help but be pleased with the bond that was forming between father and son.

Among responsible people there was always a nagging fear that a child wouldn't survive infancy during those days prior to the discovery of antibiotics, and Vivian found herself often muttering a prayer of gratitude and one for protection. This child was more precious to her than anything had ever been.

Vivian had always loved gardening, and she wrote home to Donda describing in detail her efforts in the islands. She was amazed to see how quickly a seed sprouted and plants flourished in the tropical climate. She joined the garden club, thereby becoming acquainted with a whole new circle of friends. As much as she liked the crazy crowd Mickey gravitated towards, she found these people from the 'better society' of Honolulu to be a pleasant contrast. Of course, they were delighted to have such an attractive young woman join their ranks and vied with each other to give her plants and advice.

The fact that their financial situation was so unstable was a constant worry to her. Without money, daily life seemed to drain her energy in a way that frustrated ideas she had of supplementing their income.

She woke up at odd hours in the night and couldn't go back to sleep as she fretted about ideas to make money on her own. One of her pet schemes was to make a business of selling beauty secrets. She had noticed that so many of the white women in the islands had very unattractive skin. The warm climate gave them enlarged pores, and in trying to correct this skin problem, they did all the wrong things. Vivian told Mickey that she knew she could make a living giving lectures on beauty care and selling her own beauty products. He supported her whole-heartedly and helped her plan a promotion based on her first-hand knowledge of Hollywood stars. It went like this:

"Haven't you often seen a woman with her powder or rouge carelessly applied, and haven't you restrained yourself from telling her for fear of offending? Of course you have, and so have I." She pictured her audience and went on, earnestly.

"After working in motion-picture studios for eight years, and during that time constantly being associated with stars and the finest make-up artists in the world, I feel that I speak with some authority in things regarding beauty culture. The terrific lights, irregular working hours, and lack of fresh air take a heavy toll on that fresh look. Care of the skin is vitally important. Contrary to belief, grease-paint accentuates coarse pores and other blemishes ... That is unless it has been applied so heavily that it gives an unnatural appearance."

"So you see how important it is for the person wearing such a make-up to have smooth, fine-textured skin. The average star has very beautiful skin, and let me tell you, you would be astounded at the simple methods applied in keeping it so. They do not remove heavy grease paint just to apply a mask of heavy cold-cream, skin-food, or tissue cream. After working under hot lights all day, their complexion needs the same care that you living here in the sub-tropics should give yours."

"You girls and women of this island are in such crying need of skin care that as I said before, I have to tell you about it. Look at yourself in the mirror. Have you those red pimples that I have seen on so many girls? Have you a greasy, coarse-pored face? Does your make-up look unnatural? Be honest with yourselves."

"I could go ahead and open a swank shop, enclose these simple formulas in fancy bottles and cater to a select few, but I detest business. When I think of the millions of dollars needlessly spent on short-cuts to beauty by many, many women who cannot afford it and of the small amounts of money spent by stars whose salaries run in four figures a week, I cannot help but deplore it. I'm tired of deploring it, and I'll tell you why."

"You who have read '20,000 Guinea Pigs' or 'Skin Deep' know the fallacy of so-called skin foods, tissue creams, etc., but just the same most of you go ahead spending three dollars a jar for skin food."

Vivian paused and looked out the window. She felt sure she could sell women on the idea of trusting her to advise them as to what products to use. Something as simple as coconut oil would do more good than most of the expensive creams they bought. She had a clear idea of what products she could put into jars and bottles and sell. The ticket would be to market her products at home parties. She made plans in the evening, but washing diapers, tending the garden, which was, after all, furnishing them with free vegetables, and keeping tidy a less-than-practical house left her little time to pursue her ideas.

Still, it put her mind at rest to think about her plan and believe that she could be all ready to go when an opportune time came around. Whenever she saw light at the end of the tunnel, however, something came up that drew on her energy in another direction. What little spare time she had went to sewing and decorating to make the sort of home she felt would keep them from slipping out of their chosen niche in society.

The atmosphere she and Mickey had created wowed everyone who visited their place. The satisfaction she felt in homemaking and in watching Tony grow was enough to keep her happy most of the time. The rest of the time, bills continued to pile up, and there was the constant embarrassment of having to find an excuse to put groceries on the tab at the local grocery store. It was second nature to Mickey, but Vivian couldn't bear to owe money. However, time and again, just when things seemed hopeless, Mickey would come home with a check for a promotion he had done.

A visit from Elsie added to the pressure that had begun to build up the day Vivian realized that life with Mickey was not going to be a dance on roses.

It started off well enough. Elsie arrived on the Matsonia during a month when they weren't too short of money, and Vivian had knocked herself out to make the house attractive and plan a holiday that would please her sister. Mickey knew how badly Vivian wanted Elsie's stay to be unforgettable, and he did everything he could to make sure that she had fun.

However, unlike Vivian, Elsie had a pessimistic view of the world and usually noticed flaws before she spotted beauty. She wasn't the type of person who could fall into rhapsodies about a beautiful view. Mickey soon discovered that a breathtaking drive over the Pali was wasted on her. She hardly glanced out the window, and, when he pointed out something spectacular, she usually missed it because she was telling him about something even more spectacular that she had seen in California. She had come to the islands expecting to find Mickey and Vivian living the sort of glamorous life they had in Hollywood, and she was bound to be disappointed.

She was afraid of water, and that more or less ruled out the fun he thought she would have at the beach. She didn't take to native food and dubbed Vivian's favorite fruit 'pukey papayas,' but at least she was interested in learning the hula. Desperate to please her, they lined her up with hula lessons and kept her busy partying it up with their most colorful friends, something which cost more than they could afford.

Knowing how fiercely loyal Vivian could be, Elsie was careful not to criticize Mickey openly, but her opinion of the way in which he managed his economy was clear enough. She liked Mickey, too, but she couldn't understand how Vivian could put up with some of his shenanigans. He baffled her – She could see that he was smarter than average, but in her book, a man was not quite up to par if he didn't have a nine-to-five job. How could a person who was having a struggle getting ahead waste money on subscriptions to 'Time' and 'Fortune' magazines? And, even more disturbing, take the time to read them?

Most of all, she didn't approve of a dreamer. She had learned to face the hard realities of life and make her way cautiously. She could see no virtue in pursuing dreams, for she had learned that the unhappiness she felt when she was disappointed would always be greater than the pleasure she might feel at succeeding.

Mickey could sense that she was a soft person inside a hard shell, and the only way she knew how to bring the outside world inside that shell was to lighten up with a few drinks. At least in that respect she couldn't have been disappointed in Mickey's efforts.

As so often is the case with people who are difficult to please, everyone tries harder, when common sense should tell them the job is hopeless. Mickey liked Elsie, and he wanted this trip to be a memory for life. As one last great effort, he planned a going away party on the day before her departure. He invited all the people Elsie had met and liked, and told them to meet up at a restaurant where there was music from a steel band, on the beach at Waikiki.

When Mickey planned a party, he made sure things were right. The food was good, and there was plenty to drink. Vivian was grateful, seeing Elsie have such a good time. She was enjoying herself, too, and started to feel a bit fuzzy from what she had of drinks. When it came time to settle the bill and drive home, she excused herself to make a trip to the powder room.

The owner of the restaurant presented the bill, and Mickey slapped his back pocket to get his wallet. After fumbling around and turning to look at whether it had fallen out on his chair, he said convincingly, "Damn! I must have left it at home. Hey, Elsie, could you lay out some cash for me until we get back to the house?"

In her purse, Elsie had the money that she was saving for tips on the trip home, and she needed every penny. No one who took the Matsonia would want to be a cheapskate when it came time to tip the staff. "Okay, Mickey," she said, "but that's all my money for tips. Don't let me leave without it." By now she knew Mickey well enough to have a strong feeling that he didn't have any money back at the house either.

Mickey crashed as soon as they got home, and Vivian was unaware of what had transpired when the bill was paid. In the morning, he showed no signs of remembering that he owed Elsie, and she knew that if she asked for it in her sister's presence, and he didn't have any money, Vivian would be mortified. The hints Elsie was able to drop to Mickey when Vivian was out of earshot didn't have any effect.

Elsie had a memory like an elephant, and she never forgave him his negligence. It was difficult for her to say her good-byes at the ship with the right amount of affection, and Vivian had a nagging feeling that something had gone wrong.

Elsie's presence had been like a mirror held up to Vivian's new life, and she started to lose faith in their chances to succeed. Worse, their strained economy began to take a toll on their relationship. In order to avoid upsetting Vivian with his failures, Mickey assumed the same habits with her as he had with his mother. He told white lies, small ones that became more and more complicated as he wove them together to match the ones that preceded, and she never knew when he was coming home. It was so much more pleasant to take one more drink and linger with the many friends he had found, pretending that everything was rosy, than it was to come home and face the music. Once he did get home, he always had such a plausible story about what he had done that day to drum up business that it was difficult to accuse him of bar hopping.

Then it happened that Mickey stayed out all night, coming home in the morning in an alcoholic fog with an incoherent account of what had detained him. Vivian's furious assaults rolled off him. He was always too affable to quarrel with her, and he left her feeling that she was turning into a harpy towards someone who didn't deserve it. Haranguing a person as good-natured as Mickey was like whipping a devoted dog who didn't understand why you were angry.

She decided that he lived so much in the moment that basically he was incapable of worrying about where the money was going to come for paying for that moment. She could see that the only hope for her and Mickey was if she had an income that could take care of their immediate needs, and the thought that this would make her just like Jane. That was something she didn't even want to contemplate.

Hard Times

When Tony was a little over a year old, Vivian decided to throw in the towel. As much as she loved the islands, she felt sure that the only hope for a secure future was for her to return to the mainland and go back to working in movies. Tony was weaned, and she knew her mother could take care of him while she was at work. Her more conservative side had been pushed aside long enough. Right now she craved a semblance of order in her life.

She knew she couldn't tell Mickey her plans. He would always be able to talk her out of making a move. Instead, she left a letter for him, and was on the boat for the mainland before he got home. During the long voyage back to California, she tried not to think about Mickey, but it was hard with Tony asking for his dad and looking at her with a puzzled expression. She knew he would miss his father.

At first she didn't tell her family she had left Mickey. She explained her sudden trip home as an urge to show off her son, and he was so adorable they were thrilled to see him. Doc and Poli, Marcia and her second husband, Eddie, and Elsie and Guy were all childless, and seeing how happy they were with Tony in their arms, Vivian was glad she had come. She had to confide in Donda, however, and she knew her mother would understand. After all, she had to leave Pa and Dave, Vivian thought.

She waited until they were alone that night, both in their robes, talking like mothers and daughters do when they have been apart for more than a year. It felt so good to be at Donda's where she could always count on one hundred per cent understanding and love.

"I don't think I'm going back, Ma," Vivian said and looked at her mother to see her reaction. "In fact, I've made up my mind. I can't go back to Mickey. It's no use pretending to myself that things can get better. When he had plenty of money to spend, I had no way of knowing that he couldn't manage it. Money runs through his fingers like water, and you know me…I can't live from hand to mouth, and I can't stand to have unpaid bills. Where money is concerned, he's every bit as bad for me as Dave Martin was for you."

Donda listened, and her heart went out to Vivian. She knew what it was like to discover that real life could be a far cry from one's dreams. She didn't want to tell Vivian what to do, but she knew from experience that getting a divorce didn't solve all the problems.

Again she thought about her decision to leave Charles when she did, and wondered what her family's fate would have been if they had stuck it out. It was ironic that the piece of land they had in Lomita turned out to be a site for an oil well. Jeb told her all about it, when the price of land in Lomita went sky high. Seems that the spiritualist who claimed she had visions of a "very black substance underneath the ground" and was worried that it would contaminate their drinking water had been right! Maybe she and Charles would be rich if they had stayed on a few years longer.

"Darn it all, sweetheart, I wish I was rich and could make everything right for you. I can well imagine what it's like to live with Mickey. Some people just seem to be born irresponsible where money is concerned. I blame it on his mother. She only had Mickey to care about, and he grew up not knowing what it's like to manage his own money."

They were both quiet with their own thoughts for a moment, each woman turning the problem over in her head, in relation to her own experience. Donda spoke first, and she chuckled, thinking about her first meeting with her son-in-law. "I have to admit, Vi, he is someone special, and he's head over heels in love with you. I wonder if you would ever find anyone else like him. It seems to me that people without any faults aren't nearly as much fun."

"Right now I'm not even thinking of anyone else, Ma. I'm just worn out trying to cope with what I've got. I know you like him, and I know he is someone special. The trouble is that I get so hopping mad at him. I don't like what I'm turning into. I sometimes wonder if I'll end up being just like Jane – keeping tabs on him and him telling me lies. I've never known anything like it. To stay out of trouble, he can spin lies faster than you can unwind them, and, afterwards, he looks perfectly innocent and makes me feel like I'm a battleaxe for scolding him. He's so clever and so intelligent, but he's like a child who will never grow up. My life was so much simpler when I was on my own."

Donda didn't reply. She didn't want to say anything that would make it more difficult for Vivian to figure out what to do. Besides, she had come to the realization that she herself wasn't clever in plotting her own life. It was painful to think about the months during which she decided to leave Charles, and she hadn't forgotten how desperate she was to get out of that unhappy marriage. She was nagged by the thought that her family would have been a happier one if she had tried harder to help Charles, but her hindsight couldn't serve Vivian.

She had always known Mickey was crazy, but she couldn't help but like him from the first moment she met him. She pictured him with his open, alert face, his quick smile and the way he seemed to like just about everybody. The two years with Dave Martin were enough to give Donda a clear idea of what Vivian was going through. She felt grieved that her daughter was unhappy, but thinking of Dave reminded her of how much nicer Mickey was. A hard life had taught Donda a lot about people, and one thing she had learned is that, basically, they don't change. You just have to take them the way they are and make the best of it. Mickey would always get himself into trouble pursuing the pleasure of the moment and naturally would lie to try to avoid making Vivian mad.

"Well, honey, it seems to me the only real fault Mickey has is that he can't manage money. I know all about what that leads to, but maybe you'll find a way to cope. Do you think things would be better if you both came back to Hollywood?"

"Oh, Ma. You don't know how difficult that would be. There are plenty of people who owe Mickey favors, but in Hollywood memories are short."

Seeing how sad Donda looked, Vivian gave her a hug and said, "Don't worry, dear, I'll work it out. I have to think about Tony, too. He absolutely adores his dad. Right now, though, I thought maybe you could look after Tony, and I would check out the studios to see whether they still want me."

* * * * *

Back in Honolulu, Mickey was frantic. He couldn't think straight and was obsessed with going after Vivian. He was flat broke, and, for once, he knew it mattered. He didn't have to pace the floor long before he got the brainstorm of going to the harbor to bum a place on the first freighter headed for Los Angeles.

A cattle ship was sailing that week, and Mickey pleaded with the captain to let him work his way to the mainland. The captain could see Mickey was desperate and took pity on him, saying he could sail with them if he could help loading and swabbing decks, and otherwise stay out of the way.

He rushed home and sweet-talked a neighbor into storing their furniture in her garage, telling her that it might be for a month or more.

"Sure, Mickey. We never seem to have enough money to buy a car anyway. It's no problem."

He went onboard the ship the very next night, too anxious to risk missing the hour of departure. He made himself useful during the crossing, and he slept on a hard bunk in steerage. It was a slow freighter, and he thought he would go crazy waiting to get to LA.

When they docked at San Pedro, he hitched a ride to Los Angeles and showed up at Donda's late at night, wearing the crumpled white tropical suit he had worn when he left the islands. He had never in his life felt more miserable. He knew he could count on Donda to give him a chance, but he wasn't the least bit sure about her daughter.

There was a light in the living room, and he knocked on the screen door. Donda and Vivian were in their nightclothes, ready to go to bed. Vivian felt a pang of guilt when she saw him on the doorstep, looking so wretched. Luckily, Tony was asleep, or he would have headed straight for Mickey's arms, making it even more difficult to talk things over.

Donda went into the kitchen to make a cup of coffee and give them a chance to be alone. Mickey slumped into a chair, unsure of how he should begin. Vivian remained standing, not within his reach. He looked up at her and his eyes filled with tears, but he was afraid to ask her to come back.

"How's Tony?" he asked, as he carefully felt his way through the minefield of emotions that seemed to lie between him and the one woman in the world he wanted.

"He's fine," she said. Unable to lie, she added, "He misses you."

Given this slight bit of encouragement, the words came tumbling out. "I understand why you left, darling, but believe me, I'll do anything I can to get you to come back. If you don't want to go back to the islands, I'll go wherever you choose." His voice was choked when he stammered, "As long as I can be with you, nothing else matters. Just give me another chance."

She wavered, touched by seeing him so utterly broken in spirit. She never thought she would see Mickey Owen indifferent to his appearance. Somehow he seemed more convincing when he was so disheveled. If he had touched rock bottom perhaps this would be a turning point, and he would be a changed man.

Donda stood in the kitchen, careful not to disturb them at a crucial point. She knew her own daughter well enough to figure she wouldn't take Mickey back without giving it considerable thought, but it seemed to her that he had won some time. At least Vivian wasn't throwing him out.

A silence followed, and she came in with coffee and some sandwiches for Mickey. "Looks like you could use something to eat," she said in her kind voice as she handed him a plate. She started to leave the room again, but Vivian stopped her with a look.

They sipped their coffee in an awkward silence. Mickey was too worn out to think, and Donda decided it wouldn't be any easier if he spent the night. Vivian clearly needed time to think this one out. It was late, but she suggested that they call Guy and Elsie and asked if he could stay with them.

Vivian looked relieved when Donda suggested Mickey staying elsewhere. If Tony woke up and found his father in the house, they would be right back where they started. Tony was crazy about him. The first word he had learned to say was "Dada," and he jumped with joy whenever he saw Mickey.

Elsie's big, jovial husband, Guy, came to pick up Mickey. When they left, Vivian flopped onto the sofa and pulled her legs up under her to keep her feet warm. She had forgotten how nippy it could be in California and didn't have slippers. She and Donda sat up far into the night.

With her mother, Vivian could speak freely. Donda had been through so much herself during her lifetime. There wasn't anything that could surprise her. She didn't readily give advice, but for once Vivian wished someone would tell her what to do; however, Donda knew there were no cut and dried solutions to life's problems, at least not where feelings were involved. When they finally went to bed, Vivian was too tired to think. "I'll just have to see what happens, Ma."

When Tony saw his father the next day, he was so happy that Vivian didn't have the heart to tell Mickey to go away and give her more time to think.

As it turned out, her fate was decided by the powers above, or so she claimed to Donda. A few days after Mickey's arrival, she discovered she was pregnant again, and it was almost with relief that she decided that she no longer had a choice. Now she knew that leaving Mickey would be out of the question. At times like this, she always renewed her belief in a God who meant for some things to happen.

She couldn't help but laugh when she saw how happy he was when she told him. He really was hopelessly unrealistic. If they were struggling financially now, how did he imagine it would be with two children?

Eyes shining, he promised her the pot of gold at the end of the rainbow. "I'm going to turn over a new leaf, darling. I'll do anything you want, live anywhere you like."

Jane learned that they were at Donda's and asked them to come to Reno, sending them the money for train tickets. She wanted to see her grandson. The tone of her letter was in sharp contrast to the last one. She knew about their financial troubles, and she hoped she could talk them into settling down up there. She felt sure they would never do well in the islands, and that with her to guide them they could build up a perfect family home. She already had a couple of good job offers lined up for Mickey. He had only to choose.

Some of her business associates were starting up an outfit they planned to call 'Nevada Unlimited', and they all agreed that Mickey was just the sort of man they needed for their promotions. All they wanted was to meet his wife and see whether she was presentable.

Guy and Elsie put them on a train heading north, with a stopover along the way to show Tony off to his Grandfather Charles, whose birthday was the date of Tony's birth.

Charles was back in Upland, after having written to Donda, asking her not to press charges for all the back alimony he owed if he returned to California. He was old and ill, and she readily agreed. She was glad that Vivian and Mickey were going to visit him. She was genuinely sorry when she learned that he was terminally ill, and no one could say how much time he had left.

It was difficult for Vivian to conceal her feelings when she saw how frail her father looked. A dressing covered half of his face. All the fire had gone out of him, leaving just his gentle side. He seemed so alone. Strange to think that a man who had sired seven children should end his days all by himself, she thought. She watched him when he held Tony. He had the gift of appealing to a small child, and she understood that despite his faults, he had given her the love a child needs in order to love in return.

"Whatever a person does with his own life is unimportant if he passes on love to the next generation," Vivian said to Mickey afterwards.

He looked at her, surprised. His life with a divorced mother had not inspired him to think about the importance of family in that way.

A few months later, Charles died, his face half-eaten away with cancer.

They arrived in Reno in December. Vivian was determined to do her best to get along with Jane, but they hadn't been together more than an hour before she was seething mad.

"Your mother can get my goat like no one else can," she lamented to Mickey. "We were hardly in the house before she was telling me how to raise our kid. I promise I'll try to be good, but it sure won't be easy."

Mickey had developed a knack for floating above discord when he was with his mother, and Jane cleverly waited until she and Vivian were alone when she got in her little digs. Everything Vivian did she criticized in a backhand way, and she blamed her daughter-in-law for everything that had gone wrong.

Vivian wrote to Donda that she had never been involved in so many common brawls. "If this woman ever comes your way, please keep in mind how she has behaved towards your brat, Mom. She feels so high and mighty, but I told her that at least my mother knows how to behave like a lady."

To make matters worse, Vivian wasn't feeling well. She was dizzy and headachy, not at all like she had felt when she was carrying Tony.

The two women clearly couldn't live under the same roof. Mickey found a furnished bungalow to move into, and Jane paid the rent. She didn't want them to have an excuse to leave Reno before she had secured something for Mickey.

Despite her dislike of Jane, Vivian could see they would have some security. Mickey decided on the job that seemed to promise the best chance for advancement, and Jane promised to stake them until he got his first paycheck.

He arranged to start working the following week; however, right now he was worried about Vivian and talked her into seeing a doctor. It only took a few minutes for the doctor to figure out that Vivian was suffering from the high altitude. It was affecting her blood pressure, and he didn't think it advisable for her to stay in Reno, unless she could be confined to bed.

Jane gloated and gladly paid the train fare when it was decided that Vivian should take Tony and go to stay with Bobbie and Armand in San Francisco. With Vivian out of the way, Jane knew she could control Mickey and get him started in the right direction. She smiled, thinking how much easier everything would be, without Vivian to influence Mickey. Why she could even find a suitable house for them and shell out the down payment. With two babies to take care of Vivian would have plenty to keep her busy, and she, Jane, could start building a future for Mickey's family without interference.

* * * * *

With Tony asleep on her lap, Vivian watched the scenery pass by as the train approached San Francisco. It had been years since she had seen Bobbie and Armand, and she was eager to show Tony to Bobbie. She remembered those terrible days when her first baby was stillborn, and Bobbie had a healthy baby boy. Of course, she had been happy for Bobbie, but it had made her own loss all the more poignant.

She hoped that her blowing in on them wouldn't make for an awkward situation. So much water had passed under the bridge since the days in San Francisco when she was married to Rudy, and they had been so close. Bobbie and Armand had never criticized her, but she knew how they must have felt about her leaving Rudy, their being Catholic. Their lives had taken such different turns. It would be nice to get re-acquainted, and now that Vivian was a mother, too, she felt like they had a new bond. Rudy could be forgotten at last, but she wondered what they would think of someone as unconventional as Mickey.

Bobbie and Armand had climbed steadily up the ladder to a secure future and lived in a typical San Francisco house, with a small backyard where the children could play. They managed their money wisely, and with good taste they had gradually acquired a timeless elegance in their home. They now had three boys, and Tony was only a few months younger than their youngest son.

They welcomed Vivian warmly and made a great fuss over Tony, but she was uncomfortable right from the start. Even as a girl, Bobbie had a lady-like reserve, and now that their relationship was changed, it was hard to imagine that her quiet demeanor wasn't covering up a hint of disapproval.

Bobbie had always felt that Vivian had an advantage because she was older, but everything had altered. From where they stood now, their fates offered a tangible comparison of where life leads you if you choose different roads. Bobbie's choices had given her success, American-style, while Vivian's took her in directions unknown and clearly not paved with gold so far. It had been fun, and Vivian had no regrets, but here she could clearly see the consequences of her choices. It was wonderful to be a nonconformist if you're well dressed and prosperous, but not too appealing if you're living from hand to mouth, she thought.

At any rate, it bothered her that she had arrived without any pocket money, and on the second day of her visit, she asked Bobbie to take care of Tony while she made a quick trip to town. Nothing had changed much in San Francisco, and it was easy for her to find a pawn-shop that she had passed on her way to work in the old days when she worked in the offices for the Southern Pacific.

The bell that jingled over the door when she stepped inside was the only sound in the murky shop. The glass-topped showcase was crowded with a motley array of valuables, each trinket a statement of anonymous misery. A portly, bald man stood behind a counter and watched her as she approached. From her handbag, she took a jade ring in a handsome gold setting, wrapped in a linen handkerchief. It was the one Rudy gave her when they were courting. She put it on the counter and asked the proprietor what he would give her for it.

He looked at it through a jeweler's eyepiece, dropped it back on the handkerchief, and said, "Five dollars."

"You can't be serious. It cost far more than that, and jewelry hasn't gotten cheaper. That's 18 karat gold, and a choice piece of jade."

"I know, lady, but what am I gonna do? Everybody seems to be in need of cash these days, and I can't sell half of the stuff I get in here. Sorry, but it's take it or leave it," he said, looking at the disappointment on her face.

"Alright, it's a deal," Vivian said reluctantly. She didn't feel she had any choice. She thought about the compliments she received the last time she had worn it, with a white dress that had a silk-print green pattern on the bodice. Ironically, she knew that Bobbie would love to have that ring and would pay a lot more than that to get it, but she mustn't know that things were that bad.

Truth was that Bobbie didn't disapprove of Vivian. She loved her sister dearly, but she had never dreamed that Vivian would end up living the life she did. She knew so well how much

Vivian loved luxurious clothes and a nice home. She was just as attractive as ever, and her clothes always did look like a million dollars on her; however, no detail escaped Bobbie's notice, and she could see that it had been a long time since Vivian had been able to treat herself to something new.

It was beyond Bobbie's understanding that her sister would have ended up with a character like Mickey. She and Armand hadn't actually met him, but it's a small world, and they knew plenty of people who had. He sounded like a playboy, and at that, one who no longer had any money. Besides, there was all that stuff Elsie said when she got back from the islands.

Meanwhile, back in Reno, that desperate feeling of longing hit Mickey full force as soon as Vivian left with Tony, and he panicked and changed his plans. He never could take a hassle, and he could see the writing on the wall. Living close to Jane would always be a pain in the neck. Besides, Reno could never match the islands for reaching the good life. He longed for the sea and for the carefree climate. He knew Vivian felt the same way about the islands, and that if he buckled down and was a good provider, he would have a stronger hold on her in the islands.

Without consulting Vivian or Jane, he wired Mac, telling him of their situation and asking for one more chance. He poured out his heart, telling that he had learned his lesson and was returning a reformed man. He had a hunch that Mac's affection for Vivian was strong enough that he would help them out, despite Mickey's having let him down.

True to character, Mac shot back a reply, telling Mickey he would give him a job in his real estate office, and he guaranteed that he would foot the bill for Vivian's birth expenses.

Mickey called Vivian and told her a cock and bull story about not having got the job in Reno after all, and then broke the news that they would be going back to the islands. He told her to wait in San Francisco, and he would join her as soon as he rustled up the cash.

By now Vivian was convinced that no town was big enough for both her and Jane, and the thought of returning to their tropical paradise was too exciting to resist, even though they were still broke. She didn't know whether to trust Mickey's story about Mac promising him a job, but, knowing Mac, she decided to believe it.

That night, when they went to bed, Bobbie and Armand talked about the latest development, keeping their voices low as they lay side by side in their four-poster bed. Armand had kept his peace all evening when he heard of Mickey's plans, but he was fuming that Vivian and her baby didn't have any security. "I don't care how charming everyone says that guy is, he doesn't deserve someone like your sister."

"Well, calm down," Bobbie said. "I've told Vivian that Mickey can come here, and you'll help him get passage out to Honolulu. They're determined to go back, and she's convinced that everything is going to turn out alright."

As for Jane, she was furious with Mickey for leaving, and for having contacted Mac. "After all he's done for you, I don't see how you have the nerve to ask that man for help, Mickey. How could you turn down that job offer I lined up for you? Vivian isn't the first woman to have a baby, and she could just as well have gone back to Donda's until it's over. When are the two of you going to settle down and realize that life isn't about having fun, but about making enough money to meet your responsibilities?" It grieved her to see what a bad influence Vivian was. If only Mickey had married someone who could encourage him to stay where he belonged – there where Jane could provide a safety net.

Alternately, she fumed and raised her voice or she cajoled and poured on her sweet southern accent. She used all the techniques that had worked in the past. However, Mickey was deaf to her arguments. He was desperate to keep Vivian now that she had taken him back. It would never work if they stayed near Jane.

He got on the first bus to San Francisco, got cleaned up at the train station when he arrived in San Francisco, and spent the last dollar left from Jane's handout to take a cab to Bobbie's and Armand's.

When Mickey joined them and sketched out his plans, Armand agreed to find passage for him on a ship, but they talked Vivian into taking Tony back down to Donda's where she could stay until everything was in apple pie order back in the islands.

"After all you've been through, Sis, you had better make sure that Mickey can set things right before you return to the islands," Bobbie said to Vivian when they were alone.

Vivian was only too happy to leave a few days later, for she sensed that Armand disapproved of Mickey, and she knew he wasn't likely to change his mind. The two men couldn't have been more different in attitudes.

Once Vivian was gone, the atmosphere was more strained. Armand wasn't impressed with Mickey's plans, and Bobbie wasn't surprised. "Still, I can see why Vi fell for him. He's certainly charming and good-looking," she said. Trying to lighten the mood, she added, "He has offered to take Ronnie to the zoo tomorrow. It will be a treat for Ron to have a day on his own without his little brothers getting all the attention."

"Well let's hope we can trust the guy. He hadn't been here more than an hour before he was bumming a cigarette off me. If a fellow can't afford to buy his own cigarettes, he has no business smoking."

However, Mickey's upbringing hadn't conditioned him to pick up on signals of hostility.

Their lifestyle was so unlike what he wanted, that he was insensitive to what thoughts they would have about Vivian's future with him. Their sort of success couldn't hold a candle to his pipe dreams. Throughout his stay with Bobbie and Armand, he remained cheerful and affable, oblivious to their disapproval. In fact, he was so incapable of appreciating the goals of greater America that he fancied his presence in their home probably was a bright spot in what he considered a very monotonous existence.

He took Ronnie to the zoo, as planned, and conned the little guy out of a quarter Bobbie had given him for ice cream. It was enough to buy a pack of cigarettes and still have change for Ronnie's treat. They came home late in the afternoon. Ronnie's eyes were shining when he told his mother about the animals they had seen, and he had clearly taken a liking to Mickey.

As planned, Armand got a job for Mickey as deck hand on a ship sailing to the islands. He did it for Vivian's sake, for his opinion of Mickey had only become more firmly cemented during the last days of Mickey's stay.

As soon as Mickey got back to the islands, he wholeheartedly went about the task of getting things ready for Vivian's return. He avoided the pitfalls of congenial friendship and went to work in earnest. While he tried to sell real estate for Mac, he knocked himself out selling papaya nectar for the Dillinghams.

He had promised Vivian that he would find a decent place for them to live, and that she wouldn't have to lift a finger when she came back to the islands. He was delighted when he found a little dream house out in Lanakai, with a wooden pier off a green lagoon. It was furnished and had brand new appliances.

The same friends who usually got him into trouble all rallied around to help him make a go of it. Also, Vivian's friends from the garden club proved to be warm and caring. Mickey had thought they were pretty stodgy, but he had to admit they were bricks when it came to helping him get ready for her return.

The woman, who had their furniture, took the crib Tony had used and gave it fresh paint for the new baby. Vivian's friend, Meg Atkins, came over with a new mattress for the crib, and other friends brought boxes of canned goods and stocked the refrigerator brimming full for the day Vivian was to arrive.

A Fresh Start

Vivian sailed back to Honolulu in May. She felt sure she was doing the right thing, going back to the islands, but there was enough of a nagging doubt left to convince her she should leave her big diamond and platinum and diamond wristwatch in Donda's safekeeping.

The entire family saw her off. The months she had spent at Donda's made her realize how much she loved each of her brothers and sisters, and she said a prayer that one day they would all head out to the islands where life had so much to offer. She watched them with pride as the ship set out to sea. They were a handsome bunch, standing on the pier, blowing kisses, and waving. She couldn't give up her longings for the islands, but her heart would always pull in their direction. Sometimes she wished she were a stay-at-home person, but mostly she wished that she could have everyone she loved all in one place. Wouldn't it be wonderful, she thought, if what Mickey said was true and that someday there would be a plane big enough to take passengers the long distance in no time at all?

The baby gave a kick as she stood leaning against the railing, and she smiled blissfully. There was nothing like being pregnant to make everything else seem secondary. It was good that they were going back to the islands. Life would never be the same anywhere else.

Tony was too lively to keep confined to a cabin, and he caught everyone's attention, sitting on a high chair alongside Vivian when she dined. She beamed with pride as people fussed over him. One of the waiters was a former Hollywood stuntman. He recognized her and showered her with special attention during the crossing. After the months spent with Donda whose house was like Grand Central Station, the quiet hours spent with Tony opened her eyes to how much he had developed. Luckily, all the attention he got didn't seem to spoil him.

The third day at sea, a German cruiser, named Reliance, passed. She was the same size as the Lurline, and she flew a Swastika. There was something ominous about her. She didn't toot a greeting, and the American passengers, who stood silently watching by the railing, felt the same way about her.

When Vivian arrived in Honolulu, she was overwhelmed by the welcome she and Tony got. There was a huge crowd of well-wishers on the pier, all carrying leis to give to her, and Mickey was dancing around like a madman, too happy to stand still.

Vivian felt a surge of optimism. The crowd that had turned out was the sort of people Mickey needed if they were to make a go of it. She was pleased that she had dressed Tony in a dear little peach-colored suit given to her by Bobbie. He looked adorable.

As they were waiting to dock, Tony filled his diaper with a big job, and Vivian couldn't help but laugh. It serves me right for trying to be so perfect, she thought. Everything was packed, and she had to swipe a Matson Line towel to use as a diaper. As it turned out, everyone covered him from head to toe with flower leis, and he could just as well have been naked.

Mickey stood back, enjoying the sight of his wife and son buried in flowers. When the last lei had been hung around Vivian's neck, Mickey took her in his arms. Through the leis, he could feel the swell of the baby she was carrying. He buried his face in the curve of her neck, feeling the cool petals of the fragrant flowers.

"I'll never let you leave my side, darling," he whispered in her ear. Tony was trying to climb up Mickey's leg, like a little monkey, and Mickey laughed with joy as he stooped down, to pick him up, while Vivian fussed that Tony's makeshift diaper might fall off.

* * * * *

As soon as Vivian saw the cottage Mickey had found for them, she realized that he would never change. He was so impractical. The place was like a dollhouse, far too small for a family with two kids. The living room was an adequate size, but there wasn't a separate bedroom. It was in a beautiful location with a lagoon a stone's cast from the house, something that made alarm bells ring when she thought of watching out for two small children in such a setting.

She bit her tongue though and didn't say what was on her mind. Mickey was so pleased with himself for having found something so pretty that she didn't want to spoil things just yet. When she decided to come back to the islands, she had made up her mind to make things work, and that would simply require creative thinking on her part. She had given a lot of thought to what Jane said about Mickey. He really did need a strong woman to manage him, and she would have to make sure that she could do the job – without Jane, and hopefully, without nagging.

The next day, when Mickey left for work, Vivian checked the ads for a larger house. She had decided that when she found one, she would make the arrangements to rent it without Mickey's help. She knew he would agree, and it was so much simpler than relying on him.

Besides, he was working so hard, trying to make a fresh start. I just pray things will go smoothly from now on, Vivian thought.

They moved just in time. Vivian had false labor pains and went to the hospital in Kahuku where Tony had been born. They wanted to keep her there until after the birth, but Tony came down with whooping cough.

What started out seemingly just as a cold lingered on and Tony developed a dry, hacking cough. It kept him awake at night; eight or ten coughs in one breath, and a whooping noise when he tried to catch his breath. He reached the stage when he vomited after one of these spells, filling Vivian with fear of losing him. She knew from tales her mother had told that it could be a fatal disease when it hit such a young child. Vivian didn't trust Mickey to find someone reliable to take care of him during the daytime. It was the canning season, and most available maids were busy at the canneries. What she could pay them couldn't compete with what they could earn canning pineapples. She had to go home and take care of Tony, but the doctor warned her that she would have to take good care of herself if she hoped to go full term with the baby.

A few days later, Vivian was doing just what the doctor had advised. She had succeeded in hiring a maid who was puttering around in the kitchen, and she lay on the bed, resting. She had watched with amusement as Tony pretended to shave with Mickey's razor, from which she had removed the blade. He was running around in the room wearing Mickey's shoes, when Vivian's waters burst. It felt like she had been hit by a freight train, and she let out a moan. Tony started to cry, and when the ambulance came, he howled. Vivian saw the maid pick him up to comfort him as they put her in the ambulance. "Mummy go bye-bye," Tony said through his tears.

The ambulance attendants insisted on driving her to Queen's Hospital, rather than making the long drive to Kahuku. The birth went so quickly that Mickey got to the hospital just in time to be told that he was the father of a healthy baby girl. He and Vivian could hardly believe their luck. They would have been happy just for a healthy baby, but having both a boy and a girl was more than they dared hope for.

He went home and wrote a long letter to Donda, giving her all the details she would want to know. He ended it by writing, "Well, Mother, you should have seen Vivian when she came out of that delivery room. She was the loveliest thing you ever saw. Looked like she had just gone in to pour tea when it had all happened." The baby, he wrote, was perfect, with dark, curly hair, and long lashes. They planned to call her Judith Leilani.

He put pen and paper aside and went in to check on Tony whom the maid had put to bed after having fed him. Mickey watched him sleeping, sighed with happiness, and got undressed to creep into bed, too. He fell asleep as soon as his head hit the pillow, but he awoke soon afterwards with Tony's hacking cough. The poor little guy didn't seem to be getting any better. Mickey walked the floor with him and, when he was quiet, got back into bed with Tony in his arms.

The doctors warned Vivian against exposing the new baby to whooping cough, and she decided to bring the baby home and send Tony to the hospital. She had been forced to think about the money involved. Keeping Tony there cost only $2.00 a day, whereas it was $6.50 for her and the baby. Anyway, soon Tony was so much better that Mickey could tell her he was having lots of fun at the hospital.

Tony was soon home again, and Vivian was relieved to see that he was apparently unaffected by his hospital stay. He was just as lively and inquisitive as ever. With two small children, she was too busy to think about supplementing their income, and she was nagged by the knowledge that things hadn't really changed where Mickey's ability to manage was concerned. What with diaper washing and making small improvements on their rented house, Vivian was finding very little time for rest. Mickey was wonderful about giving her a hand with the children, but sometimes she got good and mad at Mickey for the way he took care of Tony. His creative thinking led to conflicts that no one could predict, like the time he bought a motorcycle to use so that Vivian could have the car at home during the daytime.

No sooner was Vivian praising herself lucky for this considerate gesture, than he hit upon the brilliant idea of tying a tricycle to the motorcycle and driving around with Tony in tow. The tricycle tipped over when they took a corner, and he brought the poor little guy home scuffed up from head to toe from having fallen off.

Vivian was furious, but she had to admit that Tony was developing into someone fearless. He doted on his dad. She tried to keep in mind that a bond like they had between father and son is the best insurance for a happy future, something more important than a few bruises and scratches.

Mickey still wasn't making enough money to afford the large expenses that always come along when you least expect them. With Jane's words about not spending more than you earn rankling in her subconscious, Vivian decided they would have to move into something cheaper for the time being. They found an apartment in Waikiki. It was on the ground floor, with only a patch of garden, but they were right on the beach.

The rent was dirt cheap, but so were the gals who occupied the other apartments. Upstairs and on all sides were haole women whose swearing would put a stevedore to shame and whose kids spoke the same language. Windows were never shut, and Vivian could hear every word. In her letters home, she regaled her folks with accounts of daily life in Waikiki.

Direct overhead was Bo, an obese bleached blonde who claimed her true love was a seaman on a submarine; however, whenever he shipped out, she invited in so many other swabbies that Vivian and Mickey couldn't see how she kept them untangled. Mickey figured she had to be one jump ahead of Admiral Nimitz on every strategic move, or she wouldn't have been able to plan her social activities.

Next door was a divorcee named Ginger, with a neglected four-year-old daughter, named Meg. Meg liked to knock on Vivian's door to be invited in when her mother had a male visitor. She once told Vivian that if she had a toilet that needed fixing, the man who came home with her mother the night before could fix it. "He fixed ours, and it doesn't pinch my bottom anymore," she said happily.

To the other side was another single mother, with five-year-old Calvin and his grandmother. Calvin's little friend from across the street, named Donald, being too young to know feminine gender curses, called the grandmother "a fuckin' old bastard." Grandmother shouted at Donald's mother, Cissy, to keep "that foul-mouthed little shit away from Calvin," while Calvin listened raptly to this attempt to keep him free of bad influences.

The schoolteacher across the street was no different than the rest of the mob. Vivian heard every word when she told the bill collector to get the hell out of her place and give her time, and her voice and demeanor were so threatening that he did the only wise thing and hightailed it out of there.

It amused the hell out of Mickey to listen to the neighborhood cacophony, but Vivian was desperate to move. After one particularly noisy night, she decided to go up to Bo, the port in every sailor's harbor, and appeal to her to limit the amount of activity upstairs. Bo was so heavy that when she heaved her body around, it sounded like the hillside was being bombed, and her voice was like a cannon.

Vivian held Judy on her hip and Tony by the hand when she knocked on the screen door. Bo waddled to the door, and her haggard face lit up with a smile when she saw Vivian standing there with the kids. "Come on in, Mrs. Owen. Would you like a cup of coffee?"

Her friendly welcome disarmed Vivian, and she could see that she wasn't going to be able to deliver the firm lecture she had planned. She had no choice but to step inside. The apartment was a mess from last night's party. Cushions were strewn around the room, and there were filled ashtrays and half-empty glasses standing on every available surface.

While Vivian tactfully tried to explain that it was difficult to sleep with so much noise from upstairs, Tony toddled around and drained the glasses within reach. Vivian didn't notice until he complained that they weren't sweet enough.

So much for my attempts to improve the neighborhood, she thought ruefully. When Mickey came home, she related the events of the day and pointed to Tony who had passed out on the sofa. Mickey's sense of humor along with the antics of the kids made life bearable, but she wracked her brain for ideas to earn some money and pay their way out of this dump.

Vivian again toyed with the idea of writing. A writing career would be the answer to my problems, she mused. I could take care of the kids and write after they are in bed. Short stories about the neighbors would be terrific material. She made several attempts, trying to capture the dialogue that prevailed in her seedy surroundings, but before she had finished, Mickey had a streak of good luck. They were able to move to something better, and she tucked away the draft of her story.

Their new home was in Mokuleia. Vivian was thrilled. There was a big garden where she had plenty of room to grow a good supply of vegetables, and the house had lots of possibilities. One of her friends from the Garden Club, Marguerite, lived right down the street, and once again things could be normal.

Vivian was feeling tired, but she didn't take time to rest. She made their first Christmas in the new house a cozy one for Tony who was two years old now and into everything. During the baby's naps, she worked in the garden, letting Tony dig happily alongside of her. She sowed tomato seeds and the black seeds from a papaya. In the moist, warm climate, they germinated almost overnight, and she excitedly watched their rapid growth. When the children were in bed at night, she wrote home enthusiastically, telling about the crops she expected.

She had an old sewing machine and found a store where there were bolts of cotton with native prints. Until they could buy more furniture, she covered the floor with inexpensive Japanese tatami mats and covered huge cushions with material in bold Hawaiian prints. She and Mickey worked hard, painting everything, and when they were through, they had a home that looked wonderful, even though they had such limited means.

After a few months at this pace, Vivian was so tired in the evenings that she didn't always have the energy to write home, and when she did, she often had to combine letters to her sisters and brothers in one long letter to Donda. Donda, who knew all there was to know about how busy a young mother could be, worried that Vivian was doing too much. However, nothing in her letters indicated the mental strain she was under as she worried about their economy.

When Judy was nine months old and liked drinking from a cup, Vivian decided to wean her. Once the baby is weaned, she thought, I can hire a girl to help out with the kids, and I'll have time to work with Mickey. She knew that his chances for making a go of it were much greater if he had someone to screen out the wild goose chases from the steady contracts. Even Mac had suggested that Mickey would do well to have Vivian as a partner.

A few days after Judy was weaned, Vivian felt a painful swelling in her breast. She went to the doctor, and he said it was undoubtedly due to a residue of milk. He told her to go home, try soaking that breast in warm water and get plenty of rest.

Vivian did as the doctor suggested, but there was no improvement, and the next day the pain was worse. This time the doctor wanted her in hospital, where she was checked over by two specialists. They advised a biopsy and kept her there to prepare her for an exploratory operation the next day.

That night she slept fitfully. She had a nightmare about Donda trying to save her from falling over a cliff and awoke the morning of her operation feeling disturbed and tired. Mickey had found someone to take care of the kids and went to the hospital to be with Vivian. While he tried to reassure her, he was desperate with worry.

The surgeons discovered cancer, and, without hesitating, they went ahead and removed the left breast and also all the lymph glands on the inside of that arm. Vivian didn't know anything until she awoke from the anesthesia.

When she came to, the awareness of what had been done to her came as a jolt to Vivian. Mercifully, the bandages made it possible to delay the agony of seeing the result of surgery, but as the anesthesia wore off, she was aware of how much had been removed by the knife. Her arm felt on fire, and she winced with each slight movement.

Mickey was by her side throughout it all, doing all he could to cheer her up and comfort her, but at first, she felt too molested for anyone, even Mickey, to be of help. It was the thought of the children needing her that forced her to turn her mind away from her own plight and face the future. The self-discipline she had practiced at every difficult turning point in her life served her well now. She mentally refused to feel sorry for herself and made a point of being grateful every morning when she opened her eyes – grateful that she could see, that she was alive, that it wasn't the children who were ill.

It seemed like every time they made a bit of progress, there was a new blow. Now there were new hospital bills to pay and, for a few weeks at least, it looked like Vivian needed some help in the house.

Afterwards, she was treated with radium, a dose that they hoped would eliminate the cancer, but one which they knew was likely to be a death sentence in itself. Of course, they didn't say that to the patient. Human beings are remarkably different in many respects, and there was always the far-out chance that one would survive and live many years afterwards.

Mickey was doing his best to be careful with expenses and staying away from the friends who tended to lead him astray. Still, they couldn't afford full-time help, and it became clear that without proper rest, Vivian's arm wasn't going to heal.

Vivian's family was devastated over the news, not least of all Doc. His belief in the benefits of proper diet had convinced him that cancer could be prevented and even cured without an operation, and he was very upset about the radiation Vivian had received.

"Damn it all," he said, "I wish I could have got hold of her before those doctors started cutting in her." He shook his head sadly, thinking that with a radiation treatment like she had undergone it wasn't uncommon for a patient to die after two years just from the radiation alone. If only he could help her to regain her health, maybe she could counteract the worst effects.

That was Doc's approach. Marcia would have liked to see her cured by religion. She didn't say so, but she was convinced that Vivian could have gotten well by using Christian Science.

They all wondered whether cancer might be contagious, since Charles had had it when they visited him, but Elsie pointed out that the breast where there was cancer was the one injured when Vivian had a car wreck while filming "Duke of Dublin."

"Remember, Ma? She was working for Paramount. She and Charlie Murray were filming on location in rainy weather, and the car she was driving skidded into a ditch. Vivian's breast was badly bruised, but she was otherwise unhurt."

Donda did remember and recalled thinking how lucky it was that Vivian wasn't seriously hurt. "It's no use talking about what should have been done or why Vivian got cancer," Donda said. "What she needs now is some help, and I would like to go over there and stay until she is stronger."

Meanwhile, Mickey was frantic with worry. He needed to work hard to earn money for the medical bills, and he was desperate to find a means for Vivian to get complete rest. Just lifting the baby was a strain for her. If only they could send for Donda, but Vivian wouldn't even let him mention it. They didn't have the money to pay for Donda's ship fare, and she didn't want her family chipping in to help them out.

Help came from an unexpected corner. In the small haole community of Oahu, there was a lot of sympathy for Vivian and a general concern about her plight. On one of her frequent trips to the mainland, a wealthy woman, named Mrs. Schofield, had visited Donda, and, now, when she heard about Vivian's condition, she offered to pay for Donda to come out to the islands.

Vivian was overwhelmed by such a kind offer, and she realized she was in no position to turn it down. Without her mother's help, she didn't see how she could cope with taking care of the kids in the way they deserved.

Donda accepted immediately. Beulah was the only problem, and she thought of Dave's remarks when she asked, "Who will take care of Beulah while I'm gone?" Elsie promptly agreed to take on Beulah, and Marcia said she would take over if Donda stayed away very long. Donda smiled with satisfaction. She always knew it would be like that in her family.

"You've got to stay as long as it takes, Ma. She shouldn't even be lifting the baby or hanging up diapers until that arm heals," Doc pointed out. "And I've made a list of things she should be eating. Sis has always been good about her diet, and I know she will follow my advice."

Donda was very busy the next few days, getting a passport and booking passage with the Panama Pacific Line. The reason for leaving was a sad one, but she couldn't help but look forward to the trip. Except for an excursion to the World Fair in Saint Louis, the arduous train trip out to California, and the unfortunate journey to San Francisco with Dave Martin, she hadn't been anywhere, and never on an ocean liner. Marcia's husband, Eddie, had worked on the Lurline as a musician for a couple of years, and he said, "You'd better learn the latest dance steps, Donda. You're gonna' have a swell time."

While Donda laughed and reminded him that she had turned sixty-one and wasn't likely to be dancing, she wondered if she had the right clothes to take along. She didn't need to worry for long though; Doc gave her a handsome check and said, "Buy yourself some new duds, Ma. Maybe you'll catch me a rich pa."

She packed her steamer trunk full with a lot of presents for Vivian, Mickey, and the children and with the clothes she imagined she would need for a long stay. She had felt very extravagant when she bought a ball gown in navy blue silk taffeta with small polka dots, a sweetheart neckline, and a circular skirt, but Eddie insisted it was a must for evenings onboard the ship. For the departure, she wore a lovely navy-blue dress in crêpe de chine with the white pikake bead necklace Vivian had sent to her for Christmas, and she had a coordinated selection of clothes for the eight days at sea, including white slacks with a smart red top. She didn't remember when she last felt so elegant.

The sea voyage was just as marvelous as she had imagined. It was the first time in Donda's life that she didn't have to do a lick of work, and she loved the ship atmosphere. She was friendly and out-going, and during the week it took to get to the islands, there was ample opportunity to make a lot of friends among her fellow passengers. In the unavoidable intimacy of shipboard routine, no detail was too small to escape her notice.

By the time she arrived in Honolulu, she was well prepared to understand what it was that Mickey and Vivian were seeking by leaving the beaten path. Life was such an adventure! No wonder they were willing to gamble for the high stakes and take some risks.

She was just as enthralled with the islands as they had been when they arrived, and her enthusiasm was balm to Vivian's soul. It was such a contrast to the undercurrent of disapproval poor Elsie couldn't help but transmit. Having her mother there with them worked magic. The children adored her, and Donda knew how to be helpful without changing the atmosphere of the household. Vivian relaxed for the first time in years.

From the start, Mickey loved Donda. Something in her nature reminded him so much of his own grandmother. They both were so calm, with such a depth of spirit, and they both could love without making demands. He wondered if it had to do with their backgrounds. After all, the Cherokees had been farmers, too, before their lands were taken from them and they were force-marched cross-country to Indian Territory. Or maybe it was the result of the hardships both had suffered. Whatever it was, he felt the same sort of happiness being near Donda, as he had with Grandma Dunaway.

Vivian grew stronger rapidly once her mother was there. However, Donda could sense that things weren't going as smoothly as they should. Mickey's business deals weren't always easy to fathom, and they seemed to constantly live on the edge. They had such a lot of friends, and Donda could recognize in Mickey the same indifference to bills as Dave Martin had.

He and Vivian got behind because of the cost of Vivian's treatments. Once they were behind, Mickey became even more careless with money, as if a big debt was no worse than a small one. He was just as apt to come home with a present for Vivian as he was to pay a bill. Donda watched, not commenting, and she was sad to see that whenever the pressure was on he spent too much time with a crazy crowd of friends, partying it up rather than coming home where he was reminded of their debts.

Vivian knew how bad things were, but there was nothing she could do but pray for a miracle. After Donda had been with them a couple of months, everything came to a head. They were behind in the rent and had been given notice that they would be evicted unless they paid up. Mickey reassured Vivian that he could collect for a layout he did for one of the better stores, and that he would pay the rent before he came home that day.

She had a sinking feeling when he didn't come home on time. When she did hear a car, it was the man who had been by the day before with the eviction notice. He didn't look like a man who could be swayed by argument, and he told her gruffly that his orders were to put them out of the house.

"Unless you want to lose your things, too, lady, you'd better get them out of the house. My orders are to put a lock on the door."

Vivian looked him straight in the eye, and tried to think what would be the best approach to warding off this disaster. "Come on, you look like a nice guy," she said. "Have a heart. My husband should be here any minute, and he'll straighten things out. There must be some sort of a misunderstanding. He said he had talked with Mr. Young about the rent." She was mortified by their predicament, but she tried hard not to upset the kids by showing her agitation.

"I've got my orders, and if you want to argue, you'll have to argue with my boss, ma'am," he said apologetically. He hated when there wasn't a man around to deal with. Putting women and children out of their home wasn't something that could make a man feel good.

In fact, he felt so badly about this job that he gave them a hand and helped them move their things out on the lawn. Finally the man locked the house and drove off, not looking back at the two women standing by their jumbled pile of belongings.

Vivian was close to tears with bottled up anger. "I'm so sorry to put you through anything like this, Ma. I just don't know what could have happened to Mickey. He promised that he was straightening everything out."

"Don't worry about me, honey. I've been through a lot worse than being put outside in a climate as nice as this one," Donda said, good-naturedly. A lifetime filled with caring had brought her so many heartaches that there didn't exist a misfortune which she couldn't imagine being worse. Instead of moaning over present circumstances, she was conditioned to count whatever blessings shined through the gloom. Nevertheless, she knew how embarrassed her daughter was, and her heart went out to her.

Vivian fluctuated between trying to make excuses for Mickey and being hopping mad. "It's not like he hasn't been trying lately, Mom. You've seen how hard he's been working, but ever since Mickey got behind because of that darned hospital bill, he can't seem to catch up."

"I know, dear. You'll see. It'll all come out all right in the end. Mickey's got his heart in the right place, and you know he adores you and the children."

That placated Vivian, for she knew it to be true. She sat down on a chair amidst their things and listened intently for the sound of a car motor, hoping he would be here any minute. He'd know what to do. He always did, she thought ruefully, remembering all the times his way of doing things got them into trouble and how easily he wiggled out of a situation that would make another person give up. If only he had been there to deal with that character who evicted them!

After awhile, however, her temper got the better of her, and she blurted out, "Damn it all, Mom. He could at least have been here on time. What the devil do you suppose he's up to?"

Donda didn't reply. She knew her son-in-law well enough to know that with his sense of time and his love of fun, he could very well be up to just about anything. Unconcerned, Tony and Judy were running around on the lawn. Tony had sensed that something major was wrong, but Vivian's matter-of-fact attitude had reassured him. She told him that it was all a mistake that Daddy was going to set right when he got back. "If you're good, I'll let you stay up real late," she said, knowing what sort of appeal that promise had.

It would soon be dark. Thank goodness the house was back from the road, hidden by the lush row of shrubs and trees at the foot of the garden. No one could see them with all their clutter. Vivian's head was beginning to throb and she wondered where she could find the aspirin in this mess. Remembering the children, she decided that she might as well be practical and make a bed for them. At least they had been fed their dinner before they were thrown out of house and home.

"Hey, you little banshees, come here and let's put you in your pajamas."

"Are we going to sleep outside, Mommy?" Tony asked, his voice full of excitement.

"Yeah, what do you think about that. Won't Daddy be surprised when we tell him?"

Tony hopped on a mattress and even felt expansive enough to let Judy hop beside him. Finally they settled down and Vivian had them say their prayers. She couldn't help but smile. Judy could only say a few words, but she put her hands together just like Tony and snuggled up happily next to him.

It was a beautiful evening. The only sound was the surf pounding on the shore, and a crescent moon was too narrow to rob the stars of their splendor. Donda and Vivian were silent, waiting for the children to fall asleep, each woman thinking her own thoughts, but sharing the same feelings.

Donda knew it all so well, the humiliation of owing money. How she had hated Dave's indifference to it. As if she had read her mother's thoughts, Vivian said, in a voice just above a whisper, "How did I let myself get into such a mess, Mom? Do you remember how well I was doing when I met Mickey? If I just had that income now, there isn't anything I couldn't do for the kids."

Donda chuckled and said, "Yes, but Vi, if you hadn't met Mickey you wouldn't have those two precious souls, and you know you're crazy about them."

"Oh, yes, Mom. Don't ever doubt that," Vivian said softly. "Sometimes I feel like my heart will burst with joy, when I look at them or feel their small arms around my neck. But what if something happens to me? Mickey loves them just as much as I do, but he never will learn to save up for a rainy day."

Donda couldn't argue about that, but she had seen a lot of life and had stopped searching for meaning in the tricks fate played on some people. She knew that right now Vivian needed reassurance in order to get on with her fate. It was no good to dwell on what could have been. Donda had learned that you just have to accept some things as hopeless and build from there.

"Have you ever tried to picture what it would have been like if Rudy were the father of your children?" she said. "He would have been a good father and made sure you had security, but he couldn't have furnished the" – She hesitated, searching for a word – "the magic."

In the darkness, the word 'magic' lingered in the air, and Vivian thought back over the whirlwind events of the past few years. How like her mother to be able to see that, she thought. It was true. Mickey was an artist, not with paints or words, but with life. He touched life with magic. The children adored him, because they accepted whole-heartedly his fantasies, and the spell he cast was making them develop into charming small creatures, liked by everyone.

"You're right, Mom. He does make life special, and you know I wouldn't have missed a minute of it. Still, I'm desperate to be able to make money of my own and not have to depend on someone as nuts as Mickey. Just as soon as I get on my feet, I hope I can go into business on my own. I could do what Mickey's doing, but without spending more than I earn."

"I'm sure you can, dear, but don't think about that right now. All you should think about is getting well." And it certainly isn't any easier when she has so much to worry about, Donda thought to herself.

The moon climbed higher in the sky, and the children slept peacefully while Vivian and Donda talked. There seemed to be nothing else they could do but wait, and they didn't know how long they had been waiting when they heard a car driving along the road and saw its lights through the line of trees. From the sound of it, the car was full of drunks. Someone was strumming a ukulele and singing a Hawaiian song, and there was a lot of laughter, male and female.

Vivian was standing with her hands on her hips and murder in her eyes when the car swung into the yard. It was the convertible of that dippy haole woman who had fallen for Kimo, the beach boy. Because the top was down, it had been possible to jam eight people into it, and they were all roaring drunk. Mickey jumped out over the side. Except for his jockey shorts, he was naked as a jaybird.

"Hi honey. We've been playing strip poker, and, guess who lost!" he said, turning around in the headlights to make a slight bow to his friends. Amidst the laughter that followed no one seemed to think it strange that Vivian and Donda were outside with such a heap of things.

Then Mickey's smile stiffened, and he mumbled, "Oh, oh," just as Vivian let out a flood of angry words.

"Damn it all, Mickey, where the hell have you been? You promised that you would talk with Mr. Young. Now look what's happened – We've been kicked out of our house. While you have been having the time of your life, we've been standing here in the dark wondering whether or not something awful had happened to you!" Vivian felt like physically assaulting Mickey, to sober him up, but Tony was awake, and she didn't want to have him witness a real row.

When he realized how angry she was, Mickey felt contrite, and wanted badly to be forgiven. "I'm sorry, honey," he said, trying to put his arms around her. She angrily pushed him away, not wanting to be sweet-talked out of what she was feeling for him right now. He reeked of booze.

"Look, sweetheart, I'm sorry I'm late, but I ran into Kimo, and when he told Irma about the spot we're in, she very kindly said we could stay in her beach house until we get back on our feet." Mickey couldn't see that it was such a problem. As long as they had a place to sleep for a few days, he knew he'd get some money to cover his tracks and make things work.

Vivian shook her head in despair. Talking with a drunk was a waste of time, and even when he was sober, the sort of problems that occupied everyone else never bothered Mickey. If he were religious, she would have to give him credit for having taken to heart the sermon on the mount, trusting God to take care of them like the birds in the air and the lilies of the field. But he wasn't religious. He was incapable of worrying about tomorrow, and somehow he always managed to make her sound unreasonable when she talked about security.

"That's just great, Mickey, but what are we supposed to do tonight. It's pitch dark, and we have a mountain of stuff here on the lawn. We can't just leave it. What if Young comes and confiscates our things? It's only because the bill collector took pity on us that we were allowed to move it all out."

By now, the motley crowd in the convertible was subdued and trying to be helpful. Kimo stepped forward and said, "Gee, Vivian, we plenty sorry you get so much pilikia. You no worry. I get my bruddah's pick-up truck and come back wiki-wiki. We fix everyting mo betta now."

As good as his word, he drove off with everyone and was soon back, with just his burly brother, ready to load the truck and move them. Finally the first load was stashed inside the bed of the pick-up, and Vivian and Donda climbed up in the cab with the children while Mickey and Kimo got up back. Vivian was grateful that it was still dark. It would be so humiliating if anyone could see them driving to the beach house with all their worldly possessions on display.

In the light of the dashboard, she glanced at her mother's face. Donda had been wonderful. She kept in the background, not being judgmental, and now she looked as peaceful as she would have if they were on their way to a first class hotel. The way she took everything in her stride had a calming effect on Vivian and kept the kids happy.

When they got to the beach house, they were so exhausted that they curled up wherever they could and fell sound asleep. Mickey, Kimo, and Kimo's brother made a couple of more trips and got all of the furniture. In the morning, the cheerful sound of the children running around excitedly in their new surroundings awakened them.

Mickey was anxious to get into Vivian's good graces again, and he worked his tail off all morning, stowing away their things and helping take care of the children.

Kimo showed up around eleven to take Mickey to the roadside café where he had left his car the night before. Kimo's girlfriend, Irma, was with him, and she had brought a couple of big grocery bags filled with food. She was a buxom blonde, somewhere in her forties, with heavy make-up to cover the tracks that hard living had left on her face. Vivian could see that she had been a knockout at one time, back when one of the wealthiest men in the islands had fallen for her. He married her in time to leave her his fortune just before he kicked off, and that explained the beach house.

She was a good-hearted soul, with an empty life, and helping Mickey's family made her very happy. She told them they could stay there as long as they liked. It was a godsend for now, but Vivian had already decided that they would be too crowded if they had to stay there very long.

Mickey kept his nose to the grindstone for the next few weeks, and he stayed away from the bars. There was enough money coming in to pay their bills, and by the end of the month they found a place on Farmers' Road. It was an old house in a big yard. Vivian was pleased, but her worries weren't over. She knew that there was very little leeway when the rent had been paid.

Throughout Donda's stay, they were living from hand to mouth, and she witnessed all the difficulties that made Vivian's marriage chaotic. Nonetheless, she thrived in the islands and would remember the year she spent there as one of the most exciting in her lifetime. She marveled over the many beautiful flowers, the frequent rainbows, and the bird life. She gathered seeds from rare flowers and helped Vivian to collect plants for her garden, instilling in Tony and Judy, as young as they were, a love of the soil and of watching things grow.

Donda was a born beachcomber. A path flanked by spider lilies led down to a beach with flawless white sand and gentle surf. She loved taking long walks along the water's edge, finding shells and pieces of coral. Sometimes she found a glass ball that had torn loose from a fishing net and floated all the way from Japan, and once she and Vivian found a piece of ambergris, a secretion from a sperm whale. Vivian knew it was used in making perfume and was worth a lot of money. Full of hope, she put it in a parcel and sent it to one of the leading perfume manufacturers, but she never heard anything from them.

The children adored Donda. She, who had worked so hard when her own children were growing up, now felt like every hour spent with a small child was a blessing. She always had time for them, and they ran to her eagerly with the many things that inspire wonder in children. Judy called her darlin' Donna and loved to climb up on her lap whenever she felt like a quiet moment, and she and Tony had arguments as to who loved Donda best.

The multitude of flowering shrubs, delicious fruit, and exotic plants were for Donda a treasure trove, and she took great pleasure in seeing the effect the islands had on her small grandchildren. They loved the stories about the mythical 'menehunes' and the small Hawaiian fairies that legend claimed lived in the flowers, in the spray from waterfalls, and in the many rainbows. The richness of their surroundings was a constant source of entertainment, and Donda had always said that children who are well entertained are seldom difficult to manage.

Eventually, Vivian felt so much stronger that Donda started thinking about going home. She had been with them nearly a year and could have gladly stayed in the islands forever, but she knew she was missed by the rest of the family. Vivian would have liked to have her there permanently, to have someone to take care of the children while she started earning money; however, Donda had too many obligations at home, not least of all Beulah who would remain a child all her life.

Elsie came out to the islands and joined them for the last two weeks of Donda's stay, and this time it was the sort of holiday she wanted. She made a mental note of everything she regarded as a potential problem, but she could see that things were looking up.

There was a big turnout to bid Donda farewell when her ship sailed. She had been very popular with every conceivable type of person. Standing on deck when they sailed was a fellow passenger, a woman from New Zealand who found it entertaining to watch the commotion around Donda's departure. The two women became shipboard friends, and it was Donda's friendship with Julia that gave her hope that Vivian's ambitions to start a career of her own would eventually pan out.

Julia Yates was a self-made woman from Auckland whose faith in herself had made her rich. She was the most remarkable person Donda had ever met, and just being with her was a tonic. She was Irish, a product of a beautiful and long-suffering mother and a handsome father who loved drinking and gambling. Julia had intelligence and spunk, and she was determined not to let any man stand in her way of getting ahead in life. With her striking good looks and her father's gift of the gab she was determined to make a name for herself.

Because she was bright, her mother wanted her to go to an elite school in Auckland and get a higher education. Even then, however, Julia, had an eye for fashion, and she found the uniform she would have to wear hideous, particularly the thick stockings and heavy shoes. When she refused to enter the school, her mother threw the newspaper down in front of her, along with tuppence for tram fares, saying, "Don't come back without a job!"

Much to her mother's surprise, Julia came home at the end of the day with three offers for office work. She took the one closest to home, but not for long. It didn't suit her to work for someone else, and she got the idea of going into business on her own, with her talented younger sister, Trilby, as a partner.

Although Julia had a flair for dressing fashionably, she couldn't thread a needle; whereas Trilby was brilliant as a milliner. The two of them rented shop space on Queen Street in the beginning of the 1920's. Their brothers helped them make the furnishings out of old kerosene boxes, and everything was painted black. A curtain divided the showroom from Trilby's workroom. They looked at their efforts with a feeling of satisfaction. All they missed was a suitable name for their new venture.

Julia favored "The Ladies' Paradise," from a favorite book title, but her brothers were sure that would make people think it was a brothel. The girls settled on "Trilby Yates, The Ladies' Paradise," and their store got off to a good start.

When Marlene Dietrich started wearing suits with slacks, Julia eyed a chance for publicity. She had a tailor make a jaunty suit in her size, and bold as brass, she donned it and sauntered down Queen Street, drawing crowds and a good many rude remarks. She was the first woman in New Zealand ever to be seen in trousers. It wasn't an altogether pleasant experience, but being brazen had the desired effect. She had everyone's attention.

She followed her stunt with an ad in the New Zealand Woman's Weekly, where there was an article describing the suit and appealing to their readers to contribute their opinions about women in slacks in a column called "Current Controversies". The four best letters were to win 10\6, but the real winner was Julia. Orders were pouring in for suits just like hers.

Later, the famous 'Trilby hat,' her sister's invention which took the world by storm, made their shop renowned throughout the British Empire, and all celebrities who visited New Zealand had to visit 'Trilby's.'

When Donda met her, Julia was a wealthy woman, on her annual trip around the world to gather new ideas and pick up on the latest trends on the international scene. With her British accent and her inexhaustible wealth of anecdotes, she could keep anyone spellbound for hours. She had been everywhere, done everything, and it sounded like she would never run out of new adventures.

The days aboard ship flew by. Donda had never met anyone so entertaining. A person like Julia made everything seem possible – If only Mickey had her common sense to match his bright ideas, Donda thought. Meanwhile, Vivian's plan to provide management for his schemes made good sense, when she saw what Julia had accomplished.

A Roll of the Dice

Back in the islands, Vivian had to adjust to life without her mother. The children talked about Donda constantly, asking when she would come back. They were so young that Vivian could tell them soon, without telling a lie, for their sense of time was inexact. Judy had become accustomed to climbing up on Donda's lap anytime she felt like it, and she wanted to cling to Vivian, now that Donda was gone.

Mickey missed her just as much as the rest of the family. Donda had not once criticized him, and she took the pressure off him while she was there. He was like a fly in a bottle when he tried too hard to succeed, but when he stopped, took stock, and made plans, his luck changed. With the fresh burst of energy Donda's help had provided, he entered into a good and productive period, with opportunities coming his way.

Just as Vivian had hoped he would do, he became associated with a shrewd businessman, a publicity man named Bob Cork. Bob lacked the savoir-vivre that could ingratiate him with the sort of client who would be sold on Mickey, but he was a man who paid his bills and made sure that the terms of a deal were put into writing. He could use Mickey out front and to handle ads and make layouts, and Vivian could be sure that Bob wouldn't give Mickey such a long rope that he was likely to hang himself.

Bob and his plump wife, Libby, were from Texas. She was a plain country gal, and she was thoroughly uncomfortable in the tropics. The first time they came by for a visit, Libby was miserable in a rayon dress that was wet with perspiration and clung to her ample curves. Her cheeks were flushed, and she sat fanning herself while she complained about the heat. Her fat legs were encased in silk stockings, and high-heeled pumps pinched her swollen feet. Gads, there wasn't space between her legs for her to ever feel a fresh breeze, Mickey thought. Just looking at her made one uncomfortable. She didn't take to island ways that would have made her situation bearable, or she would have dressed like the lovely old Hawaiian women in their loose-fitting muumuu's. The elderly Hawaiians were usually every bit as heavy, but on them the extra pounds looked good, and they were always smiling and relaxed.

Bob and Libby sat talking with Mickey when Vivian brought out a tray with cool drinks. Unlike Libby, Vivian had taken to the islands like a duck to water. She was dressed in white linen slacks with a bare midriff blouse in a Hawaiian silk print. On her feet, she wore the white cotton toed-socks, called 'tabis,' that the Japanese women wore with their tonged, platform shoes, called getas. Comparing the two women, Mickey felt sorry for Bob and could understand why he spent so much time at the office.

As the four of them sat having their drink on the shady lanai, Judy made her appearance. She had stuck her feet in a pair of Vivian's high-heeled shoes and was lugging a purse Vivian gave her. Vivian raised an eyebrow at her two-year old daughter, but she was having a difficult time not laughing.

Judy had begged for a lipstick, and to keep her happy, Vivian had given her that and a small mirror, some powder and a Kleenex. Pleased to have an audience, Judy showed off the contents of her purse. She fished around in it and produced the lipstick brush which Vivian hadn't been able to find the past few days, flipped it open and dipped it into the lipstick which she smeared from ear to ear. Then she pulled out Vivian's eyebrow pencil and proceeded to apply it, too. She flashed her biggest smile and said, "Aren't I sooo purty?"

"You little dickens!" Vivian said. "I've been looking all over for that brush!" Judy high-tailed it off, as fast as she could with the high-heels falling off her feet, with Vivian in hot pursuit.

"Don't ya'll have any help to take care of your young'uns?" Libby asked when Vivian came back after retrieving her lipstick brush. "Mine are bigger than yours, and it'd just plumb wear me out to have to take care of them in this heat."

"Well, my mother has been staying with us, and we haven't needed any help," Vivian said, dismissing the subject. She found it very difficult to find anything to say to Libby, but it didn't really matter. Libby was content to do all the talking, and she made it quite clear that her husband was earning enough money to keep her off his back about anything she considered a problem in the islands. Vivian could see that she would be wise to try to keep a polite distance to Libby. She was one of those people who seemed to drain one of energy, just by her very presence. A tropical paradise was truly wasted on someone with Libby's temperament.

After a few months of Mickey's association with Bob, Vivian could see a light at the end of the tunnel. She knew that with half the amount of money it took to keep Libby happy, she could have a wonderful life. Mickey still used money impulsively, but for the time being, it didn't make her fly off the handle. The day he bought Sophie Tucker's latest record to send to Donda, Vivian could laugh when she pointed out to him that Donda didn't even have a phonograph to play it. He sent it anyway, convinced that she could use the old crank-up gramophone she had from her bootlegging days.

Vivian had regained much of her strength with Donda's help, but Doc kept urging her to make a trip to California. He wanted to check her over and see that she was on a diet that would counteract the ill effects of the radium treatments. Mickey thought it was a good idea, and with the money he was making as Bob's partner, he could afford to send her to the mainland for a holiday.

"You ought to go, Honey. Your mother will love to see the kids, and I know how much you miss your family. It'll do you good to see them. I promise I'll stay out of trouble while you're gone," he added with a wink, "if that worries you!"

Like anyone who lives far away from family, she did have a longing to see her brothers and sisters. She was eager to see how they were doing, and, besides, only Donda and Elsie had seen Judy. She was dying to show off the kids at such a cute stage. Thinking things over, she decided it was safe to leave Mickey on his own. He was keeping his nose to the grindstone and seemed to enjoy it. She left with Tony and Judy just after Christmas in 1940.

A lot had happened in the past couple of years – Doc had acquired a reputation for straightening the kinks out of stuntmen when Vivian and Mickey were still working in movies. Word spread, and soon he also had a long list of movie stars and professional entertainers, like wrestlers and dancers, coming to him for treatments. In 1940, he moved his practice to a nice, new building on the corner of Lankersheim and Camarillo in North Hollywood and bought a house for his mother down the street from his clinic.

Donda went to live there when she came back from the islands. She thought it was a shame that so much good farmland was filling up with houses in the valley, but at least there were still fruit and walnut orchards sprinkled here and there to give her a feeling that someone appreciated the unique qualities of land in that rich valley.

Except for Bobbie, the rest of the family lived close by and constantly popped in at Donda's. It was wonderful for Vivian to be back in the bosom of her family. They all made such a fuss over the children, and Donda wouldn't let Vivian lift a finger to help with the housework.

Vivian had to admit that she had been feeling a bit fragile, and she gratefully fell into the role of the pampered daughter. In the day-to-day struggle in the islands she pushed thoughts of her own condition aside, but now that she was at her mother's, she felt her defenses slipping. In the bosom of her family, she let down her guard and found that she had not fully recovered from the emotional shock of having breast cancer.

Marcia realized the extent of Vivian's despair one day when she was at Donda's. Vivian was soaking in a bubble bath when Marcia knocked on the door and asked if she could come in and freshen up her makeup. She sat at the vanity table with her back to the tub, talking a blue streak about a mutual friend of theirs. Suddenly, she became aware of something amiss.

Turning, she saw that Vivian was crying. Alarmed, she asked, "What's the matter, honey?"

Vivian looked up, her face the picture of despair. "Look what they've done to me, Sis. I can't stand to see it, and yet I can't help but be afraid that they didn't get everything." Where the surgeon had removed her breast and the lymph glands on the inside of her arm, there was an angry red scar that extended almost to the elbow on her left arm. It stood out all the more sharply because of the satiny smoothness of the skin left intact. Her voice broke, and she fought to regain her composure to say that which bothered her most – "What will happen to the children if I die while they are so young?"

Marcia kneeled down beside the tub, trying to comfort her, and Vivian dried her tears and apologized for feeling sorry for herself. "I don't know what got into me, Marcie Pearl. Don't pay any attention. I usually don't give it a thought." Feeling embarrassed, she laughed and said, "Look at you. I'm getting you all wet."

Marcia decided not to leave it at that. When they were alone together later that afternoon, sitting in the back yard and watching Tony and Judy play in a cardboard box they pretended was a truck, she told Vivian about her faith in Christian Science and how it had helped her through that black tunnel she had found herself in when her first husband, Lester, the love of her life, shot himself.

"Do you remember how ill I was? I didn't care about living, and my body responded by withering away. When that Christian Science friend of Mother's talked me into coming back to the real world, she taught me how the spirit can heal the body. Once I accepted the principle that mind is stronger than matter, I realized that we can free ourselves of sickness and fear. Mary Baker Eddy, the founder of Christian Science, says that love and truth rule over matter, and that faith can conquer disease, and I truly believe that now."

She told Vivian about Mary Baker Eddy's interpretation of the Scriptures, and Vivian listened with interest. It appealed to her that Marcia's belief was something based on the philosophy of a woman, and that Christian Science was a religion that spoke to the intellect, rather than just feelings. The notion that good could prevail over evil was something she had always believed, and it seemed reasonable that the same principles could apply to matter.

Marcia continued, "The spirit is stronger than matter. In feeling love and putting yourself in the hands of God, you'll get well. I'm sure of it"

Marcia spoke like a person who had taken to the faith with her heart more than her mind, but she sparked in Vivian an interest in learning more about the religion. The next day Marcia gave Vivian Mary Baker Eddy's "Science and Health with Key to the Scriptures", and, after reading that book, Vivian became a devoted student. It would prove to be the strongest crutch in the years that followed.

After a month of following the diet Doc prescribed to cleanse her system and put some weight on her, plus his chiropractic treatments, Vivian felt like a new person. When she returned to the islands she was full of energy and hope.

In time, Vivian's scars faded, and with the special bra she wore, no one could see that a breast had been removed. With a deep-seated faith that this new religion could keep her out of harm's way, she even managed to deceive herself, certain that the nagging minor illnesses that plagued her were no more than discomforts to be cured by diet. She was convinced that she could maintain an equilibrium, and that her faith would keep cancer at bay.

Meanwhile, Mickey was working like a man possessed. Past failures were forgotten, and he felt like he was starting with a clean slate. He wanted desperately to hit the big time with this advertising venture, now that everything seemed to be rolling his way. He knew he would be able to make it up to Vivian for all the times she had been disappointed.

On the way home from his office, he stopped by a client's and picked up a check for an ad he had done for them. Fifty bucks. Not bad for a good idea. He felt that spine-tingling buzz of a life without limits – just like the old days when he knew he had the world at his feet. Jesus, what a great life! It takes so little to put one back on top.

Walking back to his car, a bright red Pontiac convertible he bought with a recent windfall, he bumped into Louis Chan, the press photographer for the Bulletin. Louis was a bit of a disgrace to his hard-working Chinese family. Always laid back, like a true island boy, he broke into a big smile and said, "Hey, Mickey! Long-time-no-see. How 'bout you and me what you say, wetting our whistles?"

They were standing right outside a small dive popular with Hawaiians, and Chan indicated with a toss of his head the entrance.

Mickey slapped him on the back, delighted to have someone to share his good mood with. "Chan! Good to see you. Been seeing your name under some damned good shots lately. You're doing all right for yourself. This time it'll be my treat though."

"Fair enough," Chan said amicably. "Last time I got stuck with the check. You membah daht time?" Chan threw his head back and laughed, exposing a mouth full of gold work.

When they stepped inside, there was a chorus of greetings. Everyone sitting around the bar seemed to know Mickey, and they hailed him with an eagerness born of desperation. Anyone who hangs around a bar that early in the day is trying to escape from emptiness, and Mickey was just the man to provide a bit of color to an otherwise drab world.

Mickey felt expansive. He told the bartender to give a round of drinks to the crowd, and a party mood was immediately established. In the dark interior of the bar, one loses one's sense of time, and it was after four when Mickey said no to the third refill and waved goodbye to the crowd. He stuck the remaining bills and some change in his pocket and whistled as he headed out the door.

He found himself standing right by that gift shop Vivian liked so well, and on an inspiration he went inside. He felt like sending a present to Donda. They had a line of costume jewelry made by a local artisan, attractive beads, distinctly Hawaiian.

The sales clerk was a pretty Japanese girl. He picked out a nice necklace and asked her to gift wrap it and send it to the states.

"Yes sir. Please write the address on this piece of paper. Would you like to enclose a card?" She looked at him shyly, her dark eyes nicely spaced in an honest face.

Mickey thought for a minute and then jotted 'from your drunken son-in-law' on the card, chuckling as he thought of Donda's face when she read it.

He wrote down the address for the clerk, paid, and left the store. He smiled, thinking Donda would bawl him out for spending the money, but there would be plenty more where that came from. There wasn't much left of the fifty dollars though, and he decided not to mention it to Vivian.

When he got home, she asked him if he remembered to pay the phone bill.

Damn. He'd have to remember that tomorrow, but for now it was easier to tell a white lie. He and Vivian had been invited to fly to Hilo that weekend, and Marguerite had promised to take care of the kids. They were both looking forward to it, and he didn't want to spoil the mood. "Don't worry, honey. I paid it on the way home," he said, putting his arm around Vivian's waist and breathing deeply of her perfume while he changed the subject.

Vivian's mentioning the phone bill threatened to take the spin off his good mood, but he had a remedy. "Let's drive over to Betty and Jim's and take them up on that rain check they've been reminding us of."

Vivian felt tired, but it would be fun to drop in on the Lowes. She hurried to clean up the kids, threw on a fresh blouse, and with a bit of lipstick and a brush through her hair, she felt like a new person. Tony and Judy raced to the convertible, tumbling into the back and hopping up and down with excitement.

When they arrived, the Lowes served drinks on the terrace overlooking the sea. Beyond the terrace was a smooth green lawn, fringed with hibiscus bushes, full of flowers in a variety of flamboyant colors. There was a plumeria growing on the edge of the terrace, its branches rich with fragrant pale pink blossoms. Attached to the house was a trellis, covered with a cup-of-gold vine. Brilliant against the dark green foliage, the waxy yellow petals tempted one to reach out and touch them to see whether they were real. In the soft contours of the flowerbeds around the house, there were an amazing variety of shrubs and flowers, lushly perfect in the ideal climate of Oahu.

The drink they were served quickly rekindled Mickey's optimistic mood, and as he looked around, a home like this seemed within reach. He mellowed even more after his second drink, and Vivian wished he would stop with that one. She hated when he started to elaborate on his plans. There had been so many failures, and she was aware that friends like the Lowes were too polite to show their skepticism. Best that they leave before Mickey had gone too far, she thought. Her own drink was only half empty, and it would be too obvious if she left it unfinished. She sat sipping it, ready to jump up as soon as Mickey showed signs of finishing his.

The children came running up the lawn, excitedly telling that there was a monkey chained to a tree at the base of the garden. Vivian told them not to run off, because they were going home soon. Tony asked if he could climb up the trellis while they were waiting. Not to be outdone by her brother, Judy followed after him.

The lowering sun drenched the air with a red glow, and the children discovered to their delight that their hands and arms were bathed in a warm, burnished color, as they clutched the wooden trellis where the vine wasn't too thick. Judy was half way up when she turned towards them, saying, "Look at me!" They all looked up, just in time to see her miss her grip and fall backwards, four feet down. Her head made an audible cracking sound as it hit the cement terrace.

Terrified, Vivian rushed to pick her up, but after a few minutes in her mother's arms, Judy wriggled loose, impatient to play some more. "Looks like she didn't even get hurt, Vi. Aren't children something else?" Betty said, admiringly.

Feeling uneasy, Vivian rose to leave, saying "She seems all right, Betty, but I think we'd better get the little devils home. Anyway, it'll be dark in a minute."

Always amiable, Mickey threw back his drink and picked up his car keys, saying he hoped the Lowes would come see them soon. "It's too bad we couldn't have made an evening of it."

Betty and Jim exchanged glances. They always had a good time when they were with Mickey and Vivian, but it was a weeknight. It was too grueling to meet up at work with a hangover, and Jim tried to confine his partying to the weekends.

Judy was unusually quiet during the short drive home, and when they got in the house, she headed straight for her cot. She didn't want anything to eat and said she was sleepy. Vivian tucked her in and watched her drop off to sleep as soon as she closed her eyes.

Around midnight, Vivian awoke with Judy calling her. She found her flushed with fever. "Mommy, there are bugs in my head. It hurts," she complained. Her leg hurt, too, and she kept it drawn up in a peculiar way. The rest of the night her fever continued to rise, and she talked in delirium, about walks with Aunt Marcey and that Uncle Guy and Aunt Elsie said she was pretty. She rambled on about Beulah peeling fruit for her and Tony, and she asked for her Donna and Uncle Doc to make her head stop hurting.

By morning, she was definitely worse, and Vivian rushed her to the clinic. There she was x-rayed to determine the extent of her head injuries. Her fever was one-hundred-and-three degrees, and they said she was to be kept completely quiet and hospitalized for ten days. She was to have no visitors the first week, not even her mother.

Before she left the hospital, Vivian tried to explain to Judy that she would have to stay there with the nurses. She told her to be a good girl and mind the doctor. "Is there anything you want Mommy to bring you, honey?"

Judy was so ill that she didn't even feel like talking, but such an opportunity couldn't be missed. "A dolly with real hair and a yellow dress," she mumbled before dozing off again.

Vivian took one last look at her, a tiny figure in a cot with high sides. She felt so despondent as she left the hospital. It seemed that every time things looked promising, a new piece of misfortune fell in their laps. It was going to be expensive to keep Judy hospitalized for such a long time. Then she was cross with herself for even thinking about money. The doctor had said it was a serious blow. Think if they had lost her. Thank God they said that she would be all right.

Vivian's love for her children was her greatest source of happiness, but they were also her biggest worry. It's a good thing that Mickey is so carefree, she thought, or I would be likely to wrap them up in cotton wool. She knew that her mother had too many children to coddle any of them, but it was hard to relax when you only had two and had waited so long to get them.

Mickey was waiting anxiously with Tony when she got home. They both agreed that they would drop their plans to go to Hilo that weekend.

Days passed, and Vivian looked like she had not slept a wink during the entire time. Mickey came home from work on the fifth day and found her straightening out cupboards, something she did when she was too upset to relax. He took her in his arms and buried his face in her hair. There was a scent of pikake perfume on her neck, and he wished they could be dancing instead of standing amid kitchen clutter.

"Everything will be alright, honey. Nothing can get the Owens down. Let's see a smile on that beautiful face."

She seemed far away when she replied. "You know this will be one more bill. I used nearly all the cash we had to pay the rent today."

Mickey grabbed her hand and said, "Let's drive to Children's' Hospital. You'll be a lot happier if you get a look at Judy. I'll stay in the car with Tony. To hell with doctors' orders. You can't wait two more days to see her."

On the way to the hospital, they stopped by the drugstore for Vivian to buy a present for Judy. Weeks before, Judy had seen a pink hairbrush there, and she had begged for it ever since.

The clerk was a sweet haole girl, and she took the brush out of the glass-topped counter. The price tag said two-and-a-half dollars. Vivian's face fell, and she had to say, "I'm sorry. I'll have to find something else. That's more than I have."

"I'll fix that," said the girl as she deftly scraped off the price ticket. She added a pink toothbrush and said it would come to a dollar and a half.

Flustered and full of gratitude, Vivian didn't know how to thank her. She discovered that she had forgotten her purse and went out to the car to get it. When she came back into the drugstore each present was gift-wrapped in white paper with huge pink bows, along with a box of chocolates wrapped the same way, compliments of the sales clerk and cashier.

Vivian had tears in her eyes as she thanked them and asked for their names. *Somehow I must be able to pay them back for their kindness one day. I hadn't even asked for a cheaper price,* she thought. It just proved what she always believed – that most people are good and kind.

While they waited for Judy to recover, Tony got in a scrap with a peacock. They were on the beach at Chris Holmes' island in Kaneohe Bay, where a big gray schooner was docked on a slab of cement. While the grown-ups were talking and admiring the boat, Tony decided to get a closer look at the splendid male peacock that was strutting back and forth in a volière. He let himself into the caged area, and when Mickey heard his cries and found him, Tony's hand was crosshatched with scratches, and the bird had flown to the top of his head.

That called for another trip to the hospital, but while a doctor was tending Tony's cuts, he informed Vivian and Mickey that they would be able to take Judy home.

"I think she is well enough," he said, with a twinkle in his eye. "She woke up the entire ward last night saying she wanted her mommy, and at lunch today she stood up in her crib and threw her Jell-O at the little girl in the next bed."

Embarrassed, Vivian started to apologize, but the doctor laughed and said that he was delighted when a child rebelled against being in the hospital. "It's a sure sign she's well," he said.

A half-hour later they all four walked out to the parking lot, happy to be going home. Tony was all bandaged up but bravely claiming that he could beat that peacock next time, and Judy was happily clutching her new doll as if nothing had happened. Mickey and Vivian looked at each other over the tops of their kids' heads and broke into laughter. Suddenly they felt like they didn't have a real care in the world.

Diamond Head – 1941

With just such setbacks, it became clear that Mickey never could accumulate enough capital to start a new venture on his own. Relying on Bob Cork to put up the cash meant that he had to share a good size hunk of what was made on his bright ideas, but at least the ideas were coming fast enough to insure a steady income. Past bills were arranged so that they could pay so much each month, and Vivian finally felt like a respectable part of society.

Japan was flexing muscle in the Far East, and the United States' Pacific Fleet was gathered at Pearl Harbor, ready to protect any threats to American interests in that area. There was a building boom, and servicemen became a common sight in Honolulu, a posting that seemed like Paradise for a young man who was far from home. Vivian was delighted to learn that her nephew, 'Slivers', was stationed at Pearl Harbor, on board the battleship 'Nevada'.

Along with a good many other ventures, Bob Cork had started up a newspaper called 'Our Army', a paper designed to service the soldiers stationed in the islands. It was a little gold mine, quick to turn out and sure to be read. When Mickey wasn't too busy making layouts for ads or selling them, he helped Bob with writing and editing the paper. Mickey became a familiar figure around Schofield Barracks, the army base. His easy-going manner and good sense of humor gave him access to enlisted men and officers alike. He liked to take Tony along when he checked the base for news items, and the men at Schofield responded by making Tony their five-year old mascot, furnishing him with an authentic army uniform, tailored to his size.

Then Mickey hit upon the idea of putting advertisements above the windows in busses. On his own, he got the franchise for renting the space in all the trains and busses both for the Rapid Transit Company and the O.R. and L., but he had to make a partnership with Walter to get the capital needed to pay the thousand dollars the franchise cost. Together, they formed a company and called it D & O Advertising. Walter had joined the Army Air Force, leaving Mickey with free hands to run the business. Prospects had never looked brighter.

Vivian was busy, too. The military buildup in the Pacific meant that the social lions of Honolulu were in high gear. Although the Big Five had controlled the islands ever since their forefathers, the missionaries, came there, it was a subtle control, a feeling for knowing which way the wind was blowing, coupled with a talent for controlling the wind. Once it became clear to them that Honolulu was going to become an important part of the United States' defense system, they saw the need of getting the military brass in the palm of their hands, just as they had once manipulated the important Hawaiian families. Theirs was a policy of steering events in the islands from behind the scenes, and in this case, they set about making the military feel an unofficial tie to the Big Five through social events.

The Dillinghams called upon Vivian to be hostess at big parties they threw for naval officers and for Walter's flying squadron at their beautiful Mokuleia Ranch. There were games of all sorts organized on their extensive grounds, from the mountains clear down to the sea. They threw parties that the men would never forget, sharing with them the advantages of their wealth, their thoroughbred horses, the huge swimming pool, and their tennis courts. There were well-trained maids to do the work, while Vivian circulated, making sure the guests enjoyed themselves. She loved being in the limelight, all dolled up, charming the officers with her genuine friendliness. Walter's parents were delighted with her. She was ladylike to her fingertips, yet sociable and fun.

One thing led to the next, and Vivian was asked to help Harry Owens, a popular bandleader, with his afternoon radio program that was transmitted live from the Royal Hawaiian Hotel. She loved getting out of the house and being in the swing of things, and now they had the money to hire a maid and make sure the kids weren't neglected. It was a final turning point from those dark days that came with her illness. No one who saw her would be able to guess she had battled with cancer.

Vivian felt that she was fully cured of cancer. Now she was more concerned with Mickey's health. His love for high-flying living was taking its toll, and the doctor had warned him that he should watch his diet and intake of spirits or suffer the consequences. He was already suffering from arthritic pains in his feet. He made empty promises to take it easy, but Vivian was convinced that their wisest move would be to try to get ahead financially right now and retire to the country within the next few years.

Their newfound success generated energy, re-kindling the embers of love that had remained smoldering. The old feeling of being part of a charmed world returned to Vivian and Mickey, like in their best Hollywood days. They were having fun, just like they always used to do, but now they had a sense of purpose. Their good fortune would benefit the children, and Vivian and Mickey thought they knew just what it would take to insure Tony and Judy a ticket to the good life. Theirs would be a world with all doors standing open for them.

Not only were Mickey and Vivian doing well, Jane had moved to Las Vegas and was making money hand over fist. Roosevelt had pulled America out of a recession, and a lot was happening on all fronts. Financial success on the home front made the troubles in Europe seem very far away.

The buildup of defense in the islands wasn't the only sign of global war on the horizon.

Peculiar things happened, some of them first gaining importance in retrospect. Vivian and Mickey saw Japanese naval officers, apparently sightseeing, unhindered in taking photographs from the view over Pearl Harbor. Everyone knew their ambitions, but no one took them seriously as a threat, even after they began to hear of atrocities the Japanese Imperial Army committed in China.

On one occasion, a badly crippled English cruiser limped into Honolulu. It was all the way in the harbor before the astounded spectators noticed it. Thronged on its decks were shell-shocked, half-starved British children, dressed in rags. Its crew members were no older than twelve to seventeen years old. In Honolulu, the ship was patched up as well as possible and sent to the mainland, but there was no mention of it in the newspapers.

Other British ships made stops at Honolulu. Homesick British seamen who had seen their share of action in the Far East manned them. One such vessel was an English submarine that sailed into Pearl Harbor in August. It had left England in June and had been in too many battles to keep count. Badly battered, it was on its way to Bremerton Naval Shipyard in Washington for repairs.

Two English sailors from its crew stood on the beach at Waikiki one evening, aimlessly looking out over the water. Mickey and Vivian pulled over in their open convertible and asked if they would like to come home with them for an American hamburger and a bottle of beer. The sailors were delighted and gratefully accepted. One of them had a boy Tony's age, and he couldn't keep his eyes off Tony. He had been away from home for so long, and he imagined that his boy would be about the same size.

Vivian rustled up a good meal for them, and afterwards, she and Mickey took them for a drive around Waimanalo Way, where the air was drenched with the fragrance of ginger. They continued over the Pali, and it was, as usual, windy when they stopped at the lookout point. There was a full moon, casting light on the wind-swept shrubs of the steep precipice. No one spoke as they leaned against the wall overlooking the valley far below. One of the sailors broke the silence when he said he would never forget the beauty and the peacefulness of the scene.

"We can't tell you how much we appreciate this evening," he said solemnly. "We never know when we might be blown to hell." They told Mickey and Vivian about some of the battles they had fought. Then they related something strange, about German seamen they captured whose arms were full of hypodermic marks and who went berserk for lack of whatever it was they had been shooting themselves with, seamen who turned black when they died.

A dark cloud glowing silver on top drifted past the moon, dropping a shadow like Death's cloak over the scene that had been so moon-bright seconds before. The night air was warm, but Vivian felt a shiver. She deliberately shattered the ominous mood by saying, "Hey, I'm getting cold, Mickey. Will you put the top up before we get back into the car?"

They took the men back to their ship and drove home, quiet in their own thoughts, but by morning the beauty of the islands and their feeling of success had erased the color of war.

Mickey never seemed to run out of steam. He loved leaving the house, feeling well groomed while the morning was still fresh, with anticipation for what the day had in store. Business was booming, and everything he read, in 'Time,' 'Fortune,' and 'The Honolulu Star Bulletin' indicated that this was just the beginning.

The morning after their outing with the English sailors, he made his rounds, informing several clients of the progress he was making on their orders for ads. Then he headed over to Cork's offices to work on a layout. He was in his usual good mood when he parked his convertible and was whistling when he entered the office he shared with Bob.

Bob was out with a client but had left word with their secretary to say he wanted to have a meeting with Mickey ... Something big, she said. He returned soon afterwards, and Mickey followed him into the room they used to meet with clients. Unlike Mickey, Bob was a serious type. His mind was most often fully occupied with the business at hand, and Mickey sometimes amused himself by ribbing Bob without Bob even taking notice. Today, however, his full attention seemed tuned to Mickey's reactions. Bob had an idea, and he was eager to sell it.

"Mickey, as far as I see it, this build up in the Pacific is going to last a long time, and I've been thinking...We're crazy if we don't get 'Our Army' started out in the Philippines. I was with an old buddy from Texas last night. He just got back from Manila, and he says you wouldn't believe what's happening out there. MacArthur has convinced the brass in Washington that the Philippines is the logical place to build up the biggest defense against the Japanese. A big transport is on its way there now with more troops. What do you think about asking the army for the franchise to start up a branch office of our newspaper out there?"

"Sounds great, Bob, but who'd we send to set it up? We've both got our hands full here."

"Well, here's the way I look at it. I'd go myself, but you know how Libby is. She's difficult enough just being this far from Texas. Hell...She'd never adjust to being out there. Besides, I'm up to my ears in supervising the building of our new house. But you and Vivian...You're always game for some excitement. From what I hear, it would be just your scene."

He could see that Mickey was about to object, so he quickly continued. "Just hear me out, Mickey. I could guarantee you a salary of $1000 a month, which is equivalent to $2000 in the Philippines. You would be living in style with plenty of servants and still be able to save up half of that. You could come home after a year or so and be sitting on easy street...By then you could have found someone to take over for you in Manila. That is, unless you like it too well to want to come back."

"I don't know, Bob. Don't forget what Vivian's been through...She might not like plunging into something new just yet – Especially now that there's smooth sailing. And what about my partnership with Walter? He might be called in for active duty any time now, and I'll have to take care of the business on my own."

"But Mickey, out there Vivian wouldn't have to lift a finger. Tom says white people out there don't do a lick of work, and their homes are like palaces. He had a whale of a good time. Everyone stationed there thinks of it as a luxury holiday, and there's a social life that makes this place seem like a dump. Vivian would love it. As far as D & O Advertising goes, I could keep an eye on that for you. You've already done all the leg work, and the rest is just maintenance."

"Well, I'll talk it over with Vivian, Bob, but don't get your hopes up." Mickey walked out to his car, his mind racing with the pros and cons of what Bob had just told him.

Intellectually, Mickey resented the fact that war was always so good for business, but he shrugged it off as being nothing he could do anything about. It felt good to go home at the end of the day and find Vivian relaxed and smiling. The change a steady flow of money brought about made him realize how hard it had been for her these past years. Hell, it took so little to make her happy, and she was a whiz at making things nice with even a small amount of cash. He thought about what sort of a home she could make if they hit the big times.

The Dillinghams had let them move into a house they owned on Diamond Head Drive, overlooking the ocean. It was a low rambling structure that had been built around a banyan tree, with its spreading crown covering the breadth of the roof. There was a fishpond in the living room, with frogs that croaked at night and lazy gold fish swimming among water lilies.

The house was a bit ramshackle but oozed of possibilities, and Vivian knocked herself out fixing it up. She dyed fabrics to cover old sofas, painted everything white to make the bright splashes of color stand out, and she used unusual paint effects on the walls and floors of an area in a corner where they kept a well-stocked bar. For a backdrop, she cut out pictures of birds from a collection of 'National Geographic', and Mickey pasted them on the panes of glass in the large window facing the lanai. He painted the frames white, varnished the pictures, and the effect was sensational.

Like she had done so many times before, Vivian mapped out a large garden, but this time

Mrs. Dillingham was there to give her many of the plants she needed. The older woman took a liking to her and admired her spunk. When Vivian planned a terrace on one side of the house where they could sit and eat, her enthusiasm was so contagious, that Mrs. Dillingham sent her gardener over with a truckload of flagstones and a batch of bamboo bushes to plant on the perimeter.

Mickey saw Vivian out on this new terrace, putting flowering plants in crocks when he got home that day. He blew her a kiss as he got out of the car. The kids ran to him, grabbing his knees, and he laughed, tossing Tony up in the air while Judy pulled at his trousers, saying, "Me, too!"

He waited until after the children were in bed, when he and Vivian were sitting alone out on the lanai, enjoying the black silhouettes of coconut palms etched against the silvery reflection of the moon on the still waters below, while she told him about her day. She kicked off her shoes and stretched her legs, wiggling her toes.

"How I love the sound of the surf pounding on the beach," she said, looking at him and smiling. "I think this is the first time I've been off my feet all day...The kids were full of it. I warned Judy that I was going to smack her bottom, and she said to me, 'Aren't I your little darlin'?' She sure is starting to learn the answers," Vivian said laughing. "And, by the way, today Tony said, 'Ah for Christ's sake, Maggie,' to Judy. I scolded him for swearing, but he pointed out that Daddy says that all the time!" Vivian lifted her eyebrows and looked at Mickey, with mock disapproval. "I guess I can't complain though. Ma says healthy kids are lively ones, but I wish she were here to give me a hand with them these days. They still talk about her all the time."

Seeing his opportunity, Mickey said in an offhand manner, "Well, if you can't have your mom, how'd you like to have all the servants you could use?"

"That'd be great. Are you planning to win in the Sweepstakes?" she replied, laughingly. He was silent, and she turned towards him. She saw the contours of his face lit by the glow of his cigarette, and she realized he was serious. His eyes narrowed; he seemed to be turning some scheme over in his mind as he gazed at the moonlight-white foam of the breakers rolling over the reef.

He became aware of her watching him, and he cautiously told her about Bob's proposal, mentioning that he had told Bob that he didn't think she would want to make a move right now. "But," he hurriedly added, "Remember those folks we met at Walter's last month? They loved the Philippines, and it's true that everyone out there lives the life of Riley. A friend of Bob's just came back from there, and he's the one who turned Bob onto the idea."

Alarmed at the thought of making such a drastic move when things were running so smoothly, Vivian said, "Yes, but, Mickey...It's so close to Japan, and it's so far from home. What would the family think about us taking the kids half way 'round the world, right into the laps of the Japanese?"

"From what I read, there's an even bigger build up of U.S. military power out there than there is here in Hawaii. America might be neutral, but we're sure as hell making it clear that no one better mess with us. With all the troops we have out in the Philippines, if the Japanese did decide to take on MacArthur and the U.S. Army, Navy and Marines, there would be plenty of ships to evacuate the civilian population before there is any danger. But no one seriously thinks they would be so foolish."

He discovered while talking to Vivian that the doubts that had popped into his head when Bob approached the matter had somehow been dealt with in his subconscious. Shoot – It would be a chance to make enough money to cash in on all the opportunities he saw opening up these days and retire early.

All of a sudden he was arguing persuasively for their going to Manila, and the more he talked, the rosier he painted the picture. The spirit of adventure that possessed him so often during his life was upon him now, and it was exhilarating.

It was only natural that Vivian would be hesitant. All mothers are like that while their children are small, he thought. But he also knew her other side, the gal who loved a bit of excitement and was willing to jump out into a wild adventure, just for the heck of it. They both loved to travel and dreamed of seeing as much of the world as possible. He felt sure she'd come around. And by now he was convinced that it would be good for her. It would be fun to experience the high life in the Far East that he had always read about.

She seemed to think it over carefully before speaking. "What about your good luck here? That Selective Service Act that passed in September means that the young Dillinghams will all be called in for a year of military training. It's a golden opportunity to get a big position in the family's business. Why, you know how well Harold Sr. likes you, and he knows that your trouble with arthritis will make you exempt from the draft. With war on the horizon, everything's taking off like a house-a-fire. Who will look after D. & O Advertising, now that Walter has been called in? Heck, Mickey, this is the first time I feel like we are finally getting somewhere."

"Yeah, I know," he said, nodding his head in agreement. And then he turned and looked at her eyes in that way that still made her heart skip a beat. "But we both know how hard I would be working and how little time I would have with you and the kids. Bob says he will look after D. & O. Advertising for me if we go out there. This looks like an opportunity to stack up a real bundle of money and retire to the sort of life we've always dreamed of. Buy some property, and live off the land. And it would only be for a year," he added.

She knew he was right about that. It seemed the more successful a man was in business, the less time he had to enjoy life, and she had begun to wonder how the pace he was keeping up would affect Mickey's health. Her cancer scare had made her realize how fragile life is. Mickey never complained, but lately, he had bags under his eyes, and those spurs on his heels were making it painful to walk. With wining and dining the clients, poor health seemed to be an occupational hazard, and the doctor said his arthritis would only get worse. She had heard that life out in Manila was a white man's paradise, and it did sound like the adventure of a lifetime. Besides, apparently what they could save up in a year would take ten years in Hawaii.

"How long do you have to think it over?" she asked, and he knew that she was wavering, just as he had when Bob had talked to him.

* * * * *

At the end of August, Bob received a cordial letter from MacArthur, endorsing his idea of a newspaper, saying he "would be very glad indeed to have Mr. Owen open a branch office in the Philippines in accordance with the terms of your application. My headquarters will be glad to do everything possible to assist him. Such a publication does much to improve the contentment and morale of the Army."

A letter from MacArthur himself was the last detail needed to convince Mickey that he was doing the right thing. He decided to take the job. He had sworn he wouldn't leave without Vivian by his side, but she convinced him it would be wiser if she stayed behind to wind things up in the islands and sell their car. Judy's fall and the head injury she got had made her wary of leaving the children with anyone else, even Donda, and she didn't want to travel out there without being sure it was safe.

She told Mickey to go on ahead and get settled. She and the children would fly out in December, when he had found a house for them. Bob agreed to look after Mickey and Walter's advertising business, for 25% of the profits. Mickey had set everything up. Now it was just a question of seeing that it functioned. The date was October 1941.

The Philippines

The Philippine Islands were called a tropical Eden and the 'Pearl of the Orient Seas.' Rich in natural resources, the islands had been ruled by Spain for 350 years when the Americans entered the scene and ran the Spaniards off. During their long reign, the Spaniards had refrained from plundering the rich mineral and agricultural potential of the Philippines. They preferred to patiently reap wealth from the endeavors of the natives, while they left it to the Catholic Church to harvest the natives' souls.

As a seafaring nation, bold in exploring, Spain had cast its net over a vast part of the globe, with colonies all the way from the New World to the Spice Islands of the Orient. In 1898, the United States tugged at the corner of the net closest their coastline, felt the weight of the catch and saw fit to interfere with Spanish rule in Cuba. The Americans sympathized with Cubans in their struggle for independence, and $30 million of American investments in Cuba sweetened the cause.

In reply, the Spaniards declared war on America that same year. Commodore George Dewey was ordered to proceed from Hong Kong to the Philippines where the Spanish fleet was concentrated and destroy it.

The Spanish ships were anchored in the bay off Manila, the capital of the Philippines. It was a city surrounded by thick walls. Dewey made a stealthy dawn attack, resulting in the destruction of all the Spanish ships by midnight. However, without the help of Filipinos, he could never have driven the Spaniards out of the Walled City and the many outposts they held.

The feisty Filipinos had been hankering for freedom and had revolted sporadically over the past century. Many of them were ready and willing to fight the Spaniards, but they had to decide whether the Americans were liberators or simply new masters.

Some Filipinos sided with the Spaniards, whose language and culture had been theirs for more than three centuries, but Dewey arranged a meeting with the man who led the rebels. This man, General Aguinaldo, and his revolutionary forces were committed to ridding themselves of Spanish rule and were led to believe that the Americans were their redeemers.

As a result of their meeting, Aguinaldo stormed one Spanish outpost after the other, while Dewey sat on his ship and waited for American troops to come to his aid from the United States. When General Merritt arrived with fresh American troops, Douglas MacArthur's father, Arthur MacArthur, led the spearhead of an eleven-thousand-man expeditionary force, and, together with Aquinaldo's rebels, they forced the Spanish captain-general in Manila to capitulate nine days later. Spaniards could see that defeat was eminent.

In a pattern that has been repeated throughout history, the two warring big powers then decided the fate of the smaller, native force without listening to its advice. Dewey and Merritt didn't invite Aguinaldo to join them when they negotiated with the Spaniards through the Belgian consul in Manila. Under the terms of surrender, the Spaniards ceded the Philippines to the Americans for $20 million. It became obvious that the reason for Aquinaldo being kept out was because the Spaniards had decided that no such sum could be expected from a revolutionary government. The Americans promised the Spaniards that the rebels would have nothing to say about the peace agreement that would follow, including the fate of Manila. Finally, they agreed to stage a mock battle, in order to save Spanish honor.

Aguinaldo was kept in the dark about this treachery, and his valiant Filipino forces fought side by side with the Americans when they attacked Manila. The Spaniards were defeated as expected, after a symbolic two-hour battle. The terms of the agreement were that the city was to be placed under the protection of the American Army, and the former colonial masters would be allowed to leave safely before the rebels could enter the city.

It was to mark the first time the Americans betrayed the Filipinos, a misdeed made easier by the fact that, unlike Cuba, which was on America's doorstep, the Philippine Islands were on the other side of the world.

While the American public clamored for annexation of the Philippines, not wanting the United States to be outdistanced in that part of the world by rival countries such as France and Germany, President McKinley, who was an idealist, was perturbed. When he told Congress, "The Philippines are ours, not to exploit, but to develop, to civilize, to educate, to train in the science of self-government," he implied an acceptance of the American presence in the Philippines, but that the people of the Philippines should be independent.

However, even this benevolent form of assimilation wasn't enough to placate Aguinaldo, and the Philippine-American War began in February, 1899. The fighting was fierce, with heavy losses on both sides, especially that of the Filipinos, for the American firepower was vastly superior. Brigadier General Arthur MacArthur, determined to end his career in a blaze of glory, bravely stayed at the front, leading his men to repel Aguinaldo's forces. Still, he begged his commanding officer, Major General Otis, to be forbearing in dealing with the rebels, for he had sympathy for their cause. He suggested amnesty to all rebels and a reward to those who would lay down their arms.

Otis ignored MacArthur's entreaties, and, finally, Aguilnado was forced to retreat to Bataan, the rugged peninsula embracing the Bay of Manila. It wasn't until March of 1901 that the elusive Filipino general was captured. Fortunately, by then Arthur MacArthur had been appointed Military Governor. Aguilnado was taken to Manila and graciously received by MacArthur who then befriended him and tried to win him over.

Finally, in 1916, Congress passed the Jones Law, which stated that independence would be granted to the Philippines as soon as a stable government could be established.

Arthur MacArthur and his successor were both liberal-minded governors who genuinely wanted the Philippines for Filipinos, but in 1921, their successor, Leonard Wood, reverted to colonialism. His attitude gave the popular Filipino leader, Manuel Quezon, cause to proclaim that he "would prefer a government run like hell by Filipinos to one run like heaven by Americans."

The policy implied by the Jones Law was more specifically spelled out in the Tydings-McDuffie Act of 1934 that promised full independence to the Philippines on July 4, 1946, after a ten-year transition period as a commonwealth. Quezon was elected president, with an American governor-general named Frank Murphy as the first U.S. High Commissioner.

Quezon, with an eye on the preparations necessary for the Philippines to be a sovereign country, persuaded Douglas MacArthur, whom he knew personally, to come and organize the Philippine Army as soon as MacArthur completed his tenure as chief of staff in America.

The offer came at an opportune time – MacArthur was frustrated over not ever having achieved quite enough of all the honors he thought were his due. Therefore, he leaped at the chance to continue his career far from the petty rivalries that he felt were thwarting his chances of grabbing the golden ring on life's merry-go-round.

Because of his father's stint in the Philippines and two tours of duty of his own, MacArthur arrived in Manila in 1935 with a feeling of homecoming. He started the huge task of organizing the new army, and his aides were Majors Dwight Eisenhower and James Ord.

It would prove to be of great importance that Douglas MacArthur was the man on the scene when the scenario of the Pacific arena in World War II started to unfold. The outcome might have been quite different through anyone else's influence. He was 55 years old at that time, an age where most men would long for retirement; however, this handsome, well-preserved American was unique.

To understand MacArthur's role in the battles of the Pacific, one has to know something about the conflicting character traits of this extraordinary leader. He was born into a family that placed great emphasis on their lineage, and he maintained throughout his life a romantic notion of being prominent in this lineage. He also lived his entire life under the shadow of his parents' expectations for his career.

His father, a man with the same sense of self-importance as Douglas had, was his idol, and his mother was the stern taskmaster who supervised his every thought and action well into his adult life. Unfortunately, he longed for glory by standards that became antiquated during his very long period of active service.

MacArthur's mother, "Pinky," was a Southern belle who brought to her marriage the same amount of determination that the Confederates displayed in the issue over slavery. Her ceaseless devotion to the cause of molding her son into a man of greatness was merciless. The more he excelled, the grander grew her visions and expectations. Douglas never liberated himself from her formidable influence, and, in his struggle to please her, he displayed unusual powers of intellect and determination. However, his obsession with being a hero was so great that he sometimes lied to himself and others in order to maintain the illusion of perfection.

He adapted his father's habit of blaming envious competitors for any failures in his career. Therefore, he chose to surround himself with people whose loyalty he never had to doubt, for those who opposed him stirred up a paranoia that muddled his reasoning faculties.

His actions, even when they were the result of sane military decisions, were always affected by his feelings about himself and the over-riding belief that he was to have a place in history. This relentless striving to create a heroic image of himself occasionally marred his judgment and had profound effects on the many men who served under him.

There is no arguing that Douglas MacArthur was a most remarkable man. He was clearly of superior intelligence, capable of grasping an amazing amount of information and making brilliant plans. His eloquence could hold even his detractors spellbound for hours, and each day of his life was a performance that would have vied with the greatest acting careers.

He had a flair for publicity and was always a great favorite with reporters. During World War I, when he served in Europe as chief of staff for the Rainbow Division, he was a flamboyant figure and tremendously popular with the men who served under him. He liked to stage his appearances, and dressed with an eye for image. In the First World War, he wore riding breeches, although he wasn't a cavalry officer. Thrown jauntily around his neck was a long, scarlet red scarf, which his mother had knitted. He refused to wear the regimental steel helmet, even when in the line of fire. Instead, he created his own style in hats by removing the stiffening from the top of his officer's cap, giving it a jaunty angle and setting him apart from the other officers. He was an eye-catching figure to photograph in the otherwise dreary scenes of the trench war. Dashingly handsome, his picture was soon in all the newspapers back home.

In World War I, he rushed headlong into battle, almost as if he had a death wish and had decided that the setting was right for dying with glory. Although his theatrics didn't endear him to all types of officers, he made a tremendous impression on the men who served under him, and no one questioned his bravery in the line of fire. In fact, his defiance of death gave him a reputation among his men for being invincible.

Some of the other officers christened him "the show off". In his own defense, MacArthur argued that showing off was essential to charismatic leadership. He claimed that if a high-ranking officer got "bumped off" in action, it would be a tremendous boost for doughboy morale. His attitude set him apart from the many cold-hearted officers of World War I who sent thousands of men to sure death as they sat safely and comfortably far from the front lines.

Throughout his career, he was spurred on by a fervent belief that his pursuit of greatness was part of a larger movement towards a better world. The military was for him what the church was for a man of God, and his mother encouraged him in this attitude of having been chosen to serve a greater destiny.

Although he had proved his courage in battle during the Spanish-American War and World War I, by the time he was reaching the age of retirement, he hadn't achieved his major goal – A prominent place in history. Like his father before him, he received many accolades – General of the Rainbow Division, Superintendent of West Point (where he tried without success to make visionary reforms and introduce more of the humanities into the curriculum), and Army Chief of Staff (where he promoted the idea of modernizing the armed forces and bringing them into the twentieth century); but each time he reached what appeared to be a pinnacle in his career, he eyed a dead end and imagined that his enemies were keeping the golden apple just out of reach, giving him posts that would deter him from the unknown prize. Furthermore, his ideas were too unorthodox for the run-of-the-mill people he had to convince.

From his mother, he learned the importance of courting favor with people who recognized his family as part of the establishment, but he imagined that people outside this privileged strata harbored an unfair resentment towards him for being born into it. Thus, the invitation to serve in the Philippines as Philippine Field Marshall came as a welcome last chance to do something – he knew not quite what – and to escape the confinements of the normal American formula for success. He firmly believed in the importance of the Orient, and that the United States should do everything possible to be the friend and benefactor of the richly endowed countries of that region.

Douglas MacArthur's fate was intricately woven into the story of the Philippines. Not only had his father fought and governed there, but Douglas also returned to his beloved islands for three different tours of duty in the course of his own military career. He was there in 1903 with the Engineer Brigade, as a young second lieutenant. His second tour was from 1922-25, when he mapped out Bataan and laid the groundwork for the most logical plan for defending the Philippines.

The concept of this plan was based on the prevailing theory among tacticians, that the many islands in the Philippines, with their countless coastlines, would be virtually indefensible. Therefore, efforts to repel an enemy should be concentrated around Manila, which is located on the island of Luzon and was the most likely point for an initial attack. This defense plan relied on holding off the enemy for six months until help could come from the U.S. Fleet, just as Dewey had done. The idea was to concentrate forces on Bataan and Corregidor while waiting for relief.

Bataan is a peninsula with a rugged mountain range running down the middle, as suitable a terrain as one can ask for in the almost impossible task of waging war in the jungle. Arthur MacArthur had seen the effectiveness of luring invading troops into the wilds of Bataan well illustrated – by Aquinaldo when American troops had tried to flush him out.

Corregidor is only a small island, shaped like a frog, located within the entrance to Manila Bay, but it was made into a fortress with what were considered awesome ramifications in those days, a supposedly formidable obstacle if an enemy wanted to sail into Manila Bay.

When Quezon, who was now President of the Philippines, asked MacArthur to step back into active duty in 1935 and organize the Philippine Army, MacArthur made the grave error of dismissing his own original plan for defense and devising an alternative, far more difficult plan. His new plan was to defend the thousand-mile coastline of Luzon, a task that he, as a young lieutenant, had seen was impossible.

The only explanation for this unwise move seems to be that vanity blurred his vision. Like most men capable of grand visions, he became enthused about his role in shaping a superb army in the Philippines, which would be a credit to him. He had come to see himself as a military leader equipped to astonish his peers. He knew he had to count on the arrival of massive aid, but his ego convinced him that a well-trained army, inspired by him, could hold off the enemy in the interim, by defending not only Manila Bay, but also the beachheads along the coast of Luzon. Exerting his great powers of persuasion, he was able to convince the military experts in Washington that the Philippine Islands were, indeed, defensible if given the necessary firepower.

Although MacArthur succeeded in convincing the War Department that the American troops already stationed in the Philippines and the Filipinos under his command could provide an effective defense force, the military brass in Washington were less than helpful in providing him with what he needed to build up that defense. MacArthur's persistent requests for supplies and equipment prior to the outbreak of hostilities did not meet with success. By the time Japan formed an Axis with Germany and Italy and the men in Washington decided to make the Philippines their stronghold against Japanese expansion, it was too late to get enough hardware out there. The Philippine Army turned out to be a well-organized and dedicated outfit of inadequately equipped troops.

Therefore, in 1941, while the gentleman soldier, MacArthur, was plotting strategy from the 'House on the Wall,' his elegant headquarters in Manila, an air of unreality had already descended upon the Philippines.

In the general's plans, Pearl Harbor was not even considered as the prime target of a Japanese onslaught. It was assumed that the Japanese would secretly plan a massive attack on the Philippines in order to sever the American lines of communication, safeguard the supply routes they were in the process of conquering, and deny the United States a naval base so close to Japan.

In those days of blissful ignorance, few Americans were aware of the background of American involvement in the Philippines or the role those in power assigned the Philippines. That which met the eye was sufficient to those who were posted there. Most of the men who were stationed in Manila were grateful to be far from the battlegrounds of Europe and hoped to escape the nightmare that was transpiring there. The Philippines was the Americans' dream outpost in the Far East, and both tourists and servicemen found it to be seeped with the magic of the Orient.

Ironically, in August, while Mickey and Bob were making their plans to start a newspaper in the Philippines and were encouraged by MacArthur, those leaders who plotted the venues of war had already doomed those islands. In June 1941, there were a series of high-level top-secret conferences with British officers, the result of which was War Plan 5. Although America had not entered the war, this plan was agreed upon and adopted by Roosevelt's Joint Army-Navy Board, and in essence, it stated their intention of pursuing a "Europe first policy," giving top priority to European interests.

If President Quezon had been informed of the Europe first policy, he would have known that the Filipinos, who would fight bravely to fend off the Japanese attack when it finally came, were to be sacrificed by those leaders who sit thousands of miles away and use whole countries as their pawns on the chessboard of history. The Filipinos were to be betrayed by American policy-makers a second time, but this time there was a difference: Of the 78,000 men who would surrender at Bataan, 12,000 would be Americans. This sword had a double edge.

However, it wasn't until October that MacArthur was briefed on this change of priorities, and his letter to Bob, inviting him to start a newspaper, was written at the end of August. When Mickey arrived in Manila to pave the way for Vivian to follow with the children by clipper on December 10th, the die was already cast.

* * * * *

After thirty days at sea, Mickey arrived in Manila. He was euphoric over his first impressions. It was all he imagined and then some. After checking into a hotel, he reported to MacArthur who was at his opulent penthouse suite at the top of the Manila Hotel. A Filipino servant, immaculate in a starched white uniform, opened the door and led Mickey across highly polished hardwood floors into a spacious drawing room, known as the Gold Room which was rich with red drapes and French mirrors. Leather-bound books that had belonged to the general's father lined the shelves in a library paneled with Philippine mahogany. There were maroon leather chairs and, in the center of the room, an imposing table with silver-framed, autographed photos of Pershing, Foch, and other military notables. Two large balconies overlooked the most spectacular views of the city: The lovely bay and the dramatic outlines of Corregidor and Bataan.

MacArthur greeted Mickey and dazzled him with his presence. The general's looks were striking, and his voice and diction were unforgettable. Tall, straight-backed and classically handsome, he possessed an aura of authority that he wore effortlessly. No wonder the servicemen and civilians out here felt so confident, thought Mickey. He's a textbook example of the type Hollywood would cast as a general.

The general had developed traits designed to make it evident that he came from a long line of military leaders. He carried himself with a dignified reserve that Mickey had learned to recognize as a quality akin to loneliness. The two men were diametric opposites, but, ironically, they had similar factors in their backgrounds. Both had spent their early years in the vast spaces of the west, and both had ambitious, domineering mothers with southern roots;

however, the fine old family background of the general's mother provided her with much more clout in her efforts to mold her son and furnish him with a sense of importance and a belief in his destiny.

Douglas' parents had instilled in Douglas the self-discipline to achieve any goal. He had learned to control any impulse that would interfere with his driving desire to live up to their expectations. Furthermore, his imagination was stirred by an illustrious family history that made him believe he was endowed with all the hallmarks of an aristocrat. He grew up among people with polish, beauty, and power, and he shared a common ancestor with Winston Churchill and Franklin Delano Roosevelt.

Both MacArthur and Mickey were uniquely American, but while Mickey was an enterprising, wheeling-dealing sort of American, MacArthur was an American shackled to a glorious past. Mickey wasn't inhibited by a burden of ancestral greatness and had the free spirit's lack of respect for convention. He lived for the moment and acted on impulse. He had never let his mother's ambitions interfere with an irrepressible urge to live life to the hilt. MacArthur's desire to please was intellectual; Mickey's was sensual. It was an example of the Calvinist influence versus the hedonist, both generated by the same primal desire to bring pleasure to those around them and to be loved. Society expects the most from the aristocrat, but if the chips are down, a man whose actions don't have to be channeled through an approval committee of ancestors can sometimes be relied upon to take action with more honesty. However, neither man would have changed places with the other.

MacArthur's manner was gracious, but he seemed slightly pre-occupied in his welcome, as if something were troubling him. Undaunted, Mickey poured on the charm. He was never lacking in self-confidence, even when he met a person of MacArthur's stature, and his effervescent personality appealed to the staid general.

Mickey's eyes swept the room, and he was appealingly enthusiastic when he told the general how impressed he was with his home and with the colorful capitol of the Philippines.

Pleased, MacArthur responded warmly to Mickey's openness. As is sometimes the case with people of opposite types, they immediately established a friendly rapport, sensing that they would never be competitors. MacArthur liked journalists, and this one, he thought, was in no way abrasive.

In the torpid climate, everyone was impressed with MacArthur's flawless appearance. Like a performing artist, he changed clothes several times daily, making sure that the creases were perfect in his uniform, despite the humidity of Manila. (He had twenty-three uniforms and suits and a servant to guarantee their freshness.) His impeccable grooming fit nicely with

Mickey's typecasting of a general, and the general was aware of the same attention to appearances in Mickey.

Unlike Mickey, MacArthur followed an ascetic regime that would have been worthy of a monk. His diet was perfectly balanced and he never over-indulged. He allowed himself a cocktail in the evening, but it was for the sake of the ritual, not because he needed it. Often, it was left unfinished in the glass. While he and his wife made obligatory appearances at Filipino receptions, their lives were like the precision of a Swiss watch. They spent nearly every evening viewing a movie at home, preferably a western, and MacArthur was delighted when he discovered that Mickey was formerly a casting director and knew his favorite cowboy heroes. Whenever they were to meet in the weeks to come, he showed a boyish interest in knowing how film effects were achieved and hearing anecdotes about the actors.

The general married his wife, Jean, late in life, right after his mother's death. Earlier attempts at finding someone to share his life had been thwarted by his mother's influence. His one marriage to a rich socialite had soon ended in divorce. However, Pinky would have thoroughly approved of Jean who was every inch a lady and devoted to her 'gineral,' as she called him with her Southern accent. In return, MacArthur doted on Jean and the son she produced for him so late in his life.

She came in the room now, much like a polished maid-in-waiting, to remind him of the next step in his carefully constructed schedule. She was small, with a sweet face, and holding her hand was their little boy, Arthur. MacArthur was transformed at the sight of his son. Clearly, when the boy was present, nothing else was of importance. Mickey was reminded of his family, for Arthur was close to Tony's age.

"I can hardly wait 'til my wife sees this place," Mickey said, with enthusiasm. "She will love it, and so will our kids."

At that, MacArthur seemed startled. "Is your wife going to join you here?" he asked.

"Well, just as soon as I get settled," Mickey explained, while he wondered whether the general would have any objection to that.

"You know, the military wives were sent home as a precaution, in April and May," MacArthur said, rather stiffly.

"Well, but your wife is still here, General. I think that is a good sign of how safe it is," Mickey replied.

MacArthur reverted to the distant reserve Mickey had observed when he first entered the room. He changed the subject by wishing Mickey luck and asking him to let his staff know if he needed any assistance. He then called his servant, asking him to escort Mickey to the ground floor where there was an adjutant who had been instructed to help him in setting up an office and finding a place to stay.

The adjutant's name was Frank Barnes. He was from New York City, and being in the tropics hadn't slowed his tempo. He showed Mickey regimental headquarters in the Intramuros. There, MacArthur had his office in an architectural gem from the eighteenth century, "The House on the Wall," perched atop the 350-year-old stonewall that encircled Manila's inner city. Mickey was enthralled with the atmosphere created by the grandeur of the Spanish influence and the lush plant growth, all carefully tended by the cheap labor available among the native population. It had the same sensual appeal of Oahu, but with the added allure of a Spanish heritage.

As they drove slowly along streets crowded with people, he could see why servicemen he had met raved about the place. The friendly Filipinos added a holiday air that had made this posting seem like a luxury vacation to the GIs who were sent here. In downtown Manila, a drunken sailor or soldier was a common sight, patiently tolerated by the natives. It was everything he had heard it would be. Frank confirmed the stories Mickey had heard about what sort of life a civilian could expect to live in Manila and promised to take him for a drive in Pasay where wealthy American and European families lived in beautiful homes and enjoyed the sort of social life made possible by servants working for a pittance.

"Of course, all the military wives have been evacuated, but the civilians I know living here think that was a shame. We are damned close to Japan, but you'll soon see what a defense has been built up here. The Japs would be crazy to attack us in this place."

"I figured as much, but we decided I should come out here first and get settled in before my wife comes out with the kids. They're flying from the islands on December 10th. I can hardly wait to show my wife this place. Hawaii is a paradise, but, face it, the life style there can't match this, unless you're loaded."

"Yeah, I hear ya' talkin'...It's gonna be tough to go back to a cold-water flat in the Big Apple after this stint in Manila. There's a lot of action here though, if you know what I mean. I hope I might have a bundle of cash before I leave," Frank said confidentially. Mickey perked up his ears and was about to ask him what he meant, but decided that could wait.

The next day, Mickey borrowed a jeep and drove to Baguio, the cool high country preferred by whites. That was where the Freidmans had said he and Vivian should try to find a house. It was a four-hour drive leading to roads that were green tunnels through dense walls of tropical shrubs and trees. Happily, he thought of how excited his family would be when they got a look at the place, and once in Baguio he saw plenty of the kind of spacious houses he hoped they would live in, with well-tended grounds. Maybe we should send for Donda, too. It'd be nice to make up to her for the roughing it she had to do in the islands, he thought.

During the next couple of weeks Mickey blazed a trail in Manila. With his usual zest for new challenges, he dug into the job, starting out by getting to know the layout of the place and sizing up the best contacts. Turning out a newspaper was something that opened many doors, and he soon knew a good many civilians as well as military people.

If he did this job well enough, he reasoned, no telling what sort of opportunities it might lead to later on. Not only could he earn good money with the paper, there was also a lot of action on the civilian front, as old established families lost their nerve and sold out their assets. There was wheeling dealing to do out here that would make anything back home seem like a church bazaar. Besides, with the amount of loot he could stow away during the coming year, he might just decide to buy up a big spread here in the Philippines and make this their retirement home. Unlike Vivian, he had no qualms about being so far away from his mother. The businessmen he contacted were a different breed than the ones he met in the states. Many of them had the same spirit of adventure that Mickey possessed, otherwise they wouldn't have been attracted to the Philippines. He felt like he was on the same wavelength.

'Our Army' didn't call for the sort of writing he used to dream of, but there must be material for unlimited stories out here that he could knock out later on.

The thought flashed through his mind of the Japanese warship they had passed in the waters outside the Philippines, but looking around he could see the Japs wouldn't be foolish enough to pick a fight with an operation this size. In fact, being that close to Japan would probably be an advantage. He still didn't think they would want to have a major war waged so close to their own doorstep.

It had surprised him to learn that the wives of military personnel had already been shipped out. Evidently there had been a lot of talk about all the women who were raped when the Japs took over Nanking. However, it was reassuring to see the number of attractive women who had remained. They were the wives and daughters of businessmen in the Philippines, and they said life was too darned good in Manila to want to leave. They thought it was a shame that the servicemen's wives had been sent Stateside, and they couldn't see any reason why he shouldn't go right ahead with plans to bring his family out here.

Without Vivian, he could have felt lonely in the evenings, but he soon had a flock of friends from all different walks of life. With the abundance of domestic help, people did a lot of entertaining, and when he wasn't invited out to private homes, he whiled away time in the officers' club. Those were the scenes he knew Vivian would like, dining in style with people who had been able to hone their social skills due to the perks of colonial living. The other side was the teeming nightlife of Manila, where vice had the allure of being exotically foreign.

The Filipinos loved to gamble, and the pretty Filipinas loved to latch on to an American and squeeze what they could out of an easy affair. Mickey was in his element in either world, and he smoothly established his practice of signing the chit wherever he went. People were confident that 'Our Army' would pay the bill.

He spent much of the following days talking with GIs, getting the kind of interest stories that were popular in keeping up the morale. Not that the morale was low; Manila was a serviceman's dream. Even a buck private could afford native help to keep his gear in order, leaving plenty of time for hitting the nightspots. The easy going Filipinos accepted the Yank's boisterous ways and made a lot of money catering to their vices. Whether they were on shore leave or stationed in Manila, it was the sort of place that had more of everything: Beautiful scenery, beautiful girls, and Singapore Gin Slings to make them wild and leave them blissfully foggy about how badly they had behaved when they woke up on the morning after the night before.

Occasionally, a Japanese warship on a goodwill visit docked in Manila. A great contrast to the Americans, their crew formed an orderly procession and marched to the Japanese school and shrine to pay their respects. The Filipino population watched them with an uncomfortable feeling of apprehension. Even the Japanese who lived in the Philippines were not popular with the native population, who feared that the 'Yellow Peril' would one day invade. Their adoration of MacArthur convinced them they were safe, however. When they saw him on the day that he was given the title of Field Marshall of the Philippine Army, resplendent in a uniform he had designed himself, they shouted with joy and would have followed him to the ends of the earth.

Mickey decided to visit the military outposts on Luzon, in order to get an overall view of things before Vivian and the kids arrived. He was impressed with the skill and precision demonstrated by army artillery. A civilian, he was unaware of the things that were lacking in a good defense, and if he had been aware of them, he would have figured it was unimportant. Everyone subscribed to MacArthur's theory that a Japanese attack would hit Manila Bay before if hit any place else, and right smack dab in Manila Bay was Corregidor, 'The Rock,' the presumably impregnable island fortress that would have to be passed.

While Mickey was enthusiastically embracing life in the Philippines, MacArthur was struggling with his conscience. He had been informed of the Europe first strategy and knew what that implied as to the defense of the Philippines, but his oath of loyalty to the United States

Government prevented him from revealing this information to President Quezon, a man who was not only a loyal ally, but also a personal friend.

If war came to the Philippines, MacArthur could have the chance of a lifetime to go down in history as a great military leader. However, the thought kept nagging him that unless he got fresh troops, air power and ships coming to the rescue, an invasion could only be a catastrophe. He wrapped himself in the dignified mantle that served so well to hide his inner feelings, and those who looked to him for leadership couldn't see his mind's eye. Was he reading the writing on the wall, or was he hoping for a miracle? His anguish over his own future blinded him to the scope of the disaster that loomed ahead.

Pearl Harbor

Vivian was caught up in the same nightmare she had the night before she had her operation. Her mother had been trying to reach out to her. All around were menacing cliffs, and she was falling over the edge of a deep precipice. The feeling of great danger was intensified by the terror in her mother's eyes, and she tried to reach the outstretched hands but couldn't. She awakened with her heart pounding, grateful to slip out of the hold the dream had on her. Damn those planes. She couldn't see why the military had to have a maneuver on a Sunday. They probably were the cause of her sleeping poorly.

It was Sunday morning, December 7, 1941. She swung her legs over the edge of the bed and hoped that she wasn't going to have a bad day. A single throb behind her right eye as she sat up gave a hint of a headache. There was still a lot to do before they would be packed and ready to leave for Manila. She wrapped herself in a kimono, as she made a mental list of what needed to be done.

The car had just been Simonized and looked good as new. As soon as she put an ad in the paper to sell it, people had started calling. She figured she'd grab at the offer from the guy who called last night and said he'd give her nine hundred bucks for it. That was great, because then she only had the furniture to deal with.

Tony and Judy were already awake, fighting over the Christmas card Donda had sent. Vivian padded barefoot to the front door and was peeved upon opening it to discover that neither the milk nor the Sunday's paper were there. She told Tony and Judy to cut out the racket they were making and picked up the phone to call the 'Advertiser' office and complain about the paper not being delivered.

There was a lot of commotion at the other end of the line, and a man's excited voice cut her short. "Ma'm, we're at war! Pearl Harbor is now being bombed and is on fire!" was his exasperated reply to her complaint.

"That's a hell of a way to kid a gal on a Sunday morning," she said, laughing.

"No fooling. It's a fact…Just look out the window!" he said before hanging up.

She suddenly realized that the planes she had been hearing weren't just going through their usual drills. She drew back the curtains that covered the windows facing the sea and saw great billows of black smoke by Pearl Harbor and planes engaged in fierce dog fighting. While she stood mesmerized by the scene unfolding before her eyes, Tony was out the door like a flash, running into the yard to get a better look.

Judy ran after him, and they jumped in excitement when they saw planes flying so low and so steeply banked that their pilots were clearly visible in their cockpits. Delighted, Tony and Judy waved, unaware of the fact that this was the enemy. It was the second wave of raiders sweeping over Diamond Head to start their onslaught. Two planes were engaged in a chase, one with the Japanese red sun on its wings, and the other an American fighter. The plane in pursuit fired at the other, and there was an explosive sound before they both veered off in another direction. Tony let out a yelp and threw himself down on the grass, clutching his foot.

Vivian ran out and swooped both children up in her arms to carry them back inside. A piece of shrapnel had grazed Tony's heel, and her white silk kimono was streaked with blood when she put him down inside the house. Minor though the injury was, it brought home to her the danger they faced.

She was stunned. Just her luck that when the cards were down she would be so far away from her family and not have Mickey by her side. Her mind racing with possible courses of action, she turned on the radio to try to find out what the devil was happening. With the buildup at Pearl Harbor and Hickham Field and Schofield Barracks, she wouldn't have believed the Japanese would ever have attacked. Like most Americans, she thought the United States' Pacific fleet was invincible.

Her heart froze as she thought of her nephew, Slivers. From the huge explosions and clouds of black smoke, she knew that the Japs must have made some direct hits on ships. She looked at her watch and realized with a sense of panic that he would still have been on board ship, probably sleeping off a hangover. She thought about how Slivers spent his Saturday nights, and worried that he wouldn't be in any shape to fend for himself in an emergency.

At that moment, all over the island people were facing the overwhelming reality of war, experiencing the fear, anger and shock that come with a surprise attack. Their world was turned upside down. Even those who were not racist had never conceived of the small Japanese taking on strapping big Americans.

As for the Japanese pilots, they couldn't believe their luck. Nearly all the Navy's power was lined up in the harbor – an easy target. The prevailing attitude in the War Department was that the ships were safe there, an attack from submarines having been considered the most likely scenario. Likewise, American planes were lined up wingtip to wingtip in the airfields, because the Army and Navy Air Force thought the greatest threat was sabotage, not an air attack.

In the bedlam that followed the first attack, there were heroic attempts to fight back. Even the army chaplain at Hickam Field forgot all about the outdoor mass he was preparing and mounted a machine gun on the alter to fire at the dive bombers. (His bravery was immortalized in the popular song, "Praise the Lord, and Pass the Ammunition".)

The Japanese were amazed at how quickly the Americans responded, considering how badly they were caught unawares, but these efforts were largely in vain. The onslaught lasted slightly less than two hours, but it left a toll of 2,403 dead, 1,178 wounded, 5 ships of war lost, eighteen more damaged or sunk but salvageable, and 188 aircraft destroyed and 159 damaged. The Japanese had only lost 29 planes with their pilots, five midget submarines, and one big sub.

All the Americans who were there believed that the attack would be followed up by a major offensive. Vivian was soon in touch with her network of friends. Honolulu had become a beehive of speculation and futile activity. In every house, families and friends hovered around the radio. Rumors were rampant, and one of them was that Roosevelt wanted sixty thousand civilians to evacuate to the mountains, to be in place and carry out guerilla warfare.

Recalling accounts of the atrocities that the Japanese committed against the civilian population in Nanking, Vivian panicked. The mountains sounded safe, and she ran through the house, grabbing everything she thought would be needed for hiding out – Blankets, food supplies, and practical clothing. Tony and Judy were jubilant, hopping with excitement over the prospect of camping out and pestering her with requests to bring Tony's tricycle and Judy's 'babies'. Trying not to be cross with them and relieved that they didn't seem to realize what was going on, she hurriedly loaded the car while trying to listen to the news that was coming in a steady stream from the radio.

"What about Spots?" Tony asked. He was holding their Dalmatian puppy tightly, worried that they would leave without her.

Vivian's immediate thought was that the last thing they needed in a pinch was a puppy, but one look at Tony's face convinced her that she wouldn't have the heart to leave her behind. "Okay, honey, but put her in the car. We don't want to have to chase her when we're ready to leave."

Just as she had loaded all that she thought she would need into the car and was struggling to put the top up, Mr. Yoshiga, their Japanese neighbor, came running over and asked her what she was doing.

When she told him, he urged her not to go to the mountains, because of the danger that a fifth column of spies would be there. "Japanese snipers dey come der, Missus Owen. I think so – for shoo. You no go. Come. Come with me." And taking the children by the hand, he asked her to follow him to his house. Behind the modest little bungalow that housed him and Mrs. Yoshiga and their three children, he showed her what looked like a cellar door, hidden by thick shrubbery. He opened it revealing a dugout that had been made for just such an emergency. The whole family was gathered, ready to occupy it.

"You come stay wit us," he said. "You always plenty nice to my family. Here we safe from bombs. Bimeby everything be mo bettah." He smiled at Vivian, and Mrs. Yoshiga and the children all bobbed their heads in agreement.

Realizing what this tunnel implied, Vivian looked with alarm at her neighbor, this quiet little man who raised turkeys, and asked, "But Mr. Yoshiga, did you know about the attack?"

She had never seen him so upset when he answered. "We knew dem dirty bastards would come. My bruddah – the one who works out Pearl Harbor way – he *tell* his boss, but boss say he pupule. Boss no *believe* dah kind."

The poor man looked down shamefully, wringing his work-worn hands. His voice was full of sorrow as he continued, "You must believe me, Missus Owen. We come here for mo' betta life. We no want Japanese Imperial Army here. My children American!" he said fiercely.

"I know, Mr. Yoshiga," Vivian said, patting him on the arm to comfort him. "Thank you so much for your kindness. I'll go home now, and I'll come to you if there is trouble." She squeezed Mrs. Yoshiga's hand reassuringly and took Tony and Judy back home.

She thought of all the Japanese people she knew here in the islands and how courteous and reliable they were. Surely they would never side with those Japanese whom America would be fighting. She was convinced they would be on America's side if there were an invasion. She felt calmer as she returned to the house and decided to follow the news and bide her time.

The phone was ringing when she reached the lanai. Harry Grimm was calling to ask what she planned to do, and he talked her into coming over to their place to wait out the suspense. He said he'd come help her board up the house before she left.

Helen Grimm felt sorry for Vivian for being alone with two small kids, and she figured the unknown would seem less frightening if friends were together. Soon, however, the Grimm's house was packed with relatives who had been bombed out of Pearl Harbor. They all sat around the radio, listening to reports. The news commentator furnished a flow of wild rumors, speculation, and advice, adding to the cacophony of their own exaggerated conjectures. No one had ever dreamed the Japanese would have attacked a country as powerful as the United States, but now that it had happened, people wondered whether America was all that powerful after all and where they would strike next.

Helen's sister, Eileen, was close to hysteria, and Tony and Judy were starting to get on her nerves. Vivian tried to keep them quiet, but inwardly she felt it was unfair. In the charged atmosphere, the children alternated between bursting with excitement or losing interest and wheedling her to let them go outside and play. They would be easier to keep indoors if they were home where they had their toys to play with.

Despite everyone's protests, she decided to move back to the boarded up house and wait for the moment when she would either seek refuge in Yoshiga's tunnel or head for the mountains. She tried not to think about all the talk she had heard of women being raped by invading Japanese soldiers.

Harry watched her leave, and, as usual he couldn't help but admire her. Helen was so afraid of everything, but Vivian never showed any weakness. "My God – nothing seems to knock her out," he said, as he watched her walk across their lawn.

Vivian's first thoughts upon returning were to try to notify Mickey and her family, to assure them all was well. When she finally got through on the jammed telephone lines, she was told that no telegraphs could be taken over the phone. She was afraid to take the kids into Honolulu, so she decided to ask Harry to send a wire to Donda. She then managed to get in touch with Bob Cork and ask him to try to send word to Mickey.

Next, she called the nearest army base and asked them to loan her a rifle. The prompt reply from a harassed staff officer at the other end of the line was, "Lady, we don't have enough weapons for our own men!"

Vivian knew that with this turn of events there would be no chance of them flying to the Philippines, and if they could go, she'd be afraid to. The war was sure to spread to all of the South Pacific. There was already talk of evacuating women and children, and she decided she might have to go to Mickey's mother. Everyone assumed the Japanese would invade the Pacific coastline now that they had proved their strength, but they would never reach Nevada, she reasoned. She wryly thought to herself that a choice between the Japanese Imperial Army and Mickey's mother left her little to look forward to.

After a few days, the hours of being on alert took their toll. She forced herself to stay cheerful in order not to make the children nervous, but she slept poorly and was beginning to feel the strain. The initial shock of the attack had kept everyone charged with energy, but now they were stressed with the expectation of more to come and not knowing when it would happen.

Soon things grew quieter. The civilian population learned to live with the wild rumors that were circulating and settled down to the practical business of gathering emergency stores and preparing for an evacuation. Within hours, martial law had been declared, and people became occupied with adjusting to new realities. A military court would try an ordinary traffic offence, and a speeder would likely be required to donate a pint of blood. A total blackout was ordered, and guards were posted at places considered vital, such as telegraph offices.

Slivers turned up on Vivian's doorstep, and she was so happy to see him that she didn't know what to do. She laughed, and she cried. She took off her slipper and whacked him on the bottom for having given her such a fright, and then she hugged him tightly, saying he was a sight for sore eyes.

Slivers seemed to have grown up over-night. His voice was grave as he told Vivian about the fate of his ship that had lain at the northeastern end of Battleship Row. It was struck in the bow by a torpedo, but the captain had the men seal that part off and ordered them to get the ship underway. As they tried to get out of the harbor, Jap planes were over them like a swarm of hornets. They managed to shoot two of them down, but soon the foredeck was ablaze, and a bomb smashed the starboard gun battery. There was a huge explosion below deck that threw flames high in the air. Still they managed to keep the ship surging forth, enveloped in smoke, still manning their guns and fighting back with all they had. Oil was gushing out in their wake, but Slivers looked up at one point and saw that the Stars and Stripes were still fluttering from aft.

It was then that they saw the signal flags from the Naval District water tower warning them to stay clear of the channel. If the ship went down with her great bulk, she would bottle up the entire fleet. There was nothing else to do but turn the ship and go aground at Waipio Point, leaving her a sitting duck for the attackers. Half a dozen bombs hit her, but the crew didn't give up.

"We managed to douse the fires and saved what we could, but I'll never forget the noise and the screams of the men who were hit," Slivers told Vivian.

He had been lucky and had managed to get away from the sinking hull of his ship, only to find himself in a sea full of burning oil. Diving under the flaming oil spill, he swam until he thought it was safe to surface.

Suddenly, Slivers grew quiet and grave. The effort of telling about it had drained him of all energy. He had been lost in his tale, and he had tears in his eyes as he thought of his buddies who didn't make it. Becoming again aware of Vivian, he said, "I was hardly hurt, just some burns and cuts," he said, embarrassed about his feelings.

"Yes, but surely that must qualify you for being sent home," she said hopefully.

"Not on your life," he answered fiercely. "I can hardly wait to get back on a ship and kill as many Japs as possible. We all feel that way. They were strafing us even while we were in the drink."

Vivian thought sadly of how pleased she had been that Slivers had been stationed in Honolulu, far away from the war in Europe. It just went to show how unpredictable fate is.

The week following the attack on Pearl Harbor saw World War II become a truly global conflict. Roosevelt, who had wanted to enter the war for some time, now had the population behind him, angry and resolute. On December 8th, war was declared on Japan, and because Japan was one of the Axis powers, this implied a declaration of war on Germany and Italy as well.

While she realized the enormity of her country being at war, Vivian found that, on a personal level, she was fretting about it being another Christmas when she wouldn't be able to send presents to her loved ones in California. She discovered that the convertible, which was a cinch to sell before the attack, was all but worthless now. Gas was rationed and spare parts and tires would be unobtainable. It never failed. Just when everything was the way she wanted it, something big went wrong.

Word got out that women and children were to be evacuated at the first opportunity. In order to ward off eventual epidemics, 350,000 islanders stood in lines for the largest immunization program ever attempted at one location. Vivian had to take the kids to Honolulu for a series of inoculations against diphtheria, typhoid, and small pox, and each time the streets were more and more crowded with servicemen as the military buildup accelerated.

Gas masks were distributed to the civilian population. Vivian was given hers, but for children under six years of age, a shipment of Mickey Mouse gas masks was on the way. Meanwhile, she was told to cover the children with wet blankets in case of emergency.

In the days following Pearl Harbor, they became informed of the scope of the Japanese conquests. No nation had ever acquired such a vast empire with so many riches in such a brief span of time. Within six months they had swept throughout the Pacific, and even Australia, New Zealand, and India were threatened.

And of course, just three hours after they hit Pearl Harbor, they invaded the Philippines.

Bataan and the Rock

On the 6th of December, the newsmen in Manila were invited to General MacArthur's luxurious suite in the Manila Hotel. They partook of a good lunch, and they were sitting enjoying brandy and cigars, when MacArthur said, "Gentlemen, war is eminent. I believe the attack will come sometime after January."

Mickey was relaxed, feeling like a natural part of a worldly scene and relishing the warmth that followed a sip of a good cognac when MacArthur made his announcement. As usual, the general's timing and the deep resonance of his voice struck him. This guy could have made it big on Broadway, he thought with admiration.

A wave of contained excitement passed through the gathering, charging the atmosphere. Everyone perked up his ears, each man fitting this statement into his own view of a pending war. The rest of the afternoon was spent discussing the ramifications of what the general had said, but no one should have been surprised.

As the group started to break up, each man eager to get back to his typewriter and turn this prediction into a story, MacArthur touched Mickey's arm and asked him to stay for a few minutes. During the past month they had met on various occasions, and MacArthur had taken a liking to Mickey.

He beckoned to the servant to refill Mickey's glass before he spoke. "Mickey, I think you should get on the next ship out of here. I can't feel responsible for the other reporters, because their syndicates or papers sent them out here. But I invited you out here personally, and I'm telling you, all hell is going to break loose."

Mickey smiled. He had enjoyed the lunch, and the brandy was excellent. He was touched that the general was taking a personal interest in his fate, but hell, he couldn't see how a nation the size of Japan could take on the good old United States of America. He had seen the buildup in Hawaii, and all the gear they had been sending out there during the past year. Hells afire, the Pacific Fleet would be over here like the wrath of God if the Japanese dared to launch an attack on Americans in the Philippines. Those Jap officers who were taking pictures of Pearl Harbor knew what would be in store for them if they started any trouble.

"Don't worry about me, General. I've seen plenty in my day, and I wouldn't want to miss the chance of seeing our boys beat the bejeezes out of Hirohito's hordes." Like nearly everyone else, he was convinced that the Japanese would be no match to the Americans. Even MacArthur, who had more knowledge of the Japanese than most others, had a built in prejudice that these small people would pose no real threat to a trained American soldier, and he especially doubted their skills as pilots.

Mickey was having the time of his life. He felt like everything he had liked wherever he had lived was all rolled up in one here in Manila. Thanks to his acquaintance with MacArthur, he had come to know some of the most influential businessmen in the Philippines during the brief time he had been here, and his fertile mind was already hatching out schemes in a number of different directions. Finally, he could put Vivian in the setting she deserved.

MacArthur realized that what he was saying wasn't making any impression on Mickey, and, sadly, he had to give it up. He couldn't let it slip out that American naval and air power would be diverted to protect Australia and New Zealand, leaving the Philippines in the lurch. In fact, he had an ambivalent feeling about believing it himself.

After Mickey left, MacArthur paced the floor, trying to anticipate the next move of the Japanese. Surely they wouldn't come before April, during the dry season. Maybe by then various factors would fall into place, making for a successful defense of the Philippines. In his mind, he reviewed the scenario of an attack as he envisioned it, and then he lapsed into an uncharacteristic trance, waiting. Due to the difference of time zones, he was asleep when Pearl Harbor was attacked. When he did learn of it, he was stunned.

Major General Bereton was in charge of the air force at Clark Field, just outside Manila. As soon as he received word of Pearl Harbor, he tried to talk with MacArthur to get permission to wage an attack on Formosa from where he expected a Japanese air attack, but he couldn't get past Sutherland, the general's Chief of Staff. MacArthur's unfortunate penchant for surrounding himself with yes-men had put Sutherland in a position to be a stumbling block to communication on more than one occasion, and this would prove to be the worst occasion of all.

All Bereton could do while waiting for MacArthur's go-ahead was to send his fighter planes off on patrol and put his bombers aloft in order for them not to be sitting ducks if the Japanese should hit.

It wasn't until 11 a.m. that MacArthur finally stirred and authorized a bombing mission to Formosa, but by that time all bombers and fighter planes were back on the ground, to be refueled while their crews grabbed a bite of lunch. Time was needed both for the refueling and to load bombs. Fifteen minutes later a warning was Teletyped to Clark Field that an enemy formation had been sighted heading their way.

From within the Japanese formation, Nippon pilots could hardly believe their eyes. Looking down at Clark Field, they saw all the planes neatly lined up for them to bomb.

* * * * *

Mickey was feeling good when he walked into the cool interior of the Bay View Hotel on Dewey Boulevard. He had found a house to rent that he knew Vivian would love, and the owners had left it furnished not only with tasteful furnishings, but also with a well-trained staff – cook, maid and gardener. The cute little Filipina maid who was to keep his wardrobe tidy did an excellent job, and the crease in his white linen trousers was razor sharp. He was having lunch with Russell Bates and his wife, Lilly. Russ' family had been in the Philippines for years, making a fortune in prime hardwoods. He knew Manila like the back of his hand and enjoyed showing his favorite haunts to someone like Mickey who was keenly interested in the real Manila, not just the American presence.

They were sipping martinis, looking over the menu when they heard the roar of the first wave of twenty-seven Japanese bombers as they zoomed over Clark Field in perfect V-formation, their wings gleaming in the sunlight. The American aircrews were either at mess or servicing their planes, helpless to do anything while the sirens wailed and the bombs rained down. Only four fighter planes managed to get off the ground, before the second wave of twenty-seven bombers flew over. A third wave of Japanese Zeros finished off the job by strafing the area. Simultaneously, there was an attack at Iba Field.

War was a reality, and there was no escaping getting swept up in the stream of it. While Russ saw Lilly safely home, Mickey headed for the Red Cross center. With all those bombs falling, he knew there would be need of anyone who knew something about first aid.

* * * * *

While the American air power in the Philippines went up in smoke, an adjutant in the 26th Cavalry was pleased to report to his colonel that not one horse had panicked during the raid. The same might have been said about MacArthur. During the first twenty-four hours, he took no action, and when he woke from his stupor, Luzon was already a beehive of activity, as officers and men tried to shore up their losses and prepare for the inevitable onslaught. Despite the bad start, morale was still high. The Americans displayed amazing ingenuity in coping with the problems that arose when they discovered the extent of their vulnerability, and the Filipinos were unflagging in their loyalty, convinced that their American heroes would turn the tide.

No one will ever know with certainty the reason for MacArthur's inertia. MacArthur was to claim later that his orders from Washington were that he should not initiate hostilities against the Japanese, and, furthermore that an air attack on Formosa would have been doomed to failure. However, that statement isn't valid. It would have been feasible to bomb Formosa, and the Japanese had initiated hostilities when they attacked Pearl Harbor.

As for Bereton, his Air Force colleagues had only scathing criticism for an experienced airman who would be caught with his planes down just nine hours after Pearl Harbor, but he claimed he was unable to get past the general's aid for a go-ahead to get them airborne. That seemed true enough, for everyone knew how jealously Sutherland guarded his access to the general.

In studying the mess of conflicting statements that were issued afterwards and the obvious precautions that were ignored, and in trying to decipher why MacArthur remained so passive, one is tempted to believe that the problem was of a psychological nature, unrelated to military logistics. Those who knew MacArthur well were baffled by his behavior. They noted that he was withdrawn, ashen gray, and reticent. This absolutely brilliant man, who had always impressed people with his grasp of details and his ability to encompass a variety of conflicting scenarios and eloquently put them into order for others to understand, was like a sleepwalker or a fine piece of machinery which had stalled because of overload.

MacArthur's unwillingness to face reality might have been because he was torn in two directions. He was the dedicated soldier, loved by the Filipinos who would follow him anywhere they were led, but he was also the politicians' general who was forced to accept the conditions of a plan much larger than any plans he could make. He had before him a soldier's dream of being a hero and, at the same time, the base reality of having to obey orders.

Thus, perhaps his lethargy was a subconscious rejection of the role he had been commanded to play. Since his boyhood he had dreamed of his moment of glory, and he knew he was capable of orchestrating it but how to grasp the baton? How to respond to the stirring cadences of martial music while he was so acutely aware of the fact that so much human life would be lost? And if MacArthur was the conductor of this orchestra, it was as if he had been told at the last minute to lead them in a different marching tune. The magic bond, which forms between a good conductor and his orchestra, was missing, and there was a dissonant mess of chords.

In 1936, when MacArthur had stepped into the role of Field Marshall for the adoring Filipinos, he had thrilled them with a rousing speech. Decked out in a uniform of his own design – black trousers, a white tunic festooned with medals, stars, and gold cord, and his famous braided cap – his melodious voice sent shivers down the spines of his audience as he intoned: "The military code that has come down to us from even before the age of knighthood and chivalry," he said, had found its highest expression in the soldier, who, "above all men, is required to perform the highest act of religious teaching – sacrifice."

"In battle and in the face of danger and death he discloses those divine attributes which his Maker gave when He created man in His own image. However horrible the incidents of war may be, the soldier who is called upon to offer and to give his life for his country, is the noblest development of mankind."

How was MacArthur to recapture this boyhood dream of nobility amidst the chaos and destruction that was wreaked by air power during the first few hours of the Japanese attack? In the bog mire of World War I, he had foreseen that future battles would be won by air power. How can one explain that he who was so far-sighted then would now be left with only enough planes to offer token resistance?

His failure to take command at this crucial point is made more poignant by the courage displayed by the pilots and ground crews on that fatal day. American and Filipino pilots fought back bravely and with greater skill than possessed by the Japanese pilots, but they could do little to save the planes so badly needed in order to hold the Japanese at bay. Men on the ground fought valiantly with what they had at hand and without facilities to take cover. No 'slit' trenches had been dug on the runways, and many men were slaughtered by strafing.

Afterwards, when the adrenaline was no longer pumping full force, the Americans and Filipinos realized to what extent they had been caught unprepared, and their confidence suffered a powerful blow.

The Japanese, experts at surprise attacks, were on the other hand very well organized. American pilots of the 17th Pursuit, flying Kittyhawks out of Nichols Field, climbed straight up into the sun, into waiting Zeros, the fighter planes of the Japanese. The Zeros had both their height and the sun to their advantage, and the Americans' blood ran cold when they heard themselves called by name over their radios, welcomed to the skies by English-speaking Japanese flyers.

Having so badly crippled American-Philippine air power, the Japanese had an easy task when they hit the big naval base at Cavite on the third day. Following the second bombing raid, the base was a shambles, and 500 men had been killed and another 300 wounded. After heroic attempts to put out fires and salvage what could be used, it was discovered that undercover agents had set some of the fires.

The Filipinos recalled the Japanese who marched ashore when their 'goodwill' ships paid a visit to Manila and the sense of gloom that came with them. Their premonitions had turned out to be correct; there was fifth column activity among the Japanese population, and that became apparent once war broke out. Among other things, Japanese businessmen and fishermen had carefully mapped all points of strategic interest, and they had done ingenious things, like shooting hypodermic needles filled with acid into the silk parachutes of the air force. Shipments of machine guns, sealed in the States, had been tampered with and couldn't be used.

Not only had the Japanese fifth column sabotaged military equipment, but also much of what had been shipped out by the United States defense department was unsatisfactory to begin with. It was now that the American troops began to discover the inadequacy of the weapons they had. For example, new barrels and bolts to service their machine guns had arrived, but the components didn't fit with the existing equipment.

On the 22nd of December, Homma, the Japanese lieutenant general, made his move, and 43,000 troops of the Japanese 14th Army waded ashore, uncontested, onto the beaches of Lingayen Gulf, 120 miles north of Manila. They were an army of combat soldiers who had proved their strength in China, and they were trained and equipped to fight jungle warfare.

MacArthur's combined U.S. and Philippine Army forces represented three times that amount. However, among these numbers were 100,000 raw Philippine reservists, whose fierce loyalty was not matched by adequate training. Ridiculously ill-equipped, with rotting tennis shoes, cheap papier-mâché pith helmets, and drill 'guns' made of bamboo, their training had hardly gone beyond the art of saluting when the war broke out. Even those who had been issued firearms carried ancient firearms that had been sold to the Philippine Commonwealth by the U.S. Army at a nice profit.

The pride of MacArthur's command was the Philippine Division of the U.S. Army, with the 31st Infantry Regiment and 12,000 Philippine Scouts. With American officers and native Filipino enlisted men, they were regarded as one of the finest fighting formations in the United States Army. There was also one division of the regular Philippine Army in fighting shape, and the 4th Regiment, U.S. Marines who had arrived in November from Shanghai – in all only 25,000 to 30,000 regulars who could be relied on.

However, the biggest disadvantage was that so much was lost during those crucial days when Douglas MacArthur appeared to have descended from another planet.

* * * * *

It soon became crystal clear that the beaches couldn't be held, and MacArthur decided to put into effect the old plan that he had been instrumental in forming when he was young. He would pull all his forces back to Bataan, the 30-mile peninsula of wooded mountains, dense jungle, and steep ravines, separating Manila Bay from the South China Sea. That would leave Manila to Homma, but from the island fortress of Corregidor, at the entrance to Manila Bay, MacArthur's troops could use their cannons to prevent Homma from using the harbor. With his usual flair for elocution, MacArthur exclaimed, "He may have the bottle, but I have the cork."

The success of this plan depended on General Wainwright to hold off the advancing Japanese troops in the north long enough for Major General Parker's Southern Luzon Force to retreat, past Manila, and re-organize on Bataan. Unfortunately, MacArthur's faith in being able to defend the beaches meant that valuable time had been lost in preparation. Supplies that could have made a world of difference were left in depots along the coast and in the plains of Luzon, and it was too late to gather them and move them with the retreating troops.

The logistics of this huge retreat were formidable. Every vehicle that could move was put on the road, including Manila's gaudily painted buses, carrying load after load of soldiers, food, and ammunition into the peninsula. Immense traffic jams occurred as the bizarre busses mingled with olive-drab army vehicles and the private cars and wooden oxcarts of civilians fleeing the Japanese.

Although MacArthur had emerged from his inertia, he had never felt more alone. He was haunted by his knowledge of the behind-the-scenes decisions, the so-called Europe First plan, and he was obliged to take action in a way that was contradictory to the dreams he had of his destiny.

He had already decided that he was going to withdraw with his family to Corregidor, the island fortress with its 912-foot-long tunnel, a formidable shelter. He insisted that President Quezon join him. For the Filipino leader to be captured by the Japanese would be a propaganda disaster.

When MacArthur abandoned Manila, he declared it an 'open city,' in the belief that doing so would keep this cultural pearl from being destroyed by the advancing Japanese. His wife had to leave everything intact in their magnificent apartment, taking with her only a small suitcase with a few cotton dresses, the coat she had worn on their honeymoon, and an extra pair of shoes. She grabbed the general's medals and wrapped them in a towel, cramming them into the suitcase along with food and clothes for four-year-old Arthur. Ah Cheu, the child's

Cantonese nursemaid, clutched Arthur's stuffed rabbit, 'Old Friend,' and MacArthur's aide carried his new tricycle.

Jean took one last look at the apartment. The Christmas tree stood resplendent beside the grand piano. Her eyes fell upon two vases that Emperor Hirohito's grandfather had given to MacArthur's father. Both their names were clearly engraved on them. Jean picked up the vases and placed them in the entrance hall to the penthouse, hoping that when the Japanese invaded, they would notice them and respect the surroundings.

There was an atmosphere of despair that sundown on Christmas Eve, when General MacArthur stood on the dock below Manila Hotel, with his staff, his wife and son, and the boy's amah. Trying not to think about the good days, when it was the jumping off point for pleasure cruises, he steeled himself for deserting Manila and heading for Corregidor.

In the eerie stillness they could hear dinner music floating out from the hotel's ballroom and could picture the surrealistic gathering of formally dressed guests who were unwilling to leave.

The subdued party boarded the inter-island steamer Don Esteban for the 22-mile journey to the island that they called the Rock. Looking back, beyond the scenic waterfront, they could see the flashes and hear the rumble of explosions as supplies of fuel and other stores were destroyed to prevent them from falling into Japanese hands. At Cavite Navy Yard, to the south of Manila, a million barrels of oil were put to the torch, throwing great flames upon the darkened sky. MacArthur sat by himself, a solitary figure resting his head on his hand. A clear voice sang out the first words of 'Silent Night', and one by one the others joined in as they started their tragic journey.

Once on The Rock, MacArthur coordinated what proved to be one of the most brilliant retreats in military history. There were 160 miles of rugged countryside separating the two forces heading for Bataan, and nearly two hundred bridges had to be held and dynamited at the last moment. It required exquisite precision and concentration. The lethargic, dazed MacArthur of December 8th seemed like an illusion, dispelled by the military genius.

Sleepless and haggard, with one hand on the map coordinates of the terrain and the other holding a phone, he urged on his two field commanders, General Wainwright and Major-General Albert Jones, who took over Parker's command during the retreat, as they fought a delaying action toward Bataan.

On New Year's Day they got the last guns and trucks of the Southern Luzon Force across the Pampanga River and dynamited its bridges a few hours ahead of the advancing Japanese. Several small detachments, cut off during the retreat, dispersed into the hills and jungle to form guerrilla bands. Thousands of Filipino reservists realized how unprepared and ill equipped they were and simply stopped being soldiers and went home, while many others bravely carried on despite the odds. Lost and bewildered by a war for which neither their brief training nor their cultural background had prepared them, they stuck to their duty to defend their flag. Those who had ill-fitting army boots, found that they were more miserable wearing them than going barefoot, and they threw them away as they marched into Bataan, following their American idols to an unknown fate.

The American and Filipino defenders hunkered down in one of the most hostile environments they could have chosen, their only hope being that it would be just as hostile to the enemy invaders. With the possible exception of Stalingrad, never had there been a military force fighting under worse conditions for such a long time. The Bataan Peninsula was roughly the size of greater Los Angeles, with volcanoes rising nearly five thousand feet, their steep sides covered with outcrops of sharp coral and jungle growth teeming with snakes and too dense to penetrate without machetes. There were just two roads, one dirt road and one cobble-stoned.

As for air power and naval power, the remaining B-17s had been evacuated to Australia, and the small U.S. Asiatic Fleet had withdrawn to Java. For the defense of Bataan, MacArthur deployed his forces in a twenty-mile line across the upper neck of the peninsula. One corps, under Wainwright, held the precipitous western coast, with its dense tangle of jungle. The other, under General Parker and, later, General Jones, was deployed in an entirely different terrain that stretched to the swampy eastern shore. Separating them was 4,200-foot Mt. Natib, whose foreboding, wooded slopes and snarled, nearly impassable gullies made it impossible to establish effective contact between the two corps.

Mickey spent Christmas Eve in Manila with some of the other journalists, drinking Tom and Jerrys and trying to sort out the conflicting rumors each man had gathered from various scenes of action. In the midst of this confusion, he was trying to decide what was the best move. There were so many rumors, and he didn't have the security of belonging to a unit. He still felt confident that the Japanese would be repelled, and he wanted to be close enough to the action to be able to tell his son about it all one day. So far, it seemed to Mickey like the chance of a lifetime to experience life at its most stimulating, while feeling confident that all would end well. He decided that being with the Red Cross would be his best bet for survival if the Philippines should fall, and, subsequently, he found a unit where he could make himself useful.

Looting was rampant in the city as shopkeepers boarded up their businesses and fled. Most of the loot would have been of no use to Mickey, but he was able to pick up a small cache of gems, dropped by a Filipino on the run. It might come in handy later, he thought, as he stuffed it into his pocket. He carried with him minimum of clothing, his shaving gear and a portable typewriter as he and some of the journalists headed for Bataan.

Among the hordes of people pouring out of Manila, Mickey caught sight of Russ and Lilly and ran to join them. When he caught up with them Russ tugged at Mickey's Red Cross armband and said, "Hell, Mickey, you can throw that thing away if you think it's going to save you from the Japs. We know what they did in Nanking ... They don't give a damn about Red Cross immunity. Stick with Lily and me. We know a lot of people who might help us when the chips are down."

Mickey gratefully jumped into the back seat of their convertible, which was piled high with provisions. It wasn't long, however, before he left them to make himself useful elsewhere. He was too wired to feel like sitting in the back seat of a slow-moving swank car. Jesus, it was history in the making, and he was right in the thick of it. He was seeing everything with a cameraman's eye, unfazed by the potential danger. He had always had an inborn conviction that his life was charmed, and he was too caught up by the excitement of it all to even consider that he could be at risk. Quick thinking and adventurous, he moved around where the tide took him.

Catching up with a unit he knew, he volunteered to drive a jeep with machine parts that they wanted to hide from the Japs. Afterwards, he drove the jeep in a cloud of dust over rutted roads to take a message to one of the generals in the field. Later, his Hollywood ambulance driving experience proved useful. Wounded men were pouring into the makeshift military hospitals, and he was tireless in driving trucks with medical supplies, rendering first aid or moving victims of war.

Amidst the chaos, he saw the ordinary GI's ability to ride the storm, and he was deluded by his gut instinct that all this turmoil would end when help arrived from the States. It was uplifting, after the initial shock of seeing MacArthur so unprepared, to see Wainwright and Parker in action. War was hell, but he had never felt more alive. He was blessed with an ability to doze off any old place and to awaken soon afterwards, brimming over with energy, despite the debilitating tropical heat.

When the retreat was over, some 15,000 American and 65,000 Filipino troops, altogether 80,000 men, were concentrated on Bataan. Along with them were 26,000 civilians, and all they had was a stockpile of rations sufficient to feed 100,000 people for a month: About three thousand tons of canned meat and salmon, supplemented by inadequate supplies of rice. Since the siege could last much longer, they were put on half rations from the start, while one stockpile of food reserves that could have made things more bearable, were transferred to the Rock by MacArthur's orders.

With Manila abandoned and troops concentrated on Bataan, War Plan 5 had taken shape. If reinforcements were on the way, it would be declared a brilliant strategic move. If not, MacArthur would have marched his men into a death trap. It eased the general's mind that Marshall cabled telling him, "We are doing our utmost to rush air support to you." He specified that 140 planes had been shipped to Manila, but the truth was that the shipment had already been diverted to Australia.

As the Japanese advanced on Manila, Americans and Filipinos made heroic efforts to remove or destroy anything that the Japanese could use. There were ingenious schemes to move to Bataan parts that could be used to patch up the few planes they still had for air defense. However, after a few weeks of starving on Bataan, the men were going to wish they had been hauling out food instead.

As for MacArthur's decision to declare Manila an 'open city,' when the Japanese started bombing Manila, they also revealed their attitude towards that aspect of the Geneva Convention. They blew up vast sections of that beautiful city, including MacArthur's penthouse suite at the Manila Hotel. For weeks, they raped, burned, bayoneted and massacred Filipinos and whites from neutral nations, adhering to a directive from the Japanese brass: "When killing Filipinos, assemble them together in one place, thereby saving ammunition and labor. The disposal of dead bodies will be troublesome so either collect them in houses scheduled to be burned or throw them into the river." They killed something like one hundred thousand civilians, figuring that their actions would discourage any rebellion among the remaining Filipinos.

On January 2nd, the Japanese color guard assembled beneath the sprawling acacia trees on the lawn of the imposing residence of the United States High Commissioner in Manila. A Japanese Marine hauled down the Stars and Stripes and ground it under his heel. While the band played Kimigayo, the Japanese national anthem, the flag of the Rising Sun was run up to the top of the mast.

When Homma ordered the rounding up of all British and American civilians for internment and promised that they would not be harmed, Vivian and the children were safe in Hawaii, and Mickey was already on Bataan where the other journalists had gone.

* * * * *

Mickey carefully lifted his head, his ears still ringing from the blast of the explosion. He had sand in his eyes, and spat out dirt. Through the dense cloud of dust he could see the crater the bomb had made, and all around were the shattered bodies of American soldiers. Behind him was the safety of a fringe of trees, but he felt like a man in a nightmare, struggling to awaken so he could make a run for it. The momentary silence that followed the fierce blast was broken by machine gun fire, rousing him to action. His legs felt weak as he made a dash for the trees. Once inside their shadows, he experienced the false sense of safety a child feels when ducking under the covers.

He was startled out of this dreamlike state by the thud made by something falling out of the trees. On the ground, at his feet, was the limp body of a monkey. Its tiny offspring clutched its mother's fur while looking up at Mickey with terrified, uncomprehending eyes. A stray bullet had hit the mother, and she twitched violently before dying.

The past two days' action had jaded Mickey to the sight of men dying, but somehow the death of this animal, which had nothing to do with the wars of human beings, filled him with despair. This very jungle that everyone was cursing evoked in him a sense of awe. Rare trees and many of the plants he knew from Hawaii were rampant here. There were insects and birds more beautiful than any he had ever seen. Even though he was surrounded by danger, he took note of the richness of life that thrived in these surroundings. He felt that human warfare was blasphemous in this tropical Eden.

He gently picked up the terrified baby monkey and tucked it into his shirt, holding it tightly while he made a dash for the retreating frontline. In the days that followed, he shared his rations with it, and it soon accepted him as a substitute for the parent it had lost.

"Hey, Mickey! Who's your little friend?" The guys ribbed him about his pet, but even the roughest of the lot liked to stop up and scratch it under its chin. He said he was keeping it to give his kid when the family got to Manila, and no one corrected him. None of them wanted to think that they might not ever see Manila again. That night in camp, before inky blackness covered their bivouac, he wrote to Vivian.

In the Field

Bataan Peninsula

Darling -

I do not know when this will reach you, and, of course, it is censured so I cannot say everything I would like to ... but this thing can't last forever, and I am keeping a diary of everything that happens for you to read the day we meet. I sent a wire yesterday to Harold Dillingham that will let you know that I am still alive, and that really is about all one can ask for in this fracas. Don't be alarmed as the percentage of casualties has been comparatively light, and I've had that many close calls without getting killed for me to get it at this stage of the game.

I'm trying to get a commission, as I do not know when this thing will end, and I can't go on being a civilian the rest of the war. I wouldn't care about the whole damned thing if I didn't have to be so far away from you. Because of the censor, you are about the only subject I can write about in this letter, and that suits me fine. Out here, we go to bed as soon as the sun goes down (did I say bed?), and I can't sleep more than six hours. That leaves about four hours to think of that night in Hollywood up at Bing's house, in front of the open fire, and the night we closed up the casting office at Fox and sat in the big over-stuffed chair and necked...and all the afternoons up in Vermont canyon, and the early morning sunlight on the little place in Laurel Canyon, and that night we camped out, with ashes in the beans and a smudge on the end of your nose, and Willie Best's convertible, and the first morning in Honolulu with the heavy incense of pikaki, or the evening at Kawela Bay when the copper cobwebs laced the sky. The pride of showing Tony that first time and the expression on your face when I came into the hospital that morning, the walks down the beach with you and later with Tony and the little pup and a scoop net to catch fish. Judy came, and she looked exactly like you and even had your faults, and now that I know why, I know that I love every one of them and don't want you to lose a single one, because they are a part of you that I love. I can't remember the details of the times I have been away from you, and that's what makes it all so wrong for us to be apart. Mind you - my darling - nothing is going to happen to me, but if it does I want you to remember that my last thoughts were of you. I know that, because with every close call that I've had, I was thinking about you and your happiness. (But don't worry...the closest bomb crater was only eight feet away, and I was flat on my face on open ground. I'm still here, and they can't come any closer without hitting me. That won't happen, because they are lousy shots.) We are up in the wilds of Bataan. Lovely country. I've found a baby monkey and am taming it for Tony. Counted 186 dead Japs the other day from a foxhole where I was in the front line. Was at an OP last week and saw some beautiful artillery firing by our guns, but all that news can wait until I see you. Don't worry, my dearest, whatever happens, rest assured that Tony will never be ashamed of his dad. Kiss the babies and remember I love you will all my heart.

Aloha, My Darling,

m.

He tucked the letter into a pocket, hoping for a chance to get it back to headquarters and off to the states. Things were getting more and more chaotic, and communications were very difficult.

Mickey had gravitated towards Wainwright's camp. It hadn't taken him long to figure out that his best chance for survival was to be close to Wainwright. Unaware of the Europe first policy, Wainwright was trying to protect the pilots who would be their best bet when reinforcements arrived. Consequently, the chow was better there than anywhere else on Bataan, not sufficient, but better.

Mickey's characteristic optimism hadn't failed him, and, despite the danger, he felt the exhilaration that comes with being in the eye of the storm, if you have blind faith that the storm won't harm you. So far, he was doing all right physically. He noticed that the Americans who were worst off were often the ones who were prime specimens at the beginning of the fracas, tall men with big frames. He did what he could to help out with the sick, and the men soon got used to counting on him to be cheerful and to come up with a joke for every occasion. When he came around with his little monkey clinging to his neck and a dose of gallows humor, they brightened up and were able to forget the hell of war for a brief moment.

Being a civilian and a journalist, he had better means of moving around and accessing the overall situation, and he began to realize, more than most of the foot soldiers did, what sort of a spot they were in. It became clear that the supply of ammunition was insufficient for a protracted siege. Furthermore, four out of five grenades failed to explode. Of seventeen Stokes mortar shells fired by one platoon, only four burst.

Not only was there not enough food, but also medicine was in short supply, especially quinine, the only known remedy for malaria. There were no mosquito nets or shelters, and soon soldiers by the thousands were down with chills and fever.

The men knew that MacArthur had counted on reinforcements when he sent them out on this peninsula. Mickey figured that the mountain that guarded the tip of Bataan made the seafront less vulnerable, and the terrain lent itself to defensive battles, but, Christ, without air backup and without fresh supplies, they couldn't put up much of a fight. The sturdy little Filipino soldiers were dismayed to see the GIs they worshipped buckle under in the torpid heat.

Most of these young Americans had never been away from home, and for them the tropic wilderness wasn't full of exotic beauty, but a poisoned place, full of reptiles, maddening insects, and unbearable heat. Unlike Mickey, they couldn't wonder at the beauty of vine-covered trees emerging from morning mists. For them, the first thought in the morning was a longing for bacon and eggs and a shower. Starvation numbed their senses, and there was no spiritual relief in this strange environment, nothing to make them feel secure.

Mickey was amused to see that the Japanese used the gimmicks for their propaganda that would have made for a sure-fire success in advertising back in the states. Every other day, bombers flew over dropping empty beer cans adorned with red and white streamers. Messages supposedly sent by Homma to MacArthur were inside, stating the fact that supplies were diminishing and telling him that he could surrender with honor, now that they had fought so bravely. The men started trading the leaflets like baseball cards, each with a different message. The Filipinos were lured by the promise of a safe return to the bosoms of their loved ones, the Yanks a promise that 'all this can be yours,' with a picture of a nude, voluptuous blonde. The Americans were given the standard line: That they were poor devils sacrificing their lives for a bunch of war profiteers who were making time with their girlfriends while they were gone.

There were tickets to use if one wanted to surrender, and the guarantee that they would be treated well. "Use this ticket, save your life, you will be kindly treated…Come towards our lines waving a white flag…Any number of you may surrender with this one ticket." There were plenty of those tickets. The Americans used them for toilet paper.

On January 10th, MacArthur made a lightning trip to Bataan and the front lines. During brief encounters with Parker and Wainwright's men, he lied, promising convincingly that help was on the way. He strutted about making quotable comments, while a few photographers had a field day taking pictures of him.

He then returned to his island fortress, never to reappear, though his dispatches stateside implied that he made frequent trips to the front line. 142 communiqués, all of them good reading, were sent stateside, and the only soldier mentioned in 109 of them was MacArthur, giving the impression that he was wherever there was action. Among the American fighting men on Bataan, he earned himself the nickname 'Dugout Doug', a stinging epitaph that no amount of later glory could erase.

Was this the same man who had led the 42nd Division – called The Rainbow Division – to glory in World War I? How could this be the man whose soldiers in those days idolized him for his courage and his unstinting concern for their well-being?

From the Rock, he planned bold operations with little regard to the human sacrifices he demanded, as if the thousands of men on Bataan were mere tokens to wager in a war game. MacArthur had been willing to make great human sacrifice in 1918, too, but the difference was that in those days he put his own life on the line along with his men. Perhaps

MacArthur the actor was playing to a different public at this point in the on-going creation of his life dream.

The poorly equipped and half-starved Filipinos continued to put all their faith in him, but the Americans scanned the skies for the promised air cover and turned bitter.

* * * * *

Mickey learned to dive for a foxhole whenever there was an assault, and one day he wasn't quick enough. He threw himself through the air, making a belly-landing as he skidded to the edge of the trench. Just then he felt a searing pain and yelped a curse as he landed headfirst beside a GI who looked too dazed to be of much help.

"Jesus, I think I've been hit," Mickey said.

"Where'd the bastards get you? You look alright to me," said the anxious soldier as he motioned one of his buddies to come take a look.

Mickey put his hand where he felt the pain and saw that it was soaked with blood. "Is there any way you guys can get me out of here? I've been shot in the ass!" he said, knowing they wouldn't be able to help but laugh at his predicament.

He passed out, and the next thing he knew he was at Wainwright's headquarters, lying on a stretcher under a tree. A pretty nurse came over and gave him something to drink. Not oblivious to the humorous aspect of his injury, he asked her if someone could tell him how bad his wound was.

"You're lucky. The bullet missed your spinal cord and just tore a hunk out of your flesh. You might not feel like sitting down for awhile, but I think you're gonna live," she said with a wink.

"Just my luck to get such an unheroic wound. I won't even be able to show off my scar when this three-ring circus is over."

"Oh, I don't know. You might find a way," she said with a grin.

While he was recuperating, the war took a turn. The Japanese, believing Bataan would soon be theirs, removed General Homma's best division, the 48th, for use in the planned invasion of Java. In its place, from Formosa, came the 65th Brigade, made up mostly of conscripts with barely a month's training. Uniformly small, they quickly adapted to conditions of jungle warfare. Like machines, they excelled in dutifully performing tasks on sparse rations.

Even on meager rations, a Japanese private could move much more rapidly than an American. Trained to absolute obedience, they were fearless. During their first major offense, they attacked Parker's position on the western half of Bataan. Yelling "Banzai!" the soldiers in the front line threw themselves on the barbed wire barrier, making bridges of corpses that the second wave of men could scurry over.

Despite their zeal, that first assault was repelled, with a cost to the Japanese of 300 dead. For two weeks there was fierce fighting with losses on both sides, and even though the Japanese had the advantage of air power, Parker's forces held their line. Homma had not expected to meet such heroic resistance.

He saw that he had to put in two of his best regiments. In hobnailed boots or black, split-toe tennis shoes they scurried down the slopes of Mt. Natib, turning the flanks of Wainwright and Parker's divisions, threatening to cut them off. When informed of this, MacArthur realized he had to order a withdrawal, to a new line of defense halfway down the peninsula.

This retreat was dreadful. The men were in rags, bearded and unwashed, like dead men marching. Even as they fell back, the Americans encountered a new threat to their rear. The Japanese had made four amphibious landings at narrow points of land in the southwest corner of Bataan. These areas were lightly defended by a mixed bag of Service Command troops: Marines, sailors, airmen who had lost their planes, and Philippine Constabulary. Something had to be done to mend this weak spot while the new frontline was being strengthened.

* * * * *

Being close to Wainwright, Mickey was able to get a first hand impression of what it is that makes a great officer. Tall and lean, he had affectionately been dubbed "Skinny". A career soldier in the Cavalry, he had a reputation as a drinking man who loved his horses. While maintaining an unmistakable air of command, the general was one of those rare officers who could at all times identify with the ordinary GI. He was the best sort of commander to have in a battle as hopeless as this one was proving to be, and he continually took chances by visiting the front line, calmly sitting on sandbags to converse with one of his men, while bombs crashed around him. When chided for risking his life, he replied that this personal contact was all he had left to give his men.

At this point in the siege, MacArthur demonstrated another unfortunate trait: Begrudging other commanders a share in the planning. Although the Navy represented about a third of the American military personnel in the Philippines, MacArthur had left them out of strategy. He had a personal clash with Admiral Hart, a feisty little man with forty years of experience, and had chosen to ignore him and the Navy. He even excluded Admiral

Rockwell, the commander at Cavite Naval Base, from his meetings. However, Wainwright needed naval help to put a stop to the amphibious attacks at his rear, and fortunately, he had none of MacArthur's petty quirks when he figured out strategy. He was only interested in keeping his men alive.

He sent one of his colonels to Admiral Rockwell's ship to request a naval liaison officer, and the admiral obliged by sending a quick-witted young man named Champlin who had been brave and inventive during the carnage at Cavite. Fresh over from the states, he was too green to have stayed alive very long on his own in the jungles of Bataan, but he was one of many who were plunged into the realities of the war from one day to the next and bravely lived up to the challenge. Flag Lieutenant, Bulkeley, a man who had already proved his nettle in battle, took Champlin to Wainwright's headquarters.

Mickey looked up with interest when the two of them arrived at camp. It was Bulkeley who stole the show. He looked like a pirate right off a Hollywood set. He had a long, unruly beard, his eyes were red-rimmed and bloodshot from too many nights on patrol, and he sported two pistols strapped to his hips. He already had a reputation for being brave, quick-witted and for making mincemeat of Japanese who crossed his path.

A good rapport was immediately established when Champlin pulled a bottle of Scotch out of his bags and handed it to Wainwright, saying, "General, Admiral Rockwell sends his kindest regards and has asked me to give you this to cement Army-Navy relations."

It couldn't have been appreciated more. Wainwright held the bottle of golden liquid reverently and wanted to take a snort right away, while everything was quiet. "Young man, do you realize that what you have here is the finest Scotch whisky there is…and that I haven't had a drink in almost three months?"

It was in that mood that Wainwright and Champlin made up for MacArthur's lack of contact with the Navy. They devised a plan to put a lookout in a tall treetop to be able to spot their own ships and notify the off-shore defenses not to fire on them, making it possible to co-ordinate land and sea efforts to stop the Japanese amphibian attacks.

It worked. Once the amphibian attacks were foiled, the hard-fighting Filipino Scouts reinforced the threatened areas, and gradually the Japanese were driven back to the beaches where many of them holed up in cliffside caves at the water's edge.

With their backs against the wall, these Japanese soldiers always refused to come out of their caves, choosing death over surrender. They had to be annihilated with offshore fire or with sticks of dynamite tossed down by the Scouts from above. In the eyes of the Americans and Filipinos, the enemy seemed like something inhuman, death being the final condition of their obedience. More than anything, this brought home to them what sort of a foe they were up against.

The amphibious threat was erased, but the Japanese continued to pound away at Wainwright and Parker's lines, hoping to break through them before they became strong. In the dim light of the nearly impenetrable jungle that was Wainwright's turf, the battle became a close-range infantry duel. The defenders soon discovered that a foxhole was their best defense, even if they had to dig it with knives, helmets, or their bare hands.

War from a foxhole in the tropics is like something out of Dante's Inferno. It is living in filth and the smell of sweat, and being plagued by lice. It's the nighttime terror of not knowing what else might be down in the trench, such as poisonous snakes and a nightmare's inventory of insects. It was days of tedium with dust in their eyes and the stench of dead bodies, and fear that permeated bone and marrow. By now, the men were grappling with a greater enemy than the Japanese – They were riddled by disease and malnutrition. Dysentery often rendered them too weak to leave their foxholes, and many had to crouch in their own excrement.

Meanwhile, in another kind of hell, in the stifling atmosphere of the Malinta Tunnel on Corregidor, Philippine President Quezon glimpsed what he thought would be an opportunity to save his people from further massacres by the Japanese. Cabling to Roosevelt on February 8th, he requested that the Philippines be released from their commonwealth status and be given their independence right away. He knew it was the Americans whom the Japanese considered the enemy, and if they pulled out, he figured the Filipinos could make a separate peace with the Japanese, agreeing to certain concessions in order to become neutral, like Sweden.

However, the Allies had already seen Japanese aggression in a wider perspective, and the Philippines couldn't be left out of the picture. Quezon's message hit the Pentagon and the White House like a bombshell. Not only would such an action feed the Japanese greed, but it would also hasten the timetable for their advance across the Pacific. If Australia and New Zealand were to be protected, time was needed for the buildup of an adequate defense, and keeping Homma tied up in the Philippines was the best way to buy time.

A wire was sent flatly refusing Quezon's request, but Roosevelt, always the diplomat, went on to say, "So long as the flag of the United States flies on Filipino soil…It will be defended by our men to the death. Whatever happens to present American garrison we shall not relax our efforts until the forces which are now marshalling outside the Philippine Islands return to the Philippines and drive the last remnant of the invaders from your soil."

Upon receiving this promise, Manuel Quezon, a sick and dying old man, renewed his oath of loyalty to the United States. MacArthur, who had been witness to Quezon's request and didn't discourage him from sending it, received an explicit message from Roosevelt: "The duty and the necessity of resisting Japanese aggression to the last transcends in importance any other obligation now facing us in the Philippines...It is mandatory that there be established once and for all in the minds of all peoples complete evidence that the American determination and indomitable will to win carries on down to the last unit. I therefore give you this most difficult mission in full understanding of the desperate situation to which you may shortly be reduced. The service that you and the American members of your command can render to your country in the Titanic struggle now developing is beyond all possibility of appraisement. I particularly request that you proceed rapidly to the organization of your forces and your defenses so as to make your resistance as effective as circumstances will permit and as prolonged as humanly possible."

Roosevelt's Secretary of War, Stimson, had already told Churchill that the Philippines couldn't be saved. They knew the men on Bataan were doomed, and Stimson wrote in his diary, "There are times when men have to die." However, Roosevelt's message to MacArthur meant that the men on Bataan and on the Rock would have to suffer in ways far beyond what any of them could imagine, before they could be allowed to die or be captured.

Always the optimist, Mickey was one of the last to believe that they were going to be abandoned in their hour of need. There were just too damned many men to leave them out here on the other side of the globe, he thought. Furthermore, even though he had seen some of the inadequacies of the American arsenal, he was still impressed with their skill in using what they had. On the 16th of February, he was with the provisional air corps when they were an appreciative audience for a display of firepower conducted by Winston Jones, commanding the 41st Division Artillery. On the slopes of Mount Samat, Jones moved four big guns right up to the front line to try to hit a Japanese headquarters at Balanga, six miles north of the American line. That night, twenty rounds of shrapnel shells were fired from each of the four guns, and when morning dawned, the smoke rising from Balanga was proof of their excellent ballistic skills. Therefore, Mickey was still convinced of victory when he wrote to Vivian.

Feb.

Dearest -
Got a hot rumor that some mail was going out and thought I might get this off to you. You probably know as well as I what is going on down here. I am suffering no hardship except being away from you and I would rather go without food than that. The Japs have laid off us for awhile and everything is comparatively quiet.

My commission was denied. I am sorry darling because I wanted some insurance in case anything happened but maybe I'll get through all right. I cannot tell you what I am doing, but I can tell you that I have not had any close call since the 12th and my work is not as dangerous as it was four days ago. At that time I was supplying the front lines and had to go under shellfire. Collected enough material during that time to write a book. And believe me, there is a helluva lot of difference in hearing about it and experiencing it. Tony will never have to do this if it costs me ninety cents out of every dollar in taxes.

I sure miss that kid, darling. I hope he doesn't forget about me. I hope you don't forget about me. I hope. That's about all there is to do when the Japs leave us alone. Hope and sleep. When you catch up on your sleep you lie there and think about your wife and children. Even for an idle minute, your mind mirrors back all the things you did. You know I can't remember when I wasn't happy with you. Even the disappointments we've had are forgotten now. It seems like we've spent our whole lifetime together on one big vacation. I look back on that, and it feels like the war started many years ago. Long ago when I was a kid and the world was my oyster, and we had loads of fun.

But I will be back dearest. I know it. And if we can't live on $1000 a year, I'll make 12,000, and if the tax collector gets all of that, then to hell with it, because I can live on nothing, as long as I have you. Just as long. And when this thing is done, I'll catch the first boat there, unless I can bring you down here. I won't wait a month or two months.

I do not know if this will reach you or not. If it does there should be some money in the same mail. I say money — It is only enough to pay your grocery bill, but go into debt as far as you like, dearest, because we'll have plenty as soon as this war is over. Have written some stuff I would like you to read, but there is no use to enclose it as it would be butchered by the censor. The communiqués that come out of here will give you their idea of journalism.

Don't worry about me dearest. I'll be all right.

All my aloha,

m.

P.S. You can address me care of U.S.A.F.F.E. if you write. Tell Mr. Dillingham I appreciate what he is doing. Give my regards to Mrs. Erdman.

* * * * *

The stiffness of resistance convinced Homma by the second week in February that he should call off the offensive. He had been sure he could conquer Luzon in fifty days, and he hadn't succeeded. He had lost more than 7,000 dead and wounded in the fighting on Bataan. Another 10,000 to 12,000 were down with malaria, dengue fever, dysentery, or beriberi. Yet his stubborn foe still held half the peninsula. Homma pulled his exhausted army back a few miles and asked Tokyo for reinforcements. While he waited, there was a relative lull of nearly two weeks, allowing MacArthur's army to strengthen their position, lay minefields, and reorganize their remaining artillery.

However, while the Japanese waited for reinforcements, they introduced a new element of terror into the campaign, by resorting to unconventional tactics. Infiltrating by ones and twos, they reassembled in units of up to platoon strength at predetermined points in the jungle well behind the defender's lines.

From there they raised havoc with the rear echelons, ambushing patrols, burning supplies, and stealing food and weapons. Soldiers bivouacked in supposedly secure camps frequently woke in the morning to find that men next to them had been stabbed to death in their sleep. Anyone who was unfortunate enough to be captured by the Japanese could expect to be executed by slow death, his screams running cold down the spines of those within earshot.

Equally unnerving as their stealthy attacks were the noises they made during the night, shattering the silence with firecrackers, shellfire, and taunts shouted through a megaphone.

Morale, which had risen almost feverishly when the Japanese offensive was halted, began a steady descent toward despair. Along with hunger-pangs, disease, and incessant air raids was the growing sense of having been abandoned. A war correspondent, Frank Hewlett, summed up the feeling of the men in the Philippines when he wrote a piece of doggerel that became famous:

> We are the battling bastards of Bataan
> No momma, no poppa, no Uncle Sam
> No aunts, no uncles, no nephews, no nieces
> No rifles, no guns or artillery pieces
> And nobody gives a damn!

Sickness and malnutrition were gradually paralyzing the fighting forces. Medics had to dole out quinine carefully, for they could see they would soon run out of it completely. The food supplies were so low that the men in the trenches looked like walking skeletons. The quiet that had descended on the front didn't stifle the fear of attack. Lurking nearby could be a small patrol or a sniper. Where Wainwright was holed up, the jungle was so dense that visibility was limited to 15 meters, rendering artillery useless.

Before nightfall, the men in the foxholes checked their weapons, made sure their guns were loaded, their bayonets and knives close at hand, water bottles filled, and, if they weren't too sick, they made a quick run to empty their bowels. The long nighttime in a foxhole gave them occasional catnaps, interrupted by the roar of artillery in the early part of the evening and later the chilling rattle of machine guns, followed by silence. One thing was that they had discovered that their grenades didn't work, because they were old and corroded. Worse was the knowledge that if wounded, they couldn't count on medicine to ease the pain or ward off infection.

From the foxhole they listened to the jungle noises, a snap of a twig or a rustle in the trees. Was it a night-prowling animal or a Japanese sniper? They found out at the break of day, when their darkest fantasies took shape in the murky light of a jungle dawn. It wasn't infrequent that they found victims of the Japanese, impaled, eviscerated, their privates cut off and placed in their mouths, and they tried not to imagine how long the person was conscious before death was granted.

A fighting man, especially in trenches, needs 4 – 5000 calories a day to maintain his health and strength, but the men on Bataan were cut down to 2000 calories a day by January 8th. On February 1st, they were reduced to 1500, and on March 1st they had to do with 1000 calories a day.

That was the official record. In reality, things were even worse for the men on the front line. When word got out that there were fresh supplies, all but the scrapings at the bottom of the pot were consumed by the time the front line combatants were relieved and made it to the chow line. Perhaps just as demoralizing for the men on the front line was the desire for a smoke. In camp, there was a possibility to buy cigarettes, but hardly any smokes got to the man in the line of fire.

Food was an obsession. The men hunted fresh meat in the surrounding area, devouring caribou, lizards, or even giant maggots which came from a tropical fly a half an hour after it lay eggs in a piece of meat. Connoisseurs enjoyed python meat when they could get it. Men on the front line, however, couldn't forage. They were pinned to their positions and had to make do with steadily diminishing C-rations.

As word seeped out to the American public about the plight of the Americans in the Philippines, there was a mood of anger over President Roosevelt's Europe first strategy. Roosevelt saw that he had to make an effort to unite the country behind him, and he announced a radio speech, asking the people to sit with maps in their hands, in order to understand what was at stake.

In the islands, Vivian sat glued to the radio and heard the president say, "This war is a new kind of war. It is different from all other wars in the past not only in its methods and weapons, but also in its geography. It is warfare in terms of every continent, every island, every sea, every air lane in the world."

He then asked his audience to follow him on their maps, as he explained the interdependence of the centers of power and the need to thwart the Axis powers in their objectives if the world should be free. Just as he was speaking, a Japanese submarine surfaced off the coast of California and bombarded Santa Barbara, as if to emphasize his point. As often was the case with the Japanese firepower, it fell far astray of its objective, but the psychological impact was terrific.

So was the psychological impact on the men in the Philippines as they picked up Roosevelt's broadcast on their radio sets. They now realized that they wouldn't be helped until Australia was secured. They were abandoned.

On Bataan, conditions became increasingly cruel. On one of his daily visits to the front, Wainwright found that the foxholes of one battalion were filled with dead men. They had perished with malaria and dysentery, and their officers had left many of them standing, dead eyes staring at enemy lines, guns propped up in lifeless hands, hoping the Japanese could be fooled into thinking the position was still defended. Feces littered the ground, and the foxholes were swarming with flies. The stench was overpowering. Wainwright shuddered and ordered the men with him not to breathe a word to anyone else, but to order reserves sent in to relieve that battalion.

He returned to headquarters, agonizing over the plight of his men. That afternoon, he was told there soon would be no more fodder for the horses. For once he looked tired and defeated as he turned to the cavalry officer who had brought him the news. "Yes, Captain, I knew this was coming. We've a lot of men who are also short of food, and horsemeat ain't so bad. You will begin killing the horses at once," he said and then looked off in the distance to gain control. "Joseph Conrad is the horse that you will kill first."

His eyes were filled with tears as he walked slowly to his trailer. Of all the horses, his own prize jumper, Joseph Conrad, was the one he loved most, and he rued the day he had brought her over from the States, but he reminded himself that at least that magnificent creature would feed some of his men.

In a rare mood that night, Wainwright felt like talking, and he and his aides discussed the implications of Roosevelt's speech. Off the record, he summed up what he thought had been the major errors committed by the high command, and by that he could only mean MacArthur: First was their failure to visit the front lines, especially since there were shortages of everything and all the command had to give the men was moral support. Second was their failure to obtain more troops six months before the Japanese attack, at a time when they could have been trained. Last was MacArthur's choice of a grandiose scheme to defend the beaches rather than adhering to the original plan of retreating into Bataan. It not only meant a chaotic start to the defense of the Philippines, but vast amounts of supplies had been abandoned there, making for deficiencies on Bataan, where they were needed.

It was unlike Wainwright to talk so freely and frankly, but he had seen too much to keep it all bottled up. He knew how much food was needed to keep a man going who is pumped full of adrenaline while confined to the terror of a foxhole. However, he had to give the best rations to the pilots, they being the only hope for getting out, if there really was any hope of getting out of this hellhole.

At that, by early March he saw that even the pilots were showing signs of malnutrition. Their eyesight was poor, and they were too weak to fly a plane. He had no choice but to increase their rations, even though some of the enlisted men inwardly resented it. It made matters worse that the pilots were privileged in the first place. As officers, they were provided with sleeping quarters, while the enlisted men slept on the ground with no mosquito nets.

Meanwhile, the starving men became increasingly adept at improvising and in finding food wherever they could. They shot and killed anything they could get their hands on, and even Mickey's monkey ended up in the soup kettle. He couldn't kill it himself. It was so tame, and he knew its eyes would haunt him. Stringy it was, but not worse than water buffaloes which Parker's men sometimes got. They were huge, but tough as saddles.

Within the general's camp, Mickey's wound healed without gangrene setting in. So far, he was holding up surprisingly well. Psychologically, it helped that he had a deep-seated conviction that he was a survivor, and physically, his small stature made it easier for him to get along on skimpy rations. Unlike many Americans, he was completely unprejudiced in what he was willing to eat if it could serve as meat, and he often recognized edible leaves or plants near camp.

For most of the Americans, the jungle was terrifying. Dense walls formed by huge mahogany trees, grotesque banyans, gigantic eucalyptus trees tightly woven with twisted vines and bamboo, and undergrowth of alang-alang grass crawling with snakes, including pythons.

There were menacing cliffs that could hardly be climbed, and treacherous rivers. Along with the tropical diseases most of the men had contracted could be added beriberi, pellagra, and hookworm.

Mickey's childhood experiences in the everglades of Florida made the tropics less overwhelming for him. Also, he had the advantage of his years. He had seen enough of life to know that most things pass. He was dismayed to think about how young some of these guys were, remembering how much fun he had when he was their age. Christ, a lot of them had never been laid, he thought sadly. Before the war, most of them had never even known what it was like to have to be unclean, and now they lived in filthy foxholes, in the same clothes day after day.

His wound had only strengthened Mickey's conviction that he was invincible. The starvation diet had the unexpected effect of curing his arthritis, and that balanced out the discomforts of deprivation in the grueling tropical heat. Because he was convinced it was only a matter of time before they could all get out of there, he remained cheerful, accepting the headaches and sluggishness of malnutrition as he would a hangover. Being a hustler by nature, he would always fare better than most, in any event.

* * * * *

Meanwhile, on the island fortress of Corregidor, tensions grew, as the 13,000 Filipinos and Americans tried not to go stir-crazy, holed up as they were in the tunnel that was their headquarters and living quarters. This amazing structure was 12 feet high and only 35 feet wide at its broadest point and contained the USAFFE Headquarters, the Commonwealth Government, and 1000 hospital beds. Topside there had been barracks three miles long and a number of gunning positions. More than three hundred Japanese bombing missions and daily pounding from cannon shells and howitzers demolished the barracks along with most vegetation.

MacArthur had saved the best food for those who would be holed up on The Rock, reckoning they would be facing a longer siege. Although the Japanese bombings forced everyone but the half-starved Marines who manned the guns to move underground, those confined to Corregidor were well-equipped with medicine, and had an ample staff of doctors and nurses.

The men on Bataan were worse off; however, those who were confined to the hellish underworld of Malinta Tunnel couldn't have conceived of a fate worse than their own. Life in the tunnel was like being buried alive. At first they had ample water from two artesian wells. Then a bomb struck a wall separating sea water from the water of one of these wells, and, after that, they had only water from one well. The constant bombardment drove clouds of dirt and grit down into their tunnel, and when they shut the vents to prevent that, the air was stifling, and temperatures rose above what humans can bear. Crowded in the damp, unhealthy shelter and bombed incessantly, they were too miserable to imagine what life would be like for the men on Bataan.

MacArthur seemed to be living in a fantasy world from which he thought he would be able to plot the action. Zealously guarding the opportunity for his own chosen men to be heroes, he ignored the potential of the U.S. Marines, for example. He claimed, "the Marines had gotten their share of glory in World War I, and they aren't going to get any in this one." Frustrated by not being used effectively, those Marines who were in the Philippines had to make use of their skills and courage in random places.

Eerily out of touch with reality, MacArthur sent a message to the War Department on March 9th, recommending citations to all units on Bataan and Corregidor, except the Navy and Marines, an example of petty inter-service rivalry that is difficult to equal. Heroic deeds performed by Marines and Naval personnel on Bataan and Corregidor can fill volumes. Furthermore, they were all in the same war.

It was as if MacArthur believed that war was a treasure, with heroic deeds to be jealously coveted, a strange notion to the Marine lookouts on Corregidor or the sailors who just prayed to come out of this purgatory alive.

For weeks MacArthur resisted pressure from Washington to leave the Philippines. His wife had insisted on staying with him, and their son was there on The Rock, too, but MacArthur seemed content to accept that they should share his destiny, even if that meant death. The vision he had of himself in the great story that was unfolding made him immune to a fear of death. History's heroes paraded through his mind, and he was prepared to stay to the bitter end, to be taken prisoner or die on Corregidor. Perhaps death would have seemed a noble ending for a soldier-hero and a welcome release from the demands his parents had burned into his soul.

Indeed, his behavior indicated that he had a death wish. In the beginning of the siege on Corregidor, he and his family stayed in a cottage above ground. He made it a habit to stand out in the open, verbally defying the attacking planes. During one severe air raid, he sent his wife and son below just before their cottage got a direct hit and was destroyed. Even after that, he stayed atop, and when the second bomb fell, he merely jumped behind a hedge, not bothering to seek shelter. However, once their cottage was destroyed, they were forced to join the others in the confines of the tunnel.

He then made a habit of coming to the mouth of the tunnel whenever there was a raid, staring defiance at the fighter planes, oblivious to the danger. Roosevelt, aware of MacArthur's importance in public opinion, was urging him to leave Corregidor, and perhaps the thought of being hit by a bomb was less odious to the general than the thought of sneaking off the island in the darkness of the night.

However, the day came when he could no longer call the shots. With all the press coverage he received, it was imperative for American morale that he wasn't captured or killed by the Japanese. Roosevelt had to get him out of the Philippines before it was too late. The President wanted him to assume command of American forces that were to assemble in Australia for an eventual counter-offensive.

Finally, on March 10th, MacArthur agreed to leave, and he turned command of the forces on Luzon over to Wainwright, telling him, "If I get through to Australia, I'll come back as soon as I can with as much as I can."

General Drake stood on the bombed remains of Corregidor's wharf to see General MacArthur one last time as he left The Rock. It was late evening, and Charlie Drake was one of the few who knew MacArthur was leaving. MacArthur's escape was charged with danger, for the Japanese would have dealt a tremendous blow to the Allies' confidence if they could capture or kill their most important figurehead in the Asiatic theatre.

Rocking alongside Corregidor's concrete pier were four motor-torpedo boats, and MacArthur stepped aboard one of them, with his family and their son's Chinese nanny and some of his staff. Standing ready to sail was the bearded, barrel-chested young skipper, Lt. Bulkeley, who had distinguished himself in the ill-fated Japanese amphibian attacks on Bataan. Quickly glancing at the twin pistols he had on his hips, MacArthur said, "You may cast off, Buck, when you are ready." MacArthur's face was stony, and the phrase was ringing in his head, "I shall return," as the boats slid stealthily away, through Corregidor's minefields, towards open sea and their first destination: Mindanao, 500 miles to the south.

As the general raised his cap in salute, Drake had a premonition of being abandoned. Suddenly, he saw clearly that MacArthur's hopes to stay until July had nothing to do with a belief that aid would arrive at that time. No, it was a matter of stalling the Japanese until the defense of Australia could be cemented. He slowly made his way back to the tunnel, while the bricks of a puzzle fell into place in his consciousness. The siege of Bataan and Corregidor took on new dimensions as he allowed the implications of MacArthur's departure to take form.

Meanwhile, the men on Bataan composed a new song, to the tune of "The Battle Hymn of the Republic:"

> Dugout Doug MacArthur lies ashaking on the Rock
> Safe from all the bombers and from any sudden shock
> Dugout Doug is eating of the best food on Bataan
> And his troops go starving on.
> Dugout Doug's not timid, he's just cautious, not afraid,
> He's protecting carefully the stars that Franklin made
> Four-star generals are rare as good food on Bataan
> And his troops go starving on.
> Dugout Doug is ready in his Kris Craft for the flee
> Over bounding billows and the wildly raging sea
> For the Japs are pounding on the gates of Old Bataan
> And his troops go starving on …

The men on Bataan reviled the man who was so popular with his troops in World War I, and neither did MacArthur's brief stay on Mindanao endear him to the airmen who were there. Still irked by the fact that he had allowed for so much death and destruction during the initial attacks of the Philippines, they now had an opportunity to see the man in the flesh.

While on Mindanao MacArthur stayed close to his small entourage, appearing aloof and distant to the airmen. Meanwhile, four B-17s flew out of Darwin, Australia, coming to pick up the general and his people. Only one succeeded in landing on Mindanao; two turned back with engine trouble, and the fourth crashed in the sea.

The plane that made it was piloted by Lt. Pearse who had the reputation of being one of the best pilots in the squadron, but he was also one of the youngest. The plane he flew had seen a lot of action and was flying on a wing and a prayer. After the landing, while it was being repaired, MacArthur strolled over and cast a contemptuous look at the aircraft and the young pilot.

Ignoring Pearse, he turned to General Sharp, the commanding officer, and said, "Bill, I'm not putting my family at risk in that broken-down crate and with this boy at the controls. I want three top planes flown by the best crews in the Pacific here as soon as possible." He then wired to get the newest aircraft flown in from New Zealand.

Once these planes arrived, the pilot whose plane had crashed in the sea on the first flight, went up to MacArthur as he approached the lead plane and made a request.

"General, I want to get back to Australia to get another plane and back into this war."

"I'm glad to hear it son," the general replied, "but I'm sorry, we don't have any room."

The airmen standing nearby had watched as the planes had been loaded, and they had noticed that cases of pineapples and pineapple juice were stowed aboard.

One of them, a mechanic named Osborn, overheard the exchange between the pilot and MacArthur and was furious. He walked up to the flier and told him he could get him back to Australia. Grabbing an oxygen bottle, a mask, and a parachute from the service trolley, he gave it to the young officer and led him around to the rear of the plane. With the pretence of polishing the turret, he arranged for the gunner to open the escape hatch so they could stow the pilot in there.

Shortly afterwards, the lead plane staggered into the night sky with its VIPs, its horde of pineapples, and one stowaway named Fitzgerald.

* * * * *

Drake's hunch was right. The War Department had hoped that MacArthur could hold down Corregidor until July, thinking that would allow for a big build-up in Australia; however, soon after his arrival in Australia, while crossing the continent by train to Melbourne, MacArthur received information of the actual situation: No American infantry divisions and no tanks or heavy weapons had yet been dispatched to Australia. He also learned that the Japanese were rapidly shooting up the 250 Allied planes that were in Australia. An invasion of Australia was so probable that two of their divisions were being called home from the Middle East. In his mind's eye, MacArthur tied all this information together with what he already knew to be true of the Philippines. "God have mercy on us," he murmured.

Nevertheless, an hour later, he had regained his sang-froid and optimism and could face reporters and read a short, tersely positive statement. He had come to Australia, he said, to organize the American offensive against Japan. "I came through, and I shall return," he said with the vibrant intonations of a Shakespearean player.

As always, he was a brilliant performer. The press loved it, and his words went around the world, wiping out speculation about the plight of the men lost on Bataan. Roosevelt couldn't have chosen a better man to carry out the deception. MacArthur's personality successfully blotted out all important and negative details.

MacArthur, whose most recent claim to having been on the front line in Bataan was fictitious, continued to try to cling to the command of the Philippines, but Washington named

Wainwright commander, a blessing for the men who were trapped there. Given MacArthur's vision of glory in sacrifice, he would never have allowed for the surrender that finally released the squalid forces from the duty to keep fighting.

The Fall of Bataan

By March, Mickey no longer had freedom of movement. The battle had become just a matter of survival, one day at a time. The men snatched at any information they could get, and most of it was rumor.

On the other side of the mountain where Parker had gathered his troops, the terrain was more open, but theirs was another kind of torment. Enveloped in dust and filth, with the incessant mosquitoes, they were open to air attack and became accustomed to the way the ground buckled as bombs were dropped. At nighttime, they could see their lines threatened as the Japanese set fires in forests of bamboo.

Here, the Japanese had a trick of capturing Filipina women and burying them in sand in front of the line of defense. Their heads were exposed, and the Americans and Filipinos had to watch in horror as ants made a meal of the women's faces. If they ran to the open space to help them, the Japanese gunned them down.

By March, all the men on Bataan were a ragged bunch who seldom washed and never shaved. Their clothes were threadbare, and, although the Americans still had shoes, there were hardly any shoes left for the small feet of the Filipinos. Sapped of energy by malnutrition and temperatures over 100 degrees in the shade, they had difficulty performing the simplest tasks. Tempers were frayed and there were no rest areas into which they could withdraw for relief. They lived in the trenches, deprived of all hope.

Monkeys in some parts of Bataan were close to extinction, and everyone had grown accustomed to their taste, although no one liked finding a hand or a small, impish face in his stew. The Japanese stopped dropping propaganda leaflets with voluptuous blondes engaged in love-making and instead showered the men with menus from Manila's best restaurants.

With the huge human blood pool at their disposal, malaria mosquitoes thrived and increased in number, and by early March, eighty percent of the men had malaria. By April, there were a thousand a day coming down with the disease. To add to their misery were other tropical ailments, such as 'Guam blisters,' large white blisters that covered the body, stinging, itching, and burning, driving their victims mad.

In many locations, the men had no other choice than to drink water from stagnant pools and, in the foxholes, no means of boiling it. Dysentery was ever more rampant, and the medics experimented with local remedies. A powder was made out of charcoal that had been produced from slowly burning hardwoods and added to water to be drunk. Soon men with dysentery could be spotted by their black teeth and lips.

By the end of March, barely a fourth of the original 80,000 defenders of Bataan could still hold a weapon, and most of those who could were sick or on the verge of starvation. Rations now consisted of only 8 to 10 ounces of rice a day plus an ounce or two of fish or canned meat, and for the Americans, the unseasoned rice was a pale substitute for potatoes.

Japan had seized key bases in the southern Philippines, and its navy patrolled the narrow sea-lanes from Australia and the Dutch East Indies. It was all but impossible to get supplies through. Despite elaborate and sometimes heroic efforts to run the blockade, only 3 supply ships and an occasional submarine reached the Philippines. The "Battling Bastards of Bataan" were on their own, while Homma's forces were reinforced with 21,000 fresh troops, some 150 new field guns, and 60 bombers.

All of Mickey's attempts to get a commission had failed. One thing was that he was in the thick of battle and making himself useful, but another was finding someone who could enlist him. It looked like he wasn't going to be able to provide Vivian with any sort of income.

However, he no longer concentrated on any single problem. Like the rest of the men, he had stopped thinking about much except food and trying to get through one more day. Wainwright had moved to Corregidor when he took over MacArthur's command, and without him, a lot of the feeling of being at the crossroads of history had paled. Now Mickey felt the abject misery of war, forget the echoes of glory.

April 3 dawned, and it was Good Friday, but most Americans had lost track of the date. For the Japanese it was the anniversary of the death of their legendary Emperor Jimmu, the ancestor of Hirohito, an occasion that inspired the Japanese to break the stalemate with a grueling five-hour bombardment from planes and ground artillery. 50,000 Japanese troops stormed those Americans and Filipinos entrenched at the base of Mt. Samat.

Mickey worked tirelessly, helping out with the wounded that poured into the makeshift sick bay. Dazed by the constant pounding of bombs, he registered minute details in the overall scene as the semblance of order dissolved around him. The healing effect of a full night's sleep had been denied him so long that at times he became unsure of what was reality and what appeared to be mosaic bits of a bad dream. He was luckier than most, however. He was able to crash when he was sufficiently tired, falling asleep right on the ground with all hell breaking loose all around him. After a catnap, he bounced back with renewed energy.

At first he had assumed he would be relatively safe in an area where the Red Cross marked the operating tent, but he soon realized that the Japanese seemed to enjoy singling out that symbol as a target. There were frantic attempts to evacuate as many patients as possible whenever they were attacked.

When the center of the American defense line was hit by this massive assault of armor and infantry, the Americans and Filipinos fell back, resisted, and then retreated again. The number of wounded men made it impossible for surgeons to pause in their work.

Things got more chaotic still on Saturday when the bombings recommenced, scorching the jungle and turning carefully prepared defenses into twisted wreckage. By Easter Sunday the Japanese had stormed their prime objective, the upper slopes of Mt. Samat, which provided a commanding view of the battlefields below. Two whole divisions of the Philippine Army were obliterated, and General Parker's corps was in danger of being driven into Manila Bay.

Major General King, who had replaced Wainwright in the field, made a last ditch stand on Monday, but the emaciated Americans with their pathetic firepower were no match for the Japanese. By nightfall the trails and crude roads to the south were clogged with thousands of Americans and Filipinos staggering away from the front. Hot on their heels were Japanese tanks and infantry, as Zeroes strafed the retreating men freely.

It was all crumbling to pieces. Everywhere there was chaos. American demolition teams at Mariveles, on Bataan's southern tip, began blowing up the remaining ammunition stockpiles and setting fuel supplies afire. Some 2,000 persons, including 104 nurses, managed to escape to Corregidor by small boats and barges. Hundreds of others, trying to swim the three and a half miles to the dubious shelter of Corregidor, were mercilessly strafed by Japanese planes and attacked by sharks, leaving the water coated with blood and oil.

Men who were too sick to climb out of their foxholes still tried to follow their officers' orders and continue fighting. Everywhere there were bewildered men, forced to flee in the face of the overwhelming barrage of firepower. From The Rock, Wainwright followed explicit orders from MacArthur and ordered a final counterattack, but King, in the field, decided against it. It was futile to sacrifice still more lives, and the men had fought beyond human endurance.

No one wanted to be the man to be remembered as having ordered the biggest capitulation in America's history, but King was there, on Bataan, not on Corregidor or Australia or in Washington. He was sickened by the sacrifice of human life linked with a futile attempt to delay the inevitable. General King had the courage to lift the white flag, but by then the surrendering forces were in such pathetic condition that their chances of survival during the ordeal to come were even more doubtful.

On April 9th, at dawn, King sent two emissaries across the front lines with a soiled bed sheet as a flag of truce, but the Japanese ignored this overture for a cease-fire and pressed on relentlessly. The unexpected length of time it took them to achieve victory had filled them with blood thirst. Their armored spearheads surrounded the two general hospitals. A Japanese officer descended from the lead tank, saluted the chief doctor, Paul Ashton, and asked in halting English to be shown the hospital.

Ashton told him that there were 46 Japanese prisoners among the patients and expected him to be pleased to see that although they were in a separate ward, they were given the same conditions as those of the Americans and Filipinos.

The Japanese colonel walked to the open-air ward where the Japanese lay, many of them with limbs in traction. His face stony, he unsheathed his sword and sliced the ropes rigged up to their casts, leaving the wounded Japanese in silent agony. A few hours later, two captured American trucks arrived, and the Japanese patients were dumped in the back to be hauled away. Everyone else was forbidden to leave on pain of death.

Mickey was at the other hospital when the Japanese arrived. Having known so many Japanese in the islands, he was used to their looks, but many of the other Americans were getting their first look at the enemy. To them, they looked like they had all been poured into the same mold. Uniformly short, rarely more than five feet two, they had round faces and shaved heads. Their uniforms were threadbare but clean, and they wore their peculiar jungle boots, with a cleft between the big toe and the rest of the foot, like a mitten.

Cruel fate had brought a young American woman to the hospital. She and her wealthy Filipino husband had come back to the Philippines to settle his father's estate when war broke out. They found themselves trapped on Bataan with their children, and the husband was killed in an air raid. Their little boy had also been injured, and his arm had to be amputated. The young widow and her two small children evoked everyone's sympathy, and they let her stay on, in a separate tent.

When the Japanese had finished looting everything they could find on the patients, they turned their attention to her. All night long, the Japanese took turns raping her. There was no point in even trying to protest, for the Japanese officers had ravished her first. Americans helpless to do anything at all listened to her anguished cries, while the chaplain kept her children at his side. Mercifully, they were too young to understand what was happening.

In the morning, one of the doctors was able to get her out of there and move her to the collective misery of civilian internment. Seeing what happened to her and her children made Mickey realize what might have been his family's fate had they been with him in the Philippines. He thanked his lucky stars that he was alone with the captors.

Most of the 6,000 patients in that hospital were Filipinos, and the Japanese ordered them to leave in order to establish a base facing Corregidor, for their artillery. Many of those who tried to leave died within yards of the place, others had their casts broken off and were whipped out onto the road.

General King braved enemy fire as his jeep approached the point of rendezvous for the surrender. Hurling himself out of the jeep whenever it was hit, he arrived dirty and disheveled at 11 a.m. He sat down at a field table across from General Homma's operations officer, Colonel Motoo Nakayama. King asked for a 12-hour stay to collect his wounded. Nakayama coldly refused to negotiate terms with anyone but Wainwright, and King had no choice but to settle for unconditional surrender.

"Will our troops be well treated?" King asked.

"We are not barbarians," Nakayama assured him.

Nakayama demanded that King surrender his sword, but it had been left in Manila. A general without a sword was in the eyes of the Japanese not a fit emissary. They considered him a barbarian and had to accept his pistol.

Wearily, King unstrapped his sidearm, laid it on the table, and surrendered the remaining men on Bataan. It was the first surrender by an American general in the field since the beginning of the Republic.

King again requested that he be allowed to organize the movement of his troops and the wounded to their prisons, but he was refused. He was driven in a truck to Camp O'Donnel, but the other generals were forced to march with the rest of the prisoners.

Indeed, General Homma had ordered that the prisoners should be treated humanely, but his orders were ignored. Homma was a most unusual person, in more ways than one. Considered a giant by Japanese measures during that era (he was six feet two), he was a handsome, sensitive person with a unique background. He was born on the island of Sado, where troublesome priests, politicians and writers were banished. Ironically, he was pro-Western, had traveled in America, and studied at Oxford. He attended the disarmament conference at the League of Nations after World War I, and he was committed to the ideals of democracy and moderation. The virtues of his personality and character were cause for animosity among more conservative Japanese, but they could not deny that he was a brilliant military tactician.

His present problem was that the siege of Bataan had lasted far too long for the Japanese timetable. It was imperative that he force Corregidor to surrender as quickly as possible. To ferret the Americans out of their tunnels would be a devastating task. The best plan would be to set up operations for a constant bombardment of The Rock, and the best position for the artillery would be the coast of Bataan. He had to clear everyone off the Bataan peninsula as quickly as possible, and he had to entrust that task to his officers.

With blind faith that they would respect the good intentions of his instructions, he cheerfully said to one captive American officer, "Your worries are over. Japan treats her prisoners well. You may even see my country in cherry-blossom time, and that is a beautiful sight."

However, the Japanese who believed in battle to the death had miscalculated. They had reckoned that the commanders of the Philippine Armed Forces would hold out until there were no more than 20,000 reasonably healthy captives, but what they got was close to four times that number, and most of them were sick and starving. No one knows for sure how many of the 78,000 troops (including the 12,000 Americans) who were under General King's command on Good Friday were on the march, but an educated guess is that there were at least 62,000 Filipinos and 10,000 Americans.

King knew that the thousands under his command were totally demoralized and in such poor physical condition that moving them required the utmost of planning. Their fate was in the hands of Homma whose attention was riveted to the task of defeating Corregidor, leaving him inattentive to the difficulties of marching so many prisoners to O'Donnell. For one thing, his own Japanese soldiers were capable of covering twenty-five miles a day with a full pack, sustained by just a few rice balls, a couple of sticks of dried fish, some pickled vegetables, and a quick fix of sugar.

These small Japanese soldiers were faced with moving thousands of prisoners who were like giants, albeit gaunt giants. The scene was pandemonium. Down through the ranks, the Japanese were motivated by the urgency of clearing Bataan as quickly as possible. They yelled, "Speedo," their shouts punctuated with jabs from their bayonet, as they herded these thousands of men.

The logistics were horrendous. They lacked food, water, and adequate transport to haul the prisoners to Camp O'Donnell, but no matter how weak or ill the prisoners were, they were forced to keep moving. They were divided into groups of a hundred, with about seven guards to each group. Mickey was just one ripple in a vast river of misery – sixty-five miles of torture that became known as the Bataan Death March. To the participants at the time, it was referred to, with characteristic understatement, as "The Hike".

All line of command among the captives had disintegrated in the chaos of surrender. Units were scattered, and many men found themselves among groups of strangers, without the bonds that had formed when they were trying to pull each other through the months of battle. Still, many tried to help the weaker prisoners to keep moving, for stopping usually meant death.

Many of them were too weak to walk a mile without great pain, but those who lagged behind were prodded with bayonets or, if they fell, stabbed and left alongside the road. Soon the road was littered with dead bodies, a mutilated corpse every few paces, putrid in the tropical heat. The smell of death was something the survivors would never forget. Later, Homma was to claim that he had seen nothing "extraordinary" that had taken place on this march, but there was a dead body every fifteen paces along the way, and each one represented a war crime.

The class of Japanese foot soldier who was given the task of guarding the prisoners was at the bottom of their military hierarchy. The job they were given gave them no self-esteem. Consequently, they hated their charges, and their cruelty knew no bounds. There were, of course, the rare incidents of kindness among the many tales of abuse, but they pale in the strong colors of the bestial blood lust that prevailed.

In heat that reached the 100's, a helmet was a blessing that could make the difference between life and death, but the prisoners soon discovered that they should rid themselves of a helmet. Japanese soldiers passing by on trucks amused themselves by knocking off prisoners' helmets with bamboo canes or the butts of their rifles. A soldier whose helmet was hit felt the ringing pain of it being knocked off and knew that to stoop and pick it up would be sure death. Other truckloads deliberately veered at high speeds into the lines of men, while the passengers in back laughed hilariously at the carnage they had created. Prisoners struggling to stay alive stepped over flattened corpses that became paper-thin as trucks and tanks rolled over them.

Prisoners crossing a wooden bridge looked up in horror as they saw a line of trucks approaching them head-on. Those who were strong enough jumped to the railings and hung over the sides, but those who were too weak were simply run over. The troops in the trucks laughed hilariously at the sight of those hanging from the sides of the bridge as they were shaken loose by the speeding trucks bouncing on the flimsy bridge. Afterwards, soldiers were sent down to bayonet or shoot the prisoners who lay with broken limbs on the rocky riverbed.

Mickey thought he might declare himself an officer, hoping to get favorable treatment as accorded in the Geneva Convention. However, officers were often singled out for particularly cruel treatment. Even generals were tortured, ridiculed, and subjected to perfunctory punishment. In the eyes of their conquerors, anyone who surrendered was a traitor, and an officer who surrendered was, if possible, even more disgusting than a foot soldier. Weighing this fact, Mickey decided that the best bet for now was to try not to draw attention to one's person, and he soon discovered that it was to his advantage that he wasn't tall.

Japanese soldiers had a field day collecting valuables from the prisoners. They filled buckets full of Rolex watches and Parker pens. They also took Sheaffer pens, but those prisoners who had nothing better than a Sheaffer pen got a whack on the head at the same time. They even took nail files. They frisked the men for cash and occasionally cut off officers' fingers to get their rings. Mickey had his handful of gems hidden in the sweat rim of his hat. He knew he would need whatever he had to barter for favors later on. Luckily, the guard who frisked him was satisfied with his Parker pen and hurried on to the next man, where he could get a watch.

Mickey became accustomed to the sight of severed heads, but it didn't lessen the horror of witnessing this Japanese specialty the first time he saw a decapitation actually performed. An American lieutenant had been made to get down in the dirt on his knees, and his head was sliced off with such efficiency that Mickey wondered where the guard had practiced his skill. The head rolled, and blood gushed out of the neck while the body twitched on the ground. Mickey's stomach turned, and he felt gagged.

The captors took particular pleasure in torturing Filipinos, using them to demonstrate judo, bayoneting them repeatedly while they screamed, and sometimes burying them alive. From the 91st Division, between three and four hundred Filipino noncoms and officers were bound together with telephone wire and butchered. Japanese officers started at one end of the group and killed with their swords, while the Japanese enlisted men worked at the other end with their bayonets. The death cries lasted for more than two hours. In all probability, the command to kill came from a brigade commander named Nara Akira, a Nippon who had graduated from the U.S. Army's infantry school at Fort Benning and had been a student at Amherst College.

On the march, thirst became unbearable, and when they were allowed to drink, it was often from sources that were foul with the litter of dead bodies. The men passed tauntingly close to water that bubbled up fresh from clean artesian wells and were even called to a halt at these springs, but they weren't allowed to drink from them. Having a water stain on one's clothing was enough to invite execution on the spot.

There was nothing at the rest stages along the way that would ameliorate their continuing journey, usually no food, and most often no water. Bloated, dead bodies were not removed from the trail, nor were the wastes left by the men. The prisoners soon discovered that stopping for a rest was another form of torture. A pause stiffened their legs, making it even harder for them to force their bodies to obey the command to resume the march the following day.

As Mickey willed himself to put one foot ahead of the other, blotting out the heat, the pain, and the thirst, he recalled the tales he had been told by his grandmother, about the bitter cold her grandparents had suffered when thousands of Cherokees were forced to walk nine hundred miles to Indian Territory. He tried to remember everything his grandmother had told him about the 'Trail of Tears,' the tragedy of their tribe, when white people took their farmlands in the southeast and sent them packing to a barren wilderness. The heat seemed more bearable, when he thought about how his ancestors had frozen during that record cold winter.

She had told him that it was said anger was the best aid to endurance. A fourth of her people had died or disappeared during the four months it took to walk the distance. Were they the ones who were too ill and despondent to keep a flame of anger burning? Or was it harder to survive the penetrating cold than this dehydrating heat? Thinking about something as bad or worse than his present ordeal helped. He trudged on, convinced he could survive no matter what they piled on him.

On the third night, they were blessed with rain, and Mickey was one of the lucky ones who had a canteen to catch the precious drops. At first the drenching was life giving, and they gratefully put faces to the sky, mouths open, torrents of water soaking their clothes. However, like a cruel prank, it turned out to be a tropical downpour, leaving the emaciated men dripping wet and chilled. For those with malaria, it was disastrous, and for all of them, the march became even more difficult, as the men's feet bogged down in the resulting mud.

When the captives were herded through the streets of Lubao, their guards expected the crowds who lined the streets to feel disgust for the Americans who were being humiliated in this manner. However, the loyal Filipinos suffered beatings and even death in their attempts to give the starving men food or water. They crowded close to the captives, giving many Filipino soldiers an opportunity to escape, for their ragged clothes no longer resembled a uniform.

At every village, natives tried to give the prisoners food or water. One tearful pregnant woman approached with cassava cakes in her hands and was seized by a guard. He forced her off the road and threw her on the ground. The prisoners had to continue their march helplessly while they heard her pleas for mercy and screams. The guard plunged his bayonet into her belly and cut out the fetus.

Some groups of prisoners marched the distance in six days, others took ten, depending on the guards and where in Bataan they were picked up. All along the route were decomposing bodies, and the sight of a stray dog running off with a human limb was common. The Japanese believed that a person could pass into the afterlife only if his head was attached to his body, and the many headless corpses were an extra reminder of the extent to which they hated their captives.

No one has exact figures, but an educated guess is that between 5,000 and 10,000 Filipinos and 750 Americans perished. Some were beaten to death, some executed, and others fell from disease. The danger of being killed by the victor is always greatest just after capture, but the killings went on for weeks. Even those Japanese who had not taken part in the invasion took part in the killings.

Those prisoners who reached the final trek were so ill and apathetic from dysentery that some chose to throw away their trousers and empty their bowels as they walked, knowing they would be bayoneted if they stopped to relieve themselves.

There were men who had not had water or food for five days when they reached the last town, San Fernando. By then the Filipinos who came out by the hundreds to give moral support to the captives were so angered by the Japanese treatment of these poor wretches that the guards became frightened and didn't interfere as they reached out with food or water for the men. Many more Filipinos were able to escape as the Japanese temporarily lost control.

When they reached the end of the line, countless men were barefooted, and even those who had shoes found walking painful, not only because of their wounds and ailments, but also because the road was torn up by all the trucks that had passed over it. Following the rain, the blazing heat baked the rutted mud into something hard as rock that cut into their feet and made it difficult for them to keep from stumbling.

At San Fernando, the men marched to the railroad and were shoved into boxcars marked "40 men" or "8 horses". A hundred to a hundred and twenty men were crowded into the cars meant for men, and fifty men were crammed into the wooden boxcars meant for horses, with only enough room to crouch. There were metal sides on the larger boxcars, and the metal was too hot to touch. Where there wasn't a guard, the doors were slammed shut and locked, leaving the prisoners, all of them by now suffering from dysentery, to stand shoulder to shoulder in their own excrement. Many vomited from the stench, and others died from suffocation. Wherever these trains stopped, angry Filipinos stormed the trains and threw open the doors to give the men some air.

It took four hours of excruciating stops and starts to move the trains the twenty-five miles to where they would resume marching. When they stumbled out of the boxcars, the prisoners faced a six or seven mile march to Camp O'Donnell, all depending on which part of the camp they were assigned. Along the route, the land was mercifully flat and green, covered with cogon grass and unscarred by war, but there wasn't a tree in sight.

Construction of the camp had been halted in '41 when the war broke out, but what was there were flimsy wooden barracks with grass roofs, built for Filipino infantry, with short, double-tiered bunks made out of split bamboo. Nothing was in place when the prisoners got there. The camp had been meant for 8,000 men, and at that it would have been crowded. Now there were at least 50,000.

When Mickey's group arrived, they were marched into a barren parade ground and made to stand at attention. The sun had just passed its zenith, and the shade of a porch on the command post taunted them at a distance. They had learned that any display of weakness would only drag out the agony, and they stood as straight as they could. However, each man was carrying his own burden of misery: Bruised limbs, pounding headaches, open wounds that crawled with flies now that they stood still in the heat, and all of them were tormented by hunger and thirst. By now they had considerable practice in using methods for enduring these sessions. Mickey had a small pebble under his tongue, a Cherokee trick he had learned as a kid. It distracted him from his craving for water. He tried to think about something from life outside the present torture, but his brain refused to bend to his will. The raw instinct for survival was preventing flights of fantasy and forcing him to return to thoughts of food. For once in his life he was totally void of fantasies about women.

The word had passed among the prisoners that anyone carrying Japanese coins or souvenirs should get rid of them. They were considered to be something taken as plunder. Soon after the surrender, a Japanese soldier had stopped one poor guy, a captain, and demanded some cigarettes from him. When he got them, he gave the captain a fan. This fan turned out to be the captain's death warrant. Next time the captain was searched it was found, and he was led away and shot.

Some of the men who were weakened most by illness collapsed while waiting, but finally the Japanese commander came out of headquarters. Captain Tsuneyoshi was a squat little man with a squeaky voice, and he climbed up on a table to deliver his message.

He told them that the Japanese did not sign the Geneva Convention; therefore, the men were not prisoners of war – They were guests of the Emperor. (Actually, in order not to stand out as one of the few nations not accepting the 1929 Geneva Convention, the Japanese delegates did sign it, but their government failed to ratify it.) Then he worked himself into a frenzy, telling them that the lucky ones were their comrades who died on Bataan. "You," he told them, "are dogs. Americans have always been dogs, and you will be treated like dogs." He got more and more excited as he told them that Caucasians had been the enemies of the Orientals for one hundred years and would always be enemies. In his excitement, he jumped up and down like Donald Duck in a fury. Some of the men were still in good enough shape to feel like laughing, but all of them knew that the force driving this ridiculous figure was deadly serious.

Then the men were separated: Filipinos in one part of the camp, Americans in the other. Both sections suffered from a lack of water. The 9,000 Americans were to get their water from two spigots, furnished with half-inch pipes. Twenty-four hours a day, there was the clinking of canteens, as men reached the head of the lines that formed and got their share of water. Some died waiting for their turns.

Water could also be fetched in five-gallon cans from a sluggish stream a half a mile away, but it had to be brought back to camp and boiled. American guards were posted to keep the men from throwing themselves into the foul water and drinking it on the spot.

While they lacked drinking water, there was plenty of ground water. Men who were assigned to a detail to bury the dead had to cope with the fact that a hole filled up with water as fast as they could dig it. They had to use poles or rakes to hold down the corpses long enough to be weighted down with mud. With the best of efforts, they would discover hands or feet sticking above the mud. There were so many dead that they had to straighten out the bodies that were stacked in a grave. The worst was grabbing an arm to shift a corpse and having the skin come off, like a glove, sometimes with a tattoo of propeller and wings – the insignia of the 17th Pursuit Squadron. Handling the bodies was appalling. Dysentery continued to be rampant, and most of the corpses were coated in feces saturated with blood and mucous, skin and bones covered with open sores and blowflies. Many of the prisoners were without clothing after the Death March, and a chaplain was assigned the morbid task of removing clothing from the dead and trying to wash it as well as he could in order to give it to one of the living.

Within six weeks, one out of six Americans who had survived the Death March had died at O'Donnell, and by Christmas that year, some 2,700 Americans and 29,000 Filipinos had perished in that hellhole. Still, the Japanese wouldn't allow anyone from Red Cross into the camp. Whenever the Japanese themselves entered the camp, they were likely to wear surgical masks. The air was putrid.

The camp medics were helpless, with nothing to use for treating the sick and dying. They put men with dysentery into a separate ward, for there was so little water and no soap or disinfectant to keep them clean. Men lay on the bare floor in their wastes. All that the medics could do was move the sick from one side of the room to the other and use long scrapers to push the filth out, like cleaning a barn. They then sprinkled the empty side of the room with sand and, if they could get it, slaked lime. It was excruciatingly painful when the patients were moved back to the cleaned area, and their sores came in contact with the lime.

One prisoner stood out. Ted Lewin was the only fat man in captivity and the most likely to remain that way. He was a civilian and, by rights, should have been interred in the civilian camp at St. Thomas; however, he had miscalculated and ended up on Bataan. Back in Manila, he owned The Alcazar nightclub and a whorehouse called 'The Golden Gate'. He arrived in camp carrying excess baggage, and by mysterious ways was able to keep a steady flow of supplies coming direct to him from Manila. He never had to do a lick of work, because he had enough medicine and goods to barter, not only with the prisoners, but also with the guards. He managed to move back and forth between the American and the Filipino sections of the camp, hobnobbing with the big wheels among the Filipinos and making a bundle on gambling with them.

Mickey remembered him from the old days, when Lewin ran gambling ships out of Catalina Island, off the coast of California. He watched him operate here at O'Donnell and saw an opportunity to get a piece of the action. Ted Lewin was no altruist, but he had so much of everything that he could be persuaded to give a helping hand to someone if it was convenient. Most of the enlisted men were still in their late teens or early twenties, and a lot of them were farm boys who weren't street wise. Sometimes it took so little to make a difference between life and death for one of those kids.

Mickey made contact with Lewin and made himself useful in his black market dealings. He knew that if he played his cards right, not only could he up his own chances for survival, he could also help out people who were worse off than himself. Rumor had it that there was nothing Lewin couldn't get his hands on. Thanks to the connections Mickey had made the relatively short time he was in Manila, and thanks to a real talent as a con artist, he became a key figure in the black market at O'Donnell.

Whether it was due to MacArthur's deplorable example in the Philippines or good old Yankee ingenuity, the spirit that prevailed right from the beginning was most often 'every man for himself.' Neither did the officer class set a good example. When senior officers realized that the Japanese ignored the Geneva Convention, by and large they abandoned their role as leaders, kept to themselves and left all command to the Japanese guards and officers. They used their rank only as a means to avoid hard labor. Their behavior served to be a flagrant example of what can go wrong when leadership fails. In camps with Australian or British prisoners, the officers maintained order, and chances of survival were far greater.

*****

Meanwhile, MacArthur's successor, Wainwright, still held 'the cork' on Corregidor, and the final siege of that bastion lasted nearly a month after the fall of Bataan. The bombardment was uninterrupted, day and night. It was so intense that survivors claimed it sounded like the shells were being fired from machine guns, rather than canons. From Bataan, the island looked like it was a volcano erupting, with giant clouds of smoke and dust rising thousands of feet into the blue sky. During the final stages, 400 guns were blasting the island at a rate of one shell per second, and the ground buckled and shook with their impact.

While 13,000 Americans and Filipinos huddled in Malinta Tunnel as fires raged over the surface of the island, the guns that were manned up top by the Marines fell silent, one after another. The underground refuge became a prison, filled with dust and grit and the stench of death. The constant impact of shells was enough to drive anyone mad, and when their own guns stopped, the Americans and Filipinos knew it was only a matter of time before the Japanese would take the island.

On the evening of May 5th, Homma landed on Corregidor. Japanese artillery battered five hundred sailors who were fighting as infantrymen to man the only American line of defense remaining. Within four hours, Homma was only a mile away from the mouth of the Malinta Tunnel.

The China Marines were preparing to make a last effort to hold off the advancing troops, just yards from the entrance of the tunnel, when their commander received the code words for surrender: "Execute Pontiac". He wept when he had to face the fact that he was to be the first Marine officer ever to surrender a regiment.

Shortly before noon on May 6th, Wainwright cabled President Roosevelt from within the tunnel. "With broken heart, and head bowed in sadness but not in shame, I report to Your Excellency that today I must arrange terms for the surrender of the fortified islands of Manila Bay." He radioed MacArthur in Australia: "I have fought for you to the best of my ability from Lingayen Gulf to Bataan to Corregidor. Goodbye, General."

It was a young Army radio operator, Corporal Irving Strobing, from Brooklyn, who tapped out Corregidor's last message: "Everyone is bawling like a baby. They are piling dead and wounded in our tunnel. The jig is up."

Under a white flag, Wainwright went ashore to meet Homma and negotiate a cease-fire. The Japanese general insisted that he surrender not only Corregidor, but also the entire Philippines. Wainwright agonized over the decision. The command posts in Mindanao and other islands had not been defeated, and the Americans and Filipinos there were prepared to fight on as guerillas if necessary.

Homma was adamant, and Wainwright knew that if he didn't agree to unconditional surrender the Japanese would open fire on Malinta Tunnel, slaughtering the nurses, the wounded and the terrified civilians who were trapped there. He was a man of compassion, and he hesitated no further. The next day, by Japanese radio from Manila, he told of his capitulation, instructing the commanders of all other units in the Philippines to lay down their arms. They obeyed, but thousands of them vanished into the hills to carry on the resistance as well as they could.

In the Malinta Tunnel, General Drake sat on his cot, dazed and despondent, as he listened to the movement of Japanese soldiers through the passageways, checking for whomever there was to flush out. Suddenly he found himself face to face with a Japanese soldier who had entered the room and put the point of his bayonet to the general's throat. Expecting that this might be his last moment alive, he was surprised when the soldier asked if Drake could sing.

Drake had learned to sing from his father. He was puzzled and frightened, wondering where this conversation could lead, but he answered that he could sing. Then the soldier commanded him to sing 'Old Black Joe'.

Drake started out in a quavering voice, but seeing how pleased the soldier was, he warmed up to the task and finished the song. He was asked to give an encore and did so, still unable to fathom where this bizarre scene would lead. Then the soldier sang the song himself, accurately, word for word.

Lulled off guard, Drake said kindly, "You sing very well." The soldier smiled in agreement. "Where did you learn English?" Drake asked as the soldier started to leave.

In answer the soldier turned and delivered a vicious blow to Drake's chest, knocking him to the floor, and scolded him, telling him not to ask questions to a Japanese soldier.

The pain of the blow remained with Drake for days. It was a tangible reminder of his first lesson in trying to understand the whims of the Japanese.

Those prisoners captured at Corregidor were given no food for a week, after which they were packed into freighters to be taken ashore and driven like cattle through the streets of Manila to celebrate the Japanese triumph. Next, they were shoved into trains to be hauled to Cabanatuan. Compared to the survivors of Bataan, they were in pretty good shape, but one can't compare two types of nightmare.

Unknown to the people of the Philippines and the American soldiers who had fought there, their heroic resistance turned the tide of war. Without it, the Japanese could have easily conquered Australia and New Zealand. Their contribution has yet to be fully appreciated by the powers that trapped them in the Philippines, thereby delaying the Japanese onslaught and giving America time to build up an industry geared for war.

Evacuation

Without any knowledge of Mickey's circumstances, Vivian decided there was no choice but to return to the mainland. She had to get rid of all the furniture, because she would have to be ready to evacuate as soon as her turn came. Many other women were in the same predicament, but for most of them there was some form of security once they got to the mainland.

She found a small apartment on the Alawai, a place where they would accept children and where she could move out with a day's notice. The rent was accordingly set very high, and it wasn't long before she had come close to using up the reserves that she had managed to pile up when things started to go well for Mickey. Old man Dillingham offered his help, but she didn't feel right about accepting it.

The last word she had received from Mickey was a letter written in the field, in Bataan. She had read it, over and over again, while biding time during the days of waiting, but it was a love letter. It didn't give her a picture of Mickey's ordeal in the Philippines. Reality was here, in Honolulu, with the children. Knowing Mickey, she brushed away her worries. If anyone can pull through, he can, she thought.

Finally, at the end of February, they were notified that there would be passage on a ship. They would be part of a convoy of three ships in order that they would be safer if a submarine should attack them. The voyage to California normally took eight days, but because they would have to follow a zigzag course it could take three times as long.

The pier was crowded with women and children who were leaving and husbands seeing them off. In the midst of the confusion, Vivian caught sight of Aiolani, the lei vendor, and the big Hawaiian woman spread out her arms and smiled in greeting. She was loaded down with leis, and she edged her way through the crowd to throw leis around Vivian and Tony and Judy's necks. Vivian buried her nose into the cool petals and breathed deeply of the sweet scent of carnations, hiding her tears. She fumbled with her handbag to find money to pay for the leis, but Aiolani stopped her, insisting that she accept them as a gift.

Vivian recalled happier times when Aiolani had greeted her or seen her off. The circle of the lei was a symbol, and Vivian wondered when this circle would be complete. Both women had tears in their eyes as they hugged a farewell.

"Aloha nuiloa, Missus Owen," Aiolani said in the melodious way Vivian loved with Hawaiians. "I pray you come back."

"I pray too, Aiolani. Take care of yourself and that handsome son you have."

Vivian and the children were swept away with the crowd, up the gangplank and on board the ship. As they sailed out the harbor, they could see Aiolani standing on the pier, her bare feet planted firmly, and her muumuu billowing around her expansive figure. With her generous nature and quick smile, she embodied much of that which Vivian loved about the island and the islanders.

As the ship rounded Diamondhead and reached the open sea, Vivian threw her lei into the deep water and told the children to do the same. Judy clutched hers greedily. She wanted to keep it, but she obeyed when her mother told her that if their leis floated in to land, it would mean that they would come back again.

They stood close together by the railing, watching the brightly colored leis bob on the surface until they were too small to follow. Vivian remembered the sensation of excitement and anticipation on other occasions when she had set off on a journey. There had been so much movement during the relatively few years she had been with Mickey, but even during the bad times, she had been buoyed up by a feeling that something better was always just around the corner. For once, she felt tired and discouraged, and she realized that without Mickey some of the poetry had gone out of her life. It struck her that even though his visions often turned out to be pipe dreams, the magic they created was more wonderful than the disappointment of not realizing them. Besides, she thought with a smile, he was always able to conjure up a new dream.

The ship was equipped with triple decked steel bunks, and while Vivian worried about whether or not the kids would fall out of bed onto the hard floor, they immediately started to bicker over who should get to sleep on the top bunk. It was a madhouse, with tired mothers and children of all ages, crammed in together for what could be a slow journey. However, once they settled in, the trip was blessedly uneventful for the first few days, except for the unavoidable squabbling that takes place when women from vastly different backgrounds are squeezed together in small quarters.

Then, early one morning, the lead ship was torpedoed, and the rescued wounded were taken aboard Vivian's ship. She shooed Tony and Judy away from the scene, but not before she had a glimpse of limp sailors being laid out on the deck, their white uniforms soaked with seawater and blood. Tony turned his head as Vivian led him away, and his eyes went wide as he took in the scene. A strange silence prevailed. The women were too terrified to be hysterical. Fortunately, it was the only incident of its kind.

During the last week at sea, there was an epidemic of dysentery, and Vivian had to cope with two children with runny stomachs. At least it meant that they were listless and content to spend much of the day in their bunks. She fretted over them, unaware that had they been on the other side of the world as planned, they would soon be struggling to stay alive in a makeshift concentration camp under the brutal control of Japanese guards.

When the ship finally docked in San Francisco, the pier was mobbed with family and friends who had come to meet the evacuees. Aboard ship, crowds of women and children pushed against the railing, where they hoped to catch a glimpse of a familiar face. They were pushed and crushed into a human stream flowing towards the exits. Small children cried, while adults who had persevered the tension of the voyage felt drained, knowing they had to face dull prospects of an unsettled future.

Tony and Judy looked peaked, but thank goodness, they were being good as gold. Vivian worried about how she would manage with Judy if it took too long to disembark. She still had a bad bout of diarrhea, and Vivian hadn't dared let her eat anything but a piece of dry toast for breakfast.

There was military precision to the processing of passengers once they had left the ship. Vivian headed for the table designated for passengers whose last name began with 'O' and was relieved to find that the people checking lists were sympathetic and kind, despite the crush.

Soon Vivian and the children were on a train heading south. When they arrived in Los Angeles, she caught sight of Donda and Doc and Poli in the crowd at the train station. She pulled back her shoulders and straightened her back. She had groomed as carefully as the cramped quarters onboard ship would allow, fooling herself that this was an ordinary homecoming. The day had begun at the crack of dawn, and it would be hours before she could get out of her girdle and relax.

Everyone talked at once as they hugged each other. Donda held back tears, choked by the emotion of seeing her daughter safely home. As they all headed through the imposing terminal building, someone took Vivian by the arm. "Vi! How're ya doing?"

She turned and saw that it was Bert Longwerth, a cameraman she knew from her Hollywood days. He had a camera on a strap over his shoulder and appeared to be looking for subjects. She gave him a warm smile. She had always liked Bert. She was holding Tony and Judy by the hand and pulled them close to her to show them off. "Well, Bert, you can see what I've been doing since I left Hollywood!"

"Gee, they sure are cute, Vi. But what happened to Mickey? Is he back in the islands?"

"Worse than that, Bert...He might have been captured by the Japs. He was at Bataan last I heard. He went out there to start up 'Our Army', just in time to get caught in the thick of things. With no money coming in, I had no choice but to head back to California and stay with my family until I figure out what's going to happen."

"Hey, that really makes me feel bad. This war is splitting up so many families," Bert said, sympathetically.

Brushing off Bert's pity, Vivian turned her attention to him. She figured he must have had some bad luck himself, because she couldn't imagine he would earn as much money running around out here as a press photographer as he did at the studios. "What about you? Did you get tired of the primadonnas at Fox?" she asked diplomatically.

"Ah, a lot has happened at the studios. Things aren't like they were when you and Mickey were there. Remember how much fun we used to have? Heck, we were just a bunch of kids." He still had a slow boyish grin, but he looked care-worn. Vivian wondered what the story was…He had been a real talent in her days at the studios.

"I've been working as a press photographer for the LA Times the past couple of years," he went on to explain. "At least my contacts at the studios make it easier for me to move around and be the first on the scene for a good shot. After Zanuck took over, things tightened up at Fox, and it was more like a factory. It never was as fun as in the days when Mickey was there. Hey, how 'bout you giving me a nice pose with the kids? I'll make sure it gets in the paper."

The thought crossed Vivian's mind that a bit of publicity might not hurt. Maybe it could open a door at the studios. Who knows? Anyway she could count on Bert not to run it if it turned out poorly.

Bert snapped a picture and gave her a hug before she hurried on to meet her family. He watched her walking away and thought about her with Mickey, remembering what an attractive pair they made. No one ever thought it would last though. Mickey was such a character. Well, it looks like it took a war to tear them apart, he mused.

*****

Bobbie was shocked when she saw Vivian. Outwardly, she seemed as cheerful as ever, but there was an unaccustomed gravity that gave even more depth to her beautiful eyes, and she was thin and frail. Even Donda had to admit that Vivian's color wasn't as good as usual and, without talking about it, they all feared she might be facing a new bout with cancer.

Vivian could see it herself in the mornings, after her bath, when she wiped away the steam and looked in the mirror above Donda's cluttered vanity table, but she told herself she would soon be the picture of health, with the rest and care she was getting at her mother's. She had mastered self-discipline in repressing the fears that sometimes boiled up from deep inside.

Like a chant for a magic spell, she mentally recited the lines from the Book of John that she had written in her copy of Mary Baker Eddy's Keys to the Scriptures: "There is no fear in love; but perfect love casteth out fear, because fear hath torment."

The stilted language of the King James Version of the Bible lent power to the words, and when they popped into her head, they had a calming effect, like a rabbit foot in a child's pocket. She had learned to cancel out the very concept of cancer and regarded her ailments as passing discomfort, to be flushed out by a good diet or rest.

The excitement of the first few days at her mother's cheered her up. The kids loved all the attention they were getting, and they quickly settled in. Everyone was so happy to see her safely back, but once the newness had worn off, she began to take stock of her present situation.

If anything, Pearl Harbor had reminded her of how lucky one was just to be alive; however, being back with her family, she was sensitive to their attitudes. No one said anything critical about Mickey, but she knew that they all thought it was typical of him to put her in this sort of a predicament, world war or not. Only her mother understood what makes a character like Mickey tick, she thought.

Her first concern was money. Because of Mickey's status as civilian, there was no sort of allotment from the army like some of the wives who were evacuated could count on. She couldn't bear to let her family support her. She was especially sensitive to what she imagined Bobbie and Armand would be thinking. Thank goodness Mickey had earned good money just before Pearl Harbor, and Vivian had been able to spruce up her wardrobe. Bobbie was so elegant.

Bobbie and Armand had continued to do well since Vivian visited them in San Francisco. Armand had kept his good job in shipping, and Bobbie had opened up a nice little gift shop in San Francisco and was able to make a nest egg of her own while doing an admirable job of running their home. Because of his youthful bout with tuberculosis, Armand was exempt for the draft, but he was offered a plum of a job in the defense industry when war broke out. They had moved down south and bought a lovely home in Burbank. Vivian knew they didn't approve of Mickey, and, as much as she loved them, her pride prevented her from sharing her worries and problems with them. She was pleased with the way things had turned out for them, but it reminded her of how far out of the pale she had come. They were pictures of success, with bright prospects for the future.

Looking at their life style, she was reminded that the girl she had been would want to change places with her younger sister and not have to worry about what tomorrow had in store; but then she thought about Mickey, and she always found herself dwelling on the good times they had together, not the bad. And the children – they were so much Mickey's kids that she could not conceive of them existing without his part in it all. What would life be without her two babies? I guess Ma is right, she thought. You have to take things as they come and make the best of them. Still, her pride kept her from showing any signs of discontent with her own lot when Bobbie was around.

Donda's cooking and looking after the children was powerful medicine, and Vivian soon look rested and healthy; however, plans she had about contacting the studios seemed more and more unrealistic. Bert's press photo had turned out well and was run in the Los Angeles Times, but she had lost her nerve. Though she kept her guild card up to date through thick and thin, the people she had known at the studios were either long gone or had risen to positions where a barrage of secretaries screened out old friends asking for favors.

Donda kept in touch with Lillian Gish, and when Lillian heard about Vivian's plight, she called and said she could put in a word for Vivian at the studio. She knew they were hiring extras for a light comedy being shot at Palm Springs.

Vivian was at the hairdressers when Lillian called. When she returned, Donda thought she looked very pretty. Pleased that she could give her some good news, Donda told her about the phone call just as soon as she came in the door.

At first, Vivian was excited, but by the time they had put Tony and Judy to bed and were in their nightclothes themselves, Vivian broke down and told Donda that she'd wasn't going to the try-outs.

"Who am I kidding, Ma? For a movie like that, you know I'll have to wear summer dresses and probably a bathing suit. I won't be able to hide this damned scar on my arm, and you know they won't have me then. Good-looking women are a dime a dozen in this town."

Donda's heart filled with pity. She felt terrible that she had even made a suggestion that caused her daughter to think about her drawbacks, but whenever she looked at Vivian, with her flawless skin, her beautiful dark hair and those eyes that captivated everyone who saw her, she forgot about the operation. Vivian had kept her lovely figure, the small waist and full hips, and no one would know that one breast was false, but in a bathing suit the scar on her arm couldn't be hidden.

Vivian sighed. "Face it. I never was a great actress. I did well as an extra and bit actress, but even then I had to hide the fact that I was past thirty," she said, her ready smile crinkling the corners of her eyes. "Besides, I don't think it would be good for the kids if I got back in movies. It would be so irregular, and I would be away for days on end if I landed a good job. There are plenty of other ways to make money if I just figure out what to do."

The stay with Donda was balm for the soul, but once Vivian felt restored, she wanted to have a place of her own and a plan for the future. As soon as it became clear Mickey wasn't coming back right away, Jane wrote, offering Vivian a job running some cottages she rented out. Besides the salary she could earn, she and the kids could live rent-free in one of the cottages. As time passed by, Vivian decided that this was her best option.

Everyone objected loudly to the idea of Vivian going to Las Vegas. They all knew how awful Jane could be, but Vivian refused to listen, claiming there was good in everyone, and that if it was unbearable, she could always leave and come back to Donda's. She knew better than anyone how unpredictable Jane was. One minute she could be sugary sweet and generous, and the next conniving and sarcastic. Maybe worrying about Mickey would bring out the best in her, thought Vivian. Anyway, she knew there was very little choice right now.

Jane had written glowing reports of her financial progress in Las Vegas and promised that what she was building up there would provide Vivian and the children with a good income as long as they needed it. More important was her promise they would have a place of their own. Vivian knew she and Jane couldn't spend one night under the same roof without getting in a row.

What finally convinced Vivian was the day of surrender in the Philippines. She no longer could hope that Mickey had avoided capture, and even if he was safe, she knew it might be a long time before he got home. Also, she knew that, with all her faults, Jane was a devoted mother. It only seemed fair that she should get to know her grandchildren well, now that she had to face the fear that she might lose her only son.

Jane does have a flair for business, she mused. It won't hurt me to see what kind of a living I can make for the kids and me where she is. Whether Mickey comes home safely or not, it is high time I start building up something for our future. His unfortunate decision to try his luck in the Philippines was just one more proof that I'm going to have to provide this family with some security, she thought. Mickey's ideas were brilliant, but he sure as heck didn't have good sense.

She tried not to fret over the career opportunities she had lost since she married Mickey. It did no good to think about what could have been, and lord knows, money easily disappears when the heart rules. Still, every time she was nagged by thoughts of plans she had to abandon, she was left with a frantic sense of urgency. Most good ideas are good because the timing is right, and how many times hadn't she cooked up a scheme and had to give it up until later? Her life in the islands had simply been too full of moving from house to house, fixing up places on a shoestring, tending babies and coping with Mickey's crazy friends while trying to run a normal household. She lay awake at nights remembering the ideas she had to make money and ticked them off as things done since then by someone else.

The morning she was to leave for Vegas, Doc came to drive her and the children to the train. Vivian was smartly dressed in a lightweight navy blue gabardine suit with white trim and a navy and white hat with a jaunty tilt to the rim, and Doc and Donda put on a good face, acting like it was a festive occasion. Doc had even bought her a gardenia and awkwardly handed it to her saying, „Here Sis, I know you like these weeds."

She busied herself with pinning it on her lapel, being careful not to touch the petals and turn them brown, grateful for the chance to look down and not let him see the tears that threatened to spill over. She would miss Doc. He was like a shelter in the storm.

Doc and Donda waved until the train was well out of sight and then walked back to the car where the fragrance of the gardenia lingered. It was a balmy day in Los Angeles, with a gentle breeze, but they knew that when Vivian's train arrived in Las Vegas, even though it would be evening, it would be like stepping into an oven when she and the kids disembarked.

"What do you think, son?" said Donda. "I still don't like her color. Do you suppose there's something wrong? She never complains, but I notice that she winces sometimes. She said it's just a stitch in her side, but I feel uneasy."

Doc looked sideways at his mother's troubled face. She had aged fretting about Vivian. Deep down inside he knew what his sister's chances were, but he didn't think it would do any good to worry the rest of the family about it. "She'll be alright, Ma. I gave her a good supply of those B complex pills, and I think that will help her if her liver is acting up. Don't forget, it was a long, hard voyage over here, and all three of them were sick with dysentery part of the time."

Once the train had pulled out of the station, Vivian tried to relax. The children's excitement over the train ride and the new coloring books was a pleasant distraction from the thought of what might await them on the other end. Always the optimist, she had allowed herself to picture a nice place for Tony and Judy to spend the next couple of years, and, hopefully, a good opportunity for her to earn enough money to make a fresh start in the islands when Mickey came home.

She tried to imagine Las Vegas and remembered hearing about the ranch Rex Bell and Clara Bow had bought there years ago. They raved about the place so it had to be something special. In fact, a number of friends from her Hollywood days had moved to Las Vegas and bought ranches. Maybe they could get together like in the good old days, she thought, with a smile.

Las Vegas – 1942

In the tinny glitter of the modern city of Las Vegas, one loses sight of the true treasures of the Las Vegas Valley. Cradled within a ring of rugged mountains, the blistering desert was blessed with a string of natural springs that have all but been forgotten under the clutter that inevitably follows in the white man's trail. Indians revered the springs for thousands of years, but these sources of pure water didn't start to figure in the history of white men until the riches of California lured them to find a way across the Mojave Dessert. It wasn't until John Frémont blazed a well-defined trail that Las Vegas became a place on the map, but the life-giving water made it an interesting spot long before gambling spread its fame all over the world.

One of the shrewdest decisions Jane made was to move from Reno to Vegas, even though she had done well with rentals in Reno. In the thirties everyone went to Reno for a divorce, but things were settling down there. Her years in Hollywood had opened her eyes to the attraction that Las Vegas held as the population expanded in the Los Angeles area. She knew that people who wanted a divorce or wanted to gamble would rather travel the relatively short distance to Las Vegas than the long haul to Reno.

Nevada's liberal laws regarding matrimony dated back to the days when the state was a territory. People from all over the United States came to Nevada where it wasn't necessary to wait for blood tests to tie the knot. Or they could get divorced in just six weeks time if they stayed there and had a witness to the fact that they had not seen their spouses during that period.

She felt right at home in this man's town. Men were easy if you knew how to treat them, and Jane appreciated the raw, Western honesty about the way men were in Vegas. She was too smart to have had to make her living in bed, but she was pragmatic about those who did. Everyone in Las Vegas accepted that men had their needs, and the red light district was in the block right next to the town's most prestigious financial institution, the First State Bank. Well into the thirties, the upstairs of the honky-tonks of Block 16 were brothels, and the showcase of the block was the Arizona Club.

About the time Jane made her entrance in Las Vegas, notorious block 16 was on its last leg. Times were changing. The city commissioners cancelled the beer licenses and permits for slot machines which were the mainstay of the prostitution bars in that part of town, but anyone who was too straight-laced wouldn't have wanted to buy property in a town like Vegas in any case. (The military brass threatened to make the city off-limits unless these places were closed down. The town leaders simply moved the whore house outside city limits and kept it under control but still open, Roxie's being the most well-known bordello.)

Jane's options weren't limited when she decided to make Vegas a base. There was money to make off gambling, but for those who were pioneers in the development of Las Vegas, gambling wasn't the prime factor. There were also ranchers – cattlemen or farmers, attracted by the reliable water, and there were opportunists who pictured Las Vegas as a health resort, an alternative to Palm Springs, and hoped to get rich off of tourists. Last, but not least, there was the money to be made on marriages and divorces.

The first place Jane acquired when she arrived in Vegas was on North Seventh Street, with courts that she rented out to women who were seeking a divorce, charging them an extra fee for her services as witness that they had not seen their husbands during the six weeks of their stay. There were between three and four thousand divorcees a year going through Las Vegas in those days, and she was soon making money hand over fist.

Jane also saw an opportunity to rent out sleeping accommodations for the men who worked at a titanium plant in nearby Hendersen. Housing was limited, and prices sky-high. Most of the men who came to Vegas chose to leave their families back home. They worked hard in sweltering heat, and all they wanted was a place to hang their hats and a bed to sleep in. They weren't fussy about the decor, as long as the place was clean, and they could be sure of not getting rolled. Jane leased two big halls and turned them into flophouses. The only investment she had to make was to buy sturdy cots, mattresses, and bedding. An electric heater was all the comfort provided for cold desert nights. She ran her places with an iron hand, and money started rolling in from that operation, too.

Las Vegas took on a new importance with the building of an air force base northwest of the city when the United States entered World War II. Workers streamed to the area in droves in order to build Nellis Air Force Base. They all needed a place to stay, and Jane opened a third flophouse and a motel.

One more factor added to this boom: The war in Europe had driven tourism inland, and people who took vacations were flocking to the west like they never had before. It was clear that for those who got in on the ground floor, there were all the opportunities you could dream of, and a lot of those people who were hustling a living didn't have Jane's rock-solid convictions about not spending more than you earn. That gave her an advantage that made up for her being a woman on her own.

She thought about Mickey all the time and felt that maybe her thoughts would be keeping him alive somewhere. It was ironic that the same war that had taken her only son was the reason for her getting rich. She wouldn't allow herself to even think of him being dead. It was only when she was tired that her spirits flagged, and she wondered whether he really was alive out there in those jungles. And if he were, what sort of shape would he be in when he got back? What got her over moments like that were her plans to build something up for the day he came home, and if he never came home, she wanted to make sure her grandchildren never had to do without the best in everything.

Funny, she thought, how much money she could make when Mickey wasn't around to distract her. She bought a big black Packard and became a familiar figure about town, always flawlessly dressed in black, with a hint of flirtatiousness behind a stern demeanor. Power intoxicated her, but at the same time, success made her see things crystal clear, not blurred like they sometimes got when emotions drain your energy. Where business was concerned, she had the self-discipline to be even-tempered, unlike her shifting moods when she dealt with friends or relations. Because of her iron-clad reserve, it was impossible to fathom what triggered off her changes of mind, but her sister, Flossie, knew her well enough to be aware of the grudges she harbored against people she imagined had slighted her.

Of course, the move to Vegas meant that she saw more of Pete, someone she had met in Reno. He was a handsome cowboy who owned a tackle store by the railroad station, on South First Street, where he sold leather goods, horseshoes, saddles, and chaps, whatever a cowboy could need. Their romance kept her feeling young and took her mind off Mickey. Pete spent most of his time out on his ranch, but when he was in town, he took to staying at her place. When Jane bought a place on North Fourth Street, Pete kicked in half the sales sum, but remained a silent partner.

They sometimes had rows, but when things were 'that-a-way,' as Jane coyly expressed it, she purred with contentment. It suited her fine that he had his own place, because she loved her independence. As for Pete, he never could have given his heart completely to anyone as hard as Jane could be.

Pete and Jane shared a love for Indian crafts and Western art. Both of them bought Western paintings and Navajo blankets that served as carpets and bedspreads. Some things they bought jointly, and a lot of what he bought was left at Jane's, but with the understanding that he could move it out whenever he wanted.

Everyone knew and liked Pete, and all the old-timers traded in his store. Pete had been a respected cowhand before the war, when Las Vegas was a place for ranchers. Now he was president of the Cattleman's Association. Through Pete, Jane became an accepted member of that ranching community, accepted that is, by the men, but she felt less at ease with the women.

With bitter amusement, she saw how quickly people forgot their origins. Yesterday's down and out settler only had to stick around long enough to start to think they were better than anyone else. On the one hand, she really didn't care for most of these women from the crowd who felt superior, but on the other, she would have preferred to feel like she was in a position to reject them, rather than the other way around.

"Hells bells, Pete," she complained, "It's not like the old biddies are the least bit better than I am. Matter of fact, I 'magine none of them would be able to hold a candle to me in the business world."

"Well, honey, I hate to say it, but probably none of 'em would give a hoot," replied Pete laconically. "And I just don't see why you should care."

However, she did care. Her childhood experience with being a sharecropper had marked her for life. She was too vain not to care, but she fooled herself that she cared on her grandchildren's behalf. Besides, if she wanted to get the power she dreamed of, she had to get in thick with the Republican Party, and that meant being accepted by the men's wives. She convinced herself that once that hurdle was taken, she could make her family one that would make folks sit up and take notice. She wasn't happy when Mickey married Vivian, but she could see that there was good enough material there to make something out of those children.

That's why she got the idea of joining the Daughters of the American Revolution, and now she had plenty of money to hire someone who could trace the family tree. She knew for sure that her family had been in America back when the Founding Fathers were alive and was willing to gamble that at least one of her ancestors must have carried a gun in the battle for independence.

Ironically, organizations had mushroomed up all over America that would stratify the land of equality. Jane proved herself to be so American that she didn't see the humor in this tendency to re-create the class society that her ancestors had opposed when they fled from the Old World. She shelled out a small fortune to an expert in genealogy with orders to trace the family tree. It was so much money that she should have been suspicious of the glowing results.

Her mother's side was quickly abandoned – There the genealogist found Indians of whose history they were ignorant and horse thieves – but she hit pay dirt when they investigated the ancestors of her shifty-looking father. His lineage took her all the way back to the signers of the Magna Carta, but most importantly it turned up more than one ancestor who fought in the Revolution. It served her purpose adequately and got her into the D.A.R., the key to open all doors, she reckoned.

It had cost her a pretty penny to have the family tree traced, but she felt that the results were well worth the investment. Once she had membership in the Daughters of the American Revolution, she was all set to yield some power in the Republican Party, and everyone knew that they were the ones who ruled Nevada. She was proud to call Pat McCarran, the Republican U.S. Senator, a close friend, a person she could call anytime she needed a favor.

Despite her aspirations to be part of an elite, she continued to take a great interest in her extended family, and several times a year she drove a huge circuit in the western states, visiting relatives both on her mother's side of the family and her father's. When Jordan's son, Knox, was fifteen, she brought him up to Vegas to help her clean up one of the flophouses that had become infested with bed bugs. She had turned the management of that flophouse over to a man she had known for years. He was honest, but he had let it get run down, and the clientele was getting pretty run-down, too. It was still an operation that earned $300 a month, nine months out of the year, but she could see that she needed to step back in and put things right if she wanted to continue seeing a profit. The rooms had to be stripped of inventory and painted with calcimine, making sure that every crack was coated. For a couple of weeks she worked hard, with the help of Knox and a hired man, cleaning up the dorm and giving everything fresh paint. She was proud of the result: Nice clean dormitories, freshly painted in white and gray, with colorful Indian blankets on each bed. She renamed it 'The Desert Inn Beds' and hired a couple to keep it clean so it wouldn't revert to being inhabited by bums and bugs.

It was during Knox's Easter holiday, and she took him to Cave Springs, Red Rock Canyon, Lake Mead, and Boulder Dam. He soaked up a wealth of impressions, and everywhere they went, he noticed that she always knew the person in charge. They visited places in the dam where the public never went. The last night of his visit, she took him out on the town to the place of his choice. Knox wanted to see the floorshow at the El Rancho Vegas, and Jane ordered an eight-course dinner to teach her nephew which fork to use first. She tried to recapture those days when she always had Mickey in tow, but the two were too different to make a comparison. Perhaps Tony would fill in that empty space, she thought, as Knox self-consciously finished his dinner under her watchful supervision.

She was proud of the way her portfolio was taking shape and felt expansive towards Vivian, now that her own fortunes were riding high. Besides, she had so many irons in the fire that she felt she could use a helping hand. When she heard that Vivian was leaving the islands, she wrote a long letter, promising her daughter-in-law a steady income and making plans for Tony and Judy's futures. No matter what happened, she said that she knew she would be able to provide for them.

She had sold the motel and the lease for one flophouse. With her two remaining flophouses, The Desert Inn Beds and The Basic Hotel, she was clearing seven hundred dollars a month, and she also had the courts on North 7th Street to manage. Her latest acquisition was a property on North 4th, and she wanted to move there and supervise the work that had to be done in order to convert it to a hotel and build an annex. She was pleased that Vivian had agreed to come to Vegas and manage the courts, and, as she said to Pete, "It won't hurt any that Mickey's wife is so attractive."

"I have those courts booked solid with divorcees, but there are still those two extra rooms in the manager's duplex that I rent out to transients. If word gets 'round that there is a good-looking gal at the front desk, there will be plenty of gamblers who would like to check in when they're in town for a weekend."

Vivian arrived in the late afternoon. It was her first trip to Vegas, and she was unprepared for the dry heat when she got off the train and saw Jane waving to get her attention. Jane had written glowing letters describing the boom that had been taking place ever since the construction of Nelson Air Force Base got under way.

To Vivian it looked very much like a movie set. Facing the railroad station was the entrance to Fremont Street that the invention of neon lights had transformed to 'Glitter Gulch'. However, behind the gaudy glamour of the pretentious neon facades were one-storied, flat-roofed buildings. It looked like the sort of place that could become a ghost town, with buildings that had very little to withstand the wind and sand of the desert.

There was a cheap carnival atmosphere, with the friendly hustle and bustle of plain folks out to have a good time. On the side streets were modest houses, typical dwellings for the people who had worked for the railroad when it was the most important source of employment. It didn't seem like the sort of place where one could make a lot of money, but if Jane was right, Vivian reminded herself, this was just the beginning for Las Vegas.

When Jane pulled up in front of the courts that were to be their home, Vivian was too tired to register much of the surroundings. The cottage in which they would be staying faced the street. A front bedroom had been converted into a manager's office, and besides that were a living room, two bedrooms and a tiny kitchen and bath. Jane had furnished it simply, but comfortably. It was small but would do nicely, since Vivian had no desire to have a social life here.

After the excitement of the train trip, Tony and Judy fell asleep as soon as they were tucked into their beds. Jane lingered on, wanting to get off on the right foot with Vivian. Small talk is the key to opening a door to friendship, but Jane never had found it easy to make small talk. Her energy was so self-contained that it didn't easily inter-react with that of another person. Normally, Vivian could get along with anyone, but there was an invisible barrier between her and her mother-in-law.

Jane was proud of her efforts to make the place homey. She moved about briskly, showing Vivian where the extra linen was and pointing out that there was a refrigerator and that it was well stocked. Making an effort to forget past differences, Vivian thanked her warmly and said that she looked forward to seeing it all in the morning. She was touched that Jane seemed so eager to please. Nevertheless, she was grateful when Jane said she would let her get a good night's sleep and left.

Vivian awoke early. Tony and Judy were still sleeping soundly. They were so used to being moved around that they didn't seem to need any time to adjust to new places. Not knowing when Jane might turn up, Vivian quickly got dressed and stepped out on the small porch to get a look at the grounds. It was only 8 a.m., but the air was already warm, and the flawless blue of the sky promised a blazing hot day. The sun had scorched what little grass there was around the courts. There were no shrubs or flowers to hold down the sandy soil, and she wondered where the kids could play in this bleak place. Out back, there was a plank fence that blocked out the view of an alleyway that ran down the middle of the block. Cottonwood trees cast their shadows in the wrong direction.

Funny how the scenery changes when human beings put their mark on it, she thought, as she remembered trips to the desert with Mickey. She recalled the wind-sculpted rocks, the majestic sweep of land skirting up to mountainsides, with the play of light undisturbed by anything man-made. They had visited Flossie at Death Valley Scotty's, when the Mojave Desert was a symphony of subtle colors from tiny spring flowers, and been awe-struck by the purity and grandeur of the land. A smile played around the corners of her lips as she thought of Mickey, stealing a kiss whenever they got near a nook or cranny he could pull her into. It seemed like ages ago.

From the outside, the cottage looked bigger than it was on the inside. Curious, she walked around to the back of the building and discovered that there were two outer doors, furnished with numbers. Those must be rentals, too, she figured. Funny, Jane didn't mention them. Going back inside, she discovered that a door in her bedroom that she had presumed to be a closet was locked, and she surmised it connected with one of the rooms at the back of the house.

By now the children were awake and bounced out of bed, eager to explore their new surroundings. Vivian remembered that there was food in the refrigerator and told them to hold their horses until they had something to eat. She noticed there wasn't any fresh fruit and gave them each a bowl of cereal, making a mental note of what to shop for as soon as Jane came around and filled her in on her duties.

Jane was oozing with charm when she showed up around nine. Vivian wished she could relax and accept her friendliness for just that, but past experience had made her wary. She was determined to make the best of the situation, but it always seemed impossible to let down one's guard when Jane was around. Darn it all – Why can't I trust her, she thought. After all, she means well, despite her faults.

After a few minutes of small talk, Jane gave Vivian a ring of keys and told her they were master keys for the various rentals. "I've got a hired man to keep them clean, but you know how that goes, honey. Your job is to make sure he does his work. Most of these rentals are for women, and when it isn't their own place they are by far sloppier than men. We don't clean up for them daily, but the places have to be spick and span when they move out."

"What about those two rooms at the back of this cottage, Jane? I noticed that there appears to be an inter-connecting door to my bedroom."

"Well, I intend to get that door walled up, sugar. I've been too busy over on 4th Street to get around to it. Those two rooms are a little gold mine. I rent them out to people passing through – folks who like to gamble and just want a bed to flop in when they can't stand on their feet anymore. If a man makes a big winning while he's staying at my place, he thinks it's lucky to come back here every time he hits the casinos. It's real easy money. I charge five bucks a night for each of those rooms, and they're filled up most of the time."

While they were talking, Tony and Judy asked if they could go outside and play. Vivian nodded yes, but told them not to go out on the street. They came back inside minutes later. It was already close to 100 degrees Fahrenheit, and the only shade was from shadows cast by the cottages.

"I miss Donda," Judy said petulantly.

"Well, honey-chile, you have me. I'm gonna take you lots of nice places, just as soon as I have the time," Jane drawled sweetly. She wanted to give so much to her grandchildren and couldn't understand why she didn't have a way with them the way that woman, Donda, did.

Judy looked at Jane without saying anything, studying her to decide whether or not this sounded like a good offer. Apparently it wasn't, for she turned back to her mother and said, "When are we going to go back to Donda's?"

"She's just tired and grumpy," Vivian said apologetically to Jane. "Why don't you kids sit over there and do some nice pictures in your new coloring books?"

They busied themselves with getting out their books and crayons, something they both liked and could spend hours doing. "It is going to be a bit difficult though," Vivian continued. "I didn't really imagine it would be this hot during the daytime. I suppose most people lie low until evening, but it will take awhile for the kids to adjust to a new schedule."

"It's good, healthy clean air here on the desert, Vi. They're a lot better off than down in that congested place where your mother lives," Jane said, letting a hint of annoyance creep into her voice.

Why couldn't Jane lay off her family? Vivian bit her tongue, determined not to get into any arguments on the very first day. Instead, she talked with Jane about her business ventures and arranged to go shopping for some more groceries. The kids were already starting to wilt by the time they got into the hot car.

The grocery store wasn't too inspiring. The fruit was shriveled and the vegetables limp. Jane was unconcerned, being from a meat and potatoes background, but Vivian chalked it up as one more obstacle if she was going to make much of a home in this place. She kept reminding herself that she had only just arrived and should wait to form any opinions.

The next couple of days were busy with getting unpacked and settled in. She tried not to let the kids get on her nerves, but it was hard, with them being cooped up indoors all day long. They found a place to dig holes out back, and with their usual fervor had imagined a network of roads and tunnels to make for a couple of small cars Tony had. They came into the house coated with grit and happy, but when she put them in the bath, she discovered that Judy had developed a rash, and she chalked it up to contact with the alkaline soil being too harsh for her skin.

"Damn it all, this is no fit place for kids," she grumbled under her breath.

Tony sensed that things weren't too easy and wanted to make his mother feel better. "Maybe there will be a real good school here," he suggested hopefully.

She immediately felt sorry that she had let down the flag. It wouldn't do to make the kids unhappy, and she had to at least give this life a try. "You're right, honey," she said.

"If Daddy was here, we'd have fun, wouldn't we? Do you think he will be back soon?" He said it casually and then looked at her with an earnest expression that reminded her of how much Mickey meant to him.

Vivian hugged him, as she replied that it really would be fun if his father were here. She missed Mickey, too. Even during hard times he could make her laugh and feel like life was a lark. She wondered how long she should go on keeping up Tony's hopes that his father was alive and would be coming home. He was such a bright little guy and pieced together a lot of what he heard about the way the war was going. It worried her that she hadn't heard anything from Mickey after the surrender, but all her inquiries indicated that things were too chaotic to jump to conclusions.

The first couple of days she saw nothing of the men who occupied the two rentals in the back of the cottage. They gambled the nights away and slept most of the day. On the third day, a tall, lanky man knocked on her screen door late in the afternoon. She went to the door to see what he wanted, and he peered with interest when she got close to the screen.

"Can I help you?" she asked.

"Well, well. I sure as hell didn't know I was staying under the same roof with such a pretty little thing," he said, as he reached for the door handle like he intended to come in.

A quick glance reassured Vivian that she had locked the screen door, but it seemed a flimsy barrier between her and a man whose looks she didn't exactly like. Under normal circumstances, she would not have been on guard, but something about the atmosphere of Jane's Vegas made her cautious. There was a whiff of whiskey on his breath and a hard look about his eyes. She didn't dignify his remark with a reply, but waited for him to state his business.

Unabashed, he asked her if she was going to invite him in. The look on her face must have made him realize he had better give her a reason for coming by. He said he wanted to settle his bill, because he would be checking out the next morning. "I thought I'd better pay up before I go out for my last night on the town," he said. "Been on a real roll this time, but my luck might change."

"Oh, I didn't realize you were a lodger. Come on in, and I'll write you a receipt," Vivian said, as she unlocked the screen door. She turned to get the book Jane had given her out of the desk. She could feel his eyes on her back and hated it. "Silly me," she mused. "If he were attractive, I probably wouldn't mind at all."

She was relieved when she was able to take his money and give him the receipt without him making a pass at her, but she shuddered at the thought of him when he had turned and left. If this is what the high rollers who rent those back rooms are like, I hope that door gets walled up real soon, she thought.

She soon got to know all the tenants. They were a mixed bag, folks from every walk of life. Of course, the rich clientele who were in Vegas for divorces checked into someplace more attractive, like the Boulderado Ranch where they could swim and ride horseback. Jane's tenants were less well heeled, but some were interesting when you got to know them, and a lot of them had had a pretty tough time in a bad marriage. Nonetheless, they all seemed to be interested in Vivian and full of sympathy over her bad luck. Most of them were lonely, whiling away time in a strange town, and they liked the distraction the kids furnished. Still, Vivian couldn't help but feel it was a rather depressing atmosphere.

Just like Jane had said, the two rooms in the back were easy to rent out, but Vivian didn't like the way most of the men who rented them eyed her. More often than not, they looked like they were considering the possibility that she might be part of the deal.

A week after their arrival, a big man from Hollywood turned up. He kept staring at her as she went through the procedure of checking him in and giving him the key.

"Hey, didn't you used to work for Paramount?" he suddenly blurted out. "I'm sure I saw you working on 'The Duke of Dublin', that film with Charlie Murray."

"I did work on that film. I was the check girl," Vivian said, pleased that someone remembered her, but wary, trying to keep some distance. "This is embarrassing, though, I should recall you."

"Name's Ned Fisher. I was a prop man back then. No reason why you would have noticed me. You people in front of the camera were in a different league."

"You still working for Paramount?" Vivian asked just to be friendly.

"No. I did like most people and ended up in real estate. With that buildup at Lockheed when the war broke out, property shot sky high. Done real well for myself. I like to come up here and try my hand at the crap tables." As if he read her thoughts, he went on to say, "I can't see blowing a lot of money on a fancy hotel when all I need is a bed and a few hours sleep."

"Well, that makes sense. Good luck to you," she said with a smile while she started to close the door.

"Hey, is there any chance you'd like to join me?"

"Oh, no thanks. I've got my two little kids to take care of. Besides, I'm a married woman," she said, showing him the plain gold band that Mickey gave her on the Lurline, what seemed like a lifetime past. He wasn't at all her type, and she thought wryly how much easier it was to lead the straight and narrow when the temptation wasn't too great. Besides, a lot of the old Hollywood crowd came to Vegas regularly, and she wouldn't want to run into any of them, now that she was down on her luck.

She went to bed early that evening, tired out from the heat. Just after midnight, someone hammered on the door. She threw on her dressing gown and rushed out of the bedroom to see who it was, annoyed that someone might wake up the kids. When she switched on the porch light and opened the inner door, she saw Ned standing there.

253

"Thought you might have changed your mind. A pretty little gal like you should be out seeing the nightlights," he said. He was flushed and looked none too steady on his feet.

Angry that she had been awakened by such a jerk, she tried not to loose her temper, keeping in mind that he was a paying tenant. "No, 'fraid not," she said, "and I'll appreciate it if you don't wake up the kids." It was amazing to see how some types of men jumped to conclusions just as soon as they saw a woman was on her own. As if she needed attention from the likes of him!

He tried to persuade her, his hand on the handle of the outer screen door, but finally he shrugged his shoulders and left her alone. It was the first of many such incidences, and Vivian got more and more hot under the collar. She felt dirty having to kowtow to people like that when she would rather be in a position to send them packing with a few choice phrases, or even call the cops. More than once, men tried the handle of the door that led into her bedroom, and she lay in bed, her heart pounding with fear that it might be forced open.

Jane thought she was making a mountain out of a molehill. "A clever young lady like you should be able to handle a situation like that with no feelings hurt," she said. "I've always been able to steer such critters and still collect the rent," she said smugly.

The point was that Vivian didn't want to be in a position to have to associate with men who thought she was an item. Those years on her own at such a young age had made her wary of contact with the seamy side of life. There was too big a risk of getting caught up in it, even if you behaved like a lady. If this was what Las Vegas had to offer for her, she didn't want any part of it.

Her thoughts took her back to those early years of struggling to get free of poverty, when the family came to California and hit bad times. She thought of the freedom she felt during the days when she was making good money in Hollywood, and the feeling of control it gave her. If only she could be that independent now and give the children the life she dreamed about with Mickey.

It wasn't just Jane's business that was getting Vivian down. She was good and disillusioned with Las Vegas. Nearly a month had passed, and the daytime temperatures had climbed steadily. By now, the children had to spend the better part of the day in the house. They looked pale, and they weren't getting the fresh vegetables and fruit that she felt was so vital for their health. For that matter, she wasn't feeling so hot herself.

She tossed and turned at night, fretting about their future. She didn't want to stay on here, but she knew she had to be dependent on Jane for the time being. After all, she couldn't just think about herself. She had to provide for Tony and Judy. Jane was in one of her good phases, and they had managed to avoid any big rows. Maybe it would be the right time to tell her she wanted to throw in the towel. Lord knows she had never been a quitter, but right now she longed for her own family. At least the kids had more fun when they were in North Hollywood.

Even though Jane was relatively reasonable these days, Vivian still couldn't feel at ease with her. She made it a habit to pop in unexpectedly and rarely failed to make a remark that could be interpreted as criticism. One morning, she came in and said right off, "Judy looks real peaked. Fussy eater, isn't she? Of course, I say kids'll eat anything if they know you won't give in to their whims."

"She eats fine usually," Vivian retorted, a bit too sharply. "To tell you the truth, Jane, I just don't think this is going to work out with the kids staying here. They never get outside during the daytime, because it's too hot, and it's not healthy for them to spend so much time indoors. It's not going to get any better until long after summer, and I don't know if I can last that long. This is just no place for small children," she said, bringing the subject back to them.

"Humph. I had to raise Mickey in a lot worse places than this, and it didn't seem to do him any harm."

Vivian refrained from commenting on that. As much as she hated it, she was pretty much at Jane's mercy for the time being. It was hell to be without means. If only Mickey hadn't gone off to the Philippines. She reminded herself that good things come from good thoughts, and she was silent, trying to distance herself from the pettiness of arguing with Jane and hope that something better was in store.

As if an answer to her prayers, Flossie blew into town. She had got a few more smile wrinkles around her green eyes since Vivian saw her last, but she still had that flaming red hair and the graceful, languid movements of a large cat. Vivian wondered how old she was. She had aged, but was not less attractive.

It was so good to see her. She was between marriages and at loose ends. Her high spirits and sharp tongue could keep Jane subdued, and she had always liked Vivian. She could immediately see that this was no sort of life for Mickey's lovely wife and his kids. When she talked with Vivian and learned how unhappy she was, she told her she thought she should go back down to her mother's and figure out some other means to get by. "I'll take over here at the courts. That way Jane won't have any argument about needing your help, and I think it would be a lot of fun to hang around here for a few months. Hell, the climate won't bother an old desert rat like me."

When Flossie got an idea, she wasted no time in taking action. "If you don't like something, change it, and if you can't change it, don't complain," she liked to say, but usually she made changes. That very same day she broached the subject of Vivian's future with Jane. When presented with Flossie's plan, Jane was robbed of any logical objections. Flossie could manipulate Jane like no one else could. With her kind heart, she could accept Jane's faults and still love her, thereby earning her trust.

"Let her go, Jane. Poor little thing – She's had a helluva a time of it, and I don't think she has ever regained her strength since she had cancer. Can't help but wonder if she's living on borrowed time. You're doing real well financially. Without Mickey around, Vivian could stick to a budget if you kept her alive with a little money each month. Just for a while. Just 'til you see what happens. Look how many times you bankrolled Mickey, and usually that was just to get him out of a scrape that was of his own making."

She ended up not only making it possible for Vivian to pack up and leave with the kids, but with Jane promising to help them out. Flossie moved right into the bungalow, and she had the time of her life that hot summer. The men who came to rent the back rooms loved having a laugh with her, and there was competition over the rentals whenever a regular customer was in town.

Vivian crept back to Donda's like a wounded doe, and gratefully let her mother take charge of the children. Donda put her in the front bedroom where she could catch up on sleep, and Tony and Judy happily fell into step in a household they knew as a second home. Everything was as it always had been, with a pot of coffee staying warm on the back of Donda's stove and all the aunts and uncles coming by daily.

The weeks in Las Vegas had taken their toll, and Vivian was thin and complained about pains in the region of her kidney. Doc promised he would get her back to her old self, and he told her not to worry about money if Jane's promises didn't pan out.

"But I just can't let my family be burdened by me, Doc. You are all so good, but somehow I've got to manage on my own. I don't feel too guilty about taking money from Jane, because you know how she is...Somehow she will get back what's coming to her. Besides, she lived on Mickey's earnings a number of years when he was doing well in Hollywood. But my folks have had to work so hard for what they get." She looked discouraged just thinking about the predicament she had landed in.

However, it turned out that Jane was as good as her word. She drove down from Vegas on her way to Dunaway's a week later to discuss Vivian's economy. As usual, she came by Donda's unannounced, bringing with her that atmosphere of tension, her smiles contradictory to the coldness of her eyes, nothing she said to be accepted purely at face value.

Her initiative was due to a decision she made right after Vivian left Vegas. In order to think things out Jane drove out to Pete's. She had to make a plan, and she didn't want Flossie to confuse her. While Pete kept busy around the place, she could ride for miles, alone with his quarter horse and her own thoughts in the pristine purity of the desert.

She couldn't be sure that Mickey was alive, and she was convinced that Vivian wouldn't live very long. She knew enough about breast cancer treated with radiation to figure out the odds for a person surviving any length of time afterwards. If Tony and Judy were orphaned, she didn't want them falling into the clutches of Donda and her family. Those people were all right, she guessed, but, except for Doc and Poli, they didn't have anything like her drive or brains. Why, she could carve out a future for Mickey's son like nothing Donda would be able to imagine. He needed the best schools and the awareness that he was someone special. Besides, Donda had her big brood. Jane's hopes for the futures could only depend on Mickey's kids. She had thought the problem would solve itself if Vivian and the children were on her turf, in Las Vegas, but that plan had been foiled when Vivian left.

She prided herself on not giving up easily, and after a day of tumbling the matter over in her mind, the solution came to her clear as a bell, and she chuckled out loud with satisfaction, amazed that she hadn't seen it right away. If she could prove she was Vivian's and the children's sole support it would be darned hard for anyone to argue against her becoming the guardian of the children in the event they were left alone. She could make sure that Vivian would agree to a set plan, and that it would be easy to document having taken care of all their expenses. She knew and understood Vivian's pride, and that she hated to rely on her family. It should be easy to talk her into such a scheme.

When she got back to town, she didn't mention any of this to Flossie. She knew from experience that it was best to keep tight about one's motives. But Flossie knew her sister well and wondered what had put her in such a good mood. "I suppose I'll find out sometime or 'nother. She never can resist crowing when something works out the way she wants it," she thought, smiling with affection for her conniving sister.

That's why Jane arrived at Donda's oozing with charm. She thought it would be best if she could get Vivian alone to talk with her and invited her out to lunch. "It'd do you good to get out of the house for a breather without the kids," she said.

Donda promptly agreed. "You go right ahead, honey. Tony and Judy can help me shelling those peas we bought from Mr. Beyers when he came by with his truck, and maybe you would like to stay for dinner, Jane."

"Thanks just the same, Donda, but I have to head on down to Hawthorne. Jordan is expecting me," Jane said, with a chill in her voice.

They drove to Hollywood to eat at The Brown Derby. The black Packard moved smoothly through light traffic. It was a sunny day and the car smelled pleasantly of warm leather. "Too bad I can't just relax and enjoy her good moods," Vivian thought, "instead of always wondering what she's up to."

The restaurant was crowded with the Hollywood crowd, and Vivian recalled bygone days, when she liked to come here with Elsie and friends from the studio. The headwaiter led them to a booth at the back of the restaurant. Across the room, Vivian spotted June Allyson, and they waved at each other. Vivian and Jane found themselves a table, and Vivian excused herself to go over and say hello to June. She had been a chorus girl when Vivian was an extra, and she seemed to have made it to the big time without getting spoiled by her success. They promised each other to get in touch, and Vivian rejoined Jane.

Jane found herself enjoying being seen with her attractive daughter-in-law. It wasn't the first time that she was aware of that special quality Mickey had fallen for. She waited until they had almost finished their lunch before she told Vivian what was on her mind.

"I've given a lot of thought to your predicament, Vi, and I've come up with a plan to help you out," she drawled with her Southern accent. "It's no sort of life for you to stay with your mother and not have a place of your own."

From the large black leather handbag she always had with her, she pulled out a sheet of paper and handed it to Vivian. "I've typed up a budget, and what I'm going to offer you is covered on this piece of paper. I want you to find a nice little place near a good school for Tony. As you can see, I'll provide you with a monthly income, and I've broken it down for food, medical expenses, and clothing. I think you should be able to get along nicely on it as long as you need to."

Vivian was overwhelmed. Maybe Jane really had changed. This was almost too good to be true. "I don't know what to say, Jane. This is so generous. I just hope I'll soon be able to make do on my own and be able to pay you back, but right now this comes like a blessing from heaven. Really, though, I can stay on at Mom's as long as I like. That would save money, and with her taking care of the kids, it shouldn't be hard for me to find a job."

There was a flicker of steel in Jane's eyes. With a barely detectable change in the tone of her voice, she said, "I hope you won't take it wrong, honey, if I say this plan depends on you finding a place of your own. You know how I feel about your family. They're good people, but they're not my kind of people. Either I help you, or you'll have to let them help you. If I come to visit you, I don't want to have to see the rest of the family. I guess it's growing up on the desert, but I never have liked crowds." I hope I haven't overplayed my hand, she thought, as she watched Vivian for signs of how she was taking it.

Vivian weighed her options quickly. The old biddy had her over a barrel, but with her in Las Vegas and me down here with my folks close by, how could it make any difference? I'll find something cheap not far from Donda's and take one day at a time. Anyway, as much as she loved her mother, she hated living out of a suitcase, and, with the clutter that was already in Donda's house, there wasn't room to settle in.

"I understand that, Jane," she said, after a pause. "I'll look for a place near St. Charles. I think Tony would get the best schooling at a parochial school, don't you?"

Pleased that their little conversation had gone so well, Jane purred that as soon as Vivian found a place there would be a check in the mail. "Meanwhile, here is something to get you started," and she handed Vivian an envelope with a check for a couple of hundred dollars in it.

Vivian hated to be in debt to someone she had such a difficult time getting along with, but she gratefully accepted the money and hoped fervently that she wouldn't need help for long. Meanwhile, she told herself, I'll have to make more of an effort to understand Jane. She must be good deep down inside when she will help us out like this, she thought. She wished she could be natural with Jane, but whenever they were together, Vivian had the feeling that each word she said was like a tennis ball that once volleyed would be hit back from a different angle. She had to be alert at all times. She didn't know anyone else like that, but maybe that was because she would naturally avoid a person like Jane under normal circumstances.

The very next week she found a duplex on Moorpark Street, right across from St. Charles Cathedral and the Catholic school. It was clean and practical, and a respectable address, but it wasn't the sort of place she would have chosen under normal circumstances. Instead of a garden there was an immaculately trimmed lawn, and a low hedge. She wished she could have stayed on with her mother and saved up the money for a start in a small business. Marcia and Eddie had a gift shop and were doing nicely with it. For now, however, she would have to do as Jane said and try to save some money out of the budget.

Men of all ages and walks of life were getting drafted, and many big homes in Hollywood were suddenly sold as wives returned to their families to wait out the war. Vivian went to house sales and was able to buy some lovely things to start a new home, but she soon discovered that her heart wasn't in it. California no longer seemed like home, and everything was a pale substitute for life in the islands. Life with Mickey, hectic though it was, had taken her into another dimension, and nothing in the California scene had the same appeal.

When she had left for the islands with Mickey, Marcia and Eddie bought her little place in Laurel Canyon, and over the years they had tamed their bit of the hillside. Eddie made terraces, and they planted fruit trees among beds of flowers. If only she had a place like that, her days would take on meaning. She had loved struggling with the garden, but she also remembered so clearly the fascination of watching the endless parade of wonders provided each day by nature itself.

As the weeks passed, the small place on Moorpark began to feel like a prison. Jane's help boxed her in, and the war was depriving her from enjoying what should have been her best years. There was restlessness in her very soul, and she toyed with the idea of buying an old jalopy, tying a mattress on the roof, and roaming the countryside with the kids, camping out and living like gypsies. Mickey would love such an idea, but when she mentioned her plan to Donda, she could hear that it sounded too crazy. The war had put people's nerves on edge, and even her own mother felt that it was a time for caution.

Despite the distance from Las Vegas, Jane continued her practice of dropping in on her at odd hours, always out of a clear blue sky. "I think she figures she'll catch me with a man," she complained to Donda.

Donda worried about her. Of all her children, Vivian was most like herself, and she knew instinctively what was bothering her. Her meeting Mickey and all her adventures since then had expanded her horizon, put her in another league – where life was a treasure trove of surprises. Now she was paying the price for having had to leave that bewitching world. Nothing in the tame surroundings of North Hollywood had the flavor of the islands. She understood, better than most, Vivian's longings for a life outside the ordinary. It was just like some birds leave the flock and fly higher than the rest.

Months turned into years, and still there was no word from Mickey. Vivian tried tracing him through the Red Cross, but no one seemed to know where he was. Obviously, she couldn't remain suspended in limbo; she needed to contemplate a future without Mickey and make plans that could replace the visions they had had together.

If only Vivian had been plain, she could have resigned herself to an ordinary fate, but repeatedly her beauty inspired someone to lay out some glorious plan for her future. Donda knew that there had been no shortage of men who wanted to step in and take care of Vivian, now that she was alone. Beautiful women make men spin dreams, and dreams stir the soul. So far, no one had caught her interest, and neither did she feel free of Mickey as long as she hoped he was alive. Donda had found that one consolation for having grown older was being resigned to life in the present. She was content to live a quiet life in the Valley and no longer longed for a mansion up in the Hollywood Hills. But it's taken me a long time and quite a few hard knocks to reach that state, she thought wryly.

On her own with the children, Vivian had a lot of time for thinking things out in depth. She lay awake at night, randomly turning ideas over in her mind while the children slept peacefully. She still believed that Mickey would be coming home, but she was sorry for each day he was out of Tony's life. More than ever she realized how important a dad is for his son, and she tried to imagine how it had been for Mickey to grow up without a father.

Vivian's concept of Jane's role in Mickey's life took on a whole new dimension now that she could picture their years alone together. Jane had given Mickey such a long leash, but domineering as she is, she never left him with the final responsibility for his actions. When the chips were down, she stepped in and took command, and Mickey, being a creature of comfort, let her do it.

With time to think, it dawned on Vivian that part of Mickey's attraction to her might have been an instinct that she would fill his mother's shoes. Didn't Ma always say that if you want to understand the way a man treats his wife, you ought to know his mother? She could easily see Jane's faults, but there was no denying that she was devoted to her son.

Vivian pondered her relation with Mickey and wondered whether her old plan of being the one to provide a safety net for the family would result in her stepping into the role Jane played. Then Mickey would just chase around and have fun more than ever! It dawned on her that she was going to have to watch out when Mickey did return. He certainly had made it clear by going to the islands and then to the Philippines that he didn't mind putting distance between himself and his mother. If I treat him like she did, I might just ruin his chance to change, and maybe Tony's, too. Worse yet, I'll end up a bitter old woman, just like she is. Gosh, Mickey has so much talent that there is no reason in the world he shouldn't be able to succeed without a woman's help, she said to herself.

Judy whimpered in her sleep, and Vivian listened to hear whether she was going to wake up. All along the street people were sleeping in their small duplexes, nice people who seemed satisfied with living in this quiet neighborhood. She knew she should be grateful to be safe and have Jane provide for her, but she had a desperate feeling that a space in time was disappearing without her being able to relish it. She would soon be forty. She felt blessed that she knew all that the world had to offer and felt cursed with the feeling that there was so little time to grasp it. If only her babies had come when she was young, like Bobbie's had, perhaps the fleeting movement of time would take on a different meaning. However, she couldn't change what has been. Tony and Judy are still too young for me to put my desires first, she thought.

Carbanatuan

On the other side of the world, Mickey's nights were just as full of anguish, but of a different nature. He would have given anything for the comfort of a soft bed. Each day at O'Donnell whittled away the veneer that separates man from beast. Now they had been informed that they were to be moved to a new camp. Already at that point, so many Filipinos had perished at O'Donnell that it was supposed the Japanese wanted to get the Americans out of there in order that they wouldn't be witnesses to the extreme cruelty dealt out to the native population.

Mickey was alarmed. He had succeeded in avoiding many of the pitfalls of Camp O'Donnell, and he benefited from all the contacts he had with the Filipino prisoners. Whenever he could wangle it, he got assigned to a duty that took him to Manila, and there he had established useful contacts with the black market. This move to Cabanatuan presented a whole new ball game.

As for the rest of the men, whenever anything was about to happen, rumors were rampant. As soon as they realized they were being moved, those of them who were still in any shape that could enable them to be optimistic began to imagine the many ways in which the new camp would be better.

"Hell, yes," Harry, the pilot who was Mickey's inseparable companion, assured them. "You know what Cabanatuan was? It's a military base, right in the middle of rice paddies. We're bound to have more to eat there, and there's got to be water."

They were soon to discover their mistake. The long march to this new prison left Mickey's already emaciated group exhausted, and the quarters they found at the end of the road were even more discouraging than they could have imagined in their wildest dreams. The stench hit them before the camp was in sight. There was a black cloud of flies, millions of them, attracted by the overwhelming reek of the latrines, the sickening sweet smell of prisoners who were mortally ill, and of the burial ground.

Cabanatuan consisted of three camps with several miles separating them. 6,066 men who were captured at Corregidor had been sent to Camp No. 3., along with the sick and wounded who had come direct from field hospitals on Bataan. The remaining 1,500 from Corregidor were put in Camp No. 2, but due to a lack of water, they were soon transferred to Camp No. 1.

Mickey's batch was put in Camp No. 1. The men who were there from Corregidor had neither been on Bataan, the Death March, nor Camp O'Donnell. In the tunnels of Corregidor, they had avoided malaria, they had sufficient food, and there was medical care. They were, by comparison, in much better shape than the new batch of arrivals, and when they saw these walking skeletons, they were appalled. They couldn't recognize those of them they had known before the invasion, and they didn't feel like welcoming the new prisoners. More men meant less food and less water, and clearly most of the men coming in were riddled with disease. It was terrifying to see the state into which a man could be reduced if he was starved long enough, and seeing them was like getting an unsolicited glimpse of the future. Because of the weakened condition of the new arrivals, the death rate rose sharply as soon as the prison population swelled with their numbers.

That first week was the hardest to get through. It was easier to contend with the dreadful conditions once their disappointment had turned to inertia. In the beginning, some tried to be brave, but life in Cabanatuan was a form of torment that was to rob them of that last vestige of manliness. Those whose lives might have been snuffed out for spitting in the face of their captors had been changed into creatures too starved and weak to think of anything beyond the moment of immediate survival. Wracked by jungle fevers and beriberi, tormented by body lice and flies, and plagued by skin ailments brought on by the filth they were forced to live with, the numb weariness from chronic hunger sapped their courage, and the constant beatings taught them to do anything humanly possible to avoid the club which every guard who didn't have a rifle carried with him. They had hit rock bottom, and that saved most of them from rash displays of bravery.

Prisoners would never be able to erase the visual impact of Cabanatuan. Nothing in the terrain softened the harsh presence of its barbed wire fences and squat buildings. Surrounded by flat fields, it offered no place to hide if one were to escape. Furthermore, if one man should escape, he knew that his group would be shot. Their only hope lay in staying together, waiting for the day American troops would come and rescue them.

They were housed in nipa-thatched, swali-sided barracks, sixty-foot long, intended to accommodate forty small Filipino soldiers. One hundred and twenty men were put in each building, sleeping in two layers on wooden slats. Harry's information that the area had once been a rice paddy was true, but that meant that the makeshift barracks rested on swampy ground. The dampness, with its resulting mosquitoes, would have made the place unhealthy during the best of times, but with so many men crowded into these disease-infested confines, death was rampant.

The first month it rained every day. Within the first two months, two thousand men died, and the soggy soil made burial of the dead just as useless a practice as it had been at O'Donnell.

No sooner were the bodies buried than rains would drench the shallow graves, exposing the decomposing remains.

Just as had been the case at Camp O'Donnel, drinking water was scarce, but there was plenty of ground water and rain. Lying on the wooden slats of the barrack floors in Cabanatuan, drenched in stinking ground water, with rain seeping through the crude roof, escape by death beckoned as a rewarding blessing. Again, Mickey remembered what his grandmother had recounted from Cherokee experience – That those who stayed alive were often driven by a hatred so great that they didn't want to give the enemy the satisfaction of doing them in. He saw that this seemed to work for some of his buddies, but hatred wasn't in his nature. It was his nature to try to understand things, adjust to them, and try to outsmart the enemy – No easy task when the enemy's behavior was so erratic. Like so many others, he perfected the practice of withdrawing into a make-believe world of his own, a place where he could spend hours imagining the makings of a feast or the details of his dream home.

While the prisoners lived in constant dampness during the rainy season, during the dry season the area was swept with dust that was saturated with traces of all the diseases that flourished in the camp. Most of the men had already contracted malaria and dengue fever during the siege of Bataan, and now they had to suffer through the recurrent attacks that invariably follow. There was no confusion as to which attack was afoot: Malaria brought severe chills, followed by vomiting, high fever and paralyzing headaches. With bouts of dengue fever, they escaped the dreaded chills of malaria, but every joint in their bodies ached to the extent that no position in which they lay was bearable more than a few minutes at a time. Dengue fever was rarely fatal, but a man longed for death during an attack of dengue. Mickey suffered from both diseases.

The third greatest menace was gangrene. In the tropics, it could turn a minor cut into a fatal wound within hours. Except for someone like Lewin, usually no medicine was available, and the best thing to do was to slash the infected flesh with a knife, let air get to the injury, and hope. Another alternative was to allow maggots to enter the wound. Left alone, they devoured the rotten flesh, hopefully before an infection spread to other parts of the body.

Hundreds, if not thousands, were saved by the brave acts of a network of civilians who smuggled goods into the camp, but the pool of misery was so deep, that a life-saving drug represented a moral dilemma for the doctor who could administer it.

The smell of Cabanatuan was overwhelming. The swampy ground made it impossible to have privies. Huge pits had been dug to use as latrines, and the men had to walk out on narrow planks breaching these open pits when they needed to relieve themselves. In their weakened conditions, this in itself presented a perilous prospect. Furthermore, they were divided into groups of ten. If anyone was missing at roll call, the remaining men in the group were shot without ceremony. During the first week, Mickey's group was actually lined up for execution, when the one missing man was found dead at the bottom of the pit that served as a latrine.

By late October that first year of captivity, nearly 2,740 men had died in Cabanatuan's Camp No. 1, the camp where Mickey was, while only sixty-one men had died in Camp No. 3. Eventually, the Japanese decided to merge the two camps, and also these men who had come from Camp No. 3 were horrified when they encountered the prisoners who had lived through the battles of Bataan and the Death March.

At some point, the men were finally officially registered as 'horyos,' prisoners of war, and given a number that they were ordered to remember, in Japanese. At the risk of death, they were never to forget that number. They were never called by anything else, and it brought home to them, more than anything else, the hopelessness of their situation.

Mickey had succeeded in hiding his diary, but it served mostly as a talisman. He rarely had the opportunity to record anything in it. He had learned to stop fretting about the passage of time and was too pre-occupied with surviving here and now to be concerned with the life he was missing out on in the outside world. It was a state of equilibrium that was vital to retaining one's sanity. Those who thought beyond the present day were more apt to go mad. Being older than the average prisoner of war, Mickey also had the advantage of having seen how much a human can endure and of knowing that the body repairs itself to a remarkable degree, once it is fed again.

The men settled into a routine as bizarre as their surroundings. Tempers flared over minor incidents. Prisoners guarded with their life their meager possessions, and those who were psychologically stronger formed cliques that sometimes determined whether another man would live or die. Out of this stockpile of humanity emerged certain individuals who epitomized the extremes of human nature. The struggle for survival brought out the worst in some men. Others, when stripped of all the ornaments bestowed upon us by society, emerged as nobility in the raw.

Mickey learned that you could not always predict who would be selfish and who would be brave and generous. When incidents arise, a man acts on impulse. Later, those who survived would agonize over actions they regretted and puzzle about other times when they rose to the occasion and acted nobly.

One officer who had been among the bravest and most effective during the Bataan siege fell ill at Cabanatuan. His men were devoted to him and did everything to try to help him through a bad time. For no reason they could fathom, he quickly gave up the ghost, while others who were too far gone to bother with could suddenly get past the crisis and pull through.

Some men could be beaten to a pulp, thrown into a sweat box in full sun, and left without food or water for days on end and survive, while others who suffered no such fate rolled over, faced the wall and gave up the ghost. It was as if an invisible force held certain individuals up, and there seemed to be no specific pattern whereby one could predict who those individuals would be.

Beatings came like tropical rain ... Often without warning and sometimes in torrents. A guard could beat a man senseless for having the wrong facial expression. Like vicious children, Japanese officers would sometimes walk around the camp, bandy-legged, dressed only in underpants and black combat boots, dragging a sword in the dirt, looking for someone to torment. They would stand shamelessly on a box or make a taller American stand in a trench in order to beat him in the face. In their world, an assignment to a prison camp was the lowest rung on a ladder of ancient design. As always is the case, those who lack self-esteem have no real respect for anyone else.

Those guards who didn't carry a sword had rifles or clubs. The clubs were the thickness of a two-by-four, shaped like a saber. The prisoners dreaded a rifle butt, because it usually hit them in the kidneys, and that could prove fatal. Most of the men knew from experience that if you passed out it was best to be conscious long enough to fall on your face; otherwise, your groin would be stomped to a pulp.

Mickey got so used to beatings that he stopped getting madder than hell and resigned himself to them. The worst immediate effect came from the beatings they administered to the back of his legs. That made walking so painful that it was hard to do the work they demanded. Beatings on the back were better because one could arch one's back and let the muscles take some of the impact; however, they always included a few blows to the head, and that could have long-term bad effects. Like so many others, he couldn't figure out what was best: To stand up to the beating and hope to earn the respect of the guard, or to fall down straight off and hope he would consider you too abject to bother with.

Longer punishments were diabolical and at random. Without explanation, they would sometimes grab a man and put him in a cage too small for him to sit up or to lie down. Or they would force him to stand in full sun, without a hat and with his eyes open, his head forced backwards, causing him to look up for hours. They liked to make a man hold a heavy rock over his head until he collapsed or to make him kneel on sharp stones, barelegged and with a log behind his knees to cut off blood circulation. Sometimes they wrapped barbed wire around a man, trussed him up so tightly he couldn't move and amused themselves by offering him a drag on their cigarettes and then shoving them, lit, down his throat or up his nose. One favorite torture method was shoving a garden hose down a person's throat and turning on the water. They filled the victim with water and then jumped on him, laughing when his innards burst.

While at Cabanatuan, Mickey became friends with a Dutch jeweler whose cosmopolitan background fascinated him. Sebastian spoke an impressive number of languages. He told Mickey modestly that learning foreign languages was just part of his Dutch heritage, a necessity for people from a small seafaring nation, but Mickey couldn't help but be impressed when he learned that Sebastian not only spoke his native language and English, he was also fluent in German, French, Italian, Spanish, Swedish and some of the dialects of the Dutch East Indies.

From the day of his capture, Sebastian made an effort to pick up words and phrases and try to learn as much Japanese as possible. He and Mickey agreed that without a language to communicate with the enemy, one was at a tremendous disadvantage.

During the first few months at Cabanatuan, before everyone became too apathetic and starved to muster any intellectual energy, there were classes of all sorts, organized by the prisoners, including language courses. Both men enrolled in the Japanese language class and got a start in the basics of the language. Mickey had a flair for mimicry, and he practiced whatever words he heard repeated often.

He came close to getting himself killed the first time he tried out his newfound skill. A buddy of his keeled over while waiting for a turn at the water faucet, and Mickey wanted to call a guard to get some help. He had heard the guards using the word 'hayako' when they called on each other to come running, and he called out "Hayako!" to the nearest guard.

The guard came running but promptly kicked Mickey in his shin with his hob-nailed boot and clouted him over the head with his club. Mickey buckled over in pain and fell to the ground where the guard kicked him repeatedly. Mickey was left with an injury that was slow in healing, but he never forgot the lesson – The word 'hayako' was not something you said to your superiors.

He dragged himself back to his barracks and could just manage to mutter to Sebastian, "Son of a gun – They kicked the bejeezus out of me," before he collapsed.

The blow to his head had been the most painful, but the broken skin where he was kicked on his shin was more serious. On a starvation diet, any sore is slow to heal, and it was almost impossible to keep it clean. Mickey hobbled around until Ted Lewin noticed he was having trouble and miraculously produced a healing salve, with a cryptic reminder that Mickey 'owed him one.'

Despite this set-back, Mickey and Sebastian made progress in learning Japanese, and before long, they were sometimes able to intervene for other prisoners and smooth out conflicts before they were settled with blows, not to mention what an aid it was in making black market deals.

Many prisoners hated the Japanese so profoundly that they refused to even try to learn the language, but for Mickey it was a revelation when he saw what a difference it made. Verbal communication gave the guards a feeling that Mickey and Sebastian were showing respect. Steeped as the Japanese were in a feeling of racial superiority, it was in their books a sign of intelligence and the desired humility when someone learned their language.

Sebastian and Mickey had another thing in common. They were both alert to what things were considered edible by the Filipinos and the Japanese. Unlike the British who had lived in the Far East much like they would have lived back in the British Isles, the Dutch adapted to the tropics and learned to eat exotic plants and to make use of native cures. Some men starved to death out of sheer stubbornness and unwillingness to try some of the more indelicate sources of protein. Those who survived the first year were men who didn't object to a maggot or boll weevil in his rice, and by the end of the war, there were men who would eat anything, even machine oil, in hopes that they could satisfy a craving for flavor.

Mickey also benefited from the friendship he had established while he was in Manila, with a man named Kirkpatrick. Kirkpatrick had a pipeline to the funds he had to leave in Manila, and he helped Mickey over some rough spots by lending him money. What he didn't have was Mickey's way with people, and Mickey was able to return his favors by keeping in line the motley crew who had volunteered to protect Kirkpatrick and his assets.

There were four 'bodyguards,' each one strong enough to wipe the floor with someone of Kirkpatrick's stature, and they kept upping the price for watching out for him. They liked Mickey, though, and he could get through to them. He convinced them that it would be self-destructive to take advantage of Kirkpatrick, comparing that to killing the goose that laid golden eggs.

For one thing, Mickey had faith that the war would soon be over, and he told them that Kirkpatrick could put them on easy street when they got back to Manila.

"Christ, you should see the spread this guy owns in Baguio," he told them. "When this shit is all behind us, we will be living high on the hog if we can keep this character alive. What you can wheedle out of him in the meantime is peanuts."

With Kirkpatrick's money and contacts on the outside, they were able to sweeten life for themselves within the limits there were, and Mickey was also able to help out some of the poor GIs who didn't have any means of their own. It was easy to spot the ones who were ready to die, and there were those on the brink of death whose eyes still burned with the will to live. A portion of quinine or a hen's egg could be enough to tip the scales, and then there was always the hope that they could hang in a bit longer and make it all the way.

Mickey and some of the officers cooked up an insurance scheme, whereby Kirkpatrick put up $25,000, issuing IOU's to men who needed to borrow from it. The plan was that whoever survived should repay the money, and it would be redistributed to the families of those who didn't survive. It was an attempt to inject a form of banking and life insurance into a camp where even a pencil to write with was a precious possession.

Because he was accepted by the officers and had access to the black market, Mickey was able to avoid some of the hard, physical work the enlisted men had to perform. One very unfortunate aspect of the surrender on Bataan was that units were scattered, and the natural bond between officers and enlisted men of the same unit no longer existed. These useless officers ended up together at O'Donnell, and they continued living like pashas at Cabanatuan. A starvation diet lasts better when a guy could save energy by sitting on the shady side of the barracks, chewing the fat with his cronies.

At Cabanatuan, there were something like three thousand officers, one to every five men, and they enjoyed two crucial privileges: They got their rice ration without having to work, and, after a few months at Cabanatuan, the Japanese bowed to the Geneva Convention in one respect and allotted the prisoners a small amount of pay. The officers got 220 pesos a month for a lieutenant colonel, down to 85 for a first lieutenant. A working private only got 3 pesos, or nothing, if he was too sick to work.

Clearly, an officer's chances for survival were multiple compared to an enlisted man's. The officers, with few exceptions, took this as being a God-given right, but for the poor Joe at the bottom of the pile, it was a lesson in how unfair things were. Mickey didn't fall into any official category and received no pay; however, he had the huge advantage of being a wheeler-dealer by nature with no qualms about using the black market or stealing – termed 'liberating' by the prisoners. Whenever he could he would finagle his way into getting on the roster for a detail going to Manila, and that wasn't infrequent when the Japanese discovered that the American prisoners were much more adept at keeping trucks running than they were and were obliged to use them as drivers for various details. For Mickey, being chosen for such a detail was double lucky. Not only could he eye new opportunities to get something he or his friends needed, he could also break the monotony of being in camp.

Because of his 'non-status', he could circulate and stay friends with people he had met during those heady days in Manila. He mingled freely with officers and ordinary GIs who felt better for having an opportunity to unload some of their gripes. In that way he benefited from the good will of many different 'tribes'. Mickey's nomadic youth made it easy to communicate with guys from many different backgrounds, and he often knew enough about their hometowns to cheer them up by talking with them about what they missed.

Just as he had always done, no matter what the circumstances, he read people like a producer would read scripts, with an open mind as to their potentials. He had no pre-conceived notion of who was worth getting to know, and this unprejudiced friendliness was medicine to men from many different barracks and a tonic to an extrovert like Mickey. He tried to keep an eye on those enlisted men he had been with and liked during the siege of Bataan or on the Death March who could use a helping hand now. He thrived on this social contact, and when he saw that he could cheer up a person who was at the end of his rope, he felt like he was serving a purpose. A sense of purpose was enough to keep a man going one day at a time, and a sense of humor was the best antidote to madness.

Another person who brought comfort to men of all ranks was a Catholic priest Mickey liked especially well. He was a Jesuit, and he had so much knowledge stored in his head that to hear him talk was as entertaining as perusing an encyclopedia. When this war is over, Mickey thought, I'm going to make sure my kids learn as much as possible. When all else is lost, you still have what's in your head.

Unlike the men of the cloth Mickey had encountered during his youth, Father Joseph seemed to respect the individual's choice of belief. He and Mickey only spoke of Christianity on one occasion. A chicken had been stolen, and the guards picked at random a kid from California to set an example. He was an especially unfortunate choice, for he was well liked by the other prisoners, and they all agreed he was too promising a youth to be wasted in a war.

The Japanese tied him to a stake, bamboo splints were shoved up under his fingernails, and two guards took turns beating him to a pulp. He was left there all day, fully exposed to the sizzling tropical sun. Guards passed by at random, adding a few blows. No one could tell how long the Japanese would continue to torment him. It seemed to be a way they had of proving they were tough, and some of them had a bigger chip on their shoulders than others. Throughout that long day, every man in the camp felt the agony of this wanton torture.

When finally he was cut down, the other prisoners were allowed to carry him inside. He was still alive, but they could see it was only a matter of time. The soldier was a Catholic, and someone went to get the priest. Father Joseph came quickly to give the young man the last rites. Mickey watched from the sidelines, overcome by the thought that someone who was only a boy – such a perfect specimen – should be leaving this life without having had a real taste of it.

Father Joseph finished the ritual just before the soldier expired. As the priest stepped aside to let the others take over, he saw the anguish on Mickey's face. He thought he could comfort Mickey, and he put a hand on his shoulder, saying, "Don't feel sad, Mickey. The boy had faith. He died at peace with the world and knew there is a better life after this."

To Mickey, the concept of heaven had never held any appeal. He had a lively imagination, but he never had been able to imagine a spiritual world that could hold a candle to the pleasures of the physical world he knew. How could Heaven take the place of the feeling that came with making love or all the other sources of joy that poor kid never would try? Mickey wanted to get out of this hole and feel the exquisite sensation of a warm bath and wrap his arms around Vivian. He wanted to hear great music and taste a luau pig.

"I hate to say this, Father Joseph, but I can't imagine a heaven that could be better than the life we have right here on Earth. This planet is Paradise, if you ask me, and those S.O.B.s just deprived that poor kid of a chance to find out what pleasures there are in this world," he said, angrily.

Father Joseph nodded. He liked Mickey and couldn't find fault with a man who was grateful for God's gifts. Besides, this war was enough to make even a firm believer have doubts. Still, the look he had seen on that boy's face just before he took his last breath renewed his own faith that there is a vision worth seeing when this life is snuffed out. Somehow these past months with their proximity to death had served to strengthen the priest's faith, rather than weaken it.

"I understand what you're saying, Mickey. This is something each man has to work out for himself. My personal problem is to try not to dwell too much on thinking about the punishment I hope God will deal out to these bastards when their turn comes."

Mickey smiled, pleased to hear Father Joseph speak like any other normal guy.

Incidents like the young man's torture were more common in the beginning. Once the guards felt they had established a tone of respect, camp life settled down into the usual pattern of lethargy broken by the all-absorbing diversions of death and disease and routine beatings. Still, they never knew when the next shock would come.

One day, a guard neatly sliced off the head of one of the men in Mickey's barracks, a skill executed so quickly that the look of the severed head as it rolled away was one of surprise, rather than fear. The prisoner who stood alongside the victim doubled over and retched convulsively from an empty stomach, drawing attention to himself. This triggered off an attack from the second guard who knocked him to the floor with the butt of his rifle. Mercifully, he was unconscious, oblivious to the blows that came from that guard's boots.

Mickey froze, along with all the other men. With all the will power they could muster, they remained in a stance that they hoped would defuse the charged atmosphere. At any moment, things could escalate into an orgy in blood. Even at this point, when the prisoners were mere shadows of their former selves, their superior size was a provocation to the small Japanese guards. Lack of self-control on the part of the prisoners could cause a sadistic guard to go amok with the fear that always lurked under the surface.

Even minor torture could prove to be dangerous for men with such weakened constitutions, like when the guards plucked the beard of a young Irish American named Flaherty. He was popular with the other men, because nothing could break his spirit, but he spooked the guards. He couldn't avoid standing out, because he was tall and, in contrast to his thick black hair, he had a flaming red beard. One day Mickey saw that the guards had Flaherty hanging by his thumbs, and they took turns plucking hairs from his beard. Afterwards, the resulting bare spots became infected and drew flies. His lower face was soon covered with a mass of sores that wouldn't heal, and he started to look like a marked man, one of those who was not going to make it.

Infections were rampant and bizarre. Ordinary skin ailments, like what was known as athlete's foot at home, invaded the hands as well, getting under the nails, or even made a ferocious attack on the scrotum or inside the penis. There were ulcers that started on the crotch and, triggered off by a vitamin deficiency and encouraged by the lack of proper hygiene and absence of medication, moved like a prairie fire, – to the eyes, the mouth, and the tongue.

Despite regular searches to make sure the men had nothing that would alleviate their misery, Mickey still managed to hide his diary, but he was very careful not to write anything that would bring down the wrath of a guard should it be discovered. It's black cover was soft from being crammed into hiding places, and when he had an opportunity to get it out, the feeling of it in his hand gave him strength. It was a link to the real world, reassurance that he would one day write a story everyone would want to read.

Mostly, however, it contained a collection of recipes, exotic dishes dreamed up by him and his pals, as they sat on the shady side of the barracks in their threadbare shorts, crawling with lice and trying not to think about the realization that their eyesight was failing or about the sharp, stabbing pains from dry beriberi.

By now, one in every four prisoners didn't even own a pair of trousers and had to wear

Japanese-style G-strings, but thanks to his connections, Mickey had a pair of shorts with pockets, a Godsend for pilfering. Stealing was called 'liberating' by the men, and many of them had become ingenious in this skill. Along with his diary, Mickey managed to hide a steadily diminishing collection of 'treasures,' things either stolen or finagled to use to barter with if he was prevented from taking his excursions outside the camp.

At some point Mickey decided to get on the detail that worked the fields of The Farm and try to steal some fresh vegetables. The dreary diet of rice not only lacked in protein and vitamins, the men were desperate for flavor. The Farm had been established, by backbreaking work, supposedly to furnish food for the camp. However, most of the vegetables were eaten by the guards or shipped out, and the only chance for something fresh was to steal it.

Work on The Farm was grueling – a long day under the sweltering hot sun. Working with short handled hoes, the men crept along the straight rows, and no one was allowed to lift his head higher than his butt. If he did, he got clubbed. To ward off the worst effects of the sun, the men wore conical straw hats, and some of the guards made up a game like golf where they whacked a man's hat off, to see how far it would fly. If they nipped it at the top, it could sail a good distance, but if the club dipped too low, the man's head got a blow. A tall man was not likely to know his own name at the end of the day.

A stolen vegetable was a coveted prize, but the prisoners were guaranteed a broken arm if caught. If a guard wasn't looking, an adroit man could pull up a carrot, pop it into his mouth, and bite off the green top to stick it back in the ground. He then had to worry about someone spotting a wilted top in the row he had been working.

Though he suffered from malaria and dengue fever, Mickey was still feeling better than most of his comrades. He looked on the bright side, noticing that the starvation diet had permanently removed his symptoms of arthritis. "This is a helluva a way to go on a special diet," he liked to say to his buddies, "but it sure is effective."

Nothing was coming through from the Red Cross where Mickey was, and the camp doctors had less and less to work with. If they had to operate, the only anesthesia was yelling louder than the patient. What little medicine they could get had to be obtained from the black market or, sometimes, by making a deal with a guard. That they could do, for example, when a guard came to them, instead of one of their own medics, with a case of the clap.

Once the Japanese were well ensconced in the Philippines, venereal diseases became epidemic among their ranks. The guards knew that they would be in big trouble if they went to their own medics and said they had gonorrhea, for they weren't supposed to be mingling with the Filipinas. They went to the American doctors instead, and these doctors started up a production of fake pills to give to unsuspecting Japanese patients. It was a win-win situation. They got real medication in trade, and the guard who got a worthless treatment couldn't complain without revealing that he had gone to the enemy for help.

Of all the prisoners of war captured by the Japanese – the Brits, the Dutch, the Australians, and the Americans – it was the American prisoner of war who was at the greatest disadvantage. In an unspeakably cruel world, men from older nations could fall back on a form of tribalism that meant they helped each other as a group. The Americans continued to follow the motto "every man for himself", and the crimes they did to each other revealed how cruel and primitive such a code of behavior can be.

The American systems of bartering which took advantage of the weak continued and got more diabolic at Cabanatuan. Those who were in control would let a man who was starving gamble away his skimpy rations for the chance to win a smoke. Their officers did nothing to try to maintain order. In fact, many of the officers demanded privileges that they considered appropriate for their rank. It was survival not just of the fittest but also of the wiliest and the most unscrupulous.

However, there were those who survived despite all odds against them. They pulled through by bonding with one or two other men they could trust or by exercising an indefinable aspect of human will power. The very best odds were for the men who formed a group of four – enough to cover for the one who was too ill to work, and hopefully a group with at least one man who didn't smoke and could be trusted to hold the tobacco the others were to share.

Mickey's winning personality made such friendships easy, and his chances of surviving were multiple compared to the man who wasn't liked.

On the Home Front

If there was one talent the Silcoxes had, it was managing money well. Donda had taught each of her girls to be inventive and capable cooks, and they all knew how to sew. Without Mickey around, Vivian did very nicely with the money Jane gave her. She was able to save a fair amount each month and even bought Liberty bonds for Tony and Judy. The checks often came late, as if Jane didn't want her to take anything for granted, but, so far, she kept them coming.

Donda had always thought it was a shame that Mickey hadn't known his father. She once asked him whether he knew what had become of his dad, and Mickey had answered in an off-handed manner that as far as he knew he had ended up somewhere in California. "Name's Ed, Donda, he might live right down the street from you," he said teasingly, knowing how she loved trying to find someone in the phone book.

After that, she often thought about Mickey's missing father and wondered whether it would be nice one day for Tony to know his grandfather, seeing as neither she nor Jane had a husband. She started to look for Ed Owen whenever she could get her hands on a different phone book, and, much to everyone's surprise, she found him in Los Angeles.

She called him up one day and was pleased to hear that he sounded like a very nice man. He was as excited about hearing about Mickey as Donda was in learning about Mickey's father. She told Elsie the news, next time she came by, and Elsie grinned and said, "Ma! You didn't! Gosh, what will Jane say if she finds out we have established contact with her ex-husband?"

"I didn't even think about that," Donda said innocently, but with an irrepressible twinkle in her eye. "Anyway, now it's too late. He wants to see Vivian and the kids, and it might just cheer her up. He sounded so nice."

Ed Owen rang on Vivian's door the very next week. When she opened it, he stood with his hat in his hand and introduced himself. He was with his second wife, Nettie, and their son, Ray, with his wife, Trudy. They spent the rest of the afternoon visiting, and, of course, most of their talk was about Mickey.

All traces of the nimble cowboy Ed had once been were wiped out by age. He wore a three-piece suit on his tall, lanky frame, and fingered his hat much like he probably once fidgeted with a lasso. He was a kind old man who was clearly touched by the situation. He couldn't take his eyes off the children. They were his first grandchildren. He and his family spoke with an Oklahoma drawl and seemed like real farm people, even though they had been in California for a long time.

Nettie only referred to her husband as Mr. Owen, and Vivian wondered what she called him in private. Mickey's half-brother, Ray, was the diametric opposite of Mickey. He was a big guy, salt of the earth type, a motorcycle cop. His shy young wife looked like she had just gotten off the train from Oklahoma, but Vivian could see that, given a bit of coaching, she could be a real beauty.

Ed Owen took a liking to Vivian from the start and thought to himself that whatever his son was like, he must have done all right for himself to get such a pretty and ladylike wife. "And, those kids are cute as buttons, don't you think?" he said happily, as he and his family drove back to Los Angeles.

Ray's wife was quiet, thinking about how glamorous Vivian seemed. It was like she and Mickey were something out of the movie magazines. She looked sideways at Ray, wishing he were more exciting, and he caught her look and gave her a hand a squeeze and smiled. They hadn't been married long, and he felt like a pretty lucky guy, being hitched to such a cute little gal.

They all four sent signed photos of themselves to Vivian and told her how happy they were to have found the rest of their family, promising that they wouldn't lose touch.

Vivian couldn't help but get a kick out of her mother's bit of detective work, and, of course, Donda wanted all the details about their first meeting.

"Poor old guy. He claims Jane wouldn't let him have anything to do with Mickey. You know Jane will be fit to be tied, if she finds out about this," Vivian said, without being able to suppress a chuckle.

"Well, she gives you such a bad time when she gets a chance. I won't let my conscience keep me awake." Donda wanted to add that it would be fun to see Mickey's face when he comes home, but she stopped herself. A whole year had passed and she was beginning to waver in her faith that he would make it through the war.

Tony started school at St. Charles. For the time being, Vivian gave up the idea of finding a job. Without a car, it would be too complicated if she were to deliver Judy to her mother's and be home when Tony was through with school. Except for the pleasure she got from having her family nearby, her days were uniformly monotonous. Elsie was the one with whom she always had had the most fun, but she had gone to beauty college and worked full time, not having had any luck with having children.

Vivian had too much pride to contact most of her old Hollywood crowd. They had all envied her when she left for the islands, and she didn't want them to see her now that her life was in shambles. Anyway, a lot of them had done well for themselves, and she knew she wouldn't be able to keep up with their life styles.

It saddened her to see how much Tony missed his dad. He looked so serious when he talked with her about how much fun he used to have with Mickey. "If my Uncle Doc and Uncle Al had time to play with me, they would be lots of fun. I know 'cause Doc has a fun look on his face sometimes. Only he's too busy, and Uncle Al is sick. Are you sure Daddy will know where to find us when he comes back?" he worried. "Can't we go back to Hawaii? I miss swimming." His dark eyes with their thick lashes were so expressive that she sometimes thought he knew everything about their predicament and was only playing the role of a little boy.

She missed the clear, warm waters of the islands, too, and the poi, the papayas, the friendly, laid-back attitude of the Hawaiians. On Saturdays, she listened to 'Hawaii Calls' on the radio, and the plaintiff sounds of the steel guitar in Harry Owens' band always brought tears to her eyes. Mainly, she missed the feeling of being alive in every fiber of her body. Being in the islands somehow lifted her out of ordinary living and placed her in a sphere that made her aware of the joy of living at every single moment.

Vivian missed seeing the kids run around in a big yard with places to hide. The duplex had only a small green lawn out front and a few boxy shrubs. In back there was a large area covered with asphalt by the garages and an area with clotheslines. Tony and Judy were just as active as ever, but they were constantly getting into trouble. Feeling cooped up like she did, she realized that the fault lay with her lack of patience.

She complained to her mother, saying that she was mad at herself for being short-tempered. "Yesterday the kids got in a pillow fight and hit that little antique porcelain bell I found at the house-sale in Pasadena," she said.

"Oh, oh. Did it break?" Donda asked.

"Yes, it did," she said sadly. "I glued it, but it doesn't ring with a nice sound anymore. I got so darned mad at them, and I felt just terrible afterwards. You should have seen them. They were so sorry."

"And I don't think it's much fun for Tony without a dad to keep him occupied. You know what the little devil did yesterday? He climbed up on the rafters in the garage, and when Judy came peddling in on her tricycle to find him, he peed on her head." Vivian couldn't help but laugh when she told it, but she had to admit that she had spanked Tony when Judy came in bawling.

"I don't know, Ma. It seems to me that I'm in jail. Nothing good is happening here. I can't make plans with Mickey in mind, and I don't want to face years of living like I am right now, but as long as Jane is breathing down my neck, I can't make many changes. "

Since her homecoming, the kids had gone through mumps and chicken pox, and they had their share of colds. Now Tony was having trouble with his ears again. He was never ill in the islands. She thought more and more often about going back there. She felt under-the-weather, too, and she became convinced that her health would improve if only she could get back to all the tropical fruit, the warm surf, and the relaxation of living where the weather was always fair. She had saved up enough that it wasn't an impossible idea.

She knew how difficult it was to get transportation back to the islands. The passenger lines had been suspended since the war broke out, and troop ships were filled with men heading for the islands and posts beyond as part of the war effort. Harold Dillingham had always been so kind to her, and, in July of '43, she decided to write to him and ask for help and advice, telling him that she longed to come back. She kept her plans to herself, knowing that she would only worry her mother if it were known that she wanted to leave.

Mr. Dillingham's response came promptly, two full pages reconfirming the difficulties involved. Even people who owned homes in the islands were stranded on the mainland, and in order to get passage on a ship coming back, she would have to prove that she had employment. He also warned her that it was difficult to get fresh food and housing was scarce. Even maids without cooking skills were earning a hundred dollars a month, and there weren't enough maids to go around, now that so many women were working. He added that he hadn't been on the mainland since Pearl Harbor and had no means of making a comparison with conditions there. He ended his letter saying that he hoped the information he sent to her would help her to decide whether or not it was wise to come back to the islands before the war was over.

Well, their old friend, Commander Billingsley had said she could have work in Ship's Service Department if she came back. If he would write a letter, that should do the trick. She had kept contact with her many friends who were still in the islands, and Scotty, the schoolteacher on the Alawai, had said they could stay with her until they found a house. All she had to do was convince Jane that it would be a good idea. With all the drawbacks mentioned in Mr. Dillingham's letter, the islands still had a hold on her.

The next time Jane blew into town, Tony was sick in bed with an earache, and Judy was coming down with a cold. Vivian was worn to a frazzle from tending sick kids. Jane started harping that they would be better off in the desert climate, but Vivian was too quick-tempered to be badgered about not wanting to live in Las Vegas.

"They would be better off in the islands, where they belong, Jane. Mickey always thought it was the ideal place to bring up a family. They never had colds out there. I've been looking into possibilities of going back, and just hear me out before you say 'no'," she said all in one breath, not wanting to give Jane an opportunity to butt in.

Jane didn't say anything. She was too surprised that her daughter-in-law would even consider leaving the security net of her family. Encouraged by her silence, Vivian went on.

"Things are booming on Oahu. I wouldn't have any trouble finding work, if I could find a place to live and someone to take care of the children. If that didn't pan out, we could go to the big island, Hawaii. You've been urging me to find a piece of income property where the kids and I could live. Mickey and I flew out to Hawaii just before he left for the Philippines, and it was an unspoiled paradise. You know, if I could pick up some property over there, that's going to be where the first class tourists will want to go, when this war is over. If I find a suitable house, I could pay expenses by renting out rooms. Why, someday you might even want a cattle ranch in the islands...You should see the Parker Ranch. It's a dream, with cattle so sleek they look like blue ribbon winners, all of them."

Jane knew that Vivian was no fool, and she listened, mentally weighing the pros and cons. As luck would have it, she was having a rough patch with Pete lately, and she was never deaf to plans of moving on when they weren't on good terms. Maybe it would be a good idea. She had never been to the islands, but the mention of a ranch struck a chord. If what Vivian said was true, it wouldn't cost her any more money to support them over there than here in California, and if Mickey did pull through prison camp, she knew he would be happy to know there was something for him in the islands. If it turned out to be a good long-term investment, she might just want to move out there herself and forget about Pete.

Her first thought was that it was crazy to let Vivian take off with two small children when, in Jane's opinion, her life was hanging by a thread. As if Vivian could read her mind, she immediately added, "I've also saved up an emergency fund which could get us back or into a hospital if anything goes wrong. Mom and I have been picking up things at house sales, and Marcia's been selling them in her shop."

Jane couldn't help but be impressed with the latter statement; she had little respect for someone who didn't know that small business was always worth the effort if it gave a profit. She thought it over for a few days and then wrote a letter, telling Vivian to go ahead with her plans. She expressly stated that she wanted her to buy a piece of property, so that she and the children would have a home at the same time as it furnished them with a means of income.

Jane had given it a lot of thought, and she had even gone so far as to draw up a will, a copy of which she enclosed with her letter. In it, she named Mickey as her sole heir. In the event of his death, Tony and Judy were to share the inheritance, with Vivian drawing a salary of $100 a month as executor of the will, until each child reached the age of twenty-one. She enclosed an inventory of all her assets, an impressive list by those days' standards of what she had scraped together in only three years time.

Vivian wondered whether Jane wrote a will because she was experiencing a sense of mortality, or whether it was something that comes with the turf when you acquire enough property to want to have a say about things after you die. She sensed in Jane a desire to control everything within her sphere of influence. Gosh, she thought to herself, Mickey must have driven her mad at times!

Just the thought of Mickey convinced her that she was doing the right thing by going back to the islands. No matter what happened, that was where she and the children belonged.

Donda was devastated when she heard that Vivian's mind was made up, and they would be leaving. Still, she knew better than to spoil her daughter's enthusiasm by arguing with her. She would end up going anyway, and it was best that she felt she had the family's blessing. They all knew how restless she was.

Finally everything was settled. A friend of Vivian's had found a place for them to stay in Lanakai. A man who knew Mickey and Vivian from the days when they lived on Diamond Head owned it. The only drawback was that it was too far out if she were to work in Honolulu, but she was all geared to go and felt that could be sorted out after she got there.

There was a lot to organize before leaving and a lot of goodbyes. Tony and Judy were all excited about the trip, but Judy kept saying that she didn't want to leave her Donda behind. They had acquired a big Persian cat, named Smokey, and Donda used it to reassure Judy, saying the cat could come to live with her and keep her company.

It was a worried family that gathered to say goodbye the day they put Vivian and the children on a train to take the trip to San Francisco from where the ship would be sailing. Luckily, Tony and Judy's enthusiasm about the train ride created a happy diversion. It was the beginning of an adventure that would provide rich memories for a lifetime.

It was April, and the children were intrigued with how much later it got dark, as the train rolled north. Vivian sat with them in the dining car, enjoying their pleasure as they discovered that it was still light and way past their bedtime. Tony wanted an explanation, as usual, and Vivian explained about the fact that the farther north one travels, the longer the sun shines during the summer months. It reminded her of something Mickey had written about sunset in the tropics, and her thoughts drifted in his direction. While we are sitting here, pleased with this long twilight, but for the grace of God we would have been captive somewhere in the jungle where nighttime falls instantly, like spilled ink, she mused. She closed her eyes and conjured up Mickey's face, taking note of the fact that she always pictured him with a smile. Two years had passed since his capture, and still there was no news. She clung to the hope that as long as he popped into her thoughts he must still be alive. Surely she would feel a premonition if he were dead, but there was no use in dwelling on when or how he would come home.

When they sailed out of San Francisco, the ship was jam-packed with servicemen, and Tony and Judy raced around deck, soon becoming acquainted with the navy staff and treated to special favors. One good thing, thought Vivian, they certainly aren't shy, and everyone seems to like them so well. All this moving around can't be doing them any harm as long as they have so much fun. They were supposed to sail on Saturday, but weren't underway until Sunday. However, after the nerve-wracking voyage during the evacuation, this trip seemed like a breeze.

When they arrived in Honolulu, Vivian was relieved to see Billie and Morris Friedman there to greet them on the crowded pier. She hadn't let anyone else know the precise date of their arrival, wanting to get her bearings before she took up the threads from her old life. Morris said he had arranged for her trunks to be sent the next day, as he took their hand luggage and lead Vivian and the children to his car. They talked up a storm all the way over the Pali to Lanakai.

Vivian breathed deeply of the ginger as they passed the upside-down waterfall and lush forest of the Nuuanu Valley before crossing the Pali. One of the island's frequent showers had brightened the colors of all the vegetation, and there was a rainbow glowing against a background of golden shower trees when they arrived at the house in Lanakai. She was overwhelmed when she saw the place where they would be staying. A Japanese gardener had spent years converting several acres into an enchanting garden that sloped downhill towards the sea. There were meandering, artificial streams, still pools, and lush flowers of every description. The house was comfortably furnished, and Billie had filled the refrigerator with what food they would need while they were settling in.

After Tony and Judy were put to bed, Billie and Morris lingered on. Vivian kicked off her shoes and walked out to the lanai, where they joined her, sitting on the rattan chairs and watching the garden while it melted into darkness.

"It's so good to be back," Vivian murmured. "I hated saying goodbye to my folks, but being here, seeing people of all races at the pier, smelling ginger and the scent of plumeria in the evening air...It's all part of a cocktail too intoxicating to forget."

"I just hope you won't be disappointed when you get a taste of Honolulu," Morris said. "The place is teeming with servicemen, and everyone is hustling around like they never used to do. As for finding a house...The Chinese have bought up every available bit of land, and at prices so high that no one could compete. Clever people, those Chinese. They must have been hoarding for years, waiting for this opportunity."

"Oh, let Vi worry about all that tomorrow, honey. Tonight is just for having fun and feeling good about having her back with us. Have you heard anything from Mickey?" asked Billie.

"Well, the last word we received was a brief, censored postcard which just told us that he was a prisoner at a place called Camp O'Donnel. The government has decided to classify him as a civilian, so they won't give us any compensation, but his mother is kindly providing me with an allowance. I hate like heck to be dependent on her though."

"Gosh, Vivian, if he's a civilian, you should be eligible for social security. That would at least give you eighty to one hundred dollars a month. They notified everyone to apply as soon as the war broke out. Didn't you hear about that?"

"I sure didn't. How can I go about getting it now?"

"You will have to supply them with Mickey's social security number. They won't give you any back pay, but let's hope they will let you qualify now."

Billie took a quick look at Morris, warning him to keep silent. She knew how annoyed he was that Mickey had left Vivian with no security, but it wouldn't help to flog a dead horse.

When they left, Vivian unpacked just enough to be sure the kids had something to wear in the morning and her nightgown. She fell asleep as soon as she put her head on the pillow.

The next morning, Tony woke up with a raging fever. There had been an epidemic of measles on the boat, but she had hoped the children wouldn't contract it. Darned the luck. By the second night, his fever was so high she had to call the doctor. She was grateful there was a phone in the place and that the Chinese doctor came so promptly. Tony was begging to explore the grounds, but the doctor said he had to stay in a darkened room for ten days.

Just as Tony was feeling better, Judy came down with measles. The doctor came again, and gave her a large pill to swallow. Vivian couldn't help but scold in the morning when she discovered that her stubborn little girl still had the pill in her mouth. "All that money for a doctor, and you won't even take his medicine," she said crossly.

At least the measles kept things quiet while they were settling in. Everyone was calling and wanting to come out, but Vivian had a perfect excuse for waiting. It gave her time to regain her strength. Funny how the slightest effort seems to knock me for a loop, she thought. I'll probably have to get to Honolulu and start taking B12 shots again.

Once they were well, the children thrived. Within a few weeks, they were brown as berries, with pink cheeks, and huge appetites. They raced around the grounds all day long, pretending that this was their farm and inventing animals to tend. They played in the artificial streams and spent hours swimming in the crystal clear waters at the beach. Vivian put on weight and felt better than she had for such a long time. If only the rest of the family could be here with us, she thought, she could wish for nothing else. She liked the neighbors, and everyone was helpful about taking care of the kids if she had an appointment in town, chasing down leads on houses she could buy or rent.

She enrolled Tony in the nearby parochial school for the last few weeks before summer break, but he proved to be too non-conformist for the nuns. One day he encouraged the other children to follow him in a game that led them off the school grounds. On another occasion, he had refused to march with his class, pointing out to the nuns that they were having the children do the goosestep. "Only Nazis march like that," he told his mother, with the earnestness that was so characteristic of him now that he was the 'man in the house'.

He was sent home with a reprimand, and Vivian decided to wait until after summer to try school again. They would have moved by then anyway, she hoped. She couldn't help but smile, thinking about her little maverick. Ruefully, she realized that this independent spirit Tony had was due to the very special relationship he had with his father. Mickey had taken the boy with him everywhere and always treated him like an equal, teaching him to think for himself. She wondered whether it was going to be difficult to find teachers that could win his respect.

The phone rang constantly, once word got out that she was back in the islands. She was surprised that so many men she and Mickey had known were so keen to take her out. It must be this damned war, she thought, makes people forget normal behavior. On the other hand, maybe it was natural. Mickey had been gone two and a half years, and all the news leaking out of Japanese territory pointed to little chance of him surviving.

She still hadn't received a reply to her application for social security benefits. She could have kicked herself for not having applied as soon as the war broke out. To make matters worse, Jane's checks were often delayed.

She also learned from one of the doctors she had been seeing that since five years had passed since she had her operation, she could have had plastic surgery on her arm. He told her it could be fixed so no one could see anything. "But we don't have anyone here in the islands capable of that sort of work," he added.

If only she had known, she could have taken care of that in California and gone back to work with the studios. However, she shrugged it off, thinking that everything usually works out for the best. Right now she was sure the best thing was being back in this island paradise, where the children were so much healthier, and life didn't grow stale.

Just as all was otherwise going well, Judy took ill with dysentery, a virulent sort that came from the milk they were getting. The doctor said that it was a problem that was rampant since the war broke out and told her that all water should be boiled and the milk boiled for five minutes. Vivian caught the same bug, and it triggered off severe problems with her kidneys.

Her letters home were cheerful and newsy, but between the lines, one could begin to read a touch of anxiety. She urged her mother to burn the letters, in order that Jane wouldn't get wind of the difficulties they were having.

There still was no luck in finding a place where Vivian could work. The man whose house they were borrowing, Tom Fields, was a frequent visitor, and it dawned on Vivian that he was more than just interested in her as a victim of circumstances. One day he finally said outright that he never had thought Mickey deserved such a beautiful wife and such nice children. "Why don't you divorce him and let me take care of you. You would have any sort of life you fancy."

Quick-tempered, Vivian started to defend Mickey. "What do you know about my life with Mickey?" she said. "We've had our ups and downs, but we've had more fun than most people."

"Vivian, everyone knows he only thinks about having a good time. And how do you figure he's going to be when he gets out of prison camp? He's going to be hell bent for election, wanting to make up for lost time. Remember that time he stayed out all night, partying it up with those characters down at Waikiki? I could never do anything like that to you or to your kids. You don't deserve that kind of life. Folks said you were madder than hops when he showed up the next morning, and that's why you left for the states."

"Well, folks would be better off not gossiping," Vivian retorted crossly, feeling embarrassed that she and Mickey had given rise to talk. "Anyway, it isn't fair to try to take over a man's family when he isn't here to defend himself. MacArthur's winning his fights with the Japs. I pray he will go all the way to the Philippines soon and free those men who were caught out there. Why, Mickey might be home before the year is out, for all we know!"

After he had left, she thought about what he had said. He was an attractive man. She could see how some people would think she was a fool not to be pleased that he was interested. Right now she had to admit to herself that a good man would be the easiest solution to all her troubles. But, darn it all, she wouldn't know how to tell Tony if she gave up on waiting for his dad, and what ever would she do if Mickey did survive to come home? Besides, so far there wasn't a man who had made her feel romantic. Out of habit, she twisted the gold band on her ring finger, recalling the day Mickey put it there as the captain of the Lurline smilingly looked on. It was such a simple ring, a far cry from the sort of thing Rudy would have given her, but the inscription Mickey had ordered written on the inside made it more special than any piece of jewelry she had. "My hopes, my ideals, my life, myself, I give unto you." Mickey was in her blood, for better or worse.

Letters from Jane were always a source of worry. Sometimes they were dripping with kindness, but they were always spoiled by chiding Vivian for having misjudged the real estate market or some snide remark about her lack of success in finding a livelihood. Vivian had a hard time being grateful for Jane's good intentions when she weighed them up with the scoldings. Most of all, Vivian felt like not replying, but she knew she had to keep Jane informed if she was to expect her continued help.

Often, Jane's letters were full of rambling plans about the future of Tony and Judy. Gradually, Vivian became aware of Jane's plans to take care of the children, should anything happen to her. A mother's instinct to protect her children put her into a state of alarm. Then she got angry with herself for even having such thoughts. She had to trust in God. Of course nothing was going to happen to her!

She tossed and turned one night, after receiving an especially troublesome letter. Damn that woman's ability to get her goat! The sum of Jane's nagging suddenly gave her a terrible thought: What would become of the children, if something happened to her? She had always assumed they would be safe in the loving care of her family, but suddenly she saw clearly that Jane would feel they should be in her care, guided by her ambitions.

All her life, she had thought of Donda as an anchor in the storm. Surely, Tony and Judy would be allowed to stay with her? Vivian fretted for days, while she outwardly appeared calm and happy. No one who knew her had any idea of the problems she faced.

Never a person to give up and let things slide, she asked a neighbor to look after the kids and got a lift to Honolulu with the woman's husband. She knew that Mac could advise her.

His offices were in the Bishop Building, and as she walked along the corridor, she remembered happier times, when she met Mickey there to go out with clients.

Mac whistled when he saw her and said, "Boy, are you a picture for sore eyes. You're as pretty as ever, Vi. How's life treating you? How are the kids?"

"I can't complain, Mac, and Tony and Judy are all a mother could wish for. Gosh it's good to see you, too," she said, as he stepped from behind his desk and gave her a bear hug.

"I hear from the grape vine that there still is no news about Mickey. Damned if I don't figure him for someone who would be able to come out of any situation alive though," he said, kindly.

"It's been more than two years since he was captured, Mac. You know what health problems he had when he left for the Philippines. I keep thinking about how tough it would be for him in a Jap concentration camp. They say they are worse than anything the Germans have thought up, though it's hard to imagine."

"Well, I can't help but think how close you came to being over there. Hell, Vi, if Pearl Harbor had been attacked three days later, you would have been on your way out to Manila, with those two cute little kids of yours. I get the shivers just thinking about it."

"That just shows that there is someone up there who looks out for us, Mac," Vivian said with a smile. "Maybe He figured He could keep Mickey out of trouble for a few years and send him home safe and sound when this war is over. Until then, I have to admit, life isn't less complicated without him."

"You know I would love to help you out, Vivian. You just say the word."

"Thanks for your offer, Mac. I know you mean it. No, I'm all right. Mickey's mother is helping us out, but I hope to goodness it's only temporary. You remember what run-ins I used to have with Jane when Mickey and I got married. She's been marvelous to take care of us financially, but I sure don't like being in her pocket. I never know what she might get up to if I don't find some means to be independent of her soon."

Mac nodded sympathetically. He knew just what Vivian meant. And he could tell that she had more than that on her heart. He listened attentively, and she continued, "That's why I've come to you for some advice."

She paused for a moment, her face pensive as she thought how best she could tell him what was on her mind. He was one of the few people who knew that she had had a bout with cancer, and it was a relief to be able to talk openly with him. "I'm feeling fine, Mac, but with Mickey gone and no one knowing whether he's dead or alive, I can't help but think about what would become of the children if anything happened to me. I would want my mother to raise them...You remember what a wonderful person she is, and the kids adore her. But if something happened to me, I think Jane would fight for them tooth and nail. She could prove that she's been supporting us for the past couple of years, though she's sometimes so late with her checks that I know I mustn't take anything for granted," Vivian said with a wry smile.

"When she wants something, she'll stop at nothing. I wouldn't put it past her to lie and say that I was a bad mother. Since Mickey's been gone, it's like she's always trying to catch me out." She looked at Mac and was encouraged to go on when she saw his understanding expression.

"Anyway, maybe I'm making a mountain out of a molehill, but I thought you might have some advice as to how I can do something which would put my mind at ease and insure that Donda gets the kids if anything should happen to me. Not that it will," she hurriedly added.

Mac had always been fond of Vivian, and he was more worried about her than she would care to know. Now, he looked out the window and chewed his lower lip, giving the matter considerable thought before he answered. "Vi, I think the wisest thing you could do is to file for divorce and request full custody of those kids." He looked at her shocked face and said, "Hear me out, before you get your dander up."

"If Mickey comes back, it will be an easy matter to explain to him why you did it and to get hitched again. If not, it would mean that his mother would be far removed from a legal hold on Tony and Judy. You might even want to get married again, and it would certainly make matters less complicated. I could take care of the divorce procedure for you, and it would be an easy matter to be awarded full custody under the circumstances."

Vivian thought about what he said. It made sense. Jane would be furious if she found out, but how would she find out if it were handled from here in the islands? She thought guiltily about all she owed Jane, but, after all, that was hopefully only temporary.

As if reading her thoughts, Mac said, "If Jane doesn't pull any dirty tricks, she need never know anything about this business, and if she does try to get custody of the kids against your wishes, she deserves to be thwarted."

"Okay, Mac. What do I do?"

They discussed what needed to be done and which documents had to be submitted. Mac said he would take care of the whole business, but he refused to take any payment from such a dear friend. To change the subject, he asked her if she would like to stay around and have dinner with him, but she said no. She had to catch her ride back to Lanakai.

He stood at the window, watching her as she left the building and crossed the street, a graceful figure in white. A group of sailors passed by and whistled, jostling each other for her attention, and Mac smiled. She might be struggling to keep her head above water, but she still has style, he thought. The scent of her perfume lingered in the room, and he felt the poignancy of remembering bygone days.

Vivian wrote a long letter to Donda, explaining what had transpired when she visited Mac. "If Mickey does come home one day, we can easily re-marry. And if he doesn't, I can be free to begin a new life. I'm beginning to realize how hard it is to have much of a life without a man, even though they sometimes turn out to be more trouble than they're worth. I owe a great deal to Jane for all her help, but she will always be a source of anguish for me where the children are concerned. Mickey and I shared your ideas about bringing up children, and you know how much Judy adores you. She would be so unhappy if she ever had to live with Jane."

"It should be relatively easy to get a divorce under the circumstances, with Mickey's fate unknown. Will you please send me that copy you have of our Reno marriage certificate? The Mexican papers wouldn't hold up in court, so they're no problem. And, please burn this letter. Jane mustn't know anything about what I'm planning."

That taken care of, Vivian waited anxiously for something to turn up by chance that might change her luck. Meanwhile, a friend from Hilo, Kay Richardson, wrote, offering to help her find a place on the big island. They had met before the war and kept in touch. She said there were no food shortages on Hawaii, and that housing was cheaper, because there was a ceiling both on rentals and real estate. Vivian booked passage on a clipper leaving at the end of July. I can always cancel if something better turns up in the meantime, she reasoned.

* * * * *

While Vivian worried, it was a magic time for Tony and Judy. They had her to themselves, and she did wonderful things, like getting them out of bed long after it grew dark, in order to sit and wait for the night-blooming cereus to open its creamy white blossom in the light of the full moon. The following morning, they scampered up on the big rock alongside of where it had bloomed, but it was wilted, and the memory of its firm petals, lustrous in the moonlight, was like a dream.

They visited people who lived in interesting places, and were received kindly wherever they went. They stayed a few days in a deserted hotel. The kids raced up and down the corridors and explored the gigantic kitchen, while Vivian investigated the possibilities of running it.

They had a quiet afternoon at the lovely mansion of the Dillinghams, a place with a pond and a small rowboat. Tony was allowed to take Judy out on the pond while their mother drank tea on the terrace. Large gold fish swam lazily in the still water, and they watched them happily, unaware of the problems their mother faced.

Judy's sixth birthday rolled around, and a big box arrived from Donda and the rest of the family. Tony and Judy jumped with excitement as Vivian parceled out the gifts. From Jane there was a check and a letter that touchingly displayed how awkward Jane's relationship was to her granddaughter. Vivian waited to read the letter to Judy when she and Tony had opened their presents and had quieted down.

Dear Darling Judith,

So our little Lady is having another birthday. So glad for you that you are in Honolulu enjoying the nice big ocean. Do hope you will always be a happy loveable girl and grow into a fine lady.

Now listen, Sugar, I had your mother draw on me this month for some extra money for you and Tony. Here is what you tell your mother. Have her take five dollars of that fund and take you down town and she is to buy you anything you want for your birthday. You see, honey, I don't have time to shop for your birthday present and send it to you. Besides there are so few things one can buy for a little lady like you. You see, I don't know what size of clothes you wear, and I don't have time to go to the post office and stand in line to send you something, and I would much rather have you pick it out yourself. I just want you to know I remembered your birthday.

Judy was starting to fidget and look out the window, and Vivian read on more quickly.

Had a very nice letter from your Donda the other day, and she told me what they were sending you.

Vivian paused and smiled, seeing clearly why Jane had sent this unexpected letter.

I know you will have a lovely time and mother will cook you a nice big cake and buy you ice cream and you will have some little friends in and have a nice time. That is what birthdays are for. When you are eating your ice cream out on the terrace, looking over the cool Pacific Ocean, just think of me out here in this hot old place. And believe me it surely is warming up. We plan on going up Reno way about the first of next month and get some cool weather. I think we'll be needing it about then.

Well honey, I have the court rentals working very nicely, and I have my fingers crossed as I really do need the good help I have down there. Everyone likes them, and they have increased my business about $100.00 per week, which is the difference between profit and loss. I am well pleased with the set-up I have now.

Tell that big boy Tony that I have a very soft spot in my heart for him, and I am rooting for him to grow into a Beeg Man with plenty of hair on his chest, and he is not to disappoint me. Oh yes, and I heard a lecture on going swimming, and this famous lecturer said that one should never go swimming alone, even the best of swimmers. There are so many things to remember as we go through life. I know your mother never lets you two kids go swimming alone, as she is so proud of you two that she wants to be near you all the time.

Vivian felt the mounting sense of irritation that Jane invariably inspired in her. What does she think I am for a mother? she thought with annoyance.

Your mother wrote me all about the "big farm" you have on the hillside and your horses Grethie and Speed and a cow named Bluebell who wears a lei and straw hat and all the kittens and puppies. It surely is nice for you two kiddies to have so many wonderful things, and your mother said there was a little boy who could not see the things you see. That is too bad, because it is wonderful to train the mind to look for the good and beautiful things of life and shut out the sordid things, and I cannot imagine anything more beautiful than a lovely farm on a hillside and stocked with so many animals. You two kiddies just go on with your playing, and when Daddy comes home, maybe that make-believe farm will develop into a real farm with hundreds of acres in it, and big men growing everything that you can imagine. How about that?!

Now, let's see, sugah, on the 19th of July, about four o'clock, there you will be eating ice cream and your birthday cake, and it will be about six here, and I'll be having dinner. I'll be with someone, possibly Pete, and I'll make believe it is your birthday dinner I am having and we will entertain you and Tony and you will be the honored guest. We'll have ice cream and cake, and I'll say to you, 'Judy, would you like some more cake?' And you will say to me, 'No thank you, Jane, I have had all I care for.' See, I can imagine things, too. It is terrible to get so old that you cannot dream dreams and see visions, don't you think? I know, my dear, that you can understand every word I am saying to you, as with that wonderful vocabulary you have you can keep up with me. You see, honey, I try to use words that are not so big as the ones you use, but they have a world of meaning.

Vivian chuckled, remembering Jane's irritation when Judy told Jane she wasn't as smart as 'my Donda'. Vivian could see that Tony and Judy were not interested in hearing the letter, and she gave them each a pat on the bottom and told them to run along. "You can hear the rest of Jane's letter at bedtime, and you'll have to make a nice drawing for her to send as a thank-you, Judy." Judy nodded happily, and they raced out the door.

She sat amid the mess of wrapping paper and cards and read the rest of Jane's letter, feeling sorry for her, because she could sense deep loneliness on the other side of the self-assured tone.

Isn't it funny how I take time out from my work and write you a big letter on your birthday? When this old world settles down to a normal existence again, I'll be sending you a lot of pretty things, and maybe I can be with you on one of your birthdays and I'll cook the cake and let mother rest up a bit.

Be a very sweet girl and grow into a lovely lady, and everyone will say, 'Isn't that Judith Owen, one of the loveliest girls on this island?' Then won't we be proud of our little Judith Leilani. Some of these days, I am going to build a cottage and the name of it is going to be the Leilani Cottage, then I am going to build a very dignified house, and it will be called the St. Alwyn. You see, honey, I can make believe, and my make believe plans will be carried out some day when this old war is over, and we can go on with our plans for living.

Well, it certainly wasn't from strangers that Mickey got his ability to spin a yarn, Vivian thought.

No more now, my darling. Tell your mother and Tony hello for me and give them my love and keep a lot of it for yourself. Aloha to you Judith.

Lovingly, Jane.

I should have told Ma not to mention Judy's birthday to her, Vivian thought, but she knew her mother probably figured it was a good way to get a present out of her. She recalled the many packages that had come from her folks over the years. They all loved to find things to give the kids, and if one had a birthday, there was sure to be something for the other one.

Tony was seven when Judy's birthday parcel arrived, and Bobbie sent him his first pocket-knife, a pearl-handled one, of which he was proud as Punch. He took Judy across the street, up the hillside where there were small trees, and they played pathfinders, nicking the bark of the trees in order to be able to find the way home. A large, friendly mastiff, owned by a neighbor, ran with the children as they played, making the adventure more exciting.

As usual, Judy tired of the activity first and started home. The Lanakai house was located on a quiet dead-end street, but this day there was a military car idling there, and a haole man in uniform sat behind the wheel. He drove slowly up alongside Judy, his window rolled down, and he asked if she would like a ride home.

She was immediately suspicious. Her mother had told her never to get into a stranger's car, and besides, she was right by her home. "No, thank you," she said primly, and continued walking.

By now, he had driven right up alongside her, and he stopped and quickly opened the door and pulled her inside. Terrified, she tried to scream, but no sound would come out. The man began tearing at her panties. The thick roll of fat over his tight collar and his pinkish white skin disgusted her. She still couldn't scream, but she started to cry, loudly, and the sound carried to her brother.

Thinking Judy was hurt, Tony came running, oblivious to the fact that he held his new pocketknife in his hand, with the blade still out. The large dog ran with him and jumped against the car, its head even with the window. Tony hopped up on the running board to see what was the matter, still clutching his pocketknife. Too frightened to work the door handle on the passenger side, Judy tumbled out the open window. The dog barked angrily and scratched at the door, snarling, and the startled man revved the engine and tore off down the street.

At first, Vivian thought Judy had been hurt when she and Tony came running into the house. Her little face was streaked with dirt and tears, and words tumbled out incoherently as Tony excitedly tried to explain what had happened. He was still waving his pocketknife about. Taking the knife from him so he wouldn't accidentally hurt himself, Vivian sat down between the children and tried to make sense of what had happened. When she understood, and saw that Judy's panties were torn, she felt the blood rush from her head. Shaking with anger, she immediately phoned the military police, giving them a description of the incident. She thanked God that nothing worse had happened.

She was asked to bring Judy to Honolulu, to see whether a little girl, only six years old, could point out her attacker in a line-up of men. None of them were like the man Judy had escaped from, and Vivian asked them not to call them in again. The streets were jammed with men in uniform, and finding him would seem like finding a needle in a haystack. "I think it best that we let her forget about such an unpleasant thing happening," she said, and they understood.

Fortunately, Judy seemed unharmed by the incident. It had only reinforced her idea of Tony as a hero who could always protect her, and aside from worrying about not being able to scream for help when she wanted to, she appeared to be her usual trusting self.

Vivian recognized that this was no longer Honolulu as she had loved it. Perhaps it was all a big mistake, her coming back to the islands. It was a paradise that had been sullied, no longer the place she once knew where she never had to worry about the children. The fright with Judy was the crowning blow. Now she had no doubts about leaving for Hawaii. Perhaps over there things would still be like they were when she and Mickey went there before the war.

While she was waiting to leave for the Big Island, she took the children to lunch at the Young Hotel. It was extravagant, but she really needed the treat. She looked lovely in a pale yellow linen dress, her dark hair swept back from her smooth brow. She had dressed the children in their Sunday best, Judy in a darling little smocked frock from Saks Fifth Avenue that Gladys DeVault had given her, and Tony in the uniform he had worn at the Catholic school. They made a pretty picture as they left the hotel, pausing briefly in the doorway in order that Vivian could take hold of their hands before they reached the street. Coming towards her was a group of officers, and in the forefront, she recognized General MacArthur. Their eyes met, and she smiled, remembering that he had been friendly to Mickey. He was even more handsome than she had imagined. She was tempted to ask him whether he could tell her anything about the last time he saw Mickey, but in a flash he was gone, followed by a busy entourage of officers. Seeing him here in Honolulu with such a look of command gave her hope that the war in the Pacific would soon be won.

Vivian and the children left several days later by clipper. Upon arriving in Hilo, she left their luggage with Kay Richardson, and took the children on a ramshackle bus trip to see the island. It was just what she needed. The children were agog at the beautiful sights. The bus was a funny little thing with no glass in the windows, crammed with good-natured Hawaiians, going to market or commuting to work. The air was drenched with moisture as they drove past a long hedge of gardenias, its white blossoms glowing against shiny green leaves. For Vivian, their heady fragrance evoked memories of eveningwear in Hollywood and dancing at the Coconut Grove. Fleetingly, she wondered whether such heady times would ever come back.

They visited the Valley of Kealeakekua, where Judy gathered armfuls of gardenias and white ginger. There was every imaginable type of flower in the cool climate. Every detail etched itself in their memories, and Vivian watched the children's rapture with a feeling of profound joy.

On more than one occasion, they ran into friends Mickey and Vivian had met when they had visited the Kona Coast before the war. They spent several heavenly days at the Parker

Ranch, pampered by the Hawaiian cowboys and treated to warm, home-baked rolls for breakfast.

They stayed at the Volcano house and saw the Kilauea Crater, where the footprint of a small boy was imbedded in lava, proof of his presence in a procession to appease Pelé, the Goddess of Fire.

When they returned to Hilo, they moved into a flimsy house on stilts. It was primitive and dirty, but Vivian rolled up her sleeves, cleaned the place spic and span, and bought a bucket of paint to decorate it with a pale blue color. For the children, everything was a special treat – the colors, the fun of peeling brush hairs out of the fresh paint, and the new tastes and scents. Money was scarce, but they were too young to be aware of that. Vivian found inexpensive local foods and presented them as special treats. They learned to like bowls of fresh green soybeans, cooked in salt water and eaten as snacks.

Everywhere she went, people took pity on her, alone in the world with two small children and a husband lost in the war. Her old stubborn pride buoyed her up, however, and she made every effort to keep the appearance of someone who didn't need help. All she wanted was an investment property or a job that could tide them over until they found one, but her first real job offer was as hostess at the Naniloa Inn.

All the celebrities that came to the big island visited the place, and it was a favorite spot with Marines on leave. Vivian was just the person the owners were looking for. She was told she could have housing in one of their bungalows, and the staff could look after the children while Vivian worked. From the first day at work, Vivian was popular with the guests and the rest of the staff, and Tony and Judy were in seventh heaven, with all the attention they were getting.

The Marines who frequented the place made Tony their mascot, gave him captain bars, and taught him to swim. There was a pool, and the servants were allowed to swim there during certain hours when the guests didn't use it. The jolly, fat waitress taught Judy to float, while flirting with the cook. Like sponges, Tony and Judy soaked up words and ideas from the kitchen help. Judy was especially pleased with a delicious new phrase: "Toe jam, Mommy. Toe jam sounds so funny." Judy said happily when her mother was putting her to bed.

Vivian smiled and chose not to comment it. She always had the children say their prayers. After 'Our Father' they each listed all their favorite people, preceded by a 'God bless'. Judy's list grew longer each day, as she explored the world of the hotel. She had been such a mother's child ever since they left Donda's, and Vivian was relieved to see that the many friendly people at the hotel kept Judy too distracted to hang on her mother's apron strings.

Alert to new adventures, Tony found wondrous places to explore: Paths, along which grew wild strawberries that were white, not red, and woods where the burnished moss that hung from the trees was called Pelé's hair. They lapped up the stories about Pelé, the Goddess of Fire, who was supposed to have red hair and green eyes and whose presence was presumed to be everywhere on the Big Island.

Judy took a shine to the wife of the owner of the hotel. She was a pretty lady who wore navy blue dresses and white collars. She patiently answered all Judy's questions and was amused when Judy worked so hard to learn the name of the splendid plant that grew in the lobby: Monstorea Deliciosa. She kept reassuring Vivian that the children weren't getting on anyone's nerves, but Vivian had a feeling that her two small monkeys were all over the place and worried that they would be a bother. Thank goodness, they know their manners, she thought. A please and a thank-you went a long way in gaining favor.

Unlike the dazzling white sand of Oahu, the beach at the Naniloa Inn was pitch black, speckled with bits of emerald-colored bits like glass, from Pelé's green eyes, the children were told. If they dragged their feet when they ran through the black sand, it barked like a dog.

The water was less inviting than the surf in Oahu. Without the white sand bottom, it wasn't crystal clear and didn't have that glorious turquoise color. The children were warned that there were sharks in the waters, with no coral reef to keep them out of the swimming area. When the tide was low, however, they liked to play on an 'island' all their own, a large rock close to shore, where a single shrub had gained a foothold. There they spent a happy hour one day, pretending to set up house.

Suddenly, Tony noticed that the tide was coming in, and he shouted to Judy to hurry and follow him safely to shore. Agilely, he took a big leap and reached safe ground with no trouble, but she froze, terrified by the water that was lapping at her feet. The longer she hesitated, the deeper it became, and Tony shouted frantically at her to jump. His shouts were heard by one of the Marines who went out to get her and waded into shore with her on his shoulders. It was an adventure that Judy proudly told her mother in the evening, giving Vivian one more thing to worry about. With a twinge of guilt, she remembered Jane's letter with the cryptic remark about knowing Judy's mother wouldn't let her swim alone.

While the children thrived in the relatively cool climate, Vivian began to suffer back trouble. She had to be on her feet from eight to four every day, except Sundays, and by the end of the first week she was suffering a great deal of pain in her back and hips. She tried to use Christian Science to make the pains go away, but 'mind over matter' didn't help at all.

She consulted a kindly old Jewish doctor who questioned her about her medical history and listened carefully to a description of her discomforts. He diagnosed her trouble as lumbago and told her she needed a special corset. He had heard that her husband was a prisoner of war, and when she opened her purse to pay for his services, he would only take two dollars.

"You'll never make a living that way," she objected.

"No, but I sleep well at nights," he replied with a gentle smile. He watched her as she got into a car from the hotel, and his face was sad. He was pretty sure her illness was too serious to treat, and he had learned enough about her to realize that extensive tests would be just one more source of worry. Lumbago was a convenient deception that would do no harm. He knew how much discomfort she was suffering, and there was really nothing he could do to help, except to give her hope that she would get better.

After the second week, Vivian was in such pain she could hardly get dressed. At the same time, she received a letter from Jane telling her that she would have to cut down her allowance for a while. Jane's letter was a long diatribe, criticizing Vivian for having gone back to the islands and implying that she wasn't fit to be the mother of Mickey's children.

Vivian was used to these shifts of mood that Jane had, but she found it hard to take when she herself was having so much trouble. The thought ran through her mind that maybe Jane was right. Would it have been wiser to stay in North Hollywood and let the hours tick away until the war was over? She wondered whether Jane had seen some of the letters she had sent to Donda. Surely that couldn't have happened. Did she know about the divorce?

Whenever the pain left her enough to be aware of other things, she was nagged by her worries about Jane. Maybe all of Jane's pique was merely brought on by her own troubles, and she didn't know about any of the things Vivian had tried to keep from her. Jane had mentioned having problems of her own with her businesses in Vegas. She had decided to sell one of her hotels and taper off. Maybe that's why she was cutting down my allowance, Vivian reasoned as the latest pain ebbed out and gave her a brief respite. If only misunderstandings weren't so much worse when one had to wait for letters to be exchanged, she thought sadly.

To add to her misery, the social security office wrote informing Vivian that they couldn't pay benefits, because they considered Mickey military personnel! She couldn't help but laugh at the red tape – No one wanted to claim responsibility for her dear husband.

She stayed in bed on her Sunday off, hoping her back would improve if she were warm all day. It had been raining most of the week, and the air was chill. There was hardly any food in the house, and Tony and Judy were hungry. She rustled up some bread, spread it with butter and sprinkled it with brown cane sugar, feeling guilty that she was giving them a meal with so little nutrition; however, they took it as an unexpected treat and eagerly asked if they could have sugar sandwiches every day.

By dinnertime, she was feeling ill from the pain. The children sensed something was very wrong, and for a change were quiet. Tony tiptoed to her bedside and asked what they were having for dinner. The only thing she could suggest was that he open a can of spinach, all by himself. Vivian was miserable, but the children experienced a newfound feeling of importance. Judy stood watching in awe as her brother managed the task of opening the can, and they both relished eating spinach he had 'fixed' himself.

Later that evening, Vivian dragged herself out of bed, dressed, and walked to the office of the hotel to give the owners notice. "I am so sorry to let you down, but I just don't know when I will be fit to start work again," she said, embarrassed by her weakness.

They were both most sympathetic and told her to get herself straightened out and that the job would be open anytime she wanted to come back. "Everyone likes you, and you just let us know whatever you need, until you feel better. The kids can have all their meals at the hotel."

All those whom she had befriended rallied around and wanted to help. She and the children were offered the use of a bungalow owned by a Sunday school teacher, not far from the hotel, where they could stay until she knew what she wanted to do. There they stayed for several days, but it was small and inconvenient.

The owners of the hotel hadn't stopped being concerned about Vivian. They made an appointment at the hospital for her to have x-rays of her kidneys, liver and gall bladder and insisted she let them help her, but while she was getting dressed to leave for the hospital, she was overwhelmed by pain and collapsed. When she came to, she was in the hospital, where she stayed for a week. Maids from the hotel took good care of Tony and Judy. Vivian got tears in her eyes, as she wondered how she ever would repay so many people for their kindness. At the same time, she was frantic with worry that Jane would find out about her predicament.

Once she was released, friends of Mickey's moved them into a cottage they owned by the Volcano House. It was beautiful. Tony and Judy were so enthralled with the natural beauty of the place that they could hardly wait to go outside in the morning, even when it was raining. Determined not to give in to fear, Vivian wrote to her mother, giving a glowing description of the place.

"You'd love it here, Ma. There are Shasta daisies taller than I am, lupines the bluest I have ever seen, wild roses of every color, poppies and dahlias in every imaginable hue, and everywhere the scent of gardenias. The milk is thick as cream, and I've never eaten more delicious vegetables. Every imaginable kind of berry grows wild here, and the mountain apples are sweet and plentiful. It's like a glimpse of Heaven." If only it didn't rain so much, and if only the pain would go away, she thought.

One day, the children found their way to a sulfur pit, and Tony told Judy that it was so hot a man could light a cigarette in it. She peered over the edge and saw a yellowish substance, with fumes rising from the surface and lingering in the still air. There was a water pipe that was suspended across the pit, and Tony fearlessly balanced on it and tripped across the pit, walking the pipe like a tight rope. Judy wanted to do the same, but she prudently crawled across on her belly, inching her way with both hands tightly grasping the pipe, her eyes shut.

They ran wild, but Vivian's worries about them were stifled by seeing that they were obviously having the time of their lives. She was relieved when they started school. It was a crummy little school with six grades all in one room and an old woman as the only teacher, but it was all so new to them that they loved it.

Her money was running low, and she didn't want to touch her emergency fund. A letter arrived from Jane, telling her that she had decided not to sell her hotel and would again be sending Vivian two hundred dollars a month. Vivian breathed a sigh of relief but again worried that her mother might have shown one of her recent letters to Jane.

Convinced that all her health problems were due to the damp climate, Vivian put an ad in the Maui newspaper, seeking housing for a woman with two small children. Scotty and the Freidmans were urging her to come back to Honolulu, where they could help her out, but she knew that things wouldn't be different there than when she left. She would still be unable to find a place like she and Jane had agreed upon. Nevertheless, she booked passage on a clipper back to Honolulu, scheduled to leave the following week – Just in case nothing else turned up.

By the end of the week, she was desperate with pain and wanted to leave, but it rained so much that the flight was cancelled. Then all her speculation was brought to an end when she had another attack of pain from the region of her kidneys. She remembered passing out, the rest was a blur. Everything was falling apart, and she was vaguely aware of the many kind hands that were picking up the pieces. People she had known such a short time were packing her things, taking care of the kids, and making arrangements for a flight to Honolulu.

She awoke in a hospital bed, on the 3rd of October, and she was scared. As soon as she was assured that the children were safe, and she took stock of her situation, she asked a nurse for pencil and paper and wrote to Doc.

Dear Doc and Poli,

Just a short letter to tell you I'm in the St. Louis Army Hospital under observation. Those cramps in the kidney area got so bad I couldn't get up and down – Just like charley horses. They took seven x-rays today and blood from my finger and arm. They say the doctors here now are the best in the world. Children are in school and staying with Mrs. Linn who teaches.

All my possessions are in storage, except for two grips and my make-up box in which I have four hundred dollars worth of government bonds for the kids. If anything unforeseen should happen, take my brief case from the trunk and get my allotment permit, which is important when the money starts coming through. (It hasn't as yet.) The trunks are at the City Transfer Co. of Honolulu, and they should be shipped via American R.R. Ex. Three trunks, one large box, and one tricycle. Don't let Jane see any of my papers.

I'd come home via clipper, but it would be suicide. Jane said to leave doctors alone, but this time I couldn't, and it is trouble that has been coming on for a long time. Three doctors just came in and tapped through the area I mentioned, and also the intestines. Asked how long the stinging had been around the right front edges of my ribs. Wish I had you with me Doc. Gosh!

Tell Mother what you think you should and for her not to worry. The children couldn't be in better hands, and Mrs. Erdman and Miss Morgan of the Red Cross are also on the job.

If anything should go wrong (it won't) I never want the kids separated. Who cares for one cares for the other. You will find by my papers I have complete legal custody of them. I never want them punished by an angry person.

Just a few days will tell the tale darlings. Don't expect mail for a while. Tell Mom.

Just lots of aloha,

Sis

Exhausted by the effort it took to lean on one elbow and write, Vivian lay aside the block of paper, put her head on the pillow, and shut her eyes, feeling tears burn against her eyelids. She heard footsteps on the floor of the ward where she was lying and wiped her eyes in time to see a team of doctors and nurses come to the side of her bed. She smiled at them and momentarily forgot her pains as she listened to what they had to say about her condition.

As soon as they left, she picked up the letter she had been writing to Doc and Poli, adding a postscript with the latest news:

P.S. The final decision – My liver is diseased. It is very large and has been pulling all the other organs down, hence the kidney situation. They attribute it to dysentery I had so badly about a year ago, as it has been a long time coming on. Remember Mother used to squawk about my yellow color? They are going to try to shrink it, and I'm on a rigid diet. No cure they say. I shall be here at least three weeks, and they will tell me whether I should leave for the mainland or not. Isn't it a hell of a mess to be in. Tell Mother only what you have to.

Lots of love,

Me

Dr. Rose came back to the bedside just as Vivian put the letter into an envelope. He knew how much pain she had been suffering, and what an effort it took to smile at him and answer his greeting. She was already looking a bit better since she had been in his care, but he knew that it was only a matter of time.

Even after years of practicing medicine, it wasn't any easier for him to watch helplessly as a lovely woman dies while still in her prime. This case was especially poignant. She was beautiful, intelligent, and as ill as she was, she still had so much spunk. Her main worry seemed to be about her two little kids. He knew she was the type of patient who didn't want pity, and he made a point of speaking to her in a cheerful tone of voice. I can only hope I can get her strong enough to make the trip back to her family, he thought sadly.

He outlined the treatment he had devised to boost her strength, and Vivian felt her spirits lifted by the confidence he inspired. Under his care, she regained enough strength to be misled by her unflagging optimism, and when she wrote her next letter, it had a different tone:

St. Louis Hospital

October 13

Dearest Folks,

Just a few lines to let you know I've really improved by leaps and bounds. They have given me injections for shrinkage of the liver, and I'm on a rigid non-fat diet. The shots always make me nauseous, but the hip pains have nearly disappeared. I had my doctor (the main one) put in for clipper passage home, but if I continue to get so well, I shall cancel it.

I have the promise of a couple of places to stay when I get out of here. The kids are swell and love their school. Would hate to think of them having colds again, and Tony with earaches. I would dread coming back there and being bothered by that person that always gets me down. This hospitalization is fine. I get all care for myself and kids, also a card for the commissary for food at rock bottom prices. Am getting tired – Lots of love and don't worry.

P.S. Scotty brings my mail. I am up in Kaimukai.

Love,
Me

Word spread through the hospital about the plucky young woman who was riddled with cancer. Busy as they were with wounded men, the doctors and nurses went out of their way to try to make her comfortable. She bravely struggled to be a good patient, insisting on feeding herself, no matter how weak she felt. They brought her special treats when they learned what she liked – fresh pineapple, cool papaya and the daily newspaper.

They learned that Judy missed her mother, and they let her come and stay in the children's ward for a few days, letting her climb into her mother's bed when Vivian was rested and felt up to having her there. Reassured by being with her mother, Judy contentedly accepted going back to Scotty's to be with Tony.

Days passed, and Vivian found it more and more difficult to stay awake. At first she thought all the rest she seemed to need was a sign that she was getting well, but when she looked in the mirror, she could no longer hide from the truth. Her skin was more jaundiced for each day that passed. She kept her Bible under her pillow, and when she was alone, she took it out and read in it, trying to chase away dark thoughts.

The cover was soft brown leather, and the tissue-thin gilded pages fell open to the passage she had found solace in so many times in the past few years:

> The Lord is my shepherd, I shall not want.
> He leadeth me beside still waters.
> He restoreth my soul.
> Ye though I walk in the shadows of the Valley of Death,
> I fear no evil.

She closed her eyes, trying to concentrate and conjure up the strength of spirit she knew she had, and forced herself to go on, recanting the words of Mary Baker Eddy that she had used for such a long time:

"There is no life, truth, intelligence, nor substance in matter. All is infinite Mind and its infinite manifestation, for God is All-in-all. Spirit is immortal truth; matter is mortal error. Spirit is the real and eternal; matter is the unreal and temporal. Spirit is God, and man is His image and likeness. Therefore, man is not material; he is spiritual."

She became aware that the words were pouring into her mind automatically, while other thoughts were nagging at her consciousness. The children. What about the children? With a growing sense of agitation, she knew she had to try to make doubly sure Jane wouldn't get them.

The next time Dr. Rose came to see her, she told him that she wanted to make a will, and that it must be as soon as possible. That very afternoon, with the chaplain, the doctor, and the Red Cross lady, Miss Morgan, as witnesses, she made her last will and testament. She left her pitiful few remaining possessions to her children and stated that Tony and Judy be put in the custody of her mother. Her diamond ring and diamond and platinum watch were to be Judy's. She wanted something for Tony to remember her by, and she thought of her ring with the turquoise stones. She had a quick flash of memory of a faraway day when she had bought it from an old Indian woman on the Mojave Desert. It would have to do. It would be years before the war bonds could be cashed in. She hoped that by then they could be a help in some small way. It was so little compared to all she had wanted to do for Tony and Judy, but she hoped they would serve as proof of her good intentions.

That being done, she began the struggle to stay alive just long enough to see her children safe in Donda's care. Each day, as the staff and those few who knew she was on her deathbed watched her strength ebb away, they prayed there would be space for her and the children on a flight out, and each day they had to resign themselves to another day's wait. There were so many wounded men to send on to San Francisco, and they came first. For them there was still hope.

She was too weak to see a lot of visitors; therefore, Scotty only told Mrs. Erdman and Gladys DeVault that Vivian was in the hospital. Vivian didn't think the children should be let in on the gravity of her situation, and she and Scotty decided it was best if they didn't see her so ill. Vivian still clung to the hope that once she got back to the states Doc would be able to pull her through. No need to frighten Tony and Judy unnecessarily.

Finally, on Sunday, the 4th of November, there was space on a hospital plane, but, by a quirk of fate, the necessary papers didn't come through, and they were unable to get her and the children aboard.

Unaware of their mother's worsening condition, the children played happily at Scotty's. There was an old jalopy on a vacant lot they loved to pretend to drive, and they could always visit the old man next door who spent most of his time in the garage he had converted to a workshop. Scotty's daughter, Jane, a pretty blonde, was going to a prom, and her powder-blue tulle dress, with billowing skirts, was on a hanger in her bedroom, making Judy think she was like a princess. In their timeless children's world, they stopped thinking it strange that their mother wasn't with them at present. Scotty had enrolled them in the neighborhood school, and their days were filled with new experiences.

* * * * *

In the tortuous purgatory of imprisonment, Mickey kept alive by clinging to the hope of seeing Vivian again, while her condition grew worse by the hour. Whenever she was conscious, she remained clear-headed and uncomplaining, but it was becoming increasingly difficult to will herself into consciousness. At long last, on the 7th of November, Tony and Judy were taken to the military air force base to join their mother for the arduous flight home in a hospital plane.

Ignorant of their mother's condition, they were excited at the prospect of their first flight in such a big plane. They rode in a jeep, out on the airfield to the waiting plane. Vivian lay on a stretcher on one side of a lift with a net around it, like a big basket. As soon as Tony and Judy were put onto the lift, it was hoisted up to the side hatch of the plane. The movement jostled Vivian into consciousness, and she saw her children. She wanted to cry out with joy and hold them to her breast, but her wasted body wouldn't obey her thoughts. Feebly, she tried to reach out her hand, smiling to them and murmuring their names.

Her hand was thin and limp, and her skin, stretched taut over her cheekbones, was the color of copper. Her eyes burned with fever and appeared large in a face from which all the soft contours had been lost. Tony and Judy shrank uncomfortably against the netting of the far side of the lift, and looked away awkwardly.

Something told them that this must be their mother, but the many weeks during which they hadn't seen her had transformed her so greatly that they rejected the knowledge. They couldn't accept that this was their pretty mother who always smelled of perfume and whose cool hands soothed their brows when they needed comfort. They avoided looking at her and felt relieved when the crewmen grabbed the swaying lift, and they were able to scamper into the plane.

Afterwards, it was easy for them to forget her, during that strange flight. The plane was a converted B-29. The inside was fitted on both sides with bunks, and stretchers with wounded men were on the floor along the aisle. If Tony and Judy were aware of their mother's presence, they didn't seek her out. Her illness was a strange creature that crouched over her bunk, making them afraid of her. Instead, they stayed close to the cheerful black soldier lying on the floor, his face pitted by shrapnel wounds and his blanket flat where there should have been a leg. He didn't frighten them. Afterwards, the memory of that brief moment of betrayal, when their mother had called their names and they didn't respond, was to haunt both of them all their days.

They were taken to the cockpit, pampered by the crew, and lulled to sleep by the drone of the engines. Vivian slept too, whenever she slipped beyond the threshold of pain. Briefly, she awoke and thankfully accepted a sip of water. A nurse told her that the children were fine, and she smiled, knowing that they were going home. The pounding headache she had suffered for so long had eased, and the feeling of relief made her experience a sense of weightlessness. She wanted to lift her head to see if the children were dressed warmly enough, but she was too weak.

She felt that it was the headache that had sapped her of all will to live, and her heart filled with gratitude to God for lifting the cloud of pain, making it possible to pursue a thought to its end. It was such a comfort to know that the children would soon be in a safe harbor. Tears stung her closed eyelids, as she thought about them and worried about what would become of them. She wondered whether things would have been different and whether she would be well if she had stayed with her family in North Hollywood, but she quickly rejected that possibility. She knew now from Doctor Rose that she had been sick for a very long time. Still, she worried that Jane would claim it was wrong of her to have spent the last six months moving from pillar to post in the islands.

As if in response to that imagined reproach, brilliant images of the sights she had shared with the children appeared in her mind. In a dreamlike state, she was with them in the garden in Lanakai, the moonlight shining on their eager faces as they watched the night-blooming cereus unfold its glory. She pictured them throwing themselves into the warm, gentle surf of the beach by Diamond Head, and she remembered their wonder at seeing the black sands of Hawaii. In a dream, she recalled the flowers of Kilakauea. She was there with her children, surrounded with rich blossoms as far as the eye could reach, and Mickey was there, too, smiling. The feeling of despair dissipated like a vapor and the hope that Doc would make her well again settled comfortably in her mind.

Sometime during the night the plane landed in San Francisco. Her body was already cold.

* * * * *

The next morning, the children woke up in the pleasant surroundings of the nurses' residence at the Presidio. There was a white-capped nurse in the room, and when Judy stirred, she came over to the bed and gently brushed Judy's hair back from her face.

When the children were dressed they were given a good breakfast, and they chattered cheerfully with the nurses who lived in this big house, surrounded by green lawns and stately trees. Judy hoped they would be staying there for a while. Everyone is so nice and pretty, she thought contentedly.

"Your grandmother is here for you," said a nurse, as she ushered the children down a long, carpeted stairway. Nurses on their way out wore navy-blue cloaks with their white dresses and caps. Judy put her hand on the banister and ran down the stairs, overjoyed at the prospect of seeing Donda. When she saw her standing in the hallway at the bottom of the stairs, she ran to hug her. Donda looked so pretty in a black dress with a picture hat and veil pushed back on the brim. Uncle Doc and Aunt Poli were there, too, looking grand, he in a suit and tie, and Aunt Poli was wearing a fur coat. Judy beamed, feeling proud that they looked so fine. It was like they were when we get a treat, and they take us someplace special, she thought.

Outside, in the fog, cypress trees loomed majestically on the vast lawn. As they walked to Doc's car, Tony was grave, like he sensed there was something wrong. Judy, oblivious of the mood, skipped happily, her hand warm in Donda's. She rubbed her cheek against Poli's fur coat. It felt cool and soft and heightened the feeling Judy had that it was a festive occasion.

It wasn't until they were on the way, comfortable in the back seat of Doc's Cadillac with

Donda sitting between them, that Tony and Judy were told what had happened. Doc pulled off the road, and he and Poli got out, leaving the children alone with Donda. With all she could muster of self-control, she quietly told them that their mother had passed away and was with the angels. Tony sat in stricken silence, but Judy immediately began to cry. She didn't want to believe what she was hearing and kept hoping it was all a dream.

For days, she cried, her sobs wracking her body and leaving her gasping for air. She stopped only to sleep or to hope it wasn't true. For Tony the news was every bit as painful, but his uncles had always said big boys don't cry, and he was an eight-year-old 'big boy'. He was old enough to have suffered the anxiety of knowing that his father was missing, and now he had to come to terms with the awful truth that his mother was gone.

There was a very large crowd at the funeral. Judy clung to Donda, crying her heart out, but when someone lifted her up to look inside the casket, she was afraid and looked away. There was the smell of gardenias, and she knew her mother was lying inside the white satin folds. She closed her eyes and only saw her mother's dark hair through a veil of tears. She told herself that her mother was an angel. Whatever was in the casket wasn't real.

After everyone else had left the funeral parlor, Bobbie remained by the coffin, choked with grief and anger. The undertaker had used all his skill to make Vivian look like she was merely sleeping, but Bobbie knew her sister would have been furious to be on display, ravished as she was by her illness. She hated these open-casket funerals.

Rudy joined her. It had been such a long time ago that she had seen him. He put a comforting arm around Bobbie, and without words, she knew what he was feeling. They both blamed Mickey for not having taken better care of Vivian. It didn't seem possible that someone who was so vibrantly alive should have her life snuffed out so young.

In the days to follow, Tony continued to keep a stiff upper lip while Judy gave vent to her misery. Each time she awoke, she began to cry, and as time passed and it felt like there were no more tears to shed, she made a solemn vow to herself that she would never forget her mother and would never stop being sad. It is difficult to say how long a promise lasts in the life of a small child. Years later, she had forgotten how to feel the anguish she felt then, but she remembered the pang of guilt that came when she forgot herself and felt happy. Her sadness faded gradually, but when she had lost the impact of that initial grief, she believed she had lost forever her last hold on her mother. The concept of forever took seed in her knowledge of the world, with quick flashes of its terrifying magnitude.

There was never any question in Donda's mind that she would take on the responsibility of raising her grandchildren. Her sixty-seven years had been filled with turmoil, and she deserved a restful retirement from responsibility. However, she knew that she was the only one who could comfort Vivian's children, and she never once thought of herself first.

Wise beyond his years, Tony was more aware of how changed their lives would be. In the weeks that followed at Donda's, Judy's grief took center stage, and, Tony bottled up his own feeling of loss and joined the others in trying to comfort his little sister.

Hell Ships

Nearly three years had passed, and so far Mickey hadn't received a single word from anyone at home. Like many others, he was tormented by the notion that he was completely forgotten, and that his part in the war would never be known. One day he got the bright idea of asking for Sebastian's help. If his jeweler friend could engrave a message on Mickey's canteen, something permanent, it would be a way of being sure that if he didn't make it, there would be something left to tell Tony where he had been. It would also serve to make sure that no one swiped his canteen.

A message on an aluminum canteen would withstand shellfire and tropical storms or burning sunshine. He chuckled wryly, thinking that he no longer dreamed of writing a bestseller or a movie script. Now he would be content with a few words on a piece of tin, something to leave a mark on the world, small but durable, like a portable tombstone.

He dictated what Sebastian should engrave on the flat side of the canteen, a message that would convey the fact that he hadn't lost his sense of humor. He wanted somehow to mention one Japanese officer he had particular reason to hate, but he had to be careful not to write anything derogatory that would get him a beating if one of the English-speaking Japs could read it.

Here was a challenge to his imagination, and he solved the problem by having Sebastian write, "DEDICATED TO THE MEMORY OF LT. YOSHIKYOSHI," with 'the memory of' in italics. That way he could wish the guy dead without actually saying so.

There was a line halfway up, indicating the level of rice, and, above that, between two vertical arrows, he had Sebastian engrave "this space reserved for dysentery flies." He smiled with satisfaction. If only the folks back home knew about what sort of diet they got! Subtle, but satisfying, he mused, and there was nothing that would be likely to ring alarm bells if he was shaken down by a guard.

He thought a lot about whose address he should put on the canteen and decided on Donda's. Somehow she was the one person he knew would always be there for him. Engraved closer to the bottom was, "Say, Bud, if you find this cup, would you send it to my mother-in-law, Mrs. Donda Martin 10804 Camarillo St., North Hollywood, California, USA."

Sebastian had done a splendid job with a nail he had stolen from the wall of their barracks and sharpened. (So many nails were 'liberated' for various purposes that the building would one day collapse.) When it was finished, Mickey took the canteen in his hand and felt the letters with his fingers. In a world where people died and rotted up, not leaving a trace, here was tangible proof of his existence. It satisfied a primal instinct to leave one's mark on something that wouldn't perish – a humble bid for immortality.

As the war escalated, the Japanese had to recruit every male citizen they could get their hands on, and they were in desperate need of laborers to keep their factories going in Japan. Since October of '42, they had been shipping prisoners of war to Japan and other destinations, where they were used as slave laborers.

Meanwhile conditions improved slightly at Camp No. 1. The many deaths had reduced the number of men sharing the water, and the Japanese decided to merge those who had not been shipped out of Camp No. 3, with those in No. 1. Along with these new inmates came their camp commander, Colonel Beecher. He offered prizes – an egg or a few cigarettes – to any man who killed a hundred flies. The breeding places for all those flies were the open latrines, and an engineering officer named Saint solved that problem. He built an experimental septic tank with scrap lumber and salvaged tin, and, within a short time, the only flies they were bothered by came from the Japanese camp where they had no septic tanks. Once the flies were eliminated, the death rate declined.

Rats had been even easier to eliminate. Drainage ditches ran around the camps, and some men spent their days sitting motionless, like vultures, in the grass that fringed the ditches, spotting the rats that ran through them. With a swift whack from a stick, they killed every rat they saw, removing it as a source of disease and furnishing their mates with meat for the 'quan' pot in the makeshift kitchens the men put together in their barracks. The medics gave two cigarettes for a rat, but rats became so scarce that they could fetch five on the black market.

Life was slightly more bearable, but by now an apathy that was almost as lethal as the threat of disease had descended over the camp. Those who weren't on labor detachments spent their days squatting on the ground, on the shady side of the barracks, staring off in space.

Any sort of mental activity was preferable to this stupor, and some men never gave up. One of the men in Mickey's barracks had a homemade radio receiver he kept dismantled and hidden in various places. So far he had avoided detection by the guards who would have killed him instantly if they discovered it. By listening to whatever he could pick up, he knew that an American invasion was due any day, and as the rumor spread, the men dared to allow themselves renewed hope of being liberated from Cabanatuan. However, with an American invasion eminent, the Japanese speeded up their evacuations of able-bodied prisoners.

People like Mickey who had means to cope with the discomforts of Cabanatuan weren't interested in being sent elsewhere, especially not now when there was hope of being saved.

Officers or anyone else with clout were able to delay being transferred to Japan, pushing the enlisted men ahead of them. By September, American planes were hitting targets in Manila, and the prisoners at Cabanatuan were so overjoyed by the sight that they would have been willing to suffer a direct hit, just to see the Japs beaten. What they didn't know was that their own planes were also hitting anything afloat, including all the unmarked ships carrying POWs.

By then, there is no question that MacArthur knew personally that POWs were being killed at sea by his planes, but he chose to ignore this fact; as a result, of all the POWs who died in the Pacific arena, one out of three was killed by 'friendly fire'. (In all fairness, one has to admit that an over-riding concern was to cut off the supply lines of the Japanese, and he was faced with a choice of sacrificing POWs or prolonging the war.)

By the time MacArthur waded ashore on the island of Leyte in the Philippines in October 1944, most of the prisoners had been shipped out of Cabanatuan. Only those who were in the civilian prison camp or those who were too ill to be moved remained to be liberated. Ironically, many of those clever prisoners who delayed their removal from Cabanatuan as long as possible ended up on the ships that were most likely to be bombed as the war effort escalated. Along with the Death March, the ordeals on these freighters were to etch themselves in the minds of the men who survived. They were called 'Hell Ships'.

Mickey hit an all-time low when he finally got marching orders. He soon discovered that he would have to leave some of his best friends behind. He congratulated them on their good luck – no one wanted to move out – but he felt more despondent than he had in months. Guys like Sebastian, Harry, and Father Joseph had helped him through thick and thin. He had never felt so close to another man, and he wondered if he would ever see them again. He would also be leaving the lucrative network he had built up in his black-market dealings and through his contacts with Ted Lewin and Kirkpatrick.

To try to snap out of that mood, he devised a plan to leave his engraved canteen behind. One of his pals had died a week previously, so Mickey had an extra canteen. A canteen was a prized possession, and now that he had two he decided he could throw his engraved one somewhere along the road on the march out of camp, hoping that someone in the American invasion force would find it. He had to be sure to pick a place where it would be likely to be seen, at the same time that it wouldn't be noticed by a fellow prisoner and snatched up.

He waited until they had a brief rest and made sure that he was last in the line of men. He would have to distract the guard at the same time he tossed the canteen aside. He looked down the road and saw a place he felt sure would be right. There was a large solitary tree, the sort of place a hot and tired GI would sit down to take a sip from his own canteen and smoke a cigarette. He smiled to himself, thinking how good it would be to be a GI who could just sit down like that and inhale a real American cigarette.

Mickey had sized up the guard who was bringing up the rear, and he knew he wouldn't flip into a rage if Mickey addressed him in Japanese. As they neared the big tree, he pointed to a mass of vines on the opposite side of the road and said he it looked like a deer had run into the thicket. The guard automatically looked in that direction, and Mickey threw the canteen into the tufts of grass at the foot of the tree just as they had passed it. It landed neatly where he had aimed, and he had not been spotted by anyone. In his mind's eye, he could see it there, proof of his being alive.

However, his sense of satisfaction didn't alleviate the pain of being marched the one hundred miles to Manila. With the guards shouting, "Speedo," and whacking them when they slowed down or fell out of line, they struggled under the scorching sun, remembering the horrors of their first long march and wondering whether they would be able to finish this one.

In Manila, they were kept at Bilibid prison until they could be herded into freight ships destined for Japan. The bay was full of ships that had been battered in battle. Mickey's group was lined up to be stowed in an old freighter with a metal deck. It had been standing in the sun all morning, and the hold was like an oven. They were shoved in like cattle and left to swelter in their own body-heat while they waited to set sail. Their numbers were so great, and they were jammed in so tightly that if a man wanted to lie down, he had to lie on his side. Except for the light coming from the open hatchway, it was dark in the hold. A bucket was placed in the middle to be used as a latrine, but by this point, some of the men were too weak to make it over to the center. A bucket full of rice and one with water were lowered down by a rope, also in the center of the hold, but the men were so hungry that distribution was largely a matter of those getting something who were closest to the source.

They waited all day in order to sail under the protection of darkness, and once they left harbor, their route was lengthened as they tried to dodge attacks. It was so-so with which bucket was used as a latrine, the so-called 'honey bucket,' and which one contained food or water. Soon, most of the men had dysentery. In the heat of the hold, some went mad, howling like animals or banging their heads against the steel bulkhead. They licked the condensed water that trickled down the walls of the hold, and a man with a canteen had to guard it with his life.

Because of Mickey's connections and his knowledge of Japanese, he was one of the lucky few who stayed topside to act as interpreter, once they were out at sea. This usually took place at night when no American planes would be able to spot them, and the fresh air was a tonic that could keep him going for hours after he went back down into the hold.

Among those who didn't have to stay in the sweltering confines of the hold at all was a man they called 'Snake'. He was an officer who had curried favor from the Japanese by ratting on his fellow prisoners. Now Mickey and some of his pals saw their chance to get rid of him the next time they went topside. It was dark, and no one was watching when three of them used a concerted effort to flip Snake over the side. They stood watching him splash about in the dark water and were unmoved by his yells for help. A guard rushed over to see what was the commotion, but they said he fell, knowing that a horyo wasn't worth fishing up. It gave Mickey a sense of satisfaction he hadn't experienced in a long time.

Unknown to Mickey, the friends he had to leave behind at Cabanatuan, the 'lucky' ones who had been able to delay their removal until last, ended up on the worst Hell Ship of all, the 'Oryokko Maru,' the ship containing the most officers, two to every one enlisted man.

On the Oryokko Maru, 1,619 prisoners were crowded into three holds, packed in like tuna – so tightly than only a few could sit down at a time. Just as the case was for Mickey's ship, there was one 'honey bucket' in the center of each hold for all the men in that section of the ship. On the first day, the guards lowered by rope a light ration of rice and some water into the hold, but there were so many men that not everyone got anything. Sitting in the bay, waiting to sail, the temperature rose to 102 degrees. Once the ship got ready to sail, the hatches were closed, cutting out air and light. By nighttime the temperature in the hold was nearly 120 degrees. The total darkness made them claustrophobic and drove them mad.

It wasn't long before the men had finished the small amount of water they had in their canteens. During that first night there were those who were so thirsty that they killed to suck blood or drank their own urine, and there were desperately hungry men who ate fingers on corpses. Men killed just to get a bit more space. Within the holds of these ships, only Americans killed each other. On other ships, under equally cruel conditions, Australians or British prisoners pulled together, kept in line by their officers and their feeling of brotherhood.

No one who was among the American prisoners would ever forget being in the hold of a hell ship, especially the Oryokko Maru. There were piercing howls of madness, until the guards threatened to fire off volleys of shots into the holds. After that, the men had no choice but to silence those who howled by killing them. Soon it was quiet, except for the odd sounds, like the scratching against the steel hull by a man who was trying to make a hole, arguing that he could hear water on the other side.

Finally, they sailed north, hugging the coast of Luzon, but by the next morning, at Olongapo in Subic Bay, American planes found the ship. First it was strafed, then it was bombed. All that day they endured the attack. The guards shot those POWs who tried to get out of the hold. The next morning the Japanese struggled to get the Japanese civilians who were being evacuated out of the ship to safety, and the planes returned in time to mow them down. During the carnage that followed the prisoners huddled in the hold, unable to do anything.

On the second onslaught, when a bomb tore a hole in the ship, POWs started to pour out. A guard opened fire on some of them, but those who could move jumped overboard into the sea to swim the short distance to shore. While they were in the water, a pilot recognized white bodies and tipped his wings to signal a retreat. It was clear that at least he had not known that American POWs were on the ship. Their troubles were far from over, however. Japanese guards stood on the beach pointing their guns at them and ordered them to take off their clothes and come ashore. There were 1320 men at this point. Three hundred were missing, of whom it was reckoned fifty had died during those first two horrible nights in the hold.

The surviving prisoners were ordered onto the tennis courts at the officers' quarters on the old American Navy base. Their leaders were put in charge of lining them up in orderly lines, and they sat there all night, naked and exposed to a cold wind, and there they remained all the next day, being blistered by the sun. Most of those who were wounded developed gangrene and died rather soon, and there was nothing to use to treat those who survived. A doctor thought he could save one young man who developed gangrene, if he amputated the fellow's arm. He performed surgery on the tennis court, with a pocketknife, the only surgical tool he had. The kid asked for a cigarette, and someone had a half of one to give him while his arm was cut off. He died a few hours later.

They went without food that first day, and the second day they were given a gunnysack of raw rice. Some got a spoonful to chew on – Others got nothing. There were those who were desperate enough to eat the leaves of a lily plant that grew on the perimeters, but it made them vomit and gave them diarrhea. Even so, men kept trying to eat it. Mercifully, there was a water spigot outside the tennis courts, and they were allowed to get water there.

After a few days, the Japs brought a truckload of what appeared to be discarded clothing, all Filipino size. Some men got a pair of socks, some a pair of tennis shoes, others a pair of pants or a shirt.

On the 20th of December, they were trucked to San Fernando. Half the men were put in a cinema, and the other half in a jail. There they stayed until Christmas Eve when they were crammed into the same trains that had taken some of them to O'Donnell, this time with men on the top of the boxcars, too. After a seventeen-hour ride to Lingayen Gulf, they were eventually put on two ships to start their journey all over again. By now they were even more starved than they were the first time around.

Mickey's best friends, Sebastian and Harry, were among the thousand prisoners who were loaded onto the 'Enoura Maru,' a vessel that had just unloaded horses. The hold was full of horse manure and urine, and teeming with horseflies with a bite like a bee. Food was just as scarce as before, and the flies never let up.

Very little rice was lowered down to the men, and whenever it was, the flies covered it in a thick layer, stinging the men as they took their share. Many were weakened and ill from the ordeal they had suffered up until this point. Those who died were hoisted topside to be dumped overboard onto a barge, and the Japanese wouldn't be bothered to supply a barge until at least ten bodies had accumulated.

When they sailed, they moved slowly up the West Coast of Luzon in a convoy, setting out for Formosa when they reached open sea. They arrived there on December 31st and were bombed by an American plane. The prisoners could recognize it by the sound of its motor. In the hold it was bedlam, with prisoners pinned down and crushed by steel girders or heavy planks. There were cries for help from all sides, and nothing anyone could do. For days the Japanese left these men trapped while the horse flies fed on their wounds. Of the 600 men in the hold, about half were dead. Those who were still in one piece spent the next three days trying to free men who were alive but pinned down by wreckage. It was not until the end of those three days that the Japanese lowered down nets into which the dead could be loaded to be dumped onto a barge that lay anchored beside the ship.

After several more days sitting, bruised and starving, in the wrecked hull, they were transferred onto the 'Brazil Maru'. Its last cargo had been sugar as well as prisoners, and now the men gorged on what sugar they could scrounge from cracks and crevices in the floor of the hold. That brought on diarrhea. It was the 12th of January. Nearly a month had passed since they first left Manila, and they were only as far as Formosa. However, now they were part of a convoy heading for Japan.

Once they were out at sea and hit the cold weather, many of them got pneumonia. Squalls blew freezing air down the hatches, and the deck was coated with ice. The men were half-naked, undernourished and exhausted. They huddled in the hold, their meager flesh not offering much of a buffer for the freezing cold temperatures. A tarpaulin was stretched over the hatch, but it couldn't keep out the icy wind. The Jesuit priest gave what small rations he got to others who were younger, and he was the first of Mickey's friends to die. The second one was the air force colonel Mickey got to know in Wainwright's camp. A falling beam had broken his arm when the bombs hit the second ship, and gangrene set in where the bone stuck out. Sebastian stayed by his side, promising him that they would soon be where he could get help, but Harry smiled knowingly and decided to give up the ghost. Sebastian remembered how badly Harry felt the day the guards marched Mickey off to be freighted out. The friends Mickey left behind thought they were the ones who had won in the lottery. Taking one last look at Harry's dead body, Sebastian sighed and shook his head. In this black universe, one could never know in advance who had drawn the shortest straw and who was the lucky one.

An average of twenty-five men died each day until they docked at Moji, on the island of Kyushu in late January. When they had left Manila, it had been humid, with temperatures in the nineties, and they arrived in Japan to one of the coldest winters in man's memory. Out of more than 1,600 men at the start of that transport, it was reckoned there were about 500 still alive, and nearly one hundred more died after their arrival in the sub-zero temperatures. The only man who was noticeably fat upon arrival was Ted Lewin, the gambler. He was rice-trading all the way from Manila to Japan, keeping up his weight at the expense of men who died of starvation. He still carried enough cash to get out of working in Japan, just as he had done at O'Donnell and Cabanatuan. He was a study in the worst side of American enterprise. Among the Australians and the British, the officers would never have allowed such activities, which mean that their survival rate was much greater.

Mickey's Hell Ship had arrived in December, also in sub-zero weather. Once it docked, those who were lucky enough to survive and could still stand were herded into pens, freezing in their skimpy clothing. They were lined up and ordered to strip. The Japanese needed their labor, but they were afraid of diseases. They hosed them down with icy cold salt water, sprayed them with disinfectant, and made them bend over for a glass-rod check-up for dysentery. Then they were issued a blanket and cast-off Japanese uniforms, and marched through the streets, past children who spat at them, to be put on trains and transported to their new imprisonment.

Mickey was sent to Osaka and from there to Narumi near the port of Nagoya on the main island of Honshu. He knew he was closer to California, but in this hostile environment, he felt farther away than ever. With a feeling of despair, he faced the task of learning how to survive in this new type of confinement and with a whole new cast of characters.

Donda's House

After Vivian's death, Tony and Judy lived with Donda, in North Hollywood, a place referred to by everyone as 'The Valley'. Residential areas had sprouted up among peach, walnut and orange orchards. The snow-capped San Bernadino Mountains were etched clearly on the horizon, and the foothills weren't yet blurred by smog.

The house was a wooden, one-story structure, with a clapboard finish, like so many of the early Californian houses. A porch ran the length of the front, shielded from the street by a privet hedge with a gigantic hydrangea in the middle. A low roof and the tall hedge kept the porch cool and shady at one end, while a sunny-yellow rose climbing on an arched trellis dappled the sunlight on the other end.

During the summer, the cloying sweet fragrance of the white blossoms on the privet hedge attracted a myriad of colorful spiders that filled the space between the hedge and the shingled roof with their lacey webs. Visitors with a fear of spiders had to contend with the fact that Donda wouldn't kill creatures that were harmless. Her attitude about black widow spiders was different. When she found one of their egg cases in the garage or dugout cellar, she put them in a glass jar and baked it in the oven after hundreds of minute spiders had hatched out.

Judy loved being with her grandmother. Donda's heart went out to her, for she remembered the pain of losing her own mother at a tender age. Donda let Judy sleep in her big bed, at considerable inconvenience to herself. The vastness of the bed disoriented the tiny child, and she usually wiggled around until she was snugly nestled into Donda's side, even when a barrier of pillows was placed between them.

Tony slept in a cot by the wall, and as he and Judy lay in their beds waiting for sleep to come, their eyes became accustomed to the darkness in the room, and they talked while looking at the odd shapes looming about them.

Donda's bedroom was an intriguing place. Her penchant for saving anything she thought someone in her large family would want to use someday had caused her to fill closets and chests with clothes of all descriptions. They had overflowed into the rest of the room – Coats on hangers and gowns draped over the backs of chairs, and headless hats. Once the children had become accustomed to the shapes in all this bedlam, nightmarish figures were no longer imagined, and they provided the comfort of familiar objects.

The large wooden headboard of Donda's bed was equipped with a double-socket light fixture, with chains to turn on the light bulbs. Always thrifty, Donda fitted only one socket with a bulb, and after a few shocks to Judy's fingers, she learned not to turn on the light.

Donda's bedroom was at the back of the house where there was no movement of air. In the winter months there was an indescribable, but very explicit cold smell of unused clothing, and a warm smell of fabrics in the summer months. The clutter in the room cast it in gloom, except for an occasional ray of afternoon sunlight in which Tony and Judy could watch minute particles of dust, floating in the still air.

Suspended between wakefulness and sleep in this undisturbed atmosphere, Judy always had the comforting presence of Tony, as his words drifted cheerfully towards her in the stillness of the room.

"Tony, are you awake?" she asked, knowing perfectly well that he couldn't hear her if he weren't awake, but also knowing that usually she could count on an answer.

"Yeah. Are you?" he said, quietly enough to avoid bringing one of their aunts to the door for a scolding.

Years later, Judy had forgotten what they talked about, but she remembered clearly the pleasant feeling of lying still in the darkness, listening to his voice as he told her wonderful things about real people and ghosts, or about things too vast for her to imagine, like the universe.

Mickey had instilled in Tony a disregard for authority, enabling him to explore ideas beyond those which he learned in school or in Sunday school. Judy was less inquisitive, but she accepted as gospel anything Tony said. It was lovely to have a hero.

In the eyes of a child, the house was full of interesting places. The bathroom was so small that a vanity table had been crammed into the space by the toilet, providing hours of entertainment while one sat on the can. Judy could admire herself in a three-way mirror, sniff the stoppers of an assortment of elaborate bottles of perfume, or rummage through the drawers, treasure troves of hair fixtures, old make-up, costume jewelry and manicuring tools. Just inside the door was a built-in linen cabinet that smelled delightfully of soap when opened.

The bathtub was an old-fashioned one on lion feet, with a nice slope at one end. Tony and Judy loved to rub soap on it for a good slide into the water, and Donda was too good-natured to scold them for getting the floor wet, but they finally got too wild and were given separate baths. She never became jaded to the convenience of having running water in the house and used the same bath water for both children. It was taken for granted that Judy, being a girl, should have it first.

Donda rose early all her life and was always in the warm kitchen when the children got up. As she read the morning paper, she sat atop a chest of drawers, where the bottom drawer was left partially open to jut out, forming a footstool. It was smack up against the high side of the gas oven, and she called it her 'throne'. She drank coffee from a large, chipped cup, which she replenished several times during the day from the percolator that stood over the pilot light at the back of the stove, to keep warm.

Years of hard work lay behind Donda, and ahead of her was the vague hope that "her ship would come in," and she could shower her loved ones with gifts. Each day she checked the newspaper for the horse races and tried to choose a winner; however, her good common sense prevented her from actually placing a bet. Meanwhile, Doc's success as a chiropractor and his wife's nose for real estate had made him a well-to-do man, and he gladly took on the extra expenses that came with the children.

In summertime, the children sat barefoot on the slanted wooden door of the dugout cellar, eating ripe fruit, the juice running down their arms, making them sticky and soon striped with dirt. Like agile, small monkeys, they climbed in the apricot tree when it was filled with clouds of white blossoms or heavy with golden fruit.

Vivian had been aware that it was to their advantage that Tony and Judy were small for their ages. Everyone felt like spoiling them, and they were judged to be more precocious than the unfortunate child who is large for his age. While Mickey and Vivian had been lenient about letting them explore, they had been strict about manners. This proved to be a real advantage when they were suddenly alone in the world and had to rely on kindness from family and friends.

Donda's world was large for an imaginative child. Every block had a vacant lot, and it was there children from near and far met to hide in the tall grass or wage battles. Uncle Doc made a playhouse for Judy, and Tony made a stagecoach out of his wagon, piled Bobbie's two youngest boys inside, and stopped by Judy's small house for ice cream. It was a time of serious play, play undisturbed by adult interference, days filled with what Judy and Tony considered important projects, without supervising adults to take away the magic. Donda respected the privacy of small children as long as they told her where they were going.

Tony was always the leader. His vivid imagination provided them with an endless variety of adventures, and the boys usually tolerated Judy tagging along with them. There was someone at home in each house on the street, and they soon learned where they would be welcome and even given a glass of lemonade or a cookie, or where they would be chased off and would come back to play a prank.

The street was long and straight. The houses and gardens became grand at the other end of the street, where fruit orchards still stretched towards the mountains. Bing Crosby lived with his wife and children in a mansion on that end, and sometimes Tony strayed far enough to play with one of the Crosby boys.

At the other end of the street, by Doc's clinic, were the A & P Market and a drugstore, and Donda let the kids go there by themselves to buy Popsicles on summer days. Buying a Popsicle at the corner drugstore gave an opportunity to sit on the piles of magazines in one corner of the store and read comics under the pretext of buying one, while the kindly storeowner tried to act like he didn't notice them.

On Tuesdays, Aunt Marcia came over to do the washing and, on Fridays, to take Donda grocery shopping in Marcia's old Ford sedan that smelled like cigars, because Eddie had bought it used. Tony longed for the days when he had Mickey to tag after, but Judy loved being fussed over by dear Aunt Marcia and going with them to shop.

Marcia was prematurely gray and had lovely blue eyes, magnified by wearing glasses. She was in her own little Christian Science world, oblivious to all evil, wreathed in smiles and only reprimanding if the children allowed themselves to use the word 'hate' or to cuss. Tony loved to tease her by saying something wicked. They were allowed certain euphemisms as curses, such as 'son-of-a-gun' and 'shoot,' but those were too tame for a boy whose father had spoken much better ones.

The washing machine in the screened-in back porch was an upright round tub with an agitator in the middle and a wringer attached to the side. Borax was added to the water, and the clothes were put in and fished out according to a system, the whites first and the dirty dungarees last. This indispensable washing powder was called Twenty-Mule-Team Borax, evoking colorful visions of mules descending a steep mountain path. Equally fascinating was the bluing that was added to the last rinse of white clothes.

Judy liked to watch this process, and she enjoyed the smell of hot, wet soap. Marcia worried that her niece would put her hands in the wringer, an accident which had left Donda's one arm badly scarred many years previously. She painted horrendous mental pictures of small children who had whole arms mangled, sending Judy scampering off until the clothes were to be brought in from the line, fragrant with fresh air. Poor Beulah loved to hang up clothes, and after the children came, she took to hiding the box of clothespins under her bed, worried that they would take them from her.

In the back yard was a stone incinerator, for burning trash, and a garage, crammed with all the things Donda didn't have room for in the house. Every imaginable sort of flower and plant was squeezed into her garden, and in one sheltered spot, Judy was given a plot to make a 'victory' garden. There she spent many happy hours, tending small plants and imagining that it was a real farm.

The radio was an important part of the world at Donda's. In the afternoons, Donda listened to her favorite 'soap operas', where love and intrigue left the audience hanging in suspense at the end of each episode. Tony and Judy eagerly looked forward to their favorite radio programs, too. On Saturday evenings one was swept into the world of "The Lone Ranger" or the "Inner Sanctum," "The Shadow", or the hilarious world of Jack Benny and Rochester. All of California was in an uproar when it was discovered that when asked to spell 'does' most children demonstrated the impact of radio commercials, by answering 'duz,' which they picked up from the catchy little jingle, "Put Duz in your washin' machine, D. U. Z. does everything!"

Sometimes the children were allowed to walk downtown, to movie matinees, or Uncle Doc and Aunt Poli took them to grand cinemas where they saw "Scudda-Hoo! Scudda-Hay!" and "Song of the South," and "Bambi," each film more wonderful than the last. Walt Disney's "Fantasia" opened up the world of classical music, and "The News of the World" presented the drama of real life.

Donda's house was like Grand Central Station, with a constant flow of aunts and uncles, great-aunts and great-uncles, old friends who were to be addressed 'aunt' and 'uncle,' and all the ex-spouses of Donda's off-spring.

Vivian's first husband, Rudy, still came to see Donda, bringing his Russian wife who was content to live with him in rooms that served as his chiropractic clinic in West Los Angeles. Elsie's first husband, Uncle Guy, had worked his way up to being captain of the vice squad in the LA Police Department and was presumably the meanest cop in town. He was always very jovial when he visited Donda whom he dearly loved. Right after the war, he liked to bring a Doberman pinscher that he had trained as an attack dog and use it to roust Tony and Judy out of bed. However, he left it with Uncle Albert one summer, and when he picked it up it was docile as a lamb.

There was also Albert's first wife, Irene, who was loved by everyone in the family, and his second wife, Helen, whom he met when Albert was Charlie Bickford's chauffeur and she was the governess to Bickford's handicapped son. Helen was from Alsace-Lorraine and slept in the nude, a fact that evoked endless conjectures about their private life.

Added to that list of characters were the strays that Donda picked up during the unsettled months at the end of the war. A couple hauling a small house trailer stopped at Donda's, looking for a place they could park for a few nights. They had little else than the old jalopy and trailer and a story about a job they had been promised in the Valley. Donda loaned them bedding and a few pots and pans to cook some food she gave them, and the next morning they had vanished without a trace.

She didn't let something like that spoil her faith in human nature, however, and the next time she helped someone on the road they were circus performers, waiting for the rest of their troop to join them for a winter in California. Tony and Judy were spellbound as they sat in the branches of the walnut tree, watching the man who ate fire dip his long-handled swab into a bucket of kerosene, light it and swallow the flames. There was an albino with pink eyes who couldn't be in the sun even for a minute, and there were two trapeze artists who practiced acrobatics on the ground.

During the winter, the children's bath day was Saturday. That was the night that Donda washed Judy's hair and rolled it up in rag curlers. Sundays, it was brushed into shiny, long curls that bounced when she walked. Doc tried to teach Tony the trick of sleeping with a nylon stocking cap on his head to make his hair smooth, but Tony preferred combing it with pomade, the sticky green stuff that kept it in place. Donda checked them over and smiled with satisfaction before sending them on their way to Sunday school.

They walked to the Christian Science Church on Morrison Street, dressed in their Sunday best, with a dime for the collection tied up in a clean, white handkerchief. Judy loved attending church and singing 'Onward Christian Soldier'. She looked forward to Sunday school afterwards, with pretty Miss Lindsay as a teacher. Tony was more skeptical and wanted to know how to explain evolution if the book of Genesis was true. The study of evolution was still in the realm of speculation in many parts of America, and he found there weren't too many people to talk with about it. Lacking someone else, he talked about his ideas to Judy. She was always amazed at what he had to say, wondering how he could remember so much, and he told her matter-of-factly that he had a photographic mind.

Donda knew Vivian would want the children to go to Sunday school, and she could see that believing in God and angels had made it easier for Judy to accept her mother's death. However, Donda herself never went to church, and that was proof to Tony and Judy that you didn't have to go to church to be good.

To get to school, they walked down Donda's street and past a peach orchard whose owner once shot rock salt at Tony's bare legs as he and his chums made a run for it with some stolen peaches. From the start, they got a lot of attention at school. Coming from the islands was something special, and all the teachers knew about their parents. They became accustomed to people making a fuss over them. For Judy, as time passed, the pain of her loss was reduced by a sense of importance. She felt like Margaret O'Brien in a tear-jerking film, taking to melodrama like a duck to water. She was the envy of her class when she was asked to be on the Art Linkletter Show, where she could tell that her daddy was a prisoner of war.

Unlike Tony who missed the stimulation of a father as imaginative and fun loving as Mickey, Judy thrived on the constant attention of her doting aunts. She loved every minute of school, whereas Tony felt that there were better things to do.

Periodically, Jane descended upon Donda's, like the witch in a fairy tale. Once Jane took Judy out to buy her a new dress and some shoes, but Judy sensed that what should have been construed as an act of kindness was really an indirect criticism of Donda. She hated the dress. It was dark blue, of excellent quality, and dismally plain.

Following Jane's lightning visits, there was a great deal of talk among the aunts and Donda, and Judy knew Jane had made Donda unhappy. She heard them whisper about Jane wanting her and Tony to go live in Vegas, and whenever she came, Judy was afraid she would try to take them away.

Donda worried about Tony. She knew he hadn't forgotten Mickey at all and how much he missed those unforgettable times they had together, so long ago, before the war. One day, Donda answered a knock at the door, and Bill, the postman was standing on the porch with something in his hand.

"What you got there, Bill?" Donda asked as she opened the screen door.

"It must be a package for you, but someone's got the last two digits in the street number turned around. 'Course, I know everybody on the street, so I knew it was supposed to come here. What'd ya' suppose it is?" he asked, shaking it.

Donda smiled, knowing how nosey Bill was. "Well, wouldn't you love to hang around and find out, Bill? Hold your horses and I'll open it up."

He looked on impatiently as she took the time to untie the string, rolling it up and putting it in her apron pocket. Puzzled, she found the parcel to contain an old GI canteen, and it had writing on it. There was a pencil-written note, signed by some man she didn't know, explaining that he was in the U.S. army and had found the canteen during a battle when the Japanese were run out of the Philippines. He wrote that apparently a POW had lost it in the jungle when he was being moved from Camp Cabanatuan to Manila.

Donda felt a shiver up her spine, as she read Mickey's message on the canteen. Somehow the words sounded just like something he would have written. Tears came to her eyes as she imagined him. Holding the canteen in her hand, there was a rush of images that ran through her mind and a feeling at the pit of her stomach that her whole world was being turned upside down. She had worked so hard at blocking out thoughts of Mickey, knowing how the Japanese supposedly treated their prisoners. Was this proof that he was alive, or that he was dead?

"Well, I'll be," Bill whistled under his breath. "Imagine that coming all this way, clear around the world. Do you suppose this means he's alive?" Bill knew all the family's business, and he always felt sad when he thought about how much Tony missed his dad.

"I don't know, Bill, but we can always hope," Donda said, not knowing whether she dare to hope or not. Why would Mickey's canteen be out in the jungle if he were all right? Still, it was such a concrete reminder of Mickey as she remembered him, something that she could feel in her hand, something solid that Tony could cherish.

Slave Labor at Narumi

While the family was puzzling over the brief message on the canteen, Mickey was still captive, not in the Philippines but in Japan.

When the prisoners arrived in Nagoya, their hopes of getting out of the war alive received a tremendous blow. Not only were they far away from the sympathetic Filipinos, they were in a new type of hostile environment, right in the heart of the country where they were hated and in a climate as cold as the Philippines had been warm.

Thin as rails and under-nourished, many of them ill with dysentery, they were completely unprepared to endure the freezing winter temperatures during one of the coldest winters ever recorded in Japan. The Japanese issued each man a threadbare blanket and a used Japanese army uniform before trucking them off to the factory where they would be making railroad stock and hauling freight. By now, they had all lost so much weight that the small uniforms hung loosely on them.

Mickey was assigned to a work detail moving railroad stock, grueling work made worse by his weakened condition. Anyone who was too slow was beaten. They froze all day long, and there was no relief when they lay on their pallets at night. The first night, shivering in an unheated barracks, with the single thin blanket and the presence of the other men the only source of warmth, Mickey was unable to sleep. He pictured Vivian, remembering in detail their last night together, a night filled with the excitement of the plans they had for their life in the Philippines. Tony had come into their room half asleep and curled up between them. He tried to imagine the warmth of the bed with Vivian and Tony, but the feeling eluded him.

They worked from 5:30 in the morning until four in the afternoon, slaving away in a factory. They were fed a fraction of what an American soldier was given if he was inactive, and the food they got was without nutritional value other than a few calories. Their diet consisted of gruel in the morning, an eight-ounce loaf of rice bread at lunch, and rice in vegetable stock with a few bits of fish or meat in it on rare occasions.

Years of practicing the art of ignoring the passage of time had steeled him to live in the present moment and not worry about how big a chunk this war was taking out of his life. The POW's could surmise that the winds of war continued to blow in the wrong direction for the Japanese. Their guards were living on rations too scrimpy to keep an army in power. They continued to be unquestioning in their allegiance to their emperor or too obedient to rebel, but there were shortages of everything.

Unlike the dutiful Japanese, the Americans who had survived thus far had become adept at pilfering everything they could get their hands on. The guards couldn't bear the shame of stealing supplies, but they were only human and couldn't resist closing their eyes to the brazen antics of their prisoners, in return for a share in the loot. They knew the prisoners kept caches of stolen goods in hiding places under the floorboards of their barracks, but they no longer were zealous in their searches, preferring to wait and be offered a bribe.

At O'Donnell and Cabanatuan, the craftiest Americans had been able to survive by bartering within their own black market, but by the time they reached Japan, the prisoners had been shaken down so many times at each station along their journey that they no longer had anything to trade except their meager daily ration of rice. Aside from stealing things, the best way to strengthen one's own chance for survival was by gambling, trading rice or trading cigarettes, or by combining and juggling all three aspects of exploiting their fellow prisoners. Evil practices begun back at Cabanatuan became a plague at Nagoya.

Anyone who didn't have the self-discipline to live with being hungry every minute of the day, or to do without nicotine, risked getting in the hands of a rice-trader or a gambler. A satanic system had evolved with loan shark interest rates. Cold and starving men with weak will power would trade their next ration of rice for the opportunity of eating two rations and having a full belly here and now. If they made a trade in the morning, they would owe double the amount by evening. Nicotine addicts were so desperate for a smoke that they would be willing to trade or gamble their next ration of rice for a cigarette, which by now was only a semblance of a cigarette – either a Japanese brand or something rolled with whatever scrap of paper was available. (The very finest paper was a page from a Bible.) Mickey was appalled at the merciless exploitation of men too weak to resist and how low some people could stoop to gratify their needs. One guy was dying of malaria while his brother was out peddling quinine for cigarettes.

As the interest rates piled up higher and higher, a man risked trading his very life for one cigarette or a full belly. However, the real challenge for the dealers and gamblers was to manage to keep the borrower alive as long as possible while milking him for his pitiful rations of rice, for if he died, the ration would no longer be dealt out by the guards. The strong preyed on the weak, and the clever gambler ripped off the strong.

One of the foxiest traders was a guy they nicknamed Sly. Mickey had watched him in action, and he saw that one of Sly's 'customers' was going to die of starvation.

"How can you take the guy's rice, Sly? He won't make it through another day without his ration," Mickey said, in disgust.

Sly had about as much warmth as a reptile. He looked at Mickey coldly and grunted, "The stupid son-of-a-bitch would die anyway. If I don't get his rice someone else will."

Maybe he was right, thought Mickey. He didn't feel inclined to argue the point, because the system was too entrenched. The worse it got, the more he stayed with his closest buddies, a couple of guys he met while on Bataan. Their strength was in sticking together, and he was grateful for the bond they had formed. If one of them got sick, the others made sure he got something to eat, and they were all three practiced thieves.

Eventually, the years of starvation numbed even Mickey's feelings. At first he tried to draw parallels to what was happening to him and his fellow Americans to what had happened to other peoples in the history of the world. Not taking his suffering personally had helped. He knew that throughout time, there had been wars, when rulers eyed a source of wealth outside their boundaries and went after it. He knew enough about economy to look behind the immediate causes for war. Japan had wanted more access to the raw materials the colonial powers were controlling. The poor suckers who were implemented in the battles had been hypnotized by religion or pride in their states, and their cruelty towards the enemy was part of the formula for success. While at Cabanatuan, puzzling over these factors had helped him in distancing himself from his fate in the present battle, but after he fell into the routine of hopelessness that was their lot in Japan, he no longer could pursue a thought to its conclusion. He just put one foot in front of the other and lived on will power.

Another source of income that cropped up in Japan was the business of maiming horyos so they wouldn't have to work. Prison doctors were appalled at the number of prisoners who showed up with a broken arm, always the left if one was right-handed, or a broken leg, always a straight break that would mend properly. Some prisoners specialized making breaks, others in bone-crushing. For the man who chose a broken limb, it was a desperate act, a choice between being beaten by a guard for not keeping up the pace of work or getting a self-inflicted injury with the risk of an infection which might lead to death.

There wasn't enough flesh on their bones to insulate them from the winter cold. Their skin felt brittle, and shifting heavy loads was agonizing. That winter in Japan, Mickey could sense that he was at the end of his line. Weakened by relapses of malaria and dengue fever, his legs like matchsticks and his private parts painfully bloated from beriberi, he found it more and more difficult to pull himself out of bed and stand at attention for roll call.

Then Mickey and his buddy, Louie, had a bit of luck. It turned out that the interpreter for the camp had been a desk clerk at the Royal Hawaiian before he was conscripted and forced into the Japanese Army. His biggest wish was that the damned war would end and he could somehow get his old job back. Because he could talk with Mickey about Oahu, and because Mickey spoke Japanese, he and Louie were assigned to work in a warehouse, doing stevedoring and general cargo handling. It was backbreaking labor, toting bags of rice that weighed one hundred pounds, but it gave them boundless opportunities to 'liberate' supplies. If they unloaded a train with supplies bound for the Imperial Army Headquarters in Manchuria, they stole what they could and hid it under the floorboards in their barracks. Minus the share they had to give the guards who knew what was going on, they were able to stiffen a starvation diet with enough to carry them through the winter.

Their supervisor at the warehouse was a kindly old civilian named Oshiko. He was a little cog in the big war machine, and he was past caring about the glory of the Empire of the Rising Sun. He was by nature a good person and couldn't turn his back on the sufferings of the POWs. Mickey was able to establish a friendship with this simple man and his family.

Each morning, when the guards came to take the work force to the streetcars that transported them to the factory, everyone in the barracks would be forced to his feet. A certain number of those who were ill or disabled would be allowed to stay back, but once that number was established, anyone who didn't move would be beaten. Not working meant half rations, but a beating administered to a man in such a weakened condition could mean death.

During one extremely cold spell, Mickey had a relapse of dengue fever and was too ill to get up when the prisoners were awakened for their daily stint at the factory. Freezing winds whistled through the cracks of the flimsy barracks as he lay shivering on a thin pallet, wrapped in the rag that served for a blanket. Louie shook him and said, "Damn it all, Mickey, you've got to get up. There are too many down for you to get on the sick list today, and you're in for a beating if you aren't on that list."

Louie helped Mickey to his feet, and they made their way together to the train that took them to work. They were packed like sardines in the train, making it easy enough for Mickey to stay on his feet. He had literally no room to fall down.

When they arrived at the drafty warehouse, the cold was even more penetrating, and Mickey looked like he wasn't going to make it. Oshiko took one look at him and knew how bad off he was. The old man's quarters were behind the warehouse, and he decided that he would have to keep Mickey there if he were to have a chance to survive.

Mickey lost consciousness and didn't remember being carried into a small room hidden by crates of machine parts. Risking his own life, Oshiko had Louie help him move Mickey to the warmth of his small home and hide him. There the man's family nursed him, gave him warm broth and kept him alive. Without Oshiko's help, Mickey would never have survived.

Louie bribed the guard who was responsible for roll call, and Mickey was able to rest and recuperate for several days.

On one occasion, Mickey and Louie thought they had found a treasure. In a corner of the warehouse, they discovered boxes of chocolate bars. It seemed too good to be true. Their mouths drooled as they tore open the wrappers, and they stuffed chocolate into their mouths greedily, feeling the sugar hit their bloodstreams like a jolt of electricity. They ate as many as they could until a guard was heard heading towards the warehouse.

Mickey hid a few bars in his sleeve, planning to give them to one of the guards who appreciated bribes. Mickey figured that chocolate would be worth at least five Japanese cigarettes. The rest of the day he and Lou felt exulted, bright-eyed and bushy-tailed like they hadn't been in years. The lingering taste of chocolate was more exciting than a four-course meal at the Ritz.

The prisoners had long since given up trying to create any diversions. They were beaten if they were found with a book or with anything that resembled a checkers or chess game. Usually, they were so weak by the end of the day that they could barely manage to wolf down their sparse rations of watery rice before they fell into a sleep like death, oblivious to the vermin that infested their blankets. However, that night, when they returned from their day's work, Mickey and Louie remained wide-awake. They felt wired and figured it must have been due to the extra energy they got from the chocolate.

Mickey had hidden the extra chocolate bars in his cache under the floorboard. He could hear the guard patrolling his beat. All was quiet, and he figured it was as good a time as any to sneak out and give him the chocolate. He whispered to Louie that he was making a run, and he padded silently off in the dark.

He headed towards the 'benjo' – the flea-infested excuse for a toilet – in case a guard spotted him, and then scurried the short distance to the guardhouse where the guard sat after he had paced off the beat. There was a light in the window, and Mickey ran around to the side of the house that was dark, stealthily tapping on a back door. The guard opened the door a crack, and, when he saw it was Mickey, let him in.

Mickey bowed, like he had learned to do, and reached in his sleeve for the chocolate, handing it to the guard ceremoniously and telling him he had more where that came from.

The Jap smiled and took the present over to the light to see what it was, but instead of making a deal with Mickey, he started to laugh. Shaking his head, he said, "This stuff is pilots' store, Mickey. Too strong. Better not to eat it."

"What do you mean? That's chocolate! It's great – Gives you plenty of energy!"

"Yes, energy. Ha! Too much energy. This chocolate for our pilots. They eat so they won't sleep. It like strong medicine. You better watch out!"

Much the wiser, Mickey went back to the barracks. Louie was still awake, and they talked about what effect the chocolate was going to have on them. They had eaten most of a box.

"Hell, Mickey, I don't know about that, but it sure felt good going down. Only thing I'm worried about is how we are going to feel at five a.m. when we have to get up."

They lay awake all night, feeling wired with nervous energy. In their weakened state, it was like leaving the lights on in a car and wearing down the battery. For two days they kept going, and on the afternoon of the second day, Mickey collapsed while carrying a sack up a ramp. He was aware of the guard kicking him in the ribs and beating him with his stave, but nothing could prevent him from falling into a deep sleep. Louie fared no better. Their fellow prisoners managed to get them back to the barracks, and when Mickey awoke it was because of a burning pain in his arm. "Christ," he said to Louie. "The damned guard has broken my arm. I won't be able to tote a sack for weeks."

His instant reaction was relief. It was easier to trade a sharp, instant pain for the unrelenting pains from blows delivered to a cold body when he couldn't keep up the tempo demanded by the guards. One thing Mickey had become hardened to was pain. He couldn't count the number of times he had been beaten by a guard, and they showed no signs of letting up.

The best way to avoid a beating was to be too disabled to go out to work, but since that meant going down to rations that could hardly keep a man alive, he had to rely on what he had stored up. From the rumors going around, he figured it was just a matter of time before they would be liberated, and he knew he had enough stolen goods stored under the floorboards to pull through the next few weeks. Of course, the beating he would get if a guard discovered his stash would be the end of him, but by now there were enough guards who relied on him for goods that he felt safe.

Not having to haul himself off to work each day, Mickey had time to think about the future. He was sure he would come out of this bog mire of human misery alive. He struggled to put words to the thoughts that flooded his mind, eager to share with Vivian the wisdom he felt he had gained during the years when all but the spark of life had been stripped from his being.

As the war drew to an end, the POW's entered the most dangerous part of their captivity. Their captors refused to capitulate, and there were daily atrocities as they vented their anger and frustration on those Americans they had under their control. Until late 1944, the official policy from Tokyo was to prevent POWs from falling into enemy hands. Back in the Philippines, at Palawan, the guards herded 150 prisoners into a bomb shelter, drenched it with gasoline, and lit it, machine-gunning, clubbing, and bayoneting those who managed to get out and flee. Similar atrocities were occurring all over the areas they occupied.

MacArthur's dramatic promise – "I shall return"– had rung out around the world, and now he could realize it as he set about retaking Corregidor. For eleven days, five thousand Japanese fought to the death. Only twenty were left alive to be captured. In Manila, they also fought to the bitter end, massacring Filipinos all the while. Civilian deaths totaled approximately one hundred thousand, and the beautiful city was ruined.

No one back home knew about the fate that fell upon the American prisoners. How would one explain the fact that MacArthur's staff had knowledge of the presence of POWs on the escaping Japanese freighters and gave the order to attack them just the same? For example, the USS Snook sunk the 'Arisan Maru' when they were crossing the China Sea. 1,800 Americans were on it. Just before they saved themselves and their civilians, the Japanese guards cut the rope ladders to the holds that contained the prisoners, trapping them inside. Only ten prisoners survived.

As the war of liberation raged all over the Eastern sphere, thousands of prisoners of war were left at the mercy of their captors as MacArthur gave highest priority to further conquests. Australians desperate to rescue some of their own on Borneo were only thirty miles from a prison camp that held twenty-four hundred British and Australian prisoners, but MacArthur refused to give them a few DC-3s to execute a rescue. Only six prisoners survived, and that was by escaping on their own.

After MacArthur recaptured the Philippines, things got even more dangerous for the prisoners in camps all over the Pacific. In many places, the Japanese moved prisoners and ordered massive digging of ditches, trenches, and tunnels. Were they getting ready to torch the prisoners, or were they preparing for a last-ditch stand like they did at Iwo Jima and Okinawa, preparing to die to the last man rather than surrender?

The POWs who had secret radios risked death as they kept their ears tuned to whatever they could pick up from the outside world, hoping they could have a plan ready to get them through this last agonizing stage of their captivity. They hoarded whatever weapons they could make or find, planning to rush their guards if necessary.

The Japanese had put themselves beyond the pale of civilization by not ratifying the Geneva Convention. Furthermore, World War II had put an end to respecting the policy of avoiding attacks on civilian targets. When the invasion of Japan was launched by America, it was with bombs unlike anything the world had seen, and much of Japanese industry was located in heavily populated cities.

The biggest bombing mission in history was initiated in the beginning of March 1945. Firebombs created an inferno in Tokyo, with temperatures as high as 1,800 degrees Fahrenheit. Along with a magnesium cluster bomb, there were bombs that released the hideous chemical called napalm, a jelly-like substance that oozed across the ground, creating a river of flames. In the wake of it all, there were miles of human corpses, twisted and charred beyond recognition. The rivers were clogged with blackened bodies. There were 80,000 Japanese dead and far more than that injured. Never had there been a man-made fire of such dimensions. It was like a solar eruption and reduced Tokyo, the capital and most populous city, to a charred graveyard. Flames from the incinerated city could be seen by the retreating pilots until they flew over the curve of the horizon, and the smell of smoke and burnt flesh stayed in their nostrils long after the attack. About two hundred POWs died during the bombing raids, and by the end of June, thirteen million Japanese were homeless.

One day Mickey saw American B-29's high in the sky over Nagoya. 285 bombers flew in formation, and black smoke marked where they had dropped their load. The amount of incendiary bombs dropped on Nagoya exceeded even those dropped on Tokyo. Though their impact was a less spectacular show, two square miles of the town were totally obliterated. POW camps were unmarked, and everyone in camp knew the bombs might fall on them, but they still cheered them on.

Then the turn came to Okinawa. After two months of bombing Okinawa, seventy thousand citizens were reduced to being cave dwellers or committing suicide. They were made prisoners by their own forces if they wanted to give up. More bombs were dropped, and 95,000 Okinawans, mostly civilians, were killed. Still they were told that the emperor wanted them to continue fighting. The white invaders, they were warned, would rape and massacre them, and destroy everything they had left.

The Japanese also fed their troops atrocity stories, telling them that the Allies would treat them the same way the Japanese had treated their POWs. On Attu, an island in the Aleutians, there were 2,500 Japanese when the Americans invaded. 1000 of them made a banzai charge against the invading force and were mowed down. Others held grenades against their bodies and blew themselves up rather than be captured. Their doctors killed the wounded. It was called 'gyokusai' or heroic death. At the end of the day there were only a couple of dozen to take as prisoners.

Firebombing continued all over Japan with devastating results, and, incredibly, the Japanese still refused to surrender. Understandably, it was a dangerous time for the hated American pilots. Airmen who had to parachute out of their planes faced torture they would never have imagined possible. Some were turned over to the mobs and torn apart. Others suffered slower deaths.

Eight pilots were given to a group of professors at Kyushu Imperial University. In a dirty room used by students to dissect corpses, the professors cut the airmen up alive. They drained blood and replaced it with seawater. They removed vital organs and experimented with blood circulation, squeezing off the flow of blood through the artery that leads into the heart to see how long it took for a man to die. They gouged out holes in skulls to poke knives into living brains and observe what would happen.

Still, the allies were not able to bring Japan to her knees. Then the world got its first taste of a monster code-named Little Boy, the bomb that opened the atomic era. On August 6th, it was dropped on Hiroshima, demolishing everything within a mile around its epicenter and sending shock waves around the world, but the Japanese did not surrender.

Three days later, the second atomic bomb, named Fat Man, was dropped on Nagasaki, killing sixty or eighty POWs and forty thousand Japanese.

At last, on August 15th, the Japanese national anthem was played on the radio, and all citizens were asked to stand as they listened to an announcement made by their emperor. It was the first time the Japanese people had ever heard the voice of Hirohito, the Son of Heaven, speaking in a high-pitched voice an ancient Japanese that was incomprehensible to most of his subjects. With his words, World War II was finally all over, except for the cleaning up.

At Pingfan in Manchuria, Ishii Shiro set about closing down the laboratories where hundreds of victims had endured scientific experiments. Six hundred Chinese and Manchurian laborers were machine-gunned and the subjects of experiments poisoned or gassed. The heap of tortured, infected and vivisected bodies was too big to burn. Ishii Shiro's parting gesture was to turn loose thousands of infected rats.

Once the peace treaty was signed, Mickey and the other prisoners had to go through the anti-climatic days of waiting for the outside world to find them. The very guards who had been beating them right up to the final moment, met up in civilian clothes, subservient and hungry. Amazingly, the prisoners soon discovered that there was no satisfaction in taking revenge on such abject enemies, and they booted them away in disgust. Most horyos didn't have the mentality to inflict the same treatment on the guards as that they had endured, and those who did soon tired of it.

While they waited to be picked up, planes that had picked out POW camps dropped tons of food and supplies. The prisoners went wild and ignored all warnings to go easy when they started to get food again. They ate themselves sick on canned fruit, Spam, and chocolate – ten thousand pounds of supplies. There were bundles of boots, bales of cigarettes, crates of tomato ketchup, Campbell's soup, beef stew, fresh-baked bread, and Pet milk, dropped from giant bombers too heavily loaded to hit their targets accurately. Prisoners and Japanese were dismembered or killed, hit by mountains of supplies or a can of pineapple. There were more POWs killed by falling treats than had been killed by the Hiroshima A-bomb. Some men died from gorging.

Strangest of all, after the capitulation, the Japanese opened up enormous stores of relief supplies sent by the Red Cross to alleviate the plight of the American prisoners – canned food, all the medicine they could have used, shoes and clothing, all untouched, even though the Japanese themselves had been starving and in need of medicine. The Americans shook their heads and were more convinced than ever that they would never understand their oriental enemy.

Bellies full, some of the POWs ran wild, stealing trains and robbing banks, tossing yen to kids and terrorizing the Japanese officers who had tormented them. Other isolated POWs had no choice but to stay where they were and wait to be liberated.

A plane flew low over Mickey's camp, flashing a signal to ask what they needed most. The camp doctor told a POW signalman to signal that they needed medicine for those who had tuberculosis and a good bourbon whiskey – also for medicinal purposes. A little later they heard the drone of a plane returning and out dropped a case of bourbon and the medication. The supplies were wrapped in two mattresses and, miraculously, landed intact. The pilot then signaled for them to indicate where the kitchen was, and he dropped two cases of corned beef through the roof, with a note on one box, "Needs to be cooked. Bon apétit!"

After three and a half years of starvation, the men went crazy celebrating. They felt they had to do something to prove that they were in power, and they hit upon the idea of buying a bull. It was owned by a Japanese civilian who came regularly to empty the latrines so he could sell the contents as fertilizer. Pulling his cart was an enormous bull that the men had eyed for months, wishing it were theirs for the eating. They called the man The Honeydipper, and the last thing he wanted to part with was his bull. Intoxicated with their new power, they forced him to give it up, foisting on him all the Japanese money they had earned for their slave labor.

There were some men from Texas who claimed they could butcher the bull, but killing it was tougher than they had bargained for. They tried knocking it out with a two-by-four, but that only made the massive creature moan. Finally the Japanese cook took pity on the beast. He stepped in and rendered the deathblow with a butcher's knife to the veins in the neck. Then the men cut the meat in small pieces and cooked it for three days, but it was still as tough as shoe leather. It didn't matter ... They still felt good about having taken charge.

They stayed in the camp, feeling safer there than they did on the outside, but they longed for the day they would be found by their compatriots. Mickey was jubilant the day he spotted a group of Americans heading towards the camp, and he ran to tell the others. This was the moment they all had dreamed of and talked about. Survivors, they would be heroes, flown home to a royal welcome to make up for all those years of misery. They had fabled about what would be in store for them, one man's vision more fantastic than the next man's. Some men thought they would be given a ticker parade and a brand new car. Others spoke of a house and pension for life. Seeing Americans as victors was like proof that it was the greatest country on earth, and they were part of it, winners all.

A long time before, Mickey had reached a stage where the mind had out-distanced the body, where he had begun to take pride in his ability to let his mind take wing while his body was beaten and shackled. Humility had been forced upon him, and like the true survivor he was, he rationalized that this state was a step on the path of a greater understanding. From that moment on, he took pride in regarding himself and his fellow horyos as men who had achieved a status reserved to a privileged few. Now his hard-earned wisdom would be put to the test.

To the approaching Americans, the prisoners seemed like they were in a trance and looked half-crazy. Strapping big soldiers were appalled at seeing these poor men, who were undernourished to the point of looking deformed. Mickey stood frozen in place, even though he was mentally rushing forward for a grand reunion. Years of starvation had robbed him of his natural impulses. It was like an out-of-body experience, a dream-like vision of the old Mickey running to greet them, while the human wreck he was stood transfixed.

Over the years, the prisoners had become accustomed to seeing each other, diseased and diminished as they were. Most of them weighed little more than half their normal weight, and they all were marred by the characteristics of malnutrition. The liberators were bigger than life, straight-backed and strong limbed, with smooth skins. They were dressed in uniforms and boots so perfect that the horyos were stunned by their splendor. So much had changed in GI issue – their helmets, the fabric of their uniforms, their weapons.

Mickey, taking it all in, felt like Rip Van Winkle and wondered whether more time had passed than they had counted on. The confrontation with the Americans they had dreamed of was overwhelming and shattered their egos. One minute they had been the strongest of strong, the POWs who had come through hell and high water, beatings and diseases, work that pushed them beyond human limitations, with the inner strength it takes to be a survivor. Their expectations of being considered heroes by their liberators vanished with the blink of an eye. Now they huddled together, sensitive to the pity and repulsion written all over the faces of those liberators. It was like a great wound had been opened up, exposing the ugliness that had become a part of their existence.

Jake, whose stump of an arm had served him well this past year and who had been so grateful that it had healed, saw himself in their eyes and felt like a poor old lop-sided bugger. Louie, who had become somewhat of a hero for his ability to steal anything that wasn't nailed down, was reminded by these well-dressed men that he was just a gutter rat back in the states. Making use of his talents when he got home would only land him in jail. Henry, whose jaw had been smashed by the rifle butt of a guard in Cabanatuan, made guttural sounds that Mickey understood as an expression of happiness, but the liberators looked away, trying not to notice him.

Until this moment Mickey had felt an immense sense of accomplishment. In the nightmare world he and his buddies had known, he was a leader, a horyo who had mastered Japanese, someone who could intervene when the guards were ready with new torment. They had learned to patch their clothes, to make jokes about lost limbs or debilitating ailments. Theirs was a fraternity unlike any he had ever experienced, where membership made the difference between life and death. Throughout their internment, they had retained their ability to laugh at things that would have reduced an outsider to tears. Now he gazed at the approaching officers and suddenly saw himself and his fellow horyos through their eyes, an emaciated group of shrunken men, eyes staring from deep sockets, clothes that had never fit hanging in tatters. They were crawling with lice and putrid from untreated sores.

The splendid liberators talked above their heads, as if the prisoners would not be capable of understanding what was being said. The officers in charge agreed that these poor creatures had to be fattened up before they were presented to the American public.

Huge, gleaming white hospital ships docked in the harbors of Japan, staffed with doctors and nurses and full of all the food the men could ever have imagined. They could eat to their heart's content, anything they wanted to, any time of the day. Many of them made themselves sick, eating two-dozen eggs or ice cream with chocolate sauce for breakfast. To the staff of the ships, some of them seemed like pack rats, looking about furtively in the mess halls, eyeing the cutlery, the plates, the salt and peppershakers, all of it spotlessly clean. They still clung to their pathetic possessions, unwilling to relinquish a battered canteen or an old pillowcase where they could hide food they pilfered from the meals.

This close encounter with the army was the first inkling they got of the fact that no one would ever believe or understand what they had been through. They had to suffer the humility of being accused of lying when they told what they had been fed and what sort of work they had to do. Young, healthy doctors scoffed and figured these human wrecks were off their rockers. No one could survive on such sparse rations, much less do hard labor in mines and foundries and factories. Men who had wanted to tell their story witnessed this disbelief and fell silent, never to try again.

Most of them were overwhelmed with an unexpected feeling of despondency and fear. Mickey's readjustment was smoother. Being older, he had seen enough of life to know that a person torn out of his environment always has to reinvent himself and adjust to the newest realities. Once the effect of nourishing food started to kick in, his brain worked full speed. Feeling came back into his fingertips and the soles of his feet, and his eyesight got back to normal. The same thing was happening to most of the men, for some faster than for others. The only thing the food couldn't do was to mend the scars they had on their souls.

Mickey was intrigued with the newness of everything they were seeing. There were new types of bandages, a wonder drug called penicillin, and DDT to wipe out in a moment all the vermin that had plagued them for years. There were new fabrics, and there was sound equipment unlike anything he had seen before the war. There were things called jet planes that flew without propellers. While he had learned to exist on the very minimum required to sustain life, the war years seemed to have been a cornucopia for the rest of the world. He could hardly wait to get home and see what America had to offer.

It was MacArthur who came to Japan to administer the peace. He was the biggest hero of the war in the Pacific, to everyone but the men from Bataan and Corregidor. Those guys knew him as the vain individual who was able to promote himself in the midst of their misery, but his performance for the rest of the world had been brilliant. Even his most critical peers had to admit that never had so much territory been regained with so little loss of life among the men he had employed in the Pacific theater.

Furthermore, it was to prove crucial to the future of Japan that he was the person in charge of the rebuilding of their shattered country. Because of his knowledge of the Orient and the conviction he had – that his destiny was to play an important role in history, he approached the problem of the occupation with wisdom quite uncharacteristic of a conqueror. In fact, he played the part of a beneficent Caesar so well that he endeared himself to the Japanese while at the same time making drastic changes in every fiber of their society.

The Japanese had prostrated themselves at the feet of their emperor and had been convinced that they would win the war through racial superiority, and they were devastated after the surrender. Their entire social structure was built up around a system of obedience. MacArthur, the erudite aristocrat, saw the importance of presenting himself as a God-like figure whom they would obey, while he reinstated their sense of self-respect.

No one else would have been so well qualified for the task ahead. He paved the way for the prosperity that would be theirs for the next half a century, at the same time totally altering the rather feudal system of the Japanese Empire. He even gave their women the vote. With none of the hatred that many of the POWs had churning inside themselves, he was able to put the fighting behind him, thereby serving the best interests of the Japanese and alienating even further the men who had served under him on Bataan. In fact, the success of his program depended on ripping a page out of history. If Japan was to be rebuilt along Western lines, no one was to be reminded of the way they treated their prisoners.

While the POWs longed to go home, the first plane out of Japan was loaded with Japanese students whom MacArthur had designated to study in America, giving the horyos even more to grumble about. The fires of war had not yet cooled, and the POWs felt they had already taken on second priority in the new world order.

As the men's bodies began to fill out, their minds started to function once more, sloughing off a protective apathy. They were all eager to get out of Japan, and a gigantic program was set in motion to get them out of there by ship or plane. The final irony for some men was that the grim reaper caught up with them on the way out. One shipload went down in a typhoon, and the same typhoon wrecked two planes full of POWs. The plane crews worked non-stop, filling their cargo space with as many of the lightweight horyos as possible. The flights became so routine that, once they were airborne, they sometimes put the planes on automatic pilot and came back to drink coffee and shoot the breeze with the men. One such plane flew into a mountain. Most horrifying of all was the story of the bomber, with the men all sitting on the floor wherever there was space. Over the Pacific, the bomb bay opened, and men fell out to be lost at sea.

Once Mickey started to regain his strength and saw that his limbs were beginning to fill out and resemble something human, his old self-assurance re-surfaced, and he could think of nothing but his reunion with Vivian. So many years without hearing a word had convinced him that she must have given up waiting, but still he harbored a hope that no matter where she was she would want him back. He pushed away any thoughts of her being committed to a new life and held on to the memories he had of her just before he left for the Philippines, trying to pretend that it was only yesterday. If she had found a new man, he was confident he could ace him out.

Finally, he decided it would be best to write to Donda first. It had always been Donda who seemed like a safe anchorage in the storm. No matter what had happened in the past four years, he knew she would be there, ready to mend the holes in the fabric of life. He was hovering on the brink of a normal existence, and like a man beside a swift stream, he looked for a shallow crossing and cautiously put a toe in the water before taking the plunge.

Donna Darling -

When the boys said I could write someone, I replied that I used to have a mother-in-law that would appreciate the first letter home from a "horyo." Notice I said "used to." I don't know if I still have the privilege of sleeping with your lovely daughter, but I hope. Have not heard a word from any of you for almost four years. Four years is a long time. It's like coming back to life.

I won't try to tell you anything about what's past. It is enough that I am alive with only a few scars. I even took my arm out of splints yesterday.

Aloha nui, My Sweetheart,

Mickey.

Bill the postman brought the letter with the morning mail. It lay within a stack of other letters that Donda had carried into the breakfast nook to sit and read with her morning paper. The sun was shining, and she poured herself a fresh cup of coffee before sitting down and lighting the one cigarette she smoked each day, a habit she had picked up from Mickey that year she was in the islands. Sifting through the envelopes, she recognized Mickey's writing, and her heart jumped to her throat.

With the end of the war in Europe, followed by the surrender of Japan, Donda had scanned the news every day, trying to learn something about what had happened to Mickey. However, it was difficult to catch sight of the individual in the turmoil of the times.

When the waves of destruction that had swept over Europe and the South Pacific had ebbed out, they left in their wake the debris of war: Shattered cities, mutilated people and barren fields. Nonetheless, with the armistice, people all over the world felt the euphoria of survival and cherished a belief that this all-consuming war had cleared the land to build a lasting peace. This feeling of optimism could easily prevail in America, where the mood was undisturbed by war's wastelands. The land was unsullied by ruins of cities, and Americans were intoxicated by the success of their mission. Politics were briefly forgotten as the American people bathed in the knowledge that industries great enough to crush the German menace and the Japanese imperial designs had been built up virtually overnight. A whole new era of technical achievements beckoned with promised prosperity.

In the States, everyone celebrated a victory. However, in all the fanfare, Donda had a nagging feeling that those men in the Philippines were deliberately forgotten, and she tried in vain to understand how they could be so unimportant. It was as if they had never existed. Now she sat with proof that Mickey was alive, and she wondered why he wasn't sent home immediately upon his release.

She read his brief letter with tears in her eyes, as she thought of Vivian and Mickey and their children and all there was to tell him. When Donda lost Vivian, her daily concern with Tony and Judy had left her little time to mourn. The sorrow she felt was held at bay and had gradually seeped into her very being, not hindering her in carrying on in a way that made life normal for the children. Now, like a tidal wave, a new flood of sadness washed over her, as she put herself in Mickey's place and imagined what he would feel when he learned that Vivian was gone – Vivian whose vibrant beauty and warmth made the memory of her so intense.

She was torn between letting Mickey come home before telling him about Vivian or writing to him now. Finally, her fear that he might find out from someone else convinced her that she must tell him herself. She dipped her pen in the bottle of ink that stood by her writing pad and slowly formed the words that she knew would bring him pain at a time when he deserved comfort and joy.

Meanwhile, Mickey had arrived in Manila, the jumping off point for many of the POWs in that part of the world. He felt so alive, and he was determined never to take for granted the joys of the free world. Along with the rest of the men, he was only frustrated about the delays in getting home. After all those years in prison, with the threat of death at every dawning day, it was baffling that they had to live in tents or barracks in Manila, nagged constantly by the fear that they would die before they reached home.

It was there he received Donda's letter. He recognized the large, rounded handwriting and felt a tremendous sense of relief. He could picture Donda as he had seen her so many times, carefully forming pages of script as she corresponded with her far-flung loved ones. Just the thought of her brought comfort. All those years of longing for freedom and the past few weeks of picturing his loved ones were reaching an end, but his happiness was tinged with caution. By now he realized that he was no longer a part of their world. The fact that the first letter was from Donda made him apprehensive, and he waited until he was inside his room before he opened it. His hands trembled as he tore open the envelope.

He had to read the letter over and over again. In all the horror of what he had been through, he had never imagined that Vivian would die. During the heady months leading up to the war, her bout with cancer had been forgotten, replaced with an impression of her as someone too strong to be afflicted. Memories of their life before the war had been a cherished vision, untouched by the reality of his four-year nightmare. His mind refused to accept the knowledge of her death, but neither could it reject Donda's heart-rending testimony. As time passed and shadows deepened in the room, he continued to sit on the edge of his bed, his eyes unseeing and his hand clutching the crumbled page with Donda's words. Snatches of melodies and phrases filled up his consciousness, and he was passive, disinterested in trying to put them together in a way that would give meaning.

The old feeling that their lives were linked together was reinforced as he realized that she had passed away at the same time that he was fighting for his life in that Hell Ship. It would have been better if he had thrown in the towel, he thought, bitterly.

A cockroach that had escaped the latest round of DDT crawled towards a crack in the floor, and he watched it, momentarily interested in this small creature, with a feeling of indifference to his own future. It scurried along the crack, seeking escape into darkness. Suddenly it disappeared where the wall met the floor, leaving his mind blessedly blank.

The others found him there when they trickled back into their quarters before mess. Years of being together in the confinement of their prisons had accustomed them to these trance-like states their buddies escaped into when problems overwhelmed them. Their jocular greetings petered out, and they left Mickey alone, knowing that any attempt to jostle him out of it could cause him to go berserk. However, when he continued to sit there, staring off into space, his face a mask, Jake cautiously took the letter from him and read it.

Jake's voice cracked when he said to the others in a hushed voice, "Hell, he's lost his wife. Go get a doctor. I think he needs help."

Mickey shook his head and became aware of Jake and the other men. Like a man who is drowning, he thrashed about for a hold on anything in reach. A cry of anguish came from somewhere deep in his chest, and he pushed frantically at his mates as they tried to hold him still, feeling a long-bottled up rage at his fate.

Two doctors and a nurse rushed into the room and managed to hold Mickey still long enough to plunge a hypodermic into him. He went limp, and they were able to put him on a stretcher and move him to the psycho ward.

He spent days in a state of complete lethargy. He felt like a person who had used his last strength to swim to a lifeboat, only to find that he was unable to climb aboard. In all this despondency, he wanted to feel the luxury of closing his eyes and experiencing the restfulness of death.

Lying between clean sheets, fed each day, he was content to remain in his present state. For the first time in his life, he was indifferent to the people around him. When he thought of anyone, it was his buddies from Cabanatuan, but they were scattered. Where? Sometimes they haunted him, seeming more real than the men he saw today.

Memories of Vivian had buoyed him up through all those years of starvation and torture, and everything he had wanted to return to were things he shared with her. Now, he was trapped in a new sort of hell, where thoughts of her filled him with anguish, and the only peace he could find was in blocking all thoughts of her and everything else from his mind.

The psychiatric ward was filled with men who either were unable to slip away from the horrors of the war or unable to face the return to a life they no longer felt a part of. The bonds they had with buddies who had shared those years of clinging to hope were severed overnight by freedom and by being dispersed. They all were to go through a feeling of anti-climax as they returned to normality.

The doctors and nurses were kind and patient. The ex-POW could see pity in their eyes, but they were like people from another planet, only serving to emphasize the void into which these haunted men found themselves. The staff's job was to try to help these poor wretches regain a sense of reality, and, in many cases, a feeling of self-esteem to counteract the systematic Japanese methods of trying to make them feel inferior, but they lacked the insight to know how to do the task.

Mickey's case caught the attention of the chief psychiatrist, Dr. Bullow. He saw in the journals that Mickey was older than the average POW, and everyone said that until the day he had received word about his wife, Mickey had been one of the prisoners who seemed most up-beat. He was known for being good at boosting morale, and some of the men who knew him were shaken in their faith in the future when they saw Mickey crack.

Dr. Bullow spent as much time as he could, asking Mickey about his past, trying to rekindle an interest in the life he had left behind when he sailed to Manila. However, there were so many to help and not much time to work with. He was convinced that Mickey would pull through, if only the right words made him want to help himself out of this vale of depression.

One day a doctor came through with a flight destined for Honolulu, and it was one of those many examples of what a small world this is. He had been an intern back when Mickey drove ambulances, and he recognized Mickey's name right away when he read the roster. The doctor's name was Sam Walsh, and he was a rangy, warm-hearted Westerner whose work in the war had aged him prematurely.

Dr. Bullow told Sam what little he knew about Mickey. "From what they say, he has been one of the prisoners who was an inspiration to the others. He was also a wheeler-dealer in prison camp, and nothing seemed to get him down. Then he gets this letter from home and learns that his wife died a year ago. Knocked him for a loop, and he hasn't been able to snap out of it yet. We don't have the resources to do much for these poor guys, and I hate to send him home in this state."

Sam found Mickey sitting on a bench outdoors, his blue eyes vacantly fixed on the cloudless sky. He focused them on Sam as he approached, but his gaze was lifeless, and his greeting perfunctory.

Sam sat down next to him. He couldn't remember ever having seen Mickey even remotely sad, and he wished to God he could help. "Remember me, Mickey," he said, leaning forward to look him in the eye. "Sam Walsh. We knew each other back in Hollywood when you were driving ambulances."

Mickey looked at him, and it was obvious he was making an effort to place the face. After a moment, he nodded, smiling, and said, "Yeah, sure I remember. You were dating that cute little nurse, named Ellie." Having said that, his attention flagged, and he seemed to be off in his own thoughts again.

"Yeah, I married that cute little nurse," Frank said with a chuckle. "I heard you went on to make it big with the studios."

"Well, that was a long time ago." Mickey who was usually so talkative seemed to be weary from even this brief conversation and didn't say anything to make it easy for Frank to continue.

"I'm just passing through and saw your name on the roster. I know you guys have had a rougher time than any of us can imagine. Now that it's over, and you're returning to the land of the living, it's only natural that you're going through a rough patch." Softly he added, "I heard about your wife, and I don't know what to say, but you're gonna be all right, Mickey.

You'll see...There's a reason for you having pulled through, and one day, you'll find out I'm right."

Not expecting any response, he went on with small talk until it was time to leave. Rising, he took his wallet out of his back pocket, and opened it to find a card with his address, telling Mickey to look him up when he got back to the states. As he did so, a snapshot fell out of the wallet, onto Mickey's lap.

Mickey picked it up, and for the first time there was a look of interest on his face. Standing in the photo, between Sam and a pretty blond woman, was a little boy, holding Sam's hand and looking up at him with a proud smile.

"That's Ellie, Mickey, and that's my kid. I can hardly wait to see him. Ellie writes that he wants me to come home and teach him how to swing a bat." Hank grinned and said, "Not sure I'm any good at that. I'm more used to swinging a scalpel, but I'll give it a try. If this damned war has taught me something, it is that I want to spend every minute I can with my kid."

Sam hesitated to take the snapshot from Mickey. It was the first time he had noticed any expression on Mickey's face. It was like he was waking up from anesthesia. His voice sounded rusty when he said, almost to himself, "My boy must be about the same age as yours. He must be eight or nine." For the first time, he looked Sam in the eye.

Sam put his hand on Mickey's shoulder and quietly said, "There's your reason for pulling through, Mickey," and he gave him a friendly punch, and walked off towards headquarters.

The rest of the day, Mickey was in a feverish state. Where he had been unwilling to face life, he now was impatient to get home. He thought with longing of Tony and Judy, and he felt that every minute of delay was time lost. He remembered all the plans he and Vivian had made, the ideas they shared about bringing up the kids. He didn't know how he could bear the time it would take to be discharged from the hospital and be allotted a place on a flight home.

He felt alive again. Vivian was gone, but he would make sure their kids were raised the way she would have wanted them to be. The transformation in him was so remarkable that at first the psychiatrist was inclined to think it was an unstable phase. He wanted more time for observation, the thought of which made Mickey so frantic that they came close to triggering off a new crisis.

At last they were convinced that he was well enough to be sent home. He was on the next flight to Honolulu, ready to face the glittering new world that had emerged like a Phoenix from the war waste.

Before he left Manila, Mickey sent off a letter to Donda. It didn't occur to him that Jane might feel miffed.

Dear Donda,

Might as well send this on and trust it to reach you first as transportation is such an indeterminate thing. I finally arranged with the Navy to get out and will probably leave tomorrow. Must stop at Honolulu for a few days and tie up some loose ends there. They had me in the Psycho ward after I got your word, and I've had a hell of a time getting them to clear me.

Don't you or my mother take the kids out of school. If they are with you, keep them there until I get there. Will wire from Honolulu date of my arrival. As soon as you hear, please wire or call my mother, as I have already lost her address.

My love to the family – and tell Marcia I want her to cook the Xmas dinner, and tell Elsie to get a bottle of champagne, for I'm going to have my first drink of it with her, and tell Guy that I lost the Jap lugar I was bringing him, but I'll get him another.

Needless to say Manila isn't anything like it was before the war, but it is still better off than Japan.

Write my mother and tell her that outside of the fact that I'm gray, I'm not changed much. Will fly up and visit her after I've seen my kids.

Love to Marcy and Doc and Al and everybody.

Mickey

Mickey was flown to Honolulu and learned all he could of Vivian's last hectic months there. He saw how much the islands had changed. Honolulu was swarming with people, and the tempo was fast. Ben had been called in, and his family had gone back to the states. D&O Advertising was a closed chapter. Nothing Mickey had before the war was still intact and the memory of Vivian was everywhere he went. He booked the first flight out.

* * * * *

Mickey was finally coming home. Judy felt the tension in Donda's house, as the aunts and uncles talked about the probability that he would want to take his children to live with him.

They stopped talking when Judy came into the room, but she sensed that something dreadful was going to happen, and it was going to affect her.

Donda looked haggard. She was torn between her feelings for Mickey, whom she loved despite his faults, and the conviction that the children were better off with her. The rest of the family had no doubts at all; they were convinced that Mickey would never be able to provide a stable home for his children. Donda knew better than anyone how irresponsible Mickey could be, and she also remembered how fervently Vivian wanted her to keep the children away from Jane. But, with the wisdom gained from a hard life, Donda wasn't as sure as the rest about what should happen with Tony and Judy.

She scrutinized her own motives and realized that her desire to keep them was partly selfish. Her life had taken on new meaning from that day when she found herself the sole guardian of Tony and Judy. She was grateful for each day, feeling blessed with the rare privilege of having children in her care, at a time in her life when she could appreciate every moment of their development. She had been so busy when her own children were small, and now she had this God-given opportunity to enjoy the rewards of having young charges, without the daily struggle to keep a roof over their heads and food on the table. She had her social security, and Doc was generous in helping out with whatever the children needed.

She decided that the best thing to do was to give Mickey the welcome he deserved, and to take one day at a time. She suppressed all thoughts of the future and put cheerfulness in her voice when she told the children that their father was coming home any day.

Of course, Tony was over the moon with happiness. He had been five when his dad left for the Philippines, and no one had been able to replace him in Tony's world. Judy had been but three years old when he left, and her uncles had become as important to her as her memory of her father. Judy's pleasure was no different from her usual enthusiasm about anyone's visit, but Tony was ecstatic.

At long last he would see the father he had missed every day since that awful one, so many years ago, when Mickey had sailed out of their lives, with a promise that it was only temporary. Tony remembered all the fun they had together...Mickey laughingly putting him up on the back of a donkey, swimming with him in the warm, clear water at Lanakai, making a swing for him, and pushing him higher than anyone else could or would. Life was so much bigger when his father was around, and now it would be like that again.

Tony impatiently counted the days, telling anyone willing to listen that his dad was coming home and bragging about him having been a prisoner of war. Briefly, he worried that Mickey had changed, but then someone sent a letter with a newspaper clipping enclosed, taken after the POWs had put some meat on their bones. It showed Mickey eating ice cream and smiling. He looked almost the same, and Tony happily relapsed into his state of bliss.

The big day came, and Donda had gathered the family to welcome Mickey. Luckily, Jane declined to come to the reunion. She was hurt that Mickey had written to Donda, and she claimed to be too busy getting ready for him to come to Las Vegas. Donda invited Mickey's father, and he brought his wife, Nettie, and their son, Ray, with his pretty little wife.

The months that had passed since the liberation had put weight on Mickey. By looking at him, a stranger could never detect what years of hell he had been through, but Donda was shocked to see how much he had aged. He was thirty-seven. His hair was gray at the temples and much thinner, and his face was lined, but he still had that jaunty air of a person who had the world at his feet.

Tony didn't leave his father's side that first day he came to Donda's, but Judy was on guard. With a natural flair for understanding children, he did nothing to rush things, waiting for Judy to come to him, but he realized then that there would be problems.

The years apart had broken the continuity in his relationship with his children. Tony asked Mickey what he and Judy should call him, and he left that up to them. The result was that Tony called him Mickey and Judy called him Daddy, a choice that well reflected Tony's tendency to be a free spirit and Judy's desire for something conventional.

His stay at Donda's was not the joyous reunion he had envisioned. Even in his darkest hours, he had been unable to foresee what it would like to go back among the living, and it didn't make it easier that no one really knew what he had been through. Overjoyed at seeing each of them, he was unprepared for the wariness he could read in the faces of Vivian's sisters. He was moved at seeing his father for the first time, and Ed Owen's obvious pleasure at greeting his son was a welcome bit of spontaneity.

Only Donda seemed unchanged. Mickey didn't register how much she had aged and didn't realize how much she had suffered. He figured she must be hitting seventy, and she still looked wonderful. She spent the next day telling him about Vivian's final days and her worries about Jane. She explained about the divorce, and she showed him the will, which appointed Donda as guardian. "She was afraid they wouldn't be happy if they ended up with your mother, Mickey. Judy was so young."

"She did the right thing, Donda, but now that I'm home, you know I'll want to take them with me."

"I understand that, Mickey," Donda said hesitatingly, "but you've got to admit that you haven't been the most reliable provider in the past. Without Vivian, how will you manage to give them a secure home?"

He had lived through four years of hell, and it had taught him how little it takes to make one happy. He wasn't yet prepared for the boom that had taken place in America during those lost years. For now, he thought it would be enough to be together with his kids, but it wouldn't be long before he would be forced back into the American mold, striving for success.

He grew silent, letting his mind wander to what life would have been if Vivian were still alive. Donda saw the pain in his face and had a twinge of conscience. Why were affairs of the heart always so difficult? She well understood his desire to take his children with him. He had proved to her many times that he was an unreliable parent, but she had never doubted how much he loved his kids, and she could see clearly that Tony worshipped him. She wished Vivian's ghost could be there by her shoulder to tell her what she wanted, now that Mickey had come home alive.

"Mickey, the kids are doing well in school, and you have a lot to get settled. Why don't we wait until you've seen your mother? Leave Tony and Judy here for now and we'll figure out what to do when the school term is over. Tony would gladly go with you today, but it would be very hard on Judy. She suffered so much when Vivian passed away."

Mickey was softhearted, and he could see that what Donda said made sense. Besides, he had a lot of business to take care of and promises to carry out. He thought of the families he had said he would contact, people who should know about the love their sons felt for them when they died out in the Philippines or in Japan. He also had to rustle up the money that had been pledged to those who didn't survive and see that it was distributed. One of the first persons he knew he had to contact was Harry's sister.

He found her address and called on her one day soon after his return. They sat in her living room, and he told her about Harry's bravery and loyalty to his friends. She listened without showing any emotion, and he began to dislike this person who seemed undeserving of Harry's love. He wanted to get out of there, but he remembered his errand and said, "His last thoughts were of you. He wanted you to have this money that was part of an insurance we cooked up in prison camp." He gave her the money, and never forgot her response:

"Is that all?" she asked.

* * * * *

Tony was crushed when he learned that they wouldn't immediately leave to be with their father, but Mickey promised it would be soon, and filled him with ideas for all the things they would do together. He spent a few more days, calling old friends to let them know he was among the living, spent a week at Dunaway's, writing reports for the War Department, and then he went to stay with his father and his father's 'new' family before going on up to Vegas.

Mickey stayed at his father's longer than he had intended. The mixed reception he got at Donda's had wounded him, and it was nice to bask in the attention he received from these simple people. Besides, L.A. was a good place to be while he was trying to wrangle some sort of compensation out of the government. He was beginning to discover how far off his buddies were when they expected a hero's welcome. In fact, those who were in the service were asked to sign a paper promising that they would not speak out publicly about what they had endured.

Ed Owen must have rued the day he became reunited with this son he had deserted. Mickey quickly won over the family with his charm, but he and his half-brother were complete opposites. Ray was big, handsome, boyishly open, and trustworthy. Ray's wife, Trudy, was fascinated by Mickey's suave sophistication and flattered by the way he talked to her. She hung on every word he said. His personality was so different than Ray's down-to-earth manner.

The problems Mickey faced with getting custody of the children and the void that Vivian's death had opened up, left him adrift, confused about his immediate goals. At least his appetite for women had come back to him along with his strength, and it amused him to see that his half-brother's young wife took a fancy to him. With characteristic disregard for social norms, he took it upon himself to teach Trudy the pleasures of the flesh. In fact, he figured that when he left, Ray should be pleased that Trudy would be more fun in bed.

What he didn't count on was the fire he kindled in Trudy. She was willing to follow him to the ends of the earth and certainly as far as Las Vegas. When Mickey finally made his way up to his impatient mother's, Trudy was in tow. She was seventeen years his junior, a real country girl, with naturally curly taffy-blonde hair and a figure that could stop traffic. Mickey had acted on impulse and hadn't really thought about marrying her. He had no qualms about taking her away from his half-brother, figuring that if he hadn't, someone else would have. She was far too hot-blooded for someone like Ray.

Jane was delighted. She couldn't think of a better way to get even with her ex-husband for having left her those many years ago, and she saw that Trudy was someone she would be able to manage.

She was hopping mad that Donda still had the kids, but she contacted her lawyer and got the ball rolling to take the case to court. Mickey didn't think that would be necessary. He trusted Donda. Jane insisted, however, and within days Donda was informed that she had better hire a lawyer if she wanted to defend the will. A pall sunk over Donda's household. When Judy said her prayers, she added something about wishing to stay with Donda, while Tony fervently hoped for the opposite.

Jane hired a female lawyer in Los Angeles, figuring that she would have an advantage in a case of this nature. The lawyer advised her that it would help matters if Mickey remarried and could thereby provide the home with a mother. It didn't sound like a bad idea. Being in Las Vegas, it was a simple matter for Trudy to get a quick divorce and marry Mickey.

Mickey didn't have any objection to getting married if it could help get the kids back. From the beginning, he had only considered her a good-looking lay, but with his usual flippancy towards life's conventions, he was untroubled by any deeper considerations about the meaning of marriage. In his mind, the only woman he had ever married was Vivian, and that was not because of a legal tie. Anyway, Trudy was refreshingly easy to please. She fit right in with the other comforts he was relishing since he came back.

Christmas was coming, but he told Donda that he wouldn't be joining them. He could see that things would be too complicated right now, and Christmas never had meant much to Mickey anyway. Jane had not made it a practice to celebrate Christmas or birthdays. Her years of hardship as a child convinced her that such celebrations were just a potential source for unhappiness, and she was content to let Donda do the honors for the children.

It was a Christmas to remember, and in the eyes of a child, the details are imprinted clearly, undisturbed by the lack of space between images in such a crowded scene. Donda's small house was packed with people. The dining table was extended to its full length and covered with a lace cloth and the best china for the big meal. The centerpiece was a mirror, meant to look like a pond of ice, with cotton all around for snow, and small Christmas figures.

That Christmas was unforgettable for most American families. The war was finally over, but there remained a special atmosphere from the war. A military uniform is probably the most becoming apparel a man can wear, and the women who had married a GI brought their new spouses home to their families that first Christmas during peacetime, dressed in khakis or blues, looking uniformly like a million dollars.

Elsie, for one, was coming home with a handsome captain in the Air Force who could croon like Bing Crosby. Judy was only seven, but she fell in love with Uncle Langley at first sight in the uncommitted way of small girls.

Donda's house was bustling with family members, and each new arrival was a heady event. Cousin 'Slivers' came home from the navy with something so exotic as an English war bride. With long blonde hair and a glass eye, only slightly different in color from her real one, she fit right into the memories of those magical days.

Uncle Albert and his wife came down from the north with a fir tree atop the car. Tony and Judy thought the tree was surely the most beautiful Christmas tree in the world, and for days the children's excitement had mounted, as presents in bright wrappings piled up under its branches. Every bed in the house was occupied, and Uncle Langley had to sleep in a sleeping bag under the Christmas tree.

The kids went to sleep on Christmas Eve knowing that their waiting had finally come to an end. It was still very dark when they awoke and tumbled out of bed, and they scurried into the living room. The big moment had come: It was Christmas morning, and they could open their presents. They kneeled quietly by Uncle Langley's head, hoping he was awake. They had to shake him a bit before they could ask him whether it was Christmas.

His dog tags clinked together as he sat up and rubbed his eyes, looking at them like he didn't really know what they were talking about. He looked at his watch in the dim light from the electric candles on the tree and said, "Hell, no, kids. It's only four o'clock in the morning. Get your fannies back to bed!"

They didn't awake again before it was daylight, and the house was filled with the smell of bacon and eggs and Donda's waffles with hot maple syrup. The turkey was in the oven, and in the midst of all the confusion, Donda was calmly rolling out pastry for the mincemeat and pumpkin pies. Everywhere Tony and Judy turned there was an uncle who wanted to bite their ears, a most unpleasant way Vivian's brothers had of showing affection, something that had to be endured because the uncles were so kind. There were so many presents and so many hugs, so many smiling people standing around, drinking eggnogs and talking while the children squeezed their way through the maze of long legs. Surely it was the most wonderful Christmas ever.

After Christmas, a date was set to settle in court the question of guardianship. Judy's aunts loved to make clothes for her, and by far the prettiest frocks were the ones from Bobbie. On the day they went to court, she gave Judy a yellow, dotted Swiss dress, with flounces in three layers. The flounces were trimmed with white eyelet, laced with narrow, black velvet ribbon, and Judy preened herself in front of the mirror while Donda brushed her hair into long ringlets. It was like getting ready for a party. Tony was cleaned within an inch of his life, his hair slicked back, and his ears scrubbed pink. Anyone would be able to see that they were children who had a good home, Donda thought, as she nervously pulled on her gloves and told Doc she was ready to go.

In the courtroom, Mickey and Donda exchanged sympathetic smiles, but Jane sat coldly ignoring those of Vivian's family who attended the hearing. The children were kept in a separate room while the case was being presented and were not involved until they were led, separately, into the judge's chambers. The judge asked them where they would like to be. Tony impressed him as being mature beyond his years and answered without hesitation that he wanted to be with his father. Afterwards, he was taken out, and Judy was brought in. She promptly answered that she wanted to be with Donda.

The decision of the court was that Mickey should be given custody of the boy, and Donda should have custody of the girl. Jane smiled, satisfied that things had gone so well, but Mickey was crushed. He thought bitterly of all those years of struggling to stay alive and the dreams he and Vivian had shared about the upbringing of their children. He looked at Donda, his face stricken with despair.

With a great deal of control, Donda turned and spoke to her lawyer. "Mr. Baltimore, please tell the judge that it was their mother's wish that the children not be separated. Judy must go to live with her father, too."

George Baltimore was an old friend of the family and had a genuine fondness for Vivian's children; he thought about the many times he had seen them happy in Donda's home, and what a transition this would be for them. "Are you quite sure, Donda? Don't you want to sleep on it?"

Donda smiled ruefully, shaking her head and saying, "That's the trouble, George, I won't be able to sleep if I don't try at least to imagine what Vivian's wishes would be."

Later, she explained to Judy that she would be going to live with her father. One more time in her short life, Judy felt her small world crashing down about her. Stricken with fear of the unknown, she threw herself in Donda's arms and begged her to not let anyone take her away.

It was a terrible day for both Donda and Mickey, the day he came to take his children to Las Vegas. Tony's happiness was marred by seeing his little sister so miserable, and Judy fought all the way to the car. While Donda stood helplessly by, knowing she had no choice but to stick to her decision, Mickey picked up his daughter and carried her kicking and screaming to the front door. Judy's fingers went white as she clutched the sharp edge of the doorway. She twisted her head to look to Donda for help, but it was too late. She was carried out to the car, the door slammed shut and Mickey drove off quickly. Judy curled up, sobbing, on the back seat, while Tony tried to comfort her.

Mickey kept the appearance of remaining calm. He understood what Judy was feeling, but with a deep-set conviction that he was doing the right thing, he kept his mind on his driving while she railed at her fate.

Trudy was in the front seat, and she turned around and tried to comfort Judy. That helped. Judy thought Trudy was pretty, and she wasn't a stranger. Tony and Judy knew Trudy and liked her, from the times that Ed Owen and his family visited their mother in North Hollywood. She'll be nice to me, Judy thought, and she won't let that horrible old Jane do anything mean to me.

After awhile Judy got tired of bawling and began to calm down. She sat up and took notice of the places they were passing, thinking that she would want to be able to find her way back to Donda's if she escaped.

Wisely, Mickey let Judy sputter and rage. He knew how quickly children forget. He smiled to himself, recalling Vivian's temper and recognizing the same trait in Judy. He knew that once a tantrum blew over, she would be good as gold.

Las Vegas – 1946

At last Mickey's homecoming was complete. Jane was too excited to sleep. She had so many ideas for his future. She was grateful that he was alive, and now she would be able to have a hand in shaping the children. All her hard work took on a new meaning. She smiled smugly as she thought about how well she had done. She would be able to support Mickey and his family even if he never did a lick of work.

Feeling expansive, she opened a bank account for Mickey and told him that he should use it to buy himself a wardrobe. He gladly went on a spending spree, buying tailor-made Western clothes for Tony and Judy, and equipping Trudy and himself with pearl-buttoned cowboy shirts, tight-fitting jeans and hand-tooled boots. The world was a stage with dozens of roles, and he wasted no time in adopting the western style right down to the last detail. He clung to his prison camp habit of rolling his own cigarettes, but now he could use real cigarette paper and always had a full pouch of Bull Durham tobacco which he closed cowboy style by pulling the yellow drawstring with his teeth. He transformed Trudy from a fresh-scrubbed country pin-up to a smartly dressed cowgirl beauty.

Jane counted on them living with her at The Anthony Hotel. She could get along swell with Trudy, and as long as she was footing the bills, it sounded like a safer bet. A room had been prepared for Judy. It was a pink and white dream of a room for a little girl. There was a fluffy white rug on the floor, and an easy chair custom-made to her size with a flowered cretonne cover in shades of pink. The bedspread was white and there was a ruffled pink skirt around a vanity table that also was scaled down to suit a small child. Jane had never seen anything so nice for a little girl and thought about how much she would have liked to have such a lovely room when she was a child.

Judy should have been thrilled, but she remained doggedly sullen. Whenever Jane pointed out something nice to her, she did it in a way that seemed like a criticism of Donda. No one is more loyal than a small child, and for Judy to be nice to Jane would have been tantamount to betraying the grandmother she loved. Besides, she had listened to her aunts' talk, and she knew how much unhappiness Jane had caused her mother and Donda. Judy held on fiercely to her dislike of Jane, and because Jane had no real understanding of children, she soon tired of trying to get in the good graces of her recalcitrant granddaughter. Jane's own childhood had been a time of growing up fast to help out with the chores, and she didn't have any insight into the mind of a child who had been the center of attention from the time of birth.

Judy's dislike of Jane undoubtedly made it easier for Mickey to win over his stubborn little girl. Jane was the evil witch, and Judy soon discovered that her father was a good-natured ally. When Jane and Judy were locked in a battle of wills, he seemed amused, and if Judy went too far and had to be punished, he never punished her in anger. That was a promise he and Vivian had made to each other when they were planning the children's future.

"You're going to have to stay in your room until you can come out all smiles, Duchess. I know it's hard when you're hopping mad, but that's the final word." And then he allowed Judy the liberty of slamming the door when she stalked off, for he claimed that everyone needs to let off steam. He called this punishment 'being ostracized' or being put in Coventry, and no one was allowed to talk to the person who was being punished. He knew that she would quickly tire of being apart from Tony and come out apologizing.

Mickey had learned the effectiveness of that punishment under grim circumstances that he hoped none of his kids would ever experience. He thought about the time that the men at Narumi ostracized a guy who worked in the Japanese commandant's office. He won favor with the Japs and got extra rations by ratting on his fellow prisoners. When the men found out what he was doing, the chaplain suggested that they punish him by not speaking to him, and not one man in the camp broke the silence. It was the worst punishment he could have received.

Secretly, Mickey was delighted to see how feisty Judy was. She was learning how to stand up to someone she had decided was a tyrant, and he hoped to teach her how to get along with the rest of the world afterwards. Without lecturing her, he was giving her enough rope to let her learn that disliking someone can be self-destructive and undesirable, if for no other reason, because it wasn't much fun.

Poor Jane didn't have a chance. The first time she fixed dinner for the children, Judy complained that she hadn't been given her vitamin pill.

"Well, honey-chile, you just eat your dinner. We're going to give you such good food that you won't need any pills," she drawled with her Southern accent.

"Uncle Doc says I have to take my vitamins," she stubbornly insisted. "You aren't taking good care of me like Donda!"

With a temper as quick as Judy's, Jane retorted, "Well, you're not a very nice little girl or you wouldn't argue with an adult!"

If Jane thought she was going to get the last word, she learned otherwise. "I want my vitamins!" Judy promptly insisted, positive that Jane could never hurt her as long as Tony was in the room.

"She's a willful, spoiled child. She should never have been left with that silly old woman," Jane fumed, after the children had been put to bed.

"Don't take it personally, Jane," Mickey said consolingly. "She'll need time for adjustment. She was very attached to Donda, even when she was tiny. Don't forget, Donda stayed with us for a year when Vivian was recovering from her operation. Anyway, you always said you like a kid with spirit, rather than some sort of a milk-toast variety."

Trying to change the subject, Mickey continued, "By the way, Trudy and I were hoping you could take care of the kids tomorrow. That guy I told you about with the army surplus jeeps is taking us for a trial run out at Lake Mead."

"I'll take care of them, but I refuse to call what Judy has 'spirit'. It's plain old brattiness, and I know how I'd teach her some manners. But I don't want to be cross. I'll take the kids to the circus while you're gone. I hope Judy will at least appreciate that."

After lunch the next day, she told Tony and Judy that they were going to the circus. She also told them that they were going to like it, and that they were lucky children for having such a generous grandmother. "I want you to take a bath and put on your Sunday clothes, and I'll check to make sure you are nice and clean."

When Judy came in wearing her favorite white organdy dress and Mary Jane patent leather shoes, she thought she was all ready to go. Reluctantly, she let Jane inspect her.

"Well, young lady, I told you to get cleaned up, and just look at those finger-nails, and your knees. You haven't used soap!"

"Yes I have!" Judy said indignantly.

"Oh no you haven't," she insisted. "We aren't leaving until I say you are presentable."

Torn between wanting to attend the circus and defending her standpoint, she did what most willful children would do: She said that she didn't want to go to the old circus anyway.

Jane looked down sternly at her granddaughter, but Judy braced her scrawny eight-year-old frame and glared right back at her. Too late, Jane realized she had painted herself into a corner by threatening to cancel the circus. She had planned this outing and didn't like to change her plans. Besides, it would be a shame for Tony who wasn't any trouble at all. Deciding to take a firm stand, she picked Judy up bodily, carried her kicking into the bathroom, took off her shoes and dumped her into the still filled tub, clothes and all.

Sputtering with rage, Judy stood up and screamed that she hated her, and wriggling out of her grasp, ran through the kitchen. Tony had decided to come to his little sister's rescue, and he was sitting on top of the refrigerator, ready to dump a pail of water on Jane's head when she ran through the door in pursuit.

Mickey tried to suppress a smile when he heard about their antics later that day. He remembered what sort of mother Jane had been when he was a child. The treats she planned were every bit as much something she did to feel good about herself, and she always was furious when she was thwarted in her plans to be benevolent.

While Judy longed for Donda and her aunts and uncles, for Tony, there was no adjustment to make. He felt liberated, back in a man's world. He didn't miss all the fussing he had rebelled against in Vivian's family. Mickey was all a boy could want in a father, and it was magic to be allowed to follow him wherever he went and be part of his life.

Once Mickey had acquired a nice wardrobe and seen everyone he used to know from Hollywood who had settled in Las Vegas, he was overcome with a loneliness that was impossible to explain. Like a person stranded in a foreign country, he longed for his compatriots, the men he had been with in captivity. No one he met now that he was free seemed to have an understanding of what life is like when you are on the brink of Hell. He missed the feeling that his caring about another person could make the difference between life and death. Life in prison camp was something he never wanted to come near repeating, but the daily struggle to stay alive had simplified things and given a sense of purpose to everything he did. The petty worries of the people around him were too insignificant to consider.

It bothered him, also, to know that nothing at all was being done for the horyos now that they were home. He counted himself lucky, because he was an articulate person who could make his way in any society. However, many of those poor horyos were just boys when they were captured, poorly educated, and not capable of verbally defining what they wanted. He knew they would end up haunted by their recurrent nightmares, not understood by those they were closest to, and too psyched out to hold down anything but the most menial jobs.

He longed to see some of them now and celebrate their freedom or cheer them up like he used to do. Jesus, we didn't even get to have a real celebration when it was all over, he thought. The survivors had spread to the winds when they got back to the states. Now that he had a life again he conceived a plan to try to locate some of the others. He would drive throughout the western states in an amphibian jeep, rigged out to get attention.

The first amphibian jeep he and Trudy took for a trial spin sank on Lake Mead, the salesman having neglected to put in the plug, but the next one fared better. Jane didn't understand what he wanted with such a contraption, but she was still willing to listen to every whim Mickey had.

To furnish the jeep with a top, he bought canvas, and he stenciled it red and white candy-striped. On the side of the jeep he carefully painted "HORYO," a word that would give a signal to anyone like himself. He knew that a lot of his old buddies came from the southwest, and he told Jane that he and Trudy would take the kids and meander through the west, looking up a parcel of relatives in Texas, Colorado, and Idaho.

Four years of living with no possessions and starvation rations made traveling seem uncomplicated. With army surplus blankets as bedrolls and canteens to cook with over an open fire, they hit the road at the end of April. Other children were still in school, and while Tony didn't give a fig, Judy found it painfully embarrassing to be doing something different than the rest of the pack. As for Mickey, he considered travel to be more enlightening than schooling.

The amphibian jeep was in itself a conversation piece, and the circus-like top announced their arrival as soon as they drove into a new town. Tourism wasn't yet part of the American way of life, and Mickey's appearance was a great novelty wherever they went. Curious people came out to watch them, and Mickey's winning personality made friends everywhere. Local people told him about the best campsites and willingly offered their help or hospitality. He chose places by a river whenever possible, in order that they would have water for cooking, drinking and washing up.

At nighttime, they threw their army blankets on the ground and rolled up close to the smoldering remains of the fire, Tony and Judy feeling their eyes grow heavy as Mickey pointed out star patterns in the big sky or told them local folklore.

One night in Utah, they camped in a wide gully by a rapid stream. They were fast asleep, curled up in their blankets, when it started to rain. A few big drops were the brief harbinger of a torrent that quickly converted the stream to a roaring river. The gully flooded and became slick with mud, making it almost impossible to get the jeep to high ground.

The nearest farmer anticipated their difficulty and came to help Mickey as he fastened the winch from the jeep to a tree, in order to haul it out of the gully. Mud flew to all sides as the wheels spun to take hold on the steep banks. Mickey laughed and cursed, and Tony and Judy stood by, shivering with cold. Their clothes and the blankets were soaked through, and everything in the jeep was drenched, making it impossible to change into something dry. That night they checked into a motel to enjoy the luxury of a hot bath and clean sheets while their clothes were hung to dry. At times like that Judy remembered Donda's and wished she were back there, but by now she didn't want to be there without Tony and Mickey. For Mickey, it was a good reminder of how lucky he was, and he was pleased that the kids could experience the ultimate pleasure of being dry and warm after a thorough soaking and being freezing cold.

They headed for the Great Salt Lake, wanting to experience first-hand the fact that you could sit up on the water. They went to Bryce Canyon, with its magnificent formations in softly colored sandstone, and had it all to themselves. They continued to Zion National Park, and on the way, Mickey noticed on the map that the river beside the road made a loop and crossed the road some miles farther ahead. The day was hot, and he asked Tony and Judy if they would like a swim. He explained what he was doing, putting them on inner tubes to pick them up farther downstream, and they were both eager to go. What he hadn't anticipated was that there were rapids as soon as they were out of sight. Tony whooped with joy, but Judy was terrified. She clung tightly to the inner tube and tried not to cry.

They arrived safely at the rendezvous and saw Mickey and Trudy standing on a bridge, with their arms leaning on the railing, smiling and waving. Mickey came down to help the kids up the bank, and he laughed when he heard what sort of a ride they had. He felt like he had a charmed life and didn't waste time imagining mishaps.

They traveled to Denver and, afterwards, visited Mickey's cousin in Boulder. He and his family lived in a big old house with a grand oak stairway to the top floor where they were assigned rooms with luxurious feather beds. While they were there, they went fishing by night, with lights to lure their catch, and everyone camped by the riverside afterwards.

They crossed the plains of Kansas. That was where Tony got a grasshopper in his eye and was cured of sitting up front on the jeep, straddling the headlight. Mickey decided to visit the men's prison in Leavenworth, wondering what it would feel like, compared to a Japanese prison. He was struck by its sterile atmosphere and the silent stares of the inmates as the guided tour passed by their cells. Men who were well fed, but pallid, looked apathetic or resentful, and he regretted being a witness to their misery. He wondered how many of them had been guilty of being at the wrong place, the wrong time. He sensed that their fate was a feeling of loneliness that was in sharp contrast to the bonding that took place in the prison camps he knew.

In Texas, they visited Uncle Deb, Grandma Dunaway's brother, an old blind man who spent his days sitting in a rocking chair. He could quote the Bible, and Tony and Judy stood in awe as he recited any passage they found in the Bible, just as if he were reading, while his blind eyes stared into emptiness.

The small sphere in which his blindness had locked him was made bearable by his faith, and he had adjusted by fine-tuning his alternative senses. The result was that he was a powerful listener. He asked Mickey about the years in prison, and for once, Mickey found himself telling about it to someone who gave the narrative his full attention and truly seemed to understand the depth of those lost years. He felt like pouring it all out but realized that the images he painted on Uncle John's mind's eye might stay there, ugly scenes to no purpose, and he stopped himself, making a light remark about his good luck in being alive.

Uncle Deb's daughter, Gardena, was the fattest lady they had ever seen, and she got stuck behind the wheel of the jeep when she tried to drive it. She had a pretty face, and roll upon roll of fat bounced merrily as she laughed while Mickey and Trudy tried pulling and pushing her out of her predicament.

They visited Trudy's family in Oak and Hickory County, Oklahoma. Her parents lived like people had in the twenties, with a big old wood stove in the kitchen, kerosene lamps, and water that had to be hand pumped from the well. There was no electricity and no new-fangled gadgets. The children took an immediate shine to Trudy's mother, Ellen, and called her Grandma. She was a pretty little woman with beautiful brown eyes and long brown hair pulled back in a knot.

Trudy's father, Bob, was a mean old coot who didn't want to foul up his land with oilrigs, which was understandable enough. The only problem was that his wife seemed to be doing nearly all the work without the help of any modern appliances. As grumpy as was the old man, Ellen was always gentle and sweet-tempered.

Their day began at 4 a.m., when Bob went out to tend the pigs and cattle, while Ellen got the wood stove going. Later there was hot breakfast, and Bob cat-napped in his rocking chair while she prepared the noon meal, a big spread of mouthwatering food with plenty of hot biscuits and fresh fruit pies for dessert.

Ellen was never idle. If she wasn't plucking a chicken she was gathering eggs or making butter by working a pole in an old wooden churn. Sometimes Judy was allowed to pat fresh butter into a form with a wooden paddle, and Ellen taught her how to iron clothes with heavy irons that were heated on the stove. Wooden handles clicked into place when a freshly hot iron was needed and the first one was placed back on the stove to heat again.

Trudy was lazy, and let the children run wild. Judy's long hair had become matted underneath, and Ellen patiently and gently combed out the knots and filled a big tub with hot water to bathe her and wash her hair.

Judy felt like she was always getting into trouble because of her temper. She adored Ellen and wished she could be just as patient and kind.

"Oh I had a temper myself when I was a girl," Ellen assured her. "Why I had five brothers, and they used to make me so mad I could spit nails. Once I got the horse whip and went after them right here in this bath house when they were too naked to defend themselves," she said with a chuckle.

Judy looked at her in amazement. If that was true, she thought, I know I can learn to be good. Still, she forgot her resolution as soon as she was scolded for sassing. Sassing was her worst offence – That and fussing about the food.

Mickey never lost his temper, but he patiently explained that she would have to stay at the table until she ate everything on her plate. Once he fixed brains and scrambled eggs, and she had to sit until everyone else had gone to bed. She hoped it would be forgotten in the morning, but there the portion was, on her plate at breakfast.

Otherwise, he punished the children by making them write something a hundred times. Usually, he tried to improve their vocabulary at the same time, like the time he had Tony write: "I am a quiet, refined young man, but my father is a bombastic, vociferous individual." Judy fervently wished to go blind, sitting by a kerosene lamp and writing, but much to her disappointment, nothing which would have extracted pity ever happened.

Ellen wore an old-fashioned cotton bonnet whenever she was outside, tending her vegetable patch or her chickens. The chickens came running when she scattered corn for them, scratching after it in the dry dust. In the evening they went to roost on poles fitted into an underground dugout that stayed frost-free during the winter and cool during the hot summer months.

Hens laying eggs sat in clean nesting boxes in the dugout, fixing their beady eyes on the children when they were allowed to come in and gather eggs in a basket. Tony wasn't afraid of them and learned to carefully slip a hand under them to feel whether there was a warm egg to pick up, but Judy preferred finding eggs in an empty nest. Once, when she was climbing back up the stone steps into the bright sunlight, a cool-skinned egg snake dropped down on Judy's neck, and she panicked, throwing it off and running screaming into the yard. It slithered off and later she learned that they weren't dangerous at all. Tony was much braver; he found garden snakes and picked them up to show Judy their bright colors.

Mickey relished eating the Southern specialties of his youth. He went fishing for catfish that were dipped in batter and fried crisp. He also went out with some other men to gig frogs, and the children watched with fascination as the legs jumped when he fried them on a big pan.

Bob didn't know what to think of a man who liked to cook, and he found Mickey to be altogether too slick. He kept his peace, though; Trudy was his favorite daughter, and he could see she was pleased with herself for catching someone fancy. Mickey seemed oblivious to critical looks and insisted that Ellen let him make a cake. His mouth watered thinking of how it would taste, with all those fresh eggs on hand. He had dreamed of such a cake when he was in prison camp.

He let Judy help him, telling her the secret was in adding as many eggs as possible. Wisely, Ellen stayed away from the kitchen when Mickey tried one of his specialties. It was just as well, because much to Judy's delight, he let the dog lick the bowls as they finished with each one. She told Ellen how clever her father had been to save on the washing-up, and Mickey laughed when he found out that only the kids were willing to eat the delicious cake when it was finished.

Bob and Ellen's farmlands were mainly used for pasture, with dirt roads that lead to places where there grew wild grapes or crab apples. The children were sent off with tin pails to gather these succulent grapes for jelly making. They stood by the road, their bare feet covered in sun-warmed dust, and gorged on the sweet fruit, pinching the tough blue skins and squeezing out the juicy insides.

The farm's cattle drank from a still pond that was near the barn. In it, Tony and Judy spent hours wading, catching small water creatures in a glass jar, or swimming where the water got deeper. They made a raft and played Huckleberry Finn, poling themselves out among floating lily pads. In the afternoon, when the sun was too hot, they liked to explore the shady wooded areas, where large boulders were scattered and thick layers of moss and small twigs provided materials for making miniature towns and gardens.

Once Mickey took Trudy to visit friends in Holdenville, and Tony and Judy were parked at a movie theater. For five cents they could see the film, and the theater wasn't emptied between showings. They saw "Hurricane" with Alan Ladd and Dorothy Lamour six times, starting with the matinee and ending with the last showing when Mickey remembered them and took them sleepy-eyed home.

On the way back to Vegas, they mainly followed Route 66, and the best places to fill up with gasoline were the Mobile gas stations. There were gaily-printed chintz curtains in the restrooms, and the toilets were clean. Sometimes there was a roadside café at the service station, and they got hamburgers and cokes with chipped ice or iced tea with sugar.

Everywhere they went, Mickey was able to tune their minds to the grandeur of the land. They went as far East as the Mississippi where they stood on the western banks, taking time to absorb the power of the river and the mystery of its name, thrilling to the great rush of its waters.

They crossed the Panhandle and headed for New Mexico to see Carlsbad Caverns. There was a handful of people, and a guide took them into the magnificent caves, filling them with wonder at the sight of the stalagmites and stalactites that had taken centuries to form.

They also stopped at any place where there was a sign announcing some strange attraction:

Snakes, Gila monsters, or a tomahawk with a scalp was enough to make it worthwhile. In New Mexico, it was a small place with a photograph of Billy the Kid and a tomahawk that was supposed to have belonged to Geronimo and was made with a human fist. There never were any other people stopping at these places, and the owner could hardly stop talking as he told everything he could about his exhibit. When they left, the road was without cars, and the empty desert stretched as far as the eye could reach in all directions. It was like being the only people on the planet.

In Arizona, they passed through the Petrified Forest, and Mickey explained the process whereby these ancient trees were preserved. To a child, the tales of more recent history that they heard when they visited Tombstone were just as romantic. They saw Hangin' Judge Roy Bean's place and the OK Corral where Wyatt Earp, "Doc" Holiday, Virgil and Morgan Earp fought the Clantons and McLaurys.

Trudy's tan deepened during their travels, and her skin was as smooth as a rose petal. Tony and Judy liked snuggling up to her full figure, remembering the sensually pleasant feeling of being held by their mother.

By the end of their odyssey, Judy was devoted to her father. He was always cheerful. He stuck adamantly to certain principles, but he was never angry. After many occasions when she had to sit for hours over a morsel of food she had refused to taste, she learned to comply with his insistence that she at least try it. To be fussy about food he considered bad breeding, and neither had he forgotten how much easier it was to survive when you are willing to eat anything at hand. All he demanded of her was that she taste the objectionable food, and, rather than wrinkling her nose or being rude, she was to politely decline a second helping. "You have to say, 'It tastes good, but I'm not hungry anymore,' Duchess," he said, his eyes crinkling in amusement.

Sometimes they stayed a bit longer at a campsite, and Tony and Judy spent hours trying to trap a prairie dog or wading in a stream while Mickey loafed around with Trudy. He still wasn't jaded to the fact that life was beautiful in the absence of a squat-legged guard to clout him with a rifle butt.

For Tony the journey was an adventure that seemed too good to be true. His mind was like blotting paper, soaking up enough impressions to last a lifetime.

They returned to Las Vegas a close-knit unit; however, it soon became clear that living under the same roof with Jane wasn't going to work out. Even she could see that. Besides, they took up space that she could otherwise rent out.

She had acquired a piece of land on the road to Red Rock Canyon and said Mickey could have it to build a place of their own, but he would have to start out on a small scale. She worked hard for what she had, and it didn't take her long to realize that prison camp hadn't made any changes in the way Mickey could go through money. On the contrary – he wanted to make up for lost time.

There were already some stables on the property, and Mickey hired a black man by the name of Clyde Walters to help him build a simple, flat-roofed house out of cinder blocks. Afterwards, they ran into trouble when they dug the cesspool, unexpectedly striking water. In an attempt to empty what had turned into a well instead of a cesspool, Tony and Judy took turns being hoisted down into the hole in a pail that they filled with water before it was hauled up again. It was dirty, hard work for Mickey and Clyde, but they laughed a lot, having the time of their lives. Races were still segregated in Las Vegas, but the white, alkaline soil that coated them during a day's labor gave them a veneer of brotherhood that was sealed by the jovial comradeship. Clyde liked Mickey so well that he named one of his large brood after him.

The black population lived over in Westside in a ramshackle mixture of flimsy hovels, some of them made out of cardboard. Clyde was lucky; he had a wooden house, with a porch. The paint was peeling off, and the yard was bare dirt, but it was a happy home for Clyde and his wife and all their children.

Sometimes Clyde invited Mickey and his family to a barbecue in the yard outside his ramshackle house. Clyde's people and some of the neighbors gathered around, and there was much laughter and good-natured joshing.

It wasn't just the mouth-watering smell of the spareribs that drew Mickey to the place. In those dismal surroundings he felt he could recapture some of the better things he had learned while being in prison camp. In the squalor of the shantytown, he found the spontaneous generosity and the joy in the moment that seems to be lost when people no longer have a hand-to-mouth struggle with poverty.

When Mickey and Trudy went to visit Clyde, Tony and Judy both straddled the headlights of the jeep, sitting on the flat hood. The roads in that part of town were in a terrible state of repair, and Mickey once hit a pothole, throwing the kids forward. Judy got a deep cut on her head and was taken into the shack of a nice old Negro woman. There was one room, dimly lit by a kerosene lamp standing on a wobbly table. Being prone to dramatize things, Judy decided that she had died and was an angel, and she felt safe and happy with the kindly woman whose chiseled features were framed by cottony white hair.

When they got home, Mickey put something called 'new skin' on the cut, one more of the fascinating new products that were available after the war. He read avidly about all the latest developments and felt that soon mankind would have the answer to all problems.

Mickey hadn't forgotten the kindness of Oshika, back in Nagoya. He bought an army surplus bicycle, a hundred-pound sack of sugar, and a hundred-pound sack of rice and had them shipped to him.

Their travels hadn't brought him in contact with any of the ex-POWs, but he continued to have a longing to meet someone with whom he could share his wartime experiences. His natural curiosity made him wonder what had become of the others. They were just kids when they were captured. He wondered how they were managing now. Most of them were in no shape to stay in the army and they returned to the states without any skills that could be used in civilian life. He knew from his own experience that there was no one who would understand or even believe what they had been through. Did they also suffer a loneliness that was overwhelming at times?

The prisoners of war who returned from the European arena were given pensions, and it irked him that nothing was done for the horyos. He was lucky, but how were some of those poor bastards going to hold down regular jobs, with their health shot all to hell? It was like no one in the government wanted to know about them. Even the VA seemed to be operating under orders that they weren't to recognize any of the many disabilities these guys had to live with the rest of their days.

He found that he even missed speaking Japanese. Words and phrases popped up in his mind, not as hated reminders of what he had suffered, but as cultural tools that had helped him to survive. Without any contact to ex-horyos, he had a feeling that all he had learned and experienced was worthless.

When Pearl Harbor was bombed, and the American government rounded up American Japanese, confiscated their property, and herded them into detention camps, many Japanese lost good farm lands and had to start all over again. Mickey heard of a family like that who lived in the desert outside Las Vegas, and he decided to look them up.

He took the kids with him, but it was a disappointing experience. Mickey tried to communicate with the man in Japanese, but either the farmer spoke another dialect or he had learned to be cautious. It hadn't occurred to Mickey that the man might no longer trust white Americans and would think it wiser to avoid speaking Japanese around this white man. Tony and Judy were disappointed, sensing that their father's Japanese wasn't much use, and Mickey discovered that this man couldn't furnish a link to those lost years.

When they were leaving, the farmer gave them delicious canned abalone and a big jar of kim-chee, an oriental relish. Mickey ate the kim-chee with gusto. It was so hot that tears rolled down his cheeks.

Mickey never tried to talk with Trudy about these longings for something that could put him in touch with such an intense part of his life. Nor, indeed, did he talk with anyone else about the war years. Sympathetic though they might be, no one would have understood. Jane was the only one who sensed the extent of his ordeal, but with her he instinctively avoided revealing his wounds, knowing that she would store them up in her arsenal of hatred, and he didn't want to hear people express hatred for the Japanese. By nature, his mental processes were concentrated on forgiveness. To talk about the past should enable one to forget the pain; whereas, Jane's driving force was remembrance as a fuel for forward action or for revenge.

Outwardly, he was the same fun loving, likeable person he always had been; however, there was a new side to him. Like a ghost, this alter ego reminded him of the flaws that are hidden under the surface in most human beings and transforms them when they are stripped of all the armor civilization provides. He never did have much respect for authority, and his prison experience showed him that the very type who is a pillar of the community can be reduced to groveling for mercy or ratting on his buddies when a Japanese guard has beaten out his sense of decency, while the small, insignificant man with nothing to lose can sometimes be stubbornly courageous in the face of brutality. This hard-earned wisdom put Mickey even farther outside the limits imposed by conventional behavior.

Thus, he found a refreshing honesty in the down-and-out flotsam of society. They were already there where we all arrive, if a catastrophe strips away our pride and possessions. "Blessed be the meek, for they shall inherit the kingdom of heaven." Well, he didn't believe in heaven, but he had learned that humility was the greatest asset in taking the sting out of evil. It was a lesson hammered home with so much pain that he didn't ever want to forget it.

He gravitated towards odd types and liked to pick up hoboes when they were hitchhiking. They often traveled in pairs, reminding him of how important it had been in prison camp to have a buddy at your side. If he was driving Jane's Packard, with Trudy in the front seat, they got in the back, looking humble and grateful. Judy and Tony were squeezed in from both sides. The hoboes' smell filled the car, and they seemed uncomfortable in the luxurious interior. Mickey was oblivious to all that and talked with them like they were long-lost friends.

The cabin that Mickey and Clyde built was primitive, and winter set in before it was properly finished. There was an open fireplace in the living room, and Mickey and Trudy slept in front of it on a big double bed. The gray cement walls weren't plastered yet, and furnishings were sparse. Tony and Judy shared a room where there was a cot and a hammock. At first, they fought over who got to sleep in the hammock, but they soon discovered that it was no treat. When it was Judy's turn, she was tucked in at night with a big safety pin to keep her from falling out, and by morning she felt like she had been curved so much she'd never be able to stand straight.

One of Jane's less fortunate investments was a mercury mine that turned out to be worthless when the miners discovered that it was too expensive to extract the mercury. All she had to show for it was a vial of mercury which Tony and Judy liked to spill out on the floor and watch as it formed heavy beads. Then they used their fingers to push the poisonous fluid back together and into the vial.

They caught colds, but Mickey didn't fuss over them like Uncle Doc had done when they had the slightest ailment. Judy's cold went into her eyes, and she had to carefully pick them clean before she could open them. Sometimes she felt sorry for herself and wished she had Donda, but those thoughts were quickly forgotten during the course of an eventful day. Days with Mickey were always eventful.

Thanksgiving came, and there was to be a feast. Mickey and Trudy were in the small kitchen all day, and wonderful things were cluttering their worktable. There were pears dyed red and flavored with cinnamon. There was Waldorf salad, crisp celery stalks, and shiny black olives. The smell of pumpkin pie was followed by roasting turkey, as Tony and Judy ran in and out of the house, playing in the cold November sunshine, excitedly asking when it would all be ready.

While he was cooking, Mickey was drinking Tom and Jerry's, with a delicious whiff of nutmeg, and he good-naturedly sent them packing, promising that it wouldn't be long. With Mickey there was a general disregard for the hour, and the much-anticipated meal was served late in the afternoon. Judy watched her father dip into the feast and was puzzled to see that after only a few bites, he lay down his fork and could eat no more.

"Why aren't you eating more turkey, Daddy? Look what I have to eat!" she said, not really complaining, because for once it was something she liked.

Mickey shrugged it off, but from then on she noticed that her father was incapable of eating more than a very small portion of food. He had an extraordinary craving for the most exotic of foods and loved preparing a feast, but once he sat down and took a bite, beads of perspiration appeared on his forehead, and he lost his appetite. It was a cruel quirk of fate after having survived all those years of dreaming of food in prison camp.

He knew how much Donda missed the children, and he was good about writing to her to keep her informed. Judy was allowed to send letters with terrible complaints and hideous drawings of Jane, but it was clear from her drawings of Mickey and Trudy that she was being treated well. Day by day, she was forgetting her vow to run away at the first good opportunity and return to Donda's. She had come to love her father and wouldn't want to make him sad.

That winter, Mickey bought a Zenith phonograph, the newest thing, with an automatic turntable, and he had a stack of records that he liked to play. He thought about one of his fellow prisoners who seemed to go into a trance and claimed he could hear the entire Fifth Symphony of Beethoven's. He had died in a world without music, at Cabanatuan. There were so many things to be grateful for, now that the war was over. It was incredible that one could hear music of that quality, without being anywhere near the great concert houses. Whether he was listening to Rimsky-Korsakov or Liszt, he felt wonder at being able to bring the world's greatest music into his living room. He loved the new music that had come on the scene during the years since the war. He was delighted that his old friend, Freddie Grofé, had turned out 'The Grand Canyon Suite'. He had always claimed to be working on something monumental.

Mickey slept a lot that winter, and one day he fell asleep with a fire in the fireplace and the gramophone playing. The records fell into place, one by one, and songs written before the war played while the logs crackled. The last record dropped onto the turntable, and the smooth voices of The Mills Brothers crooned the seductive melody of "Smoke Gets in Your Eyes." Mickey stirred and sat up, his shoulders hunched and his hands clenched between his knees, staring into the fire, with tears in his eyes. He remembered Vivian and the smoothness of her satin gown, as they slowly danced to that song, at the Coconut Grove all those years ago, her soft skin driving him mad.

Judy had come into the room, unnoticed, and was standing a few feet away, watching him with a puzzled look on her face. Noticing her, he cleared his throat and smiled. "That was your mother's and my song," he said in a gravelly voice.

Judy felt happy, hearing mention of her mother. It made a new bond between father and daughter. After that, he often told her things about her mother, keeping the memory of Vivian alive and inspiring her to try to be like Vivian.

He wanted Tony and Judy to have the same love for music, and he bought records for them. They responded enthusiastically to the joy of listening to 'Peter and the Wolf' and 'The Nutcracker Suite'. He also bought them a recording of a story that was popular that year, about the Littlest Angel. He and Vivian had dreamed of making everything possible for the children, and he vowed to himself that he wouldn't let her down.

He didn't want his kids to be unaware of the pleasure there is to be found in so many different aspects of life. He didn't make demands and say that they had to like to read; he merely assumed that they would like it. That winter on the ranch, he began reading "The Hobbit" to them, and Tolkien's fabulously vivid imagery inspired Tony with the urge to draw and paint. Whatever dreams Tony or Judy had, Mickey told them they could achieve them, and they learned to believe in their own abilities.

Whether or not you are poor depends on what comparisons you make with your neighbors. In those days, there was less to compare. The closest neighbors had a boy named Jack who sometimes walked with Tony and Judy to the school bus if Mickey didn't drive them. They talked with him about Christmas and asked what presents he got. Jack told them that he got a white shirt and a haircut, and they both felt sorry they had asked him. It sounded so sad not to get toys.

Mickey seldom laid down rules, but he told Tony to stop digging holes in the yard. Tony persisted, and Mickey devised a punishment characteristic for him.

"Okay, Butch," he said, if you feel like digging, I want you to make a hole three feet wide and long and deep – a cubic yard."

Tony lunged energetically into the task, and once he was through, he no longer had an urge to dig. However, the resulting hole was elongated and furnished with planks for a roof and a well casing for a chimney. This underground fort furnished Tony and Judy with many happy hours of make-believe.

Running wild, the children explored the surrounding area. There was a pasture nearby, and Tony showed off by climbing up on a fence to drop down on the backs of horses that grazed there, riding them bareback until they ran under the mesquite trees with their low-hanging branches, and he had to slide off. Once he wasn't fast enough and a branch knocked him off. Mickey laughed and seemed proud of him for taking chances.

With their friends, Tony and Judy sometimes sneaked out at night and dared one another to prowl the darkened corridors of Clark County Hospital, which was not too far down the road. On one occasion, a door opened, and a nurse was silhouetted against the light as she approached them. They ran and hid in a laundry room, hearts pounding, and waited until it was quiet before sneaking home. An evening like that was every bit as good as a Frankenstein film.

Wherever Mickey took the children, he made it seem like an adventure. A favorite place was Red Rock Canyon, where the wind-sculpted red sandstone provided good climbing and hiding places. The place was a national park and had a picnic table with benches, but it was always deserted and felt like their own private hideaway. They made a campfire to cook their dinner and slept on the ground under the open sky, with masses of stars shining brilliantly in the clear desert air. In the mornings, Mickey cooked bacon and eggs, and there was the smell of fresh coffee, made the way hoboes make it, the grounds thrown into boiling water and, lastly, a handful of egg shells to clear it. Afterwards, they cleaned their mess kits in sand.

During the hottest part of the day while Mickey and Trudy took a siesta in the shade of an over-hanging ledge, Tony and Judy liked to play in a small stream, where the limpid water revealed decorative salamanders.

Mickey loved to visit ghost towns, eerie places peculiar to America. Other parts of the world have their monumental ruins, which inspire romantic thoughts, but the desolation of an American ghost town was tangible, the ghosts still lingering. In the vulnerable wooden structures of a deserted western town, one could still feel the presence of those adventurous souls who suddenly had to abandon what they had built up because their dreams failed, the gold petered out, or the wells ran dry.

St. Thomas was different. The people there were forced out when Boulder Dam was built, and the houses looked more permanent. The waters of Lake Mead had blotted out the memory of St. Thomas, but for a short while after the war, the lake receded, and the town emerged, making it possible to explore the deserted houses.

Mickey knew the kids would be excited by St. Thomas. People had left in a hurry, and some places still had a few pieces of furniture or an old broken cup or plate. One man had refused to leave, claiming the waters wouldn't rise high enough to cover his house on the hill. Finally he had been rowed away in a boat, and his old jalopy was left behind. It reappeared now, a rusty relic on a slightly steeper rise.

They took off their shoes to wade through the thick mud, and Mickey stopped up suddenly, saying to Tony, "I feel something between my toes. Reach down there, kid, and see what it is." To make the outing more exciting, Mickey had slipped a coin down by his foot, one dated with the year St. Thomas was flooded. Tony fished it up, and the children's eyes were round as saucers when Mickey rubbed it with his fingers to reveal a shiny silver dollar.

They visited Rhyolite where an old woman lived all alone in the middle of nowhere. A pathway leading to her small house and all around the house was made of the bottoms of bottles, and the glass had turned iridescent from being baked in the desert sun, like oil on rainwater.

Once, they drove out to Pete's ranch at a place called Ash Meadows. Pete had taken advantage of the Homesteading Act and got himself 160 acres for raising cattle. To get there one had to leave the road and strike out across a barren wasteland.

They left late in the afternoon. The jeep was equipped with canvas bags filled with water, which were hung under the bumper and kept cool as the water slowly seeped out and evaporated. Half way there, the jeep got a flat, and while Mickey worked to change the tire, and Trudy sat filing her perfectly shaped nails, Tony and Judy explored the area to find something to do. They discovered tar pits and came back to the jeep covered in the sticky black substance. Mickey cussed good-naturedly as he cleaned them off with gasoline.

After covering the stretch of deserted road that was paved, they veered off, across the vast expanse of a dry lake, the tires hopping over the cracks of what once had been a muddy lake bottom. A full moon lit their way.

The ranch was located on an oasis. It used to be that a person's claim to the land wasn't valid until five years after a dwelling had been put up, but the law had been changed to three years, and Pete now owned it quit and free. On his property were crystal clear natural springs, turquoise blue, like jewels under the cloudless sky. They were deep, and their steep sides were coated with sulphurous deposits, ochre colored and slippery to touch. The water was pleasantly warm, and Mickey spent the better part of the day swimming with his family.

Pete's house was a low, primitive affair surrounded by large cottonwood trees, with hammocks strung up in their shade. That night, Mickey bunked Tony and Judy down in those, and they were so tired out that they fell fast asleep right away. They were awakened in the middle of the night by a violent desert storm. Wind was whipping the trees, and jagged lightning was followed up immediately by deafening thunder. Horses in the coral whinnied and reared on their hind legs before charging about in fear. Judy felt safe, knowing Tony was there, and the two of them watched the spectacular scenery as the hammocks rocked in the wind. The next morning, everything was still, and a bird was singing in the trees. There was no sign that anything had happened.

Las Vegas livened up when Helldorado rolled around. Mickey took Tony and Judy with him wherever he went, making sure they saw the big parade from grandstand seats on the roof of Trader Bill's, and letting them sit astride the corrals as he talked with cowpunchers at the big rodeo. Jane's brother, Jordan came to town to ride on his magnificent Palomino in the parade with a mounted posse, all of whom had elaborate black leather tack and chaps covered with silver.

There was a "whiskering" contest, with a prize for the longest beard. A popular event was a kangaroo court, where grown men were thrown into a cage, all in fun. Jane watched the events with civic pride. She knew everyone of importance in this unique town and felt like a part of the grand rate of development in Las Vegas. It pleased her that Jordan could see she was a person of some standing, and she told him what visions she had of Las Vegas to come.

Dunaway's visit didn't bring out the best in Mickey. He had always found his uncle to be a sanctimonious old coot, and Jordan didn't approve of his nephew. Everyone in Mickey's family was opinionated, and whenever they got together, there were fireworks. What started out as a row over politics switched over to an argument about life style. They loved to disagree, and Mickey was maddening good-natured when it came to an all-out battle.

Irritated by Mickey's cocky attitude, Dunaway turned on him and asked what he meant to do with the rest of his life. "When are you planning to write that book you used to talk about?"

Riled, Jane came immediately to Mickey's defense. "That's none of your damned business, Jordan, when you ask like that."

Mickey never was without an answer, but he didn't bother to reply. Jane watched him with concern, worried that Jordan might have unsettled him, taken the wind out of his sails. Lord knows, after all he's been through, all I want is for him to stay happy and get his bearings, she thought. I don't care how long it takes.

Mickey lay awake that night. He didn't believe he would ever take for granted the comfort of a bed, and lying awake didn't bother him. Jordan had hit a nerve, not because he cared about his uncle's opinion, but because he felt like he had exhausted all the pleasures of this desert town. He longed for the islands, and he felt a need to take his kids back to the place he and Vivian had found ideal for children. Life was good, but he was haunted by his old restlessness, that feeling that life took on so many flavors, and they all had to be tasted.

He didn't intend to go on being dependent on his mother financially, that was too confining, but nothing about his old way of life had recaptured his interest. The brief glimpse of colonial Manila had given him a taste for something more cosmopolitan than anything he would find here, even if he did have enough money to live like the rich. However, when he was in the islands he never cared about money. It was enough just to be there.

It was Vivian who had begun to long for nice things, but that was only understandable. She was a real lady, and she wanted the kids to get the best. Trudy was different. She was basically lazy and would probably love lolling around on the beach and living in a shack. He looked at her lying beside him, her features illuminated by the moonlight streaming through the curtainless window. She had the untroubled sleep of a child. He remembered Vivian, with her quick mind and fiery temper, and he smiled. There had never been a dull moment with her.

Jane had stabled a Palomino out at the ranch, and she came over the next day to ride it. Mickey talked with her about wanting to go back to the islands, and, to his surprise, she didn't flare up.

"I knew this was coming, honey. That's why I told Vivian she could buy a place over there. Just as well she didn't, as things turned out. I put the money aside though and still have it." She gave him a sly smile, pleased to see his surprised expression.

"Well, I'll be damned. You mean you don't mind?"

"Of course I'd rather you stay here, Mickey, but I don't want to see you waste your life. Why don't you write to that friend of yours, Walter Dillingham? I'll figure out how much I can afford to give you for a house. It can't be fancy, mind you. And you'll have to do with an old jalopy to start with."

She rode off pleased with herself for having made Mickey happy. *I just hope he appreciates what I'm doing for him*, she thought ruefully. *Seems to me I don't always get thanks for my good deeds.*

Mickey could hardly wait to tell Trudy and the kids his plans. He wrote to Walter, and it wasn't long before he got a letter back, telling him that there was a house available in Hauula. It sat on a hillside in an acre of land.

When Mickey told Tony and Judy about the move, he said they wouldn't have to go to school. Judy was alarmed – She loved school, it being the only place that had the normality of the life she liked at Donda's, but for Tony, it was different. Bright far beyond his years, he was bored with school and made very little effort to excel. Mickey decided he would get far more out of private tutoring.

As for Mickey, the quiet of Hauula would be just the ticket for settling down to the writing career he and Vivian dreamed of so many years ago. He was like a man possessed as he counted the days until they could pull up stakes and head for a ship sailing from San Francisco.

Post-War Hawaii

Jane went with them to San Francisco from where they would sail to Honolulu. They drove in the big Packard, stopping by a publisher's in Reno where Mickey chose a selection of textbooks for Tony and Judy, as part of his scheme to educate them at home. They were a tantalizing array with bright covers, good illustrations, and workbooks to match. Mickey was intrigued with the selection, picking up books on every subject he could imagine appealing to the kids. Jane paid the bill while Mickey arranged to have the books crated and shipped to the islands.

The deep snow along the road as they went through the Carson Pass reminded Mickey of the numbing cold in Nagoya. He thought about it without bitterness, enjoying the snug feeling of being in a comfortable car with the heat on. I don't think I will ever take comfort for granted, he thought.

It was late afternoon by the time they reached Richardson Grove where they spent the night. It was the first time the children had seen redwoods, and Mickey mastered the art of inspiring in them a sense of wonder towards the giant trees that stood like silent sentries guarding over a bottomless pool of time. Stopping the car, they walked among the majestic trees, enshrouded in mists that were thick and felt like soft rain. Light fell dimly from a great height, and ancient layers of leaf mold and redwood fronds muffled their footsteps.

They spent the night at a motel with cabins built in redwood, a place dark and charming, with burls of redwood that had been removed from trees and made to sprout with bright green, fern-like growth. There was a wishing well, with what looked to Tony and Judy like a fortune in pennies, nickels and dimes, out of reach at the bottom.

Accustomed by now to the spirit of adventure that was part and parcel of their life with Mickey, the children eagerly soaked up the many impressions, from the majesty of the redwood forest to the circus-like bright lights and crowded streets when they reached San Francisco.

There they checked into a hotel near Union Square, after they had unloaded the bulk of their luggage at the pier from which their ship would be sailing. From their hotel window, the children could watch the bustle of traffic and hear the cable cars as they ground to a stop and the clang of their bells when they started up. Trudy and Mickey had a room down the hall, and Jane shared a room with Tony and Judy.

After dinner in the restaurant of the hotel, Jane took the children to their room and put them to bed. It tired her out just to think of spending a night on the town with Mickey and Trudy. Mickey was bouncing with energy, and he wanted to squeeze in as many places as they could see while they were here in San Francisco. Most the places he mentioned sounded like something too racy for me, Jane thought. Humph – Imagine a barroom where every queer in town is likely to show up, and that place where there is a nude girl in a fish bowl. Mickey had explained how they used mirrors to make it look like she was swimming around in water, and Jane toyed with the idea of going along just out of curiosity, but her better judgment won out. Some of these places sounded just plain decadent.

After she tucked the kids in, she got out of her black, crêpe-de-chine dress and put it on a hanger, smoothing the soft pleats of the skirt. Everything she did was orderly. Judy watched her furtively, fascinated with her grandmother's evening routine. First, Jane disappeared into the bathroom, leaving the door ajar, and soaked in a hot tub, humming out of tune. She came out dressed in a pretty nightgown and donned a pink satin robe and matching, high-heeled slippers, trimmed with white fur. Then she sat at the dressing table, watching herself in the mirror while she studiously applied cold cream to her face. For a moment, she seemed to be watching her grand-daughter in the mirror, but Judy quickly shut her eyes tightly and didn't open them before she heard Jane getting ready to climb into bed, first pulling all the covers loose, and, in her usual finicky way, checking the mattress to see that it was soft enough.

The next day, Mickey gave Tony four bits and told him he could take Judy to see "Sinbad the Sailor." He knew it would be good for the kids to try being on their own in the big city, and they would be bored going on a shopping spree with Jane. She was feeling generous, and Mickey wanted to change out his and Trudy's Western duds, with clothes appropriate for the islands. Like an actor preparing for a new role, he picked out loose-fitting slacks and short-sleeved shirts, a pair of bathing trunks and polo shirts. For Trudy, Mickey chose things that would set off her stunning figure, and she complacently let him put together what she would need.

For once, Jane didn't feel impatient with Judy. It was easier to play the role of the nice grandmother when she knew it was only for a few more days. In Reno, she had bought Judy a silver charm bracelet and gave her a new charm at each place they stopped along the way. In San Francisco, she added a small silver trolley car. Judy thanked her politely and was clearly delighted with the bracelet, but Jane sensed that her granddaughter, nonetheless, remained out of reach. She shrugged it off. She had from the start felt that Judy was more Vivian's child than Mickey's, someone with a different chemistry.

That night they all went to Fisherman's Wharf for dinner. Mickey drove, and Jane nagged him as he sped over the steep streets of San Francisco. "You're driving just like you used to do those danged ambulances back in Hollywood, Mickey," she scolded. He laughed as he expertly threaded his way through traffic, liking the free feeling of speed. That had been one of the things he missed most when he was a horyo.

In the morning, while Mickey hailed down a cab to drive to the pier from which their ship was to sail, Jane said goodbye, not wanting to follow them to the ship, and she started the lonely journey back to Las Vegas. She would miss Mickey and his family, but personal relations wore her out. It was a relief to be by herself, undistracted by the constant noise and movement of a family, but the thought that Mickey usually got into trouble whenever he was out of sight gnawed at her well being. If only he had some of her practical sense. She knew so well how much better Mickey's life would be if he would just leave the managing of it to her, but now here he was – off again, with that girl who didn't seem to have a brain in her head.

In a very short time Jane had put city traffic behind her, and she breathed more freely as the car moved smoothly over scenic roads. She relaxed and thought about what she had done for Mickey and his family, wondering at her own capacity for love. She was satisfied at least that she had done everything in her power to give them a good start financially.

Thinking about finances put her mind back on track. That was the key to everything here in life, and it was with a renewed sense of purpose, that she headed home where she could continue to build up her assets. On her own again, her head cleared, and she felt confident that whatever happened to Mickey and his family, she would be able to provide the necessary financial security to make them a part of the prosperous future that she had planned for them.

* * * * *

At the pier, Mickey left Tony and Judy alone, standing by the hand luggage in the huge departure hall, while he swept Trudy off to buy some magazines. Crowds of people milled about in the drafty hall, everyone busy, checking all details before boarding the huge ship that was lying bathed in sunshine alongside the pier. There was an air of excitement that easily induces anxiety to those not used to travel.

As the two children stood waiting, all the other passengers streamed by, heading for the ship. In the thinning crowd, there was an occasional person who looked at them questionably, but Tony and Judy were used to that and reacted by glancing away, with an air of self-confidence.

Afterwards, people who had been on board to drink a glass of champagne with departing friends started to come down the gangplank and walk out on the pier to be ready to watch the ship as it sailed out of harbor. In the emptiness of the dark loading area, noises gave a hollow echo. Judy was beginning to become alarmed. It seemed that everyone else was already on board. She moved closer to Tony, trying not to cry. "Where do you think they are, Tony?" she asked with a quiver in her voice.

"They'll be here, don't worry," he said. Judy looked at Tony and felt better. He never looked scared.

After what seemed like an eternity, they caught sight of Mickey, bustling towards them with his arm around Trudy's waist and a big grin on his face.

"We're going to be left behind, Daddy," Judy scolded, as they hurried along to the gangplank, but the chilling feeling of anxiety dissipated quickly in the contagious warmth of his nonchalant air.

Mickey had a stack of comic books for the kids. The party mood was there again, and they were finally going to the place they never had stopped calling 'home'. Nothing could replace the Hawaiian Islands. "And we won't have to go to school," Tony said happily, as they sat on the floor of their cabin, the comics scattered between them.

"I like school," Judy said, unsure that she wanted to do without.

"Just wait 'til we open that big box with books. They have everything in them! We won't need any stupid old school." Tony's enthusiasm was contagious, and Judy forgot her worries.

"Can you understand grown-ups not liking comics, Judy? I'm always going to like comics. I won't ever change," Tony said, seriously, settling down with the pile Mickey had bought.

"Me, too," said Judy, contentedly, feeling completely safe again.

During the eight days onboard ship, Mickey felt in his element. He was the life of the party, with Trudy as a dependably attractive prop. He knew he had to be thankful for Jane's contribution to a life free of worries, but it would be a lot easier to appreciate it when he could again feel like a free agent.

They arrived in Honolulu on a Sunday. The streets were empty as they took a taxi to the Bishop Building, where Walter had his real estate office. There they picked up the keys to a car and instructions on how to find the house Jane had bought for them outside the small village called Hauula.

The car was a beat up old Terraplane, which Mickey promptly nicknamed 'The Turkey'.

Their new home was on the windward side of the island, and, in order to reach it, they had to drive over the Pali, passing through the enchanting Nuuanu Valley.

Trudy was always content, but quiet. Her innate laziness made it impossible to tell what effect the exotic scenery was having on her. The lush forests of tree ferns, taller than a man's height, and the heavy scent of ginger was a far cry from the life she had ever imagined for herself when she was a girl in the backwoods of Oklahoma.

When they reached the top of the Pali, the place where King Kamehameha was supposed to have waged a great battle and thrown his opponents over the sheer slope of the mountainside, they stopped and got out to enjoy the view. As they stood there, buffeted by the wind, Mickey told Tony and Judy tales about that site. One woman, he claimed, had jumped off the Pali to commit suicide, and the wind was so strong that it blew her back up, landing her safely on a ledge. A man later tried the same feat, and the treacherous wind failed him, letting him plunge to his death in the valley below.

He also said that when Judy was a very little girl, he had let her stand atop the very wall where they now stood. The wind had taken hold of her and almost blown her away, but he had grabbed her ankle and hauled her in. Judy looked sideways at him to try to see whether or not he was teasing, but he smiled back, and she stored it away in a growing file of things that might or might not be true. Mickey counted small lies as 'whiffles' and said that they were permissible. Judy was already learning that sometimes people scoffed when she repeated his fantastic tales, but she liked believing all the interesting things he told her.

As they drove towards Kaneohe, the old car strained, and the kids said in chorus, "Chug, chug, chug," all the way over the pass. Mickey told them to pipe down, but there was laughter in his voice, and they kept on, knowing that they could push the limit farther on a day like this. Their father was suspended in time, with memories awakened by the poignantly familiar sensations brought on by all the plants and fragrances and the soft caress of the island air. The comforting presence of Trudy by his side warded off sad thoughts of times before the war.

The house Jane had bought them with Walter's help was a typically flimsy island construction on a rise overlooking the sea. It sat on the far side of a plateau that was covered by a big lawn and was reached by a steep, curved cement drive. Dense jungle growth and a large avocado tree that stood by the kitchen door dwarfed the modest house. At the end of the house, facing the sea, was a screened porch that was all but hidden by a trellis filled with trumpet flowers. Where the property sloped off towards the sea, there was a hedge of croton bushes, its colors flaming against the green surroundings.

When Mickey was selling Jane on the idea of them coming to the islands, he had painted a glowing picture of the sort of life they could have in Hauula. He knew the place and had told his mother that in this quiet outpost they would be able to be largely self-sufficient. There was land enough to grow papayas and bananas and raise a few chickens. He planned to catch fresh fish each day and raise rabbits for meat. He assured her that by living this far from Honolulu, he would be able to devote his time to writing, and with all he had seen, he would never run out of ideas for stories.

She didn't care whether Mickey ever wrote anything. He had suffered enough, and now she could make sure he would have enough to live on. She told him that if he would stick to a budget, nothing could go wrong, and she knew she could secure their incomes for the future, too.

As he inspected the house, and the children raced happily around the property, he felt sure this was going to be the start of a whole new life. This was all he dreamed of during those barren years in prison camp. There was even a separate building that could be used as a studio, with a picture window overlooking the sea, and he imagined Tony spending hours there, developing an artistic talent that had already surfaced.

The floor plan of the house clearly indicated that it had been built piecemeal by the previous owner, but in that mild climate, any construction was adequate. There was a small room by the front entrance that would be fine as a bedroom for Tony. The living room opened up onto the screened porch that would make an adequate bedroom for Mickey and Trudy. The kitchen was at the back of the house and was small and dark, but it would do. Judy could have the room just off the kitchen, on the same side of the house as Tony's, with the bathroom connecting the two rooms. Outdoors, there was a handy closet for tools on one side of the house, and at the back, there was a porch for washing clothes and a shower that had been rigged up under the open sky – Primitive, but serviceable. Whatever the place lacked, Mickey provided with his imagination, painting vivid pictures of the improvements that would come with time.

Mickey couldn't help but think about how much fun Vivian would have had fixing up this place. She had been in his thoughts far too much, ever since they got off the boat. He knew Trudy would never replace Vivian, but at least she was easy-going and seemed to accept any place he wanted to call home. Her indolent nature made it easy to relax, and he found he hardly ever worried about what she might want in life. The way she responded to him in bed was enough to convince him that she was satisfied, but he knew she would never be a soul mate. If he had learned anything from being in prison, it was to appreciate whatever pleasure was on hand and not fret about those that were unobtainable.

His plans to keep Tony and Judy out of school didn't work out. A local official came by soon after they moved in and said that the law required them to be enrolled. By then, however, he had realized how difficult it would be to maintain the amount of discipline necessary for home schooling. The kids ran wild in their new surroundings and were gone for hours exploring the jungle behind the house or the tide pools at the beach.

The school at Hauula was a small country school, with a beautiful blend of races: Hawaiian, Samoan, Japanese, Chinese, Filipinos, a few Portuguese, and one family from Guam. Mickey's kids were the only stateside haoles, and they strived not to fit into the mold of white kids. Tony quickly learned to speak Pidgin English in order to carry his own weight, and school days in Hauula were rich in experience.

Mickey had an idea of what sort of young lady Judy should become, and he insisted that she wear shoes to school, but Tony could go barefoot. Thinking this unfair, Judy usually hid her shoes on the way out in the morning. Small for her age to begin with, she was put up a grade in the new school, making her even smaller in relation to her classmates. She was desperate to fit in.

The principal wanted to have Tony skip a grade, too, but Mickey decided against it, thinking that it was more important that a boy could hold his own physically. Judy was nine and Tony eleven, but a pattern was already set: Judy always anxious to please and conform, Tony in a world of his own, bright and independent. Fortunately, all the love they had received from Vivian and Mickey and the relatives had provided them both with plenty of self-confidence, and they easily adjusted to a new environment.

At school, a hot lunch was served each day at noon, and all children were expected to take part in kitchen duty by turn. They were also asked to bring a cloth mat or tatami to lie on for a nap after lunch. Stateside holidays were celebrated just as if they belonged to Hawaiian traditions. At Thanksgiving, there was a school play, and Tony wrote it and had the main part. Three days before the play was to be performed, the teacher fell ill, and Tony was left in charge of the whole affair. He brought the house down with his own performance, turning into comedy what was meant to be a simple pageant.

Back in California, Donda worried about the children and wrote to the principal of the school, asking how they were doing and what he imagined they would like for Christmas. He was touched by the grandmother's concern and wrote a kind letter back, telling her that Tony had proved to be remarkably talented and that both children were doing very well with their schoolwork. He finished his letter by giving her what he reckoned were their sizes in clothing.

For Tony and Judy, life in Hauula furnished all the distractions a child can wish for. The months flew by until May Day, when a big celebration took place. A Maypole had been constructed on the playing field, and bright colored streamers were attached to the top. Cecilia, a beautiful girl whose parents were from Guam and owned a mango orchard, was chosen as May queen. The oldest pupils learned to dance around the maypole, and the others were drilled in marching.

Judy took it very seriously. The children were to meet up on the morning of the big day wearing a lei, and she picked a basketful of Australian sweetpeas to sew into the flat lei that is traditional for that bloom. All the parents were coming to see the parade, and each child was impressed with the importance of doing everything perfectly.

The parents were to arrive at eleven o'clock, and Judy's teacher decided to put the class through its paces one more time. For nearly an hour they practiced, marching around in straight lines in full sunlight, drilled into perfect unity. When the teacher felt satisfied, they went back to the classroom to wait. Judy sat at her desk, and then she saw to her dismay that the lei was wilted, and the flowers had shrunk, exposing the white thread she had used to sew it. She wanted to cry. It was going to be such a perfect day, and now it was spoiled. The final blow was that Mickey didn't come. Nothing in his own background had provided him with a sense that parent participation was important, and the May Day parade was to be one among many disappointments.

One day a district nurse came to school and inspected heads for lice. The only children without head lice were the children from Guam, with their glistening clean hair. Tony and Judy were among the majority and got a good dose of DDT powder sprayed on their heads before being sent home.

The following day, a girl named Nani came to school with her head shaved. Nani was an orphan who lived with a large family. Her foster mother made her work hard and sometimes beat her, but Judy didn't think anyone would be so cruel as to shave off Nani's long black hair. She stole glances at the girl's ravaged head, and wondered how Nani found the courage to come to school. This was a glimpse into a harsh world, and, by comparison, Judy felt safe in a charmed circle formed by Mickey's unflagging good humor.

There were three different routes to school, each one with a special appeal. Sometimes Tony and Judy loitered as they walked along the beach, watching the morning sunrise. There were spectacular effects, with shafts of light beaming through turbulent clouds, scenes that stirred Tony's earliest yearnings to be an artist and fit Judy's notion of heaven and her mother as an angel. Barefoot, they soaked up the moods of their surroundings through their feet as well as their eyes.

Sometimes they stopped to talk with a kind Hawaiian woman who showed them how to pick a small limpet, called 'opihi,' off the rocks and use a safety pin to extract it from its black shell. She taught them to eat them raw, deliciously flavored by the salt from the sea.

They followed the paved road if they were late on the way to school, or if they were coming home and had a nickel to spend at the general store, the Ching Tong Leong Store, which was owned by a Chinese family whose pretty daughters went to the same school. There, they could buy oriental treats: Dried shrimp, sweet-sour cracked-seed, or salty semoi.

The third route was along railroad tracks that had been built by old man Dillingham for transporting sugar cane. They balanced on the rails, listening for the train. Sometimes they found hunks of sugar cane that had fallen off the open wagons and chewed on them as they walked along, chattering about the possibility of being run over by a train. The thrilling moment was when they had to cross a trestle bridge that loomed over a river gorge, and they talked about what they would do if the train came along. Tony showed Judy how he could drop below the rails and hang from the cross ties, and she knew she wouldn't be able to do that but didn't want to admit it.

In their own small world, they tested their courage, hanging from a rope that was tied to the top of a very tall ironwood tree that leaned out over the ocean, and dropping into the surf, or swimming through an underwater passageway that connected a small pond to the sea. Tony had done it many times and convinced Judy that she could follow. Not as good a swimmer as he was but determined to prove that she wasn't scared, she once dove down and swam into the murky tunnel. Rocks along the sides and bottom were slippery with seaweed. Within a second, she was too far in to turn back and frightened that she wouldn't be able to finish the distance. The brightly lit opening to the sea loomed ahead, and with a mixture of will power and terror, she frantically kicked her way through and pushed her feet hard against the bottom to shoot up to the surface, gasping for air.

Each self-inflicted trial made them feel stronger. Mickey watched the process and felt pleased with their progress. He had seen how much one's self-esteem counted when the chips are down. It was a far cry from the life they would have led in California, with Donda.

When a movie came to the village, everyone attended. There was seldom a film Mickey wanted to see, and he let the children go alone. They sat on folding chairs in the darkness under an open sky, and the film was projected onto a screen set up for the occasion. There was the sweet smell of palm oil the natives rubbed in their hair, and the whir of the projector as the story unfolded. Sometimes the film broke, causing the audience to hoot and whistle through their fingers. At the end of each reel were a series of blank frames and the rattling of the tail end of the film, signaling that the next reel had to be put onto the projector. While waiting, people put their hands into the beam of the projector, making shadow figures. Tony could make a very convincing rabbit and a howling wolf.

The scariest film was "The Mummy's Hand," but the walk home, in inky darkness unless the moon was full, was as exciting as the movie. Superstition was rampant, and Tony and Judy took dares from their Hawaiian friends, to prove that they weren't afraid, while they relished the thrill of suspense. They had to pass the "13th Corner," where there was a giant mango tree. The Hawaiian boys said that your skin would turn into greenish chicken skin if you chewed Wrigley's chewing gum while walking through the graveyard. Tony and Judy told each other that they didn't believe in superstitions, but that didn't make it less spine-tingling to try them out. Tony became a master in embroidering on the local legends, causing his sister and their friends to creep closer together as he entertained them with horror stories.

Left much on their own, they invented tales about their surroundings, imagining ghosts or demented people in the few isolated houses nearby. At one house on their road, there was a prodigious amount of stones, forming a wall around the garden and bordering a path to the front door. Tony convinced his disciples that a strange man called 'The Stone King' lived there, and from then on, the house was shrouded in mystery. They dared each other to sneak up to the porch, to cautiously open the screen door, and the boldest of them to steal into the house. Tony was the bravest and tiptoed ahead to the back of the house where he discovered a man lying asleep on a bed. Terrified, they all ran out of the house and down the hill, scattering in all directions, lest they be caught.

This adventure kept them entertained for many days. Then one evening when Mickey was on his way to Honolulu, he gave a lift to a man walking on the road towards Hauula. He turned out to be a night watchman on his way to work. He slept during the daytime and lived in the house with all the stones.

The children's disappointment in having their myth shattered didn't prevent them from letting their imaginations run wild on other occasions. Tony and Judy were alone at home and playing outside one early evening when they saw a big Hawaiian standing on the edge of their property, watching them from the tangled growth of trees and shrubs. He was wearing an old hat with a soft brim and holding a half-filled gunnysack in his hand. His eyes were bloodshot, as if he had been drinking. He stared but didn't smile. Frightened, they reacted at once, talking as if their parents were in the house and hurrying inside, where they felt safe, even though there were no locks on the doors. It was said afterwards that a man of that description had escaped from a mental hospital, and the kids liked to believe that he was the man. It made the incident so much more interesting.

Mickey had promised Donda to send the children to church, but both the ranch in Las Vegas and the place in Hauula lay too far off the beaten path for them to go to Sunday school. Judy missed it, but sometimes their play took them by the Hawaiian church, where they could hear hauntingly beautiful singing from the open windows, but they couldn't understand the words..

There was a stream that ran in the mountains behind their property, and, following it, they could climb up, past low stonewalls with straight angles – what they imagined to be the ruins of a 'heiau,' an old Hawaiian temple. As they climbed higher and reached a wide waterfall, the jungle turned to brush, but down by their house, it was dense enough to use as a playground, with vines so matted that they served as trampolines. It was an adventure park for two healthy children.

They learned to find their way around, and Tony cleverly discovered details, such as brushing one's foot over the leaves of wiki-wiki grass, so they would close over the thorns of the creeping ground cover, allowing them to walk barefooted across. They took pride in how tough their feet had become and scoffed at other haole kids whose feet were tender from wearing shoes.

There was an abundance of fruit, and they discovered all the places to find their favorite kinds. They loved eating guavas the size of lemons. They picked them slightly green and ate them before the small white worms appeared in them, or they picked them juicy and ripe and shut their eyes to the worms. There were mangoes of all shapes and sizes, more delicious than anywhere else in the islands. Tony ate them green and firm, with soy sauce, or they ate them dead ripe, soft and sweet. By a waterfall, deep in the wilderness, was a still pond, with a mountain apple tree on its brink. The fruit was unforgettable – red on the outside, snowy white on the inside, and very tasty. Near the beach was a date tree, its fronds drooping down to the sand, forming a hideaway where they sat, eating ripe dates that had fallen down.

Mickey decided to clear the steep part of the garden and sow a solid carpet of nasturtiums. He hired a couple of men who came with machetes to chop down the dense growth, setting a torch to the remains. In the rich soil that was exposed, the nasturtium seeds were sown and quickly grew and bloomed, a harlequin quilt of color. It wasn't long, however, before the jungle began to claim back the land, and, his original enthusiasm waning, he let it happen.

Seeing his kids so happy, Mickey felt good about having come back to the islands. Trudy was content to laze around the house, but he sometimes wondered whether she would get bored. He tried to start writing, setting up his typewriter in the breezy living room. There was really nothing to distract him like there had been in the old days, but he soon discovered that the very silence of the place was a distraction. There was restlessness in his very soul, and he found it impossible to concentrate on filling out the blank sheet of paper.

Sure, he had the ideas, and he had plenty of stories that could beat most of what other people were writing, but the chore of compiling the details which comprise a piece of fiction was too tedious. It had been easier when Vivian worked with him, putting the words on paper as he spun the yarn, discussing his ideas with him and criticizing or praising the results.

Seeing him sit idle, Trudy padded quietly in on bare feet, nuzzled his neck, kissed him in the ear and asked if he felt like going for a swim. Grateful for the excuse, he said, "Sure. I can start on this later when I've thought it out."

Prison camp had made him so keenly aware of creature comforts that he would lose himself in the pleasure of the moment, relishing the stream of water in a hot shower or the feeling of a clean cotton shirt on skin that felt strong and smooth. Ambition was a pale flame, compared to the physical joy of being well fed and free.

When he tried to write about his experiences in the Philippines and Japan, he found that mere words didn't seem strong enough to describe what he had seen. He was fascinated with the new slick writing styles of Mickey Spillane and Erskine Caldwell, and he thought perhaps he could develop a style that would lend itself to telling tales from the war. He sat for hours, trying to find a formula that could be used in writing about the atrocities of prison camp, but formulas seemed inadequate for something so profoundly cruel.

Furthermore, he found that in order to write, he needed to submerge himself in the details of his memory of the war. Such sessions threatened to disturb the balance he had achieved after his release. Total recall brought on either an inexplicable longing for the sort of comradeship that he experienced at O'Donnel and Cabanatuan, with the feeling of being so vitally important to those who shared his fate, or nightmares that left him bathed in a pool of sweat, his heart hammering against his ribs.

His immediate desire to put it all behind him and plunge headfirst into all life's pleasures conflicted with his need to come to terms with the feeling that his prison experience was something valuable which should somehow be utilized. Meanwhile, it was so much easier to do what he did so brilliantly, to flit about in a hectic round of activity, which was a far cry from the solitude required for writing.

Always outgoing, Mickey made friends with a few of the Hawaiian families who took him spear fishing. The sea at Hauula was full of delicious fish. Once he caught a nice-sized 'ahi,' big enough to share with friends, and he even speared squid as he paddled about with a glass-bottomed box. Judy was worried about the squid, but he told her they would go limp if one remembered to bite out their eye.

To teach the children to be fearless, he gave them a solution to any problem. Besides biting out squids' eyes, fierce dogs could be managed by shoving one's arm down their throats, and dangerous people should be hit over the head with a full coke bottle, that having the thickest glass. Whether his methods were practical or not, his breezy attitude instilled in the children a belief that fear was something to be dealt with.

Hawaiians near the beach lived in simple wooden shacks, and the only complaint they had was from rats in their houses. Some claimed that a rat would gnaw the fingers of a baby if the child were left untended. Tony and Judy couldn't imagine anything being a threat to these strong-looking people. Judy was especially impressed with their feet. The skin on the soles of their feet was like shoe leather, and even very old people walked with firm steps.

Mickey also got to know the family who lived at the bottom of the hill. The Rutherfords had kids just a few years older than Tony and Judy, and Mrs. Rutherford was part Hawaiian. They were an ambitious couple who worked hard in order to send their three children to Punahau, a private school in Honolulu. Theirs was a disciplined household, where the children had chores and homework and not much time for play.

Their house was built on stilts, a practical design in a climate where rain could otherwise rot the foundations of a wooden structure. In this sheltered area below the house, there was a large tub of water filled with pieces of the woody stalk of ti plants, soaking so they would sprout and could be planted as a hedge. The water fermented, making a start to a good portion of the potent Hawaiian firewater, 'okolehau'. One day while the Rutherfords were out, their little Cairn terrier drank from the tub and staggered out from under the house, clearly inebriated. Mickey was highly amused to see that their respectable neighbors had a drunken dog.

Among Mickey's new friends was the prodigal son of a man who owned the biggest circus in the islands. Fernandez was a tall, broad-shouldered hulk of a man whom Mickey called 'Dizzy'. On weekends, Dizzy and Oofy (the nickname Mickey gave to Rutherford) spent long afternoons, competing in playing cribbage and drinking Moscow Mules made from vodka and ginger beer, a contest which Mickey usually won.

Judy learned to recognize the signs that the grown-ups had been drinking, and like most children, she didn't like it. Otherwise, she had become devoted to Mickey and more and more uncomfortable with Trudy.

Trudy was not the stereotype of the cruel stepmother, but she was young and bored with

Judy, who clearly irritated her. She preferred the more straightforward temperament of Tony. He amused her, and she liked that he was bold. Once, when he saw a spanking coming, he put a book in his trousers, and Trudy couldn't help but laugh at his cheekiness. It irritated her that Judy would start to cry with the mere threat of a reprimand.

While Tony had an easy-going, affectionate relationship with his stepmother and a healthy indifference to trying to please her, Judy knocked herself out trying to win Trudy's approval. The more she tried, the less interested in her Trudy became. Still, Judy no longer pined for Donda or questioned the fact that this was home.

Mickey decided to build some chicken coops for a batch of Rhode Island Red hens, and they had to be made good and strong to keep out the wily mongoose he had seen scurrying through the brush. He explained to Tony and Judy that the mongoose was brought to the islands to eradicate the rats that had become plentiful in the sugar plantations. Judy wanted to know where the rats came from, and his explanation led to a brief history of the islands.

They sat spellbound as he described to them the arrival of Polynesians to these volcanic islands. "They came in big outrigger canoes and brought with them all the plants they thought they would need to feed themselves, because it must have been pretty barren, and they were damned clever at farming."

"When Captain Cook first came across the Hawaiian Islands, they were like an isolated Garden of Eden. There were no major diseases, no mosquitoes, and no rats. Back then, the islands supported a sizeable population, and the people were ruled by a unique system of 'kahunas' decreed by the royalty. A kahuna was a curse, which the ruling class could put on any object or action that they wanted to keep away from their subjects. The threat of a curse served to keep people in line, since breaking a curse was likely to be followed up by having one's brains bashed out with a club." Tony and Judy had heard about kahunas, and now the word took on a meaning they wouldn't forget.

"The nobility was called 'alii,' and they ate a lot and were much bigger than all the rest of the population. That made it easier to be the one who used the club. In old Hawaii, they had wars and some things were cruel, but within their own special system, the natives were well fed and healthy," he went on to say. "After Captain Cook discovered that the islands were a great place to stop off and get food and fresh water for his ships, whaling ships made it a practice to stop here, too, and that disturbed the old society. The natives were not used to the ways of white men, and their well-run systems were spoiled. Also, their alii started wanting the nice things that the foreigners brought to trade."

"Money became important, as the Hawaiian royalty developed a taste for European clothes and luxury items. In the beginning, sandalwood was the most valuable object for the king to barter, but when there wasn't much of that left, he let the 'haoles' gain control, and they started growing sugar cane and pineapples."

"The final blow for the Hawaiian civilization was when well-meaning missionaries came to teach the natives to live like white men. First they lost their way of life, then they lost most of their land by and large to the descendants of those missionaries."

"The ships kept coming to the islands and brought with them diseases, mosquitos, and rats. The rats thrived in the sugar cane fields. To take care of the rat problem, the mongoose was brought to the islands, and, like everything else in this climate, they thrived and became almost as big a problem as the rats. They are beautiful and agile, but these small brown creatures are clever enough to make a meal of any variety of other animals, and they like chicken meat even better than rats."

"So that's why we have to make the chicken coops mongoose-proof, and Dizzy said he'll give me a hand," Mickey told the kids.

Dizzy and Mickey rigged up a power-saw by the studio, and they were sawing lumber to make frames for the coops when Tony and Judy came home from school the next day. It was afternoon, and the two men had been drinking while they worked. Dizzy held a two-by-four as he guided it through the saw. Suddenly, above the whir of the saw, Dizzy yelled out in fright and clutched his hand. In an instant, he had lost two fingers and the tip of a third.

Mickey found the severed fingers and brought them along when he rushed Dizzy, with a towel wrapped around his injured hand, to the small hospital at Kahuku. Frightened and slightly drunk, Dizzy was belligerent and wasn't given immediate attention. While he sat in the waiting room, valuable time was wasted. It wasn't until afterwards that Mickey learned Dizzy could have been flown to Maui, where his brother was a very competent surgeon and would have been able to sew on the severed fingers.

Hours later, Mickey returned home alone. Saddened, he put away the tools they had been using, and as he was straightening the wood they had sawed, he noticed the tip of Dizzy's finger, lying in the sawdust and crawling with ants. After that, some of Mickey's old nightmares returned, and he was haunted by the vision of the fingers, drained white and sealed with clotted blood, reminding him of all the body parts he had seen strewn along the wayside during the Death March.

A few weeks later, as if part of a plot, something else stirred the residues in the murky part of his mind. It was an accident involving three sailors. Their car plowed into the side of the bridge that crossed the small river that ran through the village. The driver, who was drunk, was unscathed, but one passenger was badly hurt, and the third had been thrown through the door and lay dead on the side of the road. Help had already arrived by the time Mickey drove by, with the children in the back seat. Tony and Judy craned their necks to see what had happened, and Mickey sped past, telling them that unless you can help out, you are only in the way when there is an accident.

On the surface, he seemed unaffected by these accidents. The horrors he had seen in his years of captivity had made everything else seem pale by comparison, but his apparent passivity was also part of a learned reaction, a process he had practiced and perfected during nearly four long years when he and his fellow prisoners knew that showing emotion would only prolong the agony.

He forced himself to block out the ghosts of the past, avoiding the quiet hours when they would surface. Having survived, he still felt invincible, but, the sight of mutilation and death reminded him of his determination to live life to the full, to make up for those black years.

These two reminders of scenes that were prey to maggots fractured his peace of mind. He was losing his grasp on the dream that brought him to this quiet little place on the windward side of the island, and he started concocting a new dream. This idyllic existence in rural Oahu was too small a part of the wide world. Change beckoned, just like it always had done when the present plan faded.

With this talent for creating new dreams, it was easy to conjure up an alternative one. Even without alcohol, he was capable of being 'high', intoxicated with an idea or with a love for the richness of life and all its various people. He decided he wanted to be in the midst of it all again, to be a well-groomed part of society. Past memories merged with memories of movies he used to help create back in the thirties, when cinematic life was as smooth as Fred Astaire's dance steps. It was time to have that type of fun, at good restaurants, on smooth dance floors, and with friends who lived in beautiful surroundings. He had been afraid that those scenes would only accentuate the loss of Vivian, but time had taken the edge off the pain, and he felt ready to face his old contacts in Honolulu. Why, there were a score of things he could do to make money and pick up the old life style.

He remembered the hours he had whiled away with Vivian, talking about things they wanted for their kids. Hells bells, it was time he got cracking, if he wanted them to be in the mainstream. Jane had endowed him with a feeling of being one of God's chosen, and there was no question in his mind that his kids were better than most others. He knew plenty who couldn't hold a candle to his own, but Tony and Judy needed better schooling. He realized that his plan to tutor them himself was never going to work. His lifestyle was too undisciplined.

He rose very early the next morning. For the first time in months, he dressed in a lightweight suit, white shirt and bow tie, instead of an aloha shirt and shorts. Trudy was still sleeping when he kissed her and said he was leaving for Honolulu.

"I've got some business in town, honey. Don't expect me home early," he said. He was too impatient to fill her in on his plans, and he didn't think she would necessarily understand what he was cooking up.

He had already worked out a scheme for a fresh start. Jane had paid cash for the house, and she had sent him money for his living expenses ever since they left Las Vegas. Up to now, it had been sufficient, but it wouldn't be enough to launch a new career. The ticket would be to take out a mortgage on the house, he thought. With that kind of start capital, I can take up where I left off. Jesus, things are booming in the real estate market. It should be duck soup to make enough money to pay off a mortgage and then some.

Thanks to Jane, his credit was good, and it was easy to raise some cash. The first thing I'll have to do is get a decent car, he reasoned. This old rattletrap won't make it over the Pali on its own steam too many more times. He drove into a car lot and found a nice Packard, not a convertible like he preferred, but good enough for now. All he got for his old car was a symbolic sum. A jalopy rodeo was all the rage, and the dealer said the Terraplane would do nicely in a crash at one of their shows.

Walter Dillingham greeted Mickey warmly when he walked into his office. He was delighted that Mickey wanted to get into real estate again. He looked at his old friend with interest. Mickey had aged, but there was still that air of buoyant optimism about him. There was no denying that he could sell the Brooklyn Bridge, and his good humor was so contagious that it was great just to see him back in town.

They had lunch together at the Royal Hawaiian, and Walter filled him in on the latest Honolulu gossip. The place had gotten crowded, but apparently it was still a small world as far as social relations went. It was like old home week to be there with one of Honolulu's more notorious playboys and welcomed back to the fold by passing acquaintances.

Before Mickey headed back home, he stopped at The Liberty House and bought Trudy a linen sundress with a short jacket and a softly gathered paisley print skirt with a low-necked green blouse that picked up the green in the skirt. He had a mental picture of her hanging around the house in shorts and an old shirt, with full breasts and long legs, her skin uniformly tan. But she's going to need a new wardrobe if all goes as planned, he thought. While he was at it, he bought some bright, printed aloha shirts, and a jazzy pair of watermelon red slacks with an aloha shirt to match. Like most the other horyos, he always felt elated when he was spending money.

For the next few weeks, he worked his tail off. Walter wondered if it really could be true that the old life of the party Mickey had changed. For one thing, he headed home right after the office closed.

It was a long haul from Honolulu to Hauula, but there was talk of a tunnel being put through the Pali. Meanwhile, it was probably just as well that I'm living in the sticks, Mickey thought. As soon as he was back on the scene, everybody wanted to invite him to join in on the fun, and a lot of the people he liked most weren't the kind of folks who were interested in work.

Sometimes he got home in the early afternoon, and Judy raced to jump on the running board and get a 'smoogie', a big loud kiss on the cheek, when he got out of the car. He smiled, remembering how she had squawked when he took her from Donda's. Her birthday was coming up, and he planned a party for her and made a treasure hunt.

Tony and Judy invited the Rutherford kids and spent an hour tearing around the property, solving riddles in order to find the clues that Mickey had hidden in ingenious places. Disheveled and jubilant, they found the 'treasure' in the studio: Ice cream and an elaborate cake decorated with circus animals out of marzipan.

When he said goodnight to Judy at the end of the day, her eyes were shining, and she put her arms around his neck saying, "Daddy, that was the best birthday in the whole world!" He thought of Vivian and hoped she would have approved.

His mind went back to Judy's third birthday, when Vivian made strawberry ice cream with dry ice in a churn. He had made a swing for the kids, one that was big enough for them both to sit in, facing each other. He hung it from the branches of a huge pepper tree, and they squealed with pleasure when he pushed them higher and higher, until their heads brushed the feathery foliage that blocked out the blue sky. He had pushed them too high, and Judy fell out and bawled her head off, making Vivian scold while he laughed to see how quickly Judy bounced to her feet. It seemed like such a long time ago.

Time raced by once he started working. Walter had hired him on a commission basis, and there were prospects for big earnings. There was a real estate boom in the islands, now that the pace of life had quickened and more people were moving in permanently from the mainland.

Everywhere he went, he ran into people he knew before the war, and in the newness of it all, it was easy to go on believing in a bright future. All sorts of characters wanted to buy him a drink and hear about what he had been up to. It was exhilarating, getting back in the swing of things. However, it wasn't long before he was spending less and less time in the office. Most of his activity was showing property to potential clients, and he met them at the location.

He convinced himself that contacts meant everything in a place like Honolulu, and soon his social life became blurred with his business interests. Being back in circulation meant that he spent more money, and he fell into his old habit of spending more than he earned. He had to look presentable, and so did Trudy. He saw that bringing her along for a lunch or dinner engagement was a plus. She never interfered with business talk – Just sat there looking gorgeous and dimpling up with a smile often enough to make the client forget to be cautious.

The money that Jane continued to send him slipped through his fingers like sand in an hourglass. He missed a couple of payments on the mortgage, but he wasn't worried. There were a couple of big deals brewing on the back burner.

Despite his original intentions of devoting his energy to cultivating the sort of people who could further his career, he found himself gravitating towards the so-called losers of society. They were usually more fun and a lot less hypocritical. In the hectic scene of postwar opportunism, he could easily spot the sort of men who were the scum of Cabanatuan, and they were sometimes at the top of the pyramid in the financial world.

All together, he ruminated over the fact that so many people had to become so dull in the process of becoming a success. It was often more interesting to talk with a bum than a bank director. When Vivian was alive, he tried to keep a foot in each world, because he knew it meant something to her to associate with people who shared her love for beautiful things. But those friends who had liked Vivian so well had nothing in common with Trudy, and clearly she didn't seem to notice or care. Without Vivian, he had no incentive to keep up the old ties to the garden club crowd or the more respectable members of the Big Five families.

One afternoon, he drove up to Tantalus to see if Aliolani still lived there. The large hunks of property made available to Hawaiian homesteaders meant that this was one part of Oahu that hadn't been squeezed by development. Aliolani's unpainted shack was exactly as he remembered it, except that the trees and shrubs had grown so much that it was almost entirely hidden by them. She came out when she heard his car, and when he stopped and got out, she squinted at him a second before breaking out in a big grin.

"Mickey! You come back! Aloha nui!" she shouted, while running bare-footed down her front steps, her ample figure covered in a muumuu with a pattern of large red hibiscus flowers.

There was more gray in her hair, but she still wore it in a thick braid down her back. She threw her arms around Mickey and kept up a steady stream of Pidgin English and Hawaiian.

Mickey looked over her shoulder and saw that a huge Hawaiian had come outside and was standing on the porch. He flashed a big smile, and Mickey remembered the little boy who was Aiolani's son.

She turned her head and said, "Keoke, you memba Mickey?"

Keoke nodded happily. They all three sat down on the porch and spent the rest of the afternoon, catching up on what had happened during the past seven years. It felt so good to be with them. Nothing had changed.

Aiolani was very sad when she learned about Vivian's death, but she didn't seem surprised. She told Mickey about the last time she saw Vivian, when she was evacuated. "I had a feeling, you know da kind, that mebbe she no come back. I was so sad, Mickey. She was so pretty and so good." Aiolani shook her head sadly and brushed away a tear.

Driving home, Mickey thought about the Hawaiians he knew. Lacking the devious traits of other races who came to the islands, they had been exploited and deprived of their heritage. The funny thing was that they somehow retained dignity and generosity, while everyone else was hustling around, trying to pile up riches. One side of him wanted to live like Aiolani and Keoke, enjoying the beauty of the islands without trying to change anything, and the other side of him was the ambitious haole. Only trouble is that, without enough dough, guys who wouldn't make a pimple on a Hawaiian ass, push you around all the time, he thought.

When he got home, Trudy complained of not feeling too well. She was otherwise one of these people who never had a sick day, and he looked at her with some concern. A few days before there had been a rash of food poisoning, because some Hawaiians made poi in a bathtub that had a hole in the enamel. A few people had died. It sounded like she had eaten something that had made her sick, but as far as he knew, they got their poi from a safe source. He whipped up dinner for the kids and made some soup for Trudy, but she didn't even want to eat that.

He awoke in the middle of the night. It was windy, and avocados were falling to the ground with a thud from the tree outside the house. Trudy was moaning with pain. Mickey jumped out of bed and, on checking her over, decided she could very well have appendicitis. He threw a robe around her shoulders and carried her out to the car to get her to the hospital in Kahuku as fast as possible.

Judy woke up as they went out the door. She sensed there was something wrong with Trudy, but didn't know what. Frightened, she wanted to go to Tony, but she thought she saw a lady in a white gown standing in the doorway to the bathroom between their two rooms. She froze, afraid to approach the apparition. She imagined it looked like her mother, but as she stared in the darkness, the figure disappeared. Judy hurried past the doorway and climbed into the foot end of Tony's bed where she felt safe and fell immediately asleep.

Trudy did have to have her appendix out. While Mickey paced the corridor, his mind went back to the day he paced the floor in that same hospital when Tony was born. He had to fight back tears as he remembered his first sight of Vivian when the birth was over. God, she had been beautiful. He would never forget her smile when he walked into her room. She had looked like someone who had just won the Irish Sweepstakes.

Mickey stayed until Trudy's operation was over, and she was settled in a private room. It was dawn when he drove home. Until then, he pushed out of his mind the problem of this extra expense. It wasn't the first time he had been unlucky. Tony and Judy had to have their tonsils out just the month before. He had promised Jane he would put a little aside to cover eventual medical expenses, but he hadn't done it. He couldn't very well write now and ask her to help him out with this one. He'd just have to hope for the best and let the mortgage ride.

Once he left his rural hideaway, it didn't take long for him to create around his person the same whirlwind that had been characteristic for him all his life. People always were amazed at what he could set into motion, but he seldom stayed still long enough to see the results. The days of the week ran into each other, and in the resulting confusion overdue bills started to stack up, carelessly tossed aside unopened when he was on his way out or in.

He had a bit of luck when he sold a piece of property out near Diamond Head and received a fat check for a down payment. The money was to be turned in at the office, for him to receive his commission later, but Walter was away on the mainland at the time. Mickey cashed the check and pocketed the money, thinking of it as a short-term loan. Walter sure as hell won't miss it, he thought, and it'll be easy to pay it back when I make the next big sale. It made things easier that Walter wasn't exactly a whiz at business.

Now that he was back in touch with Aiolani, some of his happiest moments were spent with her and her friends at a luau or a "jam session". Children were always welcome, and he took Tony and Judy along when he and Trudy were invited. Jam sessions were gatherings in the pitch-blackness of a tropical night on the broad beach fringed with ironwood trees at Kaneohe Bay. A huge black iron pot hanging over a fire was filled with seawater and kept boiling, while everyone chased with flashlights or torches the small white crabs that ran madly about in the wake of retreating waves. Dropped into the cauldron, they made for delicious snacks while the Hawaiians laughed and talked Pidgin English and sang to the strumming of ukuleles.

For luaus, Trudy learned to make a hula skirt out of ti leaves, using her long fingernails to shred the big leaves and make them hang softly in a green cascade. Sometimes, she and Mickey stayed out all night, and by the time they came home, the hula skirt had shrunk, revealing even more of her shapely legs.

One night as he drove home with Trudy, an old Chinaman emerged from nowhere on a bend in the road and froze, dazed by the headlights. Mickey slammed on the brakes, but was unable to avoid hitting him, throwing him onto the hood of the car. Stopping, he jumped out to see how badly the man was hurt.

Luckily, he seemed only to be dazed, and Mickey talked him into getting into the car to be driven home. Following his directions, they found themselves bumping along a dirt road that led to the beach. In a setting that would be an inspiration to a poet, there was a tumble-down shack. Mickey wanted to give the man something to make up for the accident, but the Chinaman smiled, showing gaps where age had robbed him of some of his teeth, and shook his head. With a nod at the shack and the beach beyond, he said quite simply, "I got everything. You come see me some time. I make good fish." He laughed and stood watching them as they turned the car to drive off, lifting his hand in a feeble salute. There was an uncanny resemblance to the thin figure of Oshiko, standing by the gates of the warehouse the last time Mickey saw him, when the bombing of Nagoya made it impossible to move freight.

He felt time stand still for a moment, remembering Oshiko's kindness, and the simplicity of dealing with a man of his character. Again he was reminded of the lesson prison camp had taught him: To be humble and to admire people who had achieved that state. Back then, he thought he would aspire to a life according to the principles that had been hammered into his brain whenever he was able to abstract from gnawing hunger. He remembered the feeling of having thought he had discovered the philosophers' stone, when he understood the secret to a life that could be simple and uncluttered, self-contained, simply by omitting all things that weren't essential. But it was only a passing thought, a spark of recognition. He immediately rationalized that he would return to those ideals, just as soon as he made enough money to give his kids the kind of future he and Vivian had dreamed up for them.

The next day he was informed that unless he could raise the money due on the mortgage within twenty-four hours, the house would be put up for auction. He realized that some of those unopened bills had been dunning letters. Hells bells, he thought. Jane will be livid.

When he finally told Trudy what was happening she suggested that he hit Walter for a loan. "He's got so much money, Mickey, he wouldn't even miss such a little bitty amount."

"You're right about that, honey, but I don't think it's a good idea if Walter finds out that I'm in a bind. You remember that down payment I got for that place out by Diamond Head? I should have turned it over to Walter, but I figured I could use it for some expenses I had then and make up for of it when the next sale comes through. Jesus, it's all a matter of timing. If one more big sale came through, I wouldn't have a care in the world. Meanwhile, though, we're gonna have to move."

He wasn't used to talking about his plans with Trudy, but it was a pleasant surprise to see how well she was taking it. He even got the impression that she seemed somehow pleased.

"What are you smiling about when we are in such a mess?" he asked with a grin.

"Well, honey, don't you get upset with me, but to tell you the truth, I'm real glad we'll have to move out of this place. It's a long drive when we go out in the evenings, and I think it would be fun to live closer to town. You've got a lot of nice friends in there, and sometimes I get kinda lonely when you have to work a lot," she said wistfully in her soft Oklahoman drawl.

Once Mickey heard that, he quickly thought out a plan. There was that studio apartment in Kaneohe that he was supposed to sell. The owners had gone back stateside and left the key with him. It was fully furnished, small, but ample. He and Trudy could sleep on the double bed that served as a couch in the living room, and the kids could sleep on the screened porch. They could move in there until some money came in and they could find something else. The owners never needed to find out, and if they did, they wouldn't care, he thought. They were real nice people.

Tony and Judy were devastated when they were told they were going to move. It all happened so quickly. Perhaps worst of all was that they couldn't take their dog, Toughie, with them. Mickey assured them that he had found it a good home, but as they drove towards Kaneohe, in a borrowed pickup loaded down with their things, Tony thought he saw the dog chasing them down the road. He had a hard time forgetting it and hoped maybe Toughie would suddenly find them where they were going to stay.

Their new home was a swish place with white shag wall-to-wall carpeting and an open kitchen separated from the living room with a well-stocked bar, but there were no bedrooms. For the kids, the neighborhood was a whole new environment, tame and full of haole families with steady employment. It was close to the sea, but instead of a sandy beach, there were mud flats, with little to do but wade when the tide was out, finding small fish in shallow pools. One day they found a big Samoan crab and excitedly planned to take it home to eat, but it was dead and Mickey had to throw it out. Judy caught a minnow-size fish in a tide pool and kept it alive for weeks by changing the seawater each day in a big glass jar.

There was no garden, but around the house was a border of calla lilies. The screened porch where Tony and Judy slept was exposed to the wind, and Mickey had to cover them up with a heavy tarpaulin to protect them from the rain that blew in on them from the sea. Each day Judy picked a few calla lilies and put them in a tin can on a table by their makeshift bed. Each morning they had blown over and the water had spilled.

Mickey told the children that it was only temporary. He tried to comfort them about leaving Hauula, painting a rosy picture of what life would be like just as soon as he started hauling in big money. He had come up with an idea to build A-frame houses in a housing development that was going to make a lot of money for everyone involved. The tract was dubbed Mikiola as a nod to his idea, and one of the houses could be theirs, he said.

This plan depended on Colonel Judd who was a good-natured Texan with money to burn. Mickey exploited his own Southern background and Trudy's good looks and soft-spoken Oklahoman drawl to endear them to the old guy. He was lonely, and he liked having them along when he went out to dinner or toured the island. They saw a lot of the colonel, and Mickey got to know all about his many assets. His orchards in Texas were among the first producing pink grapefruits, and he had a fine collection of antiques in a mansion in the islands. While he was around, Mickey and Trudy milked him for a lot of his money, and he didn't seem to mind.

When school broke out for the summer vacation, Mickey put Tony and Judy on a plane and sent them to California to be with Donda. Langley was going to Arkansas to visit his family in August, and he promised to take the kids with him and leave them at Trudy's parents' farm where she would join them to take them back to Honolulu.

Donda took one look at Tony and Judy and decided that she needed to put some meat on their bones. They spent a couple of months with her, being spoiled with their favorite foods and being showered with new clothes from their aunts and uncles.

Their trip with Langley was an unforgettable one for him. It was a long haul on Highway 66. It was rare when they encountered another car, and the kids were bored. They drove Langley nuts, asking him questions. It was hotter than blazes, and when they weren't scrapping, Judy was being carsick. To distract her, he patiently tried to teach her how to sing "I'm Chiquita Banana", wishing he hadn't when he decided she was tone-deaf.

After several days on the road, they were all three exhausted when he finally drove up the dirt trail to the farm. Tony and Judy awoke the next day and raced about to all the familiar haunts. They spent every waking hour outside, too busy to quarrel. From Vivian, or from Mickey, or perhaps from Donda, they had acquired a fascination and love for all living creatures, even the most insignificant plants or the least appealing insects. Or maybe these things interested them simply because so much of their growing up had been unsupervised, and a love for things of the earth is inborn in all children. In any case, the woods, the pastures, the ponds, and the yard of the farmhouse furnished them with hours of entertainment.

Soon Trudy joined them, but her being there didn't change anything. It was still her mother who took care of Tony and Judy, and they loved everything about her.

On Sundays, the major attraction was a revival meeting in the big tent that had been pitched on a field near Tulsa. The kids attended each session eagerly, anxious to hear the next installment of a Bible story that was narrated, accompanied by illustrations cut out in cloth and placed on a felt board.

Each meeting worked towards a climax that came on the last Sunday before the show moved on. That final night, the preacher worked the crowd into a fever pitch, telling them that they could see Jesus if they let themselves be lost in the words of the Lord. In the front row, there was a thin, haggard woman with her brood of five children. Swooping down on her, the preacher lifted her up to another dimension, his rich, deep voice invoking a state of rhapsody that she had never experienced.

Ecstatic, she sobbed out her ability to see Jesus, and it was an easy matter for the preacher to reel in four of her children who were alarmed by the spectacle they were witnessing. The fifth child, a small boy with tousled blonde hair, quietly insisted that he couldn't see anything. He seemed to have represented a challenge to the preacher. At least, the preacher was determined not to let this one small fish slip away. Tony watched intently, hoping the little boy would stick to his guns.

There was pandemonium among the congregation as they let themselves be caught up in the excitement of the moment. Like the quiet spot in the eye of a storm, the small boy stood fast, stubbornly shaking his head as the preacher spoke to him in a low voice. Then, Tony heard the preacher say crossly, "Look kid, if you'll say you see Jesus, I'll buy you an ice cream after we close down." The boy nodded eagerly, and Tony laughed as he nudged Judy to follow him. They edged their way through the crowd and climbed out a flap at the back of the tent. Then they high-tailed it to where Trudy was waiting by the pickup. They were going to fly back to the islands that night, and the revival meeting had lost its interest.

Back in the islands, Mickey was working all sorts of angles in order to have the money to put Trudy and the kids up in style when they got back. Thanks to the colonel's generosity, he was able to cover his tracks and could write to Jane and tell her they were moving to Waikiki to be close to the office. Christ, he thought, in another year's time, I'll be doing well enough to stand inspection if Jane comes over here.

Jane still didn't know about the deal with the mortgage. Mickey just needed to win a bit of time, and he could make it look like the move had been intentional. With the irons he had in the fire, it wouldn't be long before he could buy a piece of property that would make Hauula seem like nothing.

When Trudy got back to the islands with the children, they moved into a bungalow in a court at Waikiki, with the Catholic Church on one side and Mrs. Bishop's Hula School down the street. The kids missed their school, but Mickey told them they were better off going to English standard schools than the little school at Hauula.

The English standard schools were a carry-over from the period in Hawaiian history when the children of oriental workers started school, and the established haole families tried to keep them out by making them pass a test in English proficiency. The unintentional result was a school system that matched the excellent abilities of these ambitious oriental students who were willing to work very hard in order to be accepted. Passing the test was still required for entry, but for Judy and Tony it was no challenge.

The new surroundings gave Tony and Judy a whole new sphere of activities. They were right across the street from the beach, and Tony and Judy went there every day, swimming out among the coral-studded shallows where they could dive and look for brightly colored sea creatures. Mickey liked to hang out at the Waikiki Tavern on the beach, and the kids discovered that while sitting in a banyon tree on the side of the tavern that faced the sea they could listen to the piano player and watch their dad in action.

They also climbed in the big banyan tree in the churchyard of the Catholic Church next door. One day Tony climbed to the top, and Judy followed him. Tony came down effortlessly, but Judy chickened out and had to be rescued by the fire department. That was how Mickey met the priest at the church. They became good friends – talking about philosophy and drinking the altar wine.

Mickey was amused to discover that his old artist friend, Ted Mundorf, and his beautiful wife, Kate, had transformed the gardener's shack belonging to the Waikiki bungalows into a tasteful dwelling. Ted told Mickey that it cost them ten bucks a month when they had moved in, but once they had fixed the place up, the owner raised the rent to fifty, a good indication of what property values were like. Tony spent hours hanging around Ted's studio, watching him paint tropical flowers with silk screens and a spray gun, and Ted, who had no children of his own, enjoyed Tony's company.

Just as easily as Mickey had fit into the village scene of Hauula, he slipped into the role of man about town once they moved to Waikiki. Old friends from show business blew into

Honolulu, and he met new people from all walks of life wherever he went. Although he was selling real estate, he gravitated back towards advertising and public relations, doing some work with Akuhead Pupule, a bizarre disc jockey who made public appearances wearing a fish head and whose radio program started off the islanders' day. Mickey felt the old buzz he used to get when he was in the thick of things, exerting his ability to charm people.

It was like Mac had predicted when Vivian turned to him for advice – Mickey was out to make up for lost time. He felt he had been robbed of some of his best years, and he would make up for it by extending himself in all directions. In doing so, he sought out experiences that skirted on the edge of danger, soaking them up as a reminder of his invincibility.

Among his many new friends was a guy who flew a small aircraft to the other islands on various missions. Mickey joined him and a press photographer to take the first close-ups of the boiling lava that spewed out of the crater of Mt. Kilauea when it erupted. They also flew to the island of Molokai to spend a couple of days at the leper colony there.

The history of leprosy in the islands was a sad one. Like all other diseases, it was unknown to the Hawaiians when the first outsiders came to the islands. The natives dubbed it 'pake sickness' – Chinese illness, because they believed Chinese immigrants brought it to the islands. Because there was at that time no cure, the only way to deal with the illness was to isolate its victims.

To be diagnosed a leper and sent to Molokai was to be given a particularly cruel death doom, especially for those victims whom the disease invaded slowly. They could appear perfectly healthy but were forced to live side by side with lepers in the final, most frightening stages of the disease. All lepers were shipped to Molokai and abandoned there, in a lawless society where the strong preyed on the weak and a beautiful girl who was as yet unmarred by the disease was likely to be sexually abused by creatures who were too repulsive to describe.

There were occasionally healthy wives or husbands who joined their diseased spouses to try to alleviate their final days. The price for this sacrifice was that they were not allowed to return to society, for the fear of contamination was so great.

Molokai was a desolate place, windswept and comparatively bleak, without the bounty found on the other islands. Food was cast overboard in crates that floated ashore to be gathered up by the lepers.

In 1873, a Belgian Jesuit priest, Father Damien, made it his mission in life to join the lepers in order to bring order to the lives of these poor souls and give them the comfort of Christianity. After his death, in 1889, others from his order followed him. The priest who lived in the leper colony now had been a friend of Father Joseph, the priest at Cabanatuan. Mickey felt like seeing him and telling him about Father's Joseph's bravery and personal sacrifices in prison camp. Father Joseph had told Mickey about the colony and that it was now known that the disease could not be spread except through an open sore. Mickey's pilot friend had a mail run at the island, and he said he could drop Mickey off there and pick him up the next day.

Mickey spent the night at the colony and bathed in the sea with the priest and some of the lepers. With a vague sense of detachment, he saw lepers in the most crippling stage of the disease and realized that some of his fellow prisoners had appeared just as repulsive to those splendid troops who liberated them in Japan. After his visit to the colony, it was with a sense of relief that Mickey plunged back into the whirlwind of activity that had become a routine.

When Mickey took Trudy out in the evening, he gave Tony and Judy a couple of quarters to buy a dinner from one of the streetside stands that sold saimen and teriyaki. They loved the thin broth and fine noodles and the tasty pieces of marinated beef barbecued on wooden skewers. Sometimes Mickey gave them a dollar, and they got a meal at a nearby diner. There, they ordered chicken fried steak and watched the regular customers who came every day for their evening meal.

One of the regulars at the diner was an elderly haole who wore very unsuitable attire for the tropics – a three-piece suit and a fedora – when he came for his evening meal. He was frail and his complexion sickly white, and every evening he had the same ritual. With his paper napkin, he meticulously wiped his utensils before he started on his dinner. He was undoubtedly suspicious of the hygiene in the diner, but, after Mickey told the kids about the trip to Molokai, they were convinced the old man was hiding leprosy under his clothes.

Trudy loved their new life style. Part of her attraction had been that she was lazy, and it suited her fine that they ate most meals out. Mickey had transformed her from a pretty farm girl to a gal who stopped traffic. Smartly dressed, a becoming cut to her naturally curly honey-blonde hair, eyes a turquoise blue, and her gorgeous skin always perfectly tanned, she started to become aware of all the attention she was getting from men. They flirted with her, and turned to watch her when she passed by on the street, but at first she gave them the cold shoulder.

Feeling sure of himself, Mickey was amused to see guys fall all over themselves trying to get her attention. With more self-awareness, her sense of style became more sophisticated, and she loved nice clothes. Mickey realized how good a protégé she was when she surprised him by going to Liberty House and buying a very chic white sharkskin suit which was a far cry from the girlish style she had sported when they met. She was picking up new skills in more ways than one: She also learned Mickey's habit of charging things.

When they moved to Waikiki, Mickey chanced to run into an army officer whom he met before the war, when he used to hang out at Schoffield Barracks. They got together, and Mickey was dismayed when he saw what sort of wife the guy was straddled with. Her name was Mary Lou, and, like Trudy, she came from a small town in Oklahoma, but Mickey wasn't impressed with her and wondered whether his friend, Bill, had married her because he had to. They had an eight-month old baby named Vicky, a beautiful child who spent most of her time lying untended in her crib. Mickey thought Mary Lou was a rotten mother, but it wasn't his style to object if Trudy liked seeing her.

One day they were witness to the mother grabbing the baby by one arm and holding her under a gush of hot water in the bathtub, yelling abuse at her, just because she was soiled. Mickey hated seeing anything like that. If anything was sacred it was a baby.

Judy was delighted with the baby, because Mary Lou gladly turned her over to anyone who would take care of her, even someone as young as Judy. One day she let Judy take her to the beach by herself. Holding Vicky tightly, Judy waded out in the surf, and a wave toppled the two of them over. Judy grabbed the baby and ran ashore, horrified at the thought of how close she was to drowning Vicky. She felt terrible, but she also had an undefined awareness that the adults in her world didn't care.

Mickey was too busy to give Bill and his wife much thought, but Trudy continued to see them. She was getting a few friends of her own, but her relationship with Mickey was as smooth as it always had been. She was still impressed with him. He seemed to know so much about everything, and he had such smart ideas. It didn't bother her that he wasn't always honest with Walter. Walter should be able to take care of himself, she thought with indifference.

As soon as they had moved to Waikiki, Mickey's nightlife accelerated, and the busier he became, the more the line between his personal income and that of Walter's firm became blurred, just as it had done in the past. What with drinking with the clients and nurturing his contacts, Mickey lost track of what was coming in and what was going out. As for Walter, his habits hadn't changed since his college days, and he was usually too busy chasing skirt to worry about what Mickey was doing. Things got worse when Mickey talked Walter into putting Trudy on the payroll. With her in the office, it was easier to juggle the accounts. He never thought of his over-spending as anything other than a sensible investment in an unending line of schemes.

Indeed, in his fertile mind, Mickey conceived of more and more ways to make money, but all his ideas needed start capital. When he read an article in TIME about the post-war boom in Las Vegas and got a notion of what property values must be like there, he thought about the place that Jane had given him when he got home from prison camp. It was still there for him, but if he could convince her he had a promising investment in the islands, she might let him sell.

A man from Ohio had just forked over a handsome sum for a house in Kailua. Walter didn't know the sale had gone through, and Mickey eyed an opportunity to buy a plane ticket to the states. He told Trudy he was going to make a quick trip to Las Vegas and try to persuade his mother into letting him sell the ranch. Walter was out of town, but if he came back and asked about whether the house in Kailua was sold, she should try to stall him.

Mickey left on the next plane he could get out of the islands. Jane had begun to get suspicious that something was wrong, and actually found herself wishing Vivian were still there to keep Mickey on the straight and narrow. When she met him at the airport, he could sense that her mood was a bit prickly. He knew instinctively he had to butter her up before he could approach her with his plan, but he also knew that she would eventually come around to whatever he wanted. She always did.

"But, Mickey, you know that piece of property is a nest egg for the future," she said with some exasperation when he broached the idea of selling it. She had more of an edge to her voice than she liked, and she felt a slight throbbing in the base of her skull. Those headaches were getting more frequent, and she couldn't afford to waste time lying in a dark room while Mickey was home. She didn't want to let him rile her, and she tried to stay calm while she talked sense to him.

"That part of Vegas has taken off like a house-afire. You should see some of the homes that are going up out there. Why in a few years time it could more than double in value. It'd be downright foolish to sell it right now when we don't even need the money, and in the meantime it's even bringing in a bit of money by being rented out."

Finally he had to play with open cards and admit to her that his finances in the islands were in a mess. "But it's only temporary, Jane," he said convincingly. "I've let my expenses get a little out of hand, but the money's all there to haul in just as soon as things fall into place."

Her common sense warned her that this was more of the same old story, but she felt so weary that she wanted to believe him. As usual, as soon as he could feel her resistance wearing down, he found himself being swept along by his own arguments, selling himself on what he was saying as much as he was convincing her. Occasionally her temper flared, but he deftly smoothed her feathers and sweet-talked her into letting him go on with his arguments. Finally she said that that property was after all in his name, and he could damned well do with it as he liked.

She wanted him to stay for a real visit, but he felt like he had to get back to Honolulu as soon as possible. Trudy had scribbled a hasty note telling him Walter was back and was asking questions.

He felt a fleeting twinge of regret when the property was sold. Anyone could see how Las Vegas was expanding. However, if it bothered Mickey momentarily, it bothered Jane tenfold. Everything she had in life was due to an astute judgment of the value of property, and now the only thing she had left was the hotel and a few parcels of undeveloped land she was holding on to for speculation. She still had the deed to that damned mercury mine, but she figured it would never be worth anything.

She felt depressed when she saw him off at the airport, and it occurred to her that she ought to fly out to the islands herself and see just what was going on out there. After all, it was her money that had made it possible for Mickey to move to the islands. Before she made any plans, however, she wanted to spend a few days out at Pete's ranch. It was easier to think straight out there where there were no distractions.

She got there in the afternoon, and she and Pete rode on out to the pools. She told him what had transpired with Mickey, and as was usually the case, she found herself trying to put Mickey's actions in a better light. No matter what his faults were, she didn't know how she could live if she stopped believing in this impractical son of hers.

Pete let her talk. He knew that it never did any good to tell someone like Jane what she should think, and as long as he had known her, she had been trying to change Mickey.

They had reached one of the pools, a blue gem in the barren wasteland. She reigned in her mount and stared down at the sulfur formations that had formed along the side of the pool. Lord knows how long they had been there, unspoiled as yet by anything built up by man. She hated the thought of tearing herself away and getting entangled in her son's world three thousand miles out in the Pacific, but suddenly she had made up her mind. As if she were talking to herself, she said, "I think I'll have to go to Honolulu and see what's going on, Pete."

Once she had stated her intention, she felt an immense weariness. Maybe I'm getting old, she thought, but she immediately checked that notion. I still sit straight in the saddle, and no one could tell my age by just looking at me. She became aware of Pete watching her and said, "I'll race you back to the house," nudging her horse to a head start.

Even though Pete liked Mickey, he thought she was wasting her time worrying about what sort of a mess he might be in now. He figured that you can't teach an old dog new tricks, and Mickey would never change. Jane had told him part of what had transpired, and he sensed that she was holding back anything that would make Mickey look bad in his eyes.

She needn't bother, he thought, laconically. Mickey could charm the rattles off a snake, and Jane would always bail him out when the going got rough. The world was full of all sorts of people, and they weren't easy to change. Someone like Mickey added a lot of color and stirred things up. It was always fun to see what was new when the dust settled. He chuckled as he galloped back to the house, thinking about the fun times he had had with Jane's son.

Jane's worries about Mickey took a back seat when Flossie and their younger sister, Joy, showed up in Vegas. Joy's husband, Jack, was laid up from work, with a broken leg. He had recovered enough to take care of himself, but he was cross as a grizzly bear. Flossie thought it would do them both good if Joy cut out for a few weeks. Joy hated to leave Jack on his own, but Flossie told her that was ridiculous. She had no patience for anyone who would sit around in an unhappy situation and not do something to bring about a change. There was never a dull moment with Flossie around.

They drove up to Death Valley Scotty's where Flossie was always welcome. Then they headed out for Jane's. Jane knew they would love it at Pete's ranch, and she liked the thought of showing him off to her sisters. Flossie was thrilled. She knew Pete had plenty of horses to ride, and she loved a chance to go skinny-dipping in a clear desert pool.

Jane packed a lot of food, and they left in her car. When they got there, Pete was in the coral, working with a quarter horse that he had just broken. "Hey, Jane...and Flossie!" he said, with a grin, when he recognized Jane's redheaded sister. He tipped his Stetson at Joy and said, "Howdy...I'll be right there."

The three sisters leaned against the fence and watched him as he dismounted and latched the gate when he left the coral. He took off his hat to wipe his brow and brush back his sandy-colored hair. He was lean, and his face and hands were tan. He looked Scandinavian, calm with gray-blue eyes. Flossie remembered his languid, easy-going attitude, but she detected a spark of something different when Pete greeted Joy. Jane recognized it, too, and felt a flush of jealousy. She thought she knew Pete in and out, but she had never seen him look that interested in a woman.

They stayed on the ranch for a couple of days, spending hours riding the range, followed up with a swim in one of the springs. A breeze rustled the cottonwood trees surrounding the ranch, making a sound like rainfall, and the sunsets were spectacular. Usually Pete busied himself around his ranch when Jane was there, but this time he spent all waking hours with them.

Joy felt refreshed like she hadn't been in years. Hers had been a hard life, starting with an early marriage to a farmer in Tennessee. There had been a lot of land and a handsome farmhouse, but that didn't compensate for the fact that the man was mean. He treated her so badly that even his own family thought she should leave him, but that was in the early thirties when a mother on her own had a tough row to hoe. A trip to California to visit Dunaway and Flossie had convinced her she could manage it. Mickey was in his heyday at the studios, and she was even able to earn good money as an extra in a crowd scene.

However, every time she felt ready to leave her husband, she discovered she was pregnant. She knew she wouldn't have a chance unless her youngest child was out of diapers at least. She had five children before she could gather all of them up and make a run for freedom.

She got to California, but life there was a struggle. Mickey had left for the islands, and she had to earn money by waiting tables. Then she met Jack, who had everything Clark Gable had, except his money. He was the love of her life and a good husband, but bad luck followed them. When she met Pete, she was still pretty, but he could see she hadn't had it easy. He took a shine to her feminine ways right from the start.

He had had a lot of good times with Jane and got a kick out of her feisty nature. She didn't make him feel tied down, and that suited him fine. Seeing Joy, however, he felt for the first time an urge to be protective towards a woman. She was so sweet and gentle that he wanted to be around her all the time.

Joy could feel Pete was attracted to her, but she didn't want Jane hurt. Besides, she loved Jack just as much as ever. It was nice, just the same, to be in this beautiful place and realize that she could still be attractive. The last day of their stay, Pete found a moment alone with her and told her that if she ever felt like a life on his ranch, she just had to whistle. Somehow it was just the medicine she needed to be able to go home and soldier through a bad patch, knowing how much Jack needed her. Any married couple with all their troubles would have a hard time staying in love.

For Jane, the experience was different. She loved her little sister, and Joy had given her no cause to be jealous. Still, it hurt her to see how Pete took to Joy. She had begun to feel bitter about her fate. Hadn't she done everything she could for those she loved all her life? And here was the result. They thought of her as the iron woman, never worrying about her feelings. It didn't bother her, all those years when she was climbing upward, but lately she no longer felt so energetic and would have liked to have the feeling that there was someone to support her when she was tired.

Jane was coy about her age, and it was only on rare occasions that she admitted to herself that she was past sixty. She had been blessed with an iron constitution, but hard work or too much tension in the desert heat gave her headaches. She found relief by going to matinees in the afternoon and relaxing to the organ music in the cool darkness of the theater. Good spells with Pete made her put on weight, and when she felt she needed to get back into shape, she left for the high country, in Utah at La Verkin Hot Springs, or Bryce Canyon, staying away for a month or so. However, she never flagged in her efforts to build up a fortune according to well-defined goals.

Flossie and Joy went back to California, and Jane turned her full attention to the problem of Mickey. With the cash injection from the sale of the property, he would be able to hold the show on the road a bit longer, but Jane was convinced his situation was more complicated than he had told her when he was in Nevada. I'll bet he had to let go of the place in Hauula, she thought, otherwise he could have mortgaged that.

The more she tried to imagine what was going on, the more convinced she was that she should fly out to the islands and help Mickey set up an investment that would secure his future. Now that he was flying high again, she wanted there to be a safety net. She remembered that he had talked about a number of schemes he had dreamed up, and one of them made real sense to her.

A new air terminal was going up in Honolulu, and Mickey had said that whoever could get in on the ground floor with a gift shop would have a little gold mine. Jane had seen how air traffic had changed things in Las Vegas, and she figured he was right there. If so, he should strike while the iron was hot, but she had learned by now that if she was going to help him out, she wanted to make sure the money went to the investment and didn't get squandered on the way.

She cabled that she was coming to Honolulu and then went on a spending spree to equip herself for a trip she had never imagined taking. She hadn't had a vacation in a long time, and she thought of all the wonderful things Vivian and Mickey had said about the islands. It was about time she saw it for herself.

* * * * *

The great changes that were set in motion during the war were accelerated by the tourist influx that came afterwards. Gone were the days when a select few came to the islands on the Lurline, mostly wealthy people who had the time to spend for the long slow trip each way or who were stopping off on their way around the world. With air traffic, a whole new breed could descend upon the islands, and the more ambitious of the locals saw good means of making a bundle off them right from the moment of their arrival. It was a good time for a person like Jane to get the lay of the land and see for herself what opportunities there were.

Trudy spruced up the bungalow when she heard that Jane was coming. Ted's wife, Kate, gave her some good ideas and Trudy bought a set of long, canary yellow curtains for the living room that made a big difference. She figured Judy and Tony could bunk together, and Jane could have Judy's room while she was there. Mickey had talked about putting his mother up at the Mauna Loa, but his credit wasn't good enough these days. For once, Trudy looked at their home objectively and could see it didn't exactly compare with the Ritz. For one thing, Judy's collection of gold fish in the bathtub would have to go! She couldn't see why Mickey always had to give in to that child's whims, and Jane might not like taking showers. When she was through with cleaning things up, she shrugged her shoulders and figured it would have to do, unless Jane wanted to find something else for them.

When Jane first saw Waikiki, she was thoroughly disappointed. The beach was beautiful, with white sand, inviting turquoise blue water as clear as a bell, and gentle surf, but she preferred the solitude of the pools on Pete's desert. She never could understand how people could like a place that was the least bit crowded, and it looked to her like Waikiki was a whole lot more crowded than it had been when Vivian and Mickey first wrote home about it. There were still only two major hotels, the gracious Royal Hawaiian and the Moana Hotel, but there was traffic along Kalakaua Boulevard, the street that skirted the beach and Kapiolani Park. By afternoon there were bathers scattered along most of the length of the stretch of white sand.

She was further disappointed when she saw Mickey's place. She thought the rent was sky high, but it didn't look like the sort of place he would be living in if things were going as well as he had described. It was cramped quarters, and although Trudy and Mickey were smartly dressed, she noticed that Tony was outgrowing his clothes and Judy looked downright scraggly.

She swelled with pride when she saw Tony. He was a chip off the old block, a handsome boy and bright enough to do well at any education she and Mickey mapped out for him. Jane hadn't forgotten the things she said to Donda about being able to provide the kids with a better home than they could have with her. She had promised herself that she wouldn't meddle in the way the kids were raised, but she never had been able to keep her opinion to herself.

"Mickey, these kids need some new clothes, and Judy looks real puny," she said bluntly. "Why don't we go out and equip them with some decent duds?"

Mickey laughed. "Yeah they're growing like weeds. Don't worry about Judy. She just had a bout of viral pneumonia, but the Doc gave her penicillin, that new wonder drug. She was back on her feet in no time, and he said that all she needs now is cod liver oil." He looked at his daughter fondly and decided he needed to tell Trudy that she should take her to the hairdressers. Trudy never bothered brushing Judy's hair, and daily swims left it looking tangled. He remembered with a pang of regret how much care Vivian took to keep Judy all dolled up, but it wouldn't be fair to expect the same from Trudy.

Jane was rather formal with her grandchildren. It was ridiculous to treat children like anything but small adults, she always maintained. It suited Tony fine that she wasn't like a lot of old ladies who gushed over kids. She had no trouble with communicating with him, but she realized it would be a waste of her precious time to try to win over Judy. Still, it pleased her to see that the child was clearly devoted to her father now. She used to wonder whether it wouldn't have been far simpler to leave her with Vivian's family. Donda had been able to influence her at a crucial age, and Jane was convinced she would take after Vivian's people more than her own.

She decided to make the most of her stay. Jane didn't want to go home without having been for a swim at the famous Waikiki Beach, and when she had changed into her swimming suit, she stepped back to admire her trim figure in the bedroom mirror. She had bought a white, one-piece swimsuit, and for a woman in her sixties, Jane knew she looked pretty good in it. Pulling in her stomach and turning sideways, she stood straight and noticed Judy watching her.

Trying to be friendly, she said, "Look at this, honey-chile. I can still put my hands flat on the floor without bending my knees, and I'm wearing high heel shoes. What do you think of that for an old granny?"

Not willing to give an inch to someone she considered a mortal enemy, and still smarting about being called 'puny,' Judy said, "You're not very tan."

Peeved, Jane retorted, "Well, my ankles are slimmer than yours, darlin', and you're only eleven years old." She immediately regretted letting Judy get her goat. What was it about that child that brings the worst out in me, she thought, annoyed. She felt a twinge of that familiar pain at the base of her skull and knew she had to make an effort to calm down.

When she left Pete in Las Vegas, she had said she didn't know how long she would be gone, but in less than a week, she had had enough. It tired her to be with Mickey's friends, and she had nothing in common with Trudy. The relaxed ways of the islanders didn't suit her at all, and she missed the feeling of being in charge that she had on her own turf.

"For the life of me, I don't understand why you still like this place, Mickey. Oh sure, it's pretty all right, but I'll take the peace and quiet of a desert any day. It's too damned crowded for me. And I can't understand how you can be around all these Japs, after all the pain and suffering they caused you," she said, petulantly.

Mickey grinned in his offhand manner and replied, "Well, Jane, honey, these weren't the Japs that caused me all 'that pain and suffering'. I guess that's why. And if some of the deals I'm cooking pan out, I can buy a spread for me and the kids that even you will fall for. I've got my eye on a piece of property on Diamond Head that I'll show you this weekend."

Jane had soon worked out what Mickey's present problems were, and, with her sure sense for business, she had decided what he should do about it.

"You're like a windswept tumbleweed, with all your deals, Mickey. The only way you're going to make some money and be able to administrate it is if you settle down with one project. Now, I've only been here for a week, but I think I know what would be best for you. If you'll listen to me, I'll put up some of the money you need to get started."

Being in no position to argue, Mickey listened contritely while she spelled out her plan.

"You told me you wanted to get the franchise for a gift shop out at the airport. Now, I think that is a sure moneymaker. But I'm only willing to put up some cash if you will agree to cut down your living expenses. I want you to give up this dinky place you're paying so much for in Waikiki and move into something cheaper, out near the airport. Don't give me any hogwash about needing to have the right address. I've been able to get ahead everywhere I've ever lived, and I learned a long time ago that rent money is money out the window. If you save enough up, you can buy a place, and that makes sense."

Mickey fought the old habit of turning off his mind to what she was saying as she droned on. She didn't understand the new trends in business and the fact that if you were going to get anywhere you had to start off with a splash, but he could use her help as things were now. It was worth trying to get along with her. A gift shop in the airport would be a real gold mine. He didn't feel like moving out of Waikiki, but it made sense to find something near the airport. Trudy might balk, but he never worried about appeasing her like he had Vivian.

Before Jane left, Mickey got the franchise, and with the energy he usually exerted on any new idea, he turned all his attention to setting up the gift shop and stocking it. With very little money, he managed to create an attractive stand that would hit everyone in the eye when they passed through the new terminal. He named it the 'Princess Pupule Gift Shop', and he had the bright idea of getting permission to run a postal service there. That way, tourists who wanted to send a gift could send it off right on the spot, an extra temptation for a quick sale.

Mickey saw the necessity of listening to his mother's advice about saving rent money, and he moved his family to Damon Track. The house was a nondescript dwelling on an unpaved street. There was a small, barren yard, with two lone palm trees flanking the front walk. It was a far cry from the sort of place he had dreamed of when he and his pals at Cabanatuan idled away the hours with plans for the future.

Accustomed by now to moving, the kids took it in their stride. Mickey told them it was only temporary, and they believed him. In fact, there was plenty of reason to be optimistic. With more air travel, the influx of tourists would increase greatly. However, there was no changing the fact that the supplies to cater to all these tourists had to be brought in by ship. Old man Dillingham still controlled the harbors, but a new breed of worker had made his appearance on the scene after the war. A man named Harry Bridges was stirring up the dockworkers, encouraging them to make demands for higher wages.

People were calling Bridges a Communist. Maybe he was, thought Mickey, but intellectually he sympathized with their cause. On the one hand, he didn't like unions or anything else that wasn't based on individualism, but he always had thought the poor guy who breaks his back for the rest of the world was underpaid. In the past, the Big Five had by and large avoided unrest by anticipating the workers demands before ground was made ready for some agitator to stir them up. Dillingham and the rest saw that a contented worker was a productive one, and they liked to brag that nowhere else were conditions so good for workers as they were in the islands. However, the war destabilized the relationships between employers and employees, and these damned union leaders were striking while the iron was hot.

Mickey knew enough about politics to foresee that in the long run the little guy usually gets the shaft anyway – if not from the bosses then from his own. What Mickey didn't anticipate was how this man, Bridges, would affect his own fortunes, for just after the gift shop opened, Bridges succeeded in organizing a strike. For six months, the freight traffic of the islands was paralyzed, and, with supplies not coming in, the flow of tourists slowed down to a trickle and then petered out.

Mickey's predicament was accentuated by his new address. At Waikiki, it was easy to live out a dream of being around the action, but Damon Track was a dump. He only touched base to shower and change clothes. It was far easier to escape the dreariness of living in dismal digs if he was in the airport with people in the same boat. Trudy was content to hang out with some of her new-found friends, and didn't complain about their changed circumstances.

He occasionally worried that Judy didn't seem happy, and he was always agreeable if she asked him a favor. Diane Carleton was the girl in Judy's class that she most admired. She said that Judy could come home with her after school, and Mickey was pleased to see his daughter so happy about an invitation. He promised to pick her up around five in the afternoon.

Everything in the Carleton's house was just like Judy imagined she would like their house to be. She could tell that they didn't move around all the time, because they had more furnishings. It was a modest home, but Diane's mother wore an apron and was busy in the kitchen, and Diane's father came home with a briefcase under his arm at the same time every day.

Like most children who have moved into many different environments, Judy had become sensitive to the moods of the grown-ups around her. As the afternoon wore on, and her father didn't show up, she was keenly conscious of the Carleton's growing disapproval even though they were kind and friendly to her.

When Mickey finally arrived at the Carleton's', it was close to nine o'clock. Judy was mortified. She could tell that he had been drinking, and much to her chagrin, he didn't even apologize for being late. In the eyes of his daughter, everything was wrong about him, from his wearing a butterfly tie like some old movie star, to the way he turned on all his charm, feeling expansive and generous towards the Carletons whom he sized up as being conventional and rather dull. He told them what a marvelous evening it had been and raved about the food at some new restaurant, like it was the most natural thing in the world that they should sit up with his daughter while he was out on the town. Judy was disappointed in him, because he didn't feel their disapproval. She wished fervently that he could be like everyone else. However, as soon as they were in the car, it was impossible to stay mad at him. He was always so even-tempered with her and never said anything unkind.

When the longshoreman's strike proved to be a lengthy siege, Mickey found he had plenty of time on his hands, but he had to stay at the airport and keep the shop open for the small trickle of people who came through. Besides, out at the airport he wasn't likely to run into Walter or anyone else he owed money. Sometimes on a Saturday night, he left Judy in charge, and for her, being allowed to stay up late was a treat. Dressed up in a muumuu, she looked cute, and things were so slow that she could easily manage the few purchases that were made.

There wasn't enough business at the gift shop to even pay the rent. In the paralyzed airport terminal, Mickey whiled away the slow hours between flights by hanging out at the 'Short Snort Bar', right next door to his shop. In the dark atmosphere of the bar, with its comfortably familiar smell of booze and stale cigarettes, he felt right at home, sitting on a leather-upholstered barstool and swapping jokes with the amiable Hawaiian bartender. The Chinese photographer and anyone else who found himself fiddling his thumbs during the standstill joined him. It was cozy, and for Mickey it was balm for the soul. One day, the gift shop cash register was empty, and he borrowed some from the box where he kept postal funds, carelessly stuffing the bills in his pocket and making a mental note that he had to remember to put it back.

Occasionally there were old friends from Hollywood passing through the islands to make a film or visit friends. Dick Powell and June Allyson showed up one day, and he borrowed a wad from the postal funds and took them to lunch at the Royal Hawaiian. Another day he saw Nat King Cole, and he closed down shop to go out on the town with him.

Trudy took a turn occasionally, but with so little turnover, there wasn't much point in them both hanging out at the airport. Mickey was relieved when she started spending a lot of time with a divorcee named Nealie, whom she got to know while she worked at Walter's, but he didn't bother to ask what they usually did during the days and evenings they spent together. It was like everything was off track, and it was easier to just let things drift.

Nealie had a little boy Mickey dubbed Pifflejits, and Tony and Judy had to let him tag around with them whenever Trudy and Nealie were busy. Like most Hawaiians, he couldn't say words like 'film', and Tony patiently coached him. "Fillum," said Pifflejits, and "tree," instead of three.

One day Mickey had borrowed a pickup truck to help Nealie move. Tony and Judy and Pifflejits sat dangling their legs over the back flap, which was left open as they drove through Honolulu. Mickey stopped for a red light, and when he started up, Pifflejits fell off and landed neatly on his bottom in the middle of Royal Hawaiian Boulevard. Tony and Judy banged frantically on the cab, trying to get Mickey's attention while Pifflejits ran behind, a tiny yelling boy pursued by a mass of cars.

Finally, Mickey became aware of what was happening and stopped, but it was characteristic of him that he was laughing his head off as he lifted Pifflejits back into the bed of the pickup and didn't worry about the kids falling off again when he continued on his way. It was the sort of thing that had made Elsie think he was irresponsible as a father, but that made each day with him something out of the ordinary.

It wasn't the friendship with Nealie that was filling up Trudy's most interesting hours, however. It was an affair with Bill, the handsome husband of Mary Lou. Being so thick with Nealie just made it easier to lie about her whereabouts.

Christmas was coming, and Trudy was complaining about them being broke. Mickey never went in for Christmas as a holiday and didn't see why anyone should make a problem out of it, but Trudy harped about how the kids would be sad if they didn't have any sort of a Christmas. Trudy loved Christmas. One thing she liked about the days when Mickey was with Walter was being able to buy presents for her folks back home and for people she liked. She fretted about what she was going to do this year. It sure would be nice to give something to Nealie and Pifflejits, but Mickey said she couldn't even charge anything.

One day a big box from Vivian's family arrived for the kids while they were away at school. Trudy opened it and found that it was filled with nicely wrapped presents from all of Tony's and Judy's aunts and uncles and from Donda. Well, they are certainly going to get enough, she thought. Two small presents from Bobbie caught her eye. She remembered other occasions, birthdays and Christmases, and Bobbie's presents were always something nice. The gift-wrapping was a bit torn on Judy's present, and there was something shiny inside.

Curious, she tore it open, thinking it would need a new wrapping any way. Inside, she found a nice piece of costume jewelry, a gold-plated bracelet with a small, jeweled perfume holder on it. Nealie would love it, and Judy's not old enough for it anyway, she thought.

Judy would think something was wrong if Tony got a present from Bobbie and she didn't, Trudy reasoned. She decided to open his gift, and in it was a pocketknife, with two blades and a nail cleaner. That will do nicely for Pifflejits, she figured, pleased with this windfall.

It wasn't just Christmas that was nagging Trudy. When she was married to Ray, she didn't worry about getting pregnant, but it hadn't happened. She had thrown all caution to the winds when she met Mickey. In the beginning, she was so crazy about him that she didn't take time to take any precautions, and later she figured it didn't matter. Nothing had happened, and she got out of the habit of thinking about it. She had no desire to have children, and Mickey was content with his two. She figured it was just her good luck that she evidently didn't get pregnant easily.

When she started her affair with Bill, she didn't let it bother her either. That was one good thing about being married, she thought. I don't have to worry about getting caught out. She liked things like they were and hadn't thought about leaving Mickey. Bill was miserable in his marriage, but if anyone believed in Mickey's pipe dreams, Trudy did, and she didn't want to throw away the kind of life she knew Mickey would be able to give her one day, for life on an army officer's pay.

When Trudy realized her period was way overdue, it finally dawned on her that she might be pregnant. She decided to wait to tell Mickey about it. Things weren't going well at the airport, and anyway, maybe it was a false alarm. The thought had occurred to her that it might be Bill's child, but she pushed that into a part of her brain where she stored anything too complicated to deal with right on the spot. Anyway, Mickey loved kids. He'd probably be thrilled. She was more worried about what having a baby would do to her figure.

They had been to a New Year's Eve party and were getting ready for bed when she broke the news to Mickey. Judy woke up hearing them talk, and she lay in the dark in the next room, listening. She heard Trudy's soft drawl and her father's replies, but she went back to sleep, not really understanding what they were talking about.

"Mickey, honey, I guess I'd better tell you, it looks like I'm gonna have a baby. I know the timing's bad, but that old strike can't go on forever," Trudy said, looking at him to see his reaction.

His eyes went wide, and a smile spread slowly across his features. He looked at her like it was a tremendous joke. Unnerved, she asked if he minded that she was pregnant.

Mickey snorted with laughter. "Well, Trudy darling, I suppose it would be preposterous if I didn't mind. What I'd like to know is who's the stud?"

Trudy's voice became petulant. "How can you say something so mean to me? Of course it's our baby!"

With studied control, Mickey replied, "Well, that's interesting, considering the fact that I'm sterile. If it's that Chinese photographer out at the airport that you've been sleeping around with, you'll have a hard time claiming me as the father."

Trudy felt the blood rush to her head. She had not foreseen this course of events.

"What do you mean you're sterile?" she asked, angrily, trying to put the battle over in the other camp. "How can you be so sure about it?"

"That's quite simple, my dear. I had a vasectomy right after Judy was born." He was amused at her obvious discomfort and his eyes danced with mischief, as he speculated over her next move.

"Why didn't you tell me you couldn't have children? That isn't fair."

"Well, honey, you never asked me, and quite frankly, I never dreamed you were the slightest bit interested." Mickey said. He was watching her with a smile, irritatingly calm. He knew how good she was at lying, and it amused him to have caught her out on this one. He always voted Republican, but he was in some ways a true communist at heart. He had no sense of property, and it didn't really bother him that Trudy had slept with another man. He knew that he himself was only interested in her for her physical attributes and, with their age difference, sooner or later he was bound to get some competition.

Trudy felt a mounting sense of alarm. Her parents would never forgive her if they knew she had cheated on Mickey. She thought about her dad and pictured his stern face if he found out. He had been furious when she left Ray. Her father liked Ray and had a hard enough time getting over the fact that she had left him for a slick fellow like Mickey. Trudy knew that if he found out she had cheated on Mickey, he'd take it out on her mother, blaming her for bad blood. Somehow she had to make this look like Mickey's baby.

Trudy changed strategy. She started to sniffle and made her voice contrite. "This never would have happened if you weren't so busy all the time. I've hardly seen you lately with all your running around at the airport. You've got to help me, Mickey. Please don't tell anyone about this. I'd just die of shame. I don't care what you do about me afterwards, but my daddy will disown me if he finds out this isn't your baby."

Mickey felt sorry for her. Hell, the kid wasn't all that bright, and he knew she couldn't exactly be pleased about the prospect of losing that gorgeous figure. He told her not to worry. "We can talk it over in the morning," he said, and he rolled over on his side and fell asleep promptly.

Trudy lay awake, trying to decide what she wanted in life. She had enough pride to resent knowing that Mickey didn't seem to care what she was doing, and there was no denying that she was crazy about Bill.

She was sure Bill would be willing to get a divorce, if she said she couldn't continue seeing him. But darn-it-all, with him just getting a captain's pay and having to pay alimony, it sure wouldn't leave much for a new family. She would rather stay with Mickey. At least his mother had money. Maybe Mickey would forgive her, and they could act like nothing was wrong.

She got up late and found Mickey out in the kitchen. He had rustled up a batch of pancakes for the kids, but, as usual, he was skipping breakfast and sipping a Screwdriver. It looked like there was more vodka in it than orange juice.

Tony and Judy went out to play. Those kids always seemed to be up to something, she thought petulantly, but for once Trudy appreciated the fact that they were never underfoot.

"So are you going to tell me who's the lucky man, or keep me guessing?" Mickey said.

"I don't want to talk about it," she replied sullenly. His off-hand manner made her cross. It was such a contrast to the passionate way that Bill regarded her. All of a sudden everything seemed so dreary: The crummy surroundings, the days of waiting for business to pick up at the gift shop, and Mickey living in his own world, seemingly immune to her attributes. It wasn't fun anymore, like it had been when they lived at Waikiki and went out every night of the week.

She went back into their room and threw on some clothes. When she came back into the kitchen, she grabbed the car keys and hurried out the door, jumped into the Packard and backed too fast out the driveway. The car bumped loudly when it hit the rut at the end of the drive, and she tore off down the road, leaving a cloud of dust.

Mickey hoped this wouldn't take all day. He needed the car to go out to the airport. In the quiet of the kitchen, nursing his Screwdriver, he took stock. He didn't mind losing Trudy. There always seemed to be plenty of women interested in making his life comfortable, and he had found out how much is missing from one as young as Trudy. Nothing could beat sleeping with someone whose conversation was as interesting as her body. The way things were going, he had enough to think about without Trudy complicating things. He realized how really easy she had been up 'til now.

When Trudy returned, hours later, the subject was avoided. Whoever she had hashed things out with took the pressure off her steamed up state, and Mickey could assume that she wanted to call a truce. Nothing seemed to matter all that much, and a showdown could wait.

Trudy gave birth to a baby girl whom Mickey wanted to name Shalimar Kawahineikeliolakakealani, but Trudy named her Nancy and bided time until her captain could get a divorce and a transfer and take her back stateside.

By the time the strike was over, and things started picking up at the airport, he was so heavily in debt that he had to sell the franchise. Worse, he had embezzled postal funds, and that was a federal offence. He decided to wait and tell the children that he and Trudy were splitting up. He was relieved that, in face of present realities, she opted for life on a captain's pay and was leaving him for Bill.

Judy was thrilled that she had a little half-sister, not realizing that the baby wasn't related. However, she didn't have many weeks to get attached to her, because soon after her birth, Mickey told Tony and Judy that they would be flying out to California.

"Kids, things aren't working out here. That strike has ruined my business, and I've got to clean up the mess. I have to stay here in the islands and wind up all the loose ends, but, Judy, I've arranged for you to go to Donda's. And, you, Tony old buddy, are going to Las Vegas to stay with Jane until I get there."

Seeing Judy's stricken face, he quickly added, "Don't worry honey. It's only temporary. As soon as I get to Las Vegas, I'll send for you and we will be together again. And you know how happy it will make Donda to have you there for a while. I know you wouldn't want to go to Jane's, but she does want Tony there."

As usual, Jane was the one who was bailing him out, paying for their return tickets, and, for now, she was calling the shots.

The Final Curtain

Pete was in town taking care of some business and buying supplies. He stopped at Jane's, and they were sitting in the office. The lounge where some of his things were tastefully displayed was seldom used. Jane seemed more at home where she had her office.

"You look mighty pleased with yourself," Pete said, eyeing Jane with amusement, and wondering what she might have done to someone else in order to be in such a good mood.

"Well, I suppose some fools would say it's bad luck, but Mickey and Trudy are splitting up. Looks like he'll be coming back here where he belongs, and I can straighten him out and see that those children get a proper home."

"That sounds like something right up your alley, honey, but how much is it going to cost you this time? Of course, it's your money." He watched her with amusement, knowing just what it took to ruffle her feathers.

"That's none of your damned business!" she said fiercely. "The only trouble with Mickey is that he lets the wrong kind of woman run his life. He'll be fine once he gets back here where I can keep an eye on him. There is far too much temptation over yonder in those islands. It'll do him good to come back to the real world."

Pete held his tongue, not wanting to argue with her when she was obviously so pleased about the latest developments. Even though he liked Mickey, he would be willing to bet his last silver dollar that it wouldn't take long after he came home before there would be trouble a-plenty.

"He's sending Tony out right away, and Judy will be going to her old grandmother in North Hollywood. I guess I shouldn't say anything bad about Donda, though. Last time I was in California and got so gall darned mad at Dunaway, I called her, and, right away, she invited me to stay with her. Anyway, they'll manage to spoil Judy rotten before she comes up here, but I don't give a hoot about that. Tony's the one I'm banking on."

The rest of that week Jane was busy getting ready for Tony's appearance and making plans for the future. She felt proud of what she had achieved since Mickey was last in Nevada. Things were booming along Fremont Street and, just like she had predicted, development was starting to take off on the Strip.

When she first blew into town, the only hotels on that stretch outside of town were the El Rancho and the Last Frontier, and people thought she was nuts when she bought that big hunk of land way down the road for two cents an acre. She smiled as she thought about how she had proved them wrong when the Flamingo was built, and she sold her stake for a nice profit. Could have gotten more for it, too, if Mickey hadn't needed some cash.

By now, she had all her assets pretty well tied up in the Anthony Hotel. She had planned things this way, figuring that she had secured Mickey a future in the islands when she bought him that franchise to the gift shop. The hotel, with its divorcees, was just the right size for her to manage and be comfortable the rest of her days. It was a nice, reliable income, not the big time like with gambling casinos, but a sure thing that provided her enough to pay her bills and Mickey's, too, with enough money left over for safe investments. The cottages she had put up in the back of her property had already paid for themselves.

No one ever suspected that she had earned a few extra dollars by bending the rules for the occasional divorcee who was in a big hurry to get it over with. Now that business was booming, it was easier than ever to fiddle the ledger and make it look like they stayed at the hotel six weeks, when it really was four. It didn't bother her conscience the first time it happened – After all, it was the customer who suggested it and was willing to pay for a full six weeks, plus an extra bonus for the special favor Jane would render if she told a little white lie. In her opinion it didn't make the least bit of difference whether a couple waited six weeks or six days to get a divorce. In fact, anything she could do to help someone out of an undesirable marriage made her feel real good.

She reminisced about the days when she had picked up a nice little bundle from those flophouses she had leased with Bob Ray as front man. Now, she thought with pride, she didn't need a man in her business affairs. She carried enough clout all on her own. The irons she had in the fire nowadays were just right for her. "Nice and manageable for a gal who's no longer a spring chicken," she thought, while glancing at herself in the mirror over the mantel and reassuring herself that she didn't look her age.

Her eyes narrowed as she thought about how shrewd she had been over the years. When she picked up the phone and said with a sugar-sweet Southern accent, "This is little Janie Jones," there were any number of VIP's in the state who sat up and listened with interest to what she had to say. And, she thought with satisfaction, she hadn't gotten her influence by lying on her back like so many other women. She was respected for predicting where the action would be and managing her affairs well, no small accomplishment for a gal who hadn't had much schooling, she mused with pride.

One side of Jane was unconditionally happy that Mickey was coming home. Lord knows she wanted him to be near her. However, the pragmatic Jane was beginning to have her doubts. She had liked making plans and following them up, seeing them give fruit. Always one to look forward, she didn't approve of people who talked about the 'if onlys,' but sometimes she slipped and found herself doing so: If only she had been in the islands with him and seen that things hadn't gone wrong. If only she hadn't let him talk her into selling that ranch land out Charleston way.

If only she had bought that house in Hauula in her own name, so that he couldn't have mortgaged it. Property, that was what mattered most, but you had to hang on to it. And, damn it all, that he didn't hang on to that gift shop. It would have been a sure thing if ever there was. If only she had been there to keep an eye on him until it was running smoothly.

She shook her head ruefully and reminded herself that she couldn't have pulled up stakes and moved to the islands. She had a life of her own, too, and she hadn't wanted to leave all she had built up here in Vegas. Besides, she liked the desert, and, most the time, she liked being near Pete.

It was easy to see the light in retrospect. With Mickey, she was always throwing good money after bad. She had been happy when she saw that he was never tempted to gamble at the tables, but he sure had a gambler's mind when it came to planning his own future.

Catching herself at thinking negatively, she thought, I've got to snap out of this mood. I can't let things get me down, now that I'm needed more than ever. From old habit, she started to think about all the reasons why Mickey should be forgiven his failures, such as all those years in prison camp and Vivian's death. At least I'm still in a position to bail him out, she thought with pride.

Tony would be arriving first, and she busied herself with getting a room ready for him. She decided to give him a room in a small cabin out back. A boy his age would soon appreciate having his own entrance, she thought.

At first she had argued with Mickey about the fact that Judy would be staying with Donda to begin with, but he was adamant. He said it was going to be hard for Judy to take being sent away. She didn't have Tony's hang-loose attitude, and being with Donda would take her mind off the changes they would have to make. Just as well, Jane thought. I'm getting too old to have to wrangle with that stubborn young lady.

Jane wasn't demonstrative, but Tony knew she was pleased to see him. She had named the hotel after him, The Anthony Hotel, and she liked to tell him about what sort of future he could plan on. She tried not to be disappointed when she saw that he wasn't all that interested. He was a bright boy, but he was an age when boys live in their own worlds. "Doing real well, too," she told Pete. "He'll go to law school one day and make us all proud."

Mickey had been wise, sending Tony on ahead to Las Vegas and telling Judy she could stay with Donda. He knew from his own experience that Jane would leave Tony pretty much on his own as long as he minded his manners. Staying at Donda's, with all the relatives, would have been a hassle for Tony, but Judy loved the fuss.

Once he got to Las Vegas, Tony took to school like a duck to water, getting in with the popular crowd right from the beginning. Everyone was impressed with his island background, and Jane saw to it that he had a nice wardrobe and a new bike. She was pleased when he said he wanted to use the bike to take care of a newspaper route and earn some money on his own.

Hank Greenspun, the firebrand editor of the Las Vegas Sun, gave Tony a job delivering his newspaper. He shared the route with a kid whose father was a local undertaker. The boys rolled their papers in the back room of the mortuary, and Tony tried to be as nonchalant as his friend was about the stiffs that were lying on slabs in the same room. Once his pal's father came in to chew the gab with them, and he casually struck a match on the coarse stubble of a dead man's day-old beard to light his pipe, watching Tony's reaction with amused eyes all the while.

Afterwards, Tony bicycled down Fremont Street where he could buy a foot-long hotdog for twenty-five cents. Eating that for breakfast, he bicycled past the yellow clapboard houses of railroad workers, tossing rolled up newspapers at their doorsteps. The route was lined with the tall poplar trees that marked the older parts of Las Vegas, and Tony liked the sound of his wheels cutting through the thick layer of their leaves when Las Vegas had its brief spell of autumn.

Judy was happy to be at Donda's, but she missed her father and Tony, and she missed the islands. At least she knew they would be together again, once Mickey came stateside. Donda found her to be pale and thin, and she had outgrown all her clothes. The family all agreed that she looked neglected and pitched in to set things right.

One good thing about neglect is that a child is unspoiled by attention and grateful for everything good that comes her way. Donda loved surprising her with foods she liked, and her aunts gave her new clothes and dancing lessons. They encouraged her to get a haircut like other girls her age and to wear the lipstick that was popular with girls just entering their teens – 'tangee,' a subtle shade that went on like chapstick.

She was defensive of her father, and they quickly learned not to make any critical remarks. Even so, Judy sensed they all disapproved, all except Donda. With Donda she knew she could share her love for her father. Donda could also see that the unsettled life she led with her father had made her way beyond her years in understanding.

An additional bond between Donda and Judy was that they had both lost their mothers at an early age. Judy trusted Donda's words of wisdom, because she knew they were based on the same trials.

A half-year passed, and Mickey still hadn't left the islands. Jane wondered, was it because he was, as he said, winding up business? Or was he sitting in prison, for having dipped his hand into postal money? She didn't want to know, and she figured that if he was in jail, it would seem like a luxury hotel, compared to Cabanatuan.

When he finally arrived in Las Vegas, he didn't send for Judy right away. He figured it was best if she finished the school year where she was, at North Hollywood Junior High, and came up to Las Vegas to start high school.

Jane didn't object at all. She soon realized she needed time to sort out a sensible arrangement with Mickey. She had been feeling poorly lately, and she couldn't take any hassle. Seemed like she had been working hard all her life. Mickey bounced in as if nothing had gone wrong. Jane couldn't help but think to herself that he hadn't learned a blessed thing from his run of bad luck.

She had reckoned that her income was plenty adequate for their needs now that Mickey was single. Of course, they would have to put something aside if Tony was to go to a good college, but, with careful management, she saw it could be done.

Mickey exasperated her by showing little interest in her budget and the profit sheets from the hotel. He talked of schemes he had been cooking up in his head while waiting to come back to Vegas. They sounded good enough, but Jane felt tired just thinking about change. She got hot under the collar when she sensed that he seemed to belittle her business interests by talking about big money to be earned elsewhere. After all, she had been a shelter in the storm during all these years since the war. She had a feeling that Mickey took her for granted, or at least he acted like he didn't need her. The things she had achieved didn't impress him the way they should have, and she felt the first nagging hint of growing old.

She worried about Mickey, but didn't know what she wanted for him. He looked drawn and tired when he arrived, but after a few days of rest, she could see that he was too full of nervous energy to just settle down and help her run the hotel. She tried to warn him to take it slow and easy. "Mickey, I wish you could learn something from my example. It all boils down to not spending more than you earn and staying clear of any riff-raff that will spoil things for you. You never have learned to stick to the right people if you want things to go your way. Besides, you know that prison camp ruined your health. Why don't you try to take better care of yourself? You probably shouldn't be drinking at all."

He didn't let himself argue with her. For now he seemed intent on not getting her goat, but he hated being dependent on her again. He needed to find the means to make some money, and it had to be big money. It was time to settle down, but he wanted to settle down in style, and he didn't want to have to kowtow to the kind of jerk who usually had the money to make more money. No matter where you go you encounter arseholes, he thought, and the worst sort were successful arseholes.

The way things were going in Las Vegas, he knew there would be opportunity galore in the fields he knew best – real estate, advertising and show business. Jane agreed about the opportunities, but she was too cautious, he thought.

"I know there is big money to make in this town, Mickey, but we have to build up free capital to make investments like you're talking about. Take it from an old timer: Real freedom is not owing anyone anything. You're always in charge if you can put down cash on the spot and don't have to borrow from anyone. I know some people have gotten rich by going out on a limb, but I've seen more cases that have gone haywire. People just don't talk about failure as much."

Jane was pleased about one thing: she didn't have to worry about him being attracted to gambling. Though he was the first to think he had led a charmed life, he had never been tempted to try his luck at the game tables. All his life he had known the kind of man who hoped to get rich that way. When they did score a win, they were sure to gamble it away trying to repeat their success, and when they lost, they piled up a debt trying to re-coup their losses. He could hang out around the casinos, relishing the pool of characters there, but he was never tempted to make a bet. Besides, gambling reminded him of how low people stooped in prison camp – gambling to get another man's portion of rice.

Mickey established a routine. In the early part of the day, he showered, shaved and dressed with great care, ("Shit, shower, and shave," he said to Tony, "is the key to a good start for the day.") Like a professional performer, he never neglected his appearance. All spiffed up, he left the house to hang around The Strip hotels. He told Jane that it was the best way to pick up connections and size up the possibilities, but what drew him like a magnate were the old time entertainers he encountered. Las Vegas was one of the best places for employment for all the acts he remembered from the pre-war days in Hollywood. It was easy to lose track of time over a drink in the perpetual twilight of a cocktail lounge with one of his many show biz acquaintances. Some of them had hit the big time, and others were still struggling, but they all loved talking about the good old days.

Another good thing about Vegas was that you could get a drink any hour of the night or day. He drank in a civilized manner, daiquiris or vodka martinis or stingers, holding his glass with a well-manicured hand, wearing a pearl-buttoned Western-style shirt or gold cufflinks nicely in place on a starched, white French cuff. In the dim lighting of a bar, his visions of the future took on a special glow, and quite ordinary people in his circle were lifted magically to a higher plane. A steady stream of evergreens, crooned by a talented barroom piano player never failed to lift Mickey onto that cloud where make-believe castles beckoned and mundane reality was transformed to sparkling visions. Artful details such as the inviting cleavage of the cocktail waitress' costume, the polished brass trim on the mahogany bar-rail, and the dazzling smile of the lounge musician, blended into a mosaic like that in a kaleidoscope, constantly shifting and creating an air of glamour.

An American bar was the ultimate in the entertainment world – a place where one became both spectator and player in an ongoing performance, the perfect vehicle for inducing people to forget or to remember. Given Mickey's attributes, he was one of those fortunate people who always forgot the unpleasant things and remembered the good.

No one liked hearing a hard-luck tale, and it suited him fine to hang around with people who preferred to be amusing and to live in the present. Effortlessly, he could spin innocuous lies tailor-made to his listener. The failures of the past few years were forgotten and he half-believed the lines he fed people about why he was back in Las Vegas. It was only on rare moments that thoughts of his Hollywood days nagged Mickey and made him want to show them that he wasn't burnt out.

Rex Bell and Clara Bow still had the swanky ranch they bought back in the thirties. They had seen Mickey when he came home from the war, that year that he lived out on the desert on a ranch with his new wife. They remembered that when Mickey left to return to the islands, he had said it was for good. Good old Rex was genuinely sorry things hadn't worked out for Mickey, but Mickey wasn't cut out for the role of being someone who needed sympathy. When he ran into Rex, he dished up a story about some big angle he was working on that should put him on easy street. He repeated the same story several times, polished it, and let it blend in with things he accepted as being true.

He never had any difficulty finding female companions. He struck up a friendship with one of the divorcees at the hotel and found that it was helpful to air his views to her when he doubted which direction to take. She was a good listener and sympathized when he told her his problems. "Jane keeps harping on me to settle down and nurture her business. There's enough income here to pay our living expenses and then some, but I know I'll be bored out of my mind."

"I know what you mean, Mickey. You've been around too much to settle down in this place.

Everyone wants to come here, but a person would have to be nuts to want to stay here. I can hardly wait 'til my divorce comes through and I can get back to the real world."

Jane had a classy new Packard, and she didn't mind that Mickey used it more than she did. He was always attune to sensual pleasures, and just sliding behind the wheel in the luxurious car put his irrepressible good spirits in high gear. For some reason all the horyos had this love for strong engines and fancy cars. Speed and power on the road was the best panacea for those years of being humbled and beaten, unable to move at all, much less to move so rapidly.

When Mickey drove off, he was invariably sure that something good was lying ahead. Las Vegas wasn't his first choice, but it was clearly the place to make a fast buck. Every time he went out, he ran into people he knew, and people were a tonic, even when he was sober. There were other good sides to a stay in Vegas – Out here in the desert there was nothing to remind him of life in the islands. Also, it felt great to have some money in his pocket. Out of old habit, he took for granted the money his mother was shelling out right now, thinking it was only a temporary arrangement.

In Jane's book, money had a life of its own and should be respected and nurtured. For Mickey, it was simply the stuff that oiled the wheels of a worldwide amusement park. He gave it away gladly when he had some of his own, and never was weighed down with a feeling of indebtedness if he got it from someone else.

Mickey decided to head out to the Last Frontier where his old friend, Nat King Cole, was performing. He would get the address of the place where Nat was staying and go see him before his show. It was incredible, thought Mickey, that Nat King Cole was good enough to get top billing at the Last Frontier, but he wasn't allowed to take a swim in the pool or even get a bed there. He had to stay at a boarding house over on Westside. One thing Mickey did hate about being back in the States was the damned prejudice.

He walked around the pool, quickly sizing up whether there was anyone there he knew. Stepping into the air-conditioned cocktail lounge, he saw that it was empty. It took a second for Mickey to adjust his eyes to the cool darkness when he came in from the outside. The bartender was behind the bar, slowly and methodically drying glasses. Time stands still in an empty cocktail lounge, and the quiet, familiar atmosphere was soothing to Mickey's soul. He noticed with amusement that he was mentally comparing it to the dimly lit interior of a cathedral he visited in Manila before the war.

The bartender knew Mickey and greeted him by name when he strolled over and straddled a barstool. "Hi Mickey! You got a good story for me today?"

Mickey smiled and put on an Irish brogue to tell him the one about Pat and Clancy and a bottle of whiskey Clancy promised to pour over Pat's grave when he was six feet under. The bartender laughed heartily when Mickey got to the punch line, and Clancy asked, "Do ye mind if I'll be a-filtering it through me kidneys first?"

It was early in the day, but he didn't like sitting there without ordering anything. He asked for a daiquiri and nursed it slowly, waiting for the lunch crowd to start showing up.

The bartender liked Mickey and gave him a steady rundown of gossip and tips on what was going down these days. When the noon customers started filing in, Mickey lingered at the bar, but kept an eye on the adjacent dining room as it filled up.

"See that guy who just came in over there?" the bartender said. "That's Wilbur Clark from the Desert Inn. Word has it he's front man for the Mob, but I don't know if that's true."

By now, Mickey had finished off a couple of drinks, and he was feeling pretty good. He had a scheme, and it occurred to him that he might be able to sell it to Clark: People were streaming to Las Vegas to gamble, but more and more casinos were opening up. Most of them had floorshows to beat the competition, but so far no one had come up with the idea of trying to get a hold of the customer before he left home. Mickey had the idea of selling champagne flights. They would entail a pre-paid booking for a trip to Las Vegas from L.A., plying the customer with drinks all the way, giving him twenty bucks worth of chips and turning him loose at the hotel that offered the booking. The price of the drinks and those twenty dollars would be peanuts compared to what a guy would spend once he got to the hotel, after being put in the right frame of mind.

He decided to approach Clark the very next day. Meanwhile, he paid for his drinks and went to the desk clerk to find out where Nat was staying. The rest of the afternoon he spent shooting the breeze with his old friend over on Westside and took in his floorshow that evening. Some great music was written during the war years, and he never tired of listening to fresh tunes and the evergreens he and Vivian had liked.

Mickey drove out to the Desert Inn the next day, hoping to see Clark without an appointment. The place was amazing. Barren desert had been transformed overnight. The grounds were covered with Bermuda grass, and full-grown palms had been planted, with taut wires to anchor them in place until they took root. It had risen like a mirage, one more playground in this make-belief world.

He spotted Clark, standing alongside the swimming pool with a group of men, and walked his way. Mickey rolled out the charm, and Clark, a very amiable guy, even if he was supposedly connected with the Mob, seemed to have plenty of time for him.

Wilbur Clark was a big, jovial-looking man. He had an open smile as he stopped up to listen to what Mickey had to say. He made Mickey feel confident, making it easy to make his move from the islands sound more glamorous than it really was. "I had my own public relations firm over there, and I think I might be able to interest you in some good ideas I have for promoting your new hotel here in Vegas," Mickey said.

The two of them talked about how much had happened in just ten years time. Now it took big money to make money, Mickey said, flattering Clark, by saying it was ingenious to have linked so many facilities to the hotel. It was the first place on the strip to have its own 18-hole golf course, there were tennis courts and there was a baby-sitting service.

"You know, my mother is an old-timer here in Vegas," he said. "Funny thing – she had a place called The Desert Inn Beds. Wasn't much more than a flophouse, but she hauled in money hand over fist. Of course, it takes more than that to succeed nowadays," Mickey said, and then he told Clark about his own idea for flights from in L.A.

Clark liked the looks of this guy. "I'll tell you what to do. I've already hired Hank Greenspun as publicist, but you go by his office and tell him I sent you. Maybe you and he could check into the feasibility of those champagne flights." He shook hands with Mickey and left with his group.

Mickey was elated. This could be just what he needed to get off the ground. He already knew Hank and had taken an immediate liking to the man. He decided to drive over to his newspaper right away. He hadn't eaten lunch, but he popped a 'Tums' in his mouth as he walked to the car. If there was one thing prison camp had done for him, it had taught him to get along on very little food.

It was early afternoon, and Mickey found Hank in his office. He told him about meeting Clark, and Hank grinned, saying, "I might as well hire you, Mickey, seeing as how you're already stepping in on my territory. Let's get together tomorrow and hammer out the details."

When he told Jane about his day, she didn't know whether to be pleased that Mickey was going to be associated with Greenspun. Rumor had it that he was busted for running guns to the Palestinians, and people were still talking about the way he stood up and gave Joe McCarthy hell when something McCarthy said during a speech at the War Memorial Building ticked Greenspun off. He was a colorful publicist who was well known about town, but he was a newcomer. However, Jane's objections to Greenspun only strengthened Mickey's first good impressions of the man. What Mickey recognized in Greenspun was the sort of intelligence that wasn't hampered by provincial attitudes. His conversation was definitely a notch above what usually took place in Las Vegas, and knowing him would put Mickey in touch with an even broader circle of acquaintances.

One day, Mickey was walking out of the Golden Nugget and ran into an old acquaintance from the islands. Emma Jo Johnson was in Las Vegas to get a quick divorce from her husband, Russ, and Mickey invited her to have a drink.

They slid into a booth in the bar at the Sal Segav Hotel on Fremont Street, and Emma Jo launched into a long-winded account of why she decided to leave Russ.

Mickey liked Russ, and, knowing Emma Jo, he thought to himself that Russ would be better off without her. As far as he knew, Russ, who had been in the navy, found her at the Senate Club, the cathouse in Honolulu, where his old pal Alec Democus used to hang out. It took Mickey back a few years, remembering Alec and James Jones from the days before the war. He smiled and shook his head, thinking about the great book Jones had written, using Democus as the inspiration for Warden, the master sergeant in the novel. Jesus, James must be rolling in dough, now that Hollywood was turning "From Here to Eternity" into a film.

Seeing Emma Jo brought those hectic years back to him. It was good to sit and have a few drinks with someone from the islands, even Emma Jo, and as the afternoon wore on, he began to think she wasn't all that bad after all. One thing about Mickey – he was tolerant of nearly everyone, and given a few drinks, his normal tendency to think positive became even more pronounced.

He learned that Emma didn't think much of the place she was staying. Always quick to help out, he said, "Hey, why don't you pack up your gear and move in at my mother's hotel? One of her divorcees moved out yesterday, and the room is still vacant."

Emma Jo jumped at the suggestion. She was feeling a bit lonely and liked the thought of staying at a place where she would see someone she knew. When Mickey gave her the address he had the awful thought that she might take a shine to him. He looked at the clock over the bar and said, "Jesus, I'd better get a move on. I have an appointment on the other side of town."

As he left the bar, Emma Jo still lingered over her drink, and he hoped maybe she would forget all about the address. However, the next morning he saw her in his mother's office and they were just closing the deal for her to rent a room and have Jane as a witness. She was sober and looked tidy in a modest dress.

Mickey didn't want to give her any encouragement. He waited until she had left before he walked into the office. Jane seemed pleased that he had brought in a customer, thinking it showed he was interested in her business. "She seems like a nice enough gal, Mickey. Did you know her well in the islands?"

Mickey knew his mother's attitude about loose women, and he decided it was best not to say too much about his acquaintance with Emma Jo. Jane could accept an honest whore, but she wouldn't want her bringing any traffic into the hotel. "Yeah, I knew her and her husband. He's a helluva nice guy, but I guess they just didn't see eye-to-eye. I'm off to the races. Is it alright if I take the car?"

"You go right ahead, sugah. I've got too much work to do to go anywhere."

Mickey was back in time for dinner. He parked the car and was relieved to discover that there was no sign of Emma Jo when he went through the lounge to his mother's quarters.

Tony was in the kitchen, and Jane was fussing at Mickey almost before he was in the door. "'Bout time you came home. I made this nice dinner for us, and I was afraid it was going to get spoiled. Where've you been all day?"

He told her that he had been talking with Hank Greenspun. Jane sniffed at the mention of his name. Hank's newspaper had been campaigning against her friend, Pat McCarran, and was again stirring up a lot of trouble in his editorials opposing Senator McCarthy. Jane didn't like a troublemaker when it was aimed at the Republicans, but she knew better than to launch into a discussion about all that with Mickey. He read the 'Sun' every day, and loved the controversy.

Jane thought to herself that she just didn't seem to have the energy these days for a good old-fashioned argument. She'd made up her mind about most things a long time ago, and it got too darned exhausting to try to talk sense to anyone else. It seemed like every time she got together with her brothers and sisters they always got into a big row over politics or something. We're just too damned independent, she mused.

Mickey made himself a vodka martini and turned his attention to Tony. The two of them had a relationship like a couple of good buddies, and Tony enthusiastically related the events of his day.

Jane was pleased watching them together. She tried not to fret about the tiny amount Mickey ate for dinner; she had come to accept that as part of the legacy of the war. Of course, living with Trudy who was too simple-minded to care about what he ate wasn't much help. I'll bet I can get his appetite to pick up, she thought.

It was hard for Jane to judge how much of Mickey's day was devoted to business and how much to pleasure. The line he was pursuing combined the two at all times. She could accept that, but it gave her an uneasy feeling that things were likely to get out of hand again.

She began to suffer more frequently from headaches, and the massages she got from a physiotherapist weren't helping much. She decided to go to the doctor to find out whether he could recommend anything.

Doc Demman had known Jane for years, and he reminded her that she always did tend to get headaches when she had too much to do. "Maybe you need to head for the high country again and get some rest," he said soothingly. "You look fit as a fiddle, but let me just check out your heart and blood pressure and see whether there is anything wrong." He had to admit to himself that she was looking a bit pasty, but she was, after all, hitting seventy.

When Jane got home, she heard hoarse laughter coming from the room she had rent out to Mickey's friend, Emma Jo. I sure hope she doesn't think she can get away with having company in there, she thought, crossly.

Jane knocked sharply on the door, and her knock was followed by silence. A moment later, she could hear someone rustling around, and Emma Jo opened the door a crack, and said, "Hello, Mrs. Jones. What can I do for you?" Whiskey was on her breath, and the room was thick with smoke.

"I just wanted to be sure you understood that if I'm going to witness for you, you have to keep your path swept clean the entire six weeks you stay with me. Do you have company in there?" she asked, trying to peer beyond Emma Jo.

"No, ma'am," she answered coolly. "I was just resting and you probably heard the radio."

Not satisfied, Jane left, but stayed nearby, ready to catch anyone that might come out of the room. A short time afterwards, she heard the door open and shut, and she saw a man heading for the front door. No one else was home, and she knew he had to have come from Emma Jo's room. She decided not to say anything this time. Maybe the woman would take her warning to heart and not invite that man to her room again.

A few days later, when Jane had been out to Pete's ranch, she came home just in time to see the two of them entering Emma Jo's room. She had taken a dislike to the woman by now and was in no mood to put up with any crap. She didn't have the impression that it would make any difference to Mickey if she chucked the woman out. In an icy tone, she informed her lodger that she would have to pay up her rent and find other accommodations.

"This isn't the sort of place where we can have that kind of coming and going," Jane said in a snooty way. "Besides, I refuse to witness for you if I have to tell a lie about you not seeing anyone while you're waiting divorce. I've been in this business too many years to think that you are going to change, so just give me your key. You can pack up and settle your bill in my office."

"You old biddy, I'm not paying you a penny," Emma Jo replied. Her speech was slurred, and she swayed slightly. Her brawny boyfriend looked menacingly at Jane.

Undaunted, Jane informed her that if need be she could call the sheriff to put her out, and until she paid up what she owed, all forthcoming post would be withheld. She had noticed that Emma Jo had received an official looking letter from Honolulu that morning. She grabbed the key they had just used to enter the room, turned sharply on her heel, leaving them looking rather befuddled.

Later, she saw them moving out Emma Jo's things. He was carrying her suitcase, his free arm around her shoulder as she drunkenly complained to him about her plight. Good riddance, thought Jane. That woman would have been nothing but trouble.

Mickey never took anything seriously, and he merely laughed that his mother was such a dragon. "Don't get your hopes up about the money she owes you, Jane. I think that guy is the bartender at the Nugget Saloon. From what I hear, she's there most the time."

Jane was hopping mad at getting gypped out of nearly a week's rent. Everything seemed to be going against her lately. A few days later, she asked Tony to go by the bar where Emma Jo was supposed to hang out and tell her that there were several letters for her, and if she wanted them she'd have to settle her bill.

"Sure, Jane. I'm on my way out anyway. Don't worry, I'll be home on time for dinner," he said, anticipating her objections. He jumped on his bike and took a short cut down the back alley to Fremont Street.

He found Emma Jo and her friend, Leo the bartender, perched on barstools, engrossed in a drunken conversation with a couple of other regulars. Leo was off duty, and it looked like they were both tanked up. Emma Jo cursed when Tony delivered his message, and he said, "Hey, don't take it out on me. See ya 'round." He hightailed it out of there, and bicycled off to football practice, not giving the incident another thought.

The two of them sat there having a few more drinks. Like most bartenders, Leo usually avoided drinking, but since he met Emma Jo, he was making up for lost time. They eventually worked themselves up into a steam and decided to go over to the Anthony Hotel and get the letters from the old battle-axe.

"I'll be damned if she can withhold United States mail," Emma Jo said drunkenly. "Isn't that right, Leo? She's breaking the law, that sanctimonious bitch."

Leo was none too bright, and he was crazy about Emma Jo. He was a big guy, and he knew how easy it was to pull someone's bluff when they thought they could be tough. They could go over to that old crow and give her a scare, make her back down and give Emma Jo her letter. He downed his beer and chaser and stood up ready to go.

Jane's lodgers usually came to her office to pay their bills or fetch their mail. It was at the back of the building, and there was a long counter separating the office from Jane's kitchen. Jane was starting to make dinner, and the room smelled of the onions she had just chopped with a big butcher knife. She put it aside and had just washed her hands, when Emma Jo and Leo came barging in, all liquored up and madder than hops. Jane looked at them with contempt and stood ground when they demanded Emma Jo's mail.

"Don't you come here and use that tone of voice on me," Jane said, imperiously. "If you want to talk to me, you pay the money you owe, and I'll forward all your mail."

In a fury, Emma Jo came to the other side of the counter and pulled a wall can-opener off its fixture. While shouting obscenities she pushed Jane against the wall and hit her in the head with the heavy can-opener. Caught off-guard, Jane could do nothing but put up her hands and try to ward off the blows. Amid the unfamiliar sensation of fear, Jane had the horrible awareness that she was involved in a degrading scuffle with a floozy, an embarrassment that she would have done anything to avoid. The shock that came with the unexpected attack immediately induced a splitting headache, one more sudden and intense than she ever remembered having.

Mickey and one of the lodgers heard the ruckus and came running from the other end of the building, but Leo picked up the butcher knife Jane had been using and held Mickey at bay. Unable to get past the burly bartender, Mickey shouted at Emma Jo to stop, but Emma Jo had a firm grip on Jane's hair and didn't let go until his mother stumbled and fell backwards, striking her head against the counter.

When Mickey's mother collapsed on the floor, Emma froze for a moment and then shook her head a few times, like she was trying to throw off her drunken stupor now that her rage was spent. She dropped the bloody can opener, and stumbled outside. Leo went after her, throwing down the knife as he left. Mickey grabbed the phone to call an ambulance. Jane was unconscious, and it struck him that it was the first time he ever could recall her looking helpless.

The police had no trouble picking up Emma Jo and her boyfriend as soon as the crime was reported. Word spread like wildfire, and all of Jane's influential friends were determined that the woman who had attacked her would pay dearly for her crime.

For several days, Jane remained in a coma. She regained consciousness once, briefly, and said smiling to Tony as he entered her room, "Well, here comes the smart-aleck." She died on the seventh day, and Emma Jo was charged with second-degree murder. The sordid story hit the news as 'The Can-Opener Murder'.

Mickey, better than most, had learned to accept death, but he felt the loss far more than showed on the surface. He couldn't honestly say he had loved his mother in the same way he had loved his grandmother or like he loved Donda. Jane was too demanding for him to have that sort of uncomplicated love and too abrasive to have been pleasant company. However, with all her faults, there was no question that she had been unstinting in her devotion to him. He couldn't remember a time when she hadn't been there for him financially, her loyalty and commitment had been unconditional, and now she was gone. However, having seen so many young people die, he had no trouble accepting the death of a woman who was well up in years. Jane had prided herself in not being sentimental, and it was fitting that her only son could take a rational view of her death.

Jordan Dunaway came up from Hawthorne to conduct her funeral, and he felt proud, seeing how many important Nevadans paid her tribute. Later he was to say that in all his years as undertaker, he had never seen so many flowers at a private funeral. Senator Pat McCarran was there, as was Judge Foley and the owners of the big clubs that were established before the mob moved in.

He and Mickey avoided each other. Jordan blamed Mickey for Jane's death and said as much to Flossie.

"It was just bad luck, Jordan. You can't blame Mickey for that," Flossie replied in her reasonable way. She knew Jane's tendency to provoke confrontations.

"No, but bad luck follows bad company. Jane had her faults, but she spent her whole life trying to do the best she could for Mickey, and he treated her just like he has treated everything else. He's been careless all his life. He should never have brought such a tramp into Jane's hotel in the first place." Jordan jutted out his chin and took a deep breath, his lips in a thin line of disapproval.

Mickey had always been a great favorite of Flossie's, and Dunaway hadn't swayed her opinion of him. However, it was food for thought. No telling what Mickey's life would have been if he had combined all his talents and that brilliant mind with a few of the old-fashioned virtues. I wonder what will become of him now, she thought, sadly.

When Donda got news of Jane's death, she hoped Mickey might decide to leave Judy down in North Hollywood. However, things had changed. Judy missed her dad and Tony and could hardly wait to join them. She didn't like North Hollywood Jr. High School very well, either. It seemed so big, without Tony being there a class ahead.

Donda didn't have a vindictive bone in her body, and she could genuinely feel sorry that Jane's life had ended the way it did. Judy had shown only curiosity when she heard the news. It was so sad to think that she had no tears to shed when Jane left this world. Donda had put behind her all the unpleasant confrontations with Jane and only felt sorrow that Mickey's mother had not been more loved. She knew there was good in everyone. It just seemed to be that it sometimes got buried pretty deep, she thought.

Judy came to Vegas after Emma Jo's trial, after talk of the murder had died down. Emma Jo was sent away for ten to twelve years, convicted by a judge and jury who were outraged by the death of a prominent citizen.

With Jane no longer there to screen lodgers, Mickey was tolerant, by and large, of everyone who showed up looking for a room. It was less of a hassle to let things happen, renting out more or less to anyone who came asking. By the time Judy arrived, there was a motley collection of roomers. A few of them, though, lent an atmosphere of stability to the hotel, because they were there most of the time when Judy and Tony came home from school. Most of the lodgers were still people who were in Las Vegas to get a divorce.

Some of them had found a job to pay for their stay while they were there. Others were just whiling away their time. There was a skinny little, good-natured nurse from Ohio, named Anne. She worked at the hospital. Veronica, whom Mickey nick-named 'The Lacquer Job,' because she wore her long, black hair swept up in an impeccable French roll, spent most of her day with her grooming, never appearing without a perfect makeup job. Then there was Archie, a timid little man who looked like a bookkeeper, and there was a cook, named Charlie.

Charlie was a periodic drunk, and when he was on a bender, he didn't go to work, but stayed in his room, sitting in an easy chair and drinking bourbon. He kept the bottle in its brown paper bag, and stashed it away whenever anyone came into his room, either because he didn't want them to know he was drinking, or because he didn't want to share it. Or maybe it was because he didn't want to know when he was getting close to the bottom of the bottle.

When Charlie was drunk, his dark hair was greasy and made stripes over his almost bald pate. He was unshaven, and he sat in his undershirt, with bare hairy arms and a potbelly. When he was drunk, he was kind, amiable, and peaceful. However, after a week in a stupor, he sobered up, cold-turkey, had a frightening session of D.T.'s, and came out of that stage a miserable, cantankerous old coot. He only worked when he was sober, but his boss must have been understanding, because he was never fired.

There was a blonde bimbo who lived in one of the rooms in a cottage out back. Mickey was very lenient with his lodgers, but he had to clamp down on her. She sat in the Packard one night, out in the driveway, and made out with her boyfriend. Mickey didn't object to that, but he was madder than hops when he discovered that they left on the radio, and the battery was dead.

Without Jane's iron hand, the place was turning into a dump, but Mickey didn't really care. He had plans for something bigger and better, and the hotel was just a means of getting start capital. He figured if he could hold on to it until the right buyer came along he would get a good price.

The location of the hotel was just a block off of "Glitter Gulch", an ideal site for a bowling alley. That would have to be out in the future, however, because there were still old-timers who liked living on the street in houses that had been built by the railway when that institution furnished most of the jobs in town, and they would have to be bought out.

Meanwhile, bills had to be paid. Jane's hospital bill alone was $430. There was plenty of money in the bank right after her death, but it was dwindling fast now that Mickey was in charge. Whenever things should have looked discouraging, Mickey took comfort in the idea that he should be getting some money from the government before long – compensation for having been a POW. Pat McCarran had promised to look into it for him, and Mickey's cousin, Jack, was on the case.

Jack had been in the war, too, but he was a parachutist in Europe. He had seen plenty of action and was with the guys who parachuted over enemy territory and got embroiled in the Battle of the Bulge. For Jack, though, the experience had been a boon. He came home to bask in glory and cash in on the G.I. Bill of Rights. It paid for law school, and now he didn't have a thing to worry about.

Mickey was happy for Jack, but he couldn't believe the government would continue to be so miserly towards the guys who had been caught in the Philippines. He thought about the pipe dreams they had back in prison camp, all the things they thought they would get from the good old U.S.A. when they got home. All they got was back pay, and Mickey hadn't qualified for that.

Ex-prisoners of war from the European arena had been given a hero's welcome, but by the time the POWs got back from the war in the Pacific, no one seemed to have a concept of what they had been through and no one wanted to know. A common question was, "Didn't you get bored eating all that rice?" Christ, Mickey thought, it would have seemed like wild luxury if they had just had a halfway decent ration of rice.

The government seemed to have a policy of ignoring the horyos, like they were hoping no one would ask any questions about this large group of Americans who had been abandoned in a hostile environment. The figures told the story, however: The death rate in Nazi prison camps was 4%, compared to a death rate of 27% in Japanese prison camps, and, at that, it was the survival rate of the Dutch that brought that figure up. The American death rate was 34%, about like it would have been if they had been caught up in the Black Plague.

They say history is written by the survivors, but Mickey had learned that people only want to hear the story told by the victorious survivors, not by the men who scraped through hell crawling on their bellies. He knew better than most what a big role was played by Hollywood in building up a myth of war that was right up MacArthur's ally. Clearly, the story of the horyos could never compete with seeing John Wayne in "The Sands of Iwo Jima". I wonder if the human race will ever learn that on the path to glory there will always be mutilated bodies, foul deeds, and a string of lies to cover up the amount of waste, or whether the myth makers will always be able to stir the embers of patriotism into a bright flame, he mused.

Mickey still felt lucky though, by comparison. He continued to have bouts of malaria and suffered the torture of a yearly relapse of dengue fever, but he claimed he felt like a million dollars when he came out on the other side of one of these attacks. He didn't suffer half the after-effects that some of the poor guys he had been with would have to endure. Injuries they had received gave permanent disabilities. He knew that some would be half crazy with nightmares or have such a compulsion to keep clean that they couldn't function in a normal society. There were guys who had everything but couldn't resist shoplifting some little item – part of a pattern of hoarding. Worse, there were guys so haunted by what they had been through that they couldn't stand to look at themselves in a mirror, guys who smashed themselves up in a one-car accident or shot themselves.

He wondered how many of the others could still get it up when they wanted a woman. God, how they used to worry about that, back then when their balls were swollen beyond recognition from wet beriberi or when they were driven half mad with a rampant infection of scabies or even athlete's foot on their dicks.

Mickey thought about those who suffered the most and knew how much they were in need of medical attention for the ailments that were surfacing now. It was like they were wired with a time bomb. The doctor told him he had cirrhosis of the liver, and he knew most of the others must be just as bad off, if not worse.

He pushed aside Doc Denham's warnings about his liver. At least prison camp had cured him of his arthritis, and, with his usual faith in science, he felt confident that cures would be found for his other ailments, but he didn't think it was fair that a lot of guys wouldn't be able to afford the doctor bills if there were a cure for their diseases.

None of these thoughts weighed Mickey down, however. He woke in the morning with the same eager inquisitiveness that he had all his life. When he went to North Hollywood to pick up Judy and all her gear, he was delighted to see how happy she was to see him when he drove into Donda's driveway.

Judy was excited about starting high school in Las Vegas, and she soon discovered that having a big brother already there was a big advantage. Tony was in with the clique that had priorities on the wide stone stairway that led up to the front entrance of the school. By unwritten law, anyone who didn't belong to that group used the other entrance. Because of Tony, Judy was accepted on the fringe and felt like nothing was more important than staying there. As usual, Mickey didn't consider the schooling they were getting up to par, but he could still remember the interest one had in being popular with one's peers at that age. He listened to Judy's opinions with an indulgent smile, pleased to see that she was striving to succeed in the trial society of high school.

To keep their backs clear from criticism about corrupting society, the people behind gambling pumped a fortune into the city school system. Las Vegas High had the best-equipped athletes, cheerleaders and marching group in the state, perhaps even in the whole of the United States' public school system.

In Vegas the wealthiest citizens were usually from two very different groups: There were rich Mormons, and there were those people who profited from the casinos. The Mormons were often professional people, and they got rich by sticking together, giving each other support in their respective business ventures. At the top of the pile in the casinos, after the owners, were the pit bosses. Their wages were set high enough to avoid their being tempted to shut their eyes to irregularities.

For the youngsters from both backgrounds and those others they let into their charmed circle, there was an enjoyable mixture of sophistication and All-American teenage rites unique to that prosperous school. They could root for a well-equipped football team, or, for the price of a coke, they could see a top-notch floorshow out on the Strip. In the wide-open spaces of the desert, they could indulge in the make-believe magic of American teenage romance, with the indispensable help of the automobile. Judy and Tony temporarily forgot all about the islands in the excitement of putting a toe into the tempting waters of the pre-adult world.

They saw relatively little of their father. He trusted them to know how to behave, and he was too busy to keep tabs on them while trying to realize his plans to build a fortune. They never worried about whether or not he was having any success, because periodically he would show signs of doing very well, and he never stopped painting elaborate visions for them of the sort of home he would build for them when he hit the big time.

He would sometimes take them out to The Thunderbird or The Desert Inn, treat them to a good steak dinner, and sign the check when they were through. Often he knew the entertainer who was billed for the evening show, and they would go backstage for a visit afterwards.

Mickey's worldly mannerisms embarrassed Judy. She wished he wouldn't ask to meet the cook when he considered the dinner to be superb or flirt with the waitress and think she appreciated it. She was too conventional to enjoy having an eccentric father. Still, she loved him fiercely. She and Tony had never seen him angry, and he treated them like worthy members of the strata he thought was their just due. They couldn't help but feel a little sorry for friends whose parents seemed to be too critical or too patronizing. Mickey was unfailingly even-tempered and fun, and they found him to be knowledgeable about anything they asked him. If they gave it any thought, they would only be able to picture him smiling…Even when he was serious, there was a smile in his eyes.

Money slipped through his fingers so easily, but he never worried about what he had already spent. Instead, he kept his eye on schemes for the future and had a never-ending arsenal of ideas nourished by a genuine flair for predicting future trends.

He wanted his kids to be well dressed, and he took Tony to the best shop in town to equip him and to buy some new duds for himself. They both came back to the hotel with Hobson jackets, nice slacks and shirts, and Tony got matching corduroy shirts and trousers and the blue suede shoes which were all the rage at school. Mickey had slipped back into his Vegas mode and had gone over almost entirely to western shirts with pearl buttons and bolo ties.

Judy was told she had a charge account at Ronzone's, the best department store in Las Vegas. Mickey smiled approval when she came home from a shopping spree with a new winter coat and two pretty blouses, with artificial flowers to pin at the neck like the other girls at school were wearing. She was going to a school dance and got her first formal gown, a fire-engine red strapless, with yards and yards of tulle. Mickey laughed and asked what she was going to hold it up with, but he took the matter seriously when at the last minute she discovered she had forgotten to buy nylon stockings to wear with her first high-heeled shoes.

For once, he was annoyed at not having been more attentive. Vivian would have made sure everything was in order. He brightened up when he got an idea: Recruiting the help of The Lacquer Job, he told Judy to paint her legs with make-up and then stood her on a chair so he could draw a seam-line down the back of her legs with an eyebrow pencil.

Just like a chip off the old block, Tony was content living in the present, but Judy took after their mother's family and fretted about unpaid bills. She was only thirteen, but she was starting to be a worrywart. She had noticed the unopened bills and Mickey's careless attitude about cash, and once she lifted a wad of bills out of his pocket when he was sleeping. In the hotel office, there was an old petroleum lamp that had been converted to electricity. She pulled out the rod that connected to a knob used to regulate the wick of the lamp, wrapped the bills around it, and pushed it back in, thinking it could be an emergency fund. Mickey, if he noticed it missing, didn't say any thing.

Jane's money was dwindling rapidly, but as far as the kids could see, nothing was any different. He still liked to take them away for weekends. Always relaxed, he never objected if they wanted to bring as many friends as could be squeezed into the car, and it was usually Tony's crowd that tagged along.

Sometimes they went to Mt. Charleston to play in the snow. On the way, they once visited an old woman who lived up Deer Canyon, far off the beaten path. She was one of the old-timers, from a background similar to Jane's, but she had stuck to the ways of the wilderness. She could boast of shooting a deer each year with a bow and arrow, and no one who was along that day had the skill to string her bow, it was so big and taut.

Mickey studied the beautiful simplicity of her cabin and could recognize in her the same attributes that were present in the Japanese he had liked – a stoic peace of mind. It wasn't too often that he encountered that sort of wisdom in modern America, but it linked together the kind old man in Japan, the old Chinaman he almost ran over, Donda, and this woman who lived all alone. Maybe it can only come with age, he mused.

One early morning they went to Frenchman flats to see a nuclear test. They drove out a dirt road until they came to a wooden barrier and could drive no farther. They got out of the car and waited, anticipating something spectacular and awe-inspiring. In the beautiful setting of a rising sun, the bomb was detonated, and following the blast, the now famous mushroom-shaped cloud took shape before their eyes, deceptively pure white against the pale blue morning sky.

Mickey watched, and the explosion yanked him back to the final days of his captivity. By comparison, the bomb at Hiroshima had been much less powerful, but later he was appalled when he saw photos showing the extent of human suffering it had brought in its wake. He remembered how he and his fellow inmates had cheered, proud to finally be saved by something far greater than what the Japanese had been able to produce. None of them had questioned the wisdom of using such a deadly device. They figured that all the conventional bombs in the world would never have made the Japanese leaders surrender, and they lived in a world void of ethics.

Standing near his car, behind the wooden barrier, he was able to witness the phenomena of the atomic bomb with an air of detachment. It seemed unreal, an invention with an impact that no man could fully imagine. Tony and Judy were very excited about seeing something not many other people had seen.

Finally, by small degrees, things went missing in their daily life. Judy learned that her charge account had been closed, but when she asked her father why, he claimed that she had over-used it. She knew that was unfair. She hadn't bought anything since that first day, but he didn't want to argue about it. She shrugged and chalked it up as a failure on his part. She had started to notice that he didn't always tell the truth and decided that drinking every day did that to people.

It was worse that there was hardly ever fresh food in the house. Mickey was often out, but one afternoon he was in when Judy got home from school.

"Hi Daddy," she said as she headed for the refrigerator. On finding it empty, she looked accusingly at the bottle of whiskey on the table. "If we can buy that stuff, why's there nothing to eat?"

Mickey shrugged and was about to make a conciliatory remark when Tony came in, giving his dad a big smile as he dumped his books on the end of the counter. "What's the matter, Mickey? Is my little seestah giving you a bad time?" He swatted Judy playfully on her behind, and she thundered out of the room, furious with them both.

"What's up kid?" Mickey asked, grateful for the distraction. "How was school today?"

"Ah, heck. It was boring. It's a waste of time. There isn't anything I couldn't learn just by reading a book."

Mickey smiled. Tony was too good for an ordinary school. "I know how you feel, kid, but if some of my deals go through, I can send you to the school of your choice. I don't want you breaking your ass trying to get by in this world, and that means you've got to get a degree. With the right kind of education, you won't have to put up with a lot of crap from people who couldn't hold a candle to you intellectually. Take it from me, without a diploma, you have to work your tail off trying to prove yourself all the time."

"Yeah, I know. At least I had a lot of laughs with Craigo today," he said, changing the subject. "Any chance we can go up to Charleston this Sunday?"

"Maybe. I had a deal cooking with a guy who needed some advertising, but if I don't hear from him, I'll have the weekend free." Mickey poured himself a drink and drummed his fingers on the counter, his mind racing over the possibilities of finding the money he needed.

Tony rummaged around in the can cupboard and found a can of smoked oysters. "Hey, is it alright if I scarf this down?" Mickey glanced at him approvingly and told him to go right ahead. That kid will never starve, he thought. He walked through the house to the front porch, leaving Tony to snack on the oysters. Darkness fell, and he turned on the porch light but stayed outside to enjoy the warm spring air.

Judy's room was a glassed-in verandah at one end of the porch. She was getting ready to go to a Girls' League meeting, and through the French doors, she could see her dad sitting in the open doorway of the hotel, facing the street. He wore Levi's and cowboy boots, and his feet were resting on the wooden planks of the porch. His eyes were fixed on a crack between the floorboards.

Feeling impatient with him, it was maddening for Judy to watch his concentration as he repeatedly let a silver dollar fall through his fingers to become wedged in the crack. The porch light gleamed on the pearl buttons of his western shirt and made the lines in his face more pronounced. His only movement was to pick up the coin and carefully let it drop. Once, it rolled under the arch of his boot, and he had to move his foot to retrieve it, but without breaking rhythm he resumed this quiet exercise. She watched him with mounting irritation. He was smiling to himself, putting himself out of reach of her anger. Everything was going to pot, and he didn't look like he had a care in the world! She decided he had been drinking, and she barely bothered to say goodbye as she flounced by him to join her friends, armed to the teeth with teenage contempt.

At that he looked up, startled by the sudden movement, and felt nostalgic, recognizing a likeness to Vivian. She had not inherited her mother's beauty, but she had the same tilt to her head as she marched off in anger. Then, with a patience learned in prison camp and an oriental stoicism beaten into him at Cabanatuan, he returned his attention to the coin and the crack, blocking out all the longings, the doubts, and the subconscious awareness that this time Jane wasn't there to pull him out of trouble.

Mickey's public relations schemes were sound, but money slipped through his fingers like water. He considered all the money he was using as an investment. That was part of public relations. Trouble was, he knew everyone in town, and he fell into his old habit of mixing business and pleasure until even he didn't know the division. When he had cash he always picked up the tab, but it was often for parties who were just out for a good time. Other times he signed the check, relying on the residue of his mother's good credit rating.

One night Judy was invited to a slumber party, one of Las Vegas High School's social highlights, and Mickey said it was all right for her to come home the following day. As soon as she left the house, he hit the casinos, hoping to see Herb Shriner, the folksy comedian from the Hoosier State, who had shown some interest in a piece of property behind the Strip. Instead, he ran into the big-time gambler, Nick the Greek, looking the picture of gloom.

"Hey Nick! What's the matter, old buddy? You look like you lost your best friend."

"Worse. I just lost that bundle I won last week at the Golden Nugget. Hell. You'd think I'd know better. I had so much I could have gone off and sat in the sun in Florida for a year." Not a man of many words, Nick turned his attention to a glass with only chipped ice left in it.

Mickey chuckled. "Well, gambling is just about the only vice I don't practice, but it's a way of life with you. Don't worry. Someone'll give you a stake, and you'll win it all back."

"Yeah, but right now I don't even have a place to stay," Nick said, dejectedly.

"Come on, you can stay at my place. My daughter is at a slumber party, the latest fad among the terrible teens. You can sack out in her room tonight."

Nick looked a bit brighter and even managed a careful smile. "Hey, thanks, Mickey. I'd like to take you up on that. Christ, I don't know when I slept last. I was gambling all night and didn't lose my last chip before an hour ago."

The next morning, Judy came home and found her father out on the front lawn with a man she didn't know. The door was open to her room, and Mickey had the garden hose in his hand. The bed was smoldering and everything inside her room was drenched. Mickey looked sheepish when he said, "Hi honey. 'Fraid there's been a little accident. Nick fell asleep with a cigarette, and your bed caught on fire."

With a flood of words that showed all those years of Mickey's working on her vocabulary had paid off, Judy launched into a tirade that left the two men speechless. "If you insist on bringing your drunken friends home with you, why can't you put them in your own room," she ended by saying.

Throughout this verbal storm, Nick the Greek stood with bowed head, but when she stopped to take a breath, he looked up at her with hangdog eyes, and she felt a stab of guilt at having been so nasty. Mickey was silent, slightly embarrassed by her outburst and lacking in words to object to what she had said. Boy, she sure had Vivian's temper, he thought, and he turned his attention to Nick, to smooth over his feelings.

That night, Judy slept in Jane's old room. Mickey had rented it out to the little nurse, but she didn't mind sharing. She could see that Judy was upset and tried to divert her by telling her about her day at work. A baby had been brought to the hospital that day by Gypsy parents. He was about two years old and had pneumonia.

"The gypsies said they think it's bad luck to change the baby's clothes, and we had to cut off three layers of old clothing. Can you imagine how dirty the poor little guy was?" she said.

Judy felt better with someone like Anne being there, but she knew Anne would be moving on as soon as she got her divorce. Never had Judy felt more dejected about not having a mother, and as soon as the lights were out, she buried her face in her pillow and had a good cry. This time, however, she was old enough to become aware of the fact that she was wallowing in self-pity, and she pulled herself together and went to sleep.

One day when she came home from school, everything smelled clean. There were red apples in a big bowl in the lounge, and as she walked back to the kitchen, there was a delicious smell of food. On the other side of the counter, she could see red curls on the top of someone's head. A tall woman slammed a cupboard door and stood up. She had a wonderful smile and lively green eyes framed by smile wrinkles.

"Hi there, sugar," she said in a slightly gravelly voice. "I'm your Great Aunt Flossie. You were such a little tyke the last time I saw you that you won't remember me."

Flossie stayed a couple of weeks, and while she was there everything was perfect. She made Southern food the kids hadn't eaten before, like hominy grits and wheat grains boiled like rice. For breakfast she fried cold slices of hominy mush and laced it with syrup.

She went through Judy's wardrobe and decided that she needed a new summer dress, and by the time Judy came home from school on the third day of Floss's visit, there was a turquoise-green cotton shirt-dress hanging in her room. Judy was thrilled and couldn't wait to try it on.

Flossie, dyed in the wool nudist, laughed heartily as her skinny great-niece pulled the shade in her bedroom to try on the dress.

With Flossie there life seemed normal, and Judy was happy. Jane's sister hadn't come just to take care of them, however. She had made an appointment with Rowenda Greer who had a certain notoriety for her miracle skin treatments.

Rowenda used her own formulas to peel off as much of the outer layers of one's skin as possible, bringing to the surface a new layer that would hopefully be as smooth as a baby's bottom. Her treatment was illegal in the state of Nevada, but she got enough business by way of the grapevine to earn a handsome living.

Years of sun worshipping had wrinkled Flossie's face, and she was determined to do something about it. Rowenda, a gorgeous woman with Titian-red hair, was a walking advertisement for her own products, and she came to the hotel to treat Flossie while the kids were at school.

Judy was horrified when she came home and discovered Flossie peeling like a snake. First her skin went stiff and formed a slick, yellowish scab, sealing her lips until she had but a small opening to her mouth and could only take in liquids through a straw. She ran a raging fever when the process was at its peak, but she shook her head fiercely when Judy asked if they should call a doctor.

Mickey, who never took anything seriously, made light of his aunt's predicament, and she had to wave him away. She was so afraid he would make her laugh, and at this point she knew she needed to avoid breaking the scabs.

It was a hideous procedure, but by the end of her stay, Flossie emerged reborn. She had achieved just what she wanted. She was delighted with the result and tenderly stroked her smooth new skin. Of course, the woman had warned her not to get it out in the sun and wind again, but for now, she looked years younger.

Jordan blew into town for the Helldorado Parade like he always had. He had a splendid, bad-tempered Palomino that only he could ride, and he cut a handsome figure, tall in the saddle, with a big, white Stetson hat. He eyed The Lacquer Job approvingly, and Mickey was amused to see how he played up to her.

Jordan had just about everything he wanted now, and he crowned his lifework by having a western-style mansion built in Rolling Hills, with white-faced Hereford cattle grazing on the grassy slopes that faced the blue Pacific. He was a prominent Republican, proud of the fact that he rode in the inaugural parade when Eisenhower took office. People respected him, and he always got what he wanted.

It was galling that his nephew needled him all the time. Anyone could see that Mickey was never going to amount to anything. What right did the damned fool have to always look so pleased with life? It irritated Dunaway that Mickey didn't show more respect and that he poked fun in a smart-ass way that threw Jordan off guard.

Jordan could see right away that Mickey had let Jane's business go to the dogs, but he looked like a person without a care in the world. He complained to Flossie, saying that it was a gawldarned shame that Mickey didn't do an honest day's work. "What kind of a world would this be if everyone behaved like that?" he asked rhetorically.

Flossie didn't think it mattered. "Look at the way he can light up a room, Jordan," she drawled. "Why, it would be a dull old world if there weren't a handful of people like that. I swear, Mickey's just as entertaining as a movie. The only difference is that he isn't getting rich performing."

Well, thought Jordan, not only is he not getting rich, if he keeps going like he is, he'll end up down and out. That fella's got a knack at squandering his assets. Jordan curried his horse, making sure the long tail and mane were flawless. He stroked her muzzle, and thought of Jane and how much she loved a good piece of horse flesh. It just wasn't the same without her. She always understood him and appreciated what he had achieved.

The lilac bush that Jane planted alongside the driveway to the hotel was in bloom, its heady fragrance an incongruous element in the desert climate. Jordan was not a man to spend much time philosophizing, but he thought about his sister's dreams of leaving her mark on the world, of building up something solid. Now her son was throwing it all to the winds, and soon the only thing left to remember her by might be this scraggly lilac.

Flossie left right after Jordan's visit. She could hardly wait to show off her new skin and find herself a beau, and she was gone just as suddenly as she had appeared.

Judy was devastated. She missed Flossie and the feeling of stability that she brought with her. Mickey tried to be comforting, explaining that Flossie never stayed put very long.

"She must have been married about eight times by now, and I can't imagine her ever slowing down. Good old Floss," he said smiling, "she sure knows how to have fun."

It was after Flossie left that everything started to go wrong fast. When school broke up, Mickey sent the kids to North Hollywood, and while Judy was content to stay the entire summer with Donda, Tony soon headed back to Vegas to hang around with his friends and pick up some money as a bus boy.

People who knew Mickey kept telling him that he would be a natural as an entertainment director for one of the strip hotels, and he started to toy with that idea. They were right – It would be duck soup to put together a floorshow. He was always running into entertainers he knew. He also noticed familiar names showing up on television programs from L.A., among them Ralph Bellamy. Ralph would be a good man to contact in order to get back in touch with the talent pool in Hollywood.

Thinking of Ralph transported Mickey back to the good days in Hollywood, and he reminisced about all the great times he had spent with James Cagney, Ralph, and their Irish crowd. Mickey had always thought it was ironic that Hollywood kept casting Cagney as a gangster. He had never met a kinder or more decent guy than Jim. Besides that, he was a brilliant song and dance man. Of course anything Jim did he did well, but comedy and dance gave him so much more satisfaction than playing the street-wise crook he had worked so hard to avoid becoming in real life. Mickey knew that while Jim was growing up, he not only stayed clear of trouble in a tough part of New York, he did so well with his stage career that he pulled his whole family out of poverty. It was typical for the big cheeses in Hollywood that they insisted on using him in gangster films just because they had such good box office results.

From his vaudeville days, Cagney knew every good act that came along when they were in Hollywood, and he had introduced many of them to Mickey, hoping they could be cast in a film. Some of them must still be around now, Mickey thought.

With that in mind, he drove out to the Desert Inn, and it didn't take him long to convince Clark that he should hire him on a temporary basis, just to see how things would work out.

As soon as Clark gave him the go-ahead and an expense account, Mickey got back his old sense of freedom. He could sign a tab and be sure that Clark would pay for it. With Clark's approval, he decided to make a trip down to Hollywood, contact Bellamy, and get back in touch with the people he needed for a live floorshow.

He and Ralph went to see a clever act done by a French couple out on the Sunset Strip. Mickey knew it would be sensational in Vegas. They performed on a stage plunged in total darkness, artfully manipulating a fluorescent feather boa scarf and a high hat, creating the illusion of a sexy routine between a man and woman. Mickey booked them for an opening number. It turned out to be an expensive evening, but he figured Clark would think it was worth it when he saw their number.

The next day, he arranged to pick up Judy at Donda's and bring her back with him. Things were slack in the hottest part of the summer, and he knew he could get a free room for her at the Desert Inn.

Donda listened to his latest schemes, taking them with a grain of salt. She always hoped that someday he would prove everyone wrong and land on his feet, but she had her doubts.

Back at the Desert Inn, Mickey put Judy up in a room by the pool and introduced her to the staff and the entertainers. The owners of the Palladium and their teenage daughter were staying in the adjacent room. In the hotel setting, Judy was on neutral ground and didn't have to feel ashamed of the makeshift life she led with Mickey. The girls were equals, hanging out together and enjoying the pool.

Everyone knew she was Mickey's daughter, and made a fuss over her. Jerry, the lifeguard at the pool was a former Olympic diving champion, and Judy spent hours practicing diving with his coaching and Mickey's encouragement. She wished they could just go on living at the hotel when she went back to school. Her father's ways didn't seem eccentric in that setting.

She was sad when it came time for him to take her back to North Hollywood, but Mickey reminded her that summer would soon be over. As he drove back up to Vegas, he felt his usual optimism flow back. Being able to put Judy up in style for a week had been a boost to his spirits, and he knew something big would come along any time now.

That summer he sold Jane's Packard and replaced it with a used Pontiac convertible. He taught Tony to drive it by taking him out on the desert and asking him to reverse it and back five miles down the dirt road. "If you can maneuver a car backwards, driving forwards will be a breeze," he reasoned.

When it was time for Judy to start the school year, Mickey again drove down to Donda's to pick her up. She was packed and eager to go, and once they were out of the traffic, he switched places with her and let her drive the long haul back to Vegas. She was only fourteen, but before you know it she'd be old enough to have a car, he figured.

"I don't want my daughter to have to rely on some jerk to drive her home," he said to Judy.

He was pleased to see how easily she picked it up. Once they were rolling, he taught her to put on the brights and turn them off when another car approached, to ease up before a curve and accelerate when in it. Relaxed, he shifted his weight in the seat and was soon fast asleep.

When Tony started his junior year, and Judy was a sophomore, Mickey's stint at the Desert Inn petered out. He was a bit too freehanded with his signature on chits, and Clark let him know that they didn't need him any more.

Once again bills piled up on his desk, unopened, but he never let it worry him. He always figured that if his back was against the wall, he could just sell the hotel. One thing that still was missing in Las Vegas was a bowling alley, and this would be the perfect site. He had already lined up a few potential investors. Of course, he would have to buy out Pete's share.

However, when he talked with Pete about the idea of selling the hotel to someone who wants to build a bowling alley, Jane's old flame informed him that they wouldn't be able to call the shots. "The city council plans to buy up all that property around North 4th Street and tear down those old houses that were built for the railroad workers, Mickey. I thought you knew about that. They've just been waiting for some of the old-timers to die off. Hell, I don't care if you unload it now. I 'spose you'll get the same price now as later."

He could feel Mickey's disappointment. Cripes, Pete thought, Jane would turn over in her grave if she knew that Mickey was going to sell out for that price when he could have kept the hotel running for a steady income. He knew there was no use pointing that out to Mickey. Chances are that he needed some fast cash.

Mickey pondered this new information. Funny that Jane hadn't talked about it with him, but maybe she reckoned she would have been able to throw some weight around and have some influence in the planning. She and Pat McCarran were thick as thieves just before she died. Or maybe she just figured on letting things ride and investing her earnings off the hotel elsewhere. He shrugged and decided he might as well go to town hall and see what could be done.

What the city had to offer wasn't anything near what he had imagined he could get out of the property, but he decided to set everything in motion. Afterwards, he and Pete divided the money, fifty-fifty, and Mickey ended up with peanuts compared to what he had banked on. At least it was enough money to pay off his bills around town and bankroll a new venture. Meanwhile, he had to find some other digs.

Pete came to the hotel and collected the Indian pottery and woven blankets and the paintings, one of them a very large Remington. Mickey knew some of it was pretty valuable, but he wasn't going to argue with Pete about whether all of it was his. Besides, he liked to travel light. Years of living in prison camp with so few worldly possessions that he could have crammed them into a lady's evening bag had been easier for him than for the average guy. The only thing that gave him cause for regret was that somewhere along the line, in all the moving about since the war, he had lost his diary. Some zealous cleaning woman had chucked it out. He had said it didn't matter, but actually, it was like losing an old friend.

Mickey and the kids moved to the house he had found for Herb Shriner. Herb bought the property as an investment and wasn't going to be using it. When he heard of Mickey's predicament, he said he would rent it out for a reasonable rate. Luckily it was furnished, and they could move in without any hassle.

The house was on a deserted road in the flatlands behind the Flamingo Hotel, and the closest building was two miles away – a telephone relay station. Whenever Mickey couldn't take Judy and Tony to school or a school event, he let them take the car. Neither one of them had a driver's license, but it was typical of him not to worry about anything going wrong.

None of Mickey's deals were panning out. The hopes he had of selling the place for a handsome price to someone who could put up a bowling alley had been the first disappointment. Then he heard about plans for a racetrack in Las Vegas, and he had the idea of televising the races in all the bars. That way people could place bets without having to leave their favorite haunts. No sooner had he aired this plan than someone from the Mob warned him to back off, telling him that was their turf.

At this point, he decided the best bet was to put all his efforts into real estate. The population of Las Vegas was growing, and there was bound to be big money to be made on property. Suddenly he had a brainstorm. He would spend the money he had left from Jane's property on a small airplane. In Nevada, a private plane would be the ticket for showing large parcels of land. That way, people who wanted a ranch could really get a feeling for what they were buying.

As luck would have it, he had a contact out at the airport, an old acquaintance named Tom Sprach. Mickey had hired him as a stunt pilot back in his Hollywood days and ran into him again when he was setting up the 'champagne flights'. Tom was earning a living on mail runs, and Mickey figured he could interest him in going fifty-fifty on a scheme to sell property from the air.

Tom was tired of working for someone else, and he said he was game. "I can't throw in half, Mickey. I don't have that kind of dough. But I can make sure we get a good buy on a plane, if you can put up two thirds of the cost."

Mickey agreed to that, and together, they bought a twin-engine Cessna, a nifty little plane that was in perfect condition. Then Tom gave Mickey flying lessons so he could get a license.

The new plane was not only useful; it was a fabulous toy. Mickey loved the sense of freedom he got when up in the air. So far no one else had come up with the same idea for selling desert real estate and he could see that he was going to make a bundle.

One of his first clients was a peroxide blonde from Hollywood who came up to Las Vegas with her fourteen poodles, ready to start divorce procedures against her latest rich husband. Mickey had given her plenty of work when she was a chorus girl, but he thought she definitely looked worse for the wear all these years later. Still, when he found out what sort of money she was likely to bleed from her soon-to-be-ex-husband, he decided to try to sell her a spread of property where she could build a ranch.

He knew just the site for someone with enough money to spend and arranged to meet with her to show her an aerial view of the property. Shirley showed up at the airport, with four of her dogs in tow, and teetered out to the plane, wearing spike heels on feet that were too small for the pounds she had added to her waistline.

Mickey had told Judy she could come along for the ride, and they all three climbed into the plane. It didn't take long to reach their destination, and they flew low over the property which clearly couldn't have been seen very well any other way, there being no access by road for anything but the very front acreage.

Shirley flirted with Mickey and asked him if he would let her take a hand at the wheel and try landing it.

"Do you know how to fly this rig?" he asked, surprised.

"Sure I do. I only need a teeny bit before I've put in enough time to get my permit, and I need practice doing a landing."

"Okay," Mickey said, with as little concern as he had demonstrated when he let Judy drive the car the first time.

He was soon sorry he had been so agreeable, however, because the dizzy broad miscalculated the terrain and ended up making a crash landing. Fortunately, no one was hurt, and the plane looked all right. Mickey spent the next hour tinkering around to set things right again, and they got back to the airport before it started to get dark.

Tom was pacing the tarmac and waved to them as they taxied in. He looked at the woman and her dogs and shook his head. He couldn't imagine her to be a potential client.

"I'm glad you're back, Mickey. Someone has asked me to fly him down to Mexico, and he's willing to pay all expenses and a hundred bucks. Is that okay with you?"

"Hey, Tom old man, that's terrific. Didn't I tell you this would be a little gold mine?"

The gal had decided she wanted to buy the property, convinced by Mickey that it was going to go up in value ten-fold within the next few years. He drove her back to her hotel, and said he would call on her the next day when she was ready to sign the necessary papers.

After he and Judy got home, he made himself a drink and talked about what plans he had for her and Tony. One side of Judy had stopped believing these pipe dreams, but the other side loved hearing them even though their coming true was not likely. It was like a game between them with well-defined rules.

In the morning, Mickey got a call from Shirley saying she was leaving for LA. Her husband had come to Vegas and begged her to come back, giving her diamond earrings to sweeten the offer.

Damn the luck. He had been so sure she was going to buy the property. He should have known her husband would make it up with her when he got wind of how much money she would be able to flush out of him. Hell – their reconciliation probably wouldn't last a month, but meanwhile there went that deal down the tubes.

The next time he had a potential client, he called Tom to arrange to use the plane, but there was no answer at Tom's place. Mickey got into the car and drove out to the airport, thinking he might be out there.

After asking around, he found out that no one had seen Tom since he left for Mexico. Mickey was worried that his real estate deal would go up in smoke, but after a few days, he realized he had lost more than that. Tom Sprach had evidently stolen the plane, and Mickey saw neither hide nor hair of him after that. What was left of the money Jane had accumulated by always investing in property had literally taken wing and flown away.

Tony and Judy never heard their father complain about anything or speak of anything as a failure. It was natural to be swept along with his latest plans for a life in style, and now that Jane's hotel was past history, they drifted with him, supported by a vague notion that everything would come up aces.

One night Judy was alone in Herb Shriner's house. It was soon going to be Christmas, and she had found a sun-bleached tumbleweed, propped it up on a table, and decorated it with multi-colored jellybeans on each twig and thorn. She knew her father didn't care about Christmas, but she was satisfied with this as a decoration. She hummed a Christmas carol and felt the usual anticipation of the holiday that was always spent at Donda's.

Later, when she was in the kitchen washing the dinner dishes, she heard footsteps by the front door. There was no phone, and she was frightened. She took a paring knife and ran into the bathroom, the only room inside the house with a door that could be locked.

Standing in the bathroom, her heart pounding so hard that it was difficult to follow the sounds of the footprints, she held the knife tightly and wondered what to do. She knew it must be a man, because his footsteps were heavy.

When she heard him at the back of the house, she bolted, out the bathroom, through the front door and down to the road. She ran the two miles to the telephone relay station and found a man on watch there. He obligingly called the police, and a half an hour later they came to pick her up.

They drove to the house with her in the patrol car. All the lights in the house were still burning, and the door that she had left opened when she took flight was shut, but there was no one inside. With a flashlight, the one policeman could see that there had been someone walking around the house and out to a trailer that was parked out back. There were clearly footsteps under the windows, but they figured whoever had been there was long gone by now.

"We'll have to leave you here, missy, but we patrol this road every now and then, and we'll keep an eye on the place."

Great, Judy thought. She was terrified. She locked all the doors and watched them drive away. Then she put a rocking chair in the middle of the living room where she could keep an eye on all sides of the house. When Mickey and Tony came home, they found her still sitting there, trying to concentrate on reading 'Life Magazine', convinced that she had escaped from what she imagined was a grave danger. It turned out that the man who had been there owned the trailer and was just getting something out of it.

Not long after that, the electricity was cut off one night when Tony and Judy were doing their homework. When Mickey came home he had to admit that he had forgotten to pay the bill.

Unfortunately, it wasn't just the electricity that wasn't being paid. A few days later, the kids came home from school and there was a padlock on the door with a notice that they were evicted. When Mickey showed up, he already had a plan, and they moved in with a fat, kind-hearted cocktail waitress who lived in an apartment near the center of town. Except for the people he had conned out of money on some hare-brained business venture, everybody liked Mickey, and he always had plenty of people offering to help him out. However, the options were definitely getting less attractive.

The next day, Mickey drove out to the house and found a window he could force. He packed their clothes in cardboard boxes, but there really wasn't room for all their gear with the cocktail waitress. The best bet for now was to move in with Don and Inez, a couple who lived in a track house at Sunrise Acres, a part of town that looked permanently like a building site. Don worked at a print shop, hauling down good wages and drinking them up at the bar Inez tended out on the Boulder Highway. They said Mickey could rent two rooms and share the kitchen and bath.

There wasn't much room, but the arrangement functioned satisfactorily. Don and Inez worked nights, slept late, and were seldom there when Tony and Judy were awake. As for Mickey, he no longer had anything like a normal schedule and spent most of his time out hustling.

Judy loved Las Vegas High School and was satisfied with any kind of dwelling as long as it meant she could continue going to school there. It was a school where you could be popular with personality, but otherwise money meant a lot. If a girl's father was a pit boss, he was earning enough money to buy her a fancy car, cashmere sweaters, and Lanz dresses. In the casinos, a pit boss earned fifty bucks a day, and a dealer hauled down twenty-five. Even Tony earned, with tips, eight bucks an hour as a bus boy, but it never crossed Mickey's mind to get a regular job. You could buy a tract house in Vegas for five thousand dollars, but his idea of living was not settling for anything like a tract house.

Mickey's little family was down and out, but somehow, Mickey succeeded in making Tony and Judy feel like they belonged to a privileged class. They were blessed with the optimism denied youngsters whose parents didn't have Mickey's self-confidence.

School was a microcosm, and Judy was all wrapped up in being in with the right crowd. Unlike Tony who always did his own thing, Judy was a social creature who loved trying to fit in. Mickey didn't think they would get into trouble, because he could see they both had minds of their own and enough ambition to avoid making mistakes. However, Tony had outgrown the need to fit in with his peers. It had been a brief phase at the most, and he returned to the role of someone who marched to his own tune. After they moved out of Shriner's house, he stopped attending classes and got a job at the same print shop where Don worked.

Jane had given Tony a box of oil paints when he came to Las Vegas, and she had been pleased when he turned out a desert landscape for her. Now he took up painting again, and, inspired by Van Gogh, he spent hours teaching himself to do portraits.

Judy was making good money babysitting – In a town like Vegas, people who hired her usually stayed out half the night and came home seven sheets to the wind and ready to over-tip. She was able to buy all of her own clothes with her babysitting money, but her biggest wish was a horsehair petticoat that would make her dirndl skirts stand out. All the rich girls were wearing them, and the cotton petticoats that Judy starched so stiff they could stand alone were a poor substitute. Tony was paying his own way, too, but he it was typical of him that he spent his first paycheck from the typographer's on the desired petticoat.

Inez was very kind to Mickey's kids, but she was always quiet and a little sad. Judy thought that might have been because she had a problem with a five-o'clock shadow. She carefully shaved her face before she left for work in the afternoon, but she looked terrible the next day.

One Sunday morning Judy got up late, and Inez was already in the kitchen, her head bent over a cup of coffee. When Inez looked up, Judy saw that her right eye was swollen shut, and that half of her face was black and blue with red streaks where the skin had ruptured.

"Poor you, Inez. What happened?" Judy managed to ask, while she tried not to show how shocked she was.

Inez had been crying and she didn't want to answer, but Tony came in and said with contempt that Don had given her the shiner.

Later, when Judy saw Don she told him off, sarcastically saying that it must take a really strong man to be able to beat up a woman. Before he had time to reply, she went into the bathroom and slammed the door.

She filled the tub with hot water and bubbles and had just lowered herself in, when the door was flung open. Don threw a pitcher-full of ice cubes at the water, glared at Judy and said in a threatening tone, "Don't you ever speak to me in that tone." And he was out the door before she could reply.

When Judy came out of the bathroom, Don had left the house. Tony said, "Hey sis, watch out for that guy. He's a mean S.O.B."

She shrugged it off. Life with Mickey had made her think she could handle any situation. The school year was coming to an end, and she was satisfied that it had gone well. She was already looking forward to her junior year, but she had learned not to think too much about where they would be living.

As soon as school was out, Mickey drove her down to North Hollywood. They packed all her clothes, because things didn't look too permanent with Don and Inez. The rent was overdue, and none of the deals he made after he lost the plane had panned out yet.

Judy told Donda excitedly about her friends at school and the classes she liked, leaving out a description of the places they had been staying. She didn't want to worry her. It was nice being back at Donda's. As usual, Aunt Elsie and Aunt Marcia made a fuss over her and Poli and Doc gave her some new clothes. She liked to hang out next door with a nice family whose son was her own age, and she dated a boy down the street. Donda felt her age, worrying about whether she was giving her granddaughter too much leeway.

Back in Vegas, things came to a head late one night when Mickey and Tony were awakened by Don coming home drunk. He was loud and belligerent and worked himself into a fury about the overdue rent. They could hear Inez trying to calm him down, but she didn't seem to be having much luck.

Mickey's old habits from prison camp were just under the surface, and he quietly told Tony what to do if Don came into their room. "Play dead, son, and maybe the jerk will just fade away. If worse comes to worse, he'll go for me first, and you take this coke bottle and clout him over the head when he does. Just be sure you hit him hard enough to put him out of action, or we'll have a hell of a fight on our hands."

Tony took the full coke bottle and put it under his pillow, not giving thought to the fact that Mickey had one on hand. The door opened, letting a pool of light fall into the room. Mickey and Tony lay completely still with eyes shut, apparently sound asleep. It worked. Don muttered under his breath and shut the door. They heard him stagger through the kitchen and into his room.

The next morning, while Don was still out like a light, they got ready to make a move. Inez stopped them and said they would have to leave their things there until they paid their rent. Embarrassed, Tony started heading for the car, but Mickey lingered.

"I'll get the money, Inez. Jesus, I really am sorry to put you out like this, and you're right about keeping our stuff. Could you do me a favor though and let me have the kid's paints? I feel like a heel, letting him down."

She shrugged and went to get the oil paints, giving them to Mickey as she looked over her shoulder to make sure Don wasn't up. He would be good and mad if he knew she went soft.

Mickey gave her a kiss on her cheek and thanked her before he jumped into the car. He gave the paint box and easel to Tony and took off fast down the road.

He had just enough money to get them some breakfast and pick up a paper to look for a place to stay. It crossed his mind that it was good luck he had taken Judy down to Donda's. Hell, he and Tony could always manage.

To begin with, Tony stayed with Craig and his family while Mickey bummed around with friends. Once he had raised enough money to get their things from Inez, he found rooms to rent in a house on the other side of town, and Tony moved in with him. Tony didn't want to go back to the print shop where Don worked, but there were plenty of jobs for anyone who was willing to work. Mickey got a job for him with Martinolich, at the construction site of The Colonial House, a place going up by the Desert Inn.

Mickey also landed a contract to put advertising on bus benches, and he found an old barn where Tony could paint them. The barn was a labyrinth of cubbyholes where a motley collection of derelicts bedded down. They seemed to like having Tony there, painting benches, and their company made the job more interesting.

When The Colonial House was finished, among the first people to stay there was Joe Venutti, the violinist, an old friend of Mickey's. Joe was making a bundle, doing a stint at the Golden Nugget, and Mickey suggested to him that Tony do his portrait.

Joe took to the idea right away when he saw that Tony had talent, and he grandly proclaimed that when the painting was done, he would send Tony to the conservatory of art in Parma. Tony got Venutti to pose once, in shorts and a shirt, by The Colonial House pool. The painting was a study in blue, and Tony had finished all but the face when he realized that everything Venutti earned by playing violin at the Golden Nugget, he was throwing away on their craps tables. Art school was just another flight of fantasy.

It was about that time that Mickey and Tony were thrown out of the second house for overdue rent. By now they were used to the routine, and Tony laughed, flipping the bird at the stone-faced owner and his sons, as he and Mickey drove away from a barrage of rude remarks.

They checked into a rooming house with communal johns and showers and lived on deviled meat and Ritz crackers. It was a place for has-beens or sad characters who couldn't aspire to anything better, but it didn't occur to Mickey or Tony to think they were like the rest of the clientele. They were rolling with the punches, feeling closer than most fathers and sons ever do.

Where they lived didn't matter for now...They were together, shored up by mutual, nonjudgmental affection. They shared the same values, and they were sustained by an unflagging belief in their own worth. Jane had instilled in Mickey the feeling of being unique and valuable, and Mickey passed that feeling on to his son. It was an attitude as effective as a mackintosh in a rainstorm. So when they hit the skids, they knew the situation was only temporary, something they would look back on one day and laugh about.

Whenever one of Mickey's deals panned out, he slipped right into high gear and told Tony to get cleaned up for a night on the town. They would have a steak dinner at the Last Frontier and sometimes let themselves be photographed, Mickey, the obviously proud father, and Tony, the chip off the old block, both dressed in tailored jackets with Western style string ties. Or they would hit Mickey's favorite haunt, Mickey proudly presenting his son to the bartender, saying, "Ain't he a handsome kid?" While they were out on the town, it was a grand life.

In the morning, waking up in the dismal surroundings of the rooming house, padding down the poorly lit hallway to the bathroom, with its chipped and rusting fixtures, Mickey switched into his horyo habit – Blocking everything out except a feeling of satisfaction that he was alive, and there was another day to be unveiled.

When it came time for Judy to come back to Las Vegas and start the school year, Mickey called Donda and asked if she could stay longer. "Right now Tony and I are living out of a suitcase, Donda. It's only temporary, but at the present time there isn't anywhere for Judy to stay."

Donda was sure that this time things had really gone bad, and her first worry was about Tony. "What about Tony's schooling, Mickey?" she asked.

"He quit, Donda. He doesn't feel motivated. A friend of mine wants to send him to art school in Italy, and I have to admit that I think that would be more of an opportunity than anything he can get in the public high school."

Mickey could guess what Donda would be thinking about Tony quitting school when he only had one year left to go, and he added, "Of course, a kid as bright as Tony can always get into the better colleges by passing the entrance exams. It probably won't matter that he doesn't get a high school diploma."

Donda could hear that Mickey had already rationalized an excuse for the way things were going, and nothing she said would make any difference. She knew what a disadvantage it had been for herself and her girls that their schooling was limited, and surely Mickey must know that, too. Instead of arguing with him, though, she tried to comfort him, knowing that behind the optimistic facade there must be some pain.

"Well, I guess you're right, Mickey. As bright as Tony is, I'm sure everything will come out all right in the end."

There was a pause, like Mickey was lost in his thoughts, then he continued, "Hell, sweetheart, I'm afraid I've let things get out of hand here. I wish to God Vivian had stayed alive and could have helped me keep this show together."

Donda was sad, thinking that she couldn't recall him ever having admitted a sense of failure. Then he checked himself and again sounded cheerful. "But don't you worry your pretty head.

It's just a matter of time before things will start looking up. I want to haul in enough money to give the kids the kind of education they deserve, and I've plenty of irons in the fire."

While Donda talked with Mickey, Judy was with a new crowd of friends at the house of a girl who lived in the Hollywood hills and had a swimming pool. When she came back in high spirits, Donda hated to break the news to her that she wouldn't be able to return to Vegas. She was sure Judy would be terribly disappointed.

"Your dad called, dear, and he won't be able to take you back up to Las Vegas. Tony's not going to school, and your dad says they have no place to stay right now."

Judy was very upset. It was only a few weeks until she was supposed to start her junior year. She felt like her whole world was falling apart, and she started to argue. "He always figures out something, Donda. He has to! I don't want to go to North Hollywood High School. It's so big, and all my friends are in Las Vegas."

Donda understood why Judy was so distressed. There had been too many changes over the years. She decided it was best to let the matter drop for now, but she knew instinctively that Mickey wasn't going to work things out. Not this time.

"Well, this weekend we won't think about it. Elsie and Langley are taking us up to Carpinteria to see Bobbie and Armand and the boys."

Judy could hardly wait to see her Aunt Bobbie and Uncle Armand. Everything about them had always seemed so special. During the war they had lived right around the corner from Donda, and in Judy's mind they represented the perfect American family. What she didn't realize was that they had had their share of bad luck after the war and had to rebuild their lives.

Armand earned a lot of money while the government was pouring millions into the war effort, but afterwards, whole sections of industry were closed down. Still, it seemed like he had nothing to worry about, because two of his friends wanted him to go into a business venture with them, pooling their resources to start a factory of their own.

It had seemed like a sure bet. A scientist had developed a new technique, a process whereby they could silver-plate utensils made out of aluminum. They invested in good designs and all the necessary machinery, but they ran into technical problems, and the silver-plating blistered after awhile, leaving a marred surface.

The inventor kept reassuring them, and the associate who was best at selling continued to line up potential customers, wining and dining them on anticipated earnings.

Armand was as honest as they come, and he began to get very nervous, watching the cash flow all in the wrong direction. By the time they decided to give up on their venture, the deficits were so great that he had lost everything, even their home. He had a nervous breakdown and was sent to the state mental hospital in Camarillo to recuperate.

Bobbie proved to be a pillar of strength. Their oldest son was in the Navy, and one of his buddies said that his parents were going to sell a tiny store in Carpinteria, a sleepy small town south of Santa Barbara. Bobbie still had the money from the gift shop she had sold in San Francisco when they moved down south, and with it she bought this shop with its inventory of notions – ribbons, buttons, zippers, thread, elastic, and sensible underwear. She found a cheap house they could rent in Summerland, and once their good furniture was moved in, there was still the atmosphere of a nice home, albeit in a shabby setting.

When Armand was able to work again, he got a job with Sears Roebuck, in Ventura, a big step down from what he had been doing, but an honest start. They still had two boys in school and had to face building up a future all over again, basically from scratch.

Not long afterwards, a storefront on Carpinteria's main street was available to lease. It was a men's haberdashery, and the owner wanted to sell the fixtures. They were well-made, attractive wooden counters, shelves, racks, and open closets, stained olive green. Bobbie could see right away that they would lend class to any shop. In her mind's eye she could picture the store stocked with ladies and children's clothing. It was a gamble, but she was sure she could make a go of it. They would have to borrow money, but during the few months they had been in Carpinteria, they had already established a good reputation.

She and Armand made the plunge, and they soon had established a nice little business, catering to the wives of local farmers and small business people of Carpinteria Valley. Bobbie had a real flair for buying, and Armand kept a strict account of their economy. They were a distinguished looking couple, respectable church-going people, and welcome additions to the small community. They rented a more spacious house in the foothills near Santa Barbara and found an architect who could draw plans for the dream-house of the fifties, to be built farther up the road.

Judy could see that Bobbie and Armand's family scene was all that was desirable for Americans of the fifties, with uncomplicated goals like the ones projected by the movies and the favorite television programs of the times. She loved the way Bobbie had fixed up their home, and dinner at their house was always so special. It wasn't like at Donda's, where they ate on TV trays, except for Thanksgiving and Christmas. Things were the way Judy imagined they would have been if her own mother had stayed alive. She was too young to appreciate the sophisticated dreams her father had.

Bobbie and Armand's oldest son was married now, but Judy had always liked Alan and

Philip, the two handsome cousins who still lived at home. They took Judy outside to pitch a baseball while Armand served a pre-dinner drink. When Donda told them about Mickey's predicament, Armand lifted an eyebrow and said he wasn't the least bit surprised.

"People like that never change. It's just a crying shame that the kids have had to be batted around from pillar to post," he said, as he mixed the dry martinis he was famous for.

Donda wanted to defend Mickey, but she could see that she wouldn't be able to change Armand's mind. He stood for the exact opposite in every way. She thought about how things could have been, if Mickey hadn't squandered the assets they all figured Jane must have had. It was a puzzle to Donda, who could get by on so little, that someone like Mickey could go through money like water through a sieve. She knew how much it had meant to Jane to build up security for the future. Now all that was wasted, and Tony and Judy would never benefit from her carefully laid plans.

Still, a long life had taught her that it is what one has in one's heart and in one's head that is true wealth. With all his faults, she thought, Mickey had given his children what it takes to be a whole person. She wasn't the least bit worried about their future, but she wanted desperately for Judy to be happy in the present moment, too.

"Of course, I love having Judy back with me," Donda said, "but I know she is going to be unhappy about her school. All she talks about is the high school in Las Vegas, and now she will have to make all new friends again."

Bobbie glanced at Armand and looked like she was about to speak, but she didn't. She had always wished for a daughter but gave up after she had three sons. She thought it was a shame that Judy was growing up without her mother's guidance. They didn't really look alike, but Judy resembled her mother so much in other ways, Bobbie thought.

Even though she had only boys, she knew very well what a girl Judy's age would like, and she couldn't imagine that it would be much fun for her to live at Donda's. Bobbie thought about the last time she had spent an afternoon at her mother's. There was more clutter than ever, and it was so depressing to see Beulah. She spent her entire day sitting in a rocking chair, poor thing, and she was starting to smell bad. Bobbie knew that it was a struggle for Marcia and Donda to get her in the bath, and she wondered how often they succeeded.

It was all in all a madhouse in Bobbie's opinion. She never had been able to understand how her mother could put up with so many characters. Donda's house was like a wharf, with bits and pieces of flotsam that came in with the tide. She thought about Bertha, the latest lame duck, a lonely Polish woman who was devoted to Donda and came around every day to gather garden snails in a bucket so they could be killed with boiling water. She always seemed to be crawling around in Donda's garden, barefooted, with her large breasts hanging loose in a sack of a dress. Bobbie was sure she didn't wear any underwear. She spoke such broken English and had so many teeth missing. Why in the world doesn't Mother just put out snail poison like anyone else would do, she thought. Bless her for being so kind to all sorts of people, but it would drive me nuts to live there, and she knew Vivian would have wanted a nicer home for Judy. She wondered what Armand would think about taking on the job of letting her come to live with them.

She decided to broach the subject after the family had left. It wasn't a decision to be made lightly, and it would also have to be all right with the boys. Armand had been through enough with worries about their economy that she didn't want to put an unwanted burden on him.

She didn't need to put the suggestion to him. He had been having the same thoughts and said so as soon as the family had driven. Once he and Bobbie had decided they were willing to ask Judy to come stay with them, they talked with the boys.

"It means that one of you will have to give up his room," Armand said. "Are you two sure you don't mind bunking in the same room?"

The boys readily agreed to the plan, and already the next day Bobbie phoned Donda and asked her to talk with Judy. It was with a touch of sadness that Donda saw how readily Judy jumped at the idea of staying with Bobbie. Donda loved having her in North Hollywood, but she could see that Bobbie and her family would appeal to any girl.

Maybe it is just as well, Donda thought. She worried about Judy when she was out with her friends, but she didn't want to hold her back and spoil her fun. Besides, I guess I'm getting old, and so is poor Beulah. It's an uphill struggle just to manage her. Donda chuckled, thinking about the latest problem with Beulah. She was by now so sedentary that she didn't like to have to get up and go to the toilet. The doctor said she had kidney trouble, and needed to drink lots of water, but Beulah stubbornly refused, saying it would only make her have to pee.

Someone knocked at the door, and Donda rose wearily from her chair. Bertha was standing on the porch, grinning from ear to ear, with a bucketful of snails. Donda smiled at her and said, "Aren't you the clever one! I'll put a kettle of water over so we can do them in. Seems a shame, but there are so darned many snails this year I don't think I would have any plants left if you didn't catch them, Bertha. Put down that pail for now and come on in. Wouldn't you like a cup of coffee?"

She opened the door wide for Bertha. She felt sorry for her the first time she saw her, wandering aimlessly down the street, so far away from some little village in Poland. Too bad her English is so limited, Donda mused. I'd love to hear her story.

* * * * *

When Mickey found out that Judy was going to Carpinteria, he was surprised and momentarily thrown off balance. Leaving Judy with Donda didn't threaten his plans for her future, but Bobbie and Armand had always impressed him as being too rigid, even narrow-minded. He felt a twinge of regret, like something precious was slipping out of his grasp. He was convinced that he was the best person to shape the future of his daughter, and now it looked like she would be going into the camp of people who were his exact opposites.

Donda explained to him that Judy didn't want to go to North Hollywood High School, but Mickey wasn't concerned about Judy's preference for schools. In his opinion, none of them were worth much. Some of the most interesting people he had known were self-educated.

"Ah, hell, Donda," he said finally. "I guess it isn't going to hurt her to be there. I don't think Armand has much sense of humor, but a teenage girl only seems to be interested in her peers anyway."

He decided to treat this separation like he would a brief holiday. He was on to some pretty hot deals, and with a bit of luck he should have a nice set-up for her to come back to. Maybe by next year, he could afford to take Judy on a trip that would broaden her mind and make up for the past couple of years where he didn't think he had spent enough time with the kids. He envisioned a jaunt to Mexico, giving her a taste for the language and the sort of sophistication that can only come with contact with other cultures. The plan took shape in his mind so quickly that it made him forget his feelings of frustration over temporarily losing his hold on Judy.

* * * * *

For Judy, life in the household of her aunt was like a dream come true. There was only one hurdle to get over. That was a serious talk with Uncle Armand. Judy had always looked up to him. He was a handsome man, with dark hair and distinguished touches of gray on his temples. He was tall and elegant in his dress, even when casual. His serious demeanor was very unlike Mickey's cocky attitude.

He made Judy a little nervous, but she wasn't timid, and she looked him in the eye as he lay down some rules. The main thing he wanted her to understand was what he expected of her.

"You have to remember, Judy, that Carpinteria is a small town, and it is important for us to be respected since we rely on Carpinterians to trade in our store. I'll ask you to keep that in mind and not do anything that would embarrass us."

Judy certainly could see that this made sense. She had become painfully aware of how embarrassed one can be when someone in the family is too unconventional.

Armand smiled when she agreed and said he knew that wasn't really necessary to say to her. Then he resumed a stern countenance and continued, "Of course you may communicate with your father, but I don't want him ever coming to visit you here. That is all I will say about it, and I hope you understand."

With a fleeting pang of guilt, Judy readily agreed. She could easily picture the scene if her father came for a visit, and she knew good and well that it would be a disaster. He would do all the wrong things in such a proper setting, and she had already learned that Armand and Bobbie's type of people didn't mix with the sort her father liked. The memory of having been asked to leave the home of one of her Las Vegas' girlfriends came to mind. That friend's father had said that he didn't want anything to do with anyone connected with Mickey. It didn't make Judy love her dad any less, but she had learned that he was persona non grata in some circles. I won't tell Daddy what Uncle Armand said, she thought, figuring that it wouldn't be likely he would drive all the way to Carpinteria to visit anyway.

If Mickey knew anything about Armand's terms, he never let on. The fact that he addressed his first letter to Judy "c/o Mr. Or Mrs. Armand Bas (Whichever the case may be)" was typical of him. It made Judy wince, but Armand didn't dignify the sarcasm with a comment.

For Judy, life at her aunt and uncle's was a turning point. She never again had to worry about having something nice to wear. Bobbie loved setting aside the prettiest clothes from their store for her niece. Judy had always thrived on the orderliness of school, but now she could bask in the comfort of a smoothly run home. Bobbie had learned to cook like her French mother-in-law, and the food was delicious. Meals were always served at a nicely set table. It was a household where everything ran like clockwork. Judy loved the predictability of the routine, the tidy house, the punctual meals, the fact that beds were always made, clothes were always clean, and nothing was left in disrepair.

She loved the sound of Bobbie's stockings rubbing against silk linings as she walked briskly down the carpeted hallway, pulling on white cotton gloves on her way to the front door, a whiff of Machiabelli, Bobbie's favorite perfume, lingering in the air after she left for the store. She loved Mondays when Bobbie stayed home, doing the wash and pursuing her hobbies – sewing a new dress for Judy or making a lampshade, or upholstering an antique chair that she picked up on a bargain. On Mondays, there was likely to be the smell of pot roast mingling with that of a cake and the fragrance of freesias, picked in the garden and gathered in a bouquet on Judy's night table.

She missed Tony, but Alan and Philip were just like brothers, too. At first she worried about annoying Uncle Armand. He never scolded, but he had a way of rattling his newspaper when something irritated him. In time, she learned that he was a very fine person and witty, with a good sense of humor. He was a man of exceptionally high principles, but he made a habit of living by them, not preaching about them. As much as she loved her father with his faults, she also learned to love Uncle Armand with all his perfection.

Unlike Mickey who was in the habit of saying with a smile, "For God's sake, don't do as I do. Do what I say," Armand practiced what he preached, but his saving grace was that he demanded more of himself than of others. With his penchant for perfection, there was an air of tension about him, but when he smiled, Judy was overjoyed.

He never scolded, but the example he set made those around him do their utmost to please and excel. Ironically, it was just the right point in Judy's development to instill in her the self-discipline she needed to realize some of Mickey's visions. Despite the clash of personality of the two men, Mickey's emphasis on tolerance made it possible for Judy to become part of Armand's world without rejecting Mickey's. She decided that behavior is a game. You play it differently, all according to what goals you want to achieve. Learning the ways of Bobbie and Armand didn't make her a different person, but their ways opened up different doors.

The teachers at the small high school were devoted to their work, kind-hearted and determined to get the best out of their pupils. Bobbie and Armand were pleased to see that Judy came home with top grades and plunged whole-heartedly into student government. Bobbie thought about Vivian nearly every day, and, with all she was doing for Judy, she felt like she had re-established a bond to the sister she once loved so much. She knew how much it would have meant to Vivian to see Judy given the opportunity to be well groomed and well educated, and to see how healthy she was now that she was getting three square meals a day.

Judy wrote to Mickey regularly, being careful not to say anything that might hurt his feelings or make him think she preferred the life she was leading to what he could offer her.

She needn't have worried. Mickey was out of touch with reality, on a merry-go-'round that was lubricated with screwdrivers in the morning, bloody Mary's at noon, and Stingers, which he preferred to pronounce 'Stingahs,' or Daiquiris in the evening. However, his drinking was a superficial need, something he did to convey the message that he was 'in tune'. It was a prop, a badge one wears to tip off like-minded peers, a signal that the party was on-going, and that he was happy. He was never seen drunk, but he didn't spend a day without drinking. In the artificial environment of Las Vegas, it was easy to let day run into night and turn back to day again, without taking notice of the change.

His liver was kicking up, and, again, Doc Denham warned him that if he didn't stop drinking his days were numbered. Mickey decided that he could worry about that later. The ailments he had suffered in prison camp made everything afterwards seem minor by comparison. Hell, his liver was ruined then, and he was still going strong.

All the former Japanese POWs suffered health problems. It was nearly seven years since the end of the war, and the government still wasn't doing a damned thing for them. He wondered whether Jack was making any progress with his suit. If only the government would pay out some money, all his problems would be over, or at least his immediate problems.

Meanwhile, Las Vegas was taking on more and more of the characteristics of life in Cabanatuan. His possessions were down to a minimum, and he lived in the moment. The twilight zone of the casinos and nightclubs and the monotony of the climate served to rob the scene of the feeling of anguish that can come when nightfall and dawn or spring and autumn make a man aware of time slipping by, his days being squandered. Just like he had in the prison camp, he got to know every Tom, Dick and Harry who wound up in this self-inflicted prison, this make-believe place to which people were drawn because of an addiction to action. It was the one place in America where the wheel of fortune went spinning night and day, and one did not have to stop up and deal with memories.

While Jane was alive, he had renewed his membership in Kiwanas, thinking it would be useful in his plans to make deals in advertising or public relations. There he had encountered the kind of man who came across as thinking of himself as the best thing since sliced bread, just because he was a success in the business world. An attractive wife of a smug man was someone Mickey considered fair game, and his success rate in cuckolding potential clients ruined his chances of being part of the better society, but he didn't care.

The type of home he had imagined creating with Vivian was by now so far out of reach that he stored it away in the dim recesses of his mind along with other dreams, put on a back burner but not abandoned. He had no home, but, uncomplaining, he settled for the spontaneous fellowship one meets as a regular customer at a popular bar or nightclub. He was known wherever he went, but he gravitated towards piano bars, where a crooner could create the mood of love. In the dim light, he could easily lose sight of the tawdriness of the scene and spend an evening seducing a woman who was just as adrift as he was. Others like him welcomed such a likeable addition, and he was momentarily fulfilled, feeling their welcome. He was still a dazzling performer, but the audience had shrunk considerably.

The ability he had honed in prison camp, of warding off anxieties about the time slipping through his fingers, served him well, and his talent for scoring with the opposite sex kept him from brooding about whether he would wake up lonely. Nothing was more reassuring than being able to function well in bed.

Still, he could establish an immediate rapport with people whose intelligence enabled them to recognize a kindred spirit, albeit one that was a bit tarnished. He made friends with Bill Moore who was the architect and for years the general manager of The Last Frontier, one of the first hotels out on the Strip. Back in the 40's, Moore had the brilliant idea of putting a swimming pool in front of that hotel, reasoning that it would beckon to the hot, dusty tourist who drove into town. He was right, and The Last Frontier became a success story that paved the way for the fabulous places that sprouted up afterwards.

Mickey told Bill about his latest idea. "The Strip is all filled up with glitzy hotels, Bill, and now property is ten times cheaper on the Boulder Highway. You ought to build a hotel out there that will cater to the locals. It should be the sort of place where run-of-the-mill Vegans would like to go just to hang out."

Mickey showed Moore a watercolor he had asked Tony to do. It was a sketch of his idea for a hotel designed to look like a Mississippi steamboat, anchored in a swimming pool. "You could call it 'The Showboat'. It could be touted as 'Las Vegas' first resort hotel', because all those places on The Strip are outside city limits! You could even incorporate a bowling alley – the first resort hotel to have that facility." Mickey's enthusiasm was contagious.

Bill had been around a long time, and he could read people better than most. He had heard from others about Mickey's ordeal in the Philippines and Japan. He wasn't blind to the fact that Mickey was a character who needed to be kept on a short lead, but there was no question about the man's talent, he thought. Like most people, he also found Mickey's salesmanship and cheerful disposition to be irresistible.

Moore said, "You've sold me on the idea, Mickey! Let's look into it."

Mickey was elated. For the first time in years, he felt like he had found someone who would give him fair due for his good ideas. Moore got an architect on the task and decided to pour a couple of million dollars into what he figured might be his last big project.

Tony was working for Martinolich's construction firm when it was contracted to build The Showboat. Moore had a deadline for the opening, and Mickey had a lot of publicity lined up for the event. When things got really busy, Mickey pitched in to help out with the construction and knocked himself out, laying pipes, giving a hand with the carpentry, and helping move materials. It was hard physical work for a man out of condition, but he felt good about it. It was a whole new ball game – working like he had in prison camp, but with a full belly and no one beating him. The only trouble was that he wasn't officially a worker, and his day was a blur of conflicting activities. One hour he would be in with Moore, hashing over plans for the opening and throwing back a few drinks, or he would jump in his car and drive across town to line up some materials for the interior, with a stop at a bar on his way back to the building site.

There was grumbling that he wasn't a member of the union, and he thought any objections would disappear if he made himself indispensable by working fast on things that needed to be done here and now. The result was that one hot day that summer he was operating a power saw with too much alcohol in his blood. While guiding a piece of lumber through the rotating blade, he lost the tips of two fingers on his left hand, and at first he didn't comprehend what had happened to him. Cursing himself for having made the same stupid blunder as Dizzy had done years before, he grabbed his wrist and put pressure on it to try to stop the bleeding. His mind reeled with images of injuries he had seen in prison camp, and he was furious with himself for having been so careless.

That night he hit an all-time low. The hours after his accident, when he was rushed to emergency and kept up a running dialogue with the medical staff, weren't too bad. Much later, when the effect of the shock and the painkillers had worn off, he allowed himself to think about the implications of this injury. He prided himself for having learned humility from the Japanese, but he realized now that he had not rid himself of vanity.

Thinking about prison camp reminded him of how grateful he had been to come out without being maimed. He looked ruefully at his bandaged hand, wishing he could turn back the clock and undo this miserable day. Ah hell, he thought, that will just have to be one more lesson for me to tackle. He tried to think about how lucky it was that it was his left hand, but his mind kept going back to that split second of carelessness that he felt marked him for life.

After that, he couldn't work on the construction, but Bill Moore assured him that it wouldn't be long before he could be in charge of the promotions and putting together a floorshow for the opening night which was scheduled for September. Mickey bustled around, always cheerful, not wanting Tony to get the impression that he was bothered about his maimed fingers.

The hotel was finished on time, and Tony had to find another job. Martinolich liked him and offered him work on one of his merchant ships. It sounded like an adventure, and Tony said he would like that. When he told Mickey he was leaving, Mickey didn't show any signs of being sad. Rather, he suggested Tony take his paints along and some books. "Try to do some serious reading, too, son. You'll have plenty of time on board a ship, and there is a wealth of classics that you should read before you get too busy with something else."

The next day, Tony got a lift to San Diego in one of Martinolich's trucks. When he was settled inside the cab, ready to go, Mickey walked over to the truck to say goodbye.

"Well, Butch, take care of yourself!" Mickey said, with a smile. They said goodbye, and Tony was taken back when he noticed that for the first time he could recall, his father had tears in his eyes.

The hotel opened on time. They got "Pop" Squires, owner and publisher of Las Vegas' first newspaper to christen the Showboat by breaking a bottle of champagne over its 'prow' and pouring ten gallons of water from the Mississippi, compliments of the St. Louis Chamber of Commerce, into the pool. Mickey got Minsky's Follies of '55, a New York burlesque show, for the opening night, and things were off to a roaring start.

Meanwhile, Judy continued to do well in high school and graduated with honors. It didn't occur to her to worry about inviting her father to the graduation ceremony. She had been miserable when he didn't show up for school events when she was in grammar school and, by now, she took for granted that he wouldn't be interested in this one.

Neither would it have occurred to Mickey to show up. He had blocked out her stay with Bobbie and Armand, Judy's life in their household not being a part of his grander visions. He was noticeably proud to hear about her high school career, though, and to read the newspaper clippings Judy sent. For her graduation, he sent her Nina Farewell's book, "The Unfair Sex," with the inscription, "To my daughter on the occasion of her matriculation from high school, in the confident expectation that it has not arrived too late. From her father, a Lecherous Old Goat."

Nothing in Judy's life had taught her to make plans for the future. From her experience, she had learned to roll with the punches, but not to take an initiative. As luck would have it, a wealthy woman in Carpinteria, Mrs. Woods, made scholarships available to the graduates of the high school, and Miss Holmes, Judy's English teacher, made sure that she applied for one.

When Mickey heard the news that Judy was awarded a full scholarship to go to the University of California at Santa Barbara he wasn't impressed. The pace of Mickey's life had rubbed out the line between his flights of fancy and reality. He had always planned on her going to Steven's, a finishing school for young ladies in the South, and if she didn't want that, he wanted her to go to the University of Hawaii. He preferred to envision his daughter attending a school more for the atmosphere and the contacts she could make than for the actual studies. A small university like the one at Santa Barbara wouldn't serve to broaden her horizons, he thought, dismissing it as a provincial institution where she would never meet the kind of man he pictured her marrying.

With an intolerance towards the middle class just as pronounced as theirs was towards his type of character, he wanted passionately for Judy to move into cosmopolitan circles. He wanted her back as his kid, before she got too muddled up with what he imagined to be Bobbie and Armand's class of people. Christ, they would turn her into some opinionated, middle-class housewife, married to a nine-to-five man. He wanted to open her eyes to the wide world and all the treasures it contained before it was too late.

He had perks at the Showboat, just like he had when he was working at the Desert Inn, and he invited Judy to Las Vegas for a stay at the hotel that summer before she was to start studying at the university. He was relieved when he saw her. She didn't seem to have changed at all, except for being more self-confident. She spent the days lounging by the pool and, in the evenings, accompanied Mickey when he helped out on last-minute details for the burlesque show.

Judy watched the girls with interest as Mickey introduced them. There was a sensational stripper who called herself Patti Wagon, a beautiful girl who was working her way through college, and a number of others who were just as pretty and very friendly. While Judy chatted with the strippers, he bustled around trying to locate some adhesive tape or glue. It was hotter than blazes, and the dancers were having a problem with keeping the sequins attached to their tits when they did their number. Bill had said to Mickey, "For Chris sakes, sort that out or the cops will close down our show."

The week that Judy was there flew by. She was used to her father being someone with a life of his own, and she kept busy seeing friends and enjoying the pool. Tony showed up on ship-leave, and Judy fell for one of his friends. She was seventeen, and her romance overshadowed everything else. It was a wonderful week, but she saw very little of her father. She had promised to be back in Carpinteria to work in the store that summer, and when it came time to go, Mickey was very upset and tried to talk her into staying.

"But I promised Uncle Armand I would work this summer, Daddy. I can't let them down." She didn't want to point out to him that he didn't have a place where she would be able to stay. It wasn't until the end of her visit that she had discovered her father was sleeping in the boiler room of the hotel on a chaise lounge borrowed from the pool area. Mickey didn't have an apartment, and the room she was in was surely too expensive for her to tie it up all summer, she thought.

"Okay, but next summer you're going to come up here and make a pile of loot babysitting," Mickey told her. "Remember how much you made when you were going to school in Las

Vegas? Remember those tips? You can't beat that kind of money. And you can sit in an easy chair and read a good book while you're at it. I've talked with Bill, and we would make it part of the hotel service."

He took her to the Greyhound bus and made a stink about sending her back on a goddamn bus instead of a plane. She kissed him on the cheek and laughed, telling him not to worry about that.

"I'll write, Daddy. Thanks for everything. I had a terrific time." She found a good seat, the doors shut with a whine, and as suddenly as she came, she was on her way to what she now considered home. Mickey had managed to conceal from her the injury to his hand, and, as usual, it never occurred to her to worry about whether he was happy.

Mickey went back to the Showboat, nagged with a feeling that the visit wasn't what he had expected. He had imagined so many things he had wanted to say and to do, but the days had disappeared in a typically Las Vegas blur. Had she really been there for a little over a week? He tried to remember the days, but gave up the effort when he couldn't think back past the night before.

The bartender greeted him with a smile when he walked into the lounge. Mickey remembered a good story he knew the bartender would get a kick out of, and as he sipped his drink, his inner barometer rose to its usual 'fair weather' level. He could already picture how next summer would take shape. He would take Judy down to Mexico, maybe Tony could join them, and when they were through traveling around, Judy could work at the hotel. For now, he'd just have to plug away and make sure it all worked out.

* * * * *

After that summer, Judy moved into the dorm at Santa Barbara and started studies as an English major with minors in history and French. She wrote ecstatic letters to Mickey, and he was relieved that she seemed to be following the direction he had mapped out for her. He wrote back, advising her "to correlate European history in your mind with what was happening elsewhere in the world. Dates you will forget, but if you really remember how it happened and why, it will be not only much easier, but it runs more like any other narrative or TV show."

She took his advice seriously like she always did when it came to subjects that reflected on his intellect. She never questioned the disparity between his potential and his performance. He was like the whims of nature, to be enjoyed but not relied on.

When Judy started college, Tony decided to join the Navy. Las Vegas had no appeal, and by joining up he would be guaranteed a college education under the G.I. Bill of Rights when he decided what he wanted in life. He was in and out of Vegas when he could get leave, but Mickey never knew when he was coming. In fact, for a while there was no way of knowing where Mickey was sleeping, but Bill Moore always knew where Mickey could be contacted. Usually Tony stayed with his pal, Craig.

In November, Mickey received a letter from the Navy, stating that Tony had earned the distinction of being the Honor Man with the highest grades in the graduating class from the IC Electricians School. The commanding officer ended his letter by writing, "You have every reason to be exceedingly proud of your son, as we are proud of having had the privilege of being associated with him these past weeks. His performance reflects the splendid efforts which you put forth in the early years of his life." Mickey smiled, thinking about the unorthodox elements that went into those early years. He decided to sit right down to write Tony a letter.

Dear Tony,

Just got a letter from your seestah so I suppose I will be hearing from you pretty soon asking why I haven't written.

Wanted to be sure it was set before I wrote. I am going into the Showboat as director of publicity, which, of course, means with Bill Moore. I am glad I got the job although it changes my plans considerably. I wanted to take Judy on a bumming trip to Mexico this summer but we cannot make it now as I am going to keep my nose on that grindstone until Judy gets through college. She wrote me that she was going to work in the store this summer but one of the first things I am going to set up is a baby-sitting service at the hotel and Judy is my girl. She will not only get more than she can earn there but her tokes will run plenty with a smart kid like she is. I am taking an apartment out by there if there isn't room at the hotel with the heavy season coming up.

She wants to go to the University of Hawaii so if that is what she wants I guess it is the word. Now she can go anyplace she wants to. I don't think I'll ever get fired as no one ever has that worked for Bill Moore.

Please let me know exactly when you are coming up so that I can plan accordingly. Saw Craigo the other night and he is anxious to find out also. I guess he is really set on going to Hawaii.

It sure is good news that you are doing so well. Of course, I really expect it of you so there is no reason for me to con you that I am surprised, only mildly elated, and awfully damn proud. I am not going to try to influence your choice of career but I think you should seriously consider the State Department. You have the temperament and you should have the background by the time you get out of Columbia. Of course, everyone views things in the light of their own experience, but I know that in my own case it would have been much better if I had. You kids would have had an international education and I would certainly have acquired the discipline that somehow I've missed. I know that I wouldn't have gone to pot after your mother died. So give it some thought, will ya? You are not learning anything in the Navy that wouldn't do you some good if you picked such a career. And for gawdsakes bone up on languages. I lost a good deal last week because I didn't have anything but a superficial knowledge of a certain Latin-American country.

It would make me very happy if you were well-grounded in the humanities, and it is important to learn to be good at expressing yourself. Which reminds me of a story:

The little Jew walked into the bank and hefted an old canvas sack up on the teller's cage and said, "My name is Rabinowitz and I want to deposit this money."

The teller opened the sack and there's thousands and thousands in it. He says, "Well Sir, I think you should go in and see our president. He always likes to open new accounts of particularly large amounts." And he leads this little Jew into the president's office.

The president counts out the money – $127,000 – takes one look at the shabby, run-down little Jew and says, "Mr. Rabinowitz, how in the world have you managed to accumulate this money in these days of such high taxes. I know that you haven't stolen it, because you look so very honest."

Rabinowitz says, "Vell I'll tell you. I was born in Monsk. Vun of sefen children and my parents were poor so I heard from this cousin of mine I should come to America. So I came and in the steerage yet there vas a girl – Rebecca and von ve landed Rebecca and me we get married. Vell ve haf no money but I get job sweeping out in this clothing factory and after ten years they make me a salesman and Rebecca she is working sewing and we are savink our money and after ten more years I am finally made manage and..."

"Say no more," says the president. "I tell you what I want you to do. I am the president of the Rotary Club and I want you to be my guest at luncheon this Wednesday and tell your story so that my fellow Rotarians will know how there is still opportunity for men to make a success in America.

So the guy goes to the luncheon and he tells his long drawn out story and when he is through one of the members rises and says, "I think this is a wonderful message and we should certainly applaud Mr. Rabinowitz for scrimping and saving $127,000. This is a lesson in thrift."

The little Jew rose and said, "No – no, Mister, I got the $127,000 from my cousin that asked me to come to America. She was a whore and she died last month."

m.

Mickey popped the letter into an envelope and dropped it off at the desk to be mailed by the clerk. He was in a great mood. Being taken in under Bill Moore's wing was the break he had been hoping for. Now he felt that he could channel his energy in one direction and be sure of a decent income.

He moved into a motel on Fremont Street just in time for his annual attack of dengue fever. When the attack was over, he didn't bounce back to his usual levels of energy. He began to feel that he was losing his grip on reality, but he attributed that to the aftermath of his illness. Strange moods possessed him at unexpected moments. On the surface, he appeared to be the same fun-loving character, but out of the corner of his eye, he would be startled by glimpses of long-gone buddies from the Philippines. In the murky lighting of a casino, he imagined he could see Harry Magnuson waving to him, a smile on his face, from the other end of the room, but the vision would be gone just as quickly as it had appeared.

It was not an unpleasant experience, more like an awareness of another dimension that had been there all along. The only drawback was that it made it even more difficult for Mickey to distinguish between reality and his flights of fancy. Plans that he made for Judy or for Tony were mere ideas one minute and were beliefs the next. He wrote letters to Judy that mapped out impossible ambitions, but she didn't worry, putting that down to his usual habit of building castles in the air. She didn't know that although he was still managing to appear center stage, he was terribly alone.

When Tony was on leave in October, someone at the Showboat told him he could find his dad at June's Motel. Tony vaguely remembered June from his days of bumming around with his dad. He and his friend, Craig, went over there and knocked on the door where Mickey was supposed to be bunking.

Mickey called out in a cheerful voice, "Come on in – The door's open."

He was in bed with a cute chorus girl who was most embarrassed about the situation. Nonplussed, he greeted them cheerfully and sat up to light a cigarette. While the young lady pulled the covers up to her chin, he chatted unabashedly with Tony and Craig.

When they got ready to make a move, he asked what they planned to do that evening. "Do you need any stash?"

Tony, who never found he had too much money with a swab's wages, grinned and said, "Thank ye kindly, Mickey."

At that, Mickey reached across the redhead and picked up her handbag, fishing out a fiver to hand to Tony. "Don't do anything I wouldn't do," he said with a wink and waved them off, immediately turning his attention to his agreeable companion.

Craig was impressed. "Well, your old man sure isn't slowing down," he said, laughing.

Actually Mickey had his hands full of problems. He was still in hot water with the unions for doing work reserved for their members when the Showboat had to be completed, and they were making sure he wasn't getting paid for it. Bill Moore assured him he would take the case to court, but that could take months. As usual, Mickey had already spent that money before he had it in his hand, and people were starting to shut off his credit. Again, he found himself fretting about the money he felt should be coming to him from the government, like he always did when all else failed.

In 1948, the other horyos had been awarded a dollar a day for each day they were interned, and in 1950, they got $1.50 extra per day. Cousin Jack was still trying to wangle something out of the government for Mickey, but so far none of it had come through.

Just after Christmas, Mickey approached Bill with an idea to link together the diversion of skiing with a trip to Las Vegas. "We could set up a package deal at that ski resort up at Snow Mountains, north of St. George. My idea is to offer people who are there for the skiing a flight to Las Vegas with an over-night stay at The Showboat. I'm not doing anything tomorrow. I could drive up there and see what they think about it." Mickey figured that if he could sell his scheme, he could also count on a kick-back from the ski resort.

Bill Moore thought it sounded like a good idea. He remembered that Mickey was given credit for coming up with the idea for the champagne flights, and this sounded like a fresh angle on the same sort of idea.

"Great idea, Mickey. Let me know as soon as you get back."

Mickey went to the parking lot and opened the door to his old Pontiac. As he started the motor, he decided he had better check the oil and fill her up with gas before he had to leave for Utah. On the way to the service station, he passed Cashman's car lot and spotted a snazzy Ford. He had just cashed his first paycheck as publicity director, and it dawned on him that this was a good time to trade in his old car for something newer. *No point paying for repairs on the Pontiac now that I can afford to replace it. I can always get a decent place to live before Judy comes up here next summer,* he rationalized.

The transaction didn't take long, and he felt great driving off the lot with a honey of a car. It had power steering and handled beautifully – *A far cry from his good old convertible,* he thought. *The Pontiac was like an old friend, but it handled like a Mac truck.*

June looked up when she heard the wheels on the gravel outside her office. She wondered where Mickey got the nice car. She watched him disappear into his room, and when he came out he had changed clothes.

The bell over the door jingled as he stepped into her office, and she put aside the newspaper, hoping he would tell her what he was up to. Mickey was always so up beat. June was a quiet type, dour to those who didn't know her better. She had been around Vegas for a long time, starting out as a cocktail waitress and ending up with enough money to buy the motel. The school of hard knocks had taught her to be able to size up a person within minutes, and Mickey was one of her favorites. He seemed to see beyond her Germanic surface and treat her like the kind person she really was: Salt of the earth and caring.

He flashed her his usual smile, but for once he looked tired. He sure as heck hasn't been getting much sleep either, she thought. She had heard he was having trouble with those crooks who had tried to take over the gambling operation at the Showboat. There is a lot going on in this town that I don't like to think about, she thought, and a guy like Mickey doesn't watch his back. She had heard that Mickey's mother was loaded when she was alive, and she had no illusions about why a person like Mickey would be staying at her motel. He sure as heck wasn't calling the shots these days.

"You're knocking yourself out, Mickey. You of all people ought to know life's too short for that. When's the last time you got a good night's sleep?"

"Yeah, you're right, sweetheart, this week's been crazy. Things are looking up though, and right now I've got a chance to get my hands on some lettuce. Christ, I don't need anything myself, but I sure as hell would like to make sure my kids get a good start in life."

June didn't say anything at first. Seemed a darned shame that things weren't going his way these days, but she had been around this town long enough to recognize the downhill slide once a hustler started to show signs of age. She had a soft spot for Mickey though. Yeah, she knew he had his faults, but she also knew he didn't have a mean bone in his body. Plenty of times she had noticed how kind he was to someone who was down and out.

For once Mickey looked like he could use a kind word himself, but June wasn't a big talker. Her voice was tight and monotone, like it wasn't used very often, but she felt like making an effort. She knew all about his kids. He was proud as punch when the Navy wrote telling him of his boy's exam results, and he showed her the newspaper clippings his girl sent.

"You don't have to worry about those kids of yours, Mickey. Look at your boy ... Highest marks in the Navy, and that girl of yours getting a full scholarship for college. Face it. They don't need you no more. Kids grow up. That's the way it is, and yours turned out all right. You did a good job on your kids. Now you need to think about yourself. You're gonna kill yourself, running around like a crazy man."

Touched that June had made such a long speech, Mickey smiled and squeezed her hand.

He regained his usual jaunty air. "Well, thanks, June. Can I take that as a proposal for marriage?"

Things were back to normal. June chuckled and went back to being her usual gruff self, and Mickey said, "I'll be out of here first thing in the morning. I'm driving up to Utah to see some friends about a deal. If I get any phone calls while I'm gone, tell 'em I'll be back tomorrow night."

The next morning, he got a very early start, and he arrived at the resort in time for lunch. Mickey knew the people who owned it from days gone by when his mother went there to relax. They liked Mickey's idea and agreed on a deal that he could start working on as soon as he got back to Vegas.

They asked him to stay on for a few days, but he said no. "Thanks for the offer, but I'm too damned busy right now. I've got more irons in the fire than you can shake a stick at. Maybe I can make it back up here when things quiet down."

On the way out to the car, his own words rang repetitive in his ears. It dawned on him that being busy was becoming a way of life for him. He didn't stop to analyze it, but the truth was that he was most comfortable when perpetually in motion. The rapid shift of backdrop kept at bay those moments of truth when he got a swift impression of dreams betrayed and goals no longer in reach, and the artificial atmosphere of Las Vegas was a perfect setting for shifting illusions. What Las Vegas embodied was so far removed from all he had once thought important, that there was nothing to inspire a moment of introspection.

He headed back the same day to the Showboat, driving non-stop, except for a cup of coffee and a sandwich at a roadside café in Mesquite. The long, straight road was empty, and the monotony of the desert by daylight drugged his senses. Much of the time he was driving with the sun in his eyes.

Jesus, I'm tired, he thought as he approached Vegas. He was suddenly aware of not having eaten dinner, and the coffee he got at that roadside joint had worn off long ago. June had warned him to take it easy.

Then he remembered what she had said about the kids. He smiled and thought about the dreams he and Vivian had talked about for the kids and reminisced about how talking with her always used to make him want to make love. He wondered where they would be if she were with him now. At least it proved right, what they thought about raising kids. The first six years were the most important, and she was there until Judy was six. That must have counted for something.

They had also agreed that the best way to broaden a child's horizon was by traveling, and

Tony and Judy had had more than their share of that. He knew she would be pleased with them now, even if their old man was a flop.

The idea of himself as a 'flop' brought him up short, and, being alone with his thoughts, he took time to dwell on that possibility. He chuckled, not being able to take seriously such an evaluation. He had 'touched bottom' during those years in prison camp and with the loss of Vivian. Nothing that happened hence took on the importance usually attached to events related to one's progress.

All at once it dawned on him that it was peculiar, his being in Las Vegas, when he had wanted so badly to get away from there after the war. Looking back, it seemed like even though he chose places where he wanted to settle down and made plans for staying in those places, he ended up drifting, using his abilities to cope with whatever conditions there were in whichever place he found himself. His real talent, he realized was in being able to adapt, but that wasn't really what Jane had wanted for him. Adapting was counteractive to ambition. She had always insisted that he should make plans, control his fate. Alone on the road, in the solitary enclosure of a moving car, he allowed himself to think a thought to its end, and he came to the conclusion that, in reality, fate had controlled him.

Pondering this notion, he asked himself whether he had any regrets, but he was doubly protected from remorse, both by his inborn good spirits and the oriental stoicism pounded into him as a horyo. Nah, he thought. What was there to regret? Some people needed a planned, charted journey, but he liked the movement itself – the fascination of not knowing what was just around the corner, even if it turned out to be a bad scene. Hell, he wouldn't trade places with anyone he knew who was driven by ambition. Look at Dunaway, or worse yet, look at poor old MacArthur – It wasn't long after the war that he was out in Korea, fighting a new one. "Old soldiers never die – They just fade away." Ain't that a fact. But what good does it do to win a battle if changing politicians keep kindling new wars? He had seen so many dreams wiped out or fade away. Right now, the thought of a warm bed at the end of the road was enough for him.

It was dark as he drove the last long haul into Las Vegas. There were hardly any cars on the road, and the lights of the few that came towards him made him wince and feel like pulling over. But he had promised Bill he would get back for the weekend, and he didn't want to let him down. With one hand on the steering wheel, he shook a cigarette out of a pack he had on the dashboard and pushed in the lighter. While he was waiting for it to heat up, he flicked on the radio.

He lit his cigarette and took a drag, and the nicotine jolted him into feeling more awake.

The voice of a disc jockey was a welcome distraction on the monotonous road, and he tried to concentrate on what the guy was saying. He shook his head and straightened his back, but everything he did only seemed to help for a few minutes. Maybe he ought to pull over, just for an hour, but the thought didn't appeal to him when he was so close to home and bed.

He reached the outskirts of Vegas. He would soon be back in the three-ring circus that absorbed all his attention. Tiredness washed over him in waves, erasing the sharp division between wakefulness and sleep. He listened absent-mindedly to the soothing voice of the disc jockey as he announced the next song.

"The next platter I'm going to spin is an evergreen that might take some of us back a few years," he said. The record was slotted smoothly into place, and Mickey's thoughts drifted to the past as he heard the familiar refrains of "Smoke Gets in Your Eyes".

Mickey smiled as he pictured himself dancing with Vivian, her dress clinging to her body and her skin like satin. Their bodies had fit perfectly together, and she followed his lead effortlessly, with the precision of a bird's flight. He remembered, like it was yesterday, that moment, as they turned slowly through the steps of a fox trot, when he felt his heart beat suspended for a fraction of eternity, and he realized that he was helplessly, hopelessly in love with her.

He thought about the years they were together, and they seemed to fill so much more space in time than the ten years since he came home from the war. Looking back, he knew he would never trade those years of excitement for a lifetime of routine contentment.

Listening to the music, he felt such a longing for her that she seemed to be in the car with him. The sensation was so persuasive that he imagined he could smell the scent of the perfume she always wore. Shaken, he looked at the passenger's seat as he reached out to knock the ashes from his cigarette into the ashtray, half thinking he would see her sitting there, her green eyes bright in the reflection of the dashboard, like they had been that night they drove to Malibu.

In that brief moment, he missed the turn where the road forked. His mind registered in slow motion the car piling into the embankment, the sound of shattered glass blending with the music on the radio. Mickey was thrown against the windshield, his throat smashed by the steering wheel. He gasped for air, and he realized his windpipe must be broken. In a state of shock, he felt the moment transformed to an hour. He was engulfed in a dreamlike state. Pleasant images floated through his mind, and Vivian was there with him, after all those years of waiting. In one last instant of awareness, he knew that this was the end of the trail and recognized the irony of having avoided death so many times, only to have his life snuffed out so easily.

The radio was still playing their song, and he smiled, feeling himself drift from consciousness, his life ebbing out into the darkness of the night. Then, like a tightrope walker whose concentration was disturbed, he lost his footing and fell effortlessly into the unexplored void.

Epilogue

My task is finished. I have succeeded in bringing them back, after all these years. I sense the blood coursing through the hand that wrote the letters. I feel the warmth of the smiles in the photos.

Studying it all, I have at times felt anguish that I can't reach out and touch them, laugh with them during all their good moments and comfort them through their tragic endings. Such is the way of life. Wisdom comes too late, wrapping us in solitude.

"Listen to me. You can learn from my experiences. Why do you have to learn the hard way?" We say this to our children, vainly, for they must learn by themselves. We wish we could throw them a rope and haul them up to where the view is so grand. I find myself wishing this for my parents, having reached a greater age than they did. Their lives lie shattered in bright bits, and I muse over the notion of putting out a magic hand and preventing the past from being past. However, that would be only for my own pleasure. Each life is a life worth living, and the unique lives of my parents are best left unchanged.

Living is a skill one learns during the course of an obstacle race, with rewards along the way and points tallied up, until the unexpected moment when the runner is jerked back to start base, for having made too many errors or choosing the wrong turn. It is like a game, where there are easy solutions to a safe landing, or difficult tasks leading to a more exciting result. My parents shot for the high scores, and I want them remembered for their daring, not for their failures.

All that matters is the love that is passed on from parent to child, blessing each life with the joy of being, and my brother and I have been abundantly blessed.

Mickey – 1940

Vivian, Tony, and Judy – 1943

Bibliography

Brown, Gene. *Movie Time.* Macmillan, 1995

Daws, Gavan. *Prisoners of the Japanese.* Quill, William Morrow. 1994

Daws, Gavan. *Shoals of Time - A History of the Hawaiian Islands -* U. of Hawaii Press 1974

Eyman, Scott. *The Speed of Sound.* Simon and Schuster. 1997

Knepp, Don. *Las Vegas, The Entertainment Capital.* Lane Publishing Co. 1987

Knox, Donald. *Death March.* Harcourt Brace & Company. 1981

Manchester, William. *American Caesar, Douglas MacArthur.* Little, Brown & Co. 1978

Morris, Eric. *Corregidor* London: Hutchinson, 1982

McCabe, John. *Cagney.* Alfred A. Knopf. 1997

Owens, Louis *Mixed Blood Messages* University of Oklahoma Press: Norman 1998

Roske, Ralph J. *Las Vegas, A Desert Paradise.* Continental Heritage Press, Inc. 1986

Sides, Hampton. *Ghost Soldiers.* Doubleday. 2001

Villarin, Mariano. *We Remember Bataan and Corregidor.* Gateway Press, Inc., 1990

Whitney, Major General Courtney. *MacArthur.* Alfred A Knopf. 1956

Zich, Arthur. *The Rising Sun.* Time-Life Books, Inc. 1977